American Government and Politics

Selected Readings

MERRILL POLITICAL SCIENCE SERIES

Under the Editorship of
John C. Wahlke
Department of Political Science
State University of New York, Stony Brook

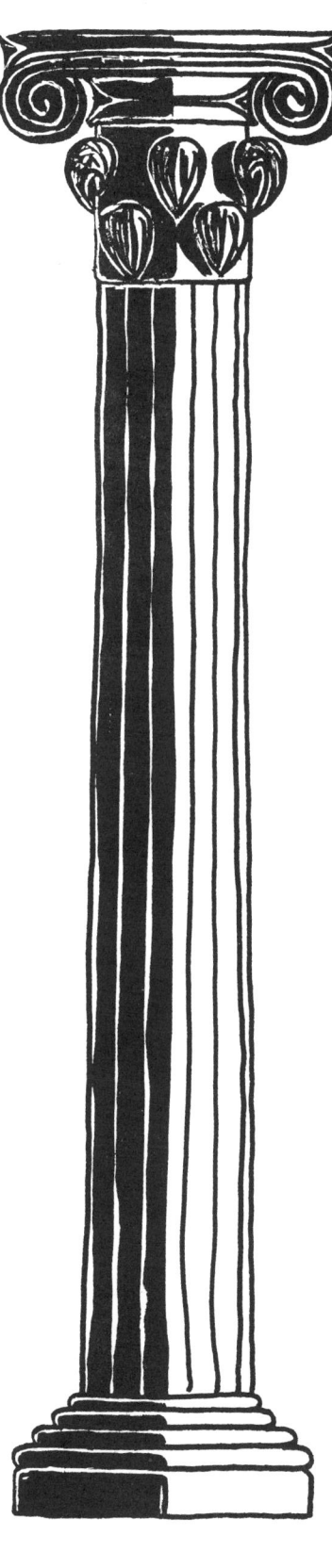

American Government and Politics

Selected Readings

Edited by

Ronald C. Moe
Office of Economic Opportunity

and

William A. Schultze
San Diego State College

Charles E. Merrill Publishing Company
A Bell & Howell Company
Columbus, Ohio

Copyright © 1971 by Charles E. Merrill Publishing Company, Columbus, Ohio. All rights reserved. No part of this book may be reproduced in any form, electronic or mechanical, including photocopy, recording, or any information storage and retrieval system, without permission in writing from the publisher.

ISBN: 0-675-09272-8

Library of Congress Catalog Card Number: 74-133959

2 3 4 5 6 7 8—76 75 74 73 72 71

Printed in the United States of America

Acknowledgments

Every professor, regardless of his discipline, enjoys playing the role of kibitzer with regard to the text material he uses in class. Somehow it rarely meets the level of scholarship that it would have achieved under his pen. It is not only easy to note the inadequacies of others' work, it is satisfying to the ego as well. Through the faith and generosity of the Charles E. Merrill Publishing Company, we were suddenly deprived of the comfort of this kibitzer role and instructed to "produce."

We found the opportunity to compile our own reader both a stimulating and challenging experience. It was stimulating in the sense that the wide latitude permitted us with regard to approach and length allowed us a certain margin for innovation. As we explain in the Introduction, we do have some thoughts on what constitutes the most useful type of supplementary text for the basic course in American Government. The experience of compiling a reader proved challenging in that the pieces did not fit together neatly by themselves. There must be a system for selecting and organizing the material. In turn, a list of priorities must be established concerning the materials as they relate to the larger priorities of deadlines, costs, and overall length of the manuscript. To satisfy these demands required of us much more in the way of judgment and revisions than we had originally anticipated.

In a real sense, this is not our book. Most of the credit for this reader must go to the authors of the essays which follow. We learned that our profession and the publishing industry are composed of many kind, efficient, and helpful individuals. Without exception, our requests for approval to re-publish materials met with a prompt and courteous reply. For the assistance of the individuals and corporations noted in the acknowledgments for each essay, we are most grateful.

The final choices of what to include were, of course, ours. But the process of paring down was made easier by the assistance received from a number of colleagues, not only at San Diego State College, but elsewhere in the nation as well. Accepting the risk of omission with regret, we are especially appreciative of the counsel given by John C. Wahlke, James H. Andrews, Kenneth Pedersen, Harlan Lewin, James Conniff, and David Johns.

We owe a special debt of gratitude to Roger Ratliff and Kip Sears of the Charles E. Merrill Publishing Company for permitting us to put our ideas in print and requiring us to "produce." They were everything a publisher's representative ought to be. For her invaluable secretarial advice and assistance, Mrs. Veva Link will not soon be forgotten. And finally, but by no means last, we wish to thank our wives and families for their encouragement, not merely in this enterprise, but throughout our careers as well.

Contents

INTRODUCTION ... 1

PART ONE – OUR CONSTITUTIONAL HERITAGE

Chapter 1   The Colonial Period and the Revolution

Origin of the Anglo-Americans
    Alexis de Tocqueville   5

The Declaration of Independence
    Carl L. Becker   17

Democracy and the American Revolution
    Merrill Jensen   25

The American Revolution as a Colonial War for Independence
    Thomas C. Barrow   39

Chapter 2   The Constitutional Period

The Founding Fathers: A Reform Caucus in Action
    John P. Roche   48

An Economic Interpretation of the Constitution
    Charles A. Beard   62

Charles Beard, the Constitution, and the Historians
    Robert Detweiler
    Raymond Starr   73

The Federalist–Number Ten
    James Madison   85

Democracy and the Federalist
    Martin Diamond   91

PART TWO – AMERICAN POLITICAL INSTITUTIONS

Chapter 3   The Legislative Branch: Congress

The Job of the Congressman
    Raymond A. Bauer
    Ithiel de Sola Pool
    Lewis Anthony Dexter   105

The Committee System
    Charles L. Clapp   115

	Conflict Management in a Congressional Committee	John F. Manley	127
	The Senate: Is There an Inner Club?	Nelson W. Polsby	141
Chapter 4	**The Executive Branch: The President**		
	The President: Leader or Clerk?	Richard E. Neustadt	150
	Presidential Advisers	Theodore C. Sorensen	164
	President–Cabinet Relations	Richard F. Fenno, Jr.	171
Chapter 5	**The Judicial Branch: The Supreme Court**		
	Judicial Review	Henry J. Schmandt	185
	The Supreme Court as a Unit of Government	Robert H. Jackson	193
	The Court and Decision-Making	Samuel Krislov	204
	Chief Justice Taft and Judicial Administration	Walter F. Murphy	211
Chapter 6	**The Administrative System**		
	The Anatomy of Bureaucracy	Charles E. Jacob	224
	Intergovernmental Relations in the Twentieth Century	Daniel J. Elazar	235
	The Bureaucracy in Pressure Politics	J. Leiper Freeman	247
	Some Lessons of Experience	Marver Bernstein	256
Chapter 7	**Political Parties**		
	The Evolution of Nominating Machinery in America	Austin Ranney Willmoore Kendall	265
	The Changing Pattern of Urban Party Politics	Fred I. Greenstein	275
	The Need for Party Government	James M. Burns	287
	On the Superiority of National Conventions	Aaron B. Wildavsky	293

CONTENTS

Our Two-Party System and the Electoral College
Ronald C. Moe   303

PART THREE—AMERICAN POLITICAL BEHAVIOR AND AMERICAN DEMOCRACY

Chapter 8 Democratic Ideals and Political Behavior

Learning Democratic Norms
Robert E. Lane
David O. Sears   315

The Malevolent Leader: Political Socialization in an American Subculture
Dean Jaros
Herbert Hirsch
Fredric Fleron, Jr.   327

Consensus and Ideology in American Politics
Herbert McClosky   342

The Fear of Equality
Robert E. Lane   364

Political Cynicism: Measurement and Meaning
Robert E. Agger
Marshall N. Goldstein
Stanley A. Pearl   378

A Critique of the Theory of Democratic Elitism
Peter Bachrach   389

Is There a Ruling Elite in America?
William A. Schultze   397

Chapter 9 Voting Behavior and Elections

The Political Behavior of the Electorate
Warren E. Miller   407

American Voting Participation
William G. Andrews   429

Electoral Myth and Reality: The 1964 Election
Philip E. Converse
Aage Clausen
Warren E. Miller   443

Continuity and Change in American Politics: Parties and Issues in the 1968 Election
Philip E. Converse
Warren E. Miller
Jerrold G. Rusk
Arthur C. Wolfe   459

PART FOUR — ISSUES OF AMERICAN POLITICS

Chapter 10   **Individual Rights**

Extension of the Bill of Rights to the States
William J. Brennan, Jr.   481

"Selective Incorporation" in the Fourteenth Amendment
Louis Henkin   490

Schenck v. United States
249 U. S. 47 (1919)   504

The First Amendment Is an Absolute
Alexander Meiklejohn   507

On the Meaning of the First Amendment: Absolutes in the Balance
Wallace Mendelson   521

Chapter 11   **The Disadvantaged and Dissenting**

Black Power: Its Need and Substance
Stokely Carmichael
Charles Hamilton   529

What Can Be Done About Air Pollution?
Edward Edelson
Fred Warshofsky   541

The Movement
Jack Newfield   555

Seedtime of the New Republic: Ideology, Identity and Social Change
Harlan Lewin   559

Responsibility and Violence in the Academy
Sidney Hook   572

Chapter 12   **Stability and Change**

Revolution and Counterrevolution
Zbigniew Brzezinski   580

A Name for Our Age
Eric Hoffer   585

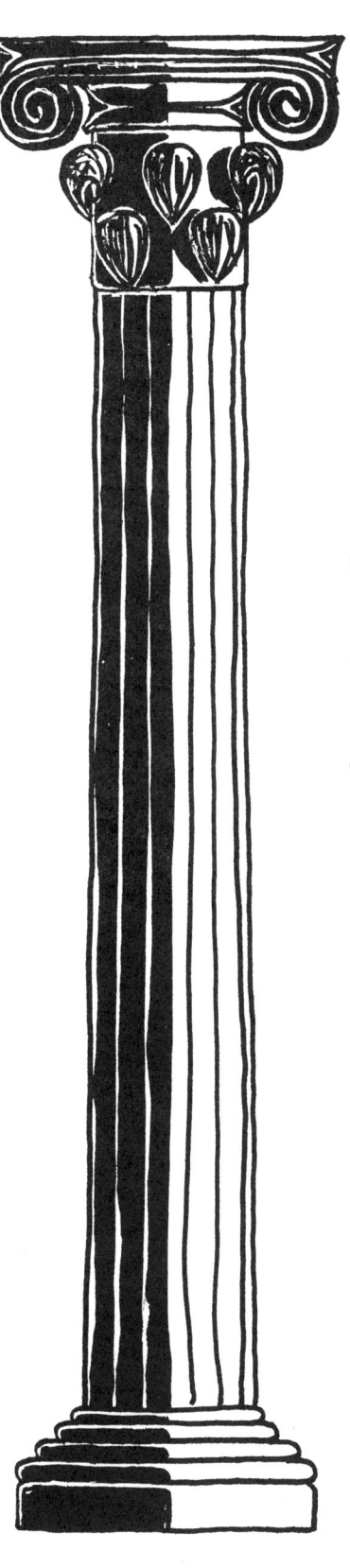

American Government and Politics

Selected Readings

Introduction

This set of readings, we believe, is distinguished from the rather large number of other readers by at least three characteristics: its comprehensiveness, its organization to highlight contrasting interpretations of the subject matter, and its inclusion of materials on contemporary political issues. It is important to explain at the outset why we feel these distinctions are not simply differences for their own sake, but are virtues.

Comprehensiveness appears to be necessary in a set of readings compiled at this stage in the development of study of American politics because there is, at present, no high level of agreement among political scientists on what the central questions are that focus our concerns. If there existed more consensus in the discipline, possibly a selection of readings more limited in scope would be appropriate. Lacking that level of agreement, we believe that to be brief is to risk being unfair to the profusion of deserving political ideas. Accordingly, we find that a comprehensive survey of the materials being written and discussed in connection with the American government would include: political history, governmental institutions and processes, political behavior, and issues.

Further, we have been guided by the view that our selections should be arranged so as to reflect, yet help focus, the grounds upon which we lack agreement on these political topics. We are keenly aware of the tendency in ourselves, as well as in our colleagues and fellow citizens, to choose to represent in the classroom and in public discussion viewpoints which reinforce our own predispositions rather than exposing the full range of relevant alternatives. Balance here, as anywhere, is difficult to achieve. We have aimed to facilitate the maintenance of balanced presentation of the American government by allowing leading exponents of particular views or schools of thought to represent themselves, and have arranged our exposition of these contrasting positions in such a way as to ease analytic comparison.

For the foregoing reasons we have not allowed any single specific conceptual framework of political analysis to guide the organization of these readings. Nonetheless, we have taken care to include materials which are adaptable to one or several such frameworks. For our organizational pattern we have taken the four central concerns described above and organized selections within each of these major topics: history, institutions and processes, political behavior, and issues.

Part One represents a modest attempt to provide the student of American government with a sense of history. All too often the tendency is to glorify the contemporary and ignore, even villify, the past. The truth is, however, that most political questions and problems are not new. We can learn something from the insights offered by those who preceded us in time. It is also true that the writing of history is frequently motivated by political questions which engage a particular generation. By introducing the subject of historiography we trust that the student will be able to see for himself that scholars often have ulterior purposes for their endeavors.

As for Part Two with its emphasis on institutions and processes, the justification seems virtually self-evident. Our polity is not an abstraction, rather it consists of concrete institutions which exist to make and enforce public policy. What are these bodies, what norms limit their internal behavior and external influence, and how do they arrive at their policy decisions? Our sections on Congress, the president, the Supreme Court, administrative agencies, and political parties were made with the intent to answer these questions.

The third major subdivision of the book deals with provocative materials produced in the scientific study of the political behavior of Americans. These materials are arranged in such a way as to highlight their relevance to democratic ideals. Readings are included which suggest the way in which democratic values are learned (or not learned); the level of political knowledge; the nature of American consensus; the sense in which political equality is endorsed; and the tendency in some of our citizens to become cynical about politics. Two overview readings discuss and theorize about the mixture of citizen participation with elite participation which the empirical findings suggest. Also included here are essays which allow sampling of the rich tradition of research on voting behavior.

The final section of the book contains three selected issues of contemporary importance: the controversy over judicial interpretation of the scope of individual rights; the growth of radical dissent; and the question, are we faced with revolution? Certain issues of our time are unquestionably fleeting, but we feel these three issues have an enduring quality. The questions they raise about the direction of our culture and government appear critical and transforming.

It is our hope that this strategy of organization and presentation will contribute, however modestly, to the convergence of perspectives on American political life.

Part One

Our Constitutional Heritage

Origin of the Anglo-Americans

Alexis de Tocqueville (1805-1859), scholar extraordinary, visited the United States in 1831 on behalf of the French government ostensibly to study America's penal institutions. He viewed his task, however, as considerably more inclusive. On his return to France he wrote Democracy in America, *the first comprehensive study of the political and social institutions of the United States. Although it was originally published in 1835, its style and scholarship, as the following selection illustrates, endow it with a contemporary quality. As de Tocqueville viewed history, the world had entered a new era. For virtually all of history human society had been aristocratic, with stratified inequality. Since the Dark Ages, however, the tide of events had steadily destroyed the foundations of the aristocratic society and a process of democratization had set in. Democracy, according to de Tocqueville, was a form of society, not a type of government. All is democracy which is not aristocracy, just as all is equality which is not inequality. Having lived through the excesses of the Napoleonic regime, he was curious to learn how America had restrained the worst features of an egalitarian society in order that these principles might be applied in France. This selection serves to introduce the reader to only his views on the origin of the Anglo-Americans and Puritanism. In the course of his two volumes, he suggests that a well-ordered democracy is most likely to occur when society is religious, where reasonable prosperity permits a middle class, where government is centralized but administration is decentralized, where public education prevails, and where individuality is encouraged. In short, democratic society is most pallatable where democratic political institutions dominate. It was France's problem, de Tocqueville concluded, that it had a democratic society without democratic institutions. America, on the other hand, had established a democratic republic.*

Alexis de Tocqueville

From *Democracy in America,* I, trans. by Henry Reeve (New York: D. Appleton and Company, 1904), pp. 11-31.

After the birth of a human being his early years are obscurely spent in the toils or pleasures of childhood. As he grows up the world receives him, when his manhood begins, and he enters into contact with his fellows. He is then studied for the first time, and it is imagined that the germ of the vices and the virtues of his maturer years is then formed. This, if I am not mistaken, is a great error. We must begin higher up; we must watch the infant in its mother's arms; we must see the first images which the external world casts upon the dark mirror of his mind; the first occurrences which he witnesses; we must hear the first words which awaken the sleeping powers of thought, and stand by his earliest efforts, if we would understand the prejudices, the habits, and the passions which will rule his life. The entire man is, so to speak, to be seen in the cradle of the child.

The growth of nations presents something analogous to this: they all bear some marks of their origin; and the circumstances which accompanied their birth and contributed to their rise affect the whole term of their being. If we were able to go back to the elements of states, and to examine the oldest monuments of their history, I doubt not that we should discover the primal cause of the prejudices, the habits, the ruling passions, and, in short, of all that constitutes what is called the national character: we should then find the explanation of certain customs which now seem at variance with the prevailing manners; of such laws as conflict with established principles; and of such incoherent opinions as are here and there to be met with in society, like those fragments of broken chains which we sometimes see hanging from the vault of an edifice, and supporting nothing. This might explain the destinies of certain nations which seem borne on by an unknown force to ends of which they themselves are ignorant. But hitherto facts have been wanting to researches of this kind: the spirit of inquiry has only come upon communities in their latter days; and when they at length contemplated their origin, time had already obscured it, or ignorance and pride adorned it with truth-concealing fables.

America is the only country in which it has been possible to witness the natural and tranquil growth of society, and where the influence exercised on the future condition of states by their origin is clearly distinguishable. At the period when the peoples of Europe landed in the New World their national characteristics were already completely formed; each of them had a physiognomy of its own; and as they had already attained that stage of civilization at which men are led to study themselves, they have transmitted to us a faithful picture of their opinions, their manners, and their laws. The men of the sixteenth century are almost as well known to us as our contemporaries. America, consequently, exhibits in the broad light of day the phenomena which the ignorance or rudeness of earlier ages conceals from our researches. Near enough to the time when the states of America were founded, to be accurately acquainted with their elements, and sufficiently removed from that period to judge of some of their results, the men of our own day seem destined to see further than their predecessors into the series of human events. Providence has given us a torch which our forefathers did not possess, and has allowed us to discern fundamental causes in the history of the world which the obscurity of the past concealed from them. If we carefully examine the social and political state of America, after having studied its history, we shall remain perfectly convinced that not an opinion, not a custom, not a law, I may even say not an event, is upon record which the origin of that people will not explain. The readers of this book will find the germ of all that is to follow in the present chapter, and the key to almost the whole work.

The emigrants who came, at different periods, to occupy the territory now covered by the American Union differed from each other in many respects; their aim was not the same, and they governed themselves on different principles. These men had, however, certain features in common, and they were all placed in an analogous situation. The tie of language is perhaps the strongest and the most durable that can unite mankind. All the emigrants spoke the same tongue; they were all offsets from the same people. Born in a country which had been agitated for centuries by the struggles of faction, and in which all parties had been obliged in their turn to place themselves under the protection of the laws, their political education had been perfected in this rude school, and they were more conversant with the notions of right and the principles of true freedom than the greater part of their European contemporaries. At the period of their first emigrations the parish system, that fruitful germ of free institutions, was deeply rooted in the habits of the English; and with it the doctrine of the sovereignty of the people had been introduced into the bosom of the monarchy of the House of Tudor.

The religious quarrels which have agitated the Christian world were then rife. England had plunged into the new order of things with headlong vehemence. The character of its inhabitants, which had always been sedate and reflective, became argumentative and austere. General information had been increased by intellectual debate, and the mind had received a deeper cultivation. While religion was the topic of discussion, the morals of the people were reformed. All these national features are more or less discoverable in the physiognomy of those adventurers who came to seek a new home on the opposite shores of the Atlantic.

Another remark, to which we shall hereafter have occasion to recur, is applicable not only to the English, but to the French, the Spaniards, and all the Europeans who successively established themselves in the New World. All these European colonies contained the elements, if not the development, of a complete democracy. Two causes led to this result. It may safely be advanced, that on leaving the mother-country the emigrants had in general no notion of superiority over one another. The happy and the powerful do not go into exile, and there are no surer guarantees of equality among men than poverty and misfortune. It happened, however, on several occasions, that persons of rank were driven to America by political and religious quarrels. Laws were made to establish a gradation of ranks; but it was soon found that the soil of America was opposed to a territorial aristocracy. To bring that refractory land into cultivation, the constant and interested exertions of the owner himself were necessary; and when the ground was prepared, its produce was found to be insufficient to enrich a master and a farmer at the same time. The land was then naturally broken up into small portions, which the proprietor cultivated for himself. Land is the basis of an aristocracy, which clings to the soil that supports it; for it is not by privileges alone, nor by birth, but by landed property handed down from generation to generation, that an aristocracy is constituted. A nation may present immense fortunes and extreme wretchedness, but unless those fortunes are territorial there is no aristocracy, but simply the class of the rich and that of the poor.

All the British colonies had then a great degree of similarity at the epoch of their settlement. All of them, from their first beginning, seemed destined to witness the growth, not of the aristocratic liberty of their mother-country, but of that freedom of the middle and lower orders of which the history of the world had as yet furnished no complete example.

In this general uniformity several striking differences were however discernible, which it is necessary to point out. Two branches may be distinguished in the Anglo-American family which have hitherto grown up without entirely commingling; the one in the South, the other in the North.

Virginia received the first English colony; the emigrants took possession of it in 1607. The idea that mines of gold and silver are the sources of national wealth was at that time singularly prevalent in Europe; a fatal delusion, which has done more to impoverish the nations which adopted it, and has cost more lives in America, than the united influence of war and bad laws. The men sent to Virginia were seekers of gold, adventurers without resources and without character, whose turbulent and restless spirit endangered the infant colony, and rendered its progress uncertain. The artisans and agriculturists arrived afterward; and, although they were a more moral and orderly race of men, they were in nowise above the level of the inferior classes in England. No lofty conceptions, no intellectual system, directed the foundation of these new settlements. The colony was scarcely established when slavery was introduced, and this was the main circumstance which has exercised so prodigious an influence on the character, the laws, and all the future prospects of the South. Slavery, as we shall afterward show, dishonours labour; it introduces idleness into society, and with idleness, ignorance and pride, luxury and distress. It enervates the powers of the mind, and benumbs the activity of man. The influence of slavery, united to the English character, explains the manners and the social condition of the Southern States.

In the North, the same English foundation was modified by the most opposite shades of character; and here I may be allowed to enter into some details. The two or three main ideas which constitute the basis of the social theory of the United States were first combined in the Northern English colonies, more generally denominated the States of New England. The principles of New England spread at first to the neighbouring States; they then passed successively to the more distant ones; and at length they imbued the whole Confederation. They now extend their influence beyond its limits over the whole American world. The civilization of New England has been like a beacon lit upon a hill, which, after it has diffused its warmth around, tinges the distant horizon with its glow.

The foundation of New England was a novel spectacle, and all the circumstances attending it were singular and original. The large majority of colonies have been first inhabited either by men without education and without resources, driven by their poverty and their misconduct from the land which gave them birth, or by speculators and adventurers greedy of gain. Some settlements can not even boast so honourable an origin; St. Domingo was founded by buccaneers; and the criminal courts of England originally supplied the population of Australia.

The settlers who established themselves on the shores of New England all belonged to the more independent classes of their native country. Their union on the soil of America at once presented the singular phenomenon of a society containing neither lords nor common people, neither rich nor poor. These men possessed, in proportion to their number, a greater mass of intelligence than is to be found in any European nation of our own time. All, without a single exception, had received a good education, and many of them were known in Europe for their talents and their acquirements. The other colonies had been founded by adventurers without family; the emigrants of New England brought with them the best elements of order and morality — they landed in the desert accompanied by their wives and children. But what most especially distinguished them was the aim of their undertaking. They had not been obliged by necessity to leave their country; the social position they abandoned was one to be regretted, and their means of subsistence were certain. Nor did they cross the Atlantic to improve their situation or to increase their wealth; the call which summoned them from the comforts of their homes was purely intellectual; and in facing the inevitable sufferings of exile their object was the triumph of an idea.

The emigrants, or, as they deservedly styled themselves, the Pilgrims, belonged to that English sect the austerity of whose principles had acquired for them the name of Puritans. Puritanism was not merely a religious doctrine, but it corresponded in many points with the most absolute democratic and republican theories. It was this tendency which had aroused its most dangerous adversaries. Persecuted by the Government of the mother-country, and disgusted by the habits of a society opposed to the rigour of their own principles, the Puritans went forth to seek some rude and unfrequented part of the world, where they could live according to their own opinions, and worship God in freedom.

A few quotations will throw more light upon the spirit of these pious adventurers than all we can say of them. Nathaniel Morton, the historian of the first years of the settlement, thus opens his subject:

"Gentle Reader — I have for some length of time looked upon it as a duty incumbent, especially on the immediate successors of those that have had so large experience of those many memorable and signal demonstrations of God's goodness, viz., the first beginners of this Plantation in New England, to commit to writing his gracious dispensations on that behalf; having so many inducements thereunto, not onely otherwise but so plentifully in the Sacred Scriptures: that so, what we have seen, and what our fathers have told us (Psalm lxxviii: 3, 4), we may not hide from our children, showing to the generations to come the praises of the Lord; that especially the seed of Abraham his servant, and the children of Jacob his chosen (Psalm cv: 5, 6), may remember his marvellous works in the beginning and progress of the planting of New England, his wonders and the judgments of his mouth; how that God brought a vine into this wilderness; that he cast out the heathen, and planted it; that he made room for it and caused it to take deep root; and it filled the land (Psalm lxxx: 8, 9). And not onely so, but also that he hath guided his people by his strength to his holy habitation and planted them in the mountain of his inheritance in respect of precious Gospel enjoyments: and that as especially God may have the glory of all unto whom it is most due; so also some rays of glory may reach the names of those blessed Saints that were the main instruments and the beginning of this happy enterprise."

It is impossible to read this opening paragraph without an involuntary feeling of religious awe; it breathes the very savour of Gospel antiquity. The sincerity of the author heightens his power of language. The band which to his eyes was a mere party of adventurers gone forth to seek their fortune beyond seas appears to the reader as the germ of a great nation wafted by Providence to a predestined shore.

The author thus continues his narrative of the departure of the first pilgrims:

"So they left that goodly and pleasant city of Leyden, which had been their resting-place for above eleven years; but they knew that they were pilgrims and strangers here below, and looked not much on these things, but lifted up their eyes to Heaven, their dearest country, where God hath prepared for them a city (Heb. xi: 16), and therein quieted their spirits. When they came to Delfs-Haven they found the ship and all things ready; and such of their friends as could not come with them followed after them, and sundry came from Amsterdam to see them shipt, and to take their leaves of them. One night was spent with little sleep with the most, but with friendly entertainment and Christian discourse, and other real expressions of true Christian love. The next day they went on board, and their friends with them, where truly doleful was the sight of that sad and mournful parting, to hear what sighs and sobs and prayers did sound amongst them; what tears did gush from every eye, and pithy speeches pierced each other's heart, that sundry of the Dutch strangers that stood on the Key as spectators could not refrain from tears. But the tide (which stays for no man) calling them away, that were thus loth to depart, their Reverend Pastor falling down on his knees, and they all with him, with watery cheeks commended them with most fervent prayers unto the Lord and his blessing; and then, with mutual embraces and many tears they took their leaves one of another, which proved to be the last leave to many of them."

The emigrants were about one hundred and fifty in number, including the women and the children. Their object was to plant a colony on the shores of the Hudson; but after having been driven about for some time in the Atlantic Ocean, they were forced to land on that arid coast of New England which is now the site of the town of Plymouth. The rock is still shown on which the Pilgrims disembarked.

"But before we pass on," continues our historian, "let the reader with me make a pause and seriously consider this poor people's present condition, the more to be raised up to admiration of God's goodness towards them in their preservation: for being now passed the vast ocean, and a sea of troubles before them in expectation, they had now no friends to welcome them, no inns to entertain or refresh them, no houses, or much less towns to repair unto to seek for succour; and for the season it was winter, and they that know the winters of the country know them to be sharp and violent, subject to cruel and fierce storms, dangerous to travel to known places, much more to search unknown coasts. Besides, what could they see but a hideous and desolate wilderness, full of wilde beasts, and wilde men? and what multitudes of them there were, they then knew not: for which way soever they turned their eyes (save upward to Heaven) they could have but little solace or content in respect of any outward object; for summer being ended, all things stand in appearance with a weather-beaten face, and the whole country full of woods and thickets, represented a wild and savage hew; if they looked behind them, there was the mighty ocean which they had passed, and was now as a main bar or gulph to separate them from all the civil parts of the world."

It must not be imagined that the piety of the Puritans was of a merely speculative kind, or that it took no cognizance of the course of worldly affairs. Puritanism, as I have already remarked, was scarcely less a political than a religious doctrine. No sooner had the emigrants landed on the barren coast described by Nathaniel Morton than it was their first care to constitute a society, by passing the following act:

"IN THE NAME OF GOD. AMEN. We, whose names are underwritten, the loyal subjects of our dread Sovereign Lord King James, &c., &c., Having undertaken for the glory of God, and advancement of the Christian Faith, and the honour of our King and Country, a voyage to plant the first colony in the northern parts of Virginia; Do by these presents solemnly and mutually, in the presence of God and one another, covenant and combine ourselves together into a civil body politick, for our better ordering and preservation, and furtherance of the ends aforesaid: and by virtue hereof do enact, constitute and frame such just and equal laws, ordinances, acts, constitutions, and officers, from time to time, as shall be thought most meet and convenient for the general good of the Colony: unto which we promise all due submission and obedience," etc.

This happened in 1620, and from that time forward the emigration went on. The religious and political passions which ravaged the British Empire during the whole reign of Charles I drove fresh crowds of sectarians every year to the shores of America. In England the stronghold of Puritanism was in the middle classes, and it was from the middle classes that the majority of the emigrants came. The population of New England increased rapidly; and while the hierarchy of rank despotically classed the inhabitants of the mother-country, the colony continued to present the novel spectacle of a community homogeneous in all its parts. A democracy, more perfect than any which antiquity had dreamed of, started in full size and panoply from the midst of an ancient feudal society.

The English Government was not dissatisfied with an emigration which removed the elements of fresh discord and of further revolutions. On the contrary, everything was done to encourage it, and great exertions were made to mitigate the hardships of those who sought a shelter from the rigour of their country's laws on the soil of America. It seemed as if New England was a region given up to the dreams of fancy and the unrestrained experiments of innovators.

The English colonies (and this is one of the main causes of their prosperity) have always enjoyed more internal freedom and more political independence than the colonies of other nations; but this principle of liberty was nowhere more extensively applied than in the States of New England.

It was generally allowed at that period that the territories of the New World belonged to that European nation which had been the first to discover them. Nearly the whole coast of North America thus became a British possession toward the end of the sixteenth century. The means used by the English Government to people these new domains were of several kinds: the King sometimes appointed a governor of his own choice, who ruled a portion of the New World in the name and under the immediate orders of the Crown; this is the colonial system adopted by other countries of Europe. Sometimes grants of certain tracts were made by the Crown to an individual or to a company, in which case all the civil and political power fell into the hands of one or more persons, who, under the inspection and control of the Crown, sold the lands and governed the inhabitants. Lastly, a third system consisted in allowing a certain number of emigrants to constitute a political society under the protection of the mother-country, and to govern themselves in whatever was not contrary to her laws. This mode of colonization, so remarkably favourable to liberty, was only adopted in New England.

In 1628 a charter of this kind was granted by Charles I to the emigrants who went to form the colony of Massachusetts. But, in general, charters were not given to the colonies of New England till they had acquired a certain existence. Plymouth, Providence, New Haven, the State of Connecticut, and that of Rhode Island were founded without the co-operation and almost without the knowledge of the mother-country. The new settlers did not derive their incorporation from the seat of the empire, although they did not deny its supremacy; they constituted a society of their own accord, and it was not till thirty or forty years afterward, under Charles II, that their existence was legally recognised by a royal charter.

This frequently renders it difficult to detect the link which connected the emigrants with the land of their forefathers in studying the earliest historical and legislative records of New England. They exercised the rights of sovereignty; they named their magistrates, concluded peace or declared war, made police regulations, and enacted laws as if their allegiance was due only to God. Nothing can be more curious, and at the same time more instructive, than the legislation of that period; it is there that the solution of the great social problem which the United States now present to the world is to be found.

Among these documents we shall notice, as especially characteristic, the code of laws promulgated by the little State of Connecticut in 1650. The legislators of Connecticut begin with the penal laws, and, strange to say, they borrow their provisions from the text of Holy Writ. "Whosoever shall worship any other God than the Lord," says the preamble of the Code, "shall surely be put to death." This is followed by ten or twelve enactments of the same kind, copied verbatim from the books of Exodus, Leviticus, and Deuteronomy. Blasphemy, sorcery, adultery, and rape were punished with death; an outrage offered by a son to his parents was to be expiated by the same penalty. The legislation of a rude and half-civilized people was thus applied to an enlightened and moral community. The consequence was that the punishment of death was never more frequently prescribed by the statute, and never more rarely enforced toward the guilty.

The chief care of the legislators, in this body of penal laws, was the maintenance of orderly conduct and good morals in the community: they constantly invaded the domain of conscience, and there was scarcely a sin which was not subject to magisterial censure. The reader is aware of the rigour with which these laws punished rape and adultery; intercourse between unmarried persons was likewise severely repressed. The judge was empowered to inflict a pecuniary penalty, a whipping, or marriage on the misdemeanants; and if the records of the old courts of New Haven may be believed, prosecutions of this kind were not infrequent. We find a sentence bearing date the 1st of May, 1660, inflicting a fine and reprimand on a young woman who was accused of using improper language, and of allowing herself to be kissed. The Code of 1650 abounds in preventive measures. It punishes idleness and drunkenness with severity. Innkeepers are forbidden to furnish more than a certain quantity of liquor to each consumer; and simple lying, whenever it may be injurious, is checked by a fine or a flogging. In other places, the legislator, entirely forgetting the great principles of religious toleration which he had himself upheld in Europe, renders attendance on divine service compulsory, and goes so far as to visit with severe punishment, and even with death, the Christians who chose to worship God according to a ritual differing from his own. Sometimes, indeed, the zeal of his enactments induces him to descend to the most frivolous particulars: thus a law is to be found in the same Code which prohibits the use of tobacco. It must not be forgotten that these fantastical and vexatious laws were not imposed by authority, but that they were freely voted by all the persons interested, and that the manners of the community were even more austere and more puritanical than the laws. In 1649 a solemn association was formed in Boston to check the worldly luxury of long hair.

These errors are no doubt discreditable to human reason; they attest the inferiority of our nature, which is incapable of laying firm hold upon what is true and just, and is often reduced to the alternative of two excesses. In strict connection with this penal legislation, which bears such striking marks of a narrow sectarian spirit, and of those religious passions which had been warmed by persecution and were still fermenting among the people, a body of political laws is to be found, which, though written two hundred years ago, is still ahead of the liberties of our age. The general principles which are the groundwork of modern constitutions—principles which were imperfectly known in Europe, and not completely triumphant even in Great Britain, in the seventeenth century—were all recognised and determined by the laws of New England: the intervention of the people in public affairs, the free voting of taxes, the responsibility of authorities, personal liberty, and trial by jury, were all positively established without discussion. From these fruitful principles consequences have been derived and applications have been made such as no nation in Europe has yet ventured to attempt.

In Connecticut the electoral body consisted, from its origin, of the whole number of citizens; and this is readily to be understood, when we recollect that this people enjoyed an almost perfect equality of fortune, and a still greater uniformity of opinions. In Connecticut, at this period, all the executive functionaries were elected, including the Governor of the State. The citizens above the age of sixteen were obliged to bear arms; they formed a national militia, which appointed its own officers, and was to hold itself at all times in readiness to march for the defence of the country.

In the laws of Connecticut, as well as in all those of New England, we find the germ and gradual development of that township independence which is the life and mainspring of American liberty at the present day. The political existence of the majority of the nations of Europe commenced in the superior ranks of society, and was gradually and imperfectly communicated to the different members of the social body. In America, on the other hand, it may be said that the township was organized before the county, the county before the State, the State before the Union. In New England townships were completely and definitely constituted as early as 1650. The independence of the township was the nucleus round which the local interests, passions, rights, and duties collected and clung. It gave scope to the activity of a real political life most thoroughly democratic and republican. The colonies still recognised the supremacy of the mother-country; monarchy was still the law of the State; but the republic was already established in every township. The towns named their own magistrates of every kind, rated themselves, and levied their own taxes. In the parish of New England the law of representation was not adopted, but the affairs of the community were discussed, as at Athens, in the market-place, by a general assembly of the citizens.

In studying the laws which were promulgated in this first era of the American republics, it is impossible not to be struck by the remarkable acquaintance with the science of government and the advanced theory of legislation which they display. The ideas there formed of the duties of society toward its members are evidently much loftier and more comprehensive than those of the European legislators at that time: obligations were there imposed which were elsewhere slighted. In the States of New England, from the first, the condition of the poor was provided for; strict measures were taken for the maintenance of roads, and surveyors were appointed to attend to them; registers were established in every parish, in which the results of public deliberations, and the births, deaths, and marriages of the citizens were entered; clerks were directed to keep these registers; officers were charged with the administration of vacant inheritances, and with the arbitration of litigated landmarks; and many others were created whose chief functions were the maintenance of public order in the community. The law enters into a thousand useful provisions for a number of social wants which are at present very inadequately felt in France.

But it is by the attention it pays to Public Education that the original character of American civilization is at once placed in the clearest light. "It being," says the law, "one chief project of Satan to keep men from the knowledge of the Scripture by persuading from the use of tongues, to the end that learning may not be buried in the graves of our forefathers, in church and commonwealth, the Lord assisting our endeavours...." Here follow clauses establishing schools in every township, and obliging the inhabitants, under pain of heavy fines, to support them. Schools of a superior kind were founded in the same manner in the more populous districts. The municipal authorities were bound to enforce the sending of children to school by their parents; they were empowered to inflict fines upon all who refused compliance; and in cases of continued resistance society assumed the place of the parent, took possession of the child, and deprived the father of those natural rights which he used to so bad a purpose. The reader will undoubtedly have remarked the preamble of these enactments: in America religion is the road to knowledge, and the observance of the divine laws leads man to civil freedom.

If, after having cast a rapid glance over the state of American society in 1650, we turn to the condition of Europe, and more especially to that of the Continent, at the same period, we can not fail to be struck with astonishment. On the continent of Europe, at the beginning of the seventeenth century, absolute monarchy had everywhere triumphed over the ruins of the oligarchical and feudal liberties of the Middle Ages. Never were the notions of right more completely confounded than in the midst of the splendour and literature of Europe; never was there less political activity among the people; never were the principles of true freedom less widely circulated; and at that very time those principles, which were scorned or unknown by the nations of Europe, were proclaimed in the deserts of the New World, and were accepted as the future creed of a great people. The boldest theories of the human reason were put into practice by a community so humble that not a statesman condescended to attend to it; and a legislation without a precedent was produced offhand by the imagination of the citizens. In the bosom of this obscure democracy, which had as yet brought forth neither generals, nor philosophers, nor authors, a man might stand up in the face of a free people and pronounce the following fine definition of liberty:

"Nor would I have you to mistake in the point of your own liberty. There is a liberty of a corrupt nature which is effected both by men and beasts to do what they list, and this liberty is inconsistent with authority, impatient of all restraint; by this liberty 'sumus omnes deteriores': 'tis the grand enemy of truth and peace, and all the ordinances of God are bent against it. But there is a civil, a moral, a federal liberty which is the proper end and object of authority; it is a liberty for that only which is just and good: for this liberty you are to stand with the hazard of your very lives, and whatsoever crosses it is not authority, but a distemper thereof. This liberty is maintained in a way of subjection to authority; and the authority set over you will, in all administrations for your good, be quietly submitted unto by all but such as have a disposition to shake off the yoke and lose their true liberty, by their murmuring at the honour and power of authority."

The remarks I have made will suffice to display the character of Anglo-American civilization in its true light. It is the result (and this should be constantly present to the mind) of two distinct elements, which in other places have been in frequent hostility, but which in America have been admirably incorporated and combined with one another. I allude to the spirit of religion and the spirit of Liberty.

The settlers of New England were at the same time ardent sectarians and daring innovators. Narrow as the limits of some of their religious opinions were, they were entirely free from political prejudices. Hence arose two tendencies, distinct but not opposite, which are constantly discernible in the manners as well as in the laws of the country.

It might be imagined that men who sacrificed their friends, their family, and their native land to a religious conviction were absorbed in the pursuit of the intellectual advantages which they purchased at so dear a rate. The energy, however, with which they strove for the acquirement of wealth, moral enjoyment, and the comforts as well as liberties of the world, is scarcely inferior to that with which they devoted themselves to Heaven.

Political principles and all human laws and institutions were moulded and altered at their pleasure; the barriers of the society in which they were born were broken down before them; the old principles which had governed the world for ages were no more; a path without a term and a field without an horizon were opened to the exploring and ardent curiosity of man: but at the limits of the political world he checks his researches, he discreetly lays aside the use of his most formidable faculties, he no longer consents to doubt or to innovate, but carefully abstaining from raising the curtain of the sanctuary, he yields with submissive respect to truths which he will not discuss. Thus, in the moral world everything is classed, adapted, decided, and foreseen; in the political world everything is agitated, uncertain, and disputed: in the one is a passive, though a voluntary, obedience; in the other an independence scornful of experience and jealous of authority.

These two tendencies, apparently so discrepant, are far from conflicting; they advance together, and mutually support each other. Religion perceives that civil liberty affords a noble exercise to the faculties of man, and that the political world is a field prepared by the Creator for the efforts of the intelligence. Contented with the freedom and the power which it enjoys in its own sphere, and with the place which it occupies, the empire of religion is never more surely established than when it reigns in the hearts of men unsupported by aught beside its native strength. Religion is no less the companion of liberty in all its battles and its triumphs; the cradle of its infancy, and the divine source of its claims. The safeguard of morality is religion, and morality is the best security of law and the surest pledge of freedom.

The reader is cautioned not to draw too general or too absolute an inference from what has been said. The social condition, the religion, and the manners of the first emigrants undoubtedly exercised an immense influence on the destiny of their new country. Nevertheless they were not in a situation to found a state of things solely dependent on themselves: no man can entirely shake off the influence of the past, and the settlers, intentionally or involuntarily, mingled habits and notions derived from their education and from the traditions of their country with those habits and notions which were exclusively their own. To form a judgment on the Anglo-Americans of the present day it is therefore necessary to distinguish what is of Puritanical and what is of English origin.

Laws and customs are frequently to be met with in the United States which contrast strongly with all that surrounds them. These laws seem to be drawn up in a spirit contrary to the prevailing tenor of the American legislation; and these customs are no less opposed to the tone of society. If the English colonies had been founded in an age of darkness, or if their origin was already lost in the lapse of years, the problem would be insoluble.

I shall quote a single example to illustrate what I advance. The civil and criminal procedure of the Americans has only two means of action—committal and bail. The first measure taken by the magistrate is to exact security from the defendant, or, in case of refusal, to incarcerate him: the ground of the accusation and the importance of the charges against him are then discussed. It is evident that a legislation of this kind is hostile to the poor man, and favourable only to the rich. The poor man has not always a security to produce, even in a civil cause; and if he is obliged to wait for justice in prison, he is speedily reduced to distress. The wealthy individual, on the contrary, always escapes imprisonment in civil causes; nay, more, he may readily elude the punishment which awaits him for a delinquency by breaking his bail. So that all the penalties of the law are, for him, reducible to fines. Nothing can be more aristocratic than this system of legislation. Yet in America it is the poor who make the law, and they usually reserve the greatest social advantages to themselves. The explanation of the phenomenon is to be found in England; the laws of which I speak are English, and the Americans have retained them, however repugnant they may be to the tenor of their legislation and the mass of their ideas. Next to its habits, the thing which a nation is least apt to change is its civil legislation. Civil laws are only familiarly known to legal men, whose direct interest it is to maintain them as they are, whether good or bad, simply because they themselves are acquainted with them. The body of the nation is scarcely acquainted with them; it merely perceives their action in particular cases; but it has some difficulty in seizing their tendency, and obeys them without premeditation. I have quoted one instance where it would have been easy to adduce a great number of others. The surface of American society is, if I may use the expression, covered with a layer of democracy, from beneath which the old aristocratic colours sometimes peep.

The Declaration of Independence

Carl L. Becker

From what source does the ethical basis of political power derive? All governments seek to provide their political power with authority, that is, to make it legitimate. Today, most nations have a government which contends that its authority rests on the consent of the governed. To trace how we have reached such a condition would require a review of our entire Western culture. It is sufficient at this point merely to say that the concept of government by authority of the governed had its origins in the social contract theory, most ably presented in the writing of Thomas Hobbes, John Locke, and Jean Jacques Rousseau. The concept of a social contract starts from the premise that man must logically, if not historically, have lived in a "state of nature," i.e., a state of co-existence with other humans but without rules imposed by any external communal authority. For various reasons, such a life was unpleasant and unsafe and men saw advantages to creating a community. They met and established a government, each giving up some of his freedom to the sovereign and in return receiving some benefits, most notably protection. What happens, however, when this sovereign, or government, which was established by consent of the governed, ceases to function for the benefit of the vast majority of the citizenry? Can such a government be overthrown? Do men have the right of rebellion? John Locke (1632-1704), a theorist closely read on this side of the Atlantic, argued that men (aristocrats) have the right to rebel, but it must be a last resort. When governments cease to provide those rights and protections for which they were constituted, the regimes may be changed. The Declaration of Independence, written by Thomas Jefferson, was an affirmation of the social contract theory with reliance on many of the ideas found in Locke's Second Treatise on Government. *The purpose of the Declaration was to provide a moral and legal justification for the rebellion embarked upon by the leaders of the colonies. Carl L. Becker (1873-1945), a noted historian, offers some background*

Reprinted by permission of the publishers, from Carl L. Becker, *The Declaration of Independence: A Study of the History of Ideas* (New York: Harcourt, Brace and Company, copyright 1922), pp. 3-23. Abridged by the editors.

on the tactical considerations which influenced Jefferson and subsequently the signers of the Declaration.

It is often forgotten that the document which we know as the Declaration of Independence is not the official act by which the Continental Congress voted in favor of separation from Great Britain. June 7, 1776, Richard Henry Lee, on behalf of the Virginia delegation, submitted to the Continental Congress three resolutions, of which the first declared that "these United Colonies are, and of right ought to be, free and independent States, that they are absolved from all allegiance to the British Crown, and that all political connection between them and the State of Great Britain is, and ought to be, totally dissolved." This resolution, which may conveniently be called the Resolution of Independence, was finally voted by the Continental Congress on the 2 of July, 1776. Strictly speaking, this was the official declaration of independence; and if we were a nation of antiquaries we should no doubt find an incongruity in celebrating the anniversary of our independence on the 4 of July.

Meanwhile, on the 10 of June, three days after Richard Henry Lee introduced the Resolution of Independence, it was voted to appoint a committee to "prepare a declaration to the effect of the said first resolution." The committee, appointed on the following day, consisted of Thomas Jefferson, John Adams, Benjamin Franklin, Roger Sherman, and Robert R. Livingston. On the 28 of June, the committee reported to Congress the draft of a declaration which, with modifications, was finally agreed to by Congress on the 4 of July. This is the document which is popularly known as the Declaration of Independence.

This title is not, strictly speaking, the official title of the document in question. The document never knew itself, in any of its various forms, by that name. Jefferson, in making the first draft, gave it the following title: *A Declaration by the Representatives of the United States of America, in General Congress assembled.* This title was retained in all the copies of the Declaration, except the engrossed parchment copy. On the 19 of July, 1776, Congress voted that the Declaration be engrossed on parchment, "with the title and stile of *The unanimous Declaration of the thirteen united States of America.*" It is true, the Declaration, in the form adopted by Congress, incorporates in its final paragraph the resolution of July 2; and so the Declaration may be said to be a declaration of independence, inasmuch as in it Congress once more declared what it had already declared two days before. Nevertheless, the primary purpose of the Declaration was not to declare independence, but to proclaim to the world the *reasons* for declaring independence. It was intended as a formal justification of an act already accomplished.

The purpose of the Declaration is set forth in the first paragraph — a striking sentence, in which simplicity of statement is somehow combined with an urbane solemnity of manner in such a way as to give that felicitous, haunting cadence which is the peculiar quality of Jefferson's best writing.

When in the course of human events, it becomes necessary for one people to dissolve the political bands, which have connected them with another, and to assume, among the powers of the earth, the separate and equal station, to which the laws of nature and of nature's God entitle them a decent respect to the Opinions of mankind requires that they should declare the causes which impel them to the separation.

The ostensible purpose of the Declaration was, therefore, to lay before the world the causes which impelled the colonies to separate from Great Britain. We do in fact find, in the Declaration, a list or catalogue of acts, attributed to the king of Great Britain, and alleged to have been done by him with the deliberate purpose of establishing over the colonies "an absolute tyranny." These "causes" which the Declaration sets forth are not quite the same as those which a careful student of history, seeking the antecedents of the Revolution, would set forth. The reason is that the framers of the Declaration were not writing history, but making it. They were seeking to convince the world that they were justified in doing what they had done; and so their statement of "causes" is not the bare record of what the king had done, but rather a presentation of his acts in general terms, and in the form of an indictment intended to clear the colonists of all responsibility and to throw all the blame on the king. From whatever causes, the colonists were in rebellion against established and long recognized political authority. The Declaration was not primarily concerned with the causes of this rebellion; its primary purpose was to present those causes in such a way as to furnish a moral and legal justification for that rebellion. The Declaration was essentially an attempt to prove that rebellion was not the proper word for what they were doing.

Rebellion against established authority is always a serious matter. In that day kings were commonly claiming to rule by divine right, and according to this notion there could be no 'right' of rebellion. The framers of the Declaration knew very well that however long their list of grievances against the king of Great Britain might be, and however oppressive they might make out his acts to have been, something more would be required to prove to the world that in separating from Great Britain they were not really engaged in rebellion against a rightful authority. What they needed, in addition to many specific grievances against their particular king, was a fundamental presupposition against kings in general. What they needed was a theory of government that provided a place for rebellion, that made it respectable, and even meritorious under certain circumstances.

Before enumerating the specific grievances against the king of Great Britain, Jefferson therefore proceeded to formulate a general political philosophy — a philosophy upon which the case of the colonies could solidly rest. This philosophy, which affirms the right of a people to establish and to overturn its own government, is formulated in the first part of the second paragraph of the Declaration.

We hold these truths to be self-evident, That all men are created equal, that they are endowed by their creator with certain unalienable rights; that among these are life, liberty & the pursuit of happiness; that to secure these rights governments are instituted among men, deriving their just powers from the consent of the governed; that whenever any form of government becomes destructive of these ends, it is the right of the people to alter or to abolish it, and to institute new government, laying its foundation on such principles and organizing its powers in such form, as to them shall seem most likely to effect their safety and happiness.

This is a frank assertion of the right of revolution, whenever "the people" are convinced that the existing government has become destructive of the ends for which all government is instituted among men. Many difficulties lie concealed in the words "the people"; but it is sufficient to note in passing that a large part of the people in the colonies, not being convinced that the British government had as yet become destructive of their liberties, or for some other reason, were either indifferently or strongly opposed to separation. Yet the leaders of the Revolution, being now committed to independence, found it politically expedient to act on the assumption that the opposition was negligible. Very naturally, therefore, Jefferson endeavored to make it appear that the people of the colonies were thoroughly united in wishing to 'institute new government' in place of the government of the king.

Accordingly, having affirmed the right of revolution under certain conditions, the Declaration goes on to state that as a matter of fact these conditions prevail in the colonies, and that 'the people' have submitted to them as long as it is humanly possible to do.

Prudence, indeed, will dictate, that governments long established should not be changed for light and transient causes; and accordingly all experience hath shewn that mankind are more disposed to suffer, while evils are sufferable than to right themselves by abolishing the forms, to which they are accustomed. But when a long train of abuses & usurpations pursuing invariably the same object evinces a design to reduce them under absolute despotism, it is their right, it is their duty to throw off such government and to provide new guards for their future security. — Such has been the patient sufferance of these colonies, and such is now the necessity, which constrains them to alter their former systems of government. The history of the present king of great Britain is a history of repeated injuries and usurpations, all having in direct object the establishment of an absolute tyranny over these states. To prove this let facts be submitted to a candid world.

So at last we come to the 'facts,' the list or catalogue of oppressive measures, the 'repeated injuries and usurpations' of the king of Great Britain.

He has refused his assent to laws the most wholesome and necessary for the public good.

He has forbidden his governors to pass laws of immediate and pressing importance, unless suspended in their operation until his assent should be obtained, and when so suspended, he has utterly neglected to attend to them.

He has refused to pass other laws for the accommodation of large districts of people, unless those people would relinquish the right of representation in the legislature, a right inestimable to them and formidable to tyrants only.

He has called together legislative bodies at places unusual, uncomfortable and distant from the depository of their public records, for the sole purpose of fatiguing them into compliance with his measures.

He has dissolved representative houses repeatedly for opposing with manly firmness his invasions on the rights of the people.

He has refused for a long time, after such dissolutions, to cause others to be elected; whereby the legislative powers incapable of annihilation have returned to the people at large for their exercise; the state remaining in the meantime exposed to all the dangers of invasion from without and convulsions within.

He has endeavored to prevent the population of these states; for that purpose obstructing the laws for naturalization of foreigners; refusing to pass others to encourage their migrations hither & raising the conditions of new appropriations of lands.

He has obstructed the administration of Justice by refusing his assent to laws for establishing judiciary powers.

He has made judges dependent on his will alone for the tenure of their offices and the amount and payment of their salaries.

He has erected a multitude of new offices, and sent hither swarms of officers to harass our people and eat out their substance.

He has kept among us in times of peace standing armies, without the consent of our legislatures.

He has affected to render the military independent of & superior to the civil power.

He has combined with others to subject us to a jurisdiction foreign to our constitution and unacknowledged by our laws, giving his assent to their acts of pretended legislation

    for quartering large bodies of troops among us;

    for protecting them by a mock trial from punishment for any murders, which they should commit on the inhabitants of these states.

    for cutting off our trade with all parts of the world;

    for imposing taxes on us without our consent;

    for depriving us in many cases of the benefits of trial by jury;

    for transporting us beyond seas to be tried for pretended offences;

    for abolishing the free system of english laws in a neighboring province, establishing therein an arbitrary government and enlarging its boundaries, so as to render it at once an example & fit instrument for introducing the same absolute rule into these colonies.

for taking away our charters, abolishing our most valuable laws and altering fundamentally the forms of our governments.

for suspending our own legislatures and declaring themselves invested with power to legislate for us in all cases whatsoever.

He has abdicated government here by declaring us out of his protection and waging war against us.

He has plundered our seas, ravaged our coasts burnt our towns & destroyed the lives of our people.

He is at this time transporting large armies of foreign mercenaries to compleat the works of death, desolation and tyranny, already begun with circumstances of cruelty and perfidy scarcely paralleled in the most barbarous ages and totally unworthy the head of a civilized nation.

He has constrained our fellow citizens taken captive on the high seas to bear arms against their country, to become the executioners of their friends and brethren or to fall themselves by their hands.

He has excited domestic insurrections amongst us and has endeavoured to bring on the inhabitants of our frontiers the merciless indian savages, whose known rule of warfare is an undistinguished destruction of all ages, sexes and conditions.

Such were the 'facts' submitted to a candid world. It is important to note that they were not submitted as being, in themselves, a justification for rebellion; they were submitted to prove that the deliberate and persistent purpose of the king was to establish an 'absolute tyranny' over the colonies. A most significant thing about this long list of the king's alleged actions is the assumption that in each case the king acted with deliberate intention and from a bad motive. It is the bad general purpose of the king, rather than his bad particular acts, that makes the indictment so effective. And this effect is enhanced by the form in which the 'facts' are presented — the steady, laborious piling up of 'facts,' the monotonous enumeration, without comment, of one bad action after another.

How could a candid world deny that the colonies were rightly absolved from allegiance to so malevolent a will!

Nevertheless, in spite of multiplied and long continued grievances, the colonies had not rushed into rebellion.

In every stage of these oppressions we have petitioned for redress in the most humble terms: Our repeated petitions have been answered only by repeated injury. A prince whose character is thus marked by every act, which may define a tyrant, is unfit to be the ruler of a free people.

Nor have we been wanting in attentions to our british brethren. We have warned them from time to time of attempts by their legislature to extend an unwarrantable jurisdiction over us. We have reminded them of the circumstances of our emigration and settlement here. We have appealed to their native justice and magnanimity and we have conjured them by the ties of our common kindred to disavow these usurpations, which would inevitably interrupt our connections & correspondence. They too have been deaf to the voice of justice & consanguinity. We must therefore acquiesce in the necessity, which denounces our separation, and hold them, as we hold the rest of mankind, enemies in war, in peace friends.

Thus, the framers of the Declaration presented their case. Having formulated a philosophy of government which made revolution right under certain conditions, they endeavored to show that these conditions prevailed in the colonies, not on account of anything which the people of the colonies had done, or had left undone, but solely on account of the deliberate and malevolent purpose of their king to establish over them an 'absolute tyranny.' The people of the colonies must, accordingly (such is the implication), either throw off the yoke or submit to be slaves. As between these alternatives, there could be but one choice for men accustomed to freedom.

We therefore the representatives of the united States of America in general Congress assembled appealing to the supreme judge of the world for the rectitude of our intentions do in the name and by authority of the good people of these colonies solemnly publish and declare—

That these united colonies are and of right ought to be free and independent States; that they are absolved from all allegiance to the british Crown, and that all political connection between them and the state of great Britain is & ought to be totally dissolved; and that as free & independent states they have full power to levy war, conclude peace, contract alliances, establish commerce, and to do all other acts & things, which independent states may of right do. And for the support of this declaration, with a firm reliance on the protection of divine providence, we mutually pledge to each other our lives, our fortunes & our sacred honor.

From the foregoing analysis it is clear that, apart from the preamble and the conclusion, the Declaration consists of two parts, apparently quite distinct. The first part is contained in the second paragraph. In these few lines the Declaration formulates, in general terms, a democratic political philosophy. The second and much longer part of the Declaration enumerates the specific grievances against the king of Great Britain, which, ostensibly, are presented as the historical causes of the Revolution. These two parts of the Declaration, apparently quite distinct, are nevertheless intimately related in the logic and purpose of the Declaration. Superficially, the Declaration seems chiefly concerned with the causes of the Revolution, with the specific grievances; but in reality it is chiefly, one might say solely, concerned with a theory of government — with a theory of government in general, and a theory of the British empire in particular. The theory of government in general is explicitly formulated; the theory of the British empire is not explicitly formulated but is implicitly taken for granted; and the second part of the Declaration was carefully phrased so that no assertion or implication might appear as a contradiction or a denial of the assumed theory.

The Declaration thus becomes interesting for what it omits as well as for what it includes. For example, it does not, in its final form, contain the word 'Parliament' — a most significant omission, considering that the controversy of the preceding decade was occasioned, not by the acts of the king, who plays the leading part in the Declaration, but by the acts of the British Parliament. In all the controversy leading up to the Revolution the thing chiefly debated was the authority of the British Parliament. What is the nature, and what precisely are the limits, of the authority of the British Parliament over the colonies? This question was in fact the central issue. Nevertheless, the Declaration does not mention the British Parliament.

So striking an omission must have been intentional. It was of course impossible to make out a list of grievances against Great Britain without referring to such acts as the Stamp Act, the Declaratory Act, the Boston Port Bill, and many other legislative measures; and the framers of the Declaration, when they brought these measures into the indictment, had accordingly to resort to circumlocution in order to avoid naming the Parliament that passed them. There are, in the Declaration, two such veiled references to the Parliament. The first is this: "He [the king] has combined with others to subject us to a jurisdiction foreign to our constitution and unacknowledged by our laws, giving his assent to their pretended acts of legislation." These 'others' who have passed pretended acts of legislation are the members of the British Parliament. The second reference is this: "We have warned them [our british brethren] ... of attempts by their legislature to extend an unwarrantable jurisdiction over us." Obviously, the framers of the Declaration make it a point of principle not on any account to pronounce the word Parliament. "Of course," we seem to hear them saying, "our British brethren have their legislature, as we have ours. But with their legislature we have nothing to do, God forbid! The very name of the thing escapes us! At least, let us pretend so."

Another significant omission is the term 'rights of British subjects.' Throughout the controversy the colonists had commonly protested against parliamentary taxation precisely on the ground that they possessed the rights of British subjects. They said that the British Parliament could not constitutionally tax British subjects without their consent, and that British subjects in the colonies were not, and in the nature of the case could not well be, represented in the British Parliament. For ten years the colonists had made the 'rights of British subjects' the very foundation of their case. Yet this is just what the framers of the Declaration carefully refrain from doing: the term 'rights of British subjects' does not appear in the Declaration. Trial by jury is mentioned, but not as a right of British subjects. 'The system of free English laws' is mentioned, but it is not stated, or even implied, that the validity of these laws arises from the fact that they are English laws. Nowhere does the Declaration say, and nowhere does it imply, that the acts of the king are intolerable because they violate the rights of British subjects.

The framers of the Declaration refrained from mentioning Parliament and the 'rights of British subjects' for the same reason that they charged all their grievances against the king alone. Being now committed to independence, the position of the colonies could not be simply or convincingly presented from the point of view of the rights of British subjects. To have said: 'We hold this truth to be self-evident, that it is a right of British subjects not to be taxed except by their own consent,' would have made no great appeal to mankind, since mankind in general could not be supposed to be vitally interested in the rights of British subjects, or much disposed to regard them as axioms in political speculation. Separation from Great Britain was therefore justified on more general grounds, on the ground of the natural rights of man; and in order to simplify the issue, in order to make it appear that the rights of man had been undeniably and flagrantly violated, it was expedient that these rights should seem to be as little as possible limited or obscured by the positive and legal obligations that were admittedly binding upon British subjects. To place the Resolution of Independence in the best light possible, it was convenient to assume that the connection between the colonies and Great Britain had never been a very close connection, never, strictly speaking, a connection binding in positive law, but only a connection voluntarily entered into by a free people. On this ground the doctrine of the rights of man would have a free field and no competitors.

The specific grievances enumerated in the Declaration were accordingly presented from the point of view of a carefully considered and resolutely held constitutional theory of the British empire. The essence of this theory, nowhere explicitly formulated in the Declaration, but throughout implicitly taken for granted, is that the colonies became parts of the empire by their own voluntary act, and remained parts of it solely by virtue of a compact subsisting between them and the king. Their rights were those of all men, of every free people; their obligations such as a free people might incur by professing allegiance to the personal head of the empire. On this theory, both the Parliament and the rights of British subjects could be ignored as irrelevant to the issue.

The specific grievances complained of in the Declaration are grievances no longer. As concrete issues they are happily dead. But the way in which the men of those days conceived of these concrete issues, the intellectual preconceptions, illusions if you like, which were born of their hopes and fears, and which in turn shaped their conduct — these make the Declaration always interesting and worthy of study. It is not my intention to search out those particular measures of the British government which served in the mind of Jefferson and his friends to validate each particular charge against the king. This could indeed be done, and has been sufficiently done already; but the truth is that when one has found the particular act to which in each case the particular charge was intended to refer, one is likely to think the poor king less malevolently guilty than he is made out to be. Yet that Jefferson and his friends, honest and good men enough, and more intelligent than most, were convinced that the Declaration was a true bill, we need not doubt. How this could be may be understood, a little at least, by seeing how the pressure of circumstances enabled the men of those days to accept as true their general philosophy of human rights and their particular theory of the British empire.

Democracy and the American Revolution

Merrill Jensen

There is no one official "history" of the United States. Rather, there are nearly as many histories of America as there are American historians. This is not to suggest, however, that the study of our history is a chaotic jumble of individual views unrelated to one another. Certain interpretations of events or periods gain wide acceptance and a "school of thought" is established. One of the most interesting and important debates in American scholarly circles is over the nature of the American Revolution. Was it primarily a social revolution on the order of the French and Russian Revolutions, albeit less bloody? Or, was it really a constitutional revolution in which the conflict was over ideas of how best to govern? The leaders of the Revolution wrote as though they were waging a constitutional revolution and the first generation historians were in agreement. Many historians at the turn of the century, however, collectively labeled "progressives," were of the opinion that our Revolution was fundamentally a social class uprising with the political arguments uttered at the time considered contrived, propaganda, designed to justify a revolution whose sources lay elsewhere. A reaction to the social-class orientation of the "progressives" began in the 1930's and gained momentum until by the 1960's the "revisionists" had achieved intellectual ascendancy. The "revisionist" view is that the evidence supports the argument that the Revolution was fought for the reasons the leaders gave, constitutional freedom. It was a revolution over ideas, not economics. Merrill Jensen argues that the Revolution was basically a democratic social movement with strong economic overtones, not so much in its origins as in its results. His views, then, are representative of the historians who follow a sophisticated version of the earlier "progressive" approach to the Revolution.

The historian who ventures to talk about democracy in early America is in danger because there are almost as many

Reprinted by permission of the author and publisher from Merrill Jensen, "Democracy and the American Revolution," *Huntington Library Quarterly,* 20 (1956-57), 321-341.

opinions as there are writers on the subject. The Puritans have been pictured as the founders of American democracy, and it is vigorously denied that they had anything to do with it. Some have seen in Roger Williams the father of American democracy, and others have denied that he was a democrat, whatever his putative progeny may be. The conflict is equally obvious when it comes to the American Revolution, and the problems of solution are far more complex than they are for the seventeenth century. The difficulty is compounded, for all too often men's emotions seem to become involved.

It is sometimes suggested that we avoid the use of the word "democracy" when discussing the seventeenth and eighteenth centuries. It seems to me that this is a flat evasion of the problem, for the Americans of those centuries used the word and they meant something by it. Our task, then, is not to avoid the issue but to try to understand what they meant, and understand what they meant in the context of the times in which they lived. What we must not do is to measure the seventeenth and eighteenth centuries in terms of our own assumptions about what democracy is or should be. This is all the more important since many of us do not seem to be too clear about our assumptions, even for the century in which we live.

A number of years ago I took the position that "in spite of the paradoxes involved one may still maintain that the Revolution was essentially, though relatively, a democratic movement within the thirteen American colonies, and that its significance for the political and constitutional history of the United States lay in its tendency to elevate the political and economic status of the majority of the people." And then, with a somewhat rhetorical flourish which I have sometimes regretted but have not as yet withdrawn, I went on to say that "the Articles of Confederation were the constitutional expression of this movement and the embodiment in governmental form of the philosophy of the Declaration of Independence."[1] One thing can be said for this statement at least: reviewers read it and quoted it, some with raised eyebrows, and some with approval, whether or not they said anything at all about the rest of the book.

During most of the present century historians have assumed that democracy was involved somehow or other in the American Revolution. They have assumed also that there were conditions within the American colonies that were not satisfactory to at least some of the American people. The causes of internal discontent were various, ranging all the way from religious to economic differences. The discontent was of such intensity that in certain colonies it led to explosive outbreaks in the 1760's such as the Regulator movements in the Carolinas, the Paxton Boys' uprising in Pennsylvania, and the tenant farmer revolt in New York, outbreaks that were suppressed by the armed forces of the colonial governments and with the help of British power.

Most historians have agreed also that the individual colonies were controlled politically by relatively small groups of men in each of them, allied by family, or economic or political interests, or by some combination of these. The colonial aristocracies owed their position to many things: to their wealth and ability, to their family connections and political allies, and to the British government which appointed them to office. As opposed to Britain, they had won virtual self-government for the colonies by 1763. Yet in every colony they were a minority who managed to maintain internal control through property qualifications for the suffrage, especially effective in the growing towns, and through refusal or failure to grant representation in any way proportional to the population of the rapidly growing frontier areas. Probably more important than either of these was the fact that in most colonies the aristocracies manned the upper houses of the legislatures, the supreme courts, and other important posts—all by royal appointment. Beyond this, their control extended down through the county court system, even in Massachusetts. In short, colonial political society was not democratic in operation despite the elective lower houses and the self-government which had been won from Great Britain.[2]

This is a brief but, I think, fair summary of a widely held point of view concerning the political actualities at the beginning of the revolutionary era.

This view has been challenged recently. A writer on Massachusetts declared that "as far as Massachusetts is concerned, colonial society and the American Revolution must be interpreted in terms something very close to a complete democracy with the exception of British restraints." It was not controlled by a wealthy aristocracy. There was little inequality of representation, and property was so widely held that virtually every adult male could vote.[3] The assumption that Massachusetts was an idyllic democracy, united in the fight against British tyranny, will be somewhat surprising to those who have read the letters of Francis Bernard and the diary of John Adams, not to mention the history of Thomas Hutchinson, and, I suspect, would be even more surprising to those gentlemen as well. Elsewhere, this writer has implied that what was true for Massachusetts was probably true for other colonies and for the United States after the Revolution.[4]

On the other hand it is asserted that democracy had nothing to do with the Revolution. Such an assertion made in connection with Pennsylvania is a little startling, for ever since C. H. Lincoln's work of more than a half century ago, down to the present, it has been held that there was a democratic movement in Pennsylvania during the revolutionary era. Not so, says a reviewer of the most recent study. He declares that "the attribution of democratic motivations and ideas to eighteenth century colonists is a common fault among many historians of the colonial period. . . ." He argues that the struggle in Pennsylvania before 1776 was one between "radical and conservative variants of whiggism," which he defines as one between "those who held privilege most dear and those who valued property above all." The Pennsylvania Constitution of 1776 itself was not democratic, but a triumph of "colonial radical whiggism."[5]

It is clear that a considerable diversity of opinion prevails. It is also clear that the time has come to set forth certain propositions or generalizations which seem to me to have a measure of validity.

First of all, a definition of democracy is called for. And just to face the issue squarely, I will offer one stated at Newport, Rhode Island, in 1641 when a meeting declared that "the government which this body politic doth attend unto . . . is a democracy or popular government; . . . that is to say: It is in the power of the body of freemen, orderly assembled, or the major part of them, to make or constitute just laws, by which they will be regulated, and to depute from among themselves such ministers as shall see them faithfully executed between man and man." That such an idea was not confined to Newport was shown six years later when the little towns in Rhode Island formed a confederation, the preamble of which states: "It is agreed, by this present assembly thus incorporate, and by this present act declared, that the form of government established in Providence Plantations is democratical; that is to say, a government held by the free and voluntary consent of all, or the greater part of the free inhabitants."

These are simple but, I think, adequate definitions. I will go even further and offer as a theoretical and philosophical foundation for democracy the statement by Roger Williams in the *Bloudy Tenent* of 1644. After describing civil government as an ordinance of God to conserve the civil peace of the people so far as concerns their bodies and goods, he goes on to say: "The sovereign, original, and foundation of civil power lies in the people (whom they must needs mean by the civil power distinct from the government set up). And if so, that a people may erect and establish what form of government seems to them most meet for their civil condition. It is evident that such governments as are by them erected and established have no more power, nor for no longer time, than the civil power or people consenting and agreeing shall betrust them with. This is clear not only in reason, but in the experience of all commonweals where the people are not deprived of their natural freedom by the power of tyrants."[6]

The central issue in seventeenth-century New England was not social equality, manhood suffrage, women's rights, or sympathy for the Levellers, or other tests which have been applied. The central issue was the source of authority for the establishment of a government. The English view was that no government could exist in a colony without a grant of power from the crown. The opposite view, held by certain English dissenters in New England, was that a group of people could create a valid government for themselves by means of a covenant, compact, or constitution. The authors of the Mayflower Compact and the Fundamental Orders of Connecticut operated on this assumption, although they did not carry it to the logical conclusion and call it democracy as did the people in Rhode Island. It is the basic assumption of the Declaration of Independence, a portion of which reads much like the words of Roger Williams written 132 years earlier.

The second proposition is that colonial governments on the eve of the Revolution did not function democratically, nor did the men who controlled them believe in democracy. Even if we agree that there was virtually manhood suffrage in Massachusetts, it is difficult, for me at least, to see it as a democracy. In 1760 the government was controlled by a superb political machine headed by Thomas Hutchinson, who with his relatives and political allies occupied nearly every important political office in the colony except the governorship. The Hutchinson oligarchy controlled the superior court, the council, the county courts, and the justices of the peace; with this structure of appointive office spread throughout the colony, it was able to control the house of representatives elected by the towns. For six years after 1760 the popular party in Boston, lead by Oxenbridge Thacher and James Otis, suffered one defeat after another at the hands of the Hutchinson machine. The popular leaders in the town of Boston tried everything from slander to mob violence to get control of the government of the colony but it was not until after the Stamp Act crisis that they were able to win a majority of the house of representatives to their side. Even then, men like James Otis did not at first realize that the Stamp Act could be turned to advantage in the fight against the Hutchinson oligarchy.[7] In terms of political support between 1760 and 1765, if Massachusetts had a democratic leader, that man was Thomas Hutchinson, a charge to which he would have been the first to issue a horrified denial.

The third proposition is that before 1774 or 1775 the revolutionary movement was not a democratic movement, except by inadvertence. The pamphleteers who wrote on political and constitutional questions, and the town and county meetings and legislatures that resolved endlessly between 1763 and 1774, were concerned with the formulation of constitutional arguments to defend the colonies and their legislatures from interference by parliament.

The colonial theorists wrote much about the British constitution, the rights of Englishmen, and even of the laws of nature, but they accepted the British assumption that colonial governments derived from British charters and commissions. Their essential concern was with the relationship that existed, or ought to exist, between the British government and the colonial governments, and not with the relationship between man as man, and government itself. Such writers showed no interest in domestic problems, and when it was suggested that the arguments against taxation by parliament were equally applicable to the taxation of under-represented areas in the colonies, or to dissenting religious groups, such suggestions were looked upon as being quite out of order.

The same indifference was displayed in the realm of political realities. The ardent leaders of the fight against British policies showed no interest in, or sympathy for, the discontent of back-country farmers or religious groups such as the Baptists. Instead, they temporarily joined with their political enemies to suppress or ignore it. Such sympathy as the discontented got, they got from the British government, or from colonial leaders charged with being tools of the British power.

The fact is that the popular leaders of the revolutionary movement had no program of domestic reform.[8] Instead, their program was a combination of a continuous assault on the local office-holding aristocracies and an ardent attack on British policies; and in the course of time they identified one with the other. It is sometimes difficult to tell with which side of the program the popular leaders were more concerned. In Massachusetts, for instance, before 1765 they were so violent in their attack on Hutchinson that they prevented Massachusetts from joining the other colonies in making formal protests against British legislation.

The fourth proposition is related to the third. It is that although the popular leaders in the colonies showed no interest in internal political and social change, they were still able to build up a political following, particularly in the seacoast towns. They were superb organizers, propagandists with a touch of genius, and possessed of an almost demonic energy in their dual fight against the local political aristocracies and British policies. After a few false starts such as that of James Otis, who at first called the Virginia Stamp Act Resolves treason,[9] the popular leaders took an extreme stand on the subject of colonial rights. The political aristocracies might object to British policies, as most of them did, but considering what they owed to British backing, they displayed an understandable caution, a caution that made it impossible for them to pose as patriotic leaders.

The popular leaders were also willing to take extreme measures in practical opposition to British policies, ranging all the way from mob violence to non-importation agreements forced upon unwilling merchants. And with ever more force and violence they accused Americans who did not agree with them or their methods of knuckling under to British tyranny and of readiness to sell the liberties of their country for a little pelf. In the course of this campaign they appealed to the people at large. Men who normally could not or did not take part in political life, particularly in the cities, were invited to mass meetings where the rules of suffrage were ignored and where they could shout approval of resolutions carefully prepared in advance by their leaders. In addition, the mob was a constant factor in political life, particularly in Boston where it was efficiently organized. Mobs were used to nullify the Stamp Act, to harass British soldiers, to hamper the operations of the customs service, and to intimidate office holders.

All these activities on the part of the disfranchised, or the hitherto politically inactive, accustomed men to taking part in public affairs as never before; and it gave them an appetite for more. From the beginning of the crisis in 1774 onward, more and more "new men," which was the politest name their opponents called them, played an ever more active role, both on the level of practical politics and on the level of political theory. They began writing about and talking about what they called "democracy." And this was a frightening experience, not only to the conservative-minded leaders of the colonies, but to many of the popular leaders as well.

For instance, when a New York mass meeting gathered in May 1774 to answer the letter of the Boston Town Meeting asking for a complete stoppage of trade with Britain as an answer to the Boston Port Act, the people talked about far more than letter writing. One alarmed observer wrote: "I beheld my fellow-citizens very accurately counting all their chickens, not only before any of them were hatched, but before above one half of the eggs were laid. In short, they fairly contended about the future forms of our government, whether it should be founded upon aristocratic or democratic principles." The leaders had "gulled" the mob for years, and now, said Gouverneur Morris, the mob was waking up and could no longer be fooled. The only salvation for the aristocracy of New York was peace with Britain at almost any price.[10]

Another witness to the stirrings among the people was John Adams. Unlike Gouverneur Morris, he never wavered in his belief in independence, but at the same time he was constantly concerned with the danger of an internal upheaval. Years later in his "Autobiography," he recalled as vividly as if it had happened the day before an event that took place while he was home in Massachusetts in the fall of 1775. While there he met a man who had sometimes been his client. "He, though a common horse jockey, was sometimes in the right, and I had commonly been successful in his favor in our courts of law. He was always in the law, and had been sued in many actions at almost every court. As soon as he saw me, he came up to me, and his first salutation to me was, 'Oh! Mr. Adams, what great things have you and your colleagues done for us! We can never be grateful enough to you. There are no courts of justice now in this province, and I hope there never will be another'." Then Adams goes on: "Is this the object for which I have been contending? said I to myself, for I rode along without any answer to this wretch. Are these the sentiments of such people, and how many of them are there in the country? Half the nation for what I know; for half the nation are debtors, if not more, and these have been, in all countries, the sentiments of debtors. If the power of the country should get into such hands, and there is great danger that it will, to what purpose have we sacrificed our time, health, and everything else? Surely we must guard against this spirit and these principles, or we shall repent of all our conduct."[11]

In May of 1776, with the talk of independence filling the air and the Virginia convention planning to draft a constitution, old Landon Carter of Virginia wrote to Washington bewailing the "ambition" that had "seized on so much ignorance all over the colony as it seems to have done; for this present convention abounds with too many of the inexperienced creatures to navigate our bark on this dangerous coast. . . ." As for independence, he said, "I need only tell you of one definition that I heard of Independency: It was expected to be a form of government that, by being independent of the rich men, every man would then be able to do as he pleased. And it was with this expectation they sent the men they did, in hopes they would plan such a form. One of the delegates I heard exclaim against the Patrolling Law, because a poor man was made to pay for keeping a rich man's slaves in order. I shamed the fool so much for it that he slunk away; but he got elected by it."[12]

One could go on endlessly giving samples like these from the hectic days between 1774 and 1776, examples of the fear among leaders of all shades of opinion that the people would get or were getting out of hand. Meanwhile there was an increasing amount of political writing in the newspapers, writing which was pointing in the direction of independence and the creation of new governments in America. More than a year before *Common Sense*, a piece which appeared first in the *Pennsylvania Packet* declared that "the history of kings is nothing but the history of the folly and depravity of human nature." "We read now and then, it is true, of a good king; so we read likewise of a prophet escaping unhurt from a lion's den, and of three men walking in a fiery furnace without having even their garments singed. The order of nature is as much inverted in the first as it was in the last two cases. A good king is a miracle."[13]

By early 1776 the debate over future governments to be adopted was in full swing. Disliking intensely the ideas of government set forth in *Common Sense*, John Adams drafted his *Thoughts on Government*. His plan was modeled on the old government of Massachusetts, with an elective rather than a royal governor, of course, but it certainly contemplated no radical change in the political structure.[14] John Adams was no innovator. He deplored what he called "the rage for innovation" which had appeared in Massachusetts by June of 1776. The projects, said he, are not for repairing the building but for tearing it down. "The projects of county assemblies, town registers, and town probates of wills are founded in narrow notions, sordid stinginess, and profound ignorance, and tend directly to barbarism."[15]

There was equal alarm in the south at demands for change and new governments. Among those who sought to defend the old order was Carter Braxton. In a long address to the Virginia convention he praised the British constitution and declared that it would be "perverting all order to oblige us, by a novel government, to give up our laws, our customs, and our manners." The spirit or principles of limited monarchy should be preserved. Yet, he said, we daily see it condemned by the advocates of "popular governments.... The systems recommended to the colonies seem to accord with the temper of the times, and are fraught with all the tumult and riot incident to simple democracy...." Braxton declared that democracies would not tolerate wealth, and that they could exist only in countries where all the people are poor from necessity. Nowhere in history could he find an example of a successful democracy. What he proposed for Virginia was a three-part government with a house of representatives elected by the voters for three years. The house, in turn, would choose a governor to serve during good behavior and a council of twenty-four to hold their places for life and to act as an upper house of the legislature.[16] Braxton in Virginia, like John Adams in Massachusetts, hoped to make the transition from dependence to independence without any fundamental political change.

But change was in the air, and writer after writer sought to formulate new ideas about government and to offer concrete suggestions for the theoretical foundations and political structures of the new states to be. In 1775, on hearing that congress had given advice to New Hampshire on the establishment of a government, General John Sullivan offered his thoughts to the revolutionary congress of his colony. All government, he wrote, ought to be instituted for the good of the people. There should be no conflicting branches in imitation of the British constitution "so much celebrated by those who understand nothing of it...." The two houses of the legislature and a governor should all be elected by the people. No danger can arise to a state "from giving the people a free and full voice in their own government." The so-called checks upon the licentiousness of the people "are only the children of designing or ambitious men, no such thing being necessary...."[17]

In the middle colonies appeared an address "To the People of North America on the Different Kinds of Government." After defining monarchy, aristocracy, oligarchy, and democracy, the anonymous writer said: "Popular government—sometimes termed democracy, republic, or commonwealth — is the plan of civil society wherein the community at large takes the care of its own welfare, and manages its concerns by representatives elected by the people out of their own body."

"Seeing the happiness of the people is the true end of government; and it appearing by the definition, that the popular form is the only one which has this for its object; it may be worth inquiring into the causes which have prevented its success in the world."

This writer then undertakes to explain the failure of former democracies. First of all, he says that past republics tried democracy too late and contained within them remnants of aristocracies and military cliques which disliked it. A second cause was that men did not have adequate knowledge of representation and that their large and tumultuous assemblies made it possible for unscrupulous men to charge all troubles to the constitution. A third cause of failure has been the political writers who from ignorance or ulterior motives have tried to discredit democracy. "This has been carried to such a length with many, that the mentioning a democracy constantly excites in them the idea of anarchy; and few, except such as have emancipated themselves from the shackles of political bigotry and prejudice, can talk of it with patience, and hearken to anything ofered in its defence." Such are the causes of the destruction of former republics, but the Americans have the best opportunity ever open to mankind to form a free government, "the last and best plan that can possibly exist."[18]

In "The Interest of America," another writer says that new governments must soon be created in America and that "the good of the people is the ultimate end of civil government." Therefore, "we should assume that mode of government which is most equitable and adapted to the good of mankind . . . and I think there can be no doubt that a well-regulated democracy is most equitable." The annual or frequent choice of magistrates is "most likely to prevent usurpation and tyranny; and most likely to secure the privileges of the people." Legislatures should be unicameral, for a plurality of branches leads to endless contention and a waste of time.[19]

In New England, where the revolutionary congresses of Massachusetts and New Hampshire were controlled by leaders along the seacoast, there was a growing discontent among the people of the back-country counties. Out of it came one of the clearest democratic statements of the times: "The People are the Best Governors." The author starts with the premise that "there are many very noisy about liberty, but are aiming at nothing more than personal power and grandeur." "God," he said, "gave mankind freedom by nature, made every man equal to his neighbor, and has virtually enjoined them to govern themselves by their own laws." Representatives in legislatures should have only the power to make laws. They should not have power to elect officials or to elect councils or senates to veto legislation. Only the people have this power. If there must be senates, they should be elected by the people of the state at large and should have only advisory powers. Representation should not be according to taxable property, for "Nature itself abhors such a system of civil government, for it will make an inequality among the people and set up a number of lords over the rest." Representation according to population also has its difficulties. The solution is for each town to have one representative, with more for larger towns if the legislature thinks fit. So far as property qualifications for representatives are concerned, there should be none. "Social virtue and knowledge . . . is the best and only necessary qualification of the person before us." If we have property qualifications "we root out virtue; and what will then become of the genuine principle of freedom?" "Let it not be said in future generations that money was made by the founders of the American states an essential qualification in the rulers of a free people." The writer proposed annual elections of a one-house legislature, of a governor, and of the judges of the superior court. The people in the counties should elect annually all their own officials—judges, sheriffs, and others—as should the inhabitants of the towns. And in all elections "any orderly free male of ordinary capacity" should have the right to vote if he has lived in a town for a year.[20]

From such discussions one may sum up certain of the essential ideas. (1) They agree that the "good" or the "happiness" of the people is the only end of government. (2) They agree that "democracy" is the best form of government to achieve that end. (3) They show a distrust of men when in power—a distrust shared with far more conservative-minded writers of the times.

As to details of government there are variations, but they do agree on fundamentals. (1) The legislatures, whether one or two houses, are to be elected by the people. (2) Public officials, state and local, are to be elected by the people or by their representatives in the legislatures. (3) There should be annual elections. (4) Some argue for manhood suffrage, and one writer even advocated that tax-paying widows should vote. (5) There should be freedom of religion, at least for Protestants; in any case, freedom from taxation to support established churches.

One may well ask: did such theoretical discussions have any meaning in terms of practical politics, or were they idle speculations by anonymous writers without influence? The answer is that they did have meaning. I have already cited the discussion of the principles of government in New York in the spring of 1774, and the litigious jockey in Massachusetts in 1775 who hoped that the courts would remain closed forever. These are not isolated examples. By the end of 1775 all sorts of organized activity was under way, ranging in place from North Carolina to New Hampshire, and from militia groups to churches.

In North Carolina the defeat of the Regulators in 1771 had not ended discontent but merely suppressed it. By September 1775 Mecklenburg County was instructing its delegates in the provincial congress to work for a plan of government providing for equal representation and the right to vote for every freeman who supported the government, either in person or property. Legislation should not be a "divided right"; no man or body of men should be "invested with a negative on the voice of the people duly collected. . . ."[21] By November 1776, when North Carolina elected a congress to write its first state constitution, Mecklenburg County was even more specific in its instructions. It told its delegates that they were to endeavor to establish a free government under the authority of the people of North Carolina, and that the government was to be a "simple democracy, or as near it as possible." In fixing fundamental principles, the delegates were to "oppose everything that leans to aristocracy or power in the hands of the rich and chief men exercised to the oppression of the poor."[22]

In the middle colonies militia organizations made demands and suggestions. Pennsylvania was in turmoil, with the assembly controlled by the opponents of independence and the revolutionary party working in large measure through a voluntary militia organization called the Associators. In February 1776 a committee of privates from the Philadelphia Associators told the assembly "that it has been the practice of all countries, and is highly reasonable, that all persons . . . who expose their lives in the defense of a country, should be admitted to the enjoyment of all the rights and privileges of a citizen of that country. . . ." All Associators should be given the right to vote.[23]

In June the committee of privates again protested to the legislature. This time they denied the right of the assembly to appoint two brigadier generals for the Associators as recommended by the Continental Congress. The privates declared that since many of them could not vote, they were not represented in the assembly. Furthermore, many counties where the Associators were most numerous did not have proportional representation. And for that matter, since many members of the assembly were members of a religious profession "totally averse to military defense," they could not possibly be called representatives of the Associators.[24]

While such ideas were being expounded in Pennsylvania, some militia in Maryland were proposing a new constitution. There was a growing discontent in Maryland with the revolutionary convention which was opposed to independence, and whose members were appointing one another to military posts. Government by convention should stop, said one writer, and regular government be instituted.[25]

Late in June 1776 deputies from the militia battalions in Anne Arundel County met and proposed a constitution to be submitted to the people of the county. They started out with the declaration that the right to legislate is in "every member of the community," but that for convenience the right must be delegated to representatives chosen by the people. The legislature must never form a separate interest from the community at large, and its branches must "be independent of and balance each other, and all dependent on the people." There should be a two-house legislature chosen annually "as annual elections are most friendly to liberty, and the oftener power reverts to the people, the greater will be the security for a faithful discharge of it." All provincial officials, including judges, should be elected annually by joint ballot of the two houses. All county officials should be chosen annually by the people of each county. Nothing is said of property qualifications for either voting or office-holding. So far as taxes are concerned, "the unjust mode of taxation by poll" should be abolished, and all monies raised should be according to a fair and equal assessment of people's estates.[26]

In New Jersey the revolutionary congress, like that in other colonies, was trying to prevent change and was maintaining the land qualification for voting for its members. But the complaints grew so loud that it was forced to yield. One petition in 1776, for instance, declared that "we cannot conceive the wise author of our existence ever designed that a certain quantity of earth on which we tread should be annexed to a man to complete his dignity and fit him for society. Was the sole design of government either the security of land or money, the possession of either or both of these would be the only necessary qualifications for its members. But we apprehend the benign intentions of a well regulated government to extend to the security of much more valuable possessions — the rights and privileges of freemen, for the defense of which every kind of property and even life itself have been liberally expended."[27]

In Massachusetts the Baptists were quick to draw a parallel between the fight for civil liberty against England and their own fight for religious liberty. Baptists were being jailed for refusal to pay taxes to support churches. Their leader, the Reverend Isaac Backus, put Sam Adams squarely on the spot in January 1774. "I fully concur with your grand maxim," wrote Backus, "that it is essential to liberty that representation and taxation go together." Hence, since the representatives in the Massachusetts legislature have only civil qualifications, how can they levy ecclesiastical taxes? "And I am bold in it," Backus goes on, "that taxes laid by the British Parliament upon America are not more contrary to civil freedom, than these taxes are to the very nature of liberty of conscience. . . ." He hopes, he says, that Adams will do something about it so that a large number of peaceable people "may not be forced to carry their complaints before those who would be glad to hear that the legislature of Massachusetts deny to their fellow servants that liberty which they so earnestly insist upon for themselves. A word to the wise is sufficient."[28]

Samuel Adams was not interested in liberty of conscience, particularly for Baptists, and he did not reply. But Backus pursued him to the first Continental Congress in Philadelphia where a four-hour meeting was held in Carpenter's Hall one night. The Massachusetts delegation met with the Baptists, but with a large audience present, among whom were the Quaker leaders James and Israel Pemberton, and members of congress like Joseph Galloway. The Backus diary gives a picture of Sam and John Adams quite literally squirming as the Baptists cited the facts of religious life in Massachusetts.[29] One can well imagine with what delight Galloway and the Pembertons looked on as the Massachusetts delegation vainly tried to wriggle out of a dilemma produced by the contradiction between their theory and their practice.

The Declaration of Independence was taken seriously by many Americans, or at least they found its basic philosophy useful in battling for change in the new states. Nowhere was this done more neatly than in Grafton County, New Hampshire. The Provincial Congress was in the control of eastern leaders and they refused to grant representation that the western towns thought adequate. In calling elections in the fall of 1776, the Congress grouped various towns together for electing representatives and told them that the men they elected must own real estate worth £200 lawful money. Led by professors at an obscure little college at Hanover, the people of Grafton County went on strike. They refused to hold elections, and town after town met and passed resolutions. The whole procedure of the Congress was unconstitutional. No plan of representation had been adopted since the Declaration of Independence. By the Declaration, said Hanover and two other towns in a joint statement, "we conceive that the powers of government reverted to the people at large, and of course annihilated the political existence of the Assembly which then was. . . ." Six other towns joined together and declared it to be "our humble opinion, that when the declaration of independency took place, the Colonies were absolutely in a state of nature, and the powers of government reverted to the people at large. . . ." Such being the case, the Provincial Congress has no authority to combine towns, each of which is entitled to representation as a corporate entity. And it has no right to limit the choice of representatives to the owners of £200, said the people of Lyme, because "every elector in free states is capable of being elected."[30]

It seems clear, to me at least, that by 1776 there were people in America demanding the establishment of democratic state governments, by which they meant legislatures controlled by a majority of the voters, and with none of the checks upon their actions such as had existed in the colonies. At the same time there were many Americans who were determined that there should be no changes except those made inevitable by separation from Great Britain.

The history of the writing of the first state constitutions is to a large extent the history of the conflict between these two ideals of government. The conflict can be exaggerated, of course, for there was considerable agreement on structural details. Most of the state constitutions worked out in written form the structure of government that had existed in the colonies, all the way from governors, two-house legislatures, and judicial systems, to the forms of local government. In terms of structure, little that is revolutionary is to be found. Even the much maligned unicameral legislature of Pennsylvania was only a continuation of what Pennsylvania had had since the beginning of the century.

The significant thing is not the continuity of governmental structure, but the alteration of the balance of power within the structure, and in the political situation resulting from the break away from the supervising power of a central government — that of Great Britain.

The first and most revolutionary change was in the field of basic theory. In May 1776, to help bring about the overthrow of the Pennsylvania assembly, the chief stumbling block in the way of independence, Congress resolved that all governments exercising authority under the crown of Great Britain should be suppressed, and that "all the powers of government [be] exerted under the authority of the people of the colonies...." John Adams described it as "the most important resolution that ever was taken in America."[31] The Declaration of Independence spelled it out in terms of the equality of men, the sovereignty of the people, and the right of a people to change their governments as they pleased.

Second: the Revolution ended the power of a sovereign central government over the colonies. Britain had had the power to appoint and remove governors, members of upper houses of legislatures, judges, and other officials. It had the power to veto colonial legislation, to review cases appealed from colonial supreme courts, and to use armed force. All of this superintending power was wiped out by independence.

Third: the new central government created in America by the Articles of Confederation was, in a negative sense at least, a democratic government. The Congress of the United States had no power over either the states or their citizens. Hence, each state could govern itself as it pleased, and as a result of some of the new state constitutions, this often meant by a majority of the voters within a state.

Fourth: in writing the state constitutions, change was inevitable. The hierarchy of appointed legislative, executive, and judicial officials which had served as a check upon the elective legislatures was gone. The elective legislature became the supreme power in every state, and the lower houses, representing people however inadequately, became the dominant branch. The appointive houses of colonial times were replaced by elective senates, which in theory were supposed to represent property. They were expected to, and sometimes did, act as a check upon the lower houses, but their power was far less than that of pre-war councils.

Fifth: the office of governor underwent a real revolution. The governors of the royal colonies had, in theory at least, vast powers, including an absolute veto. In the new constitutions, most Americans united in shearing the office of governor of virtually all power.

Sixth: state supreme courts underwent a similar revolution. Under the state constitutions they were elected by the legislatures or appointed by governors who were elected officials. And woe betide a supreme court that tried to interfere with the actions of a legislature.

What such changes meant in terms of political realities was that a majority of voters within a state, if agreed upon a program and persistent enough, could do what it wanted, unchecked by governors or courts or appeals to a higher power outside the state.

There were other areas in which changes took place, although they were only beginnings. A start was made in the direction of ending the property qualification for voting and office-holding. A few states established what amounted to manhood suffrage, and a few years later even women voted in New Jersey although that was stopped when it appeared that woman suffrage meant only a means of stuffing ballot boxes. A few states took steps in the direction of representation according to population, a process as yet unsolved in the United States. A large step was taken in the direction of disestablishing state churches, but on the whole one still had to be a Protestant, and a Trinitarian at that, to hold office.

In connection with office-holding, there is one eighteenth-century American idea that is worthy of a whole study by itself, and that is the concept of rotation in office. Many Americans were convinced that office-holding bred a lust for power in the holder. Therefore there must be frequent, if not annual, elections; and there must be a limitation on the time one might spend in certain offices. There is probably no more remarkable self-denying ordinance in the history of politics than the provision in the Articles of Confederation that no man could be a member of Congress more than three years out of any six. I have often been accused of wanting to go back to the

Articles of Confederation, which is nonsense, but there are times when I do wish that this one provision might be revived in the twentieth century.

What I have done in this paper is to set before you some of the reasons for believing that the American Revolution was a democratic movement, not in origin, but in result. Certainly the political leaders of the eighteenth century thought the results were democratic. Whether they thought the results were good or bad is another story.

Notes

[1] Merrill Jensen, *The Articles of Confederation: An Interpretation of the Social-Constitutional History of the American Revolution, 1774-1781*, reprint with new foreword (Madison, Wis., 1948), pp. 15, 239.

[2] Ibid., ch. iii, "The Internal Revolution"; Leonard W. Labaree, *Conservatism in Early American History* (New York, 1948); and Robert J. Taylor, *Western Massachusetts in the Revolution* (Providence, 1954), as examples. For methods of local control see Charles S. Sydnor, *Gentlemen Freeholders: Political Practices in Washington's Virginia* (Chapel Hill, 1952).

[3] Robert E. Brown, "Democracy in Colonial Massachusetts," *New England Quarterly*, XXV (1952), 291-313, and at length in *Middle Class Democracy and the Revolution in Massachusetts, 1691-1780* (Ithaca, N. Y., 1955).

[4] Robert E. Brown, "Economic Democracy Before the Constitution," *American Quarterly*, VII (1955), 257-274.

[5] Roy N. Lokken, review of Theodore Thayer, *Pennsylvania Politics and the Growth of Democracy, 1740-1776* (Harrisburg, 1953), in *William and Mary Quarterly*, XII (1955), 671.

[6] *English Historical Documents*, IX, *American Colonial Documents to 1775*, ed. Merrill Jensen (London and New York, 1955), pp. 168, 226, 174.

[7] See Ellen E. Brennan, *Plural Office Holding in Massachusetts 1760-1780* (Chapel Hill, 1945), and "James Otis: Recreant and Patriot," *New England Quarterly*, XII (1939), 691-725.

[8] For example, see Irving Mark, *Agrarian Conflicts in Colonial New York, 1711-1775* (New York, 1940); *The Carolina Background on the Eve of the Revolution*, ed. Richard J. Hooker (Chapel Hill, 1953); and Elisha Douglass, *Rebels and Democrats* (Chapel Hill, 1955).

[9] Brennan, "James Otis: Recreant and Patriot," p. 715.

[10] Gouverneur Morris to [John] Penn, May 20, 1774, in *English Historical Documents*, IX, 861-863.

[11] John Adams, "Autobiography," *The Works of John Adams*, ed. Charles F. Adams (Boston, 1856), II, 420-421.

[12] *American Archives*, ed. Peter Force, 4th ser. (Washington, 1837-1846), VI, 390-391. May 9, 1776.

[13] *English Historical Documents*, IX, 816-817.

[14] *Works of John Adams*, IV, 189-200.

[15] To John Winthrop, Philadelphia, June 23, 1776, in Mass. Hist. Soc. *Collections*, 5th ser. (Boston, 1878), IV, 310. This was in reply to a letter of John Winthrop, written on June 1, in which he reported to Adams on the various schemes afoot in Massachusetts. Ibid., 305-308.

[16]*The Virginia Gazette* (Dixon and Hunter), June 8, 1776. This had been printed earlier in pamphlet form. For similar ideas see the letter of William Hooper, North Carolina delegate to the Continental Congress, to the North Carolina Provincial Congress, October 26, 1776, in *The Colonial Records of North Carolina,* ed. W. L. Saunders, X (1890), 866-869.

[17]John Sullivan to Meshech Weare, Winter Hill [Mass.], December 11, 1775, in *American Archives,* IV, 241-242.

[18]*American Archives,* V, 180-183. [March 1776.]

[19]Ibid., VI, 840-843. [June 1776.]

[20]Reprinted in Frederick Chase, *A History of Dartmouth College and the Town of Hanover, New Hampshire* (Cambridge, 1891), I, Appendix D, 654-663.

[21]*Colonial Records of North Carolina,* X, 239-242. [Sept. 1775.]

[22]Ibid., 870, a-f. [Nov. 1776.]

[23]Votes and Proceedings of the Assembly, Feb. 23, 1776, in *Pennsylvania Archives,* 8th ser. [Harrisburg, 1935], VIII, 7406.

[24]Ibid., 7546-47. June 14, 1776.

[25]"An American" in "To the People of Maryland," *American Archives,* VI, 1094-96.

[26]Ibid., 1092-94. June 26-27, 1776.

[27]Richard P. McCormick, *The History of Voting in New Jersey . . . 1664-1911* (New Brunswick, 1953), pp. 66-68.

[28]To Samuel Adams, Jan. 19, 1774, in Alvah Hovey, *A Memoir of the Life and Times of the Rev. Isaac Backus* (Boston, 1859), pp. 195-197.

[29]Ibid., ch. xv.

[30]*American Archives,* 5th ser. (Washington, 1848-1853), III, 1223-24, and Chase, *History of Dartmouth,* I, 426-433.

[31]*Warren-Adams Letters,* I (Boston, 1917), 245; in Mass. Hist. Soc. *Collections,* Vols. 72, 73.

The American Revolution as a Colonial War for Independence

Frequently the American Revolution is compared with other revolutions, past and present. The results of such efforts tend to be unsatisfying, largely because there is no little confusion over what, in fact, constitutes a revolution. Thomas Barrow suggests that there are fundamental differences between a war for colonial independence and an internal social revolution such as occurred in France and Russia. Our Revolution was a colonial war for independence in which social and economic factors played a minor role. Such revolutions have been repeated in this century. Those, like the "progressive" historians, who seek to find the bases of our Revolution in the tension and divisions extant in the colonial society, as would be appropriate for the study of the French Revolution, will encounter considerable difficulties. They will be studying, according to Barrow, the wrong revolution.

Thomas C. Barrow

The current historiographical controversies over the American Revolution owe much to Carl Becker. From Becker's day to the present, historians have debated the question of the existence or non-existence of an "internal revolution" in American society. Some historians, following Becker's lead, search for traces of internal social or political turmoil. Others, disagreeing with Becker, stress the continuity of institutions and traditions during the Revolution. At issue is the basic question of just "how revolutionary was the American Revolution," and in the failure of historians to agree on an answer to that question lies the source of controversy. And so the great debate continues.[1]

Unfortunately, there is no adequate definition of a "revolution." The dictionary description of a revolution as a "total or radical change" certainly provides no effective guideline. Since history is the study of change in human society, locating a revolution according to that formula becomes a matter of appraising just how much change is involved in a given event, which inevitably comes

Reprinted by permission of the author and publisher from Thomas C. Barrow, "The American Revolution as a Colonial War for Independence," *William and Mary Quarterly*, 25 (July 1968), 452-463. Abridged by the editors.

down to a question of where one wants to place the emphasis. In any case, precise definitions are somewhat beside the point. When the word *revolution* is used today in connection with a political system, its meaning, if not its precise definition, is abundantly clear. The image called to mind is inescapably that of the French and Russian revolutions, which have provided us with our classic formulas for revolutionary re-structurings of society. A revolution in these terms represents the replacement of an archaic, repressive regime or regimes with something new, something more open, more flexible, more adaptable. In effect, in the interests of "progress," within the political system stability is replaced by instability until some new synthesis is achieved. Only then is stability restored, at which point the revolutionary drama is closed.

For generations now American historians have struggled to fit their "revolution" into this classic mold.[2] The difficulties they have encountered in doing so are reflected in the present historiographical impasse. It is a problem that might have been avoided had we remembered that the American people were, until 1776, colonials. By its very nature, a colonial society must be, in certain vital ways, unstable. Unable to exercise complete political control, subject to continual external intervention and negative interference, a colonial society cannot achieve effective "maturity" — that is, cannot create and control a political system that will be suited to the requirements of the interests indigenous to that society. A colonial society is an "incomplete" society, and consequently an inherently unstable society. This was as true of American society prior to 1776 as it is today of the colonial societies left in our world. And, consequently, if instability is the given fact in American society at the beginning of the imperial crisis, it is hard to see how the classic pattern of "stability replaced by instability" can be imposed upon it. The answer, of course, is that it cannot, that in fact colonial wars for independence or "liberation" are generically different from revolutions of the French or Russian variety. And, after all, the American Revolution was just that — a colonial war of liberation. Given the widespread existence of such wars in today's world, it is odd that for so long a time we have overlooked the full implications of this fact.

Colonial wars for independence have an inner logic of their own. The first problem is to achieve self-determination. Once that is accomplished, it then becomes a matter of organization, about which, naturally, there always will be fundamental disagreement. What course this disagreement will take, and how bitter it will be, will be determined by the nature of the particular society. In former colonies which have emerged into nationhood in this century, the determining factor has largely been the heterogeneous nature of their societies; with little internal unity or coherence, these new nations generally have fallen back at first on authoritarian centralism. When this has proved incapable of solving the complex problems confronting the society, it has been replaced usually by some kind of collective leadership, often based on the only effective national organization in existence, the military.[3] It is at this point that many of the emergent nations of today find themselves.

Americans were more fortunate in their escape from colonialism. Thanks to the nature of the First British Empire, with its emphasis on commercial growth rather than on imperial efficiency, its loose organization, and the high degree of self-government allowed to the colonists, Americans had developed effective political units which commanded the allegiance of most inhabitants and served as adequate vehicles for the transition from colonial status to nationhood. Given a common English inheritance and a common struggle against British "tyranny," these states made the transition with a minimum of disagreement and dissension. In effect, by 1760 self-government in America, while still incomplete, had gone far. A tightening of English imperial authority after the last war with France brought about a reaction within the colonies toward complete self-determination, which was achieved finally through military success.

Yet, whatever the difference of the American experience from other colonial wars of liberation, certain elements were of necessity shared in common. Within any colonial society there exists an establishment, a group of men whose interests and situation tie them to the existing structure and whose orientation is towards the preservation of the colonial status. When the issue of independence or self-determination begins to be debated, these men are caught in powerful crosscurrents. As natives to the society, they identify to some degree with its problems. At the same time, as beneficiaries of their privileged position within the existing colonial structure, they are not enthusiastic for change. Such men fall back on arguments of moderation, particularly stressing the economic benefits of association with the dominant country and also emphasizing the immaturity of their own society. The gains associated with independence are outweighed for them by the prospects of social and political disorganization. So these men cast their lot with their colonial rulers. Such a man was Thomas Hutchinson. So, too, were many of his Tory associates.

And men like Hutchinson found much to disturb them within American society. Actually, not only was American colonial society subjected to the instability normally inherent in colonial status but there were certain peculiar circumstances which complicated matters further. The melting-pot aspects of American society, the diversity of ethnic, religious, and cultural backgrounds to be found within it, created problems of communication. And, of equal importance, American colonial society was, after all, an artificial creation. Unlike most other historical colonial episodes, the American case was not a matter of an indigenous native society being expropriated and exploited by outsiders. In such instances, the pre-existing patterns of such native societies provide a degree of internal continuity and stability. But the English colonies in North America had at their disposal no such pre-existence. They were created specifically and artificially to perform certain functions in relation to the mother country. Most particularly, from the very beginning their economy was geared to production for distant markets over which they had no control and little influence.

At the same time, while there were sizeable non-English elements within the colonial population which created special problems, nevertheless the majority of the colonists were of the same national origin as their "rulers." It was not an instance of a conquered native population forced to bow fatalistically before the superior skills and power of an alien culture. Rather, it was a case in large part of Englishmen being governed and exploited by Englishmen. The result was a high degree of friction between governed and governors — an insistence by the colonists on their rights as Englishmen — that gave a special flavor and complexity to colonial politics.

Thoughtful colonials were well aware of and influenced by these problems. Thomas Hutchinson and John Adams—Tory and Whig—disagreed not so much on the question of the eventual independence of the American colonies as on the question of timing. Hutchinson's toryism sprang in part from his conviction that American society was too immature, too unstable, to stand alone. External force and authority, it seemed to him, would be required for many years to maintain internal order and stability in America. Realistically, he understood that eventually independence was probable: "It is not likely that the American Colonies will remain part of the Dominions of Great Britain another Century." But, Hutchinson added, until then, "as we cannot otherwise subsist I am consulting the best interest of my country when I propose measures for maintaining this subjection [to England]." What particularly disturbed Hutchinson about the change in English policy after 1760 was that they tended to increase the instability and disorder inherent within American society: "Sieur Montesquieu is right in supposing men good or bad according to the Climate where they live. In less than two centuries Englishmen by change of country are become more barbarous and fierce than the Savages who inhabited the country before they extirpated them, the Indians themselves."

John Adams viewed American development in a different way. Contrasting the New World with the Old, he found the former far superior. The settlement of America had produced men who "knew that government was a plain, simple, intelligible thing, founded in nature and reason, and quite comprehensible by common sense. They detested all the base services and servile dependencies of the feudal system ... and they thought all such slavish subordinations were equally inconsistent with the constitution of human nature and that religious liberty with which Jesus had made them free." The problem was that this purity of mind and behavior was always threatened by contact with the corruption of the Old World. Specifically, subordination of Americans to a distant Parliament which knew little of their needs and desires was not only frustrating but dangerous to the American experiment: "A legislature that has so often discovered a want of information concerning us and our country; a legislature interested to lay burdens upon us; a legislature, two branches of which, I mean the lords and commons, neither love nor fear us! Every American of fortune and common sense, must look upon his property to be sunk downright one half of its value, the moment such an absolute subjection to parliament is established." Independence was a logical capstone to such reasoning, although it took Adams some time to take that final step.

The differences between Hutchinson and Adams suggest that the divisions in American society between conservatives and radicals on the question of separation from Great Britain were related in part to a disagreement over the means to achieve coherence or stability within American society. For one side, continued tutelage under English authority was a necessity until such a time as maturity was achieved. For the other, it seemed that the major roadblock to maturity, to internal harmony and unity, was that self-same English authority. In effect, it was a disagreement on means, not ends. And disagreements similar to that between Hutchinson and Adams can be found within any society — whether in the eighteenth or twentieth century — which is in the process of tearing itself loose from its colonial ties.

It is possible, too, to suggest certain similarities between American intellectual development in these years and the experience of other colonial peoples. From his study of politics in eighteenth-century America, and particularly from his analysis of the pamphlet literature of the Revolutionary years, Bernard Bailyn has concluded that the "configuration of ideas and attitudes" which comprised the "Revolutionary ideology could be found intact — completely formed — as far back as the 1730's" and that these ideas had their origin in the "transmission from England to America of the literature of political opposition that furnished the substance of the ideology of the Revolution."[4] Colonial societies are both fascinated and yet antagonized by the culture of the dominant exploiting nation. They tend to borrow much from their rulers. The English background of a majority of the American colonists in their case made such borrowing a natural and easy process, particularly for those who, for one reason or another, identified themselves with British rule.

However, in colonial societies even many of those who are anxious to assert, or preserve, their native interests or culture cannot resist that fascination exerted by the dominant "mother country." These "patriots" borrow, too, but they are likely to borrow from the dissenting tradition within the dominant culture, from the literature of "opposition," to utilize in their own defense the language and literature of those elements within the ruling society which are critical, or subversive, of the governing traditions. In this way the prestige of the "superior" society can be used against that society itself. On the evidence of Bailyn's research, it seems that the Americans followed just such a line of development, fitting the "opposition" tradition into the framework of their own evolving institutions and traditions — a process which was facilitated by the natural connections between the American religious dissenting traditions and the "opposition" traditions of the eighteenth-century English society.

Again, once the movement for independence enters its final phase within a colonial society and becomes an open contest of strength, other divisions tend to become obscured. The most determined supporters of the colonial rule are silenced or forced to rely increasingly on the military strength of their rulers to maintain their position. On the other side, the advocates of independence submerge momentarily whatever differences they may have and present a common front. It is a time of common effort, of mutual support within the forces interested in achieving self-determination. At the same time the "patriot" groups develop special organizations capable of coercing those elements within society, often a majority of the population, which are inclined towards neutrality or moderation. Such were the Sons of Liberty in the American Revolution, and the evidence suggests that they performed their work effectively. Partly because of their efforts, and more generally because of the peculiar character of American colonial society and the nature of the imperial conflict, American society weathered the crisis with relative stability and harmony. As John Adams put it, "The zeal and ardor of the people during the revolutionary war, supplying the place of government, commanded a degree of order, sufficient at least for the temporary preservation of society."

With independence come altered circumstances for a former colonial society. Victorious patriots, confronted with the task of creating a permanent political structure, gradually begin to disagree among themselves as to how it can best be done. Since the only effective central direction came previously from the colonial rulers, the problem in each newly independent society is to fit the surviving local units into some coherent national structure. Here the forces of localism and centralism come into conflict. Those men or interests firmly entrenched in their positions at the local level see in increased centralism a threat to their existence and power. On the other hand, those men or interests of a more cosmopolitan nature, geared to extra-local activities and contacts, can see the benefits that would accrue to them through the introduction of the smoother flow of communications and transactions that effective centralization would bring. The disagreement pits the particularism of the entrenched local interests and individuals against the nationalism of the cosmopolitan interests and individuals. In most contemporary emergent societies these latter groups are by far the weaker. Fortunately, in America the cosmopolitan groups were stronger and more effective, partly again because of the unusual origin and nature of American colonial society. From the beginning the English colonies had been geared to production for European markets; it was the reason for their existence. The result was the development of an economy which had geographical variations but a common external orientation. Merchants and large-scale producers of items for export dominated this society. In the period after independence was achieved, these men provided a firm base for the construction of an effective national political system. Their success came with the substitution of the Constitution of 1787 for the Articles of Confederation.

Historians following the Becker-Beard approach put a different interpretation on the period following the achievement of de facto independence. For them, it was the moment of the triumph of radical democratic elements within American society. The wording of the Declaration of Independence, the constitutions of the new state governments, and particularly the drawing up of the Articles of Confederation represent for these historians the influence of a form of "radicalism." Yet, as Elisha Douglass has noted, in the formation of the governments for the new states, rather puzzlingly the one political reorganization that was subjected to the most democratic method of discussion and adoption — that of Massachusetts — turned out to be not only the most conservative of all the state constitutions but more conservative, in fact, than the previous system. Somehow in Massachusetts, at least, an excess of democracy seems to have led to an enthronement of conservatism. And, indeed, the new constitutions or systems adopted in all the states were remarkable generally for their adherence to known and familiar forms and institutions.

Obviously, given the disruption of the traditional ties to England, the interruption of the natural economic dependence on English markets, the division of American society into opposing Whig and Tory camps, and the presence on American soil of enemy troops (which occupied at different moments the most important commercial centers), some confusion and dissension was inevitable within American society. What is remarkable is how little upheaval and disagreement there actually was. Had American society been ripe for a social upheaval, had it been comprised of oppressing and oppressed classes, no better opportunity could have been offered. The conservative nature of the American response suggests that something other than a radical re-structuring of society was what was debated or desired.

Again, some historians have interpreted the decentralized political system created under the Articles of Confederation as a "triumph" of radical democracy. However, if instability, associated with colonial status and with the peculiar character of American colonial society, was a recurrent problem, and if inability to achieve positive control of their own political system was a major irritant, then the decentralization of the Articles was a logical development. In effect, if home rule was the issue and the cure, it was only natural that each local unit should seek as much autonomy within the national framework as possible. Seemingly, decentralization was the best method to bring coherence and stability, or maturity, to American society. Each local unit could look to its own needs, could arrange for the effective solution of its own special problems, could work to create that internal balance and harmony of conflicting interests that are the earmark of stability and maturity.

The problem with the Articles was not an excess of democracy. What brought about an effective opposition to them was their failure to achieve their purpose. The history of the states under the Articles, at least in the eyes of many contemporaries, suggested that decentralization, rather than being a source of stability, was a source of confusion and turmoil. James Madison explained the nature of the mistake in his Tenth Federalist. In spite of independence, under the system created by the Articles, wrote Madison, "complaints are everywhere heard from our most considerate and virtuous citizens... that our governments are too unstable." The problem, for Madison, was to control faction within society, and the most dangerous type of faction is that which includes a majority. Unfortunately, the "smaller the society, the fewer probably will be the distinct parties and interests composing it; the fewer the distinct parties and interests, the more frequently will a majority be found of the same party; and the smaller the number of individuals composing a majority, and the smaller the compass within which they are placed, the more easily will they concert and execute their plans of oppression." The solution is to enlarge the sphere, because if "you take in a greater variety of parties and interests," then "you make it less probable that a majority of the whole will have a common motive to invade the rights of other citizens ... The influence of factious leaders may kindle a flame within their particular States, but will be unable to spread a general conflagration through the other States."[5]

Nor was the opposition to the Constitution less concerned than Madison about order and stability within society. Again, disagreement was fundamentally over means, not ends. The anti-Federalists clung to the former ideas of local autonomy. They were, in fact, not more democratic than their opponents but more conservative. They were afraid of change: "If it were not for the stability and attachment which time and habit gives to forms of government, it would be in the power of the enlightened and aspiring few, if they should combine, at any time to destroy the best establishments, and even make the people the instruments of their own subjugation." The trouble was that the system created under the Articles was not yet sanctified by time: "The late revolution having effaced in a great measure all former habits, and the present institutions are so recent, that there exists not that great reluctance to innovation, so remarkable in old communities ... it is the genius of the common law to resist innovation."[6] George Clinton agreed with Madison on the dangers of faction: "The people, when wearied with their distresses, will in the moment of frenzy, be guilty of the most imprudent and desperate measures.... I know the people are too apt to vibrate from one extreme to another. The effects of this disposition are what I wish to guard against." It was on the solution to the problem, not on the nature of the problem, that Clinton differed from Madison. For Clinton, the powerful central government created by the Constitution might too easily become a vehicle for popular tyranny. It was this same sentiment which led eventually to the adoption of the first ten amendments, the Bill of Rights, with their reservations of basic rights and powers to local units and individuals.

It would not do to carry the comparison between the American Revolution and other colonial wars of liberation, particularly those of the twentieth century, too far. But there is enough evidence to suggest certain basic similarities between the American experience and that of other emergent colonial peoples — enough evidence, at least, to suggest that the efforts of historians to impose on the American Revolution the classic pattern of the French and Russian revolutions have led to a distorted view of our national beginnings. A French Revolution is the product of unbearable tensions within a society. The purpose of such a revolution is to destroy society as it exists, or at least to destroy its most objectional aspects, and to replace the old with something new. In contrast, a colonial "revolution" or war of liberation has as its purpose the achievement of self-determination, the "completion" or fulfillment of an existing society, rather than its destruction. A French Revolution is first of all destructive; a colonial revolution, first of all constructive. In either case the process may not be completed. In the instance of the French Revolution, the re-constructed society may contain more of the old than the original revolutionaries desired. And in the case of the colonial revolution, the process of winning independence and the difficulties of organizing an effective national political structure may open the gates to change, may create a radicalism that carries the original society far from its former course; the result may be more destruction than was originally envisaged. Yet, the goals of these two revolutions are fundamentally different, and their different goals determine a different process of fulfillment. The unfolding of the revolutionary drama, the "stages" of revolution, will be quite different, if not opposite.

For John Adams, the American Revolution was an epochal event, a moment of wonder for the world to behold and consider. At times his rhetoric carried him beyond the confines of his innate caution, and he sounded like a typical revolutionary: "The progress of society will be accelerated by centuries by this revolution ... Light spreads from the dayspring in the west, and may it shine more and more until the perfect day." But, as Edward Handler has noted, "The truth is that if Adams was a revolutionary, he was so in a sense very different than that produced by the other great modern revolutions." Adams did indeed feel that his revolution had a meaning for the world but it was not related to the violent re-structurings of society. Rather its message, for Adams, was that free men can decide voluntarily to limit their freedom in the interest of mutual association, that rational men can devise a system that can at once create order and preserve liberty. The American success was in contrast to the traditional authoritarian systems of the Old World: "Can authority be more amiable or respectable, when it descends from accidents or institutions established in remote antiquity, than when it springs fresh from the hearts and judgments of an honest and enlightened people?"

Most wars of liberation are not so orderly as that of the American Revolution. Most, at least in this century, have led to increasing radicalism and division within the liberated society. National unity has not been easily achieved. That the American emergence from colonialism had a different ending is significant. A firm basis for unity obviously existed within American society, which, naturally, suggests that the reverse, too, was true — that such tensions and divisions as did exist within American society were relatively minor and harmless. It is no wonder that historians determined to find an internal social or political revolution of the French variety within the American Revolution have encountered such difficulties. Nor is it a wonder that the Revolution has become so beclouded with historiographical debates and arguments. The problem has been in our approach. We have been studying, it would seem, the wrong revolution.

Notes

[1] The major statements of the Becker-Beard approach are well known: Carl L. Becker, *The History of Political Parties in the Province of New York, 1760-1776* (Madison, 1909); Charles Beard, *An Economic Interpretation of the Constitution of the United States* (New York, 1913); J. Franklin Jameson, *The American Revolution Considered as a Social Movement* (Princeton, 1926). Arthur M. Schlesinger's interpretation is summarized in his article, "The American Revolution Reconsidered," *Political Science Quarterly*, XXXIV (1919), 61-78. The Becker-Beard approach is currently carried on most sophisticatedly in the work of Merrill Jensen, particularly in *The Articles of Confederation: An Interpretation of the Social-Constitutional History of the American Revolution, 1774-1781* (Madison, 1948). For an interesting later review of his earlier position by Jensen himself see his article, "Democracy and the American Revolution," *Huntington Library Quarterly*, XX (1956-57), 321-341. The single work which most directly challenges the Becker-Beard approach is Robert E. Brown, *Middle-Class Democracy and the*

Revolution in Massachusetts, 1691-1780 (Ithaca, 1955). Bernard Bailyn, "Political Experience and Enlightenment Ideas in Eighteenth-Century America," *Amer. Hist. Rev.,* LXVII (1962-63), 339-351, accepts the argument that there was no internal political or social "revolution" but suggests that the true revolution lay in the Americans' intellectual acceptance of the "revolutionary" implications of their previous experiences concerning government and society. Some recent publications indicate a renewed emphasis on the radical social and political aspects of the American Revolution. See, for example, Gordon S. Wood, "A Note on Mobs in the American Revolution," *William and Mary Quarterly,* 3d Ser., XXIII (1966), 635-642.

[2]The classic statement of the process of "revolution" and its application is Crane Brinton, *The Anatomy of Revolution,* rev. ed. (New York, 1952). See also the formula as worked out in Alfred Meusel, "Revolution and Counter-Revolution," Edwin R. A. Seligman, ed., *Encyclopedia of the Social Sciences* (New York, 1934), XIII, 367-375. But the work that has been most influential in relating the American Revolution to the European revolutionary tradition is Robert R. Palmer, *The Age of the Democratic Revolution: A Political History of Europe and America, 1760-1800,* I (Princeton, 1959).

[3]For example, such has been the course of Ghana during and after Nkrumah, of Algiers during and after Ben Bella, and of Indonesia during and after Sukarno.

[4]Bernard Bailyn, *The Ideological Origins of the American Revolution* (Cambridge, Mass., 1967), xi.

[5]Jacob E. Cooke, ed., *The Federalist* (Middletown, Conn., 1961), 56-65. Madison considered the question of the appropriate size for political units further in Federalist 14, *ibid.,* 83-89.

[6]Quoted in Cecelia M. Kenyon, *The Antifederalists* (Indianapolis, 1966), xci-xcii. Miss Kenyon's introduction to this collection is an expansion of her provocative article, "Men of Little Faith: The Anti-Federalists on the Nature of Representative Government," *William and Mary Quarterly,* 3d Ser., XII (1955), 2-43. See also Stanley Elkins and Eric McKitrick, "The Founding Fathers: Young Men of the Revolution," *Political Science Quarterly,* LXXVI (1961), 200-216.

What were the motives of those who wrote the Constitution in 1787? Were they disinterested philosopher kings creating a new state in a grand Platonic manner, or were they selfish men intent on protecting their own economic interests? Between these extremes a number of other positions are possible to defend. John Roche, for one, feels that the extreme positions obscure the essential element in the debate over the Constitution. The most profitable way to study the Founding Fathers is to start with the notion that these men were first and foremost democratic politicians. They were interested in ideas, yes, but only as these ideas would assist in attaining the ultimate goal, a unified, national state. Roche's account of the proceedings of the Convention emphasizes the maneuverings of the participants and the high premium placed on compromise. He concludes that new countries might learn something from the study of our Constitutional Convention.

The Founding Fathers: A Reform Caucus in Action

John P. Roche

Over the last century and a half, the work of the Constitutional Convention and the motives of the Founding Fathers have been analyzed under a number of different ideological auspices. To one generation of historians, the hand of God was moving in the assembly; under a later dispensation, the dialectic (at various levels of philosophical sophistication) replaced the Deity: "relationships of production" moved into the niche previously reserved for Love of Country. Thus in counterpoint to the Zeitgeist, the Framers have undergone miraculous metamorphoses: at one time acclaimed as liberals and bold social engineers, today they appear in the guise of sound Burkean conservatives. . . . It is not my purpose here to argue that the "Fathers" were, in fact, radical revolutionaries; that proposition has been brilliantly demonstrated by Robert R. Palmer in his *Age of the Democratic Revolution*. My concern is with the further position that not only were they revolutionaries, but also they were democrats. Indeed, in my

Reprinted by permission of the author and publisher from John P. Roche, "The Founding Fathers: A Reform Caucus in Action," *American Political Science Review*, 55 (December 1961), 799-816. Article and footnotes abridged by the editors.

view, there is one fundamental truth about the Founding Fathers that *every* generation of Zeitgeisters has done its best to obscure: they were first and foremost superb democratic politicians. They were, with their colleagues, *political men* —not metaphysicians, disembodied conservatives or Agents of History—and as recent research into the nature of American politics in the 1780s confirms,[1] they were committed (perhaps willy-nilly) to working within the democratic framework, within a universe of public approval. Charles Beard *and* the filiopietists to the contrary notwithstanding, the Philadelphia Convention was not a College of Cardinals or a council of Platonic guardians working within a manipulative, predemocratic framework; it was a *nationalist* reform caucus which had to operate with great delicacy and skill in a political cosmos full of enemies to achieve the one definitive goal—popular approbation.

Perhaps the time has come, to borrow Walton Hamilton's fine phrase, to raise the Framers from immortality to mortality, to give them credit for their magnificent demonstration of the art of democratic politics. The point must be reemphasized; they *made* history and did it within the limits of consensus. . . .

In this context, let us examine the problems they confronted and the solutions they evolved. The Convention has been described picturesquely as a counter-revolutionary junta and the Constitution as a *coup d'etat*,[2] but this has been accomplished by withdrawing the whole history of the movement for constitutional reform from its true context. No doubt the goals of the constitutional elite were "subversive" to the existing political order, but it is overlooked that their subversion could only have succeeded if the people of the United States endorsed it by regularized procedures. Indubitably they were "plotting" to establish a much stronger central government than existed under the Articles, but only in the sense in which one could argue equally well that John F. Kennedy was, from 1956 to 1960, "plotting" to become President. In short, on the fundamental *procedural* level, the Constitutionalists had to work according to the prevailing rules of the game. Whether they liked it or not is a topic for spiritualists—and is irrelevant: one may be quite certain that had Washington agreed to play the De Gaulle (as the Cincinnati once urged), Hamilton would willingly have held his horse, but such fertile speculation in no way alters the actual context in which events took place.

I

When the Constitutionalists went forth to subvert the Confederation, they utilized the mechanisms of political legitimacy. And the roadblocks which confronted them were formidable. At the same time, they were endowed with certain potent political assets. The history of the United States from 1786 to 1790 was largely one of a masterful employment of political expertise by the Constitutionalists as against bumbling, erratic behavior by the opponents of reform. Effectively, the Constitutionalists had to induce the states, by democratic techniques of coercion, to emasculate themselves. To be specific, if New York had refused to join the new Union, the project was doomed; yet before New York was safely in, the reluctant state legislature had *sua sponte* to take the following steps: (1) agree to send delegates to the Philadelphia Convention; (2) provide maintenance for these delegates (these were distinct stages: New Hampshire was early in naming delegates, but did not provide for their maintenance until July); (3) set up the special *ad hoc* convention to decide on ratification; and (4) concede to the decision of the *ad hoc* convention that New York should participate. New York admittedly was a tricky state, with a strong interest in a *status quo* which permitted her to exploit New Jersey and

Connecticut, but the same legal hurdles existed in every state. And at the risk of becoming boring, it must be reiterated that the *only* weapon in the Constitutionalist arsenal was an effective mobilization of public opinion.

The group which undertook this struggle was an interesting amalgam of a few dedicated nationalists with the self-interested spokesmen of various parochial bailiwicks. The Georgians, for example, wanted a strong central authority to provide military protection for their huge, underpopulated state against the Creek Confederacy; Jerseymen and Connecticuters wanted to escape from economic bondage to New York; the Virginians hoped to establish a system which would give that great state its rightful place in the councils of the republic. The dominant figures in the politics of these states therefore cooperated in the call for the Convention.[3] In other states, the thrust towards national reform was taken up by opposition groups who added the "national interest" to their weapons system; in Pennsylvania, for instance, the group fighting to revise the Constitution of 1776 came out foursquare behind the Constitutionalists, and in New York, Hamilton and the Schuyler *ambiance* took the same tack against George Clinton.[4] There was, of course, a large element of personality in the affair: there is reason to suspect that Patrick Henry's opposition to the Convention and the Constitution was founded on his conviction that Jefferson was behind both, and a close study of local politics elsewhere would surely reveal that others supported the Constitution for the simple (and politically quite sufficient) reason that the "wrong" people were against it.

To say this is not to suggest that the Constitution rested on a foundation of impure or base motives. It is rather to argue that in politics there are no immaculate conceptions, and that in the drive for a stronger general government, motives of all sorts played a part. Few men in the history of mankind have espoused a view of the "common good" or "public interest" that militated against their private status; even Plato with all his reverence for disembodied reason managed to put philosophers on top of the pile. Thus it is not surprising that a number of diversified private interests joined to push the nationalist public interest; what would have been surprising was the absence of such a pragmatic united front. And the fact remains that, however motivated, these men did demonstrate a willingness to compromise their parochial interests in behalf of an ideal which took shape before their eyes and under their ministrations.

As Stanley Elkins and Eric McKitrick have suggested in a perceptive essay,[4] what distinguished the leaders of the Constitutionalist caucus from their enemies was a "Continental" approach to political, economic and military issues. To the extent that they shared an institutional base of operations, it was the Continental Congress (thirty-nine of the delegates to the Federal Convention had served in Congress), and this was hardly a locale which inspired respect for the state governments. Robert de Jouvenal observed French politics half a century ago and noted that a revolutionary Deputy had more in common with a non-revolutionary Deputy than he had with a revolutionary non-Deputy, similarly one can surmise that membership in the Congress under the Articles of Confederation worked to establish a continental frame of reference, that a Congressman from Pennsylvania and one from South Carolina would share a universe of discourse which provided them with a conceptual common denominator *vis à vis* their respective state legislatures. This was particularly true with respect to external affairs: the average state legislator was probably about as concerned with foreign policy then as he is today, but Congressmen were constantly forced to take the broad view of American prestige, were compelled to listen to the reports of Secretary John Jay and to the dispatches and pleas from their frustrated envoys in Britain, France and Spain. From considerations such as these, a "Continental" ideology developed which seems to have demanded a revision of our domestic institutions primarily on the ground that only by invigorating our general government could we assume our rightful place in the international arena. Indeed, an argument with great force — particularly since Washington was its incarnation — urged that our very survival in the Hobbesian jungle of world politics depended upon a reordering and strengthening of our national sovereignty.[5]

Note that I am not endorsing the "Critical Period" thesis; on the contrary, Merrill Jensen seems to me quite sound in his view that for most Americans, engaged as they were in self-sustaining agriculture, the "Critical Period" was not particularly critical.[6] In fact, the great achievement of the Constitutionalists was their ultimate success in convincing the elected representatives of a majority of the white male population that change was imperative. A small group of political leaders with a Continental vision and essentially a consciousness of the United States' *international* impotence, provided the matrix of the movement. To their standard other leaders rallied with their own parallel ambitions. Their great assets were (1) the presence in their caucus of the one authentic American "father figure," George Washington, whose prestige was enormous; (2) the energy and talent of their leadership (in which one must include the towering intellectuals of the time, John Adams and Thomas Jefferson, despite their absence abroad), and their communications "network," which was far superior to anything on the opposition side; (3) the preemptive skill which made "their" issue The Issue and kept the locally oriented opposition permanently on the defensive; and (4) the subjective consideration that these men were spokesmen of a new and compelling credo: *American* nationalism, that ill-defined but nonetheless potent sense of collective purpose that emerged from the American Revolution.

Despite great institutional handicaps, the Constitutionalists managed in the mid-1780s to mount an offensive which gained momentum as years went by. Their greatest problem was lethargy, and paradoxically, the number of barriers in their path may have proved an advantage in the long run. Beginning with the initial battle to get the Constitutional Convention called and delegates appointed, they could never relax, never let up the pressure. In practical terms, this meant that the local "organizations" created by the Constitutionalists were perpetually in movement building up their cadres for the next fight. (The word organization has to be used with great caution: a political organization in the United States—as in contemporary England—generally consisted of a magnate and his following, or a coalition of magnates. This did not necessarily mean that it was "undemocratic" or "aristocratic," in the Aristotelian sense of the word: while a few magnates such as the Livingstons could draft their followings, most exercised their leadership without coercion on the basis of popular endorsement. The absence of organized opposition did not imply the impossibility of competition any more than low public participation in elections necessarily indicated an undemocratic suffrage.)

The Constitutionalists got the jump on the "opposition" (a collective noun: opposition*s* would be more correct) at the outset with the demand for a Convention. Their opponents were caught in an old political trap: they were not being asked to approve any specific program of reform, but only to endorse a meeting to discuss and recommend needed reforms. If they took a hard line at the first stage, they were put in the position of glorifying the *status quo* and of denying the need for *any* changes. Moreover, the Constitutionalists could go to the people with a persuasive argument for "fair play" — "How can you condemn reform before you know precisely what is involved?" Since the state legislatures obviously would have the final say on any proposals that might emerge from the Convention, the Constitutionalists were merely reasonable men asking for a chance. Besides, since they did not make any concrete proposals at that stage, they were in a position to capitalize on every sort of generalized discontent with the Confederation....

II

With delegations safely named, the focus shifted to Philadelphia. While waiting for a quorum to assemble, James Madison got busy and drafted the so-called Randolph or Virginia Plan with the aid of the Virginia delegation. This was a political master-stroke. Its consequence was that once business got underway, the framework of discussion was established on Madison's terms. There was no interminable argument over agenda; instead the delegates took the Virginia Resolutions—"just for purposes of discussion"—as their point of departure. And along with Madison's proposals, many of which were buried in the course of the summer, went his major premise: a new start on a Constitution rather than piecemeal amendment. This was not necessarily revolutionary—a little exegesis could demonstrate that a new Constitution might be formulated as "amendments" to the Articles of Confederation—but Madison's proposal that this "lump sum" amendment go into effect after approval by nine states (the Articles required unanimous state approval for any amendment) was thoroughly subversive.[7]

Standard treatments of the Convention divide the delegates into "nationalists" and "states'-righters" with various improvised shadings ("moderate nationalists," etc.), but these are *a posteriori* categories which obfuscate more than they clarify. What is striking to one who analyzes the Convention as a case-study in democratic politics is the lack of clear-cut ideological divisions in the Convention. Indeed, I submit that the evidence — Madison's *Notes*, the correspondence of the delegates, and debates on ratification—indicates that this was a remarkably homogeneous body on the ideological level. Yates and Lansing, Clinton's two chaperones for Hamilton, left in disgust on July 10. (Is there anything more tedious than sitting through endless disputes on matters one deems fundamentally misconceived? It takes an iron will to spend a hot summer as an ideological *agent provocateur*.) Luther Martin, Maryland's bibulous narcissist, left on September 4 in a huff when he discovered that others did not share his self-esteem; others went home for personal reasons. But the hard core of delegates accepted a grinding regimen throughout the attrition of a Philadelphia summer precisely because they shared the Constitutionalist goal.

Basic differences of opinion emerged, of course, but these were not ideological; they were *structural*. If the so-called "states'-rights" group had not accepted the fundamental purposes of the Convention, they could simply have pulled out and by doing so have aborted the whole enterprise. Instead of bolting, they returned day after day to argue and to compromise. An interesting symbol of this basic homogeneity was the initial agreement on secrecy: these professional politicians did not want to become prisoners of publicity; they wanted to retain that freedom of maneuver which is only possible when men are not forced to take public stands in the preliminary stages of negotiation. There was no legal means of binding the tongues of the delegates: at any stage in the game a delegate with basic principled objections to the emerging project could have taken the stump (as Luther Martin did after his exit) and denounced the convention to the skies. Yet Madison did not even inform Thomas Jefferson in Paris of the course of the deliberations and available correspondence indicates that the delegates generally observed the injunction. Secrecy is certainly uncharacteristic of any assembly marked by strong ideological polarization. This was noted at the time: the *New York Daily Advertiser*, August 14, 1787, commented that the "... profound secrecy hitherto observed by the Convention [we consider] a happy omen, as it demonstrates that the spirit of party on any great and essential point cannot have arisen to any height."

Commentators on the Constitution who have read *The Federalist* in lieu of reading the actual debates have credited the Fathers with the invention of a sublime concept called "Federalism."[6] Unfortunately *The Federalist* is probative evidence for only one proposition: that Hamilton and Madison were inspired propagandists with a genius for retrospective symmetry. Federalism, as the theory is generally defined, was an improvisation which was later promoted into a political theory. Experts on "federalism" should take to heart the advice of David Hume, who warned in his *Of the Rise and Progress of the Arts and Sciences* that "... there is no subject in which we must proceed with more caution than in [history], lest we assign causes which never existed and reduce what is merely contingent to stable and universal principles." In any event, the final balance in the Constitution between the states and the nation must have come as a great disappointment to Madison, while Hamilton's unitary views are too well known to need elucidation.

It is indeed astonishing how those who have glibly designated James Madison the "father" of Federalism have overlooked the solid body of fact which indicates that he shared Hamilton's quest for a unitary central government. To be specific, they have avoided examining the clear import of the Madison-Virginia Plan,[9] and have disregarded Madison's dogged inch-by-inch retreat from the bastions of centralization. The Virginia Plan envisioned a unitary national government effectively freed from and dominant over the states. The lower house of the national legislature was to be elected directly by the people of the states with membership proportional to population. The upper house was to be selected by the lower and the two chambers would elect the executive and choose the judges. The national government would be thus cut completely loose from the states.

The structure of the general government was freed from state control in a truly radical fashion, but the scope of the authority of the national sovereign as Madison initially formulated it was breathtaking—it was a formulation worthy of the Sage of Malmesbury himself. The national legislature was to be empowered to disallow the acts of state legislatures, and the central government was vested, in addition to the powers of the nation under the Articles of Confederation, with plenary authority wherever "... the separate States are incompetent or in which the harmony of the United States may be interrupted by the exercise of individual legislation." Finally, just to lock the door against state intrusion, the national Congress was to be given the power to use military force on recalcitrant states. This was Madison's "model" of an ideal national government, though it later received little publicity in *The Federalist*.

The interesting thing was the reaction of the Convention to this militant program for a strong autonomous central government. Some delegates were startled, some obviously leery of so comprehensive a project of reform, but nobody set off any fireworks and nobody walked out. Moreover, in the two weeks that followed, the Virginia Plan received substantial endorsement *en principe;* the initial temper of the gathering can be deduced from the approval "without debate or dissent," on May 31, of the Sixth Resolution which granted Congress the authority to disallow state legislation "... contravening *in its opinion* the Articles of Union." Indeed, an amendment was included to bar states from contravening national treaties.

The Virginia Plan may therefore be considered, in ideological terms, as the delegates' Utopia, but as the discussions continued and became more specific, many of those present began to have second thoughts. After all, they were not residents of Utopia or guardians in Plato's Republic who could simply impose a philosophical ideal on subordinate strata of the population. They were practical politicians in a democratic society, and no matter what their private dreams might be, they had to take home an acceptable package and defend it — and their own political futures—against predictable attack. On June 14 the breaking point between dream and reality took place. Apparently realizing that under the Virginia Plan, Massachusetts, Virginia and Pennsylvania could virtually dominate the national government—and probably appreciating that to sell this program to "the folks back home" would be impossible — the delegates from the small states dug in their heels and demanded time for a consideration of alternatives. One gets a graphic sense of the inner politics from John Dickinson's reproach to Madison: "You see the consequences of pushing things too far. Some of the members from the small States wish for two branches in the General Legislature and are friends to a good National Government; but we would sooner submit to a foreign power than . . . be deprived of an equality of suffrage in both branches of the Legislature, and thereby be thrown under the domination of the large States." . . .

III

According to the standard script, at this point the "states'-rights" group intervened in force behind the New Jersey Plan, which has been characteristically portrayed as a reversion to the *status quo* under the Articles of Confederation with but minor modifications. A careful examination of the evidence indicates that only in a marginal sense is this an accurate description. It is true that the New Jersey Plan put the states back into the institutional picture, but one could argue that to do so was a recognition of political reality rather than an affirmation of states'-rights. A serious case can be made that the advocates of the New Jersey Plan, far from being ideological addicts of states'-rights, intended to substitute for the Virginia Plan a system which would both retain strong national power and have a chance of adoption in the states. The leading spokesman for the project asserted quite clearly that his views were based more on counsels of expediency than on principle; said Paterson on June 16: "I came here not to speak my own sentiments, but the sentiments of those who sent me. Our object is not such a Governmt. as may be best in itself, but such a one as our Constituents have authorized us to prepare, and as they will approve." . . .

The advocates of the New Jersey Plan concentrated their fire on what they held to be the *political liabilities* of the Virginia Plan—which were matters of institutional structure — rather than on the proposed scope of national authority. Indeed, the Supremacy Clause of the Constitution first saw the light of day in Paterson's Sixth Resolution; the New Jersey Plan contemplated the use of military force to secure compliance with national law; and finally Paterson made clear his view that under either the Virginia or the New Jersey systems, the general government would ". . . act on individuals and not on states." From the states'-rights viewpoint, this was heresy: the fundament of that doctrine was the proposition that any central government had as its constituents the states, not the people, and could only reach the people through the agency of the state government.

Paterson then reopened the agenda of the Convention, but he did so within a distinctly nationalist framework. Paterson's position was one of favoring a strong central government in principle, but opposing one which in fact *put the big states in the saddle*. (The Virginia Plan, for all its abstract merits, did very well by Virginia.) As evidence for this speculation, there is a curious and intriguing proposal among Paterson's preliminary drafts of the New Jersey Plan:

> Whereas it is necessary in Order to form the People of the U. S. of America in to a Nation, that the States should be consolidated, by which means all the Citizens thereof will become equally intitled to and will equally participate in the same Privileges and Rights ... it is therefore resolved, that all the Lands contained within the Limits of each state individually, and of the U. S. generally be considered as constituting one Body or Mass, and be divided into thirteen or more integral parts.
>
> Resolved, That such Divisions or integral Parts shall be styled Districts.

This makes it sound as though Paterson was prepared to accept a strong unified central government along the lines of the Virginia Plan if the existing states were eliminated. He may have gotten the idea from his New Jersey colleague Judge David Brearley, who on June 9 had commented that the only remedy to the dilemma over representation was ". . . that a map of the U. S. be spread out, that all the existing boundaries be erased, and that a new partition of the whole be made into 13 equal parts." According to Yates, Brearley added at this point, ". . . then a government on the present [Virginia Plan] system will be just."

This proposition was never pushed—it was patently unrealistic—but one can appreciate its purpose: it would have separated the men from the boys in the large-state delegations. How attached would the Virginians have been to their reform principles if Virginia were to disappear as a component geographical unit (the largest) for representational purposes? Up to this point, the Virginians had been in the happy position of supporting high ideals with that inner confidence born of knowledge that the "public interest" they endorsed would nourish their private interest. Worse, they had shown little willingness to compromise. Now the delegates from the small states announced that they were unprepared to be offered up as sacrificial victims to a "national interest" which reflected Virginia's parochial ambition. Caustic Charles Pinckney was not far off when he remarked sardonically that ". . . the whole [conflict] comes to this": "Give N. Jersey an equal vote, and she will dismiss her scruples, and concur in the Natil. system." What he rather unfairly did not add was that the Jersey delegates were not free agents who could adhere to their private convictions; they had to take back, sponsor and risk their reputations on the reforms approved by the Convention—and in New Jersey, not in Virginia.

Paterson spoke on Saturday, and one can surmise that over the weekend there was a good deal of consultation, argument, and caucusing among the delegates. One member at least prepared a full length address: on Monday Alexander Hamilton, previously mute, rose and delivered a six-hour oration. It was a remarkably apolitical speech; the gist of his position was that *both* the Virginia and New Jersey Plans were inadequately centralist, and he detailed a reform program which was reminiscent of the Protectorate under the Cromwellian *Instrument of Government* of 1653. It has been suggested that Hamilton did this in the best political tradition to emphasize the moderate character of the Virginia Plan, to give the cautious delegates something *really* to worry about; but this interpretation seems somehow too clever. Particularly since the sentiments Hamilton expressed happened to be completely consistent with those he privately—and sometimes publicly—expressed throughout his life. He wanted, to take a striking phrase from a letter to George Washington, a "strong well mounted government"; in essence, the Hamilton Plan contemplated an elected life monarch, virtually free of public control, on the Hobbesian ground that only in this fashion could strength and stability be achieved. The other alternatives, he argued, would put policymaking at the mercy of the passions of the mob;

only if the sovereign was beyond the reach of selfish influence would it be possible to have government in the interests of the whole community.

From all accounts, this was a masterful and compelling speech, but (aside from furnishing John Lansing and Luther Martin with ammunition for later use against the Constitution) it made little impact. Hamilton was simply transmitting on a different wave-length from the rest of the delegates; the latter adjourned after his great effort, admired his rhetoric, and then returned to business.[10] It was rather as if they had taken a day off to attend the opera. Hamilton, never a particularly patient man or much of a negotiator, stayed for another ten days and then left, in considerable disgust, for New York. Although he came back to Philadelphia sporadically and attended the last two weeks of the Convention, Hamilton played no part in the laborious task of hammering out the Constitution. His day came later when he led the New York Constitutionalists into the savage imbroglio over ratification—an arena in which his unmatched talent for dirty political infighting may well have won the day. . . .

IV

On Tuesday morning, June 19, the vacation was over. James Madison led off with a long, carefully reasoned speech analyzing the New Jersey Plan which, while intellectually vigorous in its criticisms, was quite conciliatory in mood. "The great difficulty," he observed, "lies in the affair of Representation; and if this could be adjusted, all others would be surmountable." (As events were to demonstrate, this diagnosis was correct.) When he finished, a vote was taken on whether to continue with the Virginia Plan as the nucleus for a new constitution: seven states voted "Yes"; New York, New Jersey, and Delaware voted "No"; and Maryland, whose position often depended on which delegates happened to be on the floor, divided. Paterson, it seems, lost decisively; yet in a fundamental sense he and his allies had achieved their purpose: from that day onward, it could never be forgotten that the state governments loomed ominously in the background and that no verbal incantations could exorcise their power. Moreover, nobody bolted the convention: Paterson and his colleagues took their defeat in stride and set to work to modify the Virginia Plan, particularly with respect to its provisions on representation in the national legislature. Indeed, they won an immediate rhetorical bonus; when Oliver Ellsworth of Connecticut rose to move that the word "national" be expunged from the Third Virginia Resolution ("Resolved that a *national* Government ought to be established consisting of a *supreme* Legislative, Executive and Judiciary"), Randolph agreed and the motion passed unanimously. The process of compromise had begun.

For the next two weeks, the delegates circled around the problem of legislative representation. The Connecticut delegation appears to have evolved a possible compromise quite early in the debates, but the Virginians and particularly Madison (unaware that he would later be acclaimed as the prophet of "federalism") fought obdurately against providing for equal representation of states in the second chamber. . . .

It would be tedious to continue a blow-by-blow analysis of the work of the delegates; the critical fight was over representation of the states and once the Connecticut Compromise was adopted on July 17, the Convention was over the hump. Madison, James Wilson, and Gouverneur Morris of New York (who was there representing Pennsylvania!) fought the compromise all the way in a last-ditch effort to get a unitary state with parliamentary supremacy. But their allies deserted them and they demonstrated after their defeat the essentially opportunist character of their objections —using "opportunist" here in a nonpejorative sense, to indicate a willingness to swallow their objections and get on with the business. Moreover, once the compromise had carried (by five states to four, with one state divided), its advocates threw themselves vigorously into the job of strengthening the general government's substantive powers—as might have been predicted, indeed, from Paterson's early statements. It nourishes an increased respect for Madison's devotion to the art of politics, to realize that this dogged fighter could sit down six months later and prepare essays for *The Federalist* in contradiction to his basic convictions about the true course the Convention should have taken. . . .

V

Drawing on their vast collective political experience, utilizing every weapon in the politician's arsenal, looking constantly over their shoulders at their constituents, the delegates put together a Constitution. It was a makeshift affair; some sticky issues (for example, the qualification of voters) they ducked entirely; others they mastered with that ancient instrument of political sagacity, studied ambiguity (for example, citizenship), and some they just overlooked. In this last category, I suspect, fell the matter of the power of the federal courts to determine the constitutionality of acts of Congress. . . .

The Framers were busy and distinguished men, anxious to get back to their families, their positions, and their constituents, not members of the French Academy devoting a lifetime to a dictionary. They were trying to do an important job, and do it in such a fashion that their handiwork would be acceptable to very diverse constituencies. No one was rhapsodic about the final document, but it was a beginning, a move in the right direction, and one they had reason to believe the people would endorse. In addition, since they had modified the impossible amendment provisions of the Articles (the requirement of unanimity which could always be frustrated by "Rogues Island") to one demanding approval by only three-quarters of the states, they seemed confident that gaps in the fabric which experience would reveal could be rewoven without undue difficulty.

So with a neat phrase introduced by Benjamin Franklin (but devised by Gouverneur Morris) which made their decision sound unanimous, and an inspired benediction by the Old Doctor urging doubters to doubt their own infallibility, the Constitution was accepted and signed. Curiously, Edmund Randolph, who had played so vital a role throughout, refused to sign, as did his fellow Virginian George Mason and Elbridge Gerry of Massachusetts. Randolph's behavior was eccentric, to say the least— his excuses for refusing his signature have a factitious ring even at this late date; the best explanation seems to be that he was afraid that the Constitution would prove to be a liability in Virginia politics, where Patrick Henry was burning up the countryside with impassioned denunciations. Presumably, Randolph wanted to check the temper of the populace before he risked his reputation, and perhaps his job, in a fight with both Henry and Richard Henry Lee. Events lend some justification to this speculation: after much temporizing and use of the conditional subjunctive tense, Randolph endorsed ratification in Virginia and ended up getting the best of both worlds.

Madison, despite his reservations about the Constitution, was the campaign manager in ratification. His first task was to get the Congress in New York to light its own funeral pyre by approving the "amendments" to the Articles and sending them on to the state legislatures. Above all, momentum had to be maintained. The anti-Constitutionalists, now thoroughly alarmed and no novices in politics, realized that their best tactic was attrition rather than direct opposition. Thus they settled on a position expressing qualified approval but calling for a second Convention to remedy various defects (the one with the most demagogic appeal was the lack of a Bill of Rights). Madison knew that to accede to this demand would be equivalent to losing the battle, nor would he agree to conditional approval (despite wavering even by Hamilton). This was an all-or-nothing proposition: national salvation or national impotence with no intermediate positions possible. Unable to get congressional approval, he settled for second best: a unanimous resolution of Congress transmitting the Constitution to the states for whatever action they saw fit to take. The opponents then moved from New York and the Congress, where they had attempted to attach amendments and conditions, to the states for the final battle.

At first the campaign for ratification went beautifully: within eight months after the delegates set their names to the document, eight states had ratified. Only in Massachusetts had the result been close (187-168). Theoretically, a ratification by one more state convention would set the new government in motion, but in fact until Virginia and New York acceded to the new Union, the latter was a fiction. New Hampshire was the next to ratify; Rhode Island was involved in its characteristic political convulsions (the Legislature there sent the Constitution out to the towns for decision by popular vote and it got lost among a series of local issues); North Carolina's convention did not meet until July and then postponed a final decision. This is hardly the place for an extensive analysis of the conventions of New York and Virginia. Suffice it to say that the Constitutionalists clearly outmaneuvered their opponents, forced them into impossible political positions, and won both states narrowly. The Virginia Convention could serve as a classic study in effective floor management: Patrick Henry had to be contained, and a reading of the debates discloses a standard two-stage technique. Henry would give a four- or five-hour speech denouncing some section of the Constitution on every conceivable ground (the federal district, he averred at one point, would become a haven for convicts escaping from state authority!); when Henry subsided, "Mr. Lee of Westmoreland" would rise and literally pole-axe him with sardonic invective (when Henry complained about the militia power, "Lighthorse Harry" really punched below the belt: observing that while the former Governor had been sitting in Richmond during the Revolution, *he* had been out in the trenches with the troops and thus felt better qualified to discuss military affairs). Then the gentlemanly Constitutionalists (Madison, Pendleton and Marshall) would pick up the matters at issue and examine them in the light of reason.

Indeed, modern Americans who tend to think of James Madison as a rather dessicated character should spend some time with this transcript. Probably Madison put on his most spectacular demonstration of nimble rhetoric in what might be called "The Battle of the Absent Authorities." Patrick Henry in the course of one of his harangues alleged that Jefferson was known to be opposed to Virginia's approving the Constitution. This was clever: Henry hated Jefferson, but was prepared to use any weapon that came to hand. Madison's riposte was superb: First, he said that with all due respect to the great reputation of Jefferson, he was not in the country and therefore could not formulate an adequate judgment; second, no one should utilize the reputation of an outsider—the Virginia Convention was there to think for itself; third, if there were to be recourse to outsiders, the opinions of George Washington should certainly be taken into consideration; and finally, he knew from privileged personal communications from Jefferson that in fact the latter *strongly favored* the Constitution. To devise an assault route into this rhetorical fortress was literally impossible.

VI

The fight was over; all that remained now was to establish the new frame of government in the spirit of its framers.

And who were better qualified for this task than the Framers themselves? Thus victory for the Constitution meant simultaneous victory for the Constitutionalists; the anti-Constitutionalists either capitulated or vanished into limbo—soon Patrick Henry would be offered a seat on the Supreme Court and Luther Martin would be known as the Federalist "bulldog." And irony of ironies, Alexander Hamilton and James Madison would shortly accumulate a reputation as the formulators of what is often alleged to be our political theory, the concept of "federalism." Also, on the other side of the ledger, the arguments would soon appear over what the Framers "really meant"; while these disputes have assumed the proportions of a big scholarly business in the last century, they began almost before the ink on the Constitution was dry. One of the best early ones featured Hamilton versus Madison on the scope of presidential power, and other Framers characteristically assumed positions in this and other disputes on the basis of their political convictions.

Probably our greatest difficulty is that we know so much more about what the Framers *should have meant* than they themselves did. We are intimately acquainted with the problems that their Constitution should have been designed to master; in short, we have read the mystery story backwards. If we are to get the right "feel" for their time and their circumstances, we must in Maitland's phrase, ". . . think ourselves back into a twilight." Obviously, no one can pretend completely to escape from the solipsistic web of his own environment, but if the effort is made, it is possible to appreciate the past roughly on its own terms. The first step in this process is to abandon the academic premise that because we can ask a question, there must be an answer.

Thus we can ask what the Framers meant when they gave Congress the power to regulate interstate and foreign commerce, and we emerge, reluctantly perhaps, with the reply that (Professor Crosskey to the contrary notwithstanding)[11] they may not have known what they meant, that there may not have been any semantic consensus. The Convention was not a seminar in analytic philosophy or linguistic analysis. Commerce was *commerce* — and if different interpretations of the word arose, later generations could worry about the problem of definition. The delegates were in a hurry to get a new government established; when definitional arguments arose, they characteristically took refuge in ambiguity. If different men voted for the same proposition for varying reasons, that was politics (and still is); if later generations were unsettled by this lack of precision, that would be their problem.

There was a good deal of definitional pluralism with respect to the problems the delegates did discuss, but when we move to the question of extrapolated intentions, we enter the realm of spiritualism. When men in our time, for instance, launch into elaborate talmudic exegesis to demonstrate that federal aid to parochial schools is (or is not) in accord with the intentions of the men who established the Republic and endorsed the Bill of Rights, they are engaging in historical Extra-Sensory Perception. . . .

The Constitution, then, was not an apotheosis of "constitutionalism," a triumph of architectonic genius; it was a patch-work sewn together under the pressure of both time and events by a group of extremely talented democratic politicians. They refused to attempt the establishment of a strong, centralized sovereignty on the principle of legislative supremacy for the excellent reason that the people would not accept it. They risked their political fortunes by opposing the established doctrines of state sovereignty because they were convinced that the existing system was leading to national impotence and probably foreign domination. For two years, they worked to get a convention established. For over three months, in what must have seemed to the faithful participants an endless process of give-and-take, they reasoned, cajoled, threatened, and bargained amongst themselves. The result was a Constitution which the people, in fact, by democratic processes, did accept, and a new and far better national government was established.

Beginning with the inspired propaganda of Hamilton, Madison and Jay, the ideological build-up got under way. *The Federalist* had little impact on the ratification of the Constitution, except perhaps in New York, but this volume had enormous influence on the image of the Constitution in the minds of future generations, particularly on historians and political scientists who have an innate fondness for theoretical symmetry. Yet, while the shades of Locke and Montesquieu *may* have been hovering in the background, and the delegates *may* have been unconscious instruments of a transcendent *telos*, the careful observer of the day-to-day work of the Convention finds no over-arching principles. The "separation of powers" to him seems to be a by-product of suspicion, and "federalism" he views as a *pis aller*, as the farthest point the delegates felt they could go in the destruction of state power without themselves inviting repudiation.

To conclude, the Constitution was neither a victory for abstract theory nor a great practical success. Well over half a million men had to die on the battlefields of the Civil War before certain constitutional principles could be defined —a baleful consideration which is somehow overlooked in our customary tributes to the farsighted genius of the Framers and to the supposed American talent for "constitutionalism." The Constitution was, however, a vivid demonstration of effective democratic political action, and of the forging of a national elite which literally persuaded its countrymen to hoist themselves by their own boot straps. American pro-consuls would be wise not to translate the Constitution into Japanese, or Swahili, or treat it as a work of semi-Divine origin; but when students of comparative politics examine the process of nation-building in countries newly freed from colonial rule, they may find the American experience instructive as a classic example of the potentialities of a democratic elite.

Notes

[1] The view that the right to vote in the states was severely circumscribed by property qualifications has been thoroughly discredited in recent years. See Chilton Williamson, *American Suffrage from Property to Democracy, 1760-1860* (Princeton, 1960). The contemporary position is that John Dickinson actually knew what he was talking about when he argued that there would be little opposition to vesting the right of suffrage in freeholders since "The great mass of our Citizens is composed at this time of freeholders, and will be pleased with it." Max Farrand, *Records of the Federal Convention,* Vol. 2, p. 202 (New Haven, 1911). (Henceforth cited as *Farrand.*)

[2] The classic statement of the *coup d'etat* theory is, of course, Charles A. Beard, *An Economic Interpretation of the Constitution of the United States* (New York, 1913), and this theme was echoed by Vernon L. Parrington, Merrill Jensen and others in "populist" historiographical tradition. For a sharp critique of this thesis see Robert E. Brown, *Charles Beard and the Constitution* (Princeton, 1956). See also Forrest McDonald, *We the People* (Chicago, 1958); the trailblazing work in this genre was Douglas Adair, "The Tenth Federalist Revisited," *William and Mary Quarterly,* Third Series, Vol. VIII (1951), pp. 48-67.

[3] A basic volume, which, like other works by Warren, provides evidence with which one can evaluate the author's own opinions, is Charles Warren, *The Making of the Constitution* (Boston, 1928). The best brief summary of the forces behind the movement for centralization is Chapter 1 of *Warren* (as it will be cited hereafter).

[4] Stanley Elkins and Eric McKitrick, "The Founding Fathers: Young Men of the Revolution," *Political Science Quarterly,* Vol. 76, p. 181 (1961).

[5] "[T]he situation of the general government, if it can be called a government, is shaken to its foundation, and liable to be overturned by every blast. In a word, it is at an end; and, unless a remedy is soon applied, anarchy and confusion will inevitably ensue." Washington to Jefferson, May 30, 1787, *Farrand,* III, 31. See also Irving Brant, *James Madison, The Nationalist* (New York, 1948), ch. 25.

[6] Merrill Jensen, *The New Nation* (New York, 1950). Interestingly enough, Prof. Jensen virtually ignores international relations in his laudatory treatment of the government under the Articles of Confederation.

[7] Yet, there was little objection to this crucial modification from any quarter—there almost seems to have been a gentlemen's agreement that Rhode Island's *liberum veto* had to be destroyed.

[8] See, *e.g.,* Gottfried Dietze, *The Federalist, A Classic on Federalism and Free Government* (Baltimore, 1960); Richard Hofstadter, *The American Political Tradition* (New York, 1948); and John P. Roche, "American Liberty," in M. Konvitz and C. Rossiter, eds., *Aspects of Liberty* (Ithaca, 1958).

[9] "I hold it for a fundamental point, that an individual independence of the states is utterly irreconcilable with the idea of an aggregate sovereignty," Madison to Randolph, cited in Brant, *op. cit.,* p. 416.

[10] Said William Samuel Johnson on June 21: "A gentleman from New-York, with boldness and decision, proposed a system totally different from both [Virginia and New Jersey]; and though he has been praised by every body, he has been supported by none." *Farrand,* I, 363.

[11] Crosskey in his sprawling *Politics and the Constitution* (Chicago, 1953), 2 vols., has developed with almost unbelievable zeal and intricacy the thesis that the Constitution *was* designed to establish a centralized unitary state, but that the political leadership of the Republic in its formative years betrayed this ideal and sold the pass to states'-rights.

An Economic Interpretation of the Constitution

Charles A. Beard

The most important, as well as the most controversial, commentator on the Constitution has been Charles A. Beard (1874-1948). In his book, An Economic Interpretation of the Constitution of the United States *(1913), he advanced the thesis that the Founding Fathers wrote the Constitution in order to arrest the apparent trend toward democracy and to protect their own economic interests. In order to prove his thesis, Beard examined the political ideas of the members of the Constitutional Convention of 1787 and the property holdings of the delegates, the purpose being to show that their ideas were actually reflections of their economic class interests. Beard also investigated the contest over ratification in each of the states in an effort to establish that the contest was fundamentally a class struggle between "substantial personalty interests" and "small farming and debtor interests." Basic to his conclusions was Beard's belief that the members of the Convention and state ratifying conventions represented wealth in "personalty"—that is, property other than real estate. Beard often misused the term, however, either using it to refer to a group of people ("All personalty was not equally interested. . . .") or in identifying personalty as primarily government securities. The excerpt which follows illustrates Beard's methodology, which was innovative, and introduces the reader to a book which has been subject to as much praise and criticism as any book published in the history of our country.*

The requirements for an economic interpretation of the formation and adoption of the Constitution may be stated in a hypothetical proposition which, although it cannot be verified absolutely from ascertainable data, will at once illustrate the problem and furnish a guide to research and generalization.

It will be admitted without controversy that the Constitution was the creation of a certain number of men, and it was opposed by a certain number of men. Now, if it were possible to have an

Reprinted from *An Economic Interpretation of the Constitution of the United States* by Charles A. Beard. Copyright 1913 by Macmillan Company. Excerpts from pages 16-18; 253-265; 268-271; 288-291; and 324-325.

economic biography of all those connected with its framing and adoption,—perhaps about 160,000 men altogether,—the materials for scientific analysis and classification would be available. Such an economic biography would include a list of the real and personal property owned by all of these men and their families: lands and houses, with incumbrances, money at interest, slaves, capital invested in shipping and manufacturing, and in state and continental securities.

Suppose it could be shown from the classification of the men who supported and opposed the Constitution that there was no line of property division at all; that is, that men owning substantially the same amounts of the same kinds of property were equally divided on the matter of adoption or rejection — it would then become apparent that the Constitution had no ascertainable relation to economic groups or classes, but was the product of some abstract causes remote from the chief business of life—gaining a livelihood.

Suppose, on the other hand, that substantially all of the merchants, money lenders, security holders, manufacturers, shippers, capitalists, and financiers and their professional associates are to be found on one side in support of the Constitution and that substantially all or the major portion of the opposition came from the non-slaveholding farmers and the debtors—would it not be pretty conclusively demonstrated that our fundamental law was not the product of an abstraction known as "the whole people," but of a group of economic interests which must have expected beneficial results from its adoption? Obviously all the facts here desired cannot be discovered, but the data presented in the following chapters bear out the latter hypothesis, and thus a reasonable presumption in favor of the theory is created.

Of course, it may be shown (and perhaps can be shown) that the farmers and debtors who opposed the Constitution were, in fact, benefited by the general improvement which resulted from its adoption. It may likewise be shown, to take an extreme case, that the English nation derived immense advantages from the Norman Conquest and the orderly administrative processes which were introduced, as it undoubtedly did; nevertheless, it does not follow that the vague thing known as "the advancement of general welfare" or some abstraction known as "justice" was the immediate, guiding purpose of the leaders in either of these great historic changes. The point is, that the direct, impelling motive in both cases was the economic advantages which the beneficiaries expected would accrue to themselves first, from their action. Further than this, economic interpretation cannot go. It may be that some larger world-process is working through each series of historical events; but ultimate causes lie beyond our horizon.

• • •

As in natural science no organism is pretended to be understood as long as its merely superficial aspects are described, so in history no movement by a mass of people can be correctly comprehended until that mass is resolved into its component parts. To apply this concept to the problem before us: no mathematically exact conclusion can be reached concerning the material interests reflected in the Constitution until "the people" who favored its adoption and "the people" who opposed it are individualized and studied as economic beings dependent upon definite modes and processes of gaining a livelihood. A really fine analytical treatment of this problem would, therefore, require a study of the natural history of the (approximately) 160,000 men involved in the formation and adoption of the Constitution; but for the present we must rely on rougher generalizations, drawn from incomplete sources.

It would be fortunate if we had a description of each of the state conventions similar to that made of the Philadelphia Convention; but such a description would require a study of the private economy of several hundred men, with considerable scrutiny. And the results of such a search would be on the whole less fruitful than those secured by the study of the Philadelphia Convention, because so many members of the state-ratifying bodies were obscure persons of whom biography records nothing and whose property holdings do not appear in any of the documents that have come down to us. In a few instances, as in the case of Pennsylvania, a portion of this work has been done in a fragmentary way—as regards economic matters; and it may be hoped that a penetrating analysis of the public security holdings and other property interests of the members of all state conventions may sometime be made—as far as the sources will allow. Nevertheless, for the purposes of this study, certain general truths concerning the conflict over the ratification of the Constitution in the several states have already been established by scholars like Libby, Harding, Ambler.

The first of these authors, Dr. Libby, has made a painstaking study of the *Geographical Distribution of the Vote on the Constitution*, in which he sets forth the economic characteristics of the areas for and against the adoption of the Constitution. These conclusions are all utilized in this chapter; but they are supplemented by reference to the later researches of Harding[1] and Ambler,[2] and by a large amount of new illustrative materials here presented for the first time. The method followed is to exhibit, in general, the conflict of economic interests in each of the several states over the adoption of the Constitution.

New Hampshire. — There were three rather sharply marked economic districts in New Hampshire which found political expression in the convention that ratified the Constitution. Two of the three were the sea-coast area and the interior or middle region. "The former," says Libby, "the coast area, represented the commercial and urban interests; here were to be found most of the professional men, leaders of thought, men of wealth and influence. The second section, the interior, was composed of those representing the small farmers; a population cut off from the outside world by lack of good roads, and which raised little for market except to exchange for the few things that could not be produced at home. The former class, progressive and liberal and familiar with the practical details of government, as a rule voted for the Constitution. The latter, conservative by environment and having little knowledge of what went on outside the narrow bounds of the home village or township, quite as generally voted against the Constitution."

The third region in New Hampshire (whose representatives favored ratification) was "the Connecticut valley or border district" whose interests were akin to those of the sea towns because it had commercial connection with the outside world through the Connecticut River. It was to this region particularly that Oliver Ellsworth must have appealed in his open letter to the citizens of New Hampshire in which he said: "New York, the trading towns on the Connecticut River, and Boston are the sources from which a great part of your foreign supplies will be obtained, and where your produce will be exposed for market. In all these places an import is collected, of which, as consumers, you pay a share without deriving any public benefit. You cannot expect any alteration in the private systems of these states unless effected by the proposed government."

Several economic facts of prime significance in the ratification of the Constitution in New Hampshire are afforded by the tax returns of 1793. These show that of the £61,711:9:5 "total value of stock in trade" in the state in that year (Vermont being then cut off) no less than £42,512:0:5 or over two-thirds was in Rockingham county, the seat of the commercial town of Portsmouth, whose citizens were the leading agitators for the new system, and whose delegates in the state convention were overwhelmingly in favor of ratification. Moreover, of the total amount of the "money on hand or at interest" in the state, £35,985:5:6, about two-thirds, £22,770:9:4 was in Rockingham county. It is of further significance that of the £893,327:16:10 worth of real estate and buildings in the state, less than one-half, £317,970:7:2, was in that county. Thus the stronghold of Federalism possessed about two-thirds of all the personalty and only about one-half of the realty values in the commonwealth.

All personalty was not equally interested in ratifying the Constitution, as pointed out above; holders of public paper multiplied their values from six to twenty times in securing the establishment of the new system. Further interesting data would be revealed, therefore, if we could discover the proportion of public securities to other personalty and their geographic distribution. The weight of the securities in New Hampshire is shown by the fact that the tax list for 1793 gives only £35,985 as the total amount of money on hand or at interest (including public securities) in the state, while the accounts of the Treasury department show that $20,000 in interest on the public debt went to the loan office of that state to discharge that annual federal obligation. It is highly probable that the tax list is very low, but even at that the public securities constituted a considerable mass of the capital of the commonwealth. The leading supporters of the Constitution in New Hampshire were large holders of public paper, and there is no doubt that as personalty was the dynamic element in the movement for the Constitution, so securities were the dynamic element in the personalty.

Massachusetts. — The vote in Massachusetts on the Constitution was clearly along class or group lines: those sections in which were to be found the commerce, money, securities—in a word, personalty—were in favor of the ratification of the new instrument of government; and those sections which were predominantly rural and possessed little personalty were against it. Libby classifies the sections on the basis of the vote as follows:—

Eastern section .... Yeas, 73 per cent
                               Nays, 27 per cent
Middle section .... Yeas, 14 per cent
                               Nays, 86 per cent
Western section .... Yeas, 42 per cent
                               Nays, 58 per cent

Speaking of this table he says: "Such striking differences as these indicate clearly that there is something fundamental lying back of the vote. Each of these sections is an economic and social unit, the first representing the coast region, the second the interior, and the third the Connecticut valley and border districts of the state. In the eastern section the interests were commercial; there was the wealth, the influence, the urban population of the state.... The middle section of Massachusetts represented the interior agricultural interests of the state — the small farmers. From this section came a large part of the Shays faction in 1786. The Connecticut valley or western district may be subdivided into the northern, most interior, and predominantly Anti-federal section, and the southern section, nearest the coast and predominantly Federal, with the trading towns of the Connecticut River in its southeastern part."

Harding, after an independent study of the opposition to the Constitution in Massachusetts, comes to substantially the same conclusion. Among the weighty elements in the struggle he places "the conflict of interest, partly real and partly fancied, between the agricultural and the commercial sections of the state." Underlying the whole opposition, he continues, "was the pronounced antagonism between the aristocratic and the democratic elements of society in Massachusetts.... Massachusetts was not alone in this experience; in most, if not all, of the states a similar contest had arisen since the war. The men who at Philadelphia had put their names to the new Constitution were, it seems quite safe to affirm, at that time identified with the aristocratic interest. . . . There can be no question that this feeling [of antagonism between democracy and aristocracy] underlay most of the opposition in the Massachusetts convention."

Of course this second element of opposition — aristocracy *versus* democracy — introduced by Harding is really nothing but the first under another guise; for the aristocratic party was the party of wealth with its professional dependents; and the democratic party was the agrarian element which, by the nature of economic circumstances, could have no large body of professional adherents. This economic foundation of the class division was fully understood by Adams and set forth with unmistakable clearness in his *Defence of the American Constitutions*. Hamilton, Madison, and all thinkers among the Federalists understood it also. To speak of a democratic interest apart from its economic sources is therefore a work of supererogation; and it does not add, in fact, to an exposition of the real forces at work. Harding himself recognizes this and explains it in a luminous fashion in his introductory chapter.

And what were the economic and social antecedents of the opponents of the Constitution in the Massachusetts convention? Harding, with his customary directness, meets the inquiry: "A half-dozen obscure men, it must be answered, whose names are utterly unknown, even to most students of this period." He continues: "William Widgery (or Wedgery) of New Gloucester, Maine, was one of these. A poor, friendless, uneducated boy, he had emigrated from England before the Revolution, had served as a lieutenant on board a privateer in that contest, had then settled in Maine, had acquired some property, and by 1788 had served one term in the Massachusetts legislature. . . . Samuel Thompson, of Topsham, Maine, was another of the anti-federalist leaders. A self-made man, he had the obstinacy of opinion which such men often show. . . . He was wealthy for the times, but inclined to be niggardly. . . . Another determined opponent of the proposed Constitution was Samuel Nasson (or Nason) of Sanford, Maine. Born in New Hampshire and a saddler by trade, he became a store keeper in Maine, served awhile in the War . . . and finally settled down as a trader at Sanford. . . . In 1787 he served a term in the General Court, but declined a re-election because he felt 'the want of a proper education.' . . . From Massachusetts proper, Dr. John Taylor, of Douglas, Worcester County, was the most prominent opponent of the new Constitution. . . . But the slightest information, it seems, can now be gathered as to his history and personality. He had been one of the popular majority in the legislature of 1787 where he had taken an active part in procuring the extension of the Tender Law. . . . Another delegate from this part of the state who was prominent in the opposition was Captain Phanuel Bishop, of Rehoboth, Bristol County. In him the Rhode Island virus may be seen at work. . . . He was a native of Massachusetts and had received a public school education. When or why he had been dubbed Captain is not now apparent. Belknap styles him 'a noted insurgent'; and he had evidently ridden into office on the crest of the Shaysite wave. His first legislative experience had been in the Senate of 1787 where he had championed the debtor's cause."

This completes the list of leaders who fought bitterly against the Constitution to the end in Massachusetts, according to a careful student of the ratification in that state: three self-made men from the Maine regions and two representatives of the debtor's cause. Nothing could be more eloquent than this description of the alignment.

Neither Harding nor Libby has, however, made analysis of the facts disclosed by the tax lists of Massachusetts or the records in the Treasury Department at Washington, which show unquestionably that the live and persistent economic force which organized and carried through the ratification was the personalty interests and particularly the public security interests. As has been pointed out, these had the most to gain immediately from the Constitution. Continental paper bought at two and three shillings in the pound was bound to rise rapidly with the establishment of the federal government. No one knew this better than the members of the federal Convention from Massachusetts and their immediate friends and adherents in Boston.

Of the total amount of funded 6 per cents in the state, £113,821, more than one-half, £65,730, was concentrated in the two counties, Essex and Suffolk, of which Boston was the urban centre—the two counties whose delegates in the state convention were almost unanimous in supporting the Constitution. Of the total amount of 3 per cents, £73,100, more than one-half, £43,857, was in these two counties. Of the deferred stock, amounting to £59,872, more than one-half, £32,973, was in these two counties. Of the total amount of all other securities of the state or the United States in the commonwealth, £94,893, less than one-third or £30,329, was in these counties. Of the total amount of money at interest in the state, £196,698, only about one-third, £63,056, was in these two counties, which supports the above conjecture that public securities were the active element.

Further confirmation for this conjecture seems to be afforded by the following tables, showing the distribution of the vote and of public securities. The first group shows the votes of the delegates from Essex and Suffolk counties — the Federalist strongholds—on the ratification, and also the amount of public securities in each as revealed by the tax lists of 1792:

ESSEX
For the Constitution ....33 votes
Against ....6 votes
SUFFOLK
For the Constitution ....34 votes
Against ....5 votes

Table of public securities listed for taxation in each of these counties:

	SUFFOLK	ESSEX
Funded, sixes	£29,228	£36,502
Funded, threes	17,096	26,761
Funded, not on interest	14,854	18,119
Other securities	14,056	16,273
Money at Interest	29,941	33,115

New let us take the vote in the convention, and the property in two counties which were heavily against the Constitution. The vote is as follows:

WORCESTER
For the Constitution ....7 votes
Against ....43 votes
BERKSHIRE
For the Constitution ....7 votes
Against ....15 votes

The tables of public securities and money in these counties follow:

	WORCESTER	BERKSHIRE
Funded, sixes	£12,924	£981
Funded, threes	8,184	665
Funded, not on interest	5,736	384
Other securities	10,903	602
Money at interest	25,594	6298

Now if we take the securities in these two counties which went heavily against the Constitution several economic facts are worthy of notice. Of the total amount of 6 per cents in the state, only £13,905, or about one-eighth is to be found in them. Of the 3 per cents, we find £8849, or about one-eighth of the total amount in the commonwealth. But if we take money at interest, we find £31,892, or about one-sixth of the total amount in the state. This is not surprising, for Worcester was the centre of the Shays rebellion in behalf of debtors, and a large portion of their creditors were presumably in the neighborhood.

"The courts were burdened with suits for ordinary debts by means of which creditors sought to put in more lasting form the obligations which their debtors could not at that time meet. In Worcester county alone, with a population of less than 50,000, more than 2000 actions were entered in 1784, and during the next year 1700 more were put on the list."

These figures, like all other statistics, should be used with care, and it would require a far closer analysis than can be made here to work out all of their political implications. We should have a thorough examination of such details as the distribution of the public securities among towns and individual holders; and such a work is altogether worthy of a Quetelet.

Meanwhile, it may be said with safety that the communities in which personalty was relatively more powerful favored the ratification of the Constitution, and that in these communities large quantities of public securities were held. Moreover, there was undoubtedly a vital connection between the movement in support of the Constitution and public security holding, or to speak concretely, among the leading men in Massachusetts who labored to bring about the ratification was a large number of public creditors.

For example, Boston had twelve representatives in the state-ratifying convention, all of whom voted in favor of the Constitution. Of these twelve men the following were holders of public securities:

Samuel Adams   John Coffin Jones
James Bowdoin, Sr.   William Phillips
Thomas Dawes, Jr.   Thomas Russell
Christopher Gore   John Winthrop

In other words, at least eight out of the twelve men representing the chief financial centre of the state were personally interested in the fate of the new Constitution. How deeply, it is impossible to say, for the Ledgers seem to have disappeared from the Treasury Department and only the Index to the funded debt remains. Supplementary records, however, show some of them to have been extensively engaged in dealing in paper. The four men who, apparently, were not security holders were John Hancock, Caleb Davis, Charles Jarvis, and Rev. Samuel Stillman.

The towns surrounding Boston in Suffolk county also returned a number of men who were holders of securities:

Fisher Ames,   Benj. Lincoln,
  Dedham   Hingham
John Baxter,   Rev. Daniel Shute,
  Medfield   Hingham
James Bowdoin,   Increase Sumner,
  Jr., Dorchester   Roxbury
Richard Cranch,   Cotton Tufts,
  Braintree   Weymouth
J. Fisher,   Ebenezer Wales,
  Franklin   Dorchester
William Heath,   Ebenezer Warren,
  Roxbury   Foxboro
Thomas Jones,   Rev. Anthony
  Hull   Wibird, Braintree

In other words, twenty-two of the thirty-four men from Boston and Suffolk county who voted in favor of the ratification of the Constitution in the Massachusetts convention were holders of public securities, and all of the twenty-two except two (Wales and Warren) probably benefited from the appreciation of the funds which resulted from the ratification.

To recapitulate. There were thirty-nine members of the Massachusetts convention from Suffolk county, which includes Boston. Of these, thirty-four voted for the ratification of the Constitution, and of the thirty-four who so voted, two-thirds, or twenty-two to be exact, were holders of public paper.

That other supporters of the Constitution from other Massachusetts counties held paper so extensively is not to be expected, and a casual glance through the records shows that this surmise is probably true. Boston was the centre of the Federalist agitation, and it supplied the sinews of war for the campaign which finally secured the adoption of the new system of government. . . .

New York.—There can be no question about the predominance of personalty in the contest over the ratification in New York. That state, says Libby, "presents the problem in its simplest form. The entire mass of interior counties . . . were solidly Anti-federal, comprising the agricultural portion of the state, the last settled and the most thinly populated. There were however in this region two Federal cities (not represented in the convention [as such]), Albany in Albany county and Hudson in Columbia county. . . . The Federal area centred about New York city and county: to the southwest lay Richmond county (Staten Island); to the southeast Kings county, and to the northeast Westchester county; while still further extending this area, at the northeast lay the divided county of Dutchess, with a vote in the convention of 4 to 2 in favor of the Constitution, and at the southeast were the divided counties of Queens and Suffolk. . . . These radiating strips of territory with New York city as a centre form a unit, in general favorable to the new Constitution; and it is significant of this unity that Dutchess, Queens, and Suffolk counties broke away from the anti-Federal phalanx and joined the Federalists, securing thereby the adoption of the Constitution."

Unfortunately the exact distribution of personalty in New York and particularly in the wavering districts which went over to the Federalist party cannot be ascertained, for the system of taxation in vogue in New York at the period of the adoption of the Constitution did not require a state record of property. The data which proved so fruitful in Massachusetts are not forthcoming, therefore, in the case of New York; but it seems hardly necessary to demonstrate the fact that New York City was the centre of personalty for the state and stood next to Philadelphia as the great centre of operations in public stock.

This somewhat obvious conclusion is reinforced by the evidence relative to the vote on the legal tender bill which the paper money party pushed through in 1786. Libby's analysis of this vote shows that "No vote was cast against the bill by members of counties north of the county of New York. In the city and county of New York and in Long Island and Staten Island, the combined vote was 9 to 5 against the measure. Comparing this vote with the vote on the ratification in 1788, it will be seen that of the Federal counties 3 voted against paper money and 1 for it; of the divided counties 1 (Suffolk) voted against paper money and 2 (Queens and Dutchess) voted for it. Of the anti-Federal counties none had members voting against paper money. The merchants as a body were opposed to the issue of paper money and the Chamber of Commerce adopted a memorial against the issue."

Public security interests were identified with the sound money party. There were thirty members of the New York constitutional convention who voted in favor of the ratification of the Constitution and of these no less than sixteen were holders of public securities:

James Duane, New York (C 6)
John DeWitt, Dutchess (N.Y. 3)
Alexander Hamilton, New York
Richard Harrison, New York (C 6)
Jonathan Havens, Suffolk (C 6 as
   Trustee for a religious society).
John Jay, New York (C 6)
Samuel Jones, Queens (C 6)
Philip Livingston, Westchester (C 6)
Robert R. Livingston, New York
   (N.Y. 3)
Nicholas Low, New York (C 6)
Richard Morris, New York (C 6)
Isaac Roosevelt, New York (R)
Gozen Ryerss, Richmond (N.Y. 3)
John Smith, Suffolk (C 6)
Melancton Smith, Dutchess (Conn.)
Philip Van Cortland, Westchester
   (C6)
Jesse Woodhull, Orange (C 6)

South Carolina.—South Carolina presents the economic elements in the ratification with the utmost simplicity.

There we find two rather sharply marked districts in antagonism over the Constitution. "The rival sections," says Libby, "were the coast or lower district and the upper, or more properly, the middle and upper country. The coast region was the first settled and contained a larger portion of the wealth of the state; its mercantile and commercial interests were important; its church was the Episcopal, supported by the state." This region, it is scarcely necessary to remark, was overwhelmingly in favor of the Constitution. The upper area, against the Constitution, "was a frontier section, the last to receive settlement; its lands were fertile and its mixed population were largely small farmers. . . . There was no established church, each community supported its own church and there was a great variety in the district."

A contemporary writer, R. G. Harper, calls attention to the fact that the lower country, Charleston, Beaufort, and Georgetown, which had 28,694 white inhabitants, and about seven-twelfths of the representation in the state convention, paid £28,081:5:10 taxes in 1794, while the upper country, with 120,902 inhabitants, and five-twelfths of the representation in the convention, paid only £8390:13:3 taxes. The lower districts in favor of the Constitution therefore possessed the wealth of the state and a disproportionate share in the convention — on the basis of the popular distribution of representation.

These divisions of economic interest are indicated by the abstracts of the tax returns for the state in 1794 which show that of £127,337 worth of stock in trade, faculties, etc. listed for taxation in the state, £109,800 worth was in Charleston, city and county—the stronghold of Federalism. Of the valuation of lots in towns and villages to the amount of £656,272 in the state, £549,909 was located in that city and county.

The records of the South Carolina loan office preserved in the Treasury Department at Washington show that the public securities of that state were more largely in the hands of inhabitants than was the case in North Carolina. They also show a heavy concentration in the Charleston district.

At least fourteen of the thirty-one members of the state-ratifying convention from the parishes of St. Philip and Saint Michael, Charleston (all of whom favored ratification) held over $75,000 worth of public securities, which amount was distributed unevenly among the following men:

John Blake	Isaac Motte
Danl. Cannon	C. C. Pinckney
Edw. Darrell	John Pringle
John F. Grimke	David Ramsay
Wm. Johnson	Nathaniel Russel
Thomas Jones	Josiah Smith
Lewis Morris	Danl. de Soussure

Georgia.—Georgia was one of the states that gave a speedy and unanimous consent to the adoption of the Constitution. If there was any considerable contest there, no record of it appears on the surface; and no thorough research has ever been made into the local unprinted records. Libby dismisses the state with the suggestion that the pressing dangers from the Indians on the frontiers, which were formidable and threatening in the summer and autumn of 1787, were largely responsible for the swift and favorable action of the state in ratifying the new instrument of government that promised protection under national arms.

Three conclusions seem warranted by the data presented in this chapter:

Inasmuch as the movement for the ratification of the Constitution centred particularly in the regions in which mercantile, manufacturing, security, and personalty interests generally had their greatest strength, it is impossible to escape the conclusion that holders of personalty saw in the new government a strength and defence to their advantage.

Inasmuch as so many leaders in the movement for ratification were large security holders, and inasmuch as securities constituted such a large proportion of personalty, this economic interest must have formed a very considerable dynamic element, if not the preponderating element, in bringing about the adoption of the new system.

The state conventions do not seem to have been more "disinterested" than the Philadelphia convention; but in fact the leading champions of the new government appear to have been, for the most part, men of the same practical type, with actual economic advantages at stake.

The opposition to the Constitution almost uniformly came from the agricultural regions, and from the areas in which debtors had been formulating paper money and other depreciatory schemes.

CONCLUSIONS

At the close of this long and arid survey —partaking of the nature of catalogue— it seems worth while to bring together the important conclusions for political science which the data presented appear to warrant.

The movement for the Constitution of the United States was originated and carried through principally by four groups of personalty interests which had been adversely affected under the Articles of Confederation: money, public securities, manufactures, and trade and shipping.

The first firm steps toward the formation of the Constitution were taken by a small and active group of men immediately interested through their personal possessions in the outcome of their labors.

No popular vote was taken directly or indirectly on the proposition to call the Convention which drafted the Constitution.

A large propertyless mass was, under the prevailing suffrage qualifications, excluded at the outset from participation (through representatives) in the work of framing the Constitution.

The members of the Philadelphia Convention which drafted the Constitution were, with a few exceptions, immediately, directly, and personally interested in, and derived economic advantages from, the establishment of the new system.

The Constitution was essentially an economic document based upon the concept that the fundamental private rights of property are anterior to government and morally beyond the reach of popular majorities.

The major portion of the members of the Convention are on record as recognizing the claim of property to a special and defensive position in the Constitution.

In the ratification of the Constitution, about three-fourths of the adult males failed to vote on the question, having abstained from the elections at which delegates to the state conventions were chosen, either on account of their indifference or their disfranchisement by property qualifications.

The Constitution was ratified by a vote of probably not more than one-sixth of the adult males.

It is questionable whether a majority of the voters participating in the elections for the state conventions in New York, Massachusetts, New Hampshire, Virginia, and South Carolina, actually approved the ratification of the Constitution.

The leaders who supported the Constitution in the ratifying conventions represented the same economic groups as the members of the Philadelphia Convention; and in a large number of instances they were also directly and personally interested in the outcome of their efforts.

In the ratification, it became manifest that the line of cleavage for and against the Constitution was between substantial personalty interests on the one hand and the small farming and debtor interests on the other.

The Constitution was not created by "the whole people" as the jurists have said; neither was it created by "the states" as Southern nullifiers long contended; but it was the work of a consolidated group whose interests knew no state boundaries and were truly national in their scope.

Notes

[1] *Massachusetts and the Federal Constitution* (Harvard Studies).

[2] *Sectionalism in Virginia.*

Charles Beard, the Constitution, and the Historians

Each successive generation of scholars sees the past mirrored through its own involvement in the present. Robert Detweiler and Raymond Starr attempt to illuminate this problem in their historiographical essay on Charles Beard and the impact produced by the publication of his An Economic Interpretation of the Constitution of the United States. *Beard, writing in 1913 during the closing years of the Progressive Era, initiated one of the great intellectual debates in our history. He did so by asserting that economic interests were determinative of the political ideas which were incorporated by the Founding Fathers into the Constitution. The debate over whether constitutional or economic motives were dominant in the minds of the early leaders continues unabated today, although the actors and substantive arguments have changed. The following essay examines the intellectual climate in which Beard's thesis was conceived, the assault launched against his conclusions and methodology by critics and then links the changing attitudes toward the theory with the shifting political concerns in recent history.*

Robert Detweiler
Raymond Starr

In the years before 1913 the American nation had shrouded its Founding Fathers in an aura of divinity — they were often remembered as *demi-gods*—and the Constitution of 1787 had become a sacred document. The development of a mythology-history during the nineteenth century had been part of the process of creating an American sense of nationhood. It had also become, by the turn of the century, an impediment to social reform, as the Constitution was held up by conservative lawyers, businessmen, and the courts as a barrier to regulation of the abuses of big business.

Into this scene a reformer-historian, Charles A. Beard, thrust *An Economic Interpretation of the Constitution of the United States* (1913). The author accused the Founding Fathers of writing the Constitution to advance their own personal economic interests. The book and its author were severely criticized by

This article was prepared especially for this volume. Permission to reprint should be obtained from Charles E. Merrill Publishing Company.

the shocked public, but in due time Beard's interpretation of the Constitution, as well as an economic approach to American history in general, became the standard one. It reached its zenith in the era of the Great Depression and, in effect, became the *new* mythology. In the years after World War II, the book has come under devastating attack by highly respected historians. The result has been that few of its particulars are accepted today, although some of the broader implications of an economic interpretation of the Constitution are being re-asserted by a new generation of Beardians.

I

The man responsible for one of the most significant books in American historiography was the son of a prosperous small town Indiana banker, publisher and farmer. As a youth, Beard moved out of his conservative background and into the mainstream of two movements which merged to shape his history—the "New History" and social reform of the Progressive Era.[1]

Beard was trained in the New History at Columbia, where he received his doctorate in 1904, and where he taught until 1917. The New History, a turn-of-the-century refinement of "scientific" history, included two tenets which Beard absorbed. One was the assumption that there were no hard and fast facts in history, but that each generation rewrote history with reference to the conditions or values most important to its own times. Thus, the present used the past to create a better future. This led logically to the second point, that the major objective of the historian was to discover "how" things happened, rather than simply to recite "what" happened.

The blending of these views of history with a concern for social reform led naturally to Beard's economic orientation as an historian. Beard first became involved in social reform as a youth, at De Pauw College, in the Chicago slums, and in England. By 1901 he was writing of his hope that "the people, instead of a few capitalists" would "reap the benefits" of the Industrial Revolution. Both in England and upon his return to the United States, he continued to be personally involved in various reform movements; Beard was a rather typical example of a Progressive intellectual of the era.

As a Progressive, Beard subscribed to a number of assumptions. For instance, questioning in the social sciences had led to a discarding of the idea that law and government were the result of "incarnate abstract principles of justice" and development of the assumption that law and government were efforts to regulate relations between interest groups. Since the Progressives tended to identify interest groups as economic groups, this new definition of political life led to investigations of American politics from an economic point of view, both by scholars and muckrakers. Beard also accepted the Progressive definition of "reality" as being not what appeared on the surface, but as the ugly, sordid and hidden truth which was seldom recognized.

Because, as one historian has noted, "Beard was not simply a scholar; he was, and remained his life long, a publicist with an urgent interest in the intellectual and political milieu in which he lived," he absorbed the assumptions of the Progressive Era and applied them to the New History he learned at Columbia. The result was *An Economic Interpretation of the Constitution*, a book designed to show that the political beliefs of the framers of the Constitution were anti-democratic and that the Constitution itself was engineered to protect the interests of a propertied minority. Hence the imposition of the document on the country constituted a counter-revolution against the democratic ideals of the Revolution.

Beard tried to prove his thesis by examining the political views of the delegates to the Constitutional Convention and then by looking into their property holdings in order to establish that the delegates were, consciously or unconsciously, operating to defend their own economic interests. His fragmentary research showed him that the dominant property interest of the delegates was personalty. After exploring the holdings of the delegates, he looked into the amount and the geographical distribution of money, public securities, and real property. He then ascribed the movement for the Constitution to the pressure of four interest groups: money, public securities, manufactures, and trading and shipping. The movement to impose the property-oriented Constitution on the country was made possible because the framers excluded the propertyless mass of people (whom Beard assumed were disfranchised) from the writing and ratifying process.

Beard found that most of the members of the Constitutional Convention were "immediately, directly, and personally interested in, and derived economic advantages from, the establishment of the new system." He said the "Constitution was essentially an economic document based upon the concept that the fundamental private rights of property are anterior to government and morally beyond the reach of popular majorities." In concluding, Beard found that the contest over the Constitution was a struggle between "substantial personalty interests" and "small farming and debtor interests."

Coming into an era fertilized with the muckrakers' works on conspiracy, sordidness, and the baseness of the economic establishment, Beard's book had immediate and lasting impact—but not until it weathered the criticisms of some shocked readers. Former President William Howard Taft accused Beard of undertaking a "muckraking investigation" to prove the "reactionary nature of the Constitution." Warren G. Harding's newspaper, the Marion *Star*, headlined its account "SCAVENGERS, HYENA-LIKE, DESECRATE THE GRAVES OF THE DEAD PATRIOTS WE REVERE," and spoke of Beard's "filthy lies and rotten perversions" and the "damnable" influence of the book. A reviewer in *Educational Review* commented on the "gap" in Beard's logic. The distinguished scholar, J. H. Latané, maintained that Beard would need much "more convincing evidence . . . to upset the traditional view" that the Founding Fathers were patriots. The most severe and persistent critic was the highly respected constitutional historian, Edward S. Corwin, who claimed that Beard's evidence was "the most unmitigated rot" and his conclusions "scarcely survive" scrutiny.[2]

Despite such criticisms, Beard's thesis concerning the making of the Constitution, and the economic interpretation of United States history in general, became the standard in American history. Most of the major historians of the period accepted the economic interpretation. In the years 1913-1935, fifty-one of sixty-one new or revised college-level textbooks presented Beard's interpretation of the Constitution. General histories of the American people continued for over a generation to reflect Beard, and over twelve million copies of Beard's own books were sold within his lifetime. As late as 1954, Richard Hofstadter could write, with little fear of contradiction, that most of Beard's thesis "has been absorbed into the main body of American historical writing." Harvey Wish accurately described Beard's position when he referred to him as "a giant in our midst."[3]

II

The primacy of Beard's economic interpretation of the Constitution came to an end in the years after World War II. A number of historians began to attack Beard's book, and unlike his contemporary critics, these historians found their criticisms accepted by most scholars and the general public. The reasons for both the increased number of critics, and for the acceptance of the attacks on Beard, undoubtedly stemmed from the changing values and assumptions of the postwar society. The economic problems of the Progressive and Depression Eras seemed less pressing in a society which had accepted a welfare state mentality and enjoyed unprecedented affluence. Developments in sociology, psychology and other disciplines had provided evidence that man's motives are very complex, and the simplistic idea of a single cause for human behavior had become difficult to accept. At the same time, the country was engaged in a life-and-death struggle with the "Red Menace" for control of men's minds throughout the world. It was no longer allowable that the world should think that the Founding Fathers of the world's greatest democracy could have been operating from base and hidden motives when they wrote and adopted the Constitution. Freed of the shackles of economic determinism and eager to reassess America's beginnings, historians began to ask penetrating questions about Beard's thesis, and to subject his evidence and methods and findings to severe scrutiny.

The parade of critics was more or less led by Robert Brown, who published *Charles Beard and the Constitution: A Critical Analysis of "An Economic Interpretation of the Constitution"* in 1956. He was joined by a host of others, all set upon re-examining the Constitutional period, usually at Beard's expense. These critics have focused on four basic aspects of Beard's economic interpretation of the Constitution: (1) they have attacked his assumptions and judgments about human motivation; (2) they have severely criticized his use of evidence; (3) the critics have challenged Beard's assumption that the Constitution was the product of an anti-democratic reaction against the principles inherent in the Revolution; and finally (4) they have questioned his assumption that America in the Constitutional period was marked by deep class cleavages and that the struggle over the Constitution was essentially a class struggle.

III

In 1956 Edmund S. Morgan angrily challenged Beard's appraisal of the motives of the Founding Fathers, denying that economic interests alone motivated them. He said that they had bought securities in a spirit of patriotism, and that the "principles they carried with them to Philadelphia would not all have fitted in their pocketbooks." He said that knowing their economic interests tells us little about the motives of the members of the convention, because human beings are "complex, unpredictable, paradoxical, compounded of rationality and irrationality, moved by selfishness and by altruism, by love and by hate and by anger — and by principle." Morgan argued that the Convention succeeded, not simply because of the common economic or class interests of the delegates, "but because they held common principles . . . learned in twenty years of British tyranny and American seeking, in colonial assemblies, in state legislatures, and in Congress."[4]

Morgan was railing against Beard's assumptions about human motivation which had grown out of the Progressive concept of "reality". Beard believed that ideas were of little importance in influencing behavior; rather man "moved" unconsciously to take action. Upon examining man's behavior, Beard came to the conclusion that the basis for it was usually (but not always) economic interests. The weakness in Beard's analysis of man and his motives was twofold: failure to recognize that ideas may shape a man's concept of his interests, and failure to account for the importance of experience. Thus, in writing about the Convention, Beard failed to note that ideas had developed in the century prior to 1787 which shaped the way in which the framers perceived their interests. He also failed to take into account the persistent influence of the Revolutionary experiences, which shaped many of the Founding Fathers' views on the structure of government. These ideas and experiences caused them to view problems of political behavior from a very different point of view than the twentieth-century Progressive concern for politics as the systemizing of relations of economic groups. As a result, most historians are inclined to accept Morgan's, rather than Beard's, interpretation of the motives of the Founding Fathers.[5]

IV

Certainly there is no more vulnerable aspect of Beard's *An Economic Interpretation* than his use of evidence. In general his evidence was of two kinds: (1) evidence to prove that the Founding Fathers' political ideas were pro-property and anti-democratic; and (2) statistical analysis of their property holdings to prove that their ideas reflected their economic interests. Beard found that it was the personalty interests — government securities, money, and commerce—which favored the Constitution and realty and debtor interests who opposed it.

In so far as the second type of evidence —that pertaining to the property holdings of the delegates—is concerned, Robert Brown made considerable headway in refuting Beard. In his chapter-by-chapter critique of *An Economic Interpretation*, Brown examined Beard's use of evidence and found many shortcomings. With reference to methodology, Brown found much irrelevant material, undue evidence often from secondary sources, and heavy reliance on uncritical biographies. He also sharply criticized Beard for trying to establish the personalty holdings of the delegates by using Treasury records which covered a period after the Convention. Brown emphasized the danger in this by proving that some of the delegates had purchased securities after the Convention adjourned. After reviewing Beard's account of the delegates' holdings and the weakness in his research methods, Brown asked whether Beard's conclusion that personal property was responsible for the Constitution was justified. He concluded "the answer must be an emphatic no." If Beard had only tried to assert that the framers represented property in general, Brown thought he would be "on firm ground."

Brown also found Beard's evidence did not support the thesis that ratification was a struggle between substantial personalty interests and the small farmer-debtor classes. He showed that some agricultural states ratified unanimously and that most of the laboring classes in the cities voted for the Constitution — both groups with no substantial holdings of personalty or public securities.[6]

While Brown's attack on Beard's use of evidence attracted much attention, his excessively critical tone was not as convincing as it might have been. Forrest McDonald produced a different type of critique of Beard; he set out to test Beard's thesis, not to destroy it. He did the research in primary sources which Beard should have done, spending years and travelling thousands of miles to fill in the details of the holdings of the members of the Convention and the state ratifying conventions. He was able, in the end, to demolish Beard's findings in a way which makes it unlikely they will ever be revived.

Upon examining the economic interests of the delegates to the Philadelphia Convention, McDonald came to the conclusion that the members were not a "consolidated economic group" with an "identity of personalty interests." Indeed, he found that only thirty-six per cent of the men signing the Constitution fitted Beard's assertion that the document was the product of personalty interests. In addition, McDonald showed that the percentages of securities held by men voting for or against an issue in the Convention was almost always the same. Likewise, the voting pattern of the state delegations, or of individuals, "by no means followed the lines of a basic economic cleavage into realty and personalty interests." McDonald's extensive research showed that the delegates did not represent a special interest group.[7]

McDonald also analyzed the economics behind ratification of the Constitution, examining the economic interests of each member of each state ratifying convention, in order to see if there was the breakdown into "substantial personalty" versus small farmers and debtors which Beard wrote about. McDonald found that in most states, the farmers and friends of paper money supported the Constitution; in Massachusetts, they provided the margin of victory. In New Hampshire, nearly all the delegates voting for ratification were small farmers. In Virginia the small farmers of the backcountry favored the Constitution, the wealthy planters were about equally divided, and the planter-debtors favored ratification by a substantial margin. Beard saw the contest in New York as a simple one between paper-money men and security holders. McDonald proved that paper-money advocates were nearly always the same men who owned the public securities. In all, McDonald, by thorough research and detailed analysis of his data, has shown that the evidence Beard presented to support his thesis that there was an economic foundation for the Constitution is not only insufficient; it is often incorrectly analyzed.[8]

The works of Brown and McDonald have effectively demonstrated that the evidence Beard used to prove his major contention — that personalty interests dominated the federal and state conventions and produced the Constitution—is inadequate. The same can be said for Beard's analysis of the delegates' supposedly anti-democratic political views. Several critiques have effectively shown Beard's sins of omission and commission in presenting this portion of his evidence. Morgan, for example, maintained that in order to support his "sordid conclusion that the delegates who held public securities also held undemocratic political views, motivated consciously or unconsciously by the desire to protect their investment," Beard "consistently overlooked contradictory evidence."[9] Undoubtedly Brown and McDonald would have agreed with Morgan.

All three critics cite specific examples to show Beard's errors. Beard's treatment of Roger Sherman will serve as an illustration. Beard asserted that Sherman had risen from poverty to wealth in public securities and that his political philosophy was undemocratic inasmuch as Sherman advocated "reducing the popular influence in the new government to the minimum" by opposing the popular election of members of the lower house of the federal legislature. Beard reported Sherman saying that "the people . . . should have as little to do as may be about the government." While this quotation from the debates in the Convention clearly supported Beard's view, Morgan, Brown and Hofstadter all have pointed out that Beard overlooked what Sherman said on other occasions, statements which indicated a greater confidence in the people than the quotation Beard used. For example, after the Convention decided the people should elect the House, Sherman opposed triennial elections, declaring: "Government is instituted for those who live under it. It ought therefore to be so constituted as not to be dangerous to their liberties. . . . Frequent elections are necessary to preserve the good behavior of rulers." As Hofstadter pointed out, the consideration of *all* that Sherman said on the floor of the convention shows that instead of being the "crusty anti democratic ideologue" Beard depicted, Sherman was a man concerned with a number of very complicated problems in the "design of government." The same can be said for Beard's treatment of many other members of the Convention; in few parts of the book has Beard looked so bad as a practitioner of the historian's craft.[10]

V

Frequently in revolutionary movements, following the change of government and the institution of a new regime, there comes a reaction — a counterrevolution—which is intended to halt the revolutionary impulses. Charles Beard took this view in the case of the American Revolution. He suggested that the drafting and ratification of the Constitution was a counter-revolution engineered by a minority of conservatives bent upon checking the democratic excesses unleashed by the Revolution. This minority of "pocketbook patriots" deliberately designed the Constitution to be the antithesis of the principles espoused in the Declaration of Independence and secured by the American rebellion. Beard pointed out various provisions in the federal document which he felt were meant to be curbs on popular government: the complex system of checks and balances, the difficult amending process, indirect elections.

Beard's critics have not denied that the framers of the Constitution often displayed a deep-seated conservatism or that they were concerned with stemming anarchy in the new nation. But they argue that the Founding Fathers were hardly the engineers of an anti-democratic counter-revolution. In 1958 Benjamin Wright suggested that most Americans were agreed as to what the fundamentals of their government should be well before the Revolution, and their basic agreement was not changed by the American insurrection. He found a consensus of opinion among the rebels: they wanted a democratic state in which they could participate and enjoy personal liberty, but at the same time they wanted a stable government strong enough to curb democratic excesses and to protect property rights. The popular attitude toward democracy remained essentially the same before, during, and after the Revolution.

Beard had noted that the Philadelphia Convention which wrote the Constitution was itself an undemocratic body inasmuch as its members had been chosen indirectly through the state legislatures and not elected directly by the people. Wright pointed out that this was no more than traditional. All such bodies were selected by the state assemblies in the Revolutionary era—the Stamp Act Congress, the Continental Congress, the Congress of the Confederation. Actually the only departure was that the Constitution was submitted for approval to the people, which was a more democratic procedure than had been followed in the past. Similarly Beard charged that the conservatives who drafted the Constitution intended to make it very difficult to amend. But, as Wright has noted, it was infinitely more amendable than the Articles of Confederation which the framers were overturning.

Beard had argued — correctly — that the Constitution attempted to check popular control by a complex system of checks and balances and indirect elections. But Wright pointed out that this was the accepted view from the colonial and Revolutionary experiences; the state constitutions did not provide for direct popular election of the upper houses, of judges, or even of governors in most instances. It was true that the Constitution was geared, in part, to make the country safe *from* democracy; Wright showed that in the eighteenth century that was the dominant American attitude, not a counter-revolutionary attitude. Wright also dismissed Beard's view that the Constitution was a conservative reaction to the radicalism of the Revolution. He found that the men who wrote the ideas of the Revolution into the various state constitutions after 1776 were also the men who framed the federal Constitution. The framers were not driven by their own interests to carry out a scheme against the majority of Americans; they were not breaking with the past on basic principles: "Where were the breaks with the past? Certainly not in the principle of the rule of law or constitutionalism. Not in the system of elections. . . . Not in the amending process, which was liberalized." In Wright's mind the framers who sought a stronger federal union were the conservators of the Revolution, not the rejectors of it.[11]

Martin Diamond has also contended that the framers were democrats rather than members of an anti-democratic reaction. He agreed with Beard that the framers were preoccupied with minority interests and that they took measures to check the power of the majority, but he pointed out that such an attitude was quite consistent with the prevailing concept of democracy in eighteenth-century America. The men of that period were fearful that the mass of men with little or no property might usurp the property rights of the minority. Hence, the men who wrote the Constitution sought to strengthen popular government by establishing the means to check its inherent defects and dangerous propensities. They "sought to alter, by certain restraints, the likelihood that the majority would decide certain political issues in a bad way." The Constitution, then, was a device to remedy the defects of democracy while preserving popular government to the degree acceptable in the era of the Revolution.[12]

While Beard argued that the framers were anti-democratic, Cecelia Kenyon has shown in a perceptive examination of the ideas of the opponents of the Constitution that they, the Anti-Federalists, were even *less* democratic than the men who supported the federal document. Her criticisim strikes at the very heart of Beard's conclusion. If the men who opposed the Constitution were less democratically inclined than the Federalists, the idea that the Founders and ratifiers were propertied men fearful of democracy has little significance. All Americans were fearful of democracy, but the men most willing to experiment with popular government on a national scale were actually those who supported the Constitution. Kenyon contended that the Anti-Federalists distrusted majority rule in any case, and that they particularly distrusted majority rule on a national level. They feared any form of representative power which transcended their own local control: "The last thing in the world they wanted was a national democracy which would permit Congressional majorities to operate freely and without restraint."[13]

Stanley Elkins and Eric McKitrick agreed with Kenyon that the opponents of the Constitution were locally oriented. After fighting for individual liberty and state autonomy, the older men were fearful of a return to centralized authority and looked upon the Constitution with dismay. But the young men who had not developed the deep distaste for central government — men whose careers were shaped during the Revolution and after —were guided by a national outlook. Elkins and McKitrick saw the framers as a group of these young men who gained power during the Revolution and drafted a federal document which institutionalized their experience; they did not design a reaction against the principles of the Revolution.[14]

The critics of Beard's assumption that the Constitution was an antidemocratic counter-revolution concentrated on two essential points. First, they argued that the Constitution, rather than being antidemocratic, was quite compatible with the basic values of the Revolutionary society: republicanism and protection of property rights. Secondly, they maintained that the debate over the Constitution was not merely a struggle between democrats and anti-democrats. It was also a struggle between localism and nationalism and between old men and young men; and in the struggle those who opposed the Constitution were often more fearful of democracy than those who supported the federal document.

VI

Charles Beard wrote at a time when Americans were keenly aware of class cleavage and his interpretation of the making of the Constitution clearly reflected this awareness by stressing class conflict. Beard had been nurtured in the intellectual climate of the Progressive reform movement and, unwittingly, he saw the past through his own involvement. As one penetrating explorer of Beard's mind has put it, Beard "could hardly fail to absorb the style of thought of the Populist-Progressive-muckraking era; the limitations, as well as the best insights of that style of thought, left their impress upon his book."[15] Beard found that the men of the propertied class grew increasingly disturbed with the threat which they thought was inherent in the Revolution, so they pushed through a Constitution geared to protect their particular interests. This propertied minority, according to Beard, was able to force their design upon the reluctant majority in a successful class struggle: "In the ratification, it became manifest that the line of cleavage for and against the Constitution was between substantial personalty interests on the one hand and small farming and debtor interests on the other."

Robert Brown has charged that Beard was quite wrong to assume that the nation was marked by a sharp class structure built along economic lines. Brown found that most men in Revolutionary America owned their own small farms and that the nation was overwhelmingly middle-class. In his view, the Constitution was the will of this great middle-class, not a self-aggrandizing scheme engineered by the upper class. Benjamin Wright agreed with Brown that the essential product of the long experience of self-government up to the time of the drafting of the federal document was consensus, not class conflict: "The consensus was there, and it was crucial. Moreover, it was not the consensus of ideology, or desperation, or crisis. . . . It was rather the consensus rooted in the common life, habits, institutions, and experience of generations." To Brown and Wright the men who exercised *de facto* self-government in colonial America were essentially agreed as to the means and the goals of their political establishment; they remained agreed when they defended their attitudes in the Revolution and they saw their attitudes safeguarded under the Constitution.[16]

In developing the thesis that the Constitution was the product of a class conflict, Beard relied heavily on James Madison's *Federalist Number Ten*, emphasizing its concern with faction and property interests. He found it to be "a masterly statement of the theory of economic determinism in politics." Douglass Adair has argued, however, that Beard carefully edited Madison's essay, selecting only those segments which served his case, the selections which emphasized economic class struggle. Madison's paper, according to Adair, was not an example of economic determinism and class conflict in early America; it was an excellent example of eighteenth-century political theory. By misuse of evidence, Beard had warped Madison into an economic creature, when actually he was an excellent illustration of post-Revolutionary democratic theory with its emphasis upon safeguards to protect minority rights against the tyrannizing proclivities of popular government.[17]

Beard seems to have written into the past a reflection of the intellectual and social climate of the nation in the 1910's. It is striking that Beard's critics may also reflect the prevailing climate of opinion of their particular time. In the 1950's when the anti-Beardian reaction reached its zenith among American historians, the nation was caught in the throes of the Cold War. Faced with the threat of communism and class struggle throughout the world, Americans concentrated on consensus and unity in their own nation. Historians seem to have sought passionately to draw an image of consensus in the American past as well. Also, the rise of the affluent society in America and new concern for the improvement of the conditions of the nation's poor made emphasis on class cleavage less significant than it had been in the Progressive Era. Thus, the works of the anti-Beardians may actually tell us something about the Cold War-affluent society of the 1950's just as Beard's work tells us something about the society of the Progressive years.

VII

Although Charles Beard's critics continue to be active today, the anti-

Beardian reaction among historians of the Constitution appears to have reached a climax. In recent years an increasing number of scholars have grown critical of the approach of the "consensus" historians with their emphasis upon unity and agreement in early America, and they have found Beard's approach to the Constitution attractive again. These "neo-Beardians" do not spell an immediate end to the anti-Beardian reaction but they have completed the full cycle of historical opinion regarding the makers of the Constitution; the men who revised Beard are now being revised.

In a sense, even Beard's most efficient critic, Forrest McDonald, was something of a Beardian; at least he did not reject the significance of economic forces in human motivation. After doing the research Beard did not do, McDonald found Beard's economic interpretation too simple. In its place he suggested a more complex economic approach to the drafting and ratification of the Constitution—one which took into account local, state, regional, and factional differences among various interest groups. This pluralistic approach was an improvement on Beard's method of inquiry, but not a rejection of the broad Beardian hypothesis that the Constitution was rooted in economics.[18]

Like McDonald, the neo-Beardians of the 1960's have found fault with Beard's method of inquiry, but they have accepted his basic assumption that the economic orientation of men is foremost in the making of political decisions and they have rejected his critics' assumption that the Federalists and Anti-Federalists did not align themselves along class lines. For example, Jackson Turner Main, who found Beard's particular economic interpretation too elementary, has advanced a more sophisticated interpretation in which he establishes an extended group of mercantile interests—merchants, shippers, craftsmen, and laborers in towns and farmers who relied on the towns as markets — which formed the backbone of support for the Constitution. By developing this extensive socio-economic breakdown in the society of the 1780's, Main has concluded that the struggle to ratify the Constitution was "primarily a contest between the commercial and non-commercial elements in the population." For Main, just as for Beard, the primary generalization to be made is that the Federalists were men of substance while among the Anti-Federalists "the rank and file were men of moderate means, with little social prestige, farmers often in debt, obscure men for the most part."[19]

E. James Ferguson has agreed that "to eliminate entirely the role of economic motive in the political affairs of the time is as doctrinaire and as unnecessary as Beard's overstatement of it." In his scholarly study of public finance in the Revolutionary and early national period, Ferguson concluded that the clearest division caused by the Constitutional controversy was that between the extended mercantile community and the non-commercial agrarians. He clearly supported Beard's thesis that creditors and men who held public securities were generally Federalists.[20]

Perhaps the attitude of the neo-Beardians is best summarized in Stoughton Lynd's appeal for historians to go "beyond Beard"—to revise and expand the old thesis. Indeed, Lynd would make economic interpretation *the* approach to history.[21] His approach represents the so-called "New Left" reaction to the "consensus" history of the post-World War II era, and is one of the earliest examples of the history that may be written in a new period of conflict and stress in American life.

While historians have widely rejected many details of Charles Beard's particular economic approach to the Constitution and have rather thoroughly mauled his scholarship, the Beard thesis and approach to history is anything but dead. For more than half a century Beard has shaped inquiry into the origin and nature of the Constitution; his work has stimulated disciples and critics alike to ask new questions about the making of that document. In the end one finds that while his critics may have demolished Beard, they have failed to destroy Beardians.

Notes

[1] For Beard's life, career and impact, see Harvey Wish, *The American Historian* (New York, 1960), 265-92; Richard Hofstadter, *The Progressive Historians: Turner, Beard, Parrington* (New York, 1968), 165-346 and "Beard and the Constitution: The History of an Idea," *American Quarterly*, II (Fall, 1950), 195-213; Howard K. Beale, ed., *Charles A. Beard: A Reappraisal* (Lexington, Ky., 1954); Cushing Strout, *The Pragmatic Revolt in American History: Carl Becker and Charles Beard* (New Haven, 1958); Bernard Borning, *The Political and Social Thought of Charles A. Beard* (Seattle, 1962); Robert A. Skotheim, *American Intellectual Histories and Historians* (Princeton, 1966), 87-109.

[2] New York *Times*, December 14, 1913; Hofstadter, *Progressive Historians*, 212; "Review of *An Economic Interpretation of the Constitution* by Charles Beard," *Educational Review*, XLVI (September, 1913), 207; John H. Latané, "Review of *An Economic Interpretation of the Constitution* by Charles Beard," *American Political Science Review*, VII (November, 1913), 697-700; Edward S. Corwin, "Review of *An Economic Interpretation of the Constitution* by Charles Beard," *History's Teacher's Magazine*, V (February, 1914), 65-8.

[3] Maurice Blinkoff, *The Influence of Charles A. Beard upon American Historiography* (Buffalo, 1936), 18-21; Richard Hofstadter, "Charles Beard and the Constitution," *Charles A. Beard*, ed. by Beale, 88; Hofstadter, "Beard and the Constitution: The History of an Idea," 195; Wish, *The American Historian*, 291-2.

[4] Edmund S. Morgan, *The Birth of the Republic, 1763-89* (Chicago, 1956), 132, 134-5.

[5] Borning, *Political and Social Thought of Beard*, 9-10; Skotheim, *Intellectual Histories*, 97; Hofstadter, *Progressive Historians*, 243-5.

[6] Robert E. Brown, *Charles Beard and the Constitution: A Critical Analysis of "An Economic Interpretation of the Constitution"* (Princeton, 1956), 89-91, 180-1.

[7] Forrest McDonald, *We the People: The Economic Origin of the Constitution* (Chicago, 1958), 92, 97-103, 110.

[8] *Ibid.*, 161-2, 254, 283, 310.

[9] Edmund S. Morgan, "The American Revolution: Revisions in Need of Revising," *William and Mary Quarterly*, 3rd Ser., XIV (January, 1957), 9-10.

[10] *Ibid.*; *Birth of the Republic*, 133-4; Brown, *Charles Beard and the Constitution*, 131-2; Hofstadter, *Progressive Historians*, 249-51.

[11] Benjamin Fletcher Wright, *Consensus and Continuity, 1776-1787* (Boston, 1958), 47-54.

[12] Martin Diamond, "Democracy and *The Federalist*: A Reconsideration of the Framers' Intent," *American Political Science Review*, LIII (March, 1959), 52-68.

[13] Cecelia Kenyon, "Men of Little Faith: The Anti-Federalists on the Nature of Representative Government," *William and Mary Quarterly*, 3rd Ser., XII (January, 1955), 3-43.

[14] Stanley Elkins and Eric McKitrick, "The Founding Fathers: Young Men of the Revolution," *Political Science Quarterly,* LXXVI (June, 1961), 202-16.

[15] Hofstadter, "Beard and the Constitution: The History of an Idea," 207. The extent to which Beard reflects a belief in class conflict in America would depend upon the extent to which he accepted economic determinism. Analysts of Beard have found an ambiguity here which mirrors a confusion in the man's own mind. Some pages of his book reflect economic forces as the prime determinant of history; others show economic forces as only one important factor which influences men in political decisions. One thing is clear, however, Beard did not subscribe to a simple, fatalistic Marxian theory of economic determinism in history. See Hofstadter, "Beard and the Constitution: The History of an Idea," 204-6 and Lee Benson, *Turner and Beard: American Historical Writing Reconsidered* (Glencoe, Ill., 1960), 96-112.

[16] Brown, *Charles Beard and the Constitution,* 20, 43-4, 54, 156, 200 and *Middle-Class Democracy and the Revolution in Massachusetts, 1691-1780* (Ithaca, 1955); Wright, *Consensus and Continuity,* 57.

[17] Douglass Adair, "The Tenth Federalist Revisited," *William and Mary Quarterly,* 3rd Ser., VIII (January, 1951), 48-67.

[18] McDonald, *We the People,* 358-417.

[19] Jackson Turner Main, *The Antifederalists: Critics of the Constitution, 1781-1788* (Chapel Hill, 1961), 280-1 and "Charles A. Beard and the Constitution: A Critical Review of Forrest McDonald's *We the People,* with a Rebuttal by Forrest McDonald," *William and Mary Quarterly,* 3rd Ser., XVII (January, 1960), 101-2. Main does not emphasize class conflict in early America in a more recent study, *The Social Structure of Revolutionary America* (Princeton, 1965). This excellent study emphasizes the large middle-class in Revolutionary America and the relative ease with which men could enter that class.

[20] E. James Ferguson, *The Power of the Purse: A History of American Public Finance, 1776-1790* (Chapel Hill, 1961), 340-1.

[21] Stoughton Lynd, "Beyond Beard," *Towards a New Past: Dissenting Essays in American History,* ed. by Barton Bernstein (New York, 1968), 46-64.

Some suggest that the United States produced three historic documents of major importance: the Declaration of Independence, the Constitution, and The Federalist. *The latter work is the product of three men: Alexander Hamilton, James Madison, and John Jay, the first two gentlemen doing the bulk of the work. There was considerable opposition to the proposed Constitution in New York state when it was published. It was evident from the outset that New York must be counted in the column of affirmative states if the Constitution was to have a chance of success. A viable Union without New York was unthinkable. Hamilton was stirred to action by his fear of defeat and enlisted Madison and Jay to assist him in writing a series of essays for New York newspapers. They wrote 85 essays under the pseudonym "Publius" which, although written for the immediate purpose of swaying knowledgeable opinion, soon acquired recognition as major works of political theory. In* Federalist 10, *the most famous of the papers, Madison inquires into the causes for failure of previous attempts at popular government. In the course of this essay he offers a psychological base on which popular government ought to rest. He describes a government circumscribed by "auxiliary precautions" which serve to make popular government possible. He discusses the virtues of large countries and the need to control what he calls "factions," particularly majority factions. In short, he describes the pluralist basis of democratic politics which still functions today.*

The Federalist — Number 10

James Madison

November 22, 1787

To the People of the State of New York.

Among the numerous advantages promised by a well constructed Union, none deserves to be more accurately developed than its tendency to break and control the violence of faction. The friend of popular governments, never finds himself so much alarmed for their character and fate, as when he contemplates their propensity to this dangerous vice. He will

From *The Daily Advertiser,* November 22, 1787. This essay appeared in *The New York Packet* on November 23 and in *The Independent Journal* on November 24.

not fail therefore to set a due value on any plan which, without violating the principles to which he is attached, provides a proper cure for it. The instability, injustice and confusion introduced into the public councils, have in truth been the mortal diseases under which popular governments have every where perished; as they continue to be the favorite and fruitful topics from which the adversaries to liberty derive their most specious declamations. The valuable improvements made by the American Constitutions on the popular models, both ancient and modern, cannot certainly be too much admired; but it would be an unwarrantable partiality, to contend that they have as effectually obviated the danger on this side as was wished and expected. Complaints are every where heard from our most considerate and virtuous citizens, equally the friends of public and private faith, and of public and personal liberty; that our governments are too unstable; that the public good is disregarded in the conflicts of rival parties; and that measures are too often decided, not according to the rules of justice, and the rights of the minor party; but by the superior force of an interested and over-bearing majority. However anxiously we may wish that these complaints had no foundation, the evidence of known facts will not permit us to deny that they are in some degree true. It will be found indeed, on a candid review of our situation, that some of the distresses under which we labor, have been erroneously charged on the operation of our governments; but it will be found, at the same time, that other causes will not alone account for many of our heaviest misfortunes; and particularly, for that prevailing and increasing distrust of public engagements, and alarm for private rights, which are echoed from one end of the continent to the other. These must be chiefly, if not wholly, effects of the unsteadiness and injustice, with which a factious spirit has tainted our public administrations.

By a faction I understand a number of citizens, whether amounting to a majority or minority of the whole, who are united and actuated by some common impulse of passion, or of interest, adverse to the rights of other citizens, or to the permanent and aggregate interests of the community.

There are two methods of curing the mischiefs of faction: the one, by removing its causes; the other, by controling its effects.

There are again two methods of removing the causes of faction: the one by destroying the liberty which is essential to its existence; the other, by giving to every citizen the same opinions, the same passions, and the same interests.

It could never be more truly said than of the first remedy, that it is worse than the disease. Liberty is to faction, what air is to fire, an ailment without which it instantly expires. But it could not be a less folly to abolish liberty, which is essential to political life, because it nourishes faction, than it would be to wish the annihilation of air, which is essential to animal life, because it imparts to fire its destructive agency.

The second expedient is as impracticable, as the first would be unwise. As long as the reason of man continues fallible, and he is at liberty to exercise it, different opinions will be formed. As long as the connection subsists between his reason and his self-love, his opinions and his passions will have a reciprocal influence on each other; and the former will be objects to which the latter will attach themselves. The diversity in the faculties of men from which the rights of property originate, is not less an insuperable obstacle to a uniformity of interests. The protection of these faculties is the first object of Government. From the protection of different and unequal faculties of acquiring property, the possession of different degrees and kinds of property immediately results: and from the influence of these on the sentiments and views of the respective proprietors, ensues a division of the society into different interests and parties.

The latent causes of faction are thus sown in the nature of man; and we see them every where brought into different degrees of activity, according to the different circumstances of civil society. A zeal for different opinions concerning religion, concerning Government and many other points, as well of speculation as of practice; an attachment to different leaders ambitiously contending for pre-eminence and power; or to persons of other descriptions whose fortunes have been interesting to the human passions, have in turn divided mankind into parties, inflamed them with mutual animosity, and rendered them much more disposed to vex and oppress each other, than to co-operate for their common good. So strong is this propensity of mankind to fall into mutual animosities, that where no substantial occasion presents itself, the most frivolous and fanciful distinctions have been sufficient to kindle their unfriendly passions, and excite their most violent conflicts. But the most common and durable source of factions, has been the various and unequal distribution of property. Those who hold, and those who are without property, have ever formed distinct interests in society. Those who are creditors, and those who are debtors, fall under a like discrimination. A landed interest, a manufacturing interest, a mercantile interest, a monied interest, with many lesser interests, grow up of necessity in civilized nations, and divide them into different classes, actuated by different sentiments and views. The regulation of these various and interfering interests forms the principal task of modern Legislation, and involves the spirit of party and faction in the necessary and ordinary operations of Government.

No man is allowed to be a judge in his own cause; because his interest would certainly bias his judgment, and, not improbably, corrupt his integrity. With equal, nay with greater reason, a body of man, are unfit to be both judges and parties, at the same time; yet, what are many of the most important acts of legislation, but so many judicial determinations, not indeed concerning the rights of single persons, but concerning the rights of large bodies of citizens; and what are the different classes of legislators, but advocates and parties to the causes which they determine? Is a law proposed concerning private debts? It is a question to which the creditors are parties on one side, and the debtors on the other. Justice ought to hold the balance between them. Yet the parties are and must be themselves the judges; and the most numerous party, or, in other words, the most powerful faction must be expected to prevail. Shall domestic manufactures be encouraged, and in what degree, by restrictions on foreign manufactures? are questions which would be differently decided by the landed and the manufacturing classes; and probably by neither, with a sole regard to justice and the public good. The apportionment of taxes on the various descriptions of property, is an act which seems to require the most exact impartiality; yet, there is perhaps no legislative act in which greater opportunity and temptation are given to a predominant party, to trample on the rules of justice. Every shilling with which they over-burden the inferior number, is a shilling saved to their own pockets.

It is in vain to say, that enlightened statesmen will be able to adjust these clashing interests, and render them all subservient to the public good. Enlightened statesmen will not always be at the helm: Nor, in many cases, can such an adjustment be made at all, without taking into view indirect and remote considerations, which will rarely prevail over the immediate interest which one party may find in disregarding the rights of another, or the good of the whole.

The inference to which we are brought, is, that the *causes* of faction cannot be removed; and that relief is only to be sought in the means of controling its *effects*.

If a faction consists of less than a majority, relief is supplied by the republican principle, which enables the majority to defeat its sinister views by regular vote: It may clog the administration, it may convulse the society; but it will be unable to execute and mask its violence under the forms of the Constitution. When a majority is included in a faction, the form of popular government on the other hand enables it to sacrifice to its ruling passion or interest, both the public good and the rights of other citizens. To secure the public good, and private rights, against the danger of such faction, and at the same time to preserve the spirit and the form of popular government, is then the great object to which our enquiries are directed: Let me add that it is the great desideratum, by which alone this form of government can be rescued from the opprobrium under which it has so long labored, and be recommended to the esteem and adoption of mankind.

By what means is this object attainable? Evidently by one of two only. Either the existence of the same passion or interest in a majority at the same time, must be prevented; or the majority, having such co-existent passion or interest, must be rendered, by their number and local situation, unable to concert and carry into effect schemes of oppression. If the impulse and the opportunity be suffered to coincide, we well know that neither moral nor religious motives can be relied on as an adequate control. They are not found to be such on the injustice and violence of individuals, and lose their efficacy in proportion to the number combined together; that is, in proportion as their efficacy becomes needful.

From this view of the subject, it may be concluded, that a pure Democracy, by which I mean, a Society, consisting of a small number of citizens, who assemble and administer the Government in person, can admit of no cure for the mischiefs of faction. A common passion or interest will, in almost every case, be felt by a majority of the whole; a communication and concert results from the form of Government itself; and there is nothing to check the inducements to sacrifice the weaker party, or an obnoxious individual. Hence it is, that such Democracies have ever been spectacles of turbulence and contention; have ever been found incompatible with personal security, or the rights of property; and have in general been as short in their lives, as they have been violent in their deaths. Theoretic politicians, who have patronized this species of Government, have erroneously supposed, that by reducing mankind to a perfect equality in their political rights, they would, at the same time, be perfectly equalized and assimilated in their possessions, their opinions, and their passions.

A Republic, by which I mean a Government in which the scheme of representation takes place, opens a different prospect, and promises the cure for which we are seeking. Let us examine the points in which it varies from pure Democracy, and we shall comprehend both the nature of the cure, and the efficacy which it must derive from the Union.

The two great points of difference between a Democracy and a Republic are, first, the delegation of the Government, in the latter, to a small number of citizens elected by the rest: secondly, the greater number of citizens, and greater sphere of country, over which the latter may be extended.

The effect of the first difference is, on the one hand to refine and enlarge the public views, by passing them through the medium of a chosen body of citizens, whose wisdom may best discern the true interest of their country, and whose patriotism and love of justice, will be least likely to sacrifice it to temporary or partial considerations. Under such a regulation, it may well happen that the public voice pronounced by the representatives of the people, will be more consonant to the public good, than if pronounced by the people themselves convened for the purpose. On the other hand, the effect may be inverted. Men of factious tempers, of local prejudices, or of sinister designs, may by intrigue, by corruption or by other means, first obtain the suffrages, and then betray the interests of the people. The question resulting is, whether small or extensive Republics are most favorable to the election of proper guardians of the public weal: and it is clearly decided in favor of the latter by two obvious considerations.

In the first place it is to be remarked that however small the Republic may be, the Representatives must be raised to a certain number, in order to guard against the cabals of a few; and that however large it may be, they must be limited to a certain number, in order to guard against the confusion of a multitude. Hence the number of Representatives in the two cases, not being in proportion to that of the Constituents, and being proportionally greatest in the small Republic, it follows, that if the proportion to fit characters, be not less, in the large than in the small Republic, the former will present a greater option, and consequently a greater probability of a fit choice.

In the next place, as each Representative will be chosen by a greater number of citizens in the large than in the small Republic, it will be more difficult for unworthy candidates to practise with success the vicious arts, by which elections are too often carried; and the suffrages of the people being more free, will be more likely to centre on men who possess the most attractive merit, and the most diffusive and established characters.

It must be confessed, that in this, as in most other cases, there is a mean, on both sides of which inconveniences will be found to lie. By enlarging too much the number of electors, you render the representative too little acquainted with all their local circumstances and lesser interests; as by reducing it too much, you render him unduly attached to these, and too little fit to comprehend and pursue great and national objects. The Federal Constitution forms a happy combination in this respect; the great and aggregate interests being referred to the national, the local and particular, to the state legislatures.

The other point of difference is, the greater number of citizens and extent of territory which may be brought within the compass of Republican, than of Democratic Government; and it is this circumstance principally which renders factious combinations less to be dreaded in the former, than in the latter. The smaller the society, the fewer probably will be the distinct parties and interests composing it; the fewer the distinct parties and interests, the more frequently will a majority be found of the same party; and the smaller the number of individuals composing a majority, and the smaller the compass within which they are placed, the more easily will they concert and execute their plans of oppression. Extend the sphere, and you take in a greater variety of parties and interests; you make it less probable that a majority of the whole will have a common motive to invade the rights of other citizens; or if such a common motive exists, it will be more difficult for all who feel it to discover their own strength, and to act in unison with each other. Besides other impediments, it may be remarked, that where there is a consciousness of unjust or dishonorable purposes, communication is always checked by distrust, in proportion to the number whose concurrence is necessary.

Hence it clearly appears, that the same advantage, which a Republic has over a Democracy, in controling the effects of faction, is enjoyed by a large over a small Republic — is enjoyed by the Union over the States composing it. Does this advantage consist in the substitution of Representatives, whose enlightened views and virtuous sentiments render them superior to local prejudices, and to schemes of injustice? It will not be denied, that the Representation of the Union will be most likely to possess these requisite endowments. Does it consist in the greater security afforded by a greater variety of parties, against the event of any one party being able to outnumber and oppress the rest? In an equal degree does the encreased variety of parties, comprised within the Union, encrease this security. Does it, in fine, consist in the greater obstacles opposed to the concert and accomplishments of the secret wishes of an unjust and interested majority? Here, again, the extent of the Union gives it the most palpable advantage.

The influence of factious leaders may kindle a flame within their particular States, but will be unable to spread a general conflagration through the other States; a religious sect, may degenerate into a political faction in a part of the Confederacy; but the variety of sects dispersed over the entire face of it, must secure the national Councils against any danger from that source: a rage for paper money, for an abolition of debts, for an equal division of property, or for any other improper or wicked project, will be less apt to pervade the whole body of the Union, than a particular member of it; in the same proportion as such a malady is more likely to taint a particular county or district, than an entire State.

In the extent and proper structure of the Union, therefore, we behold a Republican remedy for the diseases most incident to Republican Government. And according to the degree of pleasure and pride, we feel in being Republicans, ought to be our zeal in cherishing the spirit, and supporting the character of Federalists.

PUBLIUS.

Democracy and The Federalist

Martin Diamond

Charles Beard and his contemporary followers argue that theory played little or no role in the establishment of the United States. The very absence of any theory of government has been the "genius" of our system. We have pragmatically suited our institutions to our environment and hence, we have little to export to others in the way of political philosophy. Martin Diamond is a "revisionist" who accuses the followers of Beard of falling into the "naturalistic fallacy" of reading what "ought" to be from what "is." Our environment, e.g., the frontier, did not predetermine our form of government. There was no natural historical movement which preordained our democratic polity. Diamond argues that ideas do, in fact, play a role in history. By discussing Madison and Hamilton in terms of their writings in The Federalist, *he attempts to prove that our Founding Fathers did believe in and implemented a rather comprehensive theory of government. Our nation is based on a theory of government and the fact that it has remained so viable attests to the strength and validity of the theory.*

It has been a common teaching among modern historians of the guiding ideas in the foundation of our government that the Constitution of the United States embodied a reaction against the democratic principles espoused in the Declaration of Independence. This view has largely been accepted by political scientists and has therefore had important consequences for the way American political development has been studied. I shall present here a contrary view of the political theory of the Framers and examine some of its consequences. . . .

The solution of our contemporary problems requires very great wisdom indeed. And in that fact lies the greatest justification for studying anew the political thought of the Founding Fathers. For that thought remains the finest American thought on political matters. In studying them we may raise ourselves to their level. In achieving their level

Reprinted, by permission of the author and publisher, from Martin Diamond, "Democracy and *The Federalist:* A Reconsideration of the Framers' Intent," *American Political Science Review,* 53 (March 1959), 52-68. Article and footnotes abridged by the editors.

we may free ourselves from limitations that, ironically, they tend to impose upon us, *i.e.*, insofar as we tend to be creatures of the society they founded. And in so freeing ourselves we may be enabled, if it is necessary, to go beyond their wisdom. The Founding Fathers still loom so large in our life that the contemporary political problem of liberty and justice for Americans could be stated as the need to choose whether to apply their wisdom, amend their wisdom, or reject it. Only an understanding of them will tell us how to choose.

For the reflections on the Fathers which follow, I employ chiefly *The Federalist* as the clue to the political theory upon which rested the founding of the American Republic. That this would be inadequate for a systematic study of the Founding Fathers goes without saying. But it is the one book, "to which," as Jefferson wrote in 1825, "appeal is habitually made by all, and rarely declined or denied by any as evidence of the general opinion of those who framed and of those who accepted the Constitution of the United States, on questions as to its genuine meaning." As such it is the indispensable starting point for systematic study.

I

Our major political problems today are problems of democracy; and, as much as anything else, the *Federalist* papers are a teaching about democracy. The conclusion of one of the most important of these papers states what is also the most important theme in the entire work: the necessity for "a republican remedy for the diseases most incident to republican government."[1] The theme is clearly repeated in a passage where Thomas Jefferson is praised for displaying equally "a fervent attachment to republican government and an enlightened view of the dangerous propensities against which it ought to be guarded."[2] *The Federalist*, thus, stresses its commitment to republican or popular government, but, of course, insists that this must be an enlightened commitment.

But *The Federalist* and the Founding Fathers generally have not been taken at their word. Predominantly, they are understood as being only quasi- or even anti-democrats. Modern American historical writing, at least until very recently, has generally seen the Constitution as some sort of apostasy from, or reaction to, the radically democratic implications of the Declaration of Independence—a reaction that was undone by the great "democratic break-throughs" of Jeffersonianism, Jacksonianism, etc. This view, I believe, involves a false understanding of the crucial political issues involved in the founding of the American Republic. Further, it is based implicitly upon a questionable modern approach to democracy and has tended to have the effect, moreover, of relegating the political teaching of the Founding Fathers to the pre-democratic past and thus of making it of no vital concern to moderns. The Founding Fathers themselves repeatedly stressed that their Constitution was wholly consistent with the true principles of republican or popular government. The prevailing modern opinion, in varying degrees and in different ways, rejects that claim. It thus becomes important to understand what was the relation of the Founding Fathers to popular government or democracy.

I have deliberately used interchangeably their terms, "popular government" and "democracy." The Founding Fathers, of course, did not use the terms entirely synonymously and the idea that they were less than "democrats" has been fortified by the fact that they sometimes defined "democracy" invidiously in comparison with "republic." But this fact does not really justify the opinion. For their basic view was that *popular government was the genus, and democracy and republic were two species* of that genus of government. What distinguished popular government from other genera of government was that in it, political authority is "derived from the great body of the society, not from ... [any] favoured class of it."[3] With respect to this decisive question, of where political authority is lodged, democracy and republic — as *The Federalist* uses the terms — differ not in the least. Republics, equally with democracies, may claim to be wholly a form of popular government. This is neither to deny the difference between the two, nor to depreciate the importance *The Federalist* attached to the difference; but in *The Federalist's* view, the difference does not relate to the essential principle of popular government. Democracy means in *The Federalist* that form of popular government where the citizens "assemble and administer the government in person."[4] Republics differ in that the people rule through representatives and, of course, in the consequences of that difference. The crucial point is that republics and democracies are equally forms of popular government, but that the one form is vastly preferable to the other because of the substantive consequences of the difference in form. Those historians who consider the Founding Fathers as less than "democrats," miss or reject the Founders' central contention that, while being perfectly faithful to the *principle* of popular government, they had solved the *problem* of popular government.

In what way is the Constitution ordinarily thought to be less democratic than the Declaration? The argument is usually that the former is characterized by fear of the people, by preoccupation with minority interests and rights, and by measures therefore taken against the power of majorities. The Declaration, it is true, does not display these features, but this is no proof of a fundamental difference of principle between the two. Is it not obviously possible that the difference is due only to a difference in the tasks to which the two documents were addressed? And is it not further possible that the democratic principles of the Declaration are not only compatible with the prophylactic measures of the Constitution, but actually imply them?

The Declaration of Independence formulates two criteria for judging whether any government is good, or indeed legitimate. Good government must rest, procedurally, upon the consent of the governed. Good government, substantively, must do only certain things, *e.g.*, secure certain rights. This may be stated another way by borrowing a phrase from Locke, appropriate enough when discussing the Declaration. That "the people shall be judge" is of the essence of democracy, is its peculiar form or method of proceeding. That the people shall judge rightly is the substantive problem of democracy. But whether the procedure will bring about the substance is problematic. Between the Declaration's two criteria, then, a tension exists: consent can be given or obtained for governmental actions which are not right — at least as the men of 1776 saw the right. (To give an obvious example from their point of view: the people may freely but wrongly vote away the protection due to property.) Thus the Declaration clearly contained, although it did not resolve, a fundamental problem. Solving the problem was not its task; that was the task for the framers of the Constitution. But the man who wrote the Declaration of Independence and the leading men who supported it were perfectly aware of the difficulty, and of the necessity for a "republican remedy."

What the text of the Declaration, taken alone, tells of its meaning may easily be substantiated by the testimony of its author and supporters. Consider only that Jefferson, with no known change of heart at all, said of *The Federalist* that it was "the best commentary on the principles of government which was ever written."[5] Jefferson, it must be remembered, came firmly to recommend the adoption of the Constitution, his criticisms of it having come down only to a proposal for rotation in the Presidency and for the subsequent adoption of a bill of rights. I do not, of course, deny the peculiar character of "Jeffersonianism" nor the importance to many things of its proper understanding. I only state here that it is certain that Jefferson, unlike later historians, did not view the Constitution as a retrogression from democracy. Or further, consider that John Adams, now celebrated as America's great conservative, was so enthusiastic about Jefferson's draft of the Declaration as to wish on his own account that hardly a word be changed. And this same Adams, also without any change of heart and without complaint, accepted the Constitution as embodying many of his own views on government.

The idea that the Constitution was a falling back from the fuller democracy of the Declaration thus rests in part upon a false reading of the Declaration as free from the concerns regarding democracy that the framers of the Constitution felt. Perhaps only those would so read it who take for granted a perfect, self-subsisting harmony between consent (equality) and the proper aim of government (justice), or between consent and individual rights (liberty). This assumption was utterly foreign to the leading men of the Declaration.

II

The Declaration has wrongly been converted into, as it were, a super-democratic document; has the Constitution wrongly been converted in the modern view into an insufficiently democratic document? The only basis for depreciating the democratic character of the Constitution lies in its framers' apprehensive diagnosis of the "diseases," "defects" or "evil propensities" of democracy, and in their remedies. But if what the Founders considered to be defects are genuine defects, and if the remedies, without violating the principles of popular government, *are* genuine remedies, then it would be unreasonable to call the Founders anti- or quasi-democrats. Rather, they would be the wise partisans of democracy; a man is not a better democrat but only a foolish democrat if he ignores real defects in popular government. Thus, the question becomes: are there natural defects to democracy and, if there are, what are the best remedies?

In part, the Founding Fathers answered this question by employing a traditional mode of political analysis. They believed there were several basic possible regimes, each having several possible forms. Of these possible regimes they believed the best, or at least the best for America, to be popular government, but only if purged of its defects. At any rate, an unpurged popular government they believed to be indefensible. They believed there were several forms of popular government, crucial among these direct democracy and republican — or representative — government (the latter perhaps divisible into two distinct forms, large and small republics). Their constitution and their defense of it constitute an argument for that form of popular government (large republic) in which the "evil propensities" would be weakest or most susceptible of remedy....

Consider next the suffrage question. It has long been assumed as proof of an anti-democratic element in the Constitution that the Founding Fathers depended for the working of their Constitution upon a substantially limited franchise. Just as the Constitution allegedly was ratified by a highly qualified electorate, so too, it is held, was the new government to be based upon a suffrage subject to substantial property qualifications. This view has only recently been seriously challenged, especially by Robert E. Brown, whose detailed researches convince him that the property qualifications in nearly all the original states were probably so small as to exclude never more than twenty-five per cent, and in most cases as little as only five to ten per cent, of the adult white male population.[6] That is, the property qualifications were not designed to exclude the mass of the poor but only the small proportion which lacked a concrete

—however small—stake in society, *i.e.*, primarily the transients or "idlers."

The Constitution, of course, left the suffrage question to the decision of the individual states. What is the implication of that fact for deciding what sort of suffrage the Framers had in mind? The immediately popular branch of the national legislature was to be elected by voters who "shall have the qualifications requisite for electors of the most numerous branch of the State Legislature." The mode of election to the electoral college for the Presidency and to the Senate is also left to "be prescribed in each State by the legislature thereof." At a minimum, it may be stated that the Framers did not themselves attempt to reduce, or prevent the expansion of, the suffrage; that question was left wholly to the states — and these were, ironically, the very hotbeds of post-revolutionary democracy from the rule of which it is familiarly alleged that the Founders sought to escape.[7]

In general, the conclusion seems inescapable that the states had a far broader suffrage than is ordinarily thought, and nothing in the actions of the Framers suggests any expectation or prospect of the reduction of the suffrage. Again, as in the question of the amending process, I suggest that the Constitution represented no departure whatsoever from the democratic standards of the Revolutionary period, or from any democratic standards then generally recognized.[8]

What of the Senate? The organization of the Senate, its term of office and its staggered mode of replacement, its election by state legislatures rather than directly by the people, among other things, have been used to demonstrate the undemocratic character of the Senate as intended by the Framers. Was this not a device to represent property and not people, and was it not intended therefore to be a non-popular element in the government? I suggest, on the contrary, that the really important thing is that the Framers thought they had found a way to protect property *without* representing it. That the Founders intended the Senate to be one of the crucial devices for remedying the defects of democracy is certainly true. But *The Federalist* argues that the Senate, as actually proposed in the Constitution, was calculated to be such a device as would operate only in a way that "will consist . . . with the genuine principles of republican government."[9] I believe that the claim is just.

Rather than viewing the Senate from the perspective of modern experience and opinions, consider how radically democratic the Senate appears when viewed from a pre-modern perspective. The model of a divided legislature that the Founders had most in mind was probably the English Parliament. There the House of Lords was thought to provide some of the beneficial checks upon the popular Commons which it was hoped the Senate would supply in the American Constitution. But the American Senate was to possess none of the qualities which permitted the House of Lords to fulfill its role; *i.e.*, its hereditary basis, or membership upon election by the Crown, or any of its other aristocratic characteristics.[10] Yet the Founding Fathers knew that the advantages of having both a Senate and a House would "be in proportion to the dissimilarity in the genius of the two bodies."[11] What is remarkable is that, in seeking to secure this dissimilarity, they did not in any respect go beyond the limits permitted by the "genuine principles of republican government."

Not only is this dramatically demonstrated in comparison with the English House of Lords, but also in comparison with all earlier theory regarding the division of the legislative power. The aim of such a division in earlier thought is to secure a balance between the aristocratic and democratic elements of a polity. This is connected with the pre-modern preference for a *mixed* republic, which was rejected by the Founders in favor of a *democratic* republic. And the traditional way to secure this balance or mixture was to give one house or office to the suffrages of the few and one to the suffrages of the many. Nothing of the kind is involved in the American Senate. Indeed, on this issue, so often cited as evidence of the Founders' undemocratic predilections, the very opposite is the case. The Senate is a constitutional device which *par excellence* reveals the strategy of the Founders. They wanted something like the advantages earlier thinkers had seen in a mixed legislative power, but they thought this was possible (and perhaps preferable) without any introduction whatsoever of aristocratic power into their system. What pre-modern thought had seen in an aristocratic senate—wisdom, nobility, manners, religion, etc.— the Founding Fathers converted into stability, enlightened self-interest, a "temperate and respectable body of citizens." The qualities of a senate having thus been altered (involving perhaps comparable changes in the notion of the ends of government), it became possible to secure these advantages through a Senate based wholly upon popular principles. Or so I would characterize a Senate whose membership required no property qualification and which was appointed (or elected in the manner prescribed) by State legislatures which, in their own turn, were elected annually or biennially by a nearly universal manhood suffrage.

The great claim of *The Federalist* is that the Constitution represents the fulfillment of a truly novel experiment, of "a revolution which has no parallel in the annals of society," and which is decisive for the happiness of "the whole human race."[12] And the novelty, I argue, consisted in solving the problems of popular government by means which yet maintain the government "wholly popular."[13] In defending that claim against the idea of the Constitution as a retreat from democracy I have dealt thus far only with the easier task: the demonstration that the constitutional devices and arrangements do not derogate from the legal power of majorities to rule. What remains is to examine the claim that the Constitution did in fact remedy the natural defects of democracy. Before any effort is made in this direction, it may be useful to summarize some of the implications and possible utility of the analysis thus far.

Above all, the merit of the suggestions I have made, if they are accurate in describing the intention and action of the Founders, is that it makes the Founders available to use for the study of modern problems. I have tried to restore to them their *bona fides* as partisans of democracy. This done, we may take seriously the question whether they were, as they claimed to be, wise partisans of democracy or popular government. If they were partisans of democracy and if the regime they created was decisively democratic, then they speak to us not merely about bygone problems, not from a viewpoint —in this regard—radically different from our own, but as men addressing themselves to problems identical in principle with our own. They are a source from within our own heritage which teaches us the way to put the question to democracy, a way which is rejected by certain prevailing modern ideas. But we cannot avail ourselves of their assistance if we consider American history to be a succession of democratizations which overcame the Founding Fathers' intentions. On that view it is easy to regard them as simply outmoded. If I am right regarding the extent of democracy in their thought and regime, then they are not outmoded by modern events but rather are tested by them. American history, on this view, is not primarily the replacement of a pre-democratic regime by a democratic regime, but is rather a continuing testimony to how the Founding Fathers' democratic regime has worked out in modern circumstances. The whole of our national experience thus becomes a way of judging the Founders' principles, of judging democracy itself, or of pondering the flaws of democracy and the means to its improvement....

III

The Founding Fathers are often criticized for an excessive attention to, and reliance upon, mechanical institutional arrangements and for an insufficient attention to "sociological" factors. While a moderate version of this criticism may finally be just, it is nonetheless clear that *The Federalist* pays considerable and shrewd attention to such factors. For example, in *Federalist* No. 51, equal attention is given to the institutional and non-institutional strengths of the new Constitution. One of these latter is the solution to the "problems of faction." It will be convenient to examine *Federalist* No. 10 where the argument about faction is more fully developed than in No. 51. A close examination of that solution reveals something about *The Federalist's* view of the virtues necessary to the good life.

The problem dealt with in the tenth essay is how "to break and control the violence of faction." "The friend of popular governments never finds himself so much alarmed for their character and fate, as when he contemplates their propensity to this dangerous vice." Faction is, thus, *the* problem of popular government. Now it must be made clear that Madison, the author of this essay, was not here really concerned with the problem of faction generally. He devotes only two sentences in the whole essay to the dangers of *minority* factions. The real problem in a popular government, then, is *majority* faction, or, more precisely, *the* majority faction, *i.e.*, the great mass of the little propertied and unpropertied. This is the only faction that can "execute and mask its violence under the forms of the Constitution." That is, in the American republic the many have the legal power to rule and thus from them can come the greatest harm. Madison interprets that harm fairly narrowly; at least, his overwhelming emphasis is on the classic economic struggle between the rich and the poor which made of ancient democracies "spectacles of turbulence and contention." *The* problem for the friend of popular government is how to avoid the "domestic convulsion" which results when the rich and the poor, the few and the many, as is their wont, are at each others' throats. Always before in popular governments the many, armed with political power, invariably precipitated such convulsions. But the friend of popular government must find only "a republican remedy" for this disease which is "most incident to republican government." "To secure the public good and private rights against the danger of . . . [majority] faction, and at the same time to preserve the spirit and the form of popular government, is then the great object to which our inquiries are directed."

Without wrenching Madison's meaning too greatly, the problem may be put crudely this way: Madison gave a beforehand answer to Marx. The whole of the Marxian scheme depends upon the many—having been proletarianized—causing precisely such domestic convulsion and usurpation of property as Madison wished to avoid. Madison believed that in America the many could be diverted from the probable course. How will the many, *the* majority, be prevented from using for the evil purpose of usurping property the legal power which is theirs in a popular regime? "Evidently by one of two [means] only. Either the existence of the same passion or interest in a majority at the same time must be prevented, or the majority, having such co-existent passion or interest, must be rendered, by their number and local situation, unable to concert and carry into effect schemes of oppression." But "we well know that neither moral nor religious motives can be relied on" to do these things. The "circumstance principally" which will solve the problem is the "greater number of citizens and extent of territory which may be brought within the compass" of large republican governments rather than of small direct democracies.

Rather than mutilate Madison, let me complete his thought by quoting the rest of his argument before commenting on it:

The smaller the society, the fewer probably will be the distinct parties and interests, the more frequently will a majority be found of the same party; and the smaller the number of individuals composing a majority, and the smaller the compass within which they are placed, the more easily will they concert and execute their plans of oppression. Extend the sphere and you take in a greater variety of parties and interests; you make it less probable that a majority of the whole will have a common motive to invade the rights of other citizens; or if such a common motive exists, it will be more difficult for all who feel it to discover their own strength, and to act in unison with each other.

I want to deal only with what is implied or required by the first of the two means, *i.e.*, preventing the majority from having the same "passion or interest" at the same time. I would argue that this is the more important of the two remedial means afforded by a large republic. If the majority comes to have the same passion or interest and holds to it intensely for a period of only four to six years, it seems certain that it would triumph over the "extent of territory," over the barriers of federalism, and separation of powers, and all the checks and balances of the Constitution. I do not wish to depreciate the importance of those barriers; I believe they have enormous efficacy in stemming the tide Madison feared. But I would argue that their efficacy depends upon a prior weakening of the force applied against them, upon the majority having been fragmented or deflected from its "schemes of oppression." An inflamed Marxian proletariat would not indefinitely be deterred by institutional checks or extent of territory. The crucial point then, as I see it, is the means by which a majority bent upon oppression is prevented from ever forming or becoming firm.

Madison's whole scheme essentially comes down to this. The struggle of classes is to be replaced by a struggle of interests. The class struggle is domestic convulsion; the struggle of interests is a safe, even energizing, struggle which is compatible with, or even promotes, the safety and stability of society. But how can this be accomplished? What will prevent the many from thinking of their interest as that of the Many opposed to the Few? Madison, as I see it, implies that nothing can prevent it in a small democratic society where the many are divided into only a few trades and callings: these divisions are insufficient to prevent them from conceiving their lot in common and uniting for oppression. But in a large republic, numerous and powerful divisions will arise among the many to prevent that happening. A host of interests grows up "of necessity in civilized nations, and divide[s] them into different classes, actuated by different sentiments and views." "Civilized nations" clearly means here large, commercial societies. In a large commercial society the interest of the many can be fragmented into many narrower, more limited interests. The mass will not unite as a mass to make extreme demands upon the few, the struggle over which will destroy society; the mass will fragment into relatively small groups, seeking small immediate advantages for their narrow and particular interests.

If the Madisonian solution is essentially as I have described it, it becomes clear that certain things are required for the solution to operate. I only mention several of them. First, the country in which this is to take place will have to be profoundly democratic. That is, all men must be free—and even encouraged—to seek their immediate profit and to associate with others in the process. There must be no rigid class barriers which bar men from the pursuit of immediate interest. Indeed, it is especially the lowly, from whom the most is to be feared, who must feel most sanguine about the prospects of achieving limited and immediate benefits. Second, the gains must be real; that is, the fragmented interests must from time to time achieve real gains, else the scheme would cease to beguile or mollify. But I do not want to develop these themes here. Rather, I want to emphasize only one crucial aspect of Madison's design: that is, the question of the apparently narrow ends of society envisaged by the Founding Fathers. Madison's plan, as I have described it, most assuredly does not rest on the "moral and religious motives" whose efficacy he deprecated. Indeed there is not even the suggestion that the pursuit of interest should be an especially enlightened pursuit. Rather, the problem posed by the dangerous passions and interests of the many is solved primarily by a reliance upon passion and interest themselves. As Tocqueville pointed out, Americans employ the principle of "self-interest rightly understood."

The principle of self-interest rightly understood is not a lofty one, but it is clear and sure. It does not aim at mighty objects, but it attains . . . all those at which it aims. By its admirable conformity to human weaknesses it easily obtains great dominion; nor is that dominion precarious, since the principle checks one personal interest by another, and uses, to direct the passions, the very same instrument that excites them.[14]

Madison's solution to his problem worked astonishingly well. The danger he wished to avert has been averted and largely for the reasons he gave. But it is possible to question now whether he did not take too narrow a view of what the dangers were. Living today as beneficiaries of his system, we may yet wonder whether he failed to contemplate other equally grave problems of democracy, or whether his remedy for the one disease has not had some unfortunate collateral consequences. The Madisonian solution involved a fundamental reliance on ceaseless striving after immediate interest (perhaps now immediate gratification). Tocqueville appreciated that this "permanent agitation . . . is characteristic of a peaceful democracy,"[15] one might even say, the price of its peace. And Tocqueville was aware of how great might be the price. "In the midst of this universal tumult, this incessant conflict of jarring interests, this continual striving of men after fortune, where is that calm to be found which is necessary for the deeper combinations of the intellect?"[16]

IV

There is, I think, in *The Federalist* a profound distinction made between the qualities necessary for Founders and the qualities necessary for the men who come after. It is a distinction that bears on the question of the Founding Fathers' view of what is required for the good life and on their defense of popular government. Founding requires "an exemption from the pestilential influence of party animosities,"[17] but the subsequent governing of America will depend on precisely those party animosities, moderated in the way I have described. Or again, founding requires that "reason" and not the "passions," "sit in judgment."[18] But, as I have argued, the society once founded will subsequently depend precisely upon the passions, only moderated in their consequences by having been guided into proper channels. The reason of the Founders constructs the system within which the passions of the men who come after may be relied upon.

Founders need a knowledge of the newly improved "science of politics" and a knowledge of the great political alternatives in order to construct a durable regime; while the men who come after need be only legislators who are but interested "advocates and parties to the causes they determine."[19] *The Federalist* speaks, as has often been observed, with harsh realism about the shortcomings of human nature, but, as has not so often been observed, none of its strictures can characterize the Founders; they must be free of these shortcomings in order to have had disinterested and true knowledge of political things. While "a nation of philosophers is as little to be expected as the philosophical race of kings wished for by Plato,"[20] it is tempting to speculate that *The Federalist* contemplates a kind of philosopher-founder the posthumous duration of whose rule depends upon "that veneration which time bestows on everything,"[21] and in particular on a regime well-founded. But once founded, it is a system that has no necessary place and makes no provision for men of the founding kind.

It is clear that not all now regarded as Founding Fathers were thought by the authors of *The Federalist* to belong in that august company. Noting that "it is not a little remarkable" that all previous foundings of regimes were "performed by some individual citizen of pre-eminent wisdom and approved integrity,"[22] *The Federalist* comments on the difficulty that must have been experienced when it was attempted to found a regime by the action of an assembly of men. I think it can be shown that *The Federalist* views that assembly, the Federal Convention, as having been subject to all the weaknesses of multitudes of men. The real founders, then, were very few in number, men learned in the new science of politics who seized upon a uniquely propitious moment when their plans were consented to first by a body of respectable men and subsequently, by equally great good fortune, by the body of citizens. As it were, America provided a rare moment when "the prejudices of the community"[23] were on the side of wisdom. Not unnaturally, then, *The Federalist* is extremely reluctant to countenance any re-opening of fundamental questions or delay in ratifying the Constitution.

This circumstance — wisdom meeting with consent—is so rare that "it is impossible for the man of pious reflection not to perceive in it a finger of that Almighty hand."[24] But once consent has been given to the new wisdom, when the government has been properly founded, it will be a durable regime whose perpetuation requires nothing like the wisdom and virtue necessary for its creation. The Founding Fathers' belief that they had created a system of institutions and an arrangement of the passions and interests, that would be durable and self-perpetuating, helps explain their failure to make provision for men of their own kind to come after them. Apparently, it was thought that such men would not be needed.

But does not the intensity and kind of our modern problems seem to require of us a greater degree of reflection and public-spiritedness than the Founders thought sufficient for the men who came after them? One good way to begin that reflection would be to return to their level of thoughtfulness about fundamental political alternatives, so that we may judge for ourselves wisely regarding the profound issues that face us. I know of no better beginning for that thoughtfulness than a full and serious contemplation of the political theory that informed the origin of the Republic, of the thought and intention of those few men who fully grasped what the "assembly of demigods" was doing.

Notes

[1] *Federalist,* No. 10, p. 62. All references are to the Modern Library edition, ed. E. M. Earle.

[2] *Federalist,* No. 49, p. 327.

[3] *Federalist,* No. 39, p. 244. . . .

[4] *Federalist,* No. 10, p. 58.

[5] *The Works of Thomas Jefferson,* ed. Paul L. Ford (The Federal Edition), Vol. 5 (G. P. Putnam's Sons, New York, 1904), p. 434.

[6] *Middle Class Democracy and the Revolution in Massachusetts, 1691-1760.* (Cornell University Press, Ithaca, 1955).

[7] Madison must have thought that he had established this point beyond misinterpretation in *The Federalist,* No. 57. "Who are to be the electors

of the federal representatives? Not the rich, more than the poor; not the learned, more than the ignorant; not the haughty heirs of distinguished names, more than the humble sons of obscurity and unpropitious fortune. The electors are to be the great body of the people of the United States. They are to be the same who exercise the right in every State of electing the corresponding branch of the legislature of the State." (p. 371.)

[8] This is not to deny the importance of the existing property qualifications for the understanding of the Founders' political theory. The legal exclusion from the franchise of even a very small portion of the adult population may have enormous significance for the politics and life of a country. This is obvious in the case of a racial, ethnic or religious minority. And the exclusion of otherwise eligible adult males on the grounds of poverty may be equally important. The property qualification clearly praises and rewards certain virtues, implies that the voter must possess certain qualities to warrant his exercise of the franchise, and aims at excluding a "rabble" from the operations of political parties. But important, therefore, as the property qualification was, it does not demonstrate that the Founding Fathers departed radically from the most important aspects of the principle of majority rule.

[9] *Federalist,* No. 62, p. 403.

[10] *Federalist,* No. 63, p. 415.

[11] *Federalist,* No. 62, p. 403.

[12] *Federalist,* No. 14, p. 85.

[13] *Ibid.,* p. 81.

[14] *Democracy in America,* ed. Phillips Bradley (Knopf, New York, 1951) Vol. 2, pp. 122-23.

[15] *Ibid.,* p. 42.

[16] *Idem.*

[17] *Federalist,* No. 37, p. 232.

[18] *Federalist,* No. 49, p. 331.

[19] *Federalist,* No. 10, p. 56.

[20] *Federalist,* No. 49, p. 329.

[21] *Ibid.,* p. 328.

[22] *Federalist,* No. 38, p. 233.

[23] *Federalist,* No. 49, p. 329.

[24] *Federalist,* No. 38, p. 231.

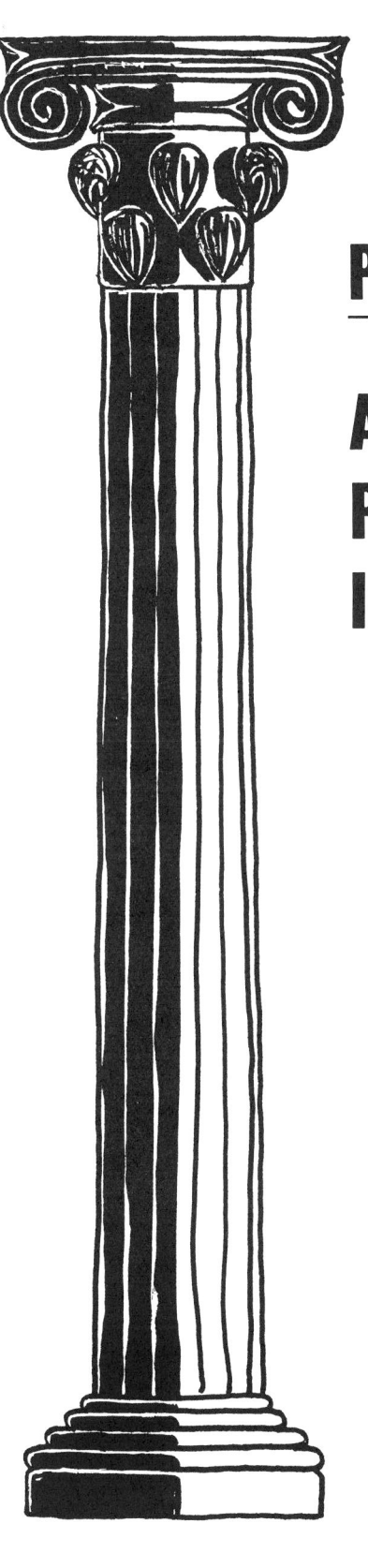

Part Two

American Political Institutions

The Job of the Congressman

Throughout American history there runs a strong sentiment against "politics" and the "politician." Politics is often viewed as a seamy activity indulged in by characters of questionable morality and omniverous material appetites. The legislator is frequently characterized as under the thumb of all-powerful lobbies. This negative perception, somewhat diminished today, provokes many interesting questions: What kind of men are actually involved in making laws and policies? What are the factors which motivate men to pursue a public career? What kind of institutional norms affect and constrain their behavior? In the following essay the authors are concerned about the problem of the representative and his relationship with his constituency. To what degree ought a representative be guided by the apparent opinion of his constituency? And to what extent ought a representative vote his own convictions? How free are congressmen, in fact, from outside groups and pressures? The conclusions offered by the authors run counter to much of the "conventional wisdom" on legislators.

Raymond A. Bauer
Ithiel de Sola Pool
Lewis Anthony Dexter

In the classical literature on democracy, notably in the writings of Burke, a lively debate concerned the question of whether the elected representative of the people should represent their interest as *he* sees it or as *they* see it. In either event, public opinion is regarded as pertinent, whether it be a constructive force guiding the representative's behavior or a corrupting force to which he makes concessions for the purpose of getting elected.

A neoclassical view of the democratic process, stemming from behavioristic political science, says in effect that it is naïve to think of legislators either as arriving independently at a decision in the general interest or as responding to the wishes of the general public. Organized special interests, according to this view, exercise the determining influence.[1] The general public, it asserts, lacks the capacity to make itself heard and, most especially, lacks the capacity to reward

Reprinted by permission of Atherton Press, Inc. from *American Business and Public Policy: The Politics of Foreign Trade* by Raymond A. Bauer, Ithiel de Sola Pool, and Lewis Anthony Dexter. Copyright © 1963, Massachusetts Institute of Technology. Pages 404-405; 414-424.

and punish legislators. The pressure groups which are articulate in presenting their views to Congress command attention because they, the pressure groups and not the general public, act to influence who will and will not be elected. In this view, organized pressure is the dynamo of politics.

One may well hold that all three models of the democratic process are correct in some instances and degrees. There are times when legislators out of their independent judgment arrive at decisions in the general interest. There are times when they respond to public opinion to the extent and in the sense they understand it, either because this corresponds to their ideal of democracy or because they wish to be re-elected. There are instances in which legislators succumb to the pressures of special-interest groups, as well as those in which they are under such pressures but resist them. A more sophisticated statement would hold that, in most legislative decisions, all three models apply to some extent. Often, the pressure of special-interest groups and of public opinion act as countervailing forces, offering the legislator independence in reaching a decision of his own choosing. Thus, what is involved is, not a single process, but a set of interacting processes.

This would, in any event, seem a sufficiently complicated way of looking at things, and it is approximately the model of the democratic process which was in our minds when we designed our study and gathered our data. Yet, even this eclectic model proved insufficient when it came to understanding just what went on in Congress. It was an inadequate representation of the forces and processes at work there.

The flaw in that model of the legislative decision-process was that it postulates certain issues and certain alternative solutions to them as given. It assumes that these issues are somehow there in the legislative arena and that the legislator finding the issues before him must pay attention to them and reach decisions on them. It pictures the legislator as much like a student before a multiple-choice examination, in which he faces fixed alternatives and selects an answer among them. The model with which we started and, for that matter, most decision theory concerns that kind of situation of defined options. The question asked by such theory is what groups or interests or forces operate to determine a choice, the alternatives being predefined.

What we actually found, on the contrary, was that the most important part of the legislative decision-process was the decision about which decisions to consider. A congressman must decide what to make of his job. The decisions most constantly on his mind are not how to vote, but what to do with his time, how to allocate his resources, and where to put his energy. There are far more issues before Congress than he can possibly cope with. There are very few of them which he does not have the freedom to disregard or redefine. Instead of choosing among answers to fixed issues, he is apt to be seeking out those issues that will meet fixed answers. He can select those issues which do not raise for him the Burkean dilemma; that is, he can select those issues on which he feels no special tension between his own views and those of his constituents.

The issues or answers the congressman chooses to deal with are largely determined by the kind of job he as an individual wishes to do. The model of the legislative decision-process toward which we inevitably moved was one dealing with the congressman's choices about his career, his professional identity, his activities, rather than one dealing primarily with choices about his policies. It was also a model which took as the relevant criterion for choice the over-all needs of his position, rather than the views on specific policies held by special groups of the public. Any model is a simplification which accounts for only a part of the observations. What we are asserting is that looking at how a congressman defined his job helped us account for his behavior on reciprocal trade as much as did looking at the foreign-trade issue or at the involvements in it of his constituents and other groups. . . . Congressmen feel much freer than most outsiders think. They need not be unduly constrained by demands from constituents, interest groups, or party. Their freedom is secured by a number of conditions. For one thing, constituents and pressure groups are often satisfied with a fair hearing, not insisting on a specific conclusion. For another thing, American political parties seldom impose discipline in regard to issues.

Among all the conditions that make congressmen free, there is one that deserves special attention; that is the fact that a congressman's own decisions largely determine what pressures will be communicated to him. Paradoxical as it may seem, their "freedom" comes from the excessive demands made on them. The complexity of their environment which seems to congressmen to rob them of initiative thrusts initiative back on them, for, when the demands on a man's resources clearly exceed his capacity to respond, he *must* select the problems and pressures to which to respond.

A CONGRESSMAN DETERMINES WHAT HE WILL HEAR

There are additional ways in which a congressman largely determines for himself what he hears from the public. Several mechanisms converge to place a congressman in a closed communication circuit. For one thing, like anyone else, a congressman indulges in selective perception and recall of what he hears. Most messages received by a congressman change saliency more than they change his attitudes on the subject with which they deal. They raise its saliency so that he thinks about it more and becomes more prone to express whatever predispositions he has regarding it. Beset by competing stimuli, he perceives the original message hurriedly, seeing in it what he expects is there. The effect of the stimulus is thus that he reacts more, but reacts in terms of his own accumulated predispositions, not in terms of the content of the communication. Messages serve more as triggers than as persuaders.[2]

Second, a congressman must select those persons within his constituency on whom he is going to build his following; he cannot react to all equally. Third, a congressman must discount as phony much of the material he receives, and the discounting process can lead to a variation of readings. Last, and perhaps most significant, the attitudes of a congressman in large measure control what messages will be sent to him, because they determine, often overdetermine, the image people have of him.

Of course, congressmen do get mail of all kinds, including some with which they are bound to disagree. Although the large bulk of issue mail is supportive, there are exceptions, and sometimes there may be large sacks of mail demanding that a congressman take a difficult or unpalatable stand. When that happens, the congressman wants to know how seriously to take those demands on him. Do they represent his constituents' deep feelings or are they the product of a slick promotion? He wants to know something of the degree of spontaneity, sincerity and urgency of these communications. The congressman's experience with other communications on the same and other issues is his touchstone of assessing the degree to which his mail is stimulated or spontaneous. Thus, a Senate mail clerk commented on one set of letters: "This mail is surprisingly unstereotyped; . . . although the stationery may have been given out, the message was not. It is quite different from other heavy pressure mail."

Lack of experience with protectionist mail probably accounted in part for the responsiveness of Southern congressmen to it in 1955. Northern congressmen, more experienced with protectionist arguments, frequently commented, "There is nothing new here."

In general, experienced congressmen and their staffs are quite tough-minded and skilled at assessing their mail. They are unlikely to feel pressure from the mere existence of numerous demands on them. That being the case, the demands that seem compelling to congressmen are apt to be those which fit their own psychic needs and their images of the world. Things interior to the congressman's mind largely determine what events he will perceive as external pressure on him. He unconsciously chooses which pressures to recognize.

One way or another, the congressman must simplify the complex world. We interviewed two congressmen from the vicinity of New Anglia. It will be remembered that there was considerable unemployment in the textile industry around New Anglia. Northern textile unemployment may be interpreted in a variety of ways — as a result of technological obsolescence, foreign competition, Southern competition, and so on. Congressman Second, in virtually these words, said: "Unemployment and the need for protection are the same issue." He saw textile unemployment as the result of foreign competition. But Congressman First, when asked about foreign-trade policy, began immediately to talk about Southern competition and about the failure of the administration to grant defense contracts to the distressed New Anglia area. Rather than seeking relief via tariffs, he was trying to get from the Office of Defense Mobilization a "certificate of necessity" for a steel mill in New Anglia. He commented: "By and large, on . . . the tariff . . . New Anglia businesses feel it is New Anglia against the South, and New Anglia is getting a raw deal every time."

We had the opportunity of observing both congressmen at a breakfast meeting organized by New Anglia textile interests. One speaker talked about foreign competition; another stressed Southern textile competition. Both Congressmen First and Second questioned the speakers. From their questioning, it might seem that Congressman First had heard one speech and Congressman Second another.

Another congressman occupied himself with doing personal favors for his constituents. The district from which the congressman came was very similar to that served by another congressman who reported a heavy influx of protectionist mail. We knew the industries in the first's district to be generally very active in favor of protectionism. But that congressman, although he frequently returned home, reported hearing little or nothing on tariff problems. Either his concentration on problems of personal service discouraged communications on tariff problems or he was so absorbed that he did not notice them.

In the Senate Office Building, the mail rooms were in the basement, a long walk from the senators' offices. That fact, added to the volume of mail a senator receives, made it far less likely for him to be aware of what was in his mail than was a representative, whose mail clerk was right in his office. In one senatorial office, the senator's administrative assistant was under the impression that they had received no mail on foreign-trade policy. One of us took a walk over to the senator's mail room. The mail clerk said that the mail on foreign-trade policy was first or second in volume of mail on any issue. However, the senator and his assistants were heavily involved in several other issues, and the mail clerk had not forwarded the reciprocal-trade mail, since, in her judgment, there was nothing that the senator could do about the issue at the moment.

In that instance, the filter against pressure was not strictly psychic. The barrier was selective communication, which, however, stemmed directly from the clerk's awareness of the senator's selective attention. We shall meet this mechanism again below. But, whatever the mechanism, the result was that effective pressure was limited to topics on which the congressman chose to recognize it.

We add another point that reinforces the notion that congressmen interpret the pressures on them. Many communications to congressmen leave the recipient in the dark as to precisely what is wanted of him. Communications to Congress are frequently ambiguous, and it is not surprising if the ambiguities are resolved in consonance with the congressman's other interests and activities. A letter reporting industrial distress might be seen as a plea for tariff protection by Congressman Second and as a plea for selective allocation of defense contracts by Congressman First. Yet, both would regard themselves as truly and effectively expressing the plea of the constituent.

The work load of the congressman and his staff reduces the precision with which congressmen interpret that high proportion of mail which is only partially on target. For example, a large volume of protectionist mail was received from employees of the Westinghouse Corporation in protest against U. S. government purchase of foreign electrical installations. Although the mail was ostensibly directed against the extension of the Reciprocal Trade Act, it is probable that the issue confronting Westinghouse — government purchasing of foreign electrical equipment—should have called for mail asking an administrative tightening-up of the Buy-American Act, not for tariff legislation. But few congressmen had the time or staff resources to investigate this problem. Our impression was that many congressmen were not clear as to what was wanted of them by the Westinghouse Corporation. The mail might have had some effect on trade-legislation votes, but the effect, if any, may have been quite unrelated to the specific situation affecting Westinghouse.

The fact that a large part of the mail, and other communications, too, are only partly on target is one which cannot be too strongly emphasized. Sometimes it makes action to meet the request impossible, for many writers ask for something that is procedurally or otherwise impracticable. They may ask a congressman to support a bill which is still in a committee of which he is not a member and where he has little influence with any member. For him to comply in any way other than by a polite reply to the correspondent would require a major investment of effort and good will. He would have to go out of his way to testify or to approach some of his better-placed colleagues.

On the other hand, the fact that petitioners are vague about what they want also helps make political action possible. Political action requires the formation of coalitions. Coalitions are held together by the glue of ambiguity which enables persons to perceive diverse goals as somehow akin. There are not enough people with an interest in the Buy-American regulations, for example, to produce Congressional action. Nor are there enough who care about oil quotas to get such action. Nor are there enough who care about specific tariff rates as such. The only way any of them could achieve legislative effectiveness was to mobilize all of them as a coalition around some issue which might serve at least as a wedge for those whom it did not serve directly. Such a bloc was organized each time against the trade acts. Had it ever succeeded, its success might have led ultimately to administrative yielding on the interpretation of Buy-American legislation too. The administration would most likely have yielded to what it would have seen as a general protectionist direction in the political atmosphere.

Indeed, it happens more often than not in public-policy debates that the issues around which mass opinion is mobilized are not the crucial ones in the minds of those who from legislative policy. This happens often enough so that congressmen are well attuned to grievances as an index to the sources of public alarm, rather than as specific guidance on legislative drafting. A congressman is concerned to allay the discontent of those who appeal to him. The complaint is a signal to him to do something, not a command as to what to do. Like a doctor, having made a diagnosis, he often has a range of choices of treatment open to him.

We consider now another range of alternatives among which a congressman must choose. Almost every district is composed of a complex of interests, and congressmen are faced with the task of deciding just whom they represent. They cannot give attention and energy equally to all. They must select some for whom they can become valued allies and from whom they can command more than passive support. They must find groups which have money, votes, media of communication, influence, and political desires which a congressman can further. A congressman must seek to make himself an important figure to some such groups within his constituency. These may change over time. A congressman elected by labor votes may throw off this harness by turning to business support. But, at any one moment, a congressman must relate to some key groups within his constituency, for a constituency is a social structure, not an amorphous mass. Thus, Rep. Henderson Lanham (D., Ga.) came from a district with both farming and business interests. He had associated himself with the business group. Their protectionist interests, rather than the farmers' stake in international trade, were communicated to him, for people write and talk more to a congressman whom they know, and he listens more to them.

Although a congressman's established relationship to a particular group may increase the probability of its members communicating with him, this established relationship does not necessarily make him more compliant to their interests on a specific issue. This is a point so important and so overlooked in the pressure-group model of the democratic process that it deserves emphasis.

In the first place, the direction of influence is as apt to be from the congressman to his closer constituents as the other way around. Citizens value a relation to a congressman and are apt to be guided by him.

Second, established favorable relationships between congressmen and groups in the constituency are invariably based on a range of issues. It is rare that any one of these is of such paramount importance that a group would renounce its allegiance to a congressman who had pleased them on many other issues. We had an illustration of this in Midwest. It will be remembered that the farmers talked to Congressman Stubborn on a range of issues on which they expected a favorable reaction from him. However, they were so certain of his opposition to trade liberalization that they did not even raise that subject. A congressman wins the allegiance of multipurpose interest groups through both legislation and services. This allegiance, then, can buy him freedom from pressure on almost any individual issue on which he has firm personal convictions.

We may thus enunciate the general principle that whether a group will communicate with a congressman and whether the congressman will respond to the interests of that group are functions of the relationship between the group and the congressman on a *range* of issues. We offer as an example our impression that some groups interested in both the St. Lawrence Seaway bill and the Reciprocal Trade Act gave priority to the former and did not communicate on the latter for fear of exhausting a finite supply of Congressional good will.

Our basic conclusion, we repeat, is that a congressman determines — consciously or unconsciously — what he hears. He hears most, for instance, from interest groups with which he is congenial; but he can cut off communication on single issues on which he is at odds with them. It is not surprising, therefore, that our old friend, Congressman Second, who interpreted textile unemployment as a foreign-trade problem, reported receiving more foreign-trade mail than did Congressman First, who saw it as a problem of Southern competition. Congressman Second reported it first or second in importance; Congressman First's assistant placed it in tenth or fifteenth position.

It is, we judge, usually truthful when two congressmen on opposite sides of an issue each say that "80 per cent of my mail supports me," for people write less to congressmen with whom they disagree.

The busyness of Congressmen First and Second forced each to specialize. Each chose a specialty congenial to himself and among the many of potential appeal to his constituents. Their specialties in turn determined what pressures were placed on them, for among the demands to which a congressman is most likely to respond are those which he has stimulated himself.

Belief that a congressman is busy with other matters will dry up the flow of communication to him on a given subject. The late Sen. Joseph McCarthy had twice succeeded in getting the Reciprocal Trade Act amended to place a quota on the importation of foreign furs. But this was before he became involved in the investigation of Communism. In 1954, an informed source commented: "None of the Wisconsin dairy or fur people would go see Joe. He's too busy and out of that world. They'd go see Wiley or Thye or Humphrey's assistant, but not Joe — he doesn't follow that sort of thing any more." The image of Senator McCarthy had become that of investigator of Communism rather than that of representative of local and state interests.

Thus, an anticipatory feedback discourages messages that may not be favorably received from even getting sent. A congressman very largely gets back what he puts out. In his limited time, he associates more with some kinds of people than with others, listens to some kinds of messages more than to others, and as a result hears from some kinds of people more than from others. He controls what he hears both by his attention and by his attitudes. He makes the world to which he thinks he is responding. Congressmen, indeed, do respond to pressures, but they generate the pressures they feel.

In making that assertion, we take leave of the traditional theory of pressure politics as expounded both by the politician and the political scientist. The political scientist observing Congress gives too much credence to the way the congressman himself describes the situation. The congressman often sees himself as buffeted by a torrent of inexorable demands on his time and effort. Like any busy executive, he sees himself responding to stimuli that come to him from without. What he does not realize is that the nature of these forces on him are largely self-made. His own sensitivities determine which demands he feels to be important and which he forgets and sloughs off. One congressman with an eye on issues will listen with concern to arguments put forward by constituents, whereas another congressman with an eye on local social groups will feel no pressure from pompous statements about issues as he tries to keep track of births, marriages, and deaths. The representative who is known to have arranged for the nonquota entrance of relatives of members of a given ethnic group will receive similar requests from other such persons. The congressman who establishes his home office in a working-class section, where his secretary gives advice on social-security cases, will get such cases, which perhaps take more time than any other service. The congressman who has interested himself in taxes will hear about taxes, and the one who has cultivated groups interested in foreign trade will hear about tariffs. The congressman's activities determine which of his constituents know him and the contexts in which they know him, and their past experience tells them to what their congressman will respond. If he has come to church suppers before, he will be invited again. If he has given speeches on foreign policy, that is what he will be invited to do. The job is largely what the congressman makes it.

A CONGRESSMAN IS RELATIVELY FREE

One implication of the fact that the congressman makes his own job and hears what he chooses to hear is that he can be a relatively free man, not the unwilling captive of interest groups or parties. There may seem to be a conflict between the two pictures we paint of the congressman harassed by many demands and of the congressman relatively free. But, as suggested above, it is precisely because the demands on him are excessive that he must be selective, and therein lies his relative freedom.

Early in our study we talked with a veteran congressman who said:

> You know, I am sure you will find out a congressman can do pretty much what he decides to do, and he doesn't have to bother too much about criticism. I've been up here where a guy will hold one economic or political position and get along all right; and then he'll die or resign, and a guy comes in (from the same district) who holds quite a different economic or political position, and he gets along all right, too. That's the fact of the matter.

The reasons for this are many. In American political practice, neither the party nor the executive branch exercises more than slight control over a member of Congress. The reader will probably note how seldom in this and the historical chapters we refer to the mechanism of party or to direct executive intervention. The weight we give them is the weight they seem to deserve. In 1953-1955, each (the Executive more than the party) played a role in forcing a few key votes at a few crucial moments, but, for the rest, theirs was a reserve power kept out of the picture. Rayburn stepped in at a breakfast described in an earlier chapter to pressure a few Democratic votes in the House in 1955. The White House did give leadership to Republican senators about how to vote on the Gore amendment, and it did have a representative meet with Senators Byrd and Millikin during the 1955 Senate committee deliberations to decide which proposed amendments would be incorporated in the bill. These were all highly important moments, but in no one of these three isolated but vital cases did the guidance affect more than a score of congressmen. Over the two years which we studied most intensively, the overwhelming majority of congressmen would have felt no more pressure toward conformity to party or administration views than that which they generated within themselves from reading the newspapers and knowing what the President and party leaders were saying.

In 1962, the White House intrusion into the life of Congress was much more direct, aggressive, and insistent. Presidential aides talked repeatedly to a large number of key congressmen and often did so in an overt bargaining manner. Yet these direct appeals did not switch the most votes. It was the indirect effect of the administration's approach to and conversion of the textile lobby and to numerous other businessmen that indirectly affected Congress. Congressmen recognized the hand of the administration in the extraordinary change whereby most of the special-interest lobbying in 1962 was for trade liberalization, not protection. But congressmen responded to this change in atmosphere because of what it showed about the shifting balance of forces in the country, not because the President asked them to go along. On the contrary, many congressmen, including Democrats, so resented the unusual intrusiveness of the Kennedy administration's tactics that they would have preferred to vote the President down. If party and administration had much direct weight at all in the House in 1962, it was precisely because congressmen had not listened to them much on a variety of issues. Congress had rebuffed the President on a whole series of proposals: long-term foreign aid, a Department of Urban Affairs, tax reform, aid to education, and the like. Both the President and numerous Democrats in Congress wished to pass some legislation that would create a party record of success for the approaching elections. To the administration, the Trade Expansion Act had the charm of something that might actually succeed in passing, so it was given a higher priority. Conversely, the selection of this bill as a Democratic show piece may have led some Democratic representatives to go along. But such mutual recognition of a chance for agreement cannot be called a result of administration pressure.

The sanction that counts much more than party or executive leadership in the Congressional picture is that of re-election by the voters of one's district. But in that regard, too, the congressman is quite free. There are limits on what is morally or sociologically conceivable. Few, if any, congressmen could announce adherence to Communism and be re-elected. But the latitude is wide and of course wider on any one given issue than on all issues put together. A congressman creates an image on the full range of issues which affects his chances of re-election, although even over the full range his freedom is much more substantial than is often realized.

SUMMARY

A congressman is free, as we have already noted, because each district is ordinarily a complex and he can choose the elements out of which he wishes to build his coalition. As Congressman Stubborn said about his district: "It is a good district, because, if the farmers are mad at you, the cities won't be; and, if the cities are, the farmers won't be; so you can be free."

He is freed from a slavish dependence on the elements in his coalition, not only because he can change it, but, even more, because, once he has built a coalition, he tends to lead it. His closest supporters, who may originally have rallied around him because they wanted him to take certain stands, come to be his men. Within very broad limits, when he shifts, they shift. They gain prestige by being close to a congressman, and they fear to break a relationship which may some day be useful for important purposes. Once the leader has committed himself, his supporters are inclined to go along.

He is free also because the voters seldom know just what they want. Mostly they want evidence that he is concerned with their problem and is addressing himself effectively to it. Often he is viewed as the doctor who should recommend the appropriate cure. The larger number of constituents, and the ones the congressman likes, are the ones who come in to say, "Congressman, this is my problem." Those, such as the League of Women Voters, who come in with a list of recommended votes are, fortunately for the comfort of the congressman, fewer.

Indeed, even where the constituent frames his appeal to his congressman as a highly specific demand, the congressman is quite free to disregard it. Few constituents deny their vote to a congressman who generally listens to them just because he differs on any one issue. Furthermore, for every demand on one side, there is a demand on the other. The congressman who saw his job in no more imaginative light than doing what his constituents or large groups of them wanted would not only face impossible problems of doing that job, but would also soon find himself offending enough other constituents to undermine his chances of remaining in office.[3] He must view the demands with a more creative eye, seeking to invent formulas that will catch the imagination of constituents rather than taking all requests at face value.

Finally, a congressman is free also because, as we shall see in the sections to come, the procedure of Congress is so complex that it is easy for him to obfuscate where he stands on any issue and what he has done about it.

[1] Cf. Schattschneider, *op. cit.;* E. P. Herring, *Group Representation Before Congress* (Baltimore: Johns Hopkins Press, 1929); and D. Truman, *Governmental Process* (New York: Knopf and Company, 1951).

[2] See Raymond A. Bauer, "The Communicator and the Audience," *Journal of Conflict Resolution,* II (March 1958), No. 1, 67-77.

[3] Cf. Anthony Downs, *An Economic Theory of Democracy* (New York: Harper & Bros., 1957), for a demonstration of the proposition that, by following the majority on each issue, a legislator is likely to court defeat by a coalition of passionate minorities.

The Committee System

Charles L. Clapp

Legislatures worldwide have experienced difficult times in this century. With the possible exception of the United States Congress, it is probably safe to argue that in all nations the legislature has declined in influence relative to the executive. Critics of Congress, of which there are many, fault it for either being a roadblock to progress as envisioned by an enlightened President or for being too weak to effectively counter the increasingly arbitrary and aggressive Executive Branch. It is condemned for being both too strong and too weak. The critics, whatever the ideological basis for their assessment of the place of Congress in the system, agree that power in Congress is fragmented among the standing committees and that this is bad. The critics tend to advocate the necessity for centralized party and chamber leadership as a prerequisite to breaking the strength of these committees. If the Congress is, as suggested previously, the exception to the trend toward weaker legislatures, what could account for its vitality? The editors believe that Congress is politically potent because of the committee system, not in spite of it. The dispersed character of power in committees, reinforced by the seniority rule, has permitted Congress to remain independent of the Executive and hence avoid the malaise that has afflicted other legislatures. Charles Clapp, as a result of a series of roundtable discussions with thirty-six congressmen, is able to present an informative view of the committee system of the House of Representatives.

"No one will be able to understand Congress unless he understands the committee system and how it functions," said one congressman at the opening session of the Brookings round table conference. The House and Senate must, of course, work their will on legislative proposals that are cleared by committees, but it is in the committee rooms that the real work is done. There, choices are made between alternative proposals and decisions are reached to pigeonhole or kill

Reprinted by permission of The Brookings Institution from *The Congressman: His Work As He Sees It* by Charles L. Clapp, copyright © The Brookings Institution, 1963, pp. 241-259.

outright other bills. The latter actions virtually eliminate the possibility of further consideration by the House or Senate; the former involve determinations that generally govern the reception of the measure in the parent body. By weighting a measure with unpalatable items though reporting it, a committee can hasten its demise. By amending a bill so as to weaken the opposition it can almost guarantee success. By endorsing a measure strongly, a committee increases significantly the likelihood that it will be accepted. Close House and Senate adherence to committee recommendations is the practice, although recommended legislation in controversial fields, such as agricultural policy, may face defeat on the floor. Normally, few substantive changes are made during floor debate. The volume and complexity of legislative proposals, the strong tradition of deferring to the "specialist," the search for ways to reconcile often conflicting pressures on congressmen, the very size of Congress — all conspire to enhance the authority of committee action. According to a congressional committee study, 90 percent of all the work of the Congress on legislative matters is carried out in committee.

The influence of committees in the legislative process is bolstered by the practice, particularly prevalent in the Appropriations Committee, of confining efforts to defeat or modify a proposal to activities within the committee itself. Once the battle has been fought and resolved there, those in the committee minority often do not press their case on the House floor. If they do intend to press it, they are careful, at the time of the committee vote, to "reserve" the right to do so. But the emphasis is on closing ranks and presenting a united front.

Committee pre-eminence and the difficulties involved in setting aside measures receiving committee endorsement have led party leaders on occasion to ignore seniority in making assignments to committees handling crucial or controversial legislation.... They also have led the Executive and the interest groups to concern themselves with the assignment process.

The central role of committees in the legislative process has also underscored the importance of strategic referral of bills to committee: by careful attention to the wording, a congressman may have his bill sent to a committee more favorably disposed to it than the one to which it might otherwise have been referred.

POWERS AND PROCEDURES

Committees are virtually autonomous bodies, hiring their own staffs, establishing their own rules of procedure, proceeding at their own pace for the most part, and resisting on occasion the urgings of the party. Chairman may openly and successfully flaunt the party leadership, or they may have such stature that they are seldom requested to follow specific courses of action. And the reports of committees or their subcommittees may become as binding on executive departments as if they were law.

Committees differ tremendously in composition and method of operation, and may change significantly from one year to the next. As one congressman said, "Each committee tends to be unique in its unwritten rules—an organism in itself. The character changes with different chairmen and with different congresses." Some rely heavily on staff, interest groups, or the executive; others are relatively free from all such influences. Some are characterized by a lack of partisanship and generally report measures to the House floor by unanimous or nearly unanimous vote; strong partisanship is typical of others. In view of the central role of committees in the legislative process, an understanding of the working relationships that exist within the various committees is very helpful—often indispensable—to those who desire to influence legislation.

Just as different personalities alter procedures, the impact of a committee on the outlook of its members may be perceptible also. For example, service on the Appropriations Committee seems to make members more conservative. This is true in part because the membership is recruited carefully from the ranks of representatives likely to be susceptible to the socialization process. Although their attitudes toward issues vary, they are considered "reasonable" and "responsible," capable of adjusting easily to committee procedures and committee thinking. The fact that there is little turnover in committee membership tends to promote a group identity that is unusual and that aids in the assimilation of new members. Explained one liberal who sits on the committee:

> The Appropriations Committee develops a strange sort of breed. As soon as you get on the committee somehow you become more responsible as a member of Congress. You find you have to justify expenditures and you cannot pass over any situation very lightly. As a result you become more conservative. I think it is fair to say that on the whole the members of the Appropriations Committee are more conservative than most members of Congress. Committee members pause long before they support various programs. They are always thinking of what additional taxes are necessary to carry these programs out. Most congressmen, on the other hand, are just thinking how worthwhile the program would be, neglecting the point of how much additional taxes would be required.

The important work of committees takes place in closed rather than open sessions. It has been estimated that in recent years from 30 percent to 40 percent of committee meetings have been held in executive session. While House committees dealing with money matters and unusually technical or sensitive legislation, such as the Appropriations, Ways and Means, and Foreign Affairs committees are concerned with, are more disposed to meet in private than most other groups, nearly every committee makes fairly extensive use of this procedure. Closed sessions facilitate compromise, promote candor and serious discussion, and eliminate the temptation to "play to the spectators," which occasionally overcomes members of Congress. Party representatives may have met together prior to a "mark-up" session in order to determine strategy and the party stand on a bill. But partisan stances are often sublimated and an atmosphere conducive to thoughtful consideration of legislation is more likely to prevail. Here representatives whose names the general public would not recognize may develop reputations among their colleagues based on their insights and their capacity for hard work. Despite the obvious advantages of holding executive sessions on many kinds of problems, there are persistent complaints, particularly from the press, that too many committee sessions are conducted behind closed doors. Far from promoting better legislation, these critics assert, closed sessions are often detrimental since, there, decisions are reached that would not be tolerated were the proceedings conducted in public.

Majority-Minority Relationships

The degree of cooperation existing between majority and minority members of a committee may be more dependent on the personal relationships between the chairman and ranking minority member than on the subject matter area involved. These two individuals usually have served together on the committee for an extended period and may have learned to work together comfortably. Retirement of one of them may alter intracommittee relationships. As one congressman illustrated:

> We had excellent relationships in our committee between the chairman and _____ [long-time ranking minority member]. But since the latter's retirement last year things have changed. I have sensed a strained relationship between the chairman and _____ [the new ranking minority member]. I don't

look for close liaison to continue. I think a sharp clash is going to develop very shortly.

Intracommittee relationships may be changed in other ways, too. The leadership may seek to alter the kind of legislation reported by a committee by deliberately "packing" it with people of different philosophy than those who have long held control. A single issue may so solidify party lines that years of cooperation and harmony will be swept aside. Or interference by the Executive in the normal committee operation may have drastic effects. One Democratic congressman described such an incident:

_____, who heads one of our subcommittees, doesn't always support our Democratic party's position. When the _____ bill came along, he supported President Eisenhower's proposal, and we had to maneuver for months and months to get him straightened out. That was the start, really, of unity among the committee Democrats. The Republicans had to be for Ike's plan because pressure was put on them. They finally stood with the administration on all parts of the bill instead of going along with the old procedure whereby we took care of committee members and other individuals. There were so many weaknesses in administration policy that we were able to unify all of the Democrats to vote against everything in the bill. In the course of considering it, interparty relationships got so bad that they have carried over into other programs. Recently, every vote on an important measure in the committee has been almost a straight party vote. That is fine with us because it is much easier when you can write the legislation among the Democrats. The Republicans started having caucuses and we started having them too.

That statement led to the following discussion regarding the cooperation between majority and minority on committees:

On our committee we have a close relationship with the ranking minority member. In House tradition the minority member is consulted in scheduling legislation, but I wonder how many committees do this. I have been critical of consultation because I think we fail to get legislation passed if we try to iron it out with the minority ahead of time. In your committee, the minority isn't consulted at all about legislation, I suppose.

It is consulted to a degree. But last year we didn't tell them in advance that we were going to vote on the TVA bill. They had hundreds of amendments to offer to it, and we suggested that they offer them all en bloc. So we had ten minutes to consider the bill. That's democracy in action! It is all contrary to the textbooks, but it is the only way we ever could have gotten a bill out of the committee.

As the first speaker noted, consultation between leading majority and minority members of a committee is not uncommon. Members of some committees and subcommittees work in such close harmony that even the questions the chairman and staff intend to put to witnesses are furnished to the minority prior to hearings.

A Republican was sharply critical of one House committee, attributing what is generally regarded as an undistinguished record on legislation to excessive partisanship and domination by the chairman.

Everything that could be wrong with a committee is wrong with that one. The chairman has all the power to schedule legislation; he won't schedule anything. He makes trades on things in which he is interested. When hearings are scheduled, he is abusive to departmental witnesses. He and the ranking member on his side take up the time; anyone below the ranking one or two members on our side has no opportunity to say anything. The committee is nothing but a propaganda agency. That is demonstrated by the fact that no substantive legislation in the areas of its jurisdiction has been passed in the time I have been in Congress. More of that committee's bills are defeated on the floor than those of any other committee. There is no discussion between Democrats and Republicans on the committee, and the Republicans never know what is going to happen.

Another Republican told of one way in which committee staffs may be used for partisan purposes.

I am on two committees which practice a good deal of partisanship. The chief clerk of one of them kept a record of how many subcommittee meetings I attended. It included not only the subcommittee on which I served but those to which I did not belong. It included the amount of time I spent in each, and what I said. The information was forwarded to my opponent. I couldn't figure how my opponent knew so much about my activities last session, or why the chairman of the committee made snide remarks about me during meetings. Finally I found out. I was in the district talking about southern domination of our committee, and it got back to the chairman.

Problems of Jurisdiction and Intercommittee Coordination

Many thoughtful members of the House are concerned about problems of overlapping jurisdiction, intercommittee coordination, lack of proper liaison and exchange of information, and situations in which committees hearing testimony and presumed to possess special competence do not actually make the decisions. Matters relating to defense and national security, foreign policy, and science are among those for which it is often difficult to determine jurisdiction. Rivalry may develop between committees with common interests as they seek to establish their primacy in a certain field or to undertake hearings or investigations which promise to arouse widespread interest and publicity. Committees are jealous of their prerogatives and resent intrusion. Information gained may not be shared with competitors. When there is duplication of effort, prospective witnesses suffer too.

The following discussion illuminates some of the jurisdictional questions that plague the House:

Conflicting committee jurisdiction is a real problem. Take the missile field, for example. The Armed Services Committee, the Appropriations Committee, the Military Affairs Subcommittee of the Government Operations Committee all have had jurisdiction. Then the space committee was organized this year and began questioning all the military leaders about the missile program. As a consequence, people from the Pentagon are testifying before four different House committees and then going over to the Senate and doing the same thing. That is time consuming and unnecessary.

Another kind of problem arises when two committees share interests, and there is no liaison between them. For example, railroad retirement and unemployment insurance for railroad workers was brought to the floor by the Interstate and Foreign Commerce Committee although Ways and Means has the bulk of unemployment insurance programing and social security. There was no liaison between the committees' staffs. It is important to have the committees in agreement on some fundamental propositions so whatever is passed on railroad retirement will be somewhat in conformity with other unemployment insurance programs and social security.

Another example is foreign trade. The Foreign Affairs Committee has an interest, as has Interstate and Foreign Commerce by its very definition. Yet I dare say Ways and Means does the bulk of the legislating in that field because it gets reciprocal trade within its jurisdiction. There is no liaison between committees. In addition to overlapping jurisdiction you have piracy. Foreign Affairs developed the idea of distributing surplus foods abroad as a means of furthering good foreign relations. The Agriculture Committee took it over.

As a result of the confusion and overlap, there is much feeling among representatives that there should be more coordination of committee activity within the House itself, even though they express little enthusiasm for joint House-Senate committees. A coordinating body is sometimes suggested, though the point is made that much of the coordination could be accomplished by the committees concerned if attention could be directed to the problem. "It wasn't by accident," said one congressman, "that when the highway bill was before the Public Works Committee, Ways and Means people sat in. Liaison was necessary, and we made sure it occurred."

Another lawmaker observed that there was very little exchange of information between the Appropriations Committee and the Government Operations Committee, "yet Government Operations' job is to follow federal expenditures to see whether they are in accordance with the law and spent efficiently. The testimony and information they get is very valuable to Appropriations." In corroboration of this observation one member of the Appropriations Committee said: "There still isn't enough of that. We seldom get members of a Government Operations subcommittee appearing before us to give us the benefit of their work. Nor do we get any staff liaison. I think it is unfortunate."

The Appropriations Committee is often resented by legislators assigned to other committees, in part because of its power over the congressional purse. Some congressmen who do not themselves take the initiative to ensure that the results of the deliberations of their committees are, where relevant, made available to the Appropriations Committee believe the latter group is negligent in failing to seek out such information. And some believe that members of other standing committees should be invited to sit in on appropriations subcommittee meetings where appropriate, as is the practice in the Senate. Commented one legislator:

> Theoretically the weapons system is authorized by the Committee on Armed Services, but that is only in theory. On the missile programs that have been permitted to go ahead, decision is made by the Appropriations Committee through the language of reports and through riders. The committee which heard all the testimony and is presumed to have special competence is not the one which makes the decision. If we are going to take the trouble to develop men with specialized knowledge in a given field, then we should give them the right to sit in and second guess on Appropriations. There is no point in having hearings before Armed Services and then have the final decision made by Appropriations.

That statement led to the following comment:

> Isn't it a little more complicated than that? Isn't it a fact that the Armed Services Committee doesn't really make decisions on major problems, that it involves itself more with housekeeping and peripheral matters? I suspect that if we had an Armed Services Committee that made substantial policy decisions rather than accommodations between the weapons systems, then the Appropriations Committee would not be in a position to do what it now does.

While many House members resent the Appropriations Committee and believe it to be somewhat arrogant in its attitude, there is wide recognition that its members work diligently. Membership on the committee is eagerly sought, but it is realized that the committee has a heavy workload which successful applicants must help to shoulder. There is, therefore, sympathy within the House for the heavy responsibilities of the committee and even for the committee itself when it is bypassed.

> Wouldn't it be better to require that bills for which there is overlapping jurisdiction be re-referred to another committee before they come to the floor? Agriculture passed a bill increasing the authorization for special school milk programs by $3,000,000, and it went directly to the floor, bypassing Appropriations. How can Appropriations have control over total government expenditures without having every bill involving expenditures re-referred to them before coming to the floor? Another ridiculous thing is that although the Foreign Affairs committee sits for weeks deciding what to put in the Mutual Security bill, the proceeds used for local currency under Public Law 480 is under Agriculture. Appropriations is bypassed.

COMMITTEE CHAIRMEN

Committee chairmen rank high among the most influential members of Congress. Sometimes respected, sometimes feared, often criticized by their colleagues, the majority have learned well the traditional privileges of their station. As men of authority and power, they are fair game for detractors who charge they often fail to discharge their duties in responsible fashion. Some appear unmoved by such criticism, regarding it as the inevitable result of power; most, at times at least, regard their actions as "misunderstood." Even House members who have words of praise for their own chairman are quick to document "arbitrary actions" of others. As one congressman said: "All committee chairmen are despots. Some of them are benevolent despots, as is the case of my chairman, but in any event they are despotic. They can run their committees as they see fit, and they usually do." In the face of such comments, it is not surprising that chairmen have a reputation in the House for moving to each other's defense if their power is threatened.

Characteristics of Success

An effective chairman is much respected in the House, earning even the grudging admiration of those who oppose him on legislative issues. In analyzing the success of one Democratic chairman, a Republican commented:

> The prime requirement for any chairman who wants to be an effective leader is to demonstrate that he is informed about the subject matter of his committee, and clearly this committee chairman is informed. And in demonstrating that he is, he commands the respect of the committee and of the House.

> But knowledge of his subject is only one of the essential attributes of a successful chairman. Realism in perceiving his support and skill in exploiting it can make a chairman strong. An awareness of the realities of a given situation — of what is possible and what is not possible — is basic. Observes one representative:

> The really skillful chairman understands where he stands on the floor. Judge Smith seems, perhaps more than anyone else among the chairmen, skillful in manipulating this relationship. He works in relation to the House as a whole. He is aware, or thinks he is aware, that he can get away with stalling a bill quietly when the House is not for it. He is aware he cannot stall a bill indefinitely if the majority is for it.

> Some chairmen have virtually no influence in the House and very little influence in committees. Others have influence out of all importance to their committees because of their personal prestige. So you have an incredible variety in the role, the position, and the power of the chairman.

The chairmen who are best liked by their committee colleagues are usually those who consult their associates on important matters, follow regularly established procedures, are amenable to reason, are not disposed to retain all committee perquisites for themselves, and do not discriminate against junior members by denying them adequate opportunity to participate fully — almost equally — in committee activities.

Sources and Uses of Power

The power of a committee chairman is impressive, varying somewhat according to committee tradition and the personal impact of the incumbent. He calls committee meetings and presides at them, exercising discretion in the recognition of his colleagues when they desire to speak. He decides the order in which bills are to be considered in the committee and when hearings should be held. Committee staffing is largely his prerogative. It is he who creates subcommittees, selects their membership, designates the chairman, and determines which legislative proposals shall be heard by each. He passes on requests for committee travel, initiates or approves special projects, acts as floor manager of legislative proposals voted out of his committee (a responsibility which carries with it the often crucial decision as to which members share in the limited debate), or designates the manager and, should such proposals go to conference, generally functions as head of the managers representing the House.

If he does not choose to have his committee governed by formal rules, his resistance may be sufficient to overcome efforts to provide for them. Should he determine to ignore established rules, it is only rarely and with great difficulty that his opponents can succeed in forcing him to acknowledge them.

In the last analysis he is, of course, responsible to his committee colleagues and can be called to account by them. Yet he often successfully avoids and sometimes flouts established procedures. Discontent may smoulder, but it seldom erupts in victorious rebellion. A freshman member of Congress says:

I knew committee chairmen were powerful, but I didn't realize the extent of the power or its arbitrary nature. Recently, when my chairman announced he planned to proceed in a particular way, I challenged him to indicate under what rules he was operating. "My rules," he said. That was it, even though there were no regularly authorized rules permitting him to function in that manner. There is great reluctance to challenge committee chairmen even though you don't agree with them. Everyone seems fearful; all members have pet projects and legislation they want passed. No one wants to tangle too much because they realize what the results would be.

Primarily, a chairman's strength rests on personal relationships undergirded by tradition. As chairman, time and again he is in a position to grant special consideration to the request of a committee member — a request which, were normal procedures to be followed, might not be acted on promptly if at all. His power is cumulative: association with his colleagues over a period of years enables him to build a strong residue of personal good will and IOU's in the face of which open revolt is most difficult.

Colleagues are grateful when he assigns them a subcommittee of their own and the right to staff it, and they want to retain this power. They know, too, that the chairman, by virtue of his position, possesses influence and leverage with other committee chairmen that on occasion, may prove helpful. In short, they recognize it is within his power to bestow certain privileges, and they hesitate to antagonize him. One Democrat describes the problem faced by would-be reformers:

The toughest kind of a majority to put together is one to reform a committee in the face of opposition from the chairman. As you get closer to the top of the hierarchy, the pressures on people who normally would be counted on to aid reformers are enormous and even people who would be classified as among the "good guys" rather than the "bad guys" tend to chicken out. It is the second and third termers who really have to lead the rebellion. The new fellows are still in a dream world and after you get beyond two or three terms you are part of the team and begin to see some merit in the system.

Another representative describes a recent attempt to bring about reform:

Our chairman is a lovable fellow but we have had no rules and no subcommittees. Inspired by the examples of some other committees last session, a number of us drew up some rules, setting up subcommittees and so on, and moved their adoption. The matter was brought to a vote after much anguish and finagling, and we were voted down. How? A couple of freshmen who had been interested in reform were "detained" in their district on this particular occasion. Some of the older people near the chairman in seniority, who nevertheless were spiritually on our side, voted against us because they had received pap from the chairman and there was more coming.

I should add a happy sequel. With this Congress came some changes in membership, and the chairman saw the handwriting. So now for the first time in history, we have a few subcommittees and a much better situation.

Majorities are Pickwickian things. You really have to have about a two-thirds majority like we now have in order to get results. Last session we had a simple majority spiritually in our favor, but they would not stand up and be counted.

A third member confirmed that many chairmen are resourceful in maintaining their power:

One chairman calls freshmen into his office and points out "if you vote for this set of rules, the chairmanships will all go to the senior members, but if you play along with me, you, as a first termer, will be selected as chairman of an important subcommittee." That gimmick has worked now for I don't know how many years. And he does appoint first termers as subcommittee chairmen.

Yet there is evidence that when contrasted with the authority of predecessors of several decades ago, the outside limits of power of today's chairmen are declining. The process has been gradual — so gradual as to be imperceptible to some congressmen. One leader in the movement to curtail the unrestricted freedom of chairmen by providing regularized procedures for committee operation explained the difference in this way:

When talking about a chairman's powers, one can differentiate between negative and positive power. Prior to the Reorganization Act when there were thirty or forty committees, you had the classical picture of what I call the negative chairman. A chairman, functioning within a system of smaller committees with narrower jurisdiction, was able to pigeonhole any bill referred to his committee to which he was opposed, provided there was not overwhelming sentiment in the House that action had to be taken. He could simply say, "There will be no hearings. We are not going to take up this bill."

This negative power of chairmen still exists today in the sense that chairmen can employ delaying tactics, by failing to call hearings, for example. But it is much more limited than it used to be, although the political scientists haven't completely caught up with that fact.

When we talk about the positive power of a chairman, we are talking about the chairman who not only is influential in his committee, but who has tremendous power and prestige on the floor. He will seldom be overruled. But the great power of pigeonholing legislation that chairmen once exercised simply by saying autocratically, "I am against this bill and there will be no hearings," has all but disappeared. Minor bills have been stalled in this fashion, but I challenge anyone to name a major bill that any chairman has killed in that way, except at the very end of a session when the time factor becomes important.

While there is considerable agreement with the views expressed above, there also is vigorous dissent. One congressman said he thought the speaker "a little too charitable and too satisfied with things as they are." He continued:

Look at all the committees that prevent consideration of legislation. Ways and Means will not consider any fiddling with oil depletion allowance. You can go on with example after example where there are taboos because of the chairman, very largely. The fact is that most of the committees, despite the valiant efforts of some members, are not reformed and the chairman is, if not omnipotent, at least the wielder of a tremendous negative influence.

In support of the position that chairmen still exert autocratic influence one lawmaker said:

The _____ committee offers a good example of complete and total dictatorship in action. The chairman runs the committee with an iron hand. He puts people on subcommittees, takes them off, and announces transfers at will. About a year ago a subcommittee was considering something to which he was strongly opposed, but which seemed likely to pass. Just as the meeting opened, in walked four additional members of the full committee, two Democrats and two Republicans. Without forewarning the subcommittee chairman, the chairman of the full committee had added four men to the group. In less than an hour there was to be a vote on a very important issue about which the four could not possibly have been fully informed. The chairman assumed that all four additions would vote with him against the legislation. It looked as though he had won until much to his distress one of the four broke ranks. But the action in increasing the subcommittee size was taken solely and arbitrarily by the chairman. Subcommittee chairmen do a lot of grumbling, but when the chips are down they vote with the chairman.

Consensus appears to be that while it probably is true that a chairman could not so flagrantly defy the will of the House today as formerly, efforts to proceed in the face of his objection depend primarily on the intensity of the pressure which can be brought to bear to get him to act, the nature of the majority aligned against him, and his own personality and conviction. Even today, opposition from a committee chairman to a proposal coming before his committee can be extremely detrimental, and sometimes fatal, to the measure. To overcome the obstinacy of a recalcitrant chairman requires a firm and determined majority strongly and skillfully led. Yet it is also true that legislators feel that fewer chairmen execute their responsibilities in the fashion of the stereotype of the autocratic committee head of old who kept his own counsel and regarded "his" committee as completely subject to his will. A definite trend in the other direction is discernible, though it would be erroneous to conclude that all chairmen are "reformed."

Today's delaying tactics are likely to be more subtle ("The judge is a much shrewder man than _____. He uses a bowie knife where _____ uses a meat axe.") and less irritating than those of the past, but the results may be the same. Observed one member, "I don't think there is a chairman in the House who will say, 'I won't give you a hearing.' They don't need to say that. A skillful chairman will schedule hearings and action on a bill in such a way that by the time it gets out of committee, it won't have time to get by the House." One chairman is drawn in this fashion:

_____ is one of the most charming and delightful chairmen in the House, and highly skillful. He doesn't sidetrack us by ever refusing anything. He just schedules a workload in other areas which makes it impossible for us to get our legislation heard. He always keeps us busy, never refusing anyone a hearing on legislation, always holding out hope. I have eternal hope. But he has one of the fullest schedules you will ever encounter.

A chairman is sometimes also criticized on the grounds that, in the words of one congressman: "Often he is trying to squirrel away information. He doesn't even want some of the committee members to be well informed, much less the average member of Congress." It is charged, too, that many of them have a lien on committee staff members, requiring them to perform assignments which should be undertaken by the chairman's personal office staff, thereby diverting hardpressed committee aides from their primary responsibilities. Although the House itself is reluctant to interfere in the activities of its committees or in committee expenditures, on occasion it has done so, generally as a rebuke to individual chairmen. For example, it reduced sharply requests of two committees for funds in the Eighty-eighth Congress, and, in one case, even specified the allocation of the funds authorized and required that the appropriate subcommittee chairman co-sign all authorizations for spending.

Preference for a Strong Chairman

As critical as some congressmen are of chairmen who seek to dominate committee proceedings and decisions, most of them seem to prefer a "strong" chairman to a "weak" one. For example, one representative stated, "I sometimes think I would prefer a despot to a man who is a pile of jelly." Another lawmaker agreed, and although a member of the minority party, had high praise for his chairman:

> The chairman of my committee is often considered a despot. I think he is a strong leader. He runs what is called in the Navy a taut ship. You know where you are headed. Sometimes you have to fight to get your point across, but if it is a good point you can get it across. I would prefer to have a committee run like that to one functioning without real leadership. Our chairman is responsible to the committee and we are very loyal to him because of the quality of his leadership. He has a record that is unparalleled for getting legislation through. Seniority, experience, and responsible leadership are the basis of his power.

Seniority and the Choice of Chairmen

There is no evidence of significant support in the House for modifying the present system for selecting committee chairmen by seniority. Though some freshmen express dissatisfaction with seniority as a test for capacity to lead a committee, nearly all of their more experienced colleagues assert there is no more satisfactory alternative. Even many freshmen support the present system. Indeed, there is some feeling that opposition to selecting chairmen by seniority is concentrated among those who write about the Congress, many of whom, it is said, possess little understanding of it. Acceptance by the Congress of seniority does not signify that members are enthusiastic about it. They are not. Rather they fear that the alternatives involve even more disadvantages. As one liberal House Democrat has written, "It is not that Congress loves seniority more but the alternatives less."

It is admitted that the present impersonal and automatic system for designating committee chairmen fails to distinguish between outstanding and mediocre House members, occasionally elevating a man incapable of leading or who possesses a record of inattention to committee responsibilities. It is also agreed that the system is not conducive to the maintenance of party discipline and that committee chairmen as a group are neither ideologically nor geographically representative of the House as a whole.

The characteristic congressional response to these criticisms is that seniority avoids the "politicking," logrolling, and factionalism that would accompany any system likely to replace it. It promotes stability by providing for an orderly transfer of authority to an heir apparent whose selection is assured. It is also suggested that to substitute another method might result in the loss of valuable talent. Said one congressman:

> Suppose you picked the number four man on a committee as a chairman. Wouldn't you immediately do away with the usefulness of the first three? They would be unhappy that they hadn't been picked and the chairman would always be regarding them as possible rivals and probably wouldn't want to give them stature. You are dealing with people, and human nature must be considered in deciding the method to be used.

Selection of a chairman by vote of committee members—more precisely, by the majority members—is thus regarded as unsatisfactory: the present impersonal system avoids the rivalries likely to develop among the more experienced committee members. In rewarding experience, the seniority system, it is asserted, generally places in positions of power men and women who through long exposure to the subject matter and to the process by which committee work is carried forward have become alert to the technicalities of legislation and its possible ramifications, and to the kinds and sources of pressures affecting the key issues before the committee. They are adept at handling relationships with the executive branch and with their own colleagues. From the minority's point of view, the present practice may result in the designation of an individual less motivated by partisanship and therefore more amenable to "reason," than election procedures would bring forward. It seems clear that many congressmen are not anxious to replace seniority with a system in which adherence to party would become a major determinant. They enjoy the flexibility of voting and degree of independence which seniority promotes. When it was suggested by one representative that where the Congress and Presidency are controlled by the same party, it is important to have committee chairmanships in the hands of legislators sympathetic to the President's program, another congressman said firmly:

I think you make a basic mistake when you assume that it is desirable for the committee chairman to be in harmony with the administration on every issue. Don't forget this is a tripartite form of government. I think it is a healthy thing sometimes to have competition if not conflict between the legislative branch and the executive branch.

An influential liberal Democrat has said that when he first was elected to Congress he shared the public image of "aging tyrannical chairmen ruling their committees with iron hands, pigeonholing bills willy-nilly and generally running Congress the way Henry VIII ran England." Eventually, however, he came to realize there was "a wide discrepancy between political folklore about the seniority system and fact about [it]."[1] He and other members believe seniority has become a popular whipping boy, unfairly charged with responsibility for many weaknesses of the committee system. Seniority, it is observed, does no more than designate the chairman; his powers and duties depend on rules of procedure adopted by the committee on which he serves. Committee inertia may produce too strong a chairman, but the remedy is clear: reform rests with the committee itself.

The tendency for committees to establish formal rules of procedure ("one man rule is on the way out") is but one of many influences that may mitigate the sometimes undesirable results of seniority. As has been demonstrated elsewhere in this volume, the seniority principle is not firmly applied in making committee assignments when there are strong reasons pointing to another choice. And the proliferation of subcommittees and select committees provides an unusual opportunity to grant early recognition to able and restive junior members of Congress who might otherwise be required to wait years to assume positions of leadership.

Though the general principle of seniority is well established as one of the basic tenets of the congressional system, there is nothing in the existing rules of the Congress to cloak it with legitimacy. It is a custom of convenience. It is clear that the elements of stability it lends to a system otherwise noted for its uncertainties and maneuverings have increased the reluctance to cast it aside. . . .

Notes

[1] Emanuel Celler, "The Seniority Rule in Congress," *Western Political Quarterly*, Vol. 14 (March 1961), pp. 160-67.

Conflict Management in a Congressional Committee

John F. Manley

There are presently twenty standing committees in the House of Representatives and sixteen in the Senate. These committees are strong, proud, and independent. Committees reduce the workload to manageable proportions by providing for a division of labor among the members of the chamber. The committee system permits a close review of the myriad of legislative proposals and the development of expertise by the members. Oversight of executive agencies is another function ably performed by committees. And finally, the committee is an excellent forum for compromise. In large bodies, compromise is often difficult to achieve. With a moderate size group, however, even the most ardent of interests can generally find some basis on which to work a compromise settlement. In recent years many scholars have turned their attention to Congress and particularly its committees. The reason for this lies, in part, in the accessibility of data on committee behavior. John Manley studies the problem of conflict management within the House Ways and Means Committee. The House has traditionally divided the fiscal and appropriations functions between two committees. The Ways and Means Committee is concerned with laws to raise money, e.g., taxation laws, while the Appropriations Committee determines how to spend money. The author discusses the methods by which the Committee strives to keep conflict within acceptable bounds on even the most controversial issues.

The House Committee on Ways and Means, according to its members, is assigned the responsibility of resolving some of the most partisan issues coming before Congress: questions of taxation, social welfare legislation, foreign trade policy, and management of a national debt which exceeds $300 billion.[1] Yet members of the Committee also contend, at the same time, that they handle most of these problems in a "responsible" way. A Republican member of Ways and Means echoed the views of his fellow Committee members when he said "it's

Reprinted, by permission of the author and publisher, from John F. Manley, "The House Committee on Ways and Means: Conflict Management in a Congressional Committee," *American Political Science Review,* 59 (December 1965), 927-939.

the issues that are partisan, not the members." A Democratic member went so far as to claim that Ways and Means is "as bipartisan a committee as you have in the House." And a Treasury Department official who has worked closely with Ways and Means for several years believes that it is a

> partisan committee in the sense that you get a lot of partisan voting. But while you get a lot of party votes the members discuss the bills in a nonpartisan way. It's a very *harmonious* committee, the members work very well and harmoniously together. Sure there is partisanship but they discuss the issues in a nonpartisan way.

The purpose of this paper is, first, to describe and analyze some of the factors which affect the Ways and Means Committee's ability to process, in a bipartisan manner, political demands which its members regard as highly partisan issues. Ways and Means is neither racked by partisanship nor dominated by nonpartisanship; conflict and consensus coexist within the Committee and the balance between them varies chiefly with the nature and intensity of the external demands which are made on the Committee. Second, an attempt is made to contribute to the development of an analytical framework, based on Fenno's study of the House Appropriations Committee, which may prove useful for the comparative analysis of congressional committees generally.[2]

For analytical purposes, the Ways and Means Committee is here conceived as a political subsystem of the House of Representatives, charged by the House with a number of tasks, but in the normal course of events enjoying a high degree of operational autonomy.[3] Its primary task *vis-à-vis* the House is the resolution of political demands, many of which involve high stakes in money, power or dogma. To perform this function the Committee must solve certain problems of internal organization and interaction, and these internal problems are inextricably linked to the nature of the environmental demands which the Committee is set up to process. The Ways and Means Committee, in other words, receives from its environment, and it generates internally, demands with which it must cope if it is to maintain itself as a viable subsystem of the House.

These internal and external demands give rise to a set of decision-making norms and roles which govern intra-Committee behavior and regularize its relations with outside actors. Committee norms and roles enable it to manage three distinct but related problems: (1) problems associated with tasks (instrumental interaction); (2) problems of personal gratifications and interpersonal relations (affective interaction); and (3) problems of integration.[4] All three are affected by the type of subject matter and the external demands placed on the Committee; the internal operations of the Committee cannot be fully understood apart from the tasks which the Committee is expected to perform for the House.

The need for internal organization of a heterogeneous group poses integrative problems for the Ways and Means Committee. Integration, as defined by Fenno, is

> the degree to which there is a working together or a meshing together or mutual support among roles and subgroups. Conversely, it is also defined as the degree to which a committee is able to minimize conflict among its roles and its subgroups, by heading off or resolving the conflicts that arise.[5]

Put in a somewhat different way, as Parsons notes,[6] the integration of roles depends on motivating *individual personalities* in the requisite ways. In order to stimulate the members of a group to contribute to the group's well-being and to the realization of its goals, they must be induced to share certain values and to behave in prescribed ways, either through the distribution of incentives or the application of sanctions, or both.[7] Members must, in a word, be socialized if the group is to be well integrated, and in congressional committees socialization depends on inducements.

Part I, below, deals with three interrelated variables and their relationship to Committee integration: the norm of restrained partisanship, the nature of the subject matter, and the external demands of the House. Part II considers the role of the chairman as an independent variable, describes how Chairman Mills directs the Ways and Means Committee, and offers some reasons why he operates as he does. Part III discusses the socialization process — the Committee's attractiveness, which predisposes the members to respond to socialization, and its ability to satisfy members' personal and political needs. The integration of four key roles, chairman-ranking minority member and newcomer-experienced member, is considered in Part IV. A final section offers some suggestions for comparative committee studies.

I

Minority reports by Republican members of the Ways and Means Committee and motions to recommit on the House floor frequently accompany the major bills reported by the Committee. In addition, the Committee members are clearly split along general ideological lines: the Democrats now overrepresent and the Republicans underrepresent their party's support for a larger federal role.[8] These indices of partisanship do not, however, reflect a critical integrative norm which governs the behavior of members in executive session: *the norm of restrained partisanship*. In the words of one experienced staff member,

I think you will find that Ways and Means is a partisan committee, there are usually minority views. But partisanship is not that high when they discuss the bill and legislate. About 95 percent of the time the members deliberate the bill in a nonpartisan way, discussing the facts calmly. Then toward the end Byrnes [the ranking Republican] and the Republicans may go partisan. The things the Committee deals with are big Administration issues, so you are bound to get minority views and partisanship. But Byrnes likes to take a nonpartisan attitude toward things and it gets partisan only toward the end. On some votes they go party line but on others they don't. It all depends on the issue.

A couple of Committee members feel that Ways and Means decides most issues on a partisan basis, but the preponderant view is that of a Democrat who declared that "most of the time we go along up to a certain point and then a sharp party vote will come. On the tax bill [Revenue Act of 1964] we went along for a long time without party votes, working very well, then the Republicans lined up at the end against it. There's very little partisanship up to a point, when the political factors come in, and then a partisan vote comes."[9] Or a Republican who said "we try to write the best legislation we can in a nonpartisan way — more so than any other committee. We work in a non-partisan way. Sure there are philosophical differences but they never become the partisan legislative fighting that they do on other committees."

The norm of restrained partisanship means that members should not allow partisanship to interfere with a thorough study and complete understanding of the technical complexities of the bills they consider. Members have a bipartisan responsibility to the House and to the nation to write sound legislation. They may disagree over what decisions the Committee ought finally to make but there is a firmly rooted consensus on *how* they ought to go about making them. Several variables affect the norm of restrained partisanship but two of them are of prime importance: (1) the nature of the Committee's subject matter; (2) the relationship between the House and the Committee.

(1) Working in a "responsible" way is valued highly by members of the Ways and Means Committee, and by "responsible" they mean being "conscientious," "thorough," "careful," and "studious." They emphasize the extreme complexity and national significance of the Committee's subject matter and this realization inclines them to constrain partisanship. "We deal with the most complicated, technical subject in the Congress, in the country for that matter, we have to be thorough on Ways and Means," according to a Democrat; a Republican said simply "you just don't mess around with taxes, it can create millionaires or paupers." All the members realize that they have to be responsible, another Democrat contended, and "this means that we don't do things on the basis of partisan or political advantage. We can reach a general consensus. Sometimes what a Republican will offer will be accepted by unanimous consent." A Republican who described the ideal GOP member in terms which made him certain to be in conflict with the Democratic members of the Committee paradoxically added that "partisanship is not too high on Ways and Means—taxes, trade, and social security should not be settled on a partisan basis."

Both partisan and nonpartisan tendencies permeate the Ways and Means Committee and are reflected in the Committee's operating style.

Those members who attend the protracted meetings go through a laborious process of illuminating the implications of arcane tax, tariff, debt and social security proposals. They are assisted by experts from the executive agencies, the House Legislative Counsel's Office, the staff of the Joint Committee on Internal Revenue Taxation, and at times by employees of the Library of Congress. Legislation is pondered line by line. When the Committee makes a decision it is translated into technical language by the experts ("technicians") and brought back to the Committee for final approval. The decision-making style varies somewhat from issue to issue but in general it is marked by caution, methodical repetition, and, most important, restrained partisanship. "We get together and go through things as twenty-five Americans all trying to do what's for the public good. It's even rare for a bill to be reported out by a 15-10 vote."

But the internal relations of the Ways and Means Committee are not devoid of partisan political or personal disputes. Restrained partisanship is the widely accepted norm governing the Committee's day-to-day operations and it does dampen partisanship and promote integration. It also, on occasion, breaks down. Not all Committee decisions are made in the full Committee meetings. Republican members frequently caucus in order to develop a united front on key pieces of legislation and party line splits are not as rare as some members imply. The norm of restrained partisanship does not stifle all dissension. A Democrat, for example, complained that the "Republicans sit there in Committee, vote for things, let things go by without saying anything, and then come out on the floor with motions to recommit, simply to surprise the Democrats." Personal feuds also erupt from time to time. On the whole, however, the Committee feels that the complex political demands which it must settle are of national importance and should be handled so far as possible on their merits.

(2) Virtually all the major bills reported to the House by the Ways and Means Committee are considered under a closed rule which precludes all floor amendments unless they are first accepted by the Committee. There is no lack of protest against this so-called "gag" rule but many members of the Committee and of the House argue that it saves the members from themselves.[10] Tax and tariff bills are so "sensitive" and "complex" that the House insulates itself from the demands of pressure groups by channeling the pressure into the committee stage of the process. On the few occasions when Ways and Means bills have

been considered under open rules, one veteran Democrat claimed, "you had chaos."

Members of the Ways and Means Committee are induced to follow the norm of restrained partisanship when they mark up a bill because of the autonomy which the closed rule gives to the Committee. A Republican, for example, expressed the common view that,

On our Committee we have a responsibility to the House, we have to do the best job we can.... The closed rule prevents amendments and changes so we have to perfect the bill. Other committees can bring a bill to the floor with provisions in it they know will be taken out on the floor. Ways and Means doesn't do this, we can't do this.

One Committee member explained that "there are congressmen who have been here for years and can't understand social security. The average congressman can't understand what we deal with and you just can't open it up on the floor. We try to report well-rounded packages of legislation, the best bills we can. We compromise a lot to get a good bill we can report out. You don't report controversies just for the sake of controversy."

A House vote on whether or not to debate Ways and Means bills under a closed rule is in a sense a vote of confidence in the Committee. The Committee is widely thought to be the master of its esoteric subject matter and almost every member has a stake in maintaining this reputation. The House expects the Committee to polish its bills to near perfection technically and, perhaps more important, to make a satisfactory adjustment of the competing demands which surround Ways and Means bills. This expectation partly explains why Ways and Means is noted for time-consuming diligence, and it also buttresses the Committee's adherence to the norm of restrained partisanship. The distinctiveness of Ways and Means was expressed by one member when he said "the House is jealous of the Committee. Many members say our bills can't be amended because we know it all, we're the experts. They are jealous." One of his colleagues sounded the same note when he observed that "the House says here are a bunch of smart guys, we won't tamper too much with what they do. The Ways and Means Committee has a reputation of being a well-balanced, level-headed group and the House respects this. . . . You just can't open a tax bill on the floor. The House knows we won't pull any fast ones."

II

If the Ways and Means Committee has been able to manage internal partisan conflict more successfully than the House Education and Labor Committee —and apparently it has—this is due in no small way to the leadership style of the chairman, Wilbur D. Mills (D., Ark.). With the exception of one member who denied that there is a leadership structure within Ways and Means (it is, he claimed, an "amalgamated mess"), members agree that Mills runs the Committee and runs it well.

Mill's fellow Democrats consider him "powerful," "prestigeful," "quite a guy," "clever," "fine," "subtle," "smart," "patient," "expert," "best mind on the Committee," "leader," "key man." Perhaps of greater significance for purposes of integration is that these views are shared by the Republican members. They say Mills is "very effective," "a good synthesizer," "leader," "real student," "master of tax affairs," "fair," "calm," "intelligent," "impartial," "able," "well educated," and "not arbitrary."

Mills promotes integration by treating everyone fairly. He is careful to protect the rights of the Republican members and he gives the Republicans, a former staff member claimed, "pride of authorship" in bills even though the minority members may ultimately oppose them on the floor. Constraints on participation, both in public hearings and in executive sessions, are very loose. One high ranking Republican said of Mills,

We deal with things on which Republicans and Democrats are in basic, fundamental disagreement and when you have something like this you are bound to get disagreement and minority reports. I think the major reason things don't disintegrate is Mills. Chairman Mills is very fair and reasonable. I can visualize disintegration and bickering if some of the members now ever become chairman, quite frankly, but all the time I've been on the Committee the chairmen have been reasonable men.

Mills recalls that as a boy he used to hear his father talk about the Ways and Means Committee with William A. Oldfield, an Arkansas congressman who was a member of the Committee during the 64th-70th congresses. When Mills was elected to the House he knew that Ways and Means was a choice assignment and he made an early attempt to get on it. His first try failed largely because he did not lay the proper foundation with the House leadership, but he tried again and with the leadership's support succeeded. Mills's attitude toward the Committee helps explain why he leads it as he does, always sensitive to threats to the Committee's status and prestige; but it is also a source of pride for some of the members. "You hear some criticism of Wilbur," said a Republican, "but he has a high regard for the Committee. *He takes care of it, respects it, and acts to insure its effectiveness on the floor.*" This commitment to the good of the Committee is a subtle factor in Committee integration but its presence is undeniable, even if there is no precise way to measure its importance.

For Mills, the Committee's reputation is dependent upon House acceptance of its bills. He does not like to lose and he usually avoids becoming so committed to an issue that he risks losing a bill on the floor. After waiting sixteen years to become chairman he lost part of the first major bill he brought to the floor; because of his bargaining skill and willingness to compromise, members feel, he has been beaten only once since then on a bill of any consequence.

Part of the reason why Mills tries to accommodate different and sometimes conflicting political demands is the internal composition of the Committee. Two or three of the Democratic members are more conservative than the rest and — before the Committee's party ratio was changed from 15-10 to 17-8 they could determine outcomes by voting with a solid Republican bloc. Conversely, one or two Republicans have been known to "go off the reservation" and vote with the Democrats. Depending on the issue, Mills may have to contain Democratic defections or lure a Republican vote. His base on the Democratic side is large and firm on most issues; even if some Democrats do not attend he can get their proxies. Neither party, however, is completely monolithic on all issues. Levels of commitment vary and in a delicately balanced situation Mills proceeds cautiously to make sure that he has the votes when he needs them. Two staff members commented: "Mills really likes to get a consensus if he can and this is one of the reasons partisanship is relatively low. He lets things settle and tries for agreement. He's just like that." "It's surprising how much Mills gets his own way. He'll sit back very quiet and let the boys thrash it out, let them go at it with their paper swords. Then he'll say we ought to do this and usually that's the way it's done." Committee integration may be positively or negatively affected by the style, ability and personality of committee chairmen.

The influence of the chairman on integration may also vary with committee structure. For example, the chairman may be a crucial factor in a committee, such as Ways and Means, that does its work in full committee rather than in subcommittees; but he may be less important or have different effects in a committee that operates through relatively autonomous subcommittees (Appropriations).

III

Political socialization is a dynamic and continuous process by which a group perpetuates its norms, values and roles. It is dynamic in that the content of what is passed on changes with new problems and demands; it is continuous in that it affects both newcomers and experienced members. To the new member socialization involves exposure to and inculcation with the norms of the group. To the experienced member it consists of the maintenance of his conformity to group norms or, if he resists, tension between his values and behavior and those of the group.

Socialization depends upon the attractiveness of the group and upon its ability to regulate behavior through the allocation of positive and negative incentives. Objectively measured, Ways and Means is the most attractive committee assignment in the House. John C. Eberhart compared House committees from 1914 to 1941 and found that Ways and Means had the highest prestige.[11] Similarly, Warren Miller has compared committee between the 80th and 88th Congresses and Ways and Means places first.

Members are attracted to Ways and Means for a variety of reasons. Most frequently mentioned are its power and prestige. Ways and Means is "tops," "the guts of government," a "real blue-ribbon committee," a "choice one." One member, who was neither especially attracted to Ways and Means nor happy with the detailed nature of the Committee's work, said you just don't leave a "blue-ribbon" committee like Ways and Means. "You just go up from Ways and Means," a Democrat said, "you don't go to another committee — Appropriations, Rules, or Interstate. You go to Senator, Governor, that sort of thing. It's a springboard and many members have gone on from it." When asked if he ever tried to shift to a different committee another Democrat replied, "are you kidding! Why leave heaven to go to hell? There's no committee in Congress, including Appropriations, that's as important as Ways and Means. Why step downward once you have reached the top?"

Group identification is high on the Ways and Means Committee and the members usually refrain from behavior that is likely to weaken the Committee's position in the House. The Committee's attractiveness buttresses the norm that outlaws such behavior. Members may disagree and they may even quarrel among themselves but, as one Democrat said, "we fight our battles in executive session and not in public." A conservative Republican member who almost never agreed with anything supported by the Democrats declared that "we keep personal things to ourselves and we stick together when someone attacks the Committee." The Committee has been criticized by its own members but this happens very rarely. Every member derives satisfaction from the Committee's reputation; they are predisposed by the Committee's attractiveness to follow the ground rules of partisan battle which place rigid constraints on the ways in which disagreement is manifested.

Socialization is also affected by the group's ability to offer the members positive incentives in return for approved modes of behavior. The Ways and Means Committee serves as the source of positive incentives in at least three important ways: (1) affective relations inside the Committee, (2) influence in the House; and (3) relations with constituents.

(1) Unlike most other congressional committees (Senate Finance is another example), the Ways and Means Committee functions in executive sessions of the full committee, and not through subcommittees. Members meet in direct face-to-face contact for weeks at a time and this style of deliberation is accompanied by a fairly well defined set of interpersonal norms. Committee meetings are not supposed to be partisan battles; some acrimony does develop but on the whole the members feel that to be effective they must maintain decorum and act in a gentlemanly way. Bitter personal disputes erupt infrequently and even public conflicts which appear to be disruptive of interpersonal relations are often played out in a benign spirit. A Republican who found it difficult to follow these norms was "talked to" by a senior Republican and told that he was losing his effectiveness by being so adamant. If a member starts to berate another member his colleagues will try to restrain him. You

"don't attack one man continually" on Ways and Means; "we spar a lot but it never gets serious." "We don't have knock-outs, maybe we are a little more clubby, more closely knit than others." Members believe that they are "responsible" men who "respect the other fellow" and who "get along pretty well with others."

These attitudes and norms help make the Committee a satisfying group to belong to. A Republican said,

Relations with the Democrats are usually harmonious. It's like a fraternity where you have different clubs with different symbols and minor disagreements. There's a spirit of *camaraderie* that prevails. Oh, we have our differences now and then, and we jab back and forth, but it never really gets too serious. We are all concerned with how the Committee looks to outsiders and if there's a lot of bickering the Committee doesn't look good. Take Banking and Currency for example after Patman took over. He's arbitrary and the Committee's prestige has sunk way down. We know that to be an effective committee we must be reasonable.

In the words of a Democrat "everyone's a moderate . . . they screen out those members who would play for publicity and make a lot of noise. . . ." Two Democrats attributed their appointments to Ways and Means to personal characteristics of their rivals as aspirants. One of these "went off half-cocked," was "controversial" and not "well-liked"; the other was "compulsive" and he would not be right for Ways and Means where members have to "contain" themselves. Another member said plainly, "we don't want any screwballs and since I've been a member we haven't had any screwballs. These men are pretty carefully selected, you know, so you don't get radicals." "Comparing Ways and Means with my former committees, and with other committees I know of, there is a spirit of cooperation between Republicans and Democrats. We are members of the 'club' now."

Personal traits are not the only consideration in the recruitment process to Ways and Means. Seniority, region, and policy orientation are important and, in many cases, decisive. When these criteria are not of overriding importance, or when more than one contestant meets them, a popular man who is "responsible" has an edge over someone who had made enemies, especially on the Democratic side where Ways and Means members are elected by a vote of all Democratic members of the House; and objective reasons can usually be found to rationalize affective predilections. These informal recruitment criteria and norms of behavior combine with the Committee's attractiveness to produce men who are inclined to follow group norms, to value harmony, and to promote integration. Members prefer to disagree amicably if they can; they feel more comfortable in a low-tension environment and they realize that to protect the Committee's status as the "queen committee" they must manage partisan dissension in a non-destructive way.

As indicated above, partisan considerations and policy orientation are important factors in determining contests over seats on the Ways and Means Committee. In 1963, for example, Phil Landrum of Georgia was denied a seat on Ways and Means largely because he was considered to be too conservative by his Democratic colleagues in the House. Landrum was elected to Ways and Means in 1965 after demonstrating more liberal inclinations by, among other things, guiding the poverty bill through the House. Republicans, on the other hand, want men on Ways and Means who "all fall within pretty much the same general philosophical area" and who will "go down the line" for the party.

(2) Membership on the Ways and Means Committee makes one a member of the House elite. Ways and Means members share in the Committee's prestige and, at a more practical level, they are in a good position to accumulate political credits with their colleagues. All

congressmen, at one time or another, are concerned with problems that relate to taxes, social security or trade. On swapping favors one Committee member explained,

Hell, I'm always being approached by members. It's important, you know. I might go to a member of Public Works once in ten years but they seek my assistance all of the time. Same with all the members of Ways and Means.... When I need a favor I can always call on Republicans whom I have helped on Ways and Means bills.

Democrats on Ways and Means have a unique source of influence because of their control over assignments to other committees.[12] Committee assignments in a political system whose life revolves around committees are of major concern to every member of the House. The Ways and Means members normally enjoy— with the exception of assignments to the Rules Committee, which are of special interest to party leaders—a high degree of influence in making appointments. The committee-on-committees function increases their contacts with members from their zone. Newly elected congressmen are indebted to them from the first day they arrive and, as a member moves up the committee hierarchy, he is continually dependent on his representative on Ways and Means. "They call you 'Mr.' and 'Sir' when you are on the committee on committees," one member said. House members "look up to me"; a third member said "*they* come to you and that's very important. Members are always coming to me for things and when I go to them, boy they remember."

In short, the members of Ways and Means stand above many of their peers in the House and they associate this preeminence with the Committee. They are, therefore, induced to follow the norms which insure the continuation of the Committee's stature: restrained partisanship, responsible law making, and reasonable behavior.

(3) Most members of the Ways and Means Committee find the Committee a good place from which to satisfy constituent demands. Not every member believes that he can serve his constituents better from Ways and Means than he could from any other House committee, but several do. Moreover, no member's district is so intimately dependent on a committee other than Ways and Means that he risks electoral defeat simply because of his committee assignment. Few members would disagree with a newly appointed member, Dan Rostenkowski (D., Ill.), who told his constituents in a newsletter,

This has been a wonderful year for me. In May I was selected to fill a vacancy on the House Ways and Means Committee. As this is the Committee on Committees, appointment must be made by a vote of the Democratic members of the House, and I am proud to say that I was unanimously chosen by my colleagues.... This is the most important committee in the House.... It is a most interesting assignment, but more important, it places me in a position whereby I can be more effective in assisting you with your needs, both personal and legislative.

Intensive bargaining surrounds the myriad parts of a major Ways and Means bill and it is often possible for a member to promote or protect constituent interests by letting it be known that he will support a position unfavorable to the Administration. Executive department representatives may even try to lure Republican support, as evidenced by the late Howard Baker's success in getting one of his favorite proposals included in the Revenue Act of 1964. "You know, you can really do things for your constituents on the Committee. Boy, if you are a horse-trader you can really move. Exports, imports, that sort of thing."

Major legislation is not the only opportunity for serving one's constituents and friends. Ways and Means also processes so-called "members' bills," which are perhaps the best examples of bipartisan cooperation on the Committee. A member's bill is supposed to be a minor piece of legislation that ameliorates the impact of some small feature in the tax laws or makes some "technical" improvement in other laws that come under the Committee's jurisdiction; it is regarded as a "little" thing, of no special interest to anyone other than the Committee member who introduced it.[13]

From time to time during the course of a Congress, Committee members are asked to list in the order of their preference (or chance of passage) those bills which they would like the Committee to consider during "members' bill time." Every member is given the opportunity to call up a bill or bills, depending on how many times they go around the table. If he can get the unanimous consent of his colleagues, his bill will be reported to the House, called up on the House floor by unanimous consent or suspension of the rules, and usually passed without objection.

On April 30, 1964, Chairman Mills stood on the floor of the House and asked unanimous consent for the immediate consideration of twelve members' bills. Eleven of these bills were passed by voice vote and one, H.R. 4198 introduced by Representative Shelley (D., Calif.), was defeated when another non-Ways and Means member, Matsunaga (D., Hawaii), objected. H.R. 4198 provided for the free importation of soluble and instant coffee and Matsunaga thought that before it was passed the Hawaiian coffee industry should be consulted. Mills had also intended to call up a bill introduced by Hale Boggs (D., La.), the third ranking Democrat on Ways and Means, but another member of the Committee, Thomas B. Curtis (R., Mo.), prevented it by indicating to Mills that he would object.

Of the eleven bills passed at this time, four were introduced by non-members of Ways and Means. The Committee reported these bills as favors to them. Two of the remaining seven were introduced by Republican members of Ways and Means, and five by Democratic members. All twelve were reported unanimously by the Committee and most were supported actively on the floor by the ranking Republican member, John Byrnes (Wis.).

A member's bill may be killed by another member of the Committee, as in the case of the Boggs bill, or it may be killed or postponed by other members of the House, as illustrated by Matsunaga's objection to H.R. 4198. Not every member's bill becomes law. But many do. If influence in the House is defined as the ability to accumulate credits and dispense them with skill then the members of the Ways and Means Committee, if they stick together, are in a good position to exert influence and satisfy the demands of their constituents and friends. Favors that are "little" in the sum total of things are often large to individual congressmen, and when small favors like these are dispensed over a period of years they amount to a considerable fund of credit on which the Committee (and its Chairman) may draw if the need arises. Ways and Means reports and passes a relative handful of major bills; it processes dozens of noncontroversial members' bills. When the Committee "cashes in its chips" to pass a major bill the chips are members' bills and other favors which it performs for members of the House.

Members' bills are important benefits which members of both parties enjoy by virtue of their membership on the Committee. They help satisfy the members' need to meet some of demands of their constituents; and they induce the members to cooperate with one another to this end. The continued success of members' bills depends on the Committee's relations with the House. Members' bills are positive incentives which emanante from the Committee and by helping to promote the members' interests they promote integration.

IV

Committee integration is also affected by the hierarchy of status and role which exists within the group. Members of the Ways and Means Committee play different roles and if the Committee is to be well integrated these roles must be legitimized and ordered. Two sets of roles are of special significance: chairman and ranking minority member, and experienced member-newcomer.

The relationship between the chairman and the ranking minority member is a potential source of conflict in the Committee. Mills, who was elected to the Committee in 1942, has been chairman since 1958. John Byrnes of Wisconsin has 18 years' experience on Ways and Means and has been the ranking Republican member since 1963. Their roles set limits to the degree of cooperation between them and they frequently oppose one another on key policy matters, both within the Committee and on the House floor. There is, however, a good deal of cooperation and mutual respect between them. Both men realize that their positions may be reversed some day and they therefore cooperate on most procedural and some substantive matters.

When the Ways and Means Committee comes to the House floor with a major bill it is often the quintessence of party conflict in the House. But the easy fraternization between Mills and Byrnes even at the height of floor battles is indicative of the spirit within which the Committee has performed its day-to-day labors.

Mills and Byrnes have jointly sponsored legislation which is referred to Ways and Means and they have collaborated on certain kinds of bills on the floor. One staff member described the two men in these words,

Mills calls the shots, he runs the show. If a member would like a Committee meeting next Monday, for example, he'd have to get Mills to call it. Every once in a while Mills is questioned about hearings and witnesses but he's very good about it. He discusses these things with Byrnes. The hearings last fall [1963] on beer concentrate were Byrnes's doing. He wanted them, so he and Mills arranged a date. It's quite informal. Mills and Byrnes are good friends. *In many ways they are very similar. Both are dedicated and have no outside life—no hobbies, never take vacations. The Committee is their life. They take work home. They remind me of guys working in a factory who punch in and out, go home and wait for the next work day to begin.*

Members of both parties are "safe" on critical issues and they are, therefore, bound to be opposed on some things. The disintegrative effect of this built-in partisanship is tempered, however, by the tendency of newly elected partisans to accept subordinate roles within the Committee until they become familiar with the subject matter and are accustomed to Committee procedure.

The apprentice role is firmly established on Ways and Means and the new member who wants to be effective does not (even if he could) try to match wits with his more experienced colleagues. This is due in part to the Committee's complex subject matter. One veteran member said that "when I first went on the Committee I used to leave the meetings with a headache, truly a headache! The stuff was just over my head. I just kept plugging along and gradually you catch on. The things we deal with are so complex!" "Detail and technical, oh there's so much detail and it's so technical! You have to take work home and study. Everything is complicated now. Social security has become complicated, tax and tariff too." A junior Democrat added,

Leadership is pretty constant. The men who sit at the head of the table naturally lead the Committee. They are knowledgeable and have been around a long time. . . . Now that doesn't mean that if I have a question I can't get my oar in. There's no problem about that. But leadership is as you go up the ladder. Neither _____ nor I will ever be fire-balls on the Committee; we are too old.

Or a junior Republican,

Byrnes and Curtis are real students, are experienced, and know more about it. They *should* lead the Committee. Yesterday, for example, I could have spoken on the Renegotiation Act but I am quite content to let Byrnes and Curtis handle it. They are the experts. I'd tell a new member to get familiar with the four or five major things the Committee deals with. To study hard.

"Jennings is a smart member and Martha Griffiths shows a lot of potential. But we are all learners and beginners, the older members are the ones we listen to." "You have to learn," a Republican said, "and I want to learn. It would be resented if I tried to talk too much or overdid it.... So keep your damn big mouth shut a while. If I tried to talk a lot it would be resented, while it wouldn't for an older member."

Newcomers to Ways and Means are expected to "attend religiously, study hard, and pay attention to what the experts are saying." And the "experts" are the experienced members. A new member may participate right away but it is a fundamentally different kind of activity from that of the senior members. Junior members are neither muzzled nor immobilized; they exist in a state of animated quiescence until they have absorbed enough information to make meaningful contributions to the policy discussion.

Friendly and cooperative relations between the chairman and the ranking minority member, plus well established norms of deference governing the degree and kind of participation by senior and junior members, constitute a system of decision-making which is marked by restrained partisanship. During their apprentice period the behavior of new partisans is controlled by the impossibility of rapidly accumulating expertise in the Committee's subject matter. They are exposed to the norms of the group; they soon detect the Committee's leaders; and they learn how to become effective members.

The socialization process is not perfect on Ways and Means but in terms of its ability to negate the influence of divisive partisan factors it compares favorably in recent years with some other committees, most notably the House Education and Labor Committee. It is doubtful if any amount of incentives derived from the Committee, or any number of years experience on the Committee, could result in the total integration of dedicated conservatives like James Utt or committed liberals like George Rhodes, but not even the most ideologically oriented members are immune from the group pressures to restrain partisanship, to articulate dissension in certain ways and not in others, and to contribute to the perpetuation of the Committee as the number one committee in the House.

The major differences in emphasis between Fenno's approach and the one adopted here are that I have stressed the influence of external House demands on the internal operations of the Committee, taken the role of chairman as an independent variable of prime importance to the Ways and Means Committee, considered socialization as a blend of attractiveness and inducements, and attempted a linkage between Parson's focus on integration and Barnard's stress on inducements. Whatever the approach, it is clear that the inner life of congressional committees, a hitherto little explored part of the workings of Congress, deserves the attention of political scientists as a way of increasing our knowledge about legislative behavior and explaining why Congress accepts or rejects the recommendations of its "little legislatures."

Notes

[1] This article is based on interviews conducted during 1964 with twenty of the twenty-five members of the Committee. The average interview ran 80 minutes. Questions were open-ended, no notes were taken during the interview, and all quotations are derived from notes made immediately after each interview. In addition, staff members, lobbyists, and executive department personnel were interviewed, some at great length. As a 1963-1964 Congressional Fellow I worked with Congressmen Thomas B. Curtis (R., Mo.) and Dante B. Fascell (D., Fla.), and was able to observe the Committee directly.

[2] Richard F. Fenno, Jr., "The House Appropriations Committee as a Political System: The Problem of Integration," *American Political Science Review*, Vol. 56 (June, 1962), pp. 310-24. Fenno's approach has been applied to two other committees. See Charles O. Jones, "The Role of the Congressional Subcommittee," *Midwest Journal of Political Science*, Vol. 6 (November, 1962), pp. 327-44; Harold P. Green and Alan Rosenthal, *Government of the Atom* (New York, 1963), ch. 2.

[3] For the general theory behind this paper see Talcott Parsons and Edward A. Shils, eds., *Toward a General Theory of Action* (New York, 1962), pp. 3-44, 190-233.

[4] Parsons and Shils, *op. cit.*, pp. 208-09. These problems are also dealt with in the literature on small groups. See Sidney Verba, *Small Groups and Political Behavior* (Princeton, 1961), pp. 117-43; Josephine Klein, *The Study of Groups* (London, 1956), pp. 115-33; George C. Homans, *The Human Group* (New York, 1950), pp. 319-20.

[5] Fenno, *op. cit.*, p. 310.

[6] Parsons and Shils, eds., *op. cit.*, pp. 24-25.

[7] Chester I. Barnard, *The Functions of the Executive* (Cambridge, 1956), pp. 139-60. Frank J. Sorauf has recently analyzed political parties from an inducement-contribution perspective; see his *Political Parties in the American System* (Boston, 1964), pp. 81-97.

[8] During the 87th Congress the Democratic members of the Committee averaged 81 percent on Congressional Quarterly's index of support for a larger federal role; the Republicans averaged 17 percent. A comparable disparity, 85 percent to 27 percent, shows up during the 88th Congress. Moreover, in both congresses the Democrats and Republicans on Ways and Means now appear to be more "liberal" and less "liberal," respectively, than the rest of their party colleagues. Data compiled from *Congressional Quarterly Weekly Report,* December 28, 1962, pp. 2290-95; October 23, 1964, pp. 2549-53. This may not have been true in earlier years.

[9] This was confirmed by the Committee's ranking Republican member, John Byrnes, in the debate over the 1964 Revenue Act: "We tried to come up with as good a bill as we could. And I say to the Speaker it was not done on a partisan basis—and that has been confirmed by the chairman. It was done on a bipartisan basis, up until the last few days. When they had almost all the drafting completed and perfected, then they said, 'Now we don't need your help any more, boys; we will put the steamroller to work.' But up until then it was on a bipartisan basis." *Congressional Record,* September 25, 1963, Vol. 109, p. 18113. Contrast this with E. E. Schattschneider's account, *Politics, Pressures and the Tariff* (New York, 1935), of the making of the Smoot-Hawley tariff in 1929-30.

[10] From 1955-1965, forty-seven bills were debated under closed rules, nine under open or modified open rules, and the rest (over 350 bills) under unanimous consent or suspension of the rules. A typical statement was made by Representative Howard W. Smith in the 1955 fight over a closed rule for the Trade Act: "Mr. Speaker, I recognize the difficulty of many Members of the House on this bill; we all have our own problems in our own districts, but this is a question that affects the whole country. . . . It has been recognized ever since I have been on the Rules Committee that bills of this type should be considered, as a practical matter, under a closed rule. The original bill setting up this program, as I recall, and the extensions in 1953 and 1954 were considered under closed rules. Nobody seemed to object at that time; as a matter of fact, both the majority and minority member of the Ways and Means Committee came before the Rules Committee and joined in the usual request that that committee makes of the Rules Committee for a closed rule."

Congressional Record, February 17, 1955, Vol. 101, p. 1676. On this occasion the closed rule was almost defeated; it was adopted by one vote only after Rayburn took the floor and told his colleagues that "the House on this last vote has done a most unusual and under the circumstances a very dangerous thing. . . . Only once in the history of the House in 42 years in my memory has a bill of this kind and character been considered except under a closed rule. How long it is going to take, how far afield you will go, I do not know. . . . So as an old friend to all of you, as a lover of the House of Representatives and its procedures, I ask you to vote down this amendment offered by the gentleman from Ohio [Mr. Brown]." p. 1678.

[11] Cited in George B. Galloway, *Congress at the Crossroads* (New York, 1946), p. 90. For some critical comments on Eberhart's methodology see James A. Robinson, "Organizational and Constituency Backgrounds of the House Rules Committee," *The American Political Arena,* ed. Joseph R. Fiszman (Boston, 1962), p. 214.

[12] On the Committee on Committees see Charles L. Clapp, *The Congressman: His Work as He See It* (Washington, 1963), pp. 183-212; also Nicholas A. Masters, "Committee Assignments in the House of Representatives," *American Political Science Review,* Vol. 55 (June, 1961), pp. 345-57.

[13] Typical members' bills alter the tariff on brooms made of broom corn, provide a credit or refund of self-employment taxes in certain cases, allow the free importation of spectrometers for universities, provide tax-exempt status for non-profit nurses' professional registries, continue the suspension of duties for metal scrap, etc.

The Senate:
Is There an Inner Club?

Nelson W. Polsby

Who really runs Congress? Such a question suggests in advance that there is some group other than the formal officers who lead the organization. Observers of differing political persuasions frequently are in agreement as to the existence of such a group, but they differ markedly on just who is in the "Inner Club." There are, in fact, two fundamental overviews of the Senate, equally true of the House, which are in competition for acceptance. One view conceives of the Senate as an organization which divides its labor and power, albeit in unequal portions, among all its members. The other conception of the Senate is that it is a body under the control of a few powerful men with everyone outside the select circle being largely ornamental. The role of the formal leadership varies over time, but it appears safe to say that the leadership does in fact lead and that the existence of a quasi-secret group operating behind the scenes has never been validated. Nelson Polsby discusses some of the differing views on Senate leadership and norms and suggests that in the most tolerant body in the world, the Senate, one must not be surprised to find all sorts of beings: sages, clowns, mavericks, and some fools.

Much ink has been spilled in recent years describing the inner workings of senatorial politics. The general feeling has been that the formal structure of the Senate has been less revealing of the actual distribution of power within the institution than is usually the case with political organizations, and so writers have attempted to capture and codify "folkways" — informal prescriptions of behavior — an understanding of which is supposed to help in disentangling the mysteries of senatorial power and influence.

The Senate, it has been argued, is really run by a small clique of interacting senators, an "inner club" of men, small in number and not necessarily the most senior in rank, who are emotionally in tune with one another, who follow the folkways and who are widely recognized

Reprinted by permission of Prentice-Hall, Inc., Englewood Cliffs, New Jersey, from Nelson W. Polsby, *Congress and the Presidency*, © 1964, pages 32-41.

as "Senate types." It is said that senators, if they aspire to this inner club, must adapt their behavior to fit the following composite description:

[He is] a prudent man, who serves a long apprenticeship before trying to assert himself, and talks infrequently even then. He is courteous to a fault in his relations with his colleagues, not allowing political disagreements to affect his personal feelings. He is always ready to help another Senator when he can, and he expects to be repaid in kind. More than anything else, he is a Senate man, proud of the institution and ready to defend its traditions and perquisites against all outsiders. He is a legislative workhorse who specializes in one or two policy areas.... He has a deep respect for the rights of others... making his institution the last citadel of individualism.... He is a man of accommodation who knows that "you have to go along to get along"; he is a conservative, institutional man, slow to change what he has mastered at the expense of so much time and patience.[1]

The picture of senatorial life which this description gives is probably less valid than its proponents recognize; indeed, in some particulars, it may be extremely misleading. In order to see why this is so, it is necessary to examine the following questions:

First, what are the "folkways," as described in the books, magazines, and journals, on which "real" senatorial leadership is supposed to be based?

Second, who are the members of the inner club?

Third, in what sense do men of power in the Senate actually follow the folkways?

Finally, what does this suggest to us about distributions of power in the Senate, and about roles available to senators who wish to share significantly in the power of the institution?

The "Folkways of the U.S. Senate" have been described most succinctly by Donald Matthews in an article which has achieved wide currency and acceptance.[2] They consist of:

1. Practices of the Senate which grant individual senators few or no opportunities for deviation. Examples include the operations of the seniority system and the rules of comity governing floor debate.

2. Prescriptions of "good behavior" which apply to freshman senators only. During his period of apprenticeship — which lasts until the next freshman class arrives 2 years later—the freshman senator is expected to perform many thankless tasks cheerfully, such as presiding over floor debate. He should seek advice from senior senators, make no speeches or remarks on the floor unless specifically invited, and take the initiative in getting acquainted with other senators.

3. Prescriptions of "good behavior" which apply to all senators in their relations one with another. Examples include the following commandments: make speeches only on subjects on which you are expert, or which concern your committee or your state; do not seek publicity at the expense of less glamorous legislative work; do favors for other senators; address your colleagues in a friendly manner; speak well of the Senate as an institution; keep your word when you make an agreement.

In truth, these folkways provide little in the way of help to nonfreshman senators who seek to unravel the secrets of the inner club. Yet freshmen are apparently not the only senators excluded, nor are nonfreshmen who conformed as freshmen necessarily "in."

Who is "in"? Who, specifically, are the "Senate men" who in the last few years are supposed to have dominated this institution? "They [are] men of the type and character," says Dean Acheson, "who, in a quiet way, are apt to dominate any male organization. The main ingredients of such men are force, likeableness and trustworthiness. Alben Barkley, Walter George and Arthur Vandenberg were, perhaps, the *beaux ideals.*"

Perhaps not. William S. White, while granting Barkley and George entrance to the inner club, says "The late Senator

Arthur Vandenberg . . . for all his influence upon foreign relations . . . was never in his career a true Senate type, no matter how formidable he was as a public man."

For White, Senate types display "tolerance toward [their] fellows, intolerance toward any who would in any real way change the Senate," and commitment to the Senate as "a career in itself, a life in itself and an end in itself." Yet certified "Senate types" such as Senators Taft or Russell (and he might have added Kerr, Humphrey, and Johnson as well) often have been discovered running for President. White's argument that they do this not because it is a higher or more preferable office, but because the Presidency is "another" ambition of theirs, is unconvincing.

Other Senate insiders can be observed tampering with the decor of the institution in a variety of ways. The consistent reformist agitations of insider Hubert Humphrey (now Majority Whip) have abated only slightly since his celebrated maiden speech suggesting the abolition of Senator Byrd's Committee on Non-Essential Expenditures in the Executive Departments. Perhaps more significant was then-Majority Leader Lyndon Johnson's successful reform of the committee assignment process on the Democratic side of the aisle, a change of "real" and undeniable significance tending to take power from senior senators and vest it in more junior ones by a man widely recognized as the most inside of insiders. As Ralph Huitt says, "One of [Johnson's] most successful political acts was his decision in 1953 to put all Democratic senators, even new ones, on at least one important committee."[3]

Johnson also was a participant in a human drama of some poignance a few years ago, when the elderly Senator Theodore Francis Green of Rhode Island, "a member of the very hierarchy of the Club"[4] was persuaded to relinquish the chairmanship of the blue-ribbon Foreign Relations Committee to the next-ranking J. William Fulbright of Arkansas, who is, White says, "not . . . quite a Senate type."

On the matter of tolerance-in-general it is very hard to judge senators from a distance. But if the habitual practice of tolerance actually separates members of the inner club from those outside, as White seems to suggest, then White is suggesting that the late Senator Walter George of Georgia, for example, was a more tolerant man than, let us say, former Senator Herbert Lehman of New York, whom White places outside the inner sanctum. It is instructive in this connection to recall the anecdote with which Mr. White introduces us to Senator George and to the "Senate type."

No skin in all the world is more easily abraded than senatorial skin. Once, for an illustration, the Attorney General of the United States, Herbert Brownell, Jr., was condemned to the pit of Senatorial displeasure for daring to permit his department to prepare a memorandum raising certain questions about a . . . proposed Amendment to the Constitution. . . . The incident struck the then Dean of the Senate, Mr. George of Georgia as [Mr. White's choice of words is exquisite] intolerable. It was his conclusion, expressed in the tragically wounded tones of which his majestic voice was capable, that Brownell was "a very *odd* Attorney General," and worse still, that his offensive paper had undoubtedly been written by "some cloik" [clerk] in the Justice Department.

"Tolerance" as such, lack of presidential ambition, undeviating acceptance of the institutional status-quo, all on closer inspection fail to differentiate members of the inner club from those who languish outside. What about acceptance of the more diffuse folkways that seem to reward agreeable men who manage their interactions with their fellows smoothly? Is there, perhaps, an identifiable personality type which foreordains membership in the inner club?

It is difficult, without an exhaustive set of identifications from those in the know, to say who is "in" the inner club and who is not at any given time; but I think we can reasonably assume that those men who over the last decade or so have been elevated by their fellows to high party posts within the Senate can be regarded as Senate types. This leaves aside the great number of self-selected leaders whose interest in particular policies might make them important in the Senate, and that group of men who may be "in" by virtue of seniority. Both groups because of the method of their selection would be likely to display personal characteristics less compatible with the folkways than senators formally selected to leadership by fellow senators.

But even in this latter group, the variation in personal characteristics is quite striking. Over the last decade observers have noted the gregariousness of the present Democratic Whip Hubert Humphrey and the diffidence of his predecessor and current Majority Leader, Mike Mansfield; the geniality of Alben Barkley and the brusqueness of Robert A. Taft; the adroitness of Everett Dirksen and the hamhandedness of Kenneth Wherry; the humorlessness of William Knowland and the wit of Eugene Millikan; the secretiveness of Styles Bridges and the openness of Arthur Vandenberg; the self-effacement of Ernest McFarland and the flamboyance of Lyndon Johnson. The list could undoubtedly be expanded indefinitely, but the point would remain the same; no clear standards of eligibility for membership in the inner club — if there is one—seem likely to emerge from an examination of personality characteristics of senators.

We must pause to ask: Is there an inner club at all? Or is power distributed in the Senate more widely? It is worthwhile to remember that there are only 100 U.S. senators. Each one enjoys high social status, great visibility, a large staff, and substantial powers in his own right. Each one has the right, by the rules of the Senate, to speak on the floor of the Senate on any subject, for as long as he desires to do so. Where a tremendous amount of business must be transacted by unanimous consent, any single senator can, if he chooses, effectively stall and harass the machinery of government. But these are ultimate sanctions, rarely employed by individuals, though more frequently by groups of senators. In any event, settled Senate practice is to take account of the wishes of each and every interested senator with respect to the convenient scheduling and disposition of most Senate business.

Senator Russell recently described this practice in debate on the floor:

I have heard questions asked [the Senate majority and minority leaders] for 30 years—Senators come up to them and say, "What time are we going to vote? What time are we going to vote?" Of course neither the majority leader nor the minority leader knows any more about the time the Senate is going to vote than does the Senator asking the question, but he is supposed to have some pleasant and reasonable answer. Another day a Senator will say, "Well, I cannot be here Thursday, so you cannot vote on such and such a bill on Thursday." Likely as not, the majority leader or the minority leader had agreed with the author of the bill to have it acted on on Thursday. That is only one instance of perhaps 10,000 different commitments that they make.

Ralph Huitt describes a striking example of the way an individual senator can have a decisive impact on legislative outcomes. His subject was William Proxmire, then freshman Senator from Wisconsin.

The provocation was a bill to allow the Metropolitan Sanitary District of Chicago to increase the amount of water it may withdraw from Lake Michigan by a thousand cubic feet per second for a three year test period. Similar bills had been passed by both houses twice before (by the Senate in the closing hours of a session with scant debate) only to be vetoed by the President because of objections raised by Canada. Once more it appeared that the bill would come up in the flood of last minute legislation, and with committee and leadership support, it seemed sure to slide through the tired Senate. Moreover, because the Canadian position was now ambiguous, the President might sign the bill. But the pressure for adjournment which was the greatest factor in favor of the bill's passage could also be its doom—if its opponents had sufficient nerve. Their hope was to stall consideration as long as possible, then make it clear that the cost of passage was extended debate. It was a simple, time-proven strategy, but not one designated to make friends. Proxmire was by no means the only man fighting the bill — there was a militant bipartisan coalition on each side—but he was probably the most determined and certainly the most conspicuous. It was he who blocked unanimous consent to allow any deviation from the rules in handling the bill. Thus he objected to a meeting of the Public Works Committee while the Senate sat, and to the bill's being reported to the Senate after the expiration of the morning hour—tactics which brought sharp rebukes from two senior members but delayed the bill a day. And it was he who held the floor from nine till midnight the last night of the session, until the water diversion bill was put aside for other business; and he who sat through the early morning hours, armed with a score of amendments and great piles of materials, ready to resume the debate. When the session ended at 4:11 in the morning the unfinished business of the Senate was a Proxmire amendment to the water diversion bill.[5]

Or consider the following excerpt from a recent news analysis:

When, at last, the Senate had voted on final passage of the battered foreign aid bill, Majority Leader Mansfield wore his habitual expression of martyred resignation. Chairman Fulbright of the Foreign Relations Committee appeared grateful to be alive.

Only Senator Morse, Democrat of Oregon, was triumphant.

The bill passed, but with $500 million less than its backers had hoped. It was largely due to Senator Morse's exertions and the exhaustion of the other Senators. Nobody wanted to take him on.

The foreign aid bill did nothing for anybody else in Washington. The Senate leadership was flouted. Secretary of State Rusk protested in vain. The President pleaded too late. The President's men in the Senate ... were too tired to fight—at least with Wayne Morse.

Senator Morse alone came out of the tedious battle with something like prestige.

His domination of the debate does not make him a leader. His forces were a motley group of defecting liberals and soured Southerners who may never march under the same banner again.

Besides he is a lone wolf.... Senator Morse combines qualities of exceptional ability, supreme egotism, self-righteousness and vindictiveness that do not make a man a favorite with his fellows....

But if he is disliked, he can no longer be discounted as a power in the Senate. He is getting mail from all over the country, hailing his attacks on foreign aid.

Presidential blandishments were of no avail. Invited to the White House, the Senator sat down with the Chief Executive for 45 minutes and went over the program.

"Then I came back up here," he told his friends with a wolfish grin, "and put in a couple of more amendments." ...

He threatened the Whip with a country-by-country review of the whole foreign aid. Senator Humphrey hastily withdrew his amendment....

Senator Morse was satisfied....

He went on to threaten "further debate of great length" if the Senate conferees on the foreign aid bill came back with a conference report that undid any of his work....

It was one time when the Senate was content to have the Senator disposing of all problems, great and small, in what the President this week called "an untidy world." The leadership was out trying to cope with Senator Mundt's sticky and inopportune amendment on the wheat sale to Russia.

So Senator Morse had a perfect day. Even the passage of the bill, against which he voted, of course, could not mar his self-satisfaction. He had left his mark on foreign aid for all the world to see.[6]

Individual senators, it is clear, can, according to the rules and customs of the Senate, play a powerful hand in the disposition of legislation reaching the floor, even without the immensely useful fortifications of seniority, membership on the relevant substantive committee, a committee chairmanship, or a position of formal leadership. But let us inquire into the distribution of these prizes, for much that happens off the floor, where so many legislative outcomes are actually settled, depends on the strategic locations of friends or foes of bills, and their diligence and skill in shaping results to suit their preferences.

There are a number of these strategic locations, as a sampling of current commentary on the senate will rapidly reveal:

[Senator Robert S.] Kerr [Democrat, of Oklahoma] was correctly rated the most powerful member of the Senate, though not one of its nominal leaders, in the last (87th) Congress.... The base of Kerr's power was never his major committees. Rather, it was his chairmanship of the Rivers and Harbors Subcommittee of the Public Works Committee, an obscure post that makes few national headlines, but much political hay. Kerr not only used it to consolidate his position in Oklahoma by festooning the state with public works but placed practically all Senators under obligation to him by promoting their pet home projects. He never hesitated to collect on these obligations later, when the votes were needed.[7]

[In the 87th Congress] ... there is a class of 21 preferred Senators, who are permitted to hold positions on more than two major committees....[8]

The office of Democratic Leader, it is true, combines all the most important elective positions — Chairman of the Conference, of the Steering Committee, of the Policy Committee (the Republicans fill these positions with four different men). Each position adds something to his influence and to the professional staff he controls. The Steering Committee handles committee transfers and assignment of new members.... As Chairman of the Policy Committee he has substantial control over legislative scheduling (in close collaboration with the Minority Leader) which gives him not only the power to help and hinder but an unequalled knowledge of legislation on the calendar and who [wants] what and why. A tactical power of importance [is] ... the right of the Majority Leader to be recognized first when he wants the floor [which can be exploited to] initiate a legislative fight when and on the terms he [wants].[9]

It is probably not possible to identify *all* the institutional nooks and crannies which are capable of providing a base of power for a U.S. senator. In any event the same base is often used differently by different men; for example, whereas Lyndon Johnson as Majority Leader pretty much ran his own show, his successor, Mike Mansfield, has been more comfortable sharing substantial power with his assistant, Hubert Humphrey, and with his party's Policy and Steering Committees. It may be useful, just the same, to see how the more obvious of the strategic positions were distributed among senators in the 88th Congress. Among these positions, one might include elective leadership posts, memberships on party policy (agenda) and steering (committee assignment) committees, committee chairmanships (or in the case of the minority, "shadow" chairmanships), chairmanships of subcommittees, membership on more than two regular legislative committees, and membership on the Appropriations Committee.

Although there are considerable inequalities in the distribution of these prizes, virtually no senator in the 88th Congress save a sprinkling of freshmen, was without some institutional base which guaranteed him a disproportionate say, either in some substantive area of public policy, or in the behind-the-scenes management of Senate business. Obviously, a senator such as Richard Russell of Georgia, member of four committees, chairman of one, sub-committee chairman of another, and a member of the Democratic Steering *and* Policy Committees, is in an institutional position more formidable than one such as John Sparkman of Alabama, who chairs one sub-committee of a major committee, sits on one other major committee, and chairs a minor committee that is powerless to offer legislation. But these disparities are easily exaggerated, for Senator Russell cannot hope to accomplish his legislative ends without the help of men like Senator Sparkman—and vice versa. The need for cooperative effort, and uncertainty about the precise composition of any particular winning coalition, makes senatorial bargaining necessary, dilutes the power of the most entrenched, and enhances tremendously the powers of all senators, however low on the totem pole.

Senators, moreover, do not agree unanimously about the relative desirability of different institutional positions. Although at the extremes it is possible to rank committees according to their apparent desirability, there are some gray areas. This can be illustrated by placing side by side two separate attempts to rank Senate committees in the order of their attractiveness to senators. In the first column, committees are ranked according to the average seniority of senators newly appointed to each committee from the 80th through the 84th Congress.[10] The reasoning here is that the committees attracting the senior men would be more desirable, first, because senior men would be likeliest to know which committees were most important, and second, because their seniority would make it possible for them to win appointment, even though competition were keen for vacant seats. In the second column, committees are ranked by another criterion—the net gain or loss sustained by committees by virtue of transfers of senators from the 81st through the 85th Congresses, corrected for the over-all size of committees.[11] The reasoning behind this tabulation is quite similar to the first; presumably senators migrate toward desirable committees and away from undesirable ones.

Part of the dissimilarities in these two lists can be explained away by the narrowness of differences in the raw data on which the rankings rest. But it is interesting to reflect that committees low on

TABLE 1. SENATE COMMITTEES RANKED ACCORDING TO CRITERIA OF DESIRABILITY*

I	II
1. Foreign Relations	1. Foreign Relations
2. Appropriations	2. Finance
3. Finance	3. Commerce
4. Agriculture	4. Judiciary
5. Armed Services	5. Appropriations
6. Judiciary	6. Armed Services
7. Commerce	7. Agriculture
8. Banking	8. Interior
9. Rules	9. Banking
10. Interior	10. Labor
11. Post Office	11. Public Works
12. Public Works	12. Government Operations
13. Government Operations	13. Rules
14. D. C.	14. Post Office
15. Labor	15. D. C.

*Space Committee, created 1958, omitted.

both lists—Government Operations, Labor, and Public Works — have provided major sources of power for senators as disparate as Kerr and Patrick McNamara, Joseph McCarthy and John McClellan, and John Kennedy and Lister Hill. There are, in other words, several ways in which a post can come to be "desirable."

When a senator brings unusual skill, resourcefulness or luck to seemingly minor posts in the institution, sometimes he is remarkably and disproportionately rewarded. Senators Joseph McCarthy and Estes Kefauver, on strikingly different missions, catapulted themselves to national prominence (which they preferred to popularity within the Senate itself) by imaginative use of minor subcommittees to which they fell heir rather early in their senatorial careers. Brian McMahon, Thomas Hennings, and Henry Jackson carved out unlikely empires, small but significant, by making themselves subject-matter specialists in atomic energy, constitutional rights, and national security policy machinery.

The division of labor in the Senate has a curiously *ad-hoc* quality, in which roles within the Senate are as much adopted by senators when it suits their interests as they are doled out by institutional forces beyond the control of individuals. There are two senses in which the term "role" may be used. In one sense, roles are job descriptions; the Senate has men who primarily investigate the Executive Branch, men who speak to the society at large, men who specialize in a wide variety of substantive policy areas, men who seek primarily to deliver federal funds to their home state, men who engage mostly in backstage politicking and legislative coalition-building, and so on. Roles also refer to the stable expectations that develop around the ways people fit into the informal society of group life; the Senate has its sages, its clowns, its mavericks, its fools. The number of senators who are distinctively placed in job roles is almost certainly quite high; the number who are distinctively located in the informal social life of the Senate is almost certainly quite low. All groups of any substantial size have their deviant members, but the existence of mavericks does not demonstrate the existence of an inner club.

Notes

[1] This composite description was drawn by Ralph K. Huitt, "The Outsider in the Senate: An Alternate Role," *American Political Science Review,* Vol. 55 (September, 1961), pp. 566-567; principally from work by William S. White, *The Citadel* (New York: Harper, 1956); and Donald Matthews, *U.S. Senators and Their World* (Chapel Hill, University of North Carolina Press, 1960). The inner-club hypothesis has many proponents. See, for examples, Joseph Kraft, "King of the U.S. Senate," *Saturday Evening Post* (January 5, 1963), pp. 26-27; Senator Joseph Clark, "The Senate Establishment," *Congressional Record* (Daily Edition), February 18-28, 1963, pp. 2413-2426, 2524-2531, 2703-2707, 2763, 2764, 2771, 2766, 2773; Allan Nevins, *Herbert H. Lehman and His Era* (New York: Scribner, 1963), especially pp. 369-370.

[2] Donald Matthews, "The Folkways of the U.S. Senate," originally in *American Political Science Review,* Vol. 53 (December, 1959), pp. 1064-1089, reprinted in Bobbs-Merrill Reprint Series, PS 189; in Joseph Fiszman (ed.), *The American Political Arena* (Boston: Little Brown, 1962), pp. 199-210; in S. Sidney Ulmer (ed.), *Introductory Readings in Political Behavior* (Chicago: Rand McNally, 1961), pp. 94-104; and, no doubt, elsewhere. It appears in Matthews, *U.S. Senators and Their World,* pp. 92-117.

[3] Ralph Huitt, "Democratic Party Leadership in the Senate," *American Political Science Review* 55 (June, 1961), p. 338. Both parties make committee assignments through their steering committees, subject to the general rule that a senator is entitled to keep whatever assignments he already has. Thus these committees handle transfers as vacancies occur, and place freshman members. Republicans generally proceed strictly according to seniority for all vacancies. Democrats under the Johnson rule have given themselves more leeway. This has, however, led to charges that committee placements are now subject to manipulation designed to affect policy outcomes. See Clark, *op. cit.*

[4] White, *op. cit.,* p. 92.

[5] Huitt, "The Outsider in the Senate: An Alternate Role," *op. cit.,* pp. 569-570.

[6] Mary McGrory, "Morse Tackles an 'Untidy World'" Washington *Evening Star,* November 17, 1963.

[7] Kenneth Crawford, "The Senate's Ways," *Newsweek* (January 14, 1963), p. 27.

[8] Senator Joseph S. Clark, *Congressional Record* (Daily Edition), February 21, 1963, p. 2704.

[9]Huitt, "Democratic Party Leadership in the Senate," *op. cit.,* pp. 337-338.

[10]Matthews, *U.S. Senators and Their World, op. cit.,* p. 153.

[11]George Goodwin, "The Seniority System in Congress," *American Political Science Review,* Vol. 53 (June, 1959), p. 433.

The President: Leader or Clerk?

Richard E. Neustadt

Every known major political system has provided for the concentration of political authority in the hands of a small leadership group. The problem of converting formal authority into actual political power has been a dilemma bedeviling political leaders and observers for centuries. At least as early as the 16th century, Nicolo Machiavelli (1469-1527), in writing his The Prince *as a "handbook" for the Medici, faced this problem squarely. He sought to have the squabbling principalities of Italy forged into a united state and viewed the Medici family as the proper leaders for such a movement. Any leader, he suggested, must understand the stakes involved and how to utilize his political resources to achieve the desired ends. A prince to be successful must not permit himself the luxury of making decisions based solely on moralistic considerations. Instead, the immediate goal of political action is to preserve and increase the Prince's own political power. In a similar, but less partisan fashion, Richard E. Neustadt has written a "handbook" for modern American Presidents. He is not concerned that a president implement a particular policy nor is he advocating that presidents possess great moral fervor or a systematic ideology. The following excerpt illustrates Neustadt's thesis concerning how a president ought to view his political environment if he seeks to maximize his impact over people and events. A great President must first be a great politician.*

The search for personal influence is at the center of the job of being President. To analyze the problem of obtaining personal power one must try to view the Presidency from over the President's shoulder, looking out and down with the perspective of *his* place. This is not the way that we conventionally view the office; ordinarily we stand outside it, looking in. From outside, or from below, a President is "many men," or one man wearing many "hats," or playing many "roles." Conventionally we divide the job of being President according to the cate-

Reprinted, by permission of the publisher, from Richard E. Neustadt, *Presidential Power* (New York: John Wiley and Sons, Inc., 1960), pp. viii; 1-2; 58-59; 63-76; 80-82; 84; 192-195.

gories such a view suggests, "Chief Legislator," "Chief Administrator," "Chief of Party," and the like, and analyze the job by treating chieftainships in turn. For many purposes this framework of analysis is valuable. For present purposes, however, it becomes a block to insight. The President himself plays every "role," wears every "hat" at once. Whatever he may do in one role is by definition done in all, and has effects in all. When he attempts to make his wishes manifest, his own will felt, he is one man, not many. To analyze this aspect of his job we need a frame of reference as unlike the usual categories as the view from inside out is unlike that from outside in. . . .

In the United States we like to "rate" a President. We measure him as "weak" or "strong" and call what we are measuring his "leadership." We do not wait until a man is dead; we rate him from the moment he takes office. We are quite right to do so. His office has become the focal point of politics and policy in our political system. Our commentators and our politicians make a specialty of taking the man's measurements. The rest of us join in when we feel "government" impinging on our private lives. In the third quarter of the twentieth century millions of us have that feeling often.

This book is an endeavor to illuminate what we are measuring. Although we all make judgments about presidential leadership, we often base our judgments upon images of office that are far removed from the reality. We also use those images when we tell one another whom to choose as President. But it is risky to appraise a man in office or to choose a man for office on false premises about the nature of his job. When the job is the Presidency of the United States the risk becomes excessive. Hopefully, this book can help reduce the risk.

We deal here with the President himself and with his influence on governmental action. In institutional terms the Presidency now includes 2000 men and women. The President is only one of them. But *his* performance scarcely can be measured without focusing on *him*. In terms of party, or of country, or the West, so-called, his leadership involves far more than governmental action. But the sharpening of spirit and of values and of purposes is not done in a vacuum. Although governmental action may not be the whole of leadership, all else is nurtured by it and gains meaning from it. Yet if we treat the Presidency as the President, we cannot measure him as though he were the government. Not action as an outcome but his impact on the outcome is the measure of the man. His strength or weakness, then, turns on his personal capacity to influence the conduct of the men who make up government. His influence becomes the mark of leadership. To rate a President according to these rules, one looks into the man's own capabilities as seeker and as wielder of effective influence upon the other men involved in governing the country. That is what this book will do.

"Presidential" on the title page means nothing but the President. "Power" means *his* influence. It helps to have these meanings settled at the start.

There are two ways to study "presidential power." One way is to focus on the tactics, so to speak, of influencing certain men in given situations: how to get a bill through Congress, how to settle strikes, how to quiet Cabinet feuds, or how to stop a Suez. The other way is to step back from tactics on those "givens" and to deal with influence in more strategic terms: what is its nature and what are its sources? What can *this* man accomplish to improve the prospect that he will have influence when he wants it? Strategically, the question is not how he masters Congress in a peculiar instance, but what he does to boost his chance for mastery in any instance, looking toward tomorrow from today. The second of these two ways has been chosen for this book. . . .

The men who share in governing this country are inveterate observers of a President. They have the doing of whatever he wants done. They are the objects of his personal persuasion. They also are the most attentive members of his audience. These doers comprise what in spirit, not geography, might well be termed the "Washington community." This community cuts across the President's constituencies. Members of Congress and of his Administration, governors of states, military commanders in the field, leading politicians in both parties, representatives of private organizations, newsmen of assorted types and sizes, foreign diplomats (and principals abroad) — all these are "Washingtonians" no matter what their physical location. In most respects the Washington community is far from homogeneous. In one respect it is tightly knit indeed: by definition, all its members are compelled to watch the President for reasons not of pleasure but vocation. They need him in their business just as he needs them. Their own work thus requires that they keep an eye on him. Because they watch him closely his persuasiveness with them turns quite as much on their informed appraisals as on his presumed advantages.

In influencing Washingtonians, the most important law at a President's disposal is the "law" of "anticipated reactions," propounded years ago by Carl J. Friedrich. The men who share in governing do what they think they must. A President's effect on them is heightened or diminished by their thoughts about his probable reaction to their doing. They base their expectations on what they can see of him. And they are watching all the time. Looking at themselves, at him, at the immediate event, and toward the future, they may think that what he might do in theory, he would not dare to do in fact. So MacArthur evidently thought before he was dismissed....

II

Ideally, any President who valued personal power would start his term with vivid demonstrations of tenacity and skill in every sphere, thereby establishing a reputation sure to stand the shocks of daily disarray until he was prepared to demonstrate again. This is no more than Franklin Roosevelt did in his first term. It is the ideal formula for others. Unfortunately, F.D.R.'s successors have not held the combination of advantages that helped him make his first-term demonstration: the public memory of his predecessor, the crisis of the Great Depression, the easy escape from foreign affairs, the eagerness of intellectuals, the patronage for partisans, the breadth of his experience in government (unmatched in this century save by the other Roosevelt). Nor is there anything to indicate that while mid-century conditions last, a future President is likely to hold comparable advantages. Emergencies in policy with politics as usual can hardly favor an effective use of Roosevelt's formula.

A contemporary President may have to settle for a reputation short of the ideal. If so, what then should be his object? It should be to induce as much uncertainty as possible about the consequences of ignoring what he wants. If he cannot make men think him bound to win, his need is to keep them from thinking they can cross him without risk, or that they can be sure what risks they run. At the same time (no mean feat) he needs to keep them from fearing lest he leave them in the lurch if they support him. To maximize uncertainties in future opposition, to minimize the insecurities of possible support, and to avoid the opposite effect in either case — these together form the goal for any mid-century President who seeks a reputation that will serve his personal power.

How can a President accomplish this result? How does he build his reputation? How does he protect it? Let me begin consideration of these questions with a classic instance of the ways in which a reputation ought *not* to be guarded. This illustration deals with the first year of Eisenhower's second term.

III

Early in 1958 a technician from the Bureau of the Budget testified before a subcommittee of the House on the provisions of a pending bill within his field of expertise. As he concluded, he remarked for emphasis that what he recommended was essential "to the program of the President." Whereupon everybody laughed. The hilarity was general and leaped party lines; to a man, committee members found the reference very funny. This incident occurred only fifteen months after Eisenhower's smashing reelection victory. Yet it is perfectly indicative, so far as can be judged from the outside, of an impression pervading all corners of the Capitol (and most places downtown), as a result of what had seemed to happen at the White House in the months between. This impression was to change somewhat with subsequent events. In 1959 a "new" Eisenhower emerged. Still, early in the second legislative session of his second term that laughter well expressed what most men thought. And why they thought it is an object lesson in how not to guard professional reputation.

On election night in 1956, knowing the dimensions of his personal triumph, but perhaps not yet aware that he had carried neither House of Congress, Eisenhower told a national television audience:

> ... And now let me say something that looks to the future. I think that modern republicanism has now proved itself. And America has approved of modern republicanism.
> And so, as we look ahead — as we look ahead to the problems in front, let us remember that a political party deserves the approbation of America only as it represents the ideals, the aspirations and the hopes of Americans. If it is anything less, it is merely a conspiracy to seize power and the Republican party is not that!
> Modern republicanism looks to the future....

For a few weeks thereafter old Washington hands of both political persuasions engaged in speculation about what, if anything, that comment might portend. They did not have to wonder very long. On January 16, 1957, the President sent to Congress his budget for Fiscal 1958, a document marked very generally by "modern" Republican touches reminiscent of the past campaign. These were evident, particularly, in the budget's relatively generous handling of resource development and welfare programs (among them general aid for school construction), in its moderate increases for defense and foreign aid, and in its bland acceptance of a spending total close to 72 billion dollars. The total was 12 billion dollars higher than the oratorical objective of the first Eisenhower campaign, four years gone but not forgotten; spending at this level heralded no further tax relief for at least two years more. Momentarily the budget seemed a clue to Eisenhower's views about the future of his party.

Then, the same day, Secretary of the Treasury George M. Humphrey held a press conference. His prepared statement struck a regretful note about the budget and its total but was mild compared to his response on being questioned. The *New York Times* account of that response is both accurate and concise:

> ... if the government cannot reduce the "terrific" tax burden of the country, "I will predict that you will have a depression that will curl your hair, because we are just taking too much money out of this economy that we need to make jobs that you have to have as time goes on." ... [Humphrey] said, "there are a lot of places in this budget that can be cut," and that he would be glad to see cuts "if Congress can find ways to cut and still do a proper job...."

"I may have gone overboard a bit this afternoon," Humphrey reportedly remarked, shortly thereafter, to the bemused Budget Director, Percival Brundage. To much of Washington that would have seemed an extraordinary understatement. Never in the history of executive budgeting since 1921 had there been anything to match the spectacle of a first-rank Cabinet officer publicly assailing the presidential budget on the very day it was sent down. Budget Bureau officials were furious; some of the aides within the White House were appalled. "Modern" Republicans in the Cabinet and their departmental staffs—and many a sharp-minded Pentagon official—took umbrage, as well they might, for obviously they were in the line of Humphrey's fire. At the Capitol and in the press corps, and among spokesmen for the private groups most vitally concerned, reactions were as unsure as the situation was unusual; everybody looked to see what Eisenhower would do.

Three days after his second inaugural, the President went before a packed press conference and, replying to the inevitable question, commented as follows:

Well, in my own instructions to the Cabinet and heads of all offices, I have told them that every place that there is a chance to save a dollar out of the money that we have budgeted . . . everybody that is examining the many details . . . ought to find someplace where they might save another dollar.

If they can, I think if Congress can, its committees, it is their duty to do it.

So with the thought behind the Secretary's statements I am in complete agreement, even though he made statements that I don't believe have a present and immediate application because, indeed, the outlook for the next few months in the economic field is very good indeed.

When these words came across the news tickers there were few laughs in Congress, or downtown, but many stricken faces, some delight, a great deal of suspicion, and considerable scorn. "Old Guard" Republicans and like-minded associates across the aisle sensed prospects brighter than they had thought possible so soon after the Eisenhower re-election. "Modern" Republicans felt the ground opening beneath their feet just when they had thought themselves secure. Democrats, both "liberal" and "moderate," sensed a deliberate squeeze-play with the middle place reserved for them. On the one hand (as they saw it) the President proposed a budget big with borrowings from their traditional stock-in-trade; on the other hand he joined in dramatizing the traditional Republican attack on Federal spending; with both hands he pointed at Congress where their party held a nominal majority. That "modern" Republicans might be caught in a comparable squeeze was insufficient recompense for many Democrats.

Right or wrong, all of these first impressions seemed to be borne out by happenings in the weeks after Eisenhower's press conference. For one, congressional in-boxes promptly became crammed with protests against spending (and demands for tax relief). "But two weeks later," wrote a Senator in retrospect, "the protesting tide swelled into an organized torrent . . . [which] gave the impression of being largely stimulated by corporations." Behind these "corporations" numbers of Washingtonians thought they perceived a prompter in the Secretary of the Treasury. On March 6 he was reported by the *New York Times* (a paper read with care in Washington) to have informed Detroit Republicans that "specific and substantial [budget] reductions were possible if the people of the country continued their 'insistence'. . . . [This] 'would not only take . . . pressure off prices . . . but would also lead the way toward another tax cut.' . . . high spending for security would be required for some time, but that is all the more reason why expenditures in other areas must be curtailed and postponed. . . ." Those last words were read with particular attention by proponents of school aid, the largest new domestic item in the budget.

Executive officials publicly identified with major spending programs did not go unnoticed as the mail campaign progressed. The Budget Director, for one, got more than letters. "Brundage wants the shirt off your back" became the slogan of some businessmen—and laundry, clean or dirty, flooded in to him by parcel post.

At the same time the Executive Branch was in the throes of one of the most hectic episodes in the whole history of central budgeting, the out-of-season "budget season" of 1957. To prove the President's sincerity the Budget Bureau spent the months of February and March extracting from the agencies reductions in his January budget. Contemporary accounts vary: budget aides counted "about" two "overall" revisions of the budget; some weary officials thought they counted five. On March 1, half in fun and half in anger, a House majority resolved that Eisenhower should inform the Congress where to cut. A week later, the Budget Director told a subcommittee of the House that at the President's behest he was already doing all he could to get an answer for them (a response so astonishing to practical politicians that some of them swore off political readings of Administration behavior). "You would have thought," remarked a legislative aide in private conversation, "that they had just come into office and were trying to clean up the outgoing crowd's budget. It was 1953 all over again, only odder."

So numbers of observers thought when, in mid-April, Eisenhower formally submitted the results of Brundage's endeavor. In a letter to the Speaker of the House, the President then proposed or accepted reductions of 1.3 billion dollars in his January request for new appropriations. He warned, however, that these would not have much effect on 1958 *expenditures* and that a "multibillion" saving in expenditures could be obtained "only at the expense of the national safety and interest." Taken alone, that warning spelled out a defense of the budget's central structure and the proffered cuts became no more than reasonable tidying by conscientious budgeteers. But in the light of what had gone before, the impact of this defense was diluted by the President's own opening remarks:

I am sure many members of the Congress are as gratified as I am to note the growing awareness of private citizens that ... Federal benefits are not free but must be paid for out of taxes collected from the people. It is good to see ... widespread insistence that Federal activity be held to the minimum consistent with the national needs.
...
The evident responsiveness of the Congress to this attitude I find equally encouraging. I assure you ... that the Executive Branch will continue to cooperate ....

If his purpose was a defense of his budget —and a cover for the Congressmen who rallied to its cause — those remarks, as the saying goes, put Eisenhower's emphasis on the wrong syllable.

This letter of mid-April marked a late stage in White House equivocation after Humphrey's outbreak. When Eisenhower thus addressed the Speaker there were signs that he was concerned lest the assault on his budget go too far. Concern was certainly justified. By April, the Administration faced a real crisis of confidence in its own ranks and, simultaneously, a prospect of deep, indiscriminate appropriation cuts which would spare neither foreign aid nor national defense. Downtown the departmental staffs responsible for programs thought to be on Humphrey's "list," felt themselves victims of a backstairs *coup*. Under cover of the decorous behavior usual in Eisenhower's neighborhood their resentments ran deep, with the White House an object no less than Humphrey or Brundage. For Brundage's economy drive seemed to be strongly seconded at every turn by Sherman Adams and the President. At the Capitol, meanwhile, the sense of public pressure coupled to suspicions of Administration "strategy" left even friends of Pentagon programs — to say nothing of welfare or of aid abroad—increasingly inclined to show themselves more holy than the pope. Among the Democratic members of the House, especially, temptation grew to make a record out-economizing the economizers downtown. On April 11, no less a personage than Speaker Rayburn voiced the hope that by June revenue prospects and spending cuts, combined, would clear the way for tax relief. And on the Senate side Senator Byrd of Virginia, dean of the professional economizers, gained an unusually attentive audience for his retrenchment pleas which he embodied, late in March, in a 5 billion-dollar list of "feasible" appropriation cuts.

From the end of March until mid-April Eisenhower shifted back and forth between defense of his budget and good words for the economizers. On March 27, at his regular press conference, the President used stronger language on the budget's behalf than any since his January budget message. Stung, apparently, by Byrd's proposals and by talk of tax reduction, Eisenhower characterized as "futile" and as "fatuous" both sorts of claims. Without eliminating programs there could be no major savings, he asserted, and he entered a defense of programs such as foreign aid. In consequence, the claims for "piecemeal" cuts were fraudulent. "... to say you are going to save millions here and a few millions there, I think is the poorest kind of economy we can find." As an acute observer noted at the time:

> The Congressional reaction to the President's strong attitude was unusually mixed. The "Eisenhower Republicans" were pleased and relieved... orthodox Republicans were glum and grumpy. The Democrats were not unhappy at the division... Sam Rayburn of Texas, Speaker of the House, pointed out that yesterday [March 26] House Republicans had passed a resolution unanimously calling for heavy budget cuts. The President's attack... "looks like a pretty good answer to what his own folks did up here yesterday."

To concern over budget prospects, the White House had to add concern for the apparent disarray in Republican ranks. On two occasions in the week that followed, Eisenhower tried to formulate a budget stand that would both calm the "orthodox" and satisfy his "modern" followers. The net effect was to reduce, somewhat, the force of his March 27 press statement. Then his letter in mid-April to the Speaker of the House blurred his position further. Shortly thereafter Congress recessed for Easter and the White House gained a chance to collect its thoughts.

In early May the White House announced that Eisenhower would deliver two nationally televised addresses rallying the country to his budget. Visits home in recess had convinced many Congressmen that calls to cut the budget, reduce taxes, were beginning to bite deep into the consciousness of usually inattentive publics. Though these are tricky things to gauge, there is considerable evidence that consonant with Humphrey's invitation "public opinion," organized and not, grew more aroused about those issues during 1957 than at any time in Eisenhower's first term (a matter no doubt bearing some relation to the climb in living costs that had begun in 1956). And whatever the facts, it is apparent that by May a wide variety of bureaucrats and politicians *thought* this was the case, which is what counts in Washington. The President's decision to address the country is a tribute to that thought.

The first of Eisenhower's "fireside chats," a general roundup on the budget, came on May 14. It was judged fairly ineffectual in Washington, a view held on the Hill and by the press corps, and quite evidently at the White House. Some notion of its public impact can be gleaned from the fact that the President's press secretary would not comment upon rumors of an adverse mail response. And its impact upon politicians was reduced materially by Eisenhower's own appearance of ambivalence at a press conference the next day:

> I don't think it is the function of a President of the United States to punish anybody for voting what he believes.... I don't see how it is possible for any President to work with the Republican group in Congress, the whole Republican group, except through their elected leadership.... When these large sums are involved, there comes a chance for both the Executive and the Congress to do a squeezing process... there is some squeezing possible and I have never kicked about that.

As Senators Knowland and Bridges, Republican leaders both, were just then in the van of the congressional economizers, those words were noted throughout Washington and appropriate conclusions drawn.

A week later all conclusions were shaken. The President's second televised address on May 21, dealt with defense and foreign aid. It was generally thought "effective" and the White House happily announced a strongly favorable mail response. Moreover at his next press conference, again the following day, his tone was confident, his fielding fast and his words relatively tough:

Well, as long as I am in a fight, I never rest until [I get] ... what ... I believe to be necessary for the operation of this Government ... I shall never stop until a decision is reached.... I do believe this: when a political party gets together and agrees upon a platform ... they should remain true to it. I believe they should stick with it through thick and thin.... I have no right and no desire to punish anybody. I just say this: I am committed to the support of people who believe, as I do, that the Republican platform of 1956 must be our political doctrine.

"In what have probably been the two most effective days of his second administration," James Reston wrote of Eisenhower's performance, "he has regained the initiative over the opposition in his own and the Democratic party." Most members of the Washington community seem to have shared that view, and it grew stronger as the initiative, once taken, was sustained. On May 22 a presidential message went to Congress outlining the plans for foreign aid which were to be supported by the dollars in the budget. The Secretary of State, John Foster Dulles, followed with an elaborate personal presentation to the Senate Committee on Foreign Relations. Both the message and his testimony emphasized Administration sponsorship of program innovations previously advanced by congressional study groups. Chief among them was a Development Loan Fund as a source of capital assistance for the less developed countries, with the implication that eventually loans would replace most outright grants abroad. The upshot of the Dulles presentation was a heartening reception for the foreign-aid program in Senate offices and a more general cordiality than had seemed possible a week before.

Two days later Eisenhower spoke by telephone to a Republican Party conference in New Jersey and strongly urged the item veto as a way to "real" economics. His aim, apparently, was to turn the gaze of the economizers from his budget toward congressional initiatives on public works. At the same conference, his assistant, Sherman Adams, made a speech demanding party unity behind the President. Since Adams, twelve days earlier, reportedly had remarked on a television program that the budget could be cut 2 billion dollars without harm, his address in New Jersey seemed another sign in Washington of new determination at the White House.

Between the first and second presidential television talks, the Secretary of Defense, Charles E. (General Motors) Wilson, had held a press conference defending in detail the military budget which the House was threatening to cut by 1.2 billion dollars. Eisenhower in his second televised address had pressed the Secretary's case. A few days later, Minority Leader Martin was enabled to announce that as a party matter, House Republicans would now seek restoration of a fourth of the projected cut. When this was then attempted on the floor it was defeated by the Democrats. In the crucial roll-call all but eleven of them voted against the restoration, which three-quarters of the House Republicans supported. Although this outcome seemed at first glance to repudiate the President's newly asserted leadership, the White House could take comfort from it nonetheless, and close observers gained from it a new respect for Eisenhower's potency. Congressional Republicans had closed ranks in a gesture to his cause, however short of his avowed objective. House Democrats had made a party record most embarrassing to defense-minded Senate colleagues. A base seemed surely laid for better fortune in the Senate and in conference.

Washingtonians quite generally responded with considerable respect to the "new" Eisenhower who had emerged in the month of May. Belatedly but definitely, he seemed to have accepted, now, the role reserved for Presidents in the time-honored play of legislative action on the budget. Downtown, men trying to rouse public support for their programs were encouraged. On Capitol Hill men trying to resist public pressure against spending were relieved. The President could now be praised or blamed for what they sought to do. Political interpretations of his conduct flourished once again, but these assigned him motives quite like those assigned in other years to other Presidents and the familiarity was reassuring to the politically minded. "Modern" Republicans were gratified. Democrats began to reassess. "Old Guard" Republicans prepared to give some ground. So far as I can ascertain, nobody laughed.

So matters stood by June of 1957. The President's own actions for the past five months, along with those of his associates, now seemed to show contrasting patterns, and the latest signs seemed to belie the relevance of what had gone before. Momentarily, a host of expectations throughout Washington were tempered or revised to suit.

In the month of June, however, there came some harbingers of new developments. For one thing, the Comptroller of the Pentagon testified on June 4 to a House subcommittee that military expenditures were runnning at an unusual rate of 4 billion dollars above January estimates—the result of rising costs and (paradoxically) of improved paper work — and that, in consequence, directives had come down from Wilson and from Brundage, late in May, to slow current spending to the rates originally projected. On the same day as this testimony, at the other end of Pennsylvania Avenue, the chairman of the Republican National Committee told the press that Eisenhower had been briefed on the adverse reaction of Republican contributors to current White House views about the budget. Three weeks later a Young Republican convention voted almost two-to-one, in Washington, against support for the Administration's proposed aid to schools. A week after that, the President in a letter to one of his most ardent House supporters said he could not "pass judgment on all the details" of the pending school aid bill, a response described by its recipients as "disappointing."

Such miscellaneous occurrences as these gained pattern restrospectively for many Washingtonians when the Administration found itself embarrassed on three notable occasions in July. Early that month the Senate passed a military appropriation bill restoring most of the funds cut by the House, as Wilson and the President had urged. With confidence, the Senate conferees prepared to battle for their version. Then on July 18, while the conference committee was in session, a letter from the Secretary of Defense announced that to hold spending at the rate of January's estimate (under his May directive from Brundage) 100,000 men would be dropped by the army and a portion of the Senate increase would be saved. That announcement not only made senators look silly — and forced the Senate conferees to drop their base for bargaining — it also seriously hampered Senate advocates of foreign aid on which debate had just begun. Nine months later, Wilson's letter still caused scathing comment on the Senate floor, and there were no defenders in the chamber.

On July 25 general aid for school construction came to a vote in the House. The measure as reported from committee compromised Administration plans for grants to states on grounds of need alone with plans by the bill's sponsors for grants proportional to school-age population. Eisenhower had not blessed the compromise, exactly. Although he had called repeatedly for action on the measure, he had evaded opportunities to put his own stamp of approval on its grant provisions. Even so, the Secretary of Health, Education and Welfare, Marion Folsom, had never ceased to represent the White House as firmly behind the bill. On the House floor, however, the Republican leadership failed to support it, even at the crucial moment when its Democratic sponsors offered to accept Administration terms for grants-in-aid. Thereupon the bill was killed in parliamentary circumstances so complex that this offer was scarcely mentioned by most press reports, while members made a record for each party on which blame could be heaped from across the aisle. But the interested lobbyists, officials, and reporters were aware, of course, that there had come a point in the debate when the Administration *might* have gained its grant provisions and secured the bill. In consequence the President was asked at his next press conference to comment on the lack of response from Republican leaders. He replied: "I never heard.... If that is true, why you are telling me something I never heard."

The impact of that comment in the Washington community was heightened by the fact that just three weeks before the President had responded somewhat similarly on a matter even closer to the heart of his program. In the first week of July, Senator Russell of Georgia had charged the Administration with a tricky, hidden intent in provisions of the civil rights bill that it had sponsored and that the House had passed. The bill was in the front rank of Administration measures; its drafting had been done by the Department of Justice; those provisions were included from the first. Yet the President, on being asked about them in press conference had said:

Well, I would not want to answer ... in detail because I was reading part of that bill this morning, and I — there were certain phrases I didn't completely understand. So, before I made any more remarks on that, I would want to talk to the Attorney General and see exactly what they do mean.... Naturally I'm not a lawyer and I don't participate in drawing up the exact language of proposals....

These three occurrences in July furnished considerable food for thought to those who watch a President professionally, but it cannot be said that there was a consensus, all at once, on their interpretation. For during August Eisenhower led a renewed White House effort on behalf of foreign aid. Reportedly, he also intervened to assure enactment of a useful compromise on civil rights. By late August when Congress adjourned, its record, although mixed, seemed no disaster for the Administration, not even on the budget (when one sets aside the cuts that Eisenhower had endorsed). In light of that outcome there were numbers of Washingtonians, especially downtown, who thought they saw the likelihood of more consistency and more determination from the White House in the year ahead. For one thing, Humphrey had left office in July. For another, as one high official told me hopefully: "I think the President knows some things now he didn't have to learn in his first term." Again, as in late May, although less markedly, there was a tendency to read two patterns into Eisenhower's past behavior and to hedge, somewhat, the expectations based on either one of them....

IV

The professional reputation of a President in Washington is made or altered by the man himself. No one can guard it for him; no one saves him from himself. His office has been institutionalized to a degree unknown before the Second World War, but as a reputation-builder he is no mere "office manager." On the contrary, everything he personally says and does (or fails to say, omits to do), becomes significant in everyone's appraisals regardless of the claims of his officialdom. For his words, his own actions, provide clues not only to his personal proclivities but to the forecasts and asserted influence of those around him. What Humphrey says gains weight as Eisenhower seems not to oppose him. What Folsom says becomes a joke as Eisenhower seems not to support him. Press secretariats and "chiefs of staff" and other aides aside, in fashioning his Washington reputation a President's own doings are decisive....

A President's decisive role in reputation-building is a source of opportunity as well as risk. In a government where Secretaries of the Treasury may go astray at press conference, where Secretaries of Defense may choose the poorest time to make announcements, where Presidents may not be briefed on legislative drafts — and ours is such a government no matter who is President — the fact that his own conduct will decide what others think of him is precious for the man inside the White House. He can steal scenes from his subordinates. He can switch roles or even open a new play. In May of 1957 when Eisenhower made and pressed a vigorous appeal for portions of his budget, he very nearly managed to switch roles himself. He also turned attention from what Humphrey, Brundage, Adams, and the like had seemed to say or do up to that time. A President can *change* his reputation. This is the essence of his opportunity. "I always must remind myself," a very senior bureaucrat once told me, looking at the White House from his office window, "that the power of that fellow over there is never the same two weeks in a row; it fluctuates almost from day to day." Had "everybody's" laughter in the early days of 1958 expressed a fixed, immutable impression, Eisenhower's own prospects for influence would have been less than actually became the case in the years after.

Few single actions on a President's part will either set or totally transform what Washington perceives of him. Eisenhower's program did not become laughable the moment he first seemed to sanction Humphrey's attack on his budget. The laughter followed a year later when that incident appeared the key to a whole pattern of equivocation. Nothing short of a contrasting pattern, equally substantial and sustained, could have transformed the view induced by the occurrences of 1957. In 1958 amidst recession difficulties, defense dilemmas, vicuña coats, hard desegregation problems, and a host of troubles overseas, Eisenhower managed no such transformation. But in 1959 he did achieve it; a "New Eisenhower" emerged that year. The newness was sustained for months on end. Impressions of equivocation were replaced by visions of tenacity and not a little skill. In his seventh year this President apparently won more respect from Washington on both these scores than he had been accorded since the time of his belated honeymoon in 1955, after the eclipse of Senator McCarthy and before the Denver heart attack. That Eisenhower could look "new" in 1959 despite his look in 1957 is a tribute to the opportunity presented by a President's own role in reputation....

The President of the United States can rarely make a choice with nothing more in mind than his professional reputation. Franklin Roosevelt sometimes asked his aides for "something I can veto" as a lesson and a reminder to congressmen. But chances for decision in these terms alone will not come often to a President. Most choices will involve him also in the institutional imperatives of being President, in the extensive duties of his clerkship. Through the first half of 1957 Eisenhower's troubles turned upon the fact that whatever he might want to be or seem, he could not escape authorship and advocacy of a budget. Both were required of the President-as-clerk in order that congressional and agency officials could carry on their jobs. Moreover, many choices will involve the President's own sense of right and wrong. Eisenhower, as we have seen, argued for economy amidst the outcry over sputniks and recession; Truman stuck to advocacy of his Fair Deal measures in the hardest months of the Korean War. Besides, each choice involves not only general reputation but particular relationships. The two considerations often clash. Although a President lacks other means to guard the way he looks, his choice-making involves him in *competing* considerations. The choice that started Eisenhower's reputation toward its downward slide in 1957 was his personal approval of a Treasury press conference on Budget Day....

THE SIXTIES COME NEXT

We are confronted by an evident necessity for government more energetic, policies more viable, than we have been enjoying in the Fifties. The areas of controversy, just described, are also fields for governmental action. But every path to action leads through controversy. Effective policy can only be created out of the material our politics provides. It is not very promising material. If policy is to be viable, ways must be found in every field to reconcile all sorts of things now called irreconcilable. This is the special province of the President-as-expert whose concern for power brings him face to face with the ingredients that make for viability in policy.

A President who knows what power is and wants it has to face irreconcilables whenever he considers his own stakes in acts of choice. The sources of his influence are such that one may suffer from whatever serves another. The move that gains him ground on some particular may scar his general Washington reputation. The move that brightens Washington impressions may raise public hopes the future cannot meet. And moves that seem imperative for reasons of high policy may threaten all three sources of his power. The essence of his expertise is an awareness that these are irreconcilable and that they must be reconciled. Viability in policy calls for the same awareness.

A President-as-expert is no cure-all. The illustrations in this book suggest his limitations. Power cannot be his sole criterion for choice, nor will his choices be the only regulators of his influence. They are the only levers in *his* hands, but other hands hold other levers. And his influence, at most, is only one of many factors shaping what eventuates as governmental action; events and men beyond his personal control are much the greater shapers. One cannot look around the world in the late Fifties with any special confidence in men or in events throughout the Sixties. It is not easy, after such a look, to quarrel with those who think that science and technology have pushed our social competence too far. Yet it seems premature to write off the adaptability and the inventiveness of American public policy. Admitting that the future is not wholly in our hands, our policy responses may make a substantial difference. Despairing views could have been voiced—and were—in 1950, or in 1940, or in 1930. At a time and in a world where rates of change accelerate, the Sixties may be the decade that finally proves too much for us. But on the record of the past, the policy responses of our political system give us grounds for hope. (In the whole perspective of this century so far, our recent pause seems relatively brief; besides, it was a pause, not a regression.) We might as well enjoy the hope; there is no present prospect that we soon shall change the system. Nor is there any prospect that a change of system would eliminate our policy dilemmas.

An expert in the White House does not guarantee effective policy, but lacking such an expert every hope is placed in doubt. If past experience is reassuring, its assurances are conveyed with that caveat. The responses of our system remain markedly dependent on the person of the President. "As matters have stood," Edward Corwin writes, "... presidential power has been at times dangerously *personalized*," and with unerring instinct for an expertise in influence he distrusts Franklin Roosevelt only less than Abraham Lincoln. But if one wants effective policy from the American system, danger does not lie in our dependence on *a* man; it lies in our capacity to make ourselves depend upon a man who is inexpert. Any human judgment is worth fearing nowadays, but save for this the expert is a boon. His expertise assures a contribution to the system and it naturally commits him to proceed within the system. The system, after all, is what he knows. The danger lies in men who do not know it.

A dangerous dependence on the expertise of the top man — dependence on his "feel" for power in the going system — is not confined to the United States. It seems to be a feature of all democratic governments (presumably of communist regimes as well) though sometimes, as in Britain, it is so disguised that numbers of Americans may not have noticed it. The British cabinet system tends to cover up the weaknesses and to show up the strengths of the top man; ours tends to do the opposite. English politics does not place amateurs on top, while ours has put an amateur in office very recently. But Britain, in this century, has not lacked for inexpert heads of government, albeit quite professional, and British policy has paid a heavy price for them; most recently in Eden's case, to say nothing of Chamberlain's. With the English, as with us, structure and conventions and traditions count for everything *within* the system since the top man's expertise is wedded to them. But the English seem to be no less dependent than Americans upon the contributions of an expert at the top. If we were to import the British system overnight, power at the White House would be personalized still — and the person might turn out to be Ramsay MacDonald. Some dangers in political society are not escaped by structure.

One of those dangers is the yearning in our national electorate for political leaders "above politics." Eisenhower, to be sure, is *sui generis*. But part of Stevenson's appeal was that he had not been in politics for long and did not seem to be a "politician." Currently, contenders for the 1960 nomination are doing all they can, each in his own way, to take the curse off their political careers by assertions of amateur standing. Desire for an amateur is not new in American politics; Wendell Willkie's instance makes that plain. Now we have had Eisenhower. Significantly, to the limited extent that Eisenhower has been criticized in public his detractors, for the most part, deal in arguments *ad homimum*. Much of the criticism is unjust. Little of it makes allowance for the words attributed to Speaker Rayburn in the spring of 1952: "No, won't do. Good man. Wrong profession." But this is the heart of the matter.

The striking thing about our national elections in the Fifties was not Eisenhower's personal popularity; it was the genuine approval of his candidacy by informed Americans whom one might have supposed would know better. A sizeable majority of voters twice elected him. And save for one brief interval, his conduct as a President has always had commensurate approval on the showing of the Gallup Poll. Why not? The popular hero in a genuine sense, the man who is both great and friend, has never been in long supply with us. In the later Forties and throughout the Fifties, Eisenhower was the only one we had. To place him in the White House without losing him as hero seems both reasonable and prudent on the part of average citizens, no matter what their general view of politics or Presidents. The same thing can be said of the Republican professionals who managed Eisenhower's nomination in 1952; their action appears reasonable and prudent in *their* terms. They twice had tried a leading politician as their candidate; this time they wanted most of all to win. But when it comes to journalists, and government officials, and business leaders, and professors, who joined in the parade or urged it on, one deals with a phenomenon decidedly less reasonable. Some of Eisenhower's sharpest critics at the present time were once among his most articulate admirers. What was their understanding then — what is it now — of our political institutions? His virtue was supposed to be that he was above politics, and disenchantment with him rarely seems a disenchantment with this odd criterion. Instead it is all Eisenhower's fault that he is not what temperament and training never equipped him to be. When one finds attitudes of this sort in the circle of articulate observers, one wonders at the meaning for American society.

Before he reached the White House Woodrow Wilson once remarked: "Men of ordinary physique and discretion cannot be Presidents and live, if the strain be not somehow relieved. We shall be obliged always to be picking our chief magistrates from among wise and prudent athletes — a small class." In the perspective of this book his formula needs some revision. The strain is vastly greater now, with no relief in sight. If we want Presidents alive and fully useful, we shall have to pick them from among experienced politicians of extraordinary temperament—an even smaller class.

Presidential Advisers

Every president has his own coterie of formal and informal advisers. His problem, in the most general terms, is to establish ways and means whereby these advisers are able to use their talents to his advantage. The president has, in fact, both an internal and external advisory system. The internal net consists of his cabinet, presidential assistants, the Bureau of the Budget, and the various special advisers operating within the general framework of the executive office of the president. In recent decades an external network of advice for the president has developed. This external network has largely escaped the attention of political scientists but includes the myriad of White House appointed advisory councils, task forces, conferences, and interagency committees. The evidence available suggests that the role of these external groups, in terms of policy initiation, is impressive and growing. These White House appointed collectivities are not only citadels of "expertise," but the prime "patronage" available to the president as well. Theodore Sorensen, assistant and confidant to President Kennedy, describes the various sources of advice presently available to a President. In so doing, he stresses their capabilities and limitations always noting the key role played by the President.

Theodore C. Sorensen

... Each President must determine for himself how best to elicit and assess the advice of his advisers. Organized meetings, of the Cabinet and National Security Council, for example, have certain indispensable advantages, not the least of which are the increased public confidence inspired by order and regularity and the increased esprit de corps of the participants.

President Kennedy, whose nature and schedule would otherwise turn him away from meetings for the sake of meeting, has sometimes presided over sessions of the full Cabinet and National Security Council held primarily for these two reasons. Regularly scheduled meetings can also serve to keep open the channels of communication. This is the primary pur-

Reprinted by permission of the publisher from Theodore C. Sorensen, *Decision-Making in the White House,* Columbia University Press, © 1963, pp. 58-76.

pose, for example, of the President's weekly breakfast with his party's legislative leaders.

But there are other important advantages to meetings. The interaction of many minds is usually more illuminating than the intuition of one. In a meeting representing different departments and diverse points of view, there is a greater likelihood of hearing alternatives, of exposing errors, and of challenging assumptions. It is true in the White House, as in the Congress, that fewer votes are changed by open debate than by quiet negotiation among the debaters. But in the White House, unlike the Congress, only one man's vote is decisive, and thorough and thoughtful debate *before* he has made up his mind can assist him in that task.

That meetings can sometimes be useful was proven by the deliberations of the NSC executive committee after the discovery of offensive weapons in Cuba. The unprecedented nature of the Soviet move, the manner in which it cut across so many departmental jurisdictions, the limited amount of information available, and the security restrictions which inhibited staff work, all tended to have a leveling effect on the principals taking part in these discussions, so that each felt free to challenge the assumptions and assertions of all others.

Everyone in that group altered his views as the give-and-take talk continued. Every solution or combination of solutions was coldly examined, and its disadvantages weighed. The fact that we started out with a sharp divergence of views, the President has said, was "very valuable" in hammering out a policy.

In such meetings, a President must carefully weigh his own words. Should he hint too early in the proceedings at the direction of his own thought, the weight of his authority, the loyalty of his advisers and their desire to be on the "winning side" may shut off productive debate. Indeed, his very presence may inhibit candid discussion. President Truman, I am told, absented himself for this reason from some of the National Security Council discussions on the Berlin blockade; and President Kennedy, learning on his return from a mid-week trip in October, 1962, that the deliberations of the NSC executive committee over Cuba had been more spirited and frank in his absence, asked the committee to hold other preliminary sessions without him.

But no President—at least none with his firm cast of mind and concept of office—could stay out of the fray completely until all conflicts were resolved and a collective decision reached. For group recommendations too often put a premium on consensus in place of content, on unanimity in place of precision, on compromise in place of creativity.

Some advisers may genuinely mistake agreement for validity and coordination for policy — looking upon their own role as that of mediator, convinced that any conclusion shared by so many able minds must be right, and pleased that they could in this way ease their President's problems. They may in fact have increased them.

Even more severe limitations arise when a decision must be communicated, in a document or speech or diplomatic note. For group authorship is rarely, if ever, successful. A certain continuity and precision of style, and unity of argument, must be carefully drafted, particularly in a public communication that will be read or heard by many diverse audiences. Its key principles and phrases can be debated, outlined, and later reviewed by a committee, but basically authorship depends on one man alone with his typewriter or pen. (Had the Gettysburg address been written by a committee, its ten sentences would surely have grown to a hundred, its simple pledges would surely have been hedged, and the world would indeed have little noted or long remembered what was said there.)

Moreover, even spirited debates can be stifling as well as stimulating. The homely, the simple, or the safe may sound far more plausible to the weary ear in the Cabinet room than it would look to the careful eye in the office. The most formidable debater is not necessarily the most informed, and the most reticent may sometimes be the wisest.

Even the most distinguished and forthright adviser is usually reluctant to stand alone. If he fears his persistence in a meeting will earn him the disapprobation of his colleagues, a rebuff by the President, or (in case of a "leak") the outrage of the Congress, press, or public, he may quickly seek the safety of greater numbers. At the other extreme are those who seek refuge in the role of chronic dissenter, confining their analytical power to a restatement of dangers and objections.

Still others may address themselves more to their image than to the issues. The liberal may seek to impress his colleagues with his caution; idealists may try to sound tough-minded. I have attended more than one meeting where a military solution was opposed by military minds and supported by those generally known as peace-lovers.

The quality of White House meetings also varies with the number and identity of those attending. Large meetings are less likely to keep secrets — too many Washington officials enjoy talking knowingly at social events or to the press or to their friends. Large meetings are also a less flexible instrument for action, less likely to produce a meaningful consensus or a frank, hard-hitting debate. President Kennedy prefers to invite only those whose official views he requires or whose unofficial judgment he values, and to reserve crucial decisions for a still smaller session or for solitary contemplation in his own office.

The difficulty with small meetings, however, is that, in Washington, nearly everyone likes to feel that he, too, conferred and concurred. For years agencies and individuals all over town have felt affronted if not invited to a National Security Council session. The press leaps to conclusions as to who is in favor and who is not by scanning the attendance lists of meetings, speculating in much the same fashion (and with even less success) as the Kremlinologists who study the reviewing stand at the Russian May Day Parade or analyze which Soviet officials sat where at the opening of the Moscow ballet.

Yet in truth attendance at a White House meeting is not necessarily a matter of logic. Protocol, personal relations, and the nature of the forum may all affect the list. Some basic foreign policy issue, for example, may be largely decided before it comes to the National Security Council — by the appointment of a key official, or by the President's response at a press conference, or by the funds allocated in the budget. Yet personnel, press conference, and budget advice is generally given in meetings outside the National Security Council.

EXPERT ADVISERS

Many different types of advisers, with differing roles and contributions, attend these meetings. President Kennedy met on his tax policy in the summer of 1962, for example, with professional economists from both inside and outside the government, as well as with department heads and White House aides. To the key meetings on Cuba were invited highly respected Foreign Service officers as well as policy appointees, retired statesmen as well as personal presidential assistants.

There is no predictable weight which a President can give to the conclusions of each type. The technical expert or career specialist, operating below the policymaking level, may have concentrated knowledge on the issue under study which no other adviser can match. Yet Presidents are frequently criticized for ignoring the advice of their own experts.

The reason is that the very intensity of that expert's study may prevent him from seeing the broader, more practical perspective which must govern public policy. As Laski's notable essay pointed out, too many experts lack a sense of proportion, an ability to adapt, and a willingness to accept evidence inconsistent with their own. The specialist, Laski wrote, too often lacks "insight into the movement and temper of the public mind.... He is an invaluable servant and an impossible master."

Thus the atomic scientist, discussing new tests, may think largely in terms of his own laboratory. The career diplomat, discussing an Asian revolt, may think largely in terms of his own post. The professional economist, in urging lower farm price supports, may think more in terms of his academic colleagues than of the next presidential election.

But not all experts recognize the limits of their political sagacity, and they do not hesitate to pronounce with a great air of authority broad policy recommendations in their own field (and sometimes all fields). Any President would be properly impressed by their seeming command of the complex; but the President's own common sense, his own understanding of the Congress and the country, his own balancing of priorities, his own ability to analyze and generalize and simplify, are more essential in reaching the right decision than all the specialized jargon and institutionalized traditions of the professional elite.

The trained navigator, it has been rightly said, is essential to the conduct of a voyage, but his judgment is not superior on such matters as where it should go or whether it should be taken at all. Essential to the relationship between expert and politician, therefore, is the recognition by each of the other's role, and the refusal of each to assume the other's role. The expert should neither substitute his political judgment for the policy-maker's nor resent the latter's exercising of his own; and the policy-maker should not forget which one is the expert.

Expert predictions are likely to be even more tenuous than expert policy judgments, particularly in an age when only the unpredictable seems to happen. In the summer of 1962, most of the top economists in government, business, and academic life thought it likely that a recession would follow the stock-market slide—at least "before the snows melted" was the cautious forecast by one economist from a cold northern state. But, instead, this year's thaw brought with it new levels of production — and, naturally, a new set of predictions.

In the fall of 1962, most specialists in Soviet affairs believed that long-range Soviet missiles, with their closely guarded electronic systems, would never be stationed on the uncertain island of Cuba, nearly 6,000 miles away from Soviet soil and supplies. Nevertheless, each rumor to this effect was checked out; increasing rumors brought increased surveillance; and when, finally, the unexpected did happen, this did not diminish the President's respect for these career servants. It merely demonstrated once again that the only infallible experts are those whose forecasts have never been tested.

CABINET ADVISERS

In short, a Cabinet of politicians and policy-makers is better than a Cabinet of experts. But a President will also weigh with care the advice of each Cabinet official. For the latter is also bound by inherent limitations. He was not necessarily selected for the President's confidence in his judgment alone — considerations of politics, geography, public esteem, and interest-group pressures may also have played a part, as well as his skill in administration.

Moreover, each department has its own clientele and point of view, its own experts and bureaucratic interests, its own relations with the Congress and certain subcommittees, its own statutory authority, objectives, and standards of success. No Cabinet member is free to ignore all this without impairing the morale and efficiency of his department, his standing therein, and his relations with the powerful interest groups and congressmen who consider it partly their own.

The President may ask for a Secretary's best judgment apart from the department's views, but in the mind of the average Secretary (and there have been many notable exceptions) the two may be hardly distinguishable. Whether he is the captive or the champion of those interests makes no practical difference. By reflecting in his advice to the President his agency's component bureaus, some of which he may not even control, he increases both his prestige within the department and his parochialism without.

Bureaucratic parochialism and rivalry are usually associated in Washington with the armed services, but they in fact affect the outlook of nearly every agency. They can be observed, to cite only a few examples, in the jurisdictional maneuvering between the Park Service and the Forest Service, between the Bureau of Reclamation and the Army Engineers, between State and Treasury on world finance, or State and Commerce on world trade, or State and Defense on world disarmament.

They can also be observed in Cabinet autobiographies complaining that the President — any President — rarely saw things their way. And they can be observed, finally, in case studies of an agency head paying more heed to the Congress than to the President who named him. But it is the Congress, after all, that must pass on his requests for money, men, and authority. It is the Congress with which much of his time will be spent, which has the power to investigate his acts or alter his duties. And it is the Congress which vested many of his responsibilities directly in him, not in the President or the Executive branch.

WHITE HOUSE STAFF ADVISERS

The parochialism of experts and department heads is offset in part by a President's White House and executive staff. These few assistants are the only other men in Washington whose responsibilities both enable and require them to look, as he does, at the government as a whole. Even the White House specialists — the President's economic advisers or science adviser, for example — are likely to see problems in a broader perspective, within the framework of the President's objectives and without the constraints of bureaucratic tradition.

White House staff members are chosen, not according to any geographical, political, or other pattern, but for their ability to serve the President's needs and to talk the President's language. They must not —and do not, in this Administration— replace the role of a Cabinet official or block his access to the President. Instead, by working closely with departmental personnel, by spotting, refining, and defining issues for the President, they can increase governmental unity rather than splinter responsibility. A good White House staff can give a President that crucial margin of time, analysis, and judgment that makes an unmanageable problem more manageable.

But there are limiting factors as well. A White House adviser may see a departmental problem in a wider context than the Secretary, but he also has less contact with actual operations and pressures, with the Congress and interested groups. If his own staff grows too large, his office may become only another department, another level of clearances and concurrences instead of a personal instrument of the President. If his confidential relationship with the President causes either one to be too uncritical of the other's judgment, errors may go uncorrected. If he develops (as Mr. Acheson has suggested so many do) a confidence in his own competence which outruns the fact, his contribution may be more mischievous than useful. If, on the other hand, he defers too readily to the authority of renowned experts and Cabinet powers, then the President is denied the skeptical, critical service his staff should be providing.

OUTSIDE ADVISERS

Finally, a President may seek or receive advice from outside the Executive branch: from members of the Congress; from independent wise men, elder statesmen, academic lights; from presidentially named high-level commissions or special agents; or merely from conversations with friends, visitors, private interest leaders, and others. Inevitably, unsolicited advice will pour in from the mass media.

This is good. Every President needs independent, unofficial sources of advice for the same reasons he needs independent, unofficial sources of information. Outside advisers may be more objective. Their contact with affected groups may be closer. They may be men whose counsel the President trusts, but who are unable to accept government service for financial or personal reasons. They may be men who are frank with the President because, to use Corwin's phrase, their "daily political salt did not come from the President's table."

Whatever the justification, outside advice has its own limitations. As national problems become more complex and interrelated, requiring continuous, firsthand knowledge of confidential data and expert analysis, very few outsiders are sufficiently well informed. The fact that some simple recommendation, contained in an editorial or political oration or informal conversation, seems more striking or appealing or attention-getting than the intricate product of bureaucracy does not make it any more valid.

Moreover, once the advice of a distinguished private citizen or committee is sought and made public, rejection of that advice may add to the President's difficulties. The appointment by the last three Presidents of special advisory committees on civil rights, world trade, and foreign aid was, in that sense, a gamble —a gamble that the final views of these committees would strengthen, not weaken, the President's purpose. Should the outside report not be made public, the Gaither report being a well-known example, a President who rejects its advice may still have to face the consequences of its authors' displeasure.

QUALIFICATIONS OF ADVISERS

Finally, a President's evaluation of any individual's advice is dependent in part on the human characteristics of both men. Personalities play an intangible but surprisingly important role. Particular traits, social ties, recreational interests or occupational backgrounds may strengthen or weaken the bonds between them. Some Presidents pay more attention to generals, some to businessmen, some to politicians, some even to intellectuals who have "never met a payroll and never carried a precinct."

In truth, a political background, not necessarily at the precinct level, is helpful. It gives the adviser a more realistic understanding of the President's needs. Those without such experience will tend to assume that the few congressmen in touch with their agency speak for all the Congress, that one or two contacts at a Washington cocktail party are an index of public opinion, and that what looms large in the newspaper headlines necessarily looms large in the public mind.

Those with a political base of their own are also more secure in case of attack; but those with political ambitions of their own—as previous Presidents discovered—may place their own reputation and record ahead of their President's. (Such a man is not necessarily suppressing his conscience and forgetting the national interest. He may sincerely believe whatever it is most to his advantage to believe, much like the idealistic but hungry lawyer who will never defend a guilty man but persuades himself that all rich clients are innocent.)

Other advisers may also be making a record, not for some future campaign, but for some future publication. "History will record that I am right," he mutters to himself, if not to his colleagues, because he intends to write that history in his memoirs. The inaccuracy of most Washington diaries and autobiographies is surpassed only by the immodesty of their authors.

The opposite extreme is the adviser who tells his President only what he thinks the President wants to hear — a bearer of consistently good tidings but frequently bad advice.

Yet there is no sure test of a good adviser. The most rational, pragmatic-appearing man may turn out to be the slave of his own private myths, habits, and emotional beliefs. The hardest-working man may be too busy and out-of-touch with the issue at hand, or too weary to focus firmly on it. (I saw firsthand, during the long days and nights of the Cuban crisis, how brutally physical and mental fatigue can numb the good sense as well as the senses of normally articulate men.)

The most experienced man may be experienced only in failure, or his experience, in Coleridge's words, may be "like the stern lights of a ship which illumine only the track it has passed." The most articulate, authoritative man may only be making bad advice sound good, while driving into silence less aggressive or more cautious advisers.

All this a President must weigh in hearing his advisers. . . .

President–Cabinet Relations

Richard F. Fenno, Jr.

While the Constitution enumerates in some detail the powers to be exercised by the Congress, no such specific list is provided for the President. It is accepted that he is responsible for whatever policies and practices are followed by agencies in the executive branch, but each President soon discovers that his voice is only one among many seeking to influence the course of the bureaucracy. The cabinet is seen by many as a primary instrument the President can use to achieve dominance in the executive branch. One recent widely used text on American government commented as follows on the role of the cabinet: "In practice, the Cabinet plays an important part in determining executive policies and coordinating administrative work." This view of the cabinet as a collectivity making policy, some argue, is inaccurate and is largely based on an unwarranted comparison with the British cabinet. Our cabinet is composed of members who feel little or no sense of loyalty to one another and who are often quite literally rivals in the inevitable conflicts of the bureaucracy. Once named to a cabinet post, the new political executive quickly finds that he must be an ambassador from his department to the president rather than the reverse. His goal is to keep the other department chiefs from "meddling" in his department's activities so he gladly joins in the "conspiracy of silence" which envelopes most cabinet meetings. The president, then, finds the cabinet a limited resource, primarily useful for administrative coherence and the interchange of ideas on basic policy problems. The limitations placed on the President by the nature of his cabinet and the bureaucracy are clearly demonstrated in the following essay by Richard Fenno.

A common generalization about the distribution of power in the American political system states that it is fragmented and decentralized. In accordance with this view, the making of public policy decisions can be explained largely in terms of the continuous interaction, com-

Reprinted, by permission of the author and publisher, from Richard F. Fenno, Jr., "President-Cabinet Relations: A Pattern and a Case Study," *American Political Science Review,* 52 (June 1958), 388-405. Abridged by the editors.

petitive or cooperative, among many diverse semi-autonomous centers of power, some governmental, others nongovernmental. Each power-holding unit —individual or group, private or public —is a discrete, describable entity existing within a plural political universe. It must be perceived and understood not in isolation but as one unit in a larger system of interrelated parts. Within such a network, multiple role-playing, group cross-pressures, and institutional rivalry must be considered normal. This paper is an attempt to apply the generally pluralistic viewpoint so expressed to a much neglected political institution, the President's Cabinet, and to the power relationships involving an individual Cabinet member.

I

The most fruitful approach to President-Cabinet relations is one already made accessible by research in tangential areas. From the angle of executive-legislative relations, Pendleton Herring has analyzed the "maze of criss-crossing relationships between the President, Congress, and the departments." He has captured the dilemma of executive officials caught between conflicting theories and practices of administrative responsibility, "vertically" to the President and "horizontally" to the Congress. Norton Long, in examining the pattern whereby executive officials establish a power base from which to operate a program, has emphasized that sufficient power *cannot* be "derived exclusively from superiors in the hierarchy." Officials must "fend for themselves and acquire support peculiarly their own." In his study of interest groups, David Truman has demonstrated that, "The patterns of interaction among officials of the executive branch . . . show . . . an accepted practice of responding to the initiative of organized interest groups, to elements in the legislature to which these have effective access, or both." Herring, Long, Truman and others have concluded that executive officials, thus Cabinet members, are involved in a pattern of power relationships which are understandable in pluralistic, quasi-feudal terms, as a "pattern of fiefs, baronies, and dukedoms," "a protean aggregation of feudalities that overlap and crisscross in an almost continual succession of changes."

Before proceeding with this line of analysis, another viewpoint, with a substantial currency both inside and outside of the profession, presents itself for consideration. Briefly stated, this alternative image pictures the President's relations with his Cabinet, collectively and individually, as essentially *hierarchical*, *helpful*, and *intimate*. Emphasis is placed upon tight presidential control from the top down, faithful Cabinet assistance from the bottom up, and harmonious cooperation at the points of interaction. For example, with respect to hierarchy, it is said that "No institution is more a body of one man's men than the American President's Cabinet." Its members are characterized as the President's "chief lieutenants," his "chief assistants," his subordinates in the chain of command. Their "daily salt" comes "from the President's table." On the assumption of helpfulness, "the rule may be laid down that the President ordinarily consults the Cabinet on matters of grave public importance." Moreover, "an able Cabinet can go far to make up for the deficiencies of a weak President." The Cabinet is frequently proposed as a natural source of institutionalized assistance for the President in his relations with the legislative and/or the executive branch. Regarding intimacy, the Cabinet is traditionally described in the press in the terminology of closest kinship, as the Chief Executive's "official family." As individuals, we read that it is "simply a matter of course that the Secretary of a new Department will become as such an intimate adviser and associate of the President." The diversity of sources from which this image emerges testifies at least to its vitality. And in recent years it has achieved added status as the professed facsimile of the Eisenhower Cabinet.

The difficulty with the emphasis on hierarchy, helpfulness and intimacy is not its irrelevance but its one-sidedness —which results in turn, from a one-sided concentration on the Cabinet as a group, on the Cabinet as a discrete institution. According to this outlook, the important features of the Cabinet are its formal, institutional ones. Thus, as a group, the Cabinet exists to help the President implement his responsibilities and his authority. It has no institutional life apart from the President. It is a group appointed by him, his to use or not to use, and to use in any way that he sees fit. It has no self-starting mechanism, no legalized group prerogatives, and no collective decision-making authority. These are basic institutional facts. Standing alone, they tend to support the hierarchical representation of President-Cabinet relations. They can be illustrated by such time-honored anecdotes as the one involving Lincoln's decision contrary to the unanimous vote of his Cabinet, *i.e.*, "Seven noes, one aye—the ayes have it." The trouble with the story is similar to that of the hierarchical viewpoint which it most readily supports. Both are concerned more with ultimate institutional prescription than with actual performance.

The approach to President-Cabinet relations which begins by concentrating on formal institutional characteristics and ends by stressing hierarchy, helpfulness, and intimacy is an inadequate one. In the first place, it carries with it the false implication that day-to-day President-Cabinet relations are, in fact, precisely what a knowledge of their special institutional properties would indicate that they are. It also implies that the relationship can somehow be understood as self-contained and unaffected by the impact of external forces upon it. The burden of this article, and of the approach which it follows, is to insist that the activity of the individual Cabinet member cannot be understood wholly in terms of the immediate President-Cabinet nexus. He cannot be treated simply as a member of a collectivity. Neither can we assume that he is a devoted keeper of the President's confidences whose career in public life is one single-minded endeavor to act as the agent and servant of his superior. The Cabinet member participates in a multiplicity of non-presidential, and hence non-Cabinet, relationships. Through the extra-Cabinet activities of its individual members, the Cabinet interacts with the larger political universe, producing significant consequences for the behavior of the group.

A Cabinet member is typically the chief executive of an administrative organization, constantly interacting with its members, with the variety of private groups which seek decisions from it, with the legislators who hold life-and-death controls over it, and with partisan factions most sympathetic to him. He is a man with a particular departmental viewpoint, responsive to particular clientele interests and pursuing a particular program. His political behavior is shaped to a large degree by the kinds of extra-presidential relationships he establishes as he seeks solutions to his particular problems — the support of his policies, the survival of his organization, the control of his environment. Where extra-presidential relationships exist, then extra-presidential — perhaps, anti-presidential—actions are not far behind. For the realities of the Cabinet member's existence are not alone his dependent, contingent, hierarchical relationship to the President, but his independent, self-regulating, polyarchical relationships to non-presidential centers of power.

The fact that he shares mutual interests with the units of his department, with special social constituencies, with legislators, and with party factions puts him in a situation fraught with ambivalence and competing demands. He has several sources of power and prestige, several focal points for his time and energy, several claimants for his loyalty and services. Conflict may, of course, be avoided; but the potentialities and uncertainties of the situation color his whole pattern of behavior. He is frequently caught and torn between alternatives of action—President-oriented or other-oriented — in an environment where the rationale, the means, and the incentives for pursuing either are readily available. Viewed from the perspective of the individual Cabinet member, there is an acute unreality to the hierarchical image. Hierarchy is subject to many countervailing influences. Opportunities to help the President are freighted with possibilities of hurting him. Intimacy is a condition to be achieved rather than assumed. The following case study is illustrative.

II

Jesse Jones's behavior as a Cabinet officer must be set in the context of his previous experience in government. A Texas Democrat, he was appointed by President Hoover in 1932 as a Director of the Reconstruction Finance Corporation. One year later, he became its Chairman, a position he held until 1939 when President Roosevelt designated him to be Federal Loan Administrator. In this post, he was given general supervision over several loan agencies in addition to the RFC. In 1940, Jones was made Secretary of Commerce, and by a special unanimous resolution of Congress was allowed to remain as Federal Loan Administrator. That agency was formally incorporated into the Department of Commerce in 1942. Three features of his RFC experience shed light on Jones's perception of his job and his pattern of behavior as Secretary of Commerce.

In the *first* place, the RFC was a creature of the Congress, a government corporation whose authority and functions were determined by the legislature. With the exception of the appointment of its Directors, it was relatively independent of the President. A statutory relationship thus bound Jones closely to the Congress during his entire thirteen years of government service. He assiduously cultivated and strengthened these ties at every opportunity in order "to make the RFC a dependable favorite of Congress." At the forefront of his accomplishments, Jones always spoke, not a bit modestly, of his smooth relationships with that body:

Throughout the entire period, we received in a manner probably unique in the history of federal agencies, the complete cooperation and confidence of each successive Congress. Not a single request that I made of Congress during those thirteen years was refused. On the other hand, Congress increased and broadened our power from year to year.

Under congressional authorization and subject only to the routine approval of the President, Jones lent, between 1940 and 1945 "anything that we think we should . . . any amount, any length of time, any rate of interest." A remark by Senator Adams bespeaks the unusual willingness of Congress to grant discretionary authority to him:

Of course, the credit you are using comes from the Congress, and we have heard it said across this table and in the Senate and House that these vast credits were being extended largely because of the confidence the Congress has in Jesse Jones. Now that has been said time after time.

Senator Taft described the incorporation of the RFC into the Commerce Department as "an extraordinary precedent, justified only by the character of the man."

For Jones, congressional hearings were not inquisitions or ordeals about which to become apprehensive. They were informal, friendly, laudatory — almost clubby — interchanges. Frequently, he would sit on the witness table and chat in an off-the-cuff manner. Or, if there happened to be a vacant seat between committee members, he would take it and the "hearing" would begin. Indeed, so comfortable did this executive official feel among congressional committees that he designed, bought, and presented to the Senate Committee on Banking and Currency a new table for their hearing room — one is tempted to say their clubroom — in order that he might see them all better while testifying. Jones pursued this cordial alliance in casual day-to-day contacts. Once a week, he would lunch on Capitol Hill with members of the legislature, in the office of Vice President Garner or Speaker Rayburn or Senate Secretary Biffle. On other occasions, he would come to Garner's office for morning or afternoon coffee. "I guess it's *our* office," commented Garner, "Jones uses it as much as I do."

A *second* crucial element in Jones's RFC experience was its non-partisan character. Like most independent agencies, its plural executive was composed of members of both political parties. Jones himself had been a very active Democrat as Director of Finance for the Democratic National Committee in 1924, as a favorite-son candidate for President in 1928, and as a faithfully heavy contributor to party causes. He had influential Democratic friends like fellow-Texan John Nance Garner and Senator Carter Glass. And though he retained these ties the RFC acquired a reputation for non-partisanship. Jones was a conservative in politics and, as the Republican-Southern Democratic coalition took shape within Congress, his Democratic politics became less of a liability. He continually stressed the non-partisan nature of his organization, and won the support of Republicans as well as Democrats. The ranking Republican member of the House Banking and Currency Committee spoke of Jones as "a man whom I so much respect for his wisdom, his intelligence, and his patriotism that without giving it much consideration, I would accept almost any proposal he might make." Or, consider this colloquy between the ranking Republican and the ranking Democrat in the Senate Appropriations Committee:

Sen. White: . . . I have to confess that there is a disposition for me to favor anything that Mr. Jones recommends.

Sen. McKellar: That is for me, too. I do not think that there is a finer man anywhere in the world.

Jones's extraordinary standing with Congress was built partly on his success in keeping his organization in close touch with that body and yet outside party conflict.

A *third* factor, intertwined with the other two, was the close *entente* between Jones's organization and a powerful social constituency — the business community. During his government service, agencies under his supervision authorized expenditures of fifty billion dollars to assist various enterprises in business, industry, and banking. He was in constant contact with representatives of this group, as consciously and as inevitably reaching out for their support as they did for his. His public speeches were aimed at this particular clientele, and the groups which gave him a forum were business groups — the Chamber of Commerce, the American Bankers Association, the National Wholesale Association Council, the Committee for Economic Development, the Department of Commerce's Business Advisory Council. Jones himself was a businessman, who had become by 1929 "the best known private citizen in Texas," due to his ownership of a newspaper, several hotels, a bank, several skyscrapers and other assorted real estate. He identified himself completely with business; and he considered the RFC to be "America's largest corporation and the world's biggest and most varied banking agency."

Jones never passed up the opportunity before Congress to attribute the success of the RFC wholly to the fact that it was a "businesslike, nonpolitical organization." Again and again he reiterated that, "Our agency is a business agency composed entirely of business people." He was tireless in his praise of his agencies as paragons of businesslike efficiency and economy, and he loved to make invidious comparisons between himself and the "do-gooders," "idealists," and "screwballs" in the government who did not possess the same virtues. His organizations were run as businesses, by businessmen, and for businessmen. Jones fastened himself to a powerful constituency which cut across party lines and gave him leverage both in and out of Congress. Moreover, his appeals to Congress and to his business constituency were mutually reenforcing. Throughout the Roosevelt Administration, the executive branch had not been especially hospitable to business, and business channels of access to government coursed mostly through the legislature. Members of Congress tended to be very sympathetic to Jones's emphasis on business and identified themselves with his efforts to help it, especially small business.

As head of the RFC, Jones developed lines of responsibility and areas of support which had few presidential dimensions. On the basis of his personal and his institutional resources, he fashioned a substantial enclave of power and, hence, a considerable degree of political independence. As Secretary of Commerce, however, he was brought into a different and theoretically more dependent relationship to the President. He joined the "official family" at Cabinet meetings; his formal responsibility now ran directly up the hierarchy to the Chief Executive; and with a closer relationship came greater opportunities for him to help the President. Jones himself had no intention of allowing either of the two patterns of relationships — least of all, the President-oriented one — to absorb the other. And as if to underscore the point, he refused to accept the Commerce post until Roosevelt agreed to let him retain all his RFC functions. However this may be, the key idea is that Jones's network of relations with Congress, with a social constituency, and with political partisans, is only an extreme case of the kind of network within which nearly every department Secretary must operate. It is the essence of his extra-Cabinet activity. The vividness, perhaps, but not the validity of this proposition depends upon Jones's peculiar RFC background and his perception of his new role. His situation, faced with alternative lines of responsibility, one to the President and one to the Congress, is a normal one in the American political system. In his first appearance before the House Appropriations Committee, he spoke as any Secretary of Commerce would when he said,

If the Department of Commerce means anything, it means as I understand it, the representation of business in the councils of the administration, at the Cabinet table, and so forth.

The duality of roles, as presidential lieutenant and departmental executive, promotes ambiguity and conflict and, as the Jones case illustrates, a pattern of behavior quite unknown to the hierarchical image of President-Cabinet relations.

In 1943, Congress was considering legislation to set up a single agency to coordinate the disposal of surplus government property. The bill provided for coordination by the President, and as a practical matter by the Bureau of the Budget. With an eye to uniformity and control, the Budget Bureau desired that all agencies in the executive branch be tied into the program. This, of course, included the RFC and its various subsidiary corporations which comprised one of the largest government purchasers and holders of property. In the Senate hearings, the Bureau expressed its wish that,

... the disposal policies of these corporations should be subject to review under this bill, for assurance that they are tied in, that there is cohesion and coordination, and that they are not out in a competitive status.

Jones was willing to listen to the advice of a unifying agency, but fought for the complete autonomy of the RFC in disposing of its property. In effect, he argued against the wishes of the Chief Executive, and did so without even consulting Roosevelt. Before the committee, Jones stated his own position, and appealed for support to his favorite constituencies, Congress and business.

Arguing from the standpoint of business, he said,

I don't see any excuse for a new agency to handle and dispose of these properties. You have a perfectly good one.... I should think that you would use the RFC and give it such additional manpower as it needs, because it is a business agency and this is a business proposition. There would be no purpose in setting up a new one, but Congress can do it if it wants.

At the suggestion of the Committee, he was "willing" even to enlarge his own domain and leave out the Budget Bureau altogether in the area of real property.

Sen. Ferguson: Could the RFC become the agency and dispose of all properties? Is that the logical place to place it, because it is a business organization?

Secretary Jones: I think that is where it belongs; that is all plants, equipment, machinery, machine tools, and so forth. *I have not discussed the matter with anyone in authority in the government.* Those are my views and they are very strong.... I do not understand why they (Budget Bureau) would be a natural agency to do this job.

Ferguson: Who would be the natural agency in the government?

Jones: The RFC.... When I say the RFC, I mean also the Department of Commerce, because they are the business end of the government.

The hearing closed on a familiar note, Jones's appeal to the Congress and reciprocated congressional sentiments of affection for him:

Chairman: (Senator Hill) You feel that your agency, having built these plants and secured this property, is the agency to make this disposition?

Jones: The RFC is your agency, an agency of the Congress.

Chairman: Mr. Jones, when you first appeared here this morning, I spoke about your many different titles. I am going to confer another title on you, and that is that you are a great diplomat, too. That was a fine way to put it. But as you say, it is Congress' agency that has secured this property. It is your feeling that it is the agency that Congress should use for the disposition of this property better than anybody else?

Jones: Yes, sir.... I do not intend to be immodest.

Chairman: We would not have you immodest. We do not want you to be.

Sen. Ferguson: The entire country is going to be very fortunate if all the other agencies feel about Congress as you do I am sure.

Chairman: I want to say this, too, since the Senator has said what he has, that Mr. Jones' actions always square with his words. He is always most considerate of the Congress.

One point at which Jones's double-barrelled efforts to mitigate presidential control were effective was in the appropriations process. In theory the major purpose of the executive budget is to provide for coordination of the expenditures of the executive branch in the name of economy and efficiency. The reverse side of the coin is the central control over programming by the President through his control over expenditures. The Budget Bureau, as a staff arm of the President, prepares a document which tries to express unity in policy as well as in finance. Reductions in agency requests represent the complex judgment of the President and his staff on matters of priority, cohesion, and purpose. Insofar as Cabinet members can make successful appeals to the Congress against this judgment, they can operate their departments with little dependence on the President and, virtually, if not literally, in defiance of him.

In drawing up the Department of Commerce budget for fiscal 1944, the decision was made to eliminate the field service of the Bureau of Foreign and Domestic Commerce. Wartime restrictions on trade had reduced the usefulness of this service, and that part of the job which needed to be done could, in the eyes of those dealing with the budget, be performed better by a wartime agency. To Jones, the reduction represented an attack upon his domain by people who were ignorant of his problems, and he lobbied strenuously before the appropriations committees in the House and Senate to restore the cut of $430,000 in the interests of his clientele.

In the House Subcommittee hearings, Jones began by stressing the efficiency and economy of his own agency while taking pot shots at others, both tactics designed to identify his aims with those of Congress.

We have a seasoned organization, which would work in cooperation with the RFC and its agencies. We have been in the government a long time. You don't hear much fuss about us. We get along pretty well and we think we know how to do the job better than some big shot that you would get in as temporary head, building up an organization which would be partly made up of volunteers and inexperienced people who do not know how to work together.... Of course, we do not spend any money which does not seem to be necessary. I believe in economy, but there are apparently not a great many people who do. There seem to be a good many in Congress who do, but not the boys on the spending line.

With a little legislative arm-twisting, Jones freely stated his position on the budget cut.

Mr. Hare: Mr. Secretary, ... we all know of your wide business experience, and I wonder if you would give us the advantage of your judgment as to what extent and in what way these district offices would be able to contribute in giving assistance to small business activity?

Jones: If we had that money, we would expand the present organization instead of closing it. *But we have had advice from the Budget Bureau that this does not fit into the President's program. Of course, we are not trying to oppose the President, but we think the Budget is wrong.*

Before the Senate Committee, Jones concluded his appeal for the restoration of the cut in terms of his particular constituency and without any reference to any overall presidential program.

I think that the Department of Commerce has got to carry the ball for business. That is what it is set up to do. If we haven't got the right people to do the job, then others should be gotten to do it. But the Department is the representative of business at the Cabinet table and in the administration whatever the administration is. So I say that I think it is of importance that we not destroy or diminish this service one iota, that it really ought to be expanded and encouraged.

Of the $430,000, Congress restored $295,000; and only four of the thirty field offices were closed.

Jones's consciousness of his high standing contributed to a psychological hypersensitivity to any attempt "to horn in on our RFC operations." He communicated this sensitivity to the Congress and they responded in kind. They were irritated when a wartime agency like the Office of Production Management or the Board of Economic Warfare infringed in any way on the discretionary authority of Jones over the money which they had appropriated. Their solicitude, while a blessing to Jones, was a distinct burden to the President. For it allowed the Secretary of Commerce to prosecute, before friendly committees, an internecine warfare with other agencies of the executive branch, casting about for non-presidential support as he went. The most obvious of these adventures was that which resulted in the "acrimonious public debate" between Jones and Henry Wallace, who was head of the BEW, in June of 1943. This quarrel between subordinates obviously hurt and annoyed the President and hampered his direction of the war effort.

At least as early as December of 1942, Jones had been engaged in sidewise combat with the BEW before Congress. In an appearance before the Senate Banking and Currency Committee, Jones allowed himself, with little encouragement, to complain that he was really "working under" the BEW and was very dissatisfied with the arrangement. One of those informal gestures which seldom break into print provided Senator Tobey with an opening.

Sen. Tobey: This matter of working with the BEW was enough to cause you to *raise your eyebrows,* as you did the first time it was mentioned here, is that right?

Jones: That is right, I suppose, but I don't quite know what you mean.

Of course, Jones knew very well, and only had to be coaxed a little more to reveal that,

We negotiate contracts and arrange financing and none of them (other agencies) except the BEW ever interferes with our negotiations. They leave it to us, feeling that we are the business organization with experience, preferring to have us negotiate the contracts; and because of our responsibility to Congress, we quite naturally prefer to do it.

Tobey: But the BEW does interfere.

Jones: They do a great deal of the negotiating, yes....

Tobey: Would you want to answer this question, having in mind the talk here this morning about the BEW and its extraordinary powers? Would you feel that if the BEW were curbed ... it would be a wise procedure?

Jones: The Executive Order is made by the President.

Tobey: Yes, I know.

Jones: I think I would not care to discuss that.

Tobey: But here is a nation and we are all striving to serve it.... *Such a thing as I suggest might contravene the President...* but whether the nation would be better served by having a better setup ... would you feel that some other arrangement would be wiser than the present arrangement?

Jones: Inasmuch as you press the question, I will say I think it could be improved.

Jones did not consider his relationship with Roosevelt in terms of subordination or hierarchy. He saw it, instead, as a marriage of convenience between co-equal potentates. "I never considered that I was working *for* him, but *with* him for the country."

In the twelve years I worked with him, we never had an argument. We did not always see alike. If he asked me to do something which in my opinion we could not or should not — and that happened only a few times — we just did not do it. For me that was the only way to operate without having a break with the President.

His biographer describes how Jones "layered" Roosevelt's proposals.

He granted such demands as he deemed wise or safe, but when Roosevelt wanted something that Jones considered wrong or clearly unwise, he listened, withheld argument, and then contrived an escape by inconspicuous inaction.

Neither was there any feeling of intimacy between the two men.

In no sense did I feel his superiority over other men except that he was President and the greatest politician our country has ever known, and ruthless when it suited his purpose.

Roosevelt, for his part, was willing to work on a relatively thin margin of loyalty, both personal and programmatic—which is doubtless one reason why their association lasted as long as it did. Ultimately, however, the personalities of the two men cannot explain the difficulties or the endurance of the relationship.

Roosevelt retained Jones in the Cabinet because his presence was helpful—not in spite of his independent strength, but because of it. The most persistent political problem facing any President is that of consolidating enough support for his policies. From this standpoint, Jones's influence with groups in and out of government was an asset on which Roosevelt could trade. He saw Jones's conservatism as "a good thing for this administration," "a good antidote for the extreme liberals, a sort of balance as it were." In 1940, Jones spoke over a nation-wide radio hookup, to his business constituency, urging that the re-election of the President was in their best interests. Roosevelt realized, too, that Jones's strength in Congress, with its hard core in the influential Texas delegation, was useful to him. It was a strength calculated by some as "ten votes in the Senate and forty in the House" on matters within Jones's area of competence. He was able on one occasion, for instance, to persuade reluctant legislators to vote a huge export-import loan to South America. Thus the total picture of the Jones-Roosevelt relationship was an admixture of help and hindrance. Neither assets nor liabilities were constants, and the ultimate judgment, of participant and observer alike, is one of subtle calculation.

As the 1944 Democratic Convention approached, Roosevelt's calculations "convinced" him that Jones's influence was being used to support a conservative revolt, and to persuade the Texas delegation to vote against a fourth term nomination. Jones denies it. Whatever the case, the decisive thing is that Roosevelt believed it was true. Moreover, it was the kind of behavior which touched his most sensitive political nerve. Jonathan Daniels writes that in 1944 the President was speaking contemptuously of "Jesus H. Jones," and that he was planning then to remove him from the Cabinet. Judge Rosenman feels that the move was a mistake and that "Roosevelt would never have made it under ordinary circumstances, but the vindictiveness aroused by the reports of Jones's activity impaired his usually clear political insight." The puzzle of the curt Roosevelt-to-Jones note after the election can best be explained in this way. It stressed Henry Wallace's "utmost devotion to the cause, travelling almost incessantly and working for the success of the ticket in a great many parts of the country." As Joseph Harris says,

Roosevelt chose this means of letting it be known that Jones was dismissed because of his failure to support Roosevelt politically. On any other grounds, the dismissal of Jones would have caused a great furor.

Jones did not go down without a fight in which he incontestably demonstrated his independent power. Divorced of the prestige of office, he nonetheless could summon enough political support to keep his base of operations, the RFC, out of the hands of his successor. His letter blasting Henry Wallace, and his testimony on the George Bill were in the nature of a valedictorian appeal to business and to the Congress. Congress responded with majorities of 400-2 and 74-12 in favor of removing the RFC from the Department of Commerce. Wallace, with that lack of perspective so common to a man who has been run over by a steamroller but with the sure knowledge that he had been thoroughly flattened, said later that "Jesse Jones wielded greater power for a longer period than any human being in the history of the United States."

A more sober and pertinent comment, perhaps, would be this: that the *denounement*, like the rest of the story, illustrates something of the fragmented, decentralized nature of power in the American political system. Jesse Jones built, inhabited, and manipulated a political fiefdom with a degree of independence which brought a heavy burden to his lord-President. But the feudal analogy is only partially correct. For within the democratic political process there are no laws of primogeniture and entail. Jones's fiefdom was, in the final accounting, a web of relationships peculiarly his, held for as long as he could hold it. It was not a transferrable property. At the very end, he boasted facetiously about his double-job that, "I do not believe there is another man in the world that will do it except me." It was an accurate assessment not alone of the man, but of the system. Power in the American system is both fragmented and, in David Riesman's term "mercurial." It can be quite easily and logically won by the Cabinet member. But as the Jones case demonstrates, no particular constellation can be held or held together permanently. The Jones case also demonstrates that the winning and the holding involve an area of activity and a kind of result which are neglected in the hierarchical-helpful-intimate image of President-Cabinet relations.

III

The pattern of extra-Cabinet activity examined here has a marked effect on the behavior of the Cabinet as a group, especially at the point where its group activity has meaning, the Cabinet meeting. Ideally, the members come together here to work as a unit, to advise, discuss, debate, coordinate and, in general to cooperate in helping the President deal with his government-wide responsibilities. Actually, however, the individual member brings to the meeting a point of view which is a derivative of his extra-Cabinet activity and which, to a varying but substantial degree, militates against the assumptions about cohesiveness and teamwork. His intra-Cabinet relationships are heavily influenced by the same centrifugal forces which operate outside of the meeting to pressure him into a kind of competitive independence *vis a vis* the President. His outlook is particularistic and departmental. His attitudes toward his colleagues scale from one of benign indifference to one of competitive distrust. His loyalty, his interest, and his contribution are tendered to the group as a group only in a very minimal sense. He comes to the Cabinet table in much the same frame of mind as a diplomat comes to an international conclave, with departmentalism rather than nationalism as the root barrier against cooperative enterprise.

The psychology of departmentalism is revealed most clearly in the reluctance of each member to raise important and controversial issues in Cabinet meeting. Each one feels that his problems, be they departmental or interdepartmental, are his private affair or, at most, the concern of but a few others whom he prefers to solicit in private. He tends not to want and hence to resent, the comment, criticism or judgment of his fellows. Jesse Jones, like many other members, evaluated his colleagues in terms of the degree to which they minded their own business. He stated the canon of behavior succinctly as follows: "I made no suggestions to other Cabinet members about their departments and asked none from them." Or, again,

My principal reason for not having a great deal to say at Cabinet meeting was that there was no one at the table who could be of help to me except the President, and when I needed to consult him I did not choose a Cabinet meeting to do so.

Sphinx-like during the meetings, Jones invariably scrambled into line afterward for a private conference with the President at which he, like the others, conducted any serious business that was on his mind. The typical post-Cabinet traffic jam at the President's chair is but one symptom of departmentalism and the lack of group identification. Others can be found in the members' eagerness to disassociate themselves from the difficulties of their fellow members (evident in the extreme during the Teapot Dome scandals), and their sometime willingness to "leak" the contents of Cabinet proceedings to the newspapers. These manifestations, coupled with the formal institutional weakness of the Cabinet, entwine cause and effect in the debilitation of the Cabinet meeting.

Since it is the President, if anyone, who wants and needs to have the Cabinet function as a unit, it is he who suffers most from the impact of enfeebling forces upon it. And though their predisposition to rely on it varies with temperament and administrative habit, all Presidents do wish to and do use it to some degree. The President is, of course, not helpless in combating the lack of a cooperative *esprit*. He hires and fires, devises new procedural techniques, exercises a control over the business content of the meetings and acts, by example, as a positive energizing force. Indeed, this is the meaning of his formal hierarchical status, that he and only he has the resources with which to exercise a centripetal influence on the Cabinet. But to say that without his help the Cabinet will do nothing is not to say that with his help the Cabinet will do everything. The elements which nourish departmentalism have their sources in the basic pluralism of American politics. They are non-presidential in origin and extra-presidential in scope. The President's power to countervail against them is limited.

His control over Cabinet appointments is restricted by the unwillingness of many to accept, by the conditions of the period, by certain normative expectations as to ability, and by a whole set of traditional criteria of selection. One such criterion, that of a "balanced" or "representative" Cabinet is nothing less than an instruction to build into the Cabinet at the very outset the pluralism of American society in terms of geography, party faction, socio-economic constituencies, personal experience, etc. This only highlights the extent to which the President is surrounded by forces over which he has limited control. As for the removal power, it is an ultimate weapon seldom used, and always, as in the Jones case, after a careful weighing of the assets and liabilities. The President may, as President Eisenhower has, make an institutional change; but its effect, too, will be modest and ameliorative. Thus, while the manifestations of departmentalism are relatively absent from the Eisenhower Cabinet meeting itself, they present themselves just as clearly at one stage removed in the procedure—in the reluctance of the Cabinet member to permit touchy items to be placed on the recently inaugurated Cabinet agenda.

Departmentalism is a political fact of life to which every President will accommodate himself. It does not render the Cabinet useless. But it is, surely, one of the forces which drives every President beyond the Cabinet meeting and beyond the advice and assistance he requires. More positively, departmentalism helps determine which, of all the hypothetically possible Cabinet functions, are the ones most likely to be performed successfully. A group activity which presumes a high degree of cohesiveness, such as that of interdepartmental coordination, is less likely to be performed well by the Cabinet than one, such as that of political sounding board, which does not. Probably the function best served by the Cabinet meeting is the provision of a small but vital measure of administrative coherence. That is to say, the infusion of a minimal sense of common purpose, of participant unity, and of some understanding by high level administrators of overall direction and emphasis. It is promoted by the very fact of a regular group meeting, however non-controversial the subject matter. It is promoted by the stimulation of the President's participation and by the communication of some of his thoughts to the group. Departmentalism has an adverse effect on the Cabinet meeting, but the meeting also serves to develop a degree of coherence and a degree of support for the President which would not exist in its absence.

It may be objected that the Jesse Jones-Franklin Roosevelt relationship is a poor one with which to prove a point, that it is an attempt to make a rule out of an exception. Probably the degree of Jones's power, and certainly its visibility, was unusual. But in terms of a basic pattern of activity, the Jones case is not exceptional. Some observers have maintained that in the Eisenhower Cabinet "separatist tendencies" have been reduced, if not eliminated. To be sure, any pattern of activity involving the Cabinet will be modified by particular presidential influences. In the case of President Eisenhower, his conviction, out of a military background, that his staff mechanisms should function as "a single mind," his repeated insistence on the virtue of team play, and the institutionalized procedures he has adopted have minimized the symptoms of departmentalism in the Cabinet meeting itself. Harmony does exist at the Cabinet table; but it exists in large part because that is what the President wants and expects, and the members know it. Outside of the meeting, one need only cite the damaging public criticism of the President's 1958 budget by one of his most helpful and intimate advisers, Secretary of the Treasury Humphrey. Or, consider Secretary of Labor Mitchell's independent behavior before his constituency and before Congress with respect to "right-to-work" and FEPC legislation. Intra-Cabinet controversies involving Weeks and Durkin, Mitchell and Weeks, Stassen and Humphrey, and Dulles and Stassen have reached the public press. Others have, in effect, been forced underground into Cabinet Committees on Water Resources and Transportation. Though its manifestations and its effects may be modified, departmentalism cannot be put to death by executive fiat, by pledges of allegiance to the team, or by a Secretariat, however able. *The conditions which a system of fragmented power sets for the success and the survival of a Cabinet officer encourage him to consolidate his own nexus of power and compel him to operate with a degree of independence from the President.*

With respect to the assumptions about *hierarchy*, the individual member engages in many non-hierarchical relationships which tend to weaken his dependent subordination to the President and to foster, instead, a pattern of independent, if not insubordinate, activity. The impact of non-presidential, centrifugal influences on its members attenuates the President's control over the Cabinet as a group. With respect to *helpfulness*, insofar as the individual member's extra-Cabinet relations tend to give him an area of operating freedom, his actions may be detrimental as well as helpful to the Chief Executive. And where the group is concerned, we might well consider reversing our conventional inquiry into why the President relies on the Cabinet so little and ask, instead, why he uses it as much as he does. It is as valid to say that the President cannot live with his Cabinet as it is to say that he cannot live without it. With respect to *intimacy*, all the non-hierarchical, non-helpful tendencies mentioned are influences against intimacy. The real problem here is to discard the sentimental myth of the "official family" and make the crucial discriminations among blood relatives, kissing cousins and black sheep. Every President, no matter how predisposed he is to utilize the group as a group, will rely more heavily on some members than others and will form, inevitably, a kind of inner Cabinet. Thus an informal hidden hierarchy may in fact be created for which some of the alternative assumptions may be more applicable.

If the line of analysis being pursued here can be put in the form of a large generalization, it is this—that we ought to appreciate the relative difficulty of promoting unity and centralizing power in the face of the dispersion and volatility of power which are so evident in the American political system. More specifically, this applies to a recognition of the limits which the system places on the President in his efforts to accumulate sufficient power to exercise the unifying functions of national leadership. Most specifically, we might examine some Cabinet-oriented reform proposals with respect to executive-legislative relations and the organization of the Presidency for their tendency to dilute the power of the President. There has been a tendency to propose more centrifugal, extra-Cabinet activities for the Cabinet member (Cabinet taken from Congress, Legislative-Executive Council, Cabinet membership in Congress) on the assumption that the President can bear the strain without additional difficulty, or, if pressed, can eliminate them by an act of will. Suggestions have also been made that the Cabinet be given more administrative functions ("center of executive coordination," "the administrative vehicle of the government") or that it be "vitalized" and "strengthened" by the addition of new machinery (Cabinet Secretariat, sub-Cabinet policy groups) on the assumption that the President will not mind either hostaging himself to one coordinating body or having his coordinating methods rigidly prescribed for him. From the point of view of his Cabinet relations, at least, the President's difficulties are more substantial than these assumptions recognize. Those who value the degree of presidential leadership which now exists in the American government should assess the assumptions and the proposals alike with considerable skepticism.

Judicial Review

Having lost the election of 1800, the Federalists turned the reins of government over to the Jeffersonian Republicans. The Federalists, however, decided that they would attempt to retain some influence over the course of events. They still controlled the courts and in the interim between the election and the inauguration they sought to strengthen their judicial position. In March 1801 President Adams named his secretary of state, John Marshall, to be chief justice. Also, the "lame duck" Congress created a number of new judgeships in the lower courts to be filled by Federalists. President Adams did not sign some of the commissions, however, until near midnight of his last night in office and Secretary of State Marshall was unable to deliver these commissions in time. One undelivered commission was intended for William Marbury and he brought suit in the Supreme Court demanding that the new secretary of state, James Madison, deliver the commission. When the case of Marbury v. Madison *was heard in 1803, Marshall realized that Madison would not obey any court order on the question so he ruled that Marbury had brought his case under an unconstitutional section of the Judiciary Act of 1789. Marshall was thus able to placate Madison while at the same time firmly establishing the right of the Supreme Court to "review" congressional acts. Since that time the subject of whether this case represented a "usurpation" of power by the Supreme Court has been hotly debated. Today, as Henry Schmandt suggests, the debate is not over whether the Supreme Court has the right of judicial review — for all now accept this as legitimate—but over the extent to which such a power shall be used. Professor Schmandt offers a summary of the three major schools of thought on this question.*

Henry J. Schmandt

Much of the literature dealing with the lawmaking function of the Supreme Court is concerned with the question of judicial review, or the authority of the High Tribunal to test acts of other gov-

Reprinted by permission of the publisher from *Courts in the American Political System* by Henry J. Schmandt, copyright 1968 by Dickenson Publishing Company, Inc., Belmont, California.

ernmental agencies for compliance with constitutional provisions. Since the Constitution does not define or mention this power, there has been much disagreement among lawyers, jurists, and historians. Almost from the Nation's beginning, there has been a running debate in legal and scholarly circles about whether the Court legitimately possesses this right. Much of the argument has centered on the intention of the Founding Fathers, but painstaking searches into the records have failed to marshall decisive evidence to prove exactly what the Constitution's authors meant. Actually, the strongest argument for the right of judicial review has been based on logic rather than history. Formulated simply the function of the judiciary is to interpret and apply law; the Constitution is law; and it is therefore the implicit duty of the courts to interpret and apply the provisions of this document regardless of who is affected.

As interesting as the debate over the right of judicial review may be from an historical and intellectual point of view, the question is no longer of practical importance. The uncontroverted fact is that the Court has been exercising this power for over 150 years, and the practice has become as integral a part of the American legal system as the assumption that one is innocent until proved guilty. Most of the legal commentators, still attracted by the question of whether judicial review was originally intended by the framers of the Constitution, are little interested in the issue as such. Their primary purpose in rummaging through records of the past is to seek historical legitimation for some present view of the Court's role in a democratic society or for some theory of the function of the review process.

The important question debated by legal scholars today is not the right of judicial review — all now accept it as legitimate—but its proper limits or the extent to which it should be used. A wide divergence of views exists, both in and out of the Court. These may be grouped into three categories: restraint, activism, and neutralism. The first argues that judges must recognize the primacy of the legislative and executive branches in policymaking and must avoid injecting their own socio-economic preferences into the judicial process. The second approach maintains that courts are policymakers and, as such, should consciously exercise their judicial power to influence the social system in the interest of justice. The third, while showing far less deference to the legislative and executive wills than the advocates of judicial restraint, holds that constitutional judgments may not be based on the court's sympathy toward litigants or their cause but on fundamental and disinterested principles of law.

These three categories are by no means precise or all-inclusive but serve as a convenient means of grouping the diverse views on the policymaking responsibilities of the judiciary. Any classification will necessarily be arbitrary because the stated positions of lawyers, judges, and legal scholars run a continuum from insistence on virtual withdrawal of the judiciary from the policymaking arena to espousal of almost total involvement in the political struggle. Internal inconsistencies in the arguments of proponents of the various viewpoints add to the difficulty of devising a satisfactory set of categories.

THE DOCTRINE OF RESTRAINT

The classic expression of judicial restraint was made by Justice Oliver Wendell Holmes in reflecting on his constitutional philosophy: "About seventy-five years ago I learned that I was not God. And so, when the people . . . want to do something I can't find anything in the Constitution expressly forbidding them to do, I say, whether I like it or not, Goddammit, let 'em do it!" Holmes' mode of pithy expression has not been emulated by other legal writers, but the philosophy embodied in his remark constitutes the basis for the self-restraint doctrine. Many shades of opinion exist among proponents of this doctrine. One of the most rigid formulations was made by James Bradley Thayer, the dean of legal scholars, at the turn of this century. As he put it, a statute can be declared unconstitutional only "when those who have the right to make laws have not merely made a mistake, but have made a very clear one—so clear that it is not open to rational question." Thirty-five years later, Justice Harlan Stone gave a more carefully phrased enunciation of the doctrine in his reaction to the invalidation of the Agricultural Adjustment Act of 1933 by a Court majority:

The power of courts to declare a statute unconstitutional is subject to two guiding principles of decision which ought never to be absent from judicial consciousness. One is that courts are concerned only with the power to enact statutes, not with their wisdom. The other is that while unconstitutional exercise of power by the executive and legislative branches of the government is subject to judicial restraint, the only check upon our own exercise of power is our own sense of self restraint. For the removal of unwise laws from the statute books, appeal lies not to the courts but to the ballot and to the processes of democratic government.

Justice Felix Frankfurter, the leading spokesman for the self-restraint wing of the "Roosevelt" court, was, like Stone, sensitive to the "undemocratic" aspect of judicial review. He viewed courts, not as representative bodies, but as inherently oligarchical institutions, poorly designed to be a good reflection of a democratic society. He felt, moreover, that they seriously jeopardize their independence when they "become embroiled in the passions of the day and assume primary responsibility in choosing between competing political, economic, and social pressures." Although he was not as emphatic as Thayer, he would "set aside the judgment of those whose duty it is to legislate only if there is no reasonable basis for it." To Frankfurter, judicial self-restraint and judicial power are on opposite sides of the same coin. He believed that the latter may be maintained only by wise use of the former. When the justices cast aside judicial restraint, efforts to weaken the Court inevitably result. Roosevelt's "court-packing" plan, for instance, followed the High Tribunal's initial invalidation of New Deal legislation in the early 1930s.

Judicial restraint manifests itself not only in the explicit refusal of the Court to interfere with decisions made by legislative and administrative agencies, but also in various practices to which it occasionally resorts in order to by-pass the direct issue confronting it. These practices fall into two categories: procedural and substantive. The first relates to the techniques employed by the Court when it wants to avoid dealing with the substantive issues in question. The simple expedient followed here is to deny certiorari (refuse to review the case); or, if an appeal is involved, to hand down a per curiam decision (brief opinion by the Court with no authorship indicated), noting that the appeal is dismissed for "want of jurisdiction" or for "want of a substantial federal question." Since the High Tribunal has almost complete control over its business, it is free to select those issues it desires to consider while side-tracking the others. Thus, in 1943, it avoided a ruling on the constitutionality of the Smith Act pertaining to communist activity by refusing to grant certiorari; and in 1950, it rejected by similar action an opportunity to pass on the legality of segregation in housing built with state aid.

The second category includes the various methods of by-passing an issue by a substantive holding that the matter is not properly one for judicial settlement. Unlike the denial of certiorari in which no reason is given for the refusal, the justices are obliged to give some explanation for their action once a case has been accepted for hearing on its merits. One tactic to avoid ruling on a troublesome issue is to invoke the familiar doctrine of "political questions." This technique was employed in early state legislative reapportionment suits and in cases in which executive action in foreign relations was constitutionally challenged.

Another substantive self-restraint device is called the doctrine of "judicial parsimony." According to this principle, courts may refuse to discuss the validity of a law if the case may be decided on technical grounds or by statutory construction. One of the more notorious examples of this occurred during World War II when the Supreme Court was faced with the constitutionality of regulations aimed at the Japanese-Americans on the West Coast. A defendant who came under this classification was convicted in a federal district court on charges of violating the curfew imposed by the military and of refusing to report to an evacuation center. He was sentenced to three months' imprisonment on each of the two counts, the sentences to run concurrently. The Supreme Court sustained the curfew conviction but refused to examine the more significant question of the validity of the evacuation order, maintaining that regardless of the ruling on this issue, the appellant would still have to serve three months on the curfew conviction.

A current example of the Supreme Court avoiding an issue is the applicability of the "one man — one vote" principle to local legislative bodies. Opportunity to rule on this matter was provided by three suits before the Court during the 1967 term, but in each case the justices evaded the question. When the appointment of a county board of supervisors was challenged, the Court reversed a ruling favorable to the plaintiffs on jurisdictional grounds, maintaining that the convening of a three-man federal district court is not authorized when the constitutionality of a local charter provision, as distinguished from a state statute, is attacked. In another case, the justices reserved the question of whether apportionment of local councils is governed by *Reynolds* v. *Simms* stating that a county board of education (which consisted of representatives of local school boards) is an administrative rather than a legislative body. The third case involved the membership of a municipal council. Here the Court found a disputed residency requirement not fatal to the apportionment plan even "assuming *arguendo* that the one man—one vote principle was applicable."

These various procedural and substantive restraints developed by the Court to guide it in questions of constitutionality were summed up by Justice Louis D. Brandeis in a 1936 opinion.

The Court will not ... decide questions of a constitutional nature unless absolutely necessary to a decision of the case. The Court will not formulate a rule of constitutional law broader than is required by the precise facts to which it is to be applied.

The Court will not pass upon a constitutional question although properly presented by the record, if there is also present some other ground upon which the case may be disposed of.

When the validity of an act of Congress is drawn in question, and even if a serious doubt of constitutionality is raised, it is a cardinal principle that this Court will first ascertain whether a construction of the statute is fairly possible by which the question may be avoided.

As Brandeis stated, the use of these rules enables the Court to avoid judgment on many of the constitutional issues it is asked to decide. The canons are still as relevant today as in the past although they are at times relaxed in civil liberty cases.

ACTIVISM

Unlike the advocates of judicial modesty, the activists view the Court as a dynamic force in resolving current social issues. To the more ardent the High Tribunal is "the American political conscience, a kind of secular papacy, a new search in every generation for what the more larger minded and more farsighted of the Founders might have meant if they were alive." Although there exist as many shades of judicial activism as restraint, adherents to this approach generally agree that the Court must apply stricter tests in examining legislation involving human rights, extend its reach to issues of constitutionality, and deal with the many socially significant questions now avoided by procedural or substantive techniques. Activism on the Court is essential to preserve a Constitution capable of adapting itself to an ever changing society. In short, keeping law abreast of life is as much a judicial as a legislative function.

Judicial activism has not been the exclusive possession of the liberals. In the past, conservative interests warmly applauded the Supreme Court for its intervention in the political order. Activism reached a high stage when the Court struck down the economic and social welfare legislation of the early 1930s in the name of freedom of contract and property rights. Although the judicial activists of that era differed profoundly in their social and political philosophy from those of today, both regarded the Court as the Nation's conscience and believed it should not hesitate to act vigorously to enforce the provisions of the Constitution. In this respect, Willis Van Devanter and George Sutherland, two of the conservative bulwarks of the pre-1937 court, were as much judicial activists as Frank Murphy and Wiley Rutledge, two of the prominent liberals of the "Roosevelt" court. The former lashed out at legislation which they believed threatened the free enterprise system, the latter at governmental action which they saw as a threat to human freedom.

The liberals, who supported greater government intervention in the economic sphere, were the most vocal critics of judicial activism before and during the early days of the New Deal. Many of them argued that judgment of the representative branches of the government may not be thwarted by Platonic guardians who hold life tenure in their public posts and who are not responsible to the electorate in a political sense. Since the late 1930s, however, liberals generally have discarded their opposition to judicial review and have supported more vigorous action by the Court particularly in the field of civil liberties. Thus their criticism of the "Vinson" court for its self-restraint in loyalty issues during the "McCarthy period" was as sharp as their attack on the High Tribunal for its activism in the early 1930s. This apparent change in position has subjected the liberals to charges of inconsistency. Justice Robert Jackson, for example, who frequently joined Frankfurter as a spokesman for judicial moderation, was among those who strongly reacted to their advocacy of activism. In his words, "A cult of libertarian judicial activists now assails the Court almost as bitterly for renouncing power as the earlier 'liberals' once did for assuming too much power."

The actions of the Court itself have come under attack in recent years for what critics say is its illogical posture toward judicial review. Since 1937, the High Tribunal's approach to most constitutional problems of economic regulation and social welfare has been characterized by a self-restraint amounting to almost complete withdrawal. In these fields, it has generally deferred to the legislative and executive branches of both the national and state governments. At the same time, however, it has increasingly reasserted a primacy of power in the protection of civil liberties. This reorientation has prompted one federal district court judge to comment that the dogma of "liberty of contract" developed for the benefit of laissez-faire capitalism has been replaced by a modern version of freedom which is concerned with the privileges of "picketers, prisoners, proselyters . . . and pigmented portions of the population." Indeed, some of the more emotional critics of the Court say that a petitioner must be from among these groups to gain recognition from the justices.

Modern supporters of judicial activism answer the charges of inconsistency in several ways. First, they note that the Court has always focused its attention on the great issues of American society, and today the critical question is not the economy of the Nation but the relationship between a constantly expanding bureaucracy and the individual's human rights. Hence, it is logical for the judiciary to place increased emphasis on this latter aspect of social life. Those who take this position criticize the pre-1937 Court not for intrusion into the economic policymaking sphere, but for the manner of its intervention and its failure to reflect the overwhelming consensus of the Nation at the time.

Second, the judicial liberals distinguish between the right of courts to play a more assertive role in civil liberties issues than in economic matters. A political majority, as they see it, should not be stopped by the judiciary from experimenting with economic arrangements. Mistakes made by government in this realm can always be corrected by future majorities—a statement that cannot be made of civil liberties because the violation of a human right can never be satisfactorily remedied by subsequent action. The careers of some indivduals, for example, were irreparably damaged during the McCarthy era by government loyalty programs which at times blatantly ignored constitutional safeguards. For this reason, majorities must not be permitted under any circumstances to tamper with the basic human freedoms guaranteed by the Nation's charter. These rights occupy a preferred position in the constitutional hierarchy of values.

Justice Stone, although basically predisposed to judicial restraint, was the first member of the Court to suggest the possibility of a preferred position for personal freedoms. In a frequently cited footnote to a case that upheld a statute involving economic regulation, Stone noted that there may be a narrowed scope for the presumption of the constitutionality of laws affecting human rights, particularly those which are necessary to preserve the integrity of a democratic political process. Implicit in his remarks was the belief that the Court must protect the rights of minorities who lack effective means of influencing popularly elected bodies by voting. The freedom of these minorities to become tomorrow's majorities through peaceful persuasion must be carefully guarded. Justice Rutledge later carried the doctrine further when he held that "the usual presumption supporting legislation is balanced by the preferred place given in our scheme to the great, the indispensable democratic freedoms secured by the First Amendment." Some activists would go still further and impose a presumption of unconstitutionality on legislation which restricts these guarantees. As Justice Murphy maintained "Human freedoms are presumed to be invulnerable and any attempt to sweep away these freedoms is prima facie invalid." As expressed by another legal commentator, "The doctrine of presumption of constitutionality should be completely eradicated in cases involving basic liberties. In that area a presumption of unconstitutionality should prevail."

A third argument advanced by those who deny any inconsistency in the Court's posture toward civil, as distinguished from economic, rights rests on purportedly logical grounds. This reasoning begins by differentiating the nature of the constitutional authority involved in the two fields. First, economic regulation is based on the enumerated powers granted to Congress, such as those pertaining to interstate commerce and taxation. These are the powers which the pre-1937 Court most often interpreted. Second, questions of civil liberties involve primarily the Bill of Rights (first ten amendments) which is not a grant of authority but a set of restrictions and prohibitions on the national government and also on the states through the due process clause of the fourteenth amendment as judicially interpreted. The more critical cases which have come before the post-1937 Court relate to this category. Activist proponents claim the distinction enables one to logically oppose judicial interference in the economic realm and support intervention in matters of civil liberties. They reason that judicial acquiescence in the judgment of the other two branches of government is more appropriate when a positive grant of authority is questioned than when an expressed constitutional limitation on their powers is at issue. Thus in the former instance, it is appropriate for the judiciary to act with modesty; but in the latter, it must discard restraint and actively intervene in the political order. This reasoning says nothing about the fact that the literal wording of the due process clause of the fourteenth amendment gives coextensive protection against the states to property rights along with those pertaining to individual liberty. If the logic of the argument seems strained, it is typical of discussions which have characterized much of the debate over judicial policymaking.

NEUTRALISM

At an indeterminate point between judicial activism and judicial passivism is a formulation of the Court's role known as "neutralism." The doctrine has generated considerable debate among legal scholars in recent years, yet it is difficult to describe precisely because of the ambiguous terms in which it is couched. Its proponents are activists and stalwart traditionalists simultaneously. They criticize judicial modesty for discouraging interference in the political order when constitutional principles are violated. Conversely, they say the courts must not overturn the value choices of the other branches of government unless intervention is based on reasons which in their "generality and neutrality transcend any immediate result that is involved." As a leading proponent of this approach has said, "Courts have the duty when a case is before them to review actions of the other branches in the light of constitutional provisions even though the action involves value choices. In doing so, however, they are bound to function otherwise than as a naked power organ; they participate as courts."[1] According to this formulation, it is essential to distinguish between legislative freedom to appraise gains and losses in projected measures of public policy and between the judicial appraisal of emergent policy in the light of constitutional principles. Presumably by recognizing and adhering to this distinction, a political system may achieve a middle ground "between a judicial House of Lords and the abandonment of any limitation on the other branches—a middle ground consisting of judicial action that embodies what are the main qualities of law, its generality and neutrality."[2]

The question arises: what is meant by "neutrality." Unfortunately, the proponents of this position do not define the term operationally.[3] Like Humpty Dumpty in *Through the Looking Glass*, they say, "When I use a word, it means just what I choose it to mean—neither more nor less." The most definite statement offered thus far is that neutral principles are standards which transcend the present case. In other words, the Court must be prepared to apply these principles in all instances uncompromisingly and with reference to the full impact of the decision upon future cases of conflicting values. This means, for example, that in ruling that the practice of racial segregation in public education is unlawful, the justices must be willing to apply the same principle to discrimination in all public facilities. If they are unwilling to do so, the principle cannot be called neutral or general. The position of the neutralists here is not unlike that of the activists, since the latter strongly urge the Court to discard the policy of case-to-case adjudication normally followed and instead to enunciate broad principles beyond the immediate controversy.

Critics of this sweeping approach note that a political system must determine some matters based on specific decisions which cannot project a straight line to the future. Courts are parts of this system and must be careful not to foreclose the consideration of future distinctions, because situations which seem the same today may appear otherwise later. From this standpoint, the doctrine that constitutional matters not be decided until their resolution is necessary to the immediate case has considerable merit and utility. Anticipating the inevitable collision of important values too far beyond the case under adjudication may preclude action altogether on the case at hand. *Shelley* v. *Kraemer*, which barred the legal enforcement of restrictive racial covenants in real estate deeds, is a case in point. If the justices had been concerned with how far the decision carried them—that is, whether all private contracts which are enforced in the courts would be subject to the rule—agreement on the opinion might never have been reached.

The formulation of the neutralists appears very similar to the older, but largely discredited, doctrine which views the courts as impartial discoverers and appliers of fundamental law. Unlike contemporary social scientists, who regard the judiciary as an integral part of the political system, the neutralists reassert the traditional theory that law is something apart and above the clash of politics. This posture, in a sense, rules out the issue of judicial activism versus judicial restraint. For if the Court is an impartial discoverer and applier of fundamental law, it has no alternative morally but to act against the other organs of government when principles of justice and equity are violated. The neutralist position implies that whereas the judiciary cannot avoid involvement in the active solution of societal problems which reach the litigation stage, it must present carefully formulated principles to support the choice it decrees. The question is no longer whether the Court should act in the political order but what rationale is legally and logically most satisfactory for its actions. The latter point is important because the tribunal's ability to influence the course of the Nation's life depends on its maintaining a public image of authority and impartiality. This image is enhanced to the degree that it is believed that the Court reaches its judgments by the application of fundamental and timeless principles of law.

Notes

[1]Herbert Wechsler, "Toward Neutral Principles of Constitutional Law," *Harvard Law Review,* 73 (November, 1959), 15.

[2]*Ibid.*

[3]The ambiguity of the doctrine is stressed in Benjamin F. Wright, "The Supreme Court Cannot Be Neutral," *Texas Law Review,* 40 (May, 1962), 599-618.

The Supreme Court as a Unit of Government

Robert H. Jackson (1892-1954) rose from a modest up-state New York background to hold a succession of important positions during the Roosevelt Administration culminating in his appointment to the Supreme Court in 1941. After World War II he was named chief American prosecutor at the controversial Nuremberg war crimes trials and was absent from the Court for 18 months. On his return he found the Court involved with the difficult problem of weighing the freedom of the individual to promote his political beliefs with the need to maintain a stable order in society under the rule of law. Jackson expressed the opinion that if democracy is to flourish in this country, over the long-term, the Supreme Court must defer to the judgment of the elective branches on matters of public policy. A primary purpose of the Court is to insure that the government does not abuse this trust. The Court's strength, according to Jackson, does not lie in its aggressive "activism," rather it is a product of the exercise of "self-restraint." In the essay that follows Jackson notes the philosophical base on which the Court was established and how the Court functions today as an actor in the general political system.

Robert H. Jackson

No sound assessment of our Supreme Court can treat it as an isolated, self-sustaining, or self-sufficient institution. It is a unit of a complex, interdependent scheme of government from which it cannot be severed. Nor can it be regarded merely as another law court. The Court's place in the combination was determined by principles drawn from a philosophy broader than mere law.

Our foundations were quarried not only from the legal ideas but also from the political, social, philosophical, scientific, and theological learnings of the eighteenth century, "the silver age of the Renaissance." All these were dominated by a belief in "the laws of nature and of nature's God." Faith in a "higher law," which had achieved a venerable place in the history of ideas through the speculations of jurists, monks, and scholars,

Reprinted by permission of the publishers from Robert H. Jackson, *The Supreme Court in the American System of Government.* Cambridge, Mass.: Harvard University Press, Copyright, 1955, by William Eldred Jackson and G. Bowdoin Craighill, Jr., Executors. Abridged by the editors.

burst forth toward the end of the eighteenth century into a fanatical creed that took over French and American liberal thinking and led in each case to a violent revolution.

Our judicial, executive, and legislative branches all were grounded in a belief that they were bound by the authority of a clear and universally acceptable natural law, revealed by man's reason and always and everywhere the same. Its fundamentals were proclaimed self-evident truths, as indisputable as the axioms of geometry, which needed only to be declared to be acknowledged as right and just by the opinion of mankind. These truths of natural law to that age stood as the ultimate sanction of liberty and justice, equality and toleration. The whole constitutional philosophy of the time was based on a system of values in which the highest was the freedom of the individual from interference by officialdom—the rights of man. To supplement this natural order, little man-made government was thought to be needed, and the less the better.

To make certain that these natural rights should have some man-made sanctions, the forefathers added ten Amendments to the original instrument, translating their version of the rights of man into legal limitations on the new government. They did not stop, as the French did, at reciting these in a preamble to the Constitution, where they served as an admonition only to a parliament that was all-powerful because there could be no judicial review of its legislation. On the contrary, the forefathers established a Bill of Rights which conferred as a matter of law, enforceable in court, certain immunities and rights upon citizens which correspondingly limited the power of the majority duly expressed through governmental action. The whole spirit of this was to make secure the liberties which were what men in that age most wanted of the law. I find little indication that they foresaw a technique by which those liberties might be used to destroy themselves by immunizing a movement of a minority to impose upon the country an incompatible scheme of values which did not include political and civil liberties. The resort to that technique in this country, however fruitless, contemporaneously with the collapse or capture of free governments abroad, has stirred American anxieties deeply.

What we face today on an intellectual level is the climax of a long-gathering conflict between opposite poles of thought. Our traditional high valuation of individual liberty conflicts with the totalitarians' higher valuation of group interest within the state. Communism, Naziism, and Fascism have each made phenomenally successful drives to capture the minds and loyalties of numerous aspiring peoples for this philosophy so antithetic to our own.

It is not possible to detail all of the American trends which, rightly or wrongly, have cooled the zeal of our own people for the principles on which our government was founded. Our own indifference, deviations, and dissatisfactions are largely the reason why our principles make so anemic and sterile an appearance in the world-wide struggle for the minds of men. The majestic phrases of the forefathers, even as they were penned, were being drained of their fervor. Men were already ceasing to ask "What must I do to be saved?" and were asking "What can I do to become rich, powerful and honored?"

As men's minds turned more to material advancement, and the industrial revolution introduced new means both to satisfy and to stimulate the acquisitive instincts, a riotous competition was touched off for the spoils of the world and for exploitation of working and consuming masses. The inherently obscure and oracular character of natural law led courts to respond to the pressure of the times by making it a sanction for *laissez faire;* and skeptics, historians, and jurists joined in discrediting it. The nineteenth century closed with Americans repeating the phrases of the Declaration of Independence about the laws of nature and of nature's God, but the real attitude was that attributed by Knickerbocker to the Connecticut Yankees, who resolved to be governed by the laws of God—until they found time to make better ones. The so-called positivists took over, and any command that some authority had physical power to enforce became law. Since the Nürnberg postmortem on the Hitler regime, few will believe that these positivist doctrines are weapons in the struggle to preserve liberty.

Meanwhile, Marx and Engels, two strangers to the actual workings of our American system, had formulated the revolutionary scheme of values which under new leadership is now our world-wide rival. Their doctrine teaches that there is no such thing as natural law or impartial justice, that the law is and should be the weapon of the class in power and administered in its interests, that law rests on the authority of force and not on any inherent rightfulness, that the object of its protection is the dominant group rather than the individual, and that it should not be administered by neutral judges but by class-conscious and class-serving judges. The Communists reject our claims to liberty as abstract intellectualism, if not hypocrisy, and claim that our free government is a sham to conceal economic exploitation of the most numerous class—the proletariat—which should be aroused to support the Communists in containment of our system and its eventual overthrow.

Our forefathers' conception of a liberal legal order had been the dynamic ideology of most of the nineteenth century. But the twentieth century has seen the depressed masses in nearly all backward countries abandon it as their hope and turn to a militant Communism radiating from the Soviet Union, which Clement Attlee once described as merely "an inverted czardom." It dawns upon us that we are in an age of almost worldwide reaction, indeed, of counterrevolution, against the teachings and philosophy of our American Revolution and our Constitution. Revolutions in our time, whether by Communists, Fascists, or Nazis, have not pretended to overthrow or moderate the power of the state over the individual, but, instead, have each aspired to concentrate in the state a more absolute power over every activity of life and leave nothing but tatters of the "rights of man." Paradoxical as it may seem, we are in an age of rebellion against liberty. The rise of this new doctrine has brought about one of the most bloody and cruel half-centuries in the annals of mankind, one which has put to death or enslaved more people solely because of racial or national origin and political or economic views or status than ever before in history. This violence that civilization has experienced was not a repetition of physical overthrow from barbarians without. Civilization is still threatened by forces generated within and perhaps by itself.

Fortunately, up to now America has escaped any catastrophic impact from this turn of events. With few exceptions these revolutionary ideas have made their appeal to those we have long deemed backward peoples. The old and the new did not confront each other in our country with such provocative contrasts as in some other lands. We entered each of the great wars late, and while our collective resources were strained, they were not exhausted. Individual living standards were depressed, but not to the point of misery. It is true that we have suffered some intellectual demoralization, which has proceeded far — to the point where speculative freedom is regarded as the equivalent of revolutionary action. But intolerance, suspicion, and hatred still resort only to verbal and legalistic weapons and have not sunk to a regime of physical violence.

Nevertheless, it would have been too much to expect that the American mind would be wholly free from the influence of counterrevolutionary currents of thought which have captivated other peoples or that each of the ideologies which have divided the rest of the world would not find some followers and sympathizers here. Unfortunately, liberal-minded citizens have sometimes become entangled with Communist teachings, while many conservative citizens have reacted by favoring some form of "strong" government controlled by themselves—the reaction which elsewhere brought about Naziism and Fascism. It is time that we reëxamine the strength and defects of our own system, for we cannot longer regard the worldwide revolt against its animating principles as a local or passing flash in the pan. The fact is that we face a rival, secularized system of faith and order spread with a religious fervor not witnessed since the tides of Islamic fanaticism receded. We are brought into sudden and bitter competition with a whole new concept of the nature and use of social and political organization, a rivalry for which we are prepared intellectually even less than militarily.

Against this background a study of the Supreme Court can hardly fail to be instructive. First, the Court is distinctively a product of our founders' philosophy in some of its most important functions, and no counterpart has existed or can exist in those areas of the world which have traded individual liberty for totalitarianism. Second, this Court, structurally and functionally, has survived an attempt by President Roosevelt to reorganize it so as to eliminate a "judicial activism" which was impairing a program supported by large popular majorities. Third, soon thereafter the Court passed, by the process of mortality and replacement, almost entirely into the hands of those who were its former critics, and they have now had over a decade of its control. Fourth, not one of the basic power conflicts which precipitated the Roosevelt struggle against the judiciary has been eliminated or settled, and the old conflict between the branches of the Government remains, ready to break out again whenever the provocation becomes sufficient.

We ought first to inquire what kind of institution the Supreme Court really is, the degree of its independence, the nature of its power, and the limitations on its capacity and effectiveness. In the second lecture we will consider it as a conventional law court administering the usual civil and criminal justice. Lastly, we will consider the Court as a political institution arbitrating the allocation of powers between different branches of the Federal Government, between state and nation, between state and state, and between majority government and minority rights.

The Supreme Court of the United States was created in a different manner from most high courts. In Europe, most judiciaries evolved as subordinates to the King, who delegated to them some of his functions. For example, while the English judges have developed a remarkably independent status, they still retain the formal status of Crown servants. But here, the Supreme Court and the other branches of the Federal Government came into existence at the same time and by the same act of creation. "We the People of the United States" deemed an independent Court equally as essential as a Congress or an Executive, especially, I suppose, to "establish Justice, insure domestic Tranquility," and to "secure the Blessings of Liberty to ourselves and to our Posterity." The status of the Court as a unit of the Government, not as an institution subordinate to it, no doubt has given it prestige, for the people do not regard the Justices as employees of the Government of the day or as civil servants, as in continental Europe. Also, federal judges enjoy two bulwarks of independence — life tenure (except for impeachable misbehavior) and irreducible salaries (except by taxation and inflation).

Nonetheless, the Constitution-makers left the Court in vital respects a dependent body. The political branches nominate and confirm the Justices, a control of the Court's composition which results in a somewhat lagging political influence over its trend of decision, and any party that prevails in the Federal Government through several presidential terms will gradually tend to impress its political philosophy on the Court. The political branches also from time to time may alter the number of Justices, and that power was used to influence the course of decision several times before it was again proposed by President Roosevelt.

The Court also is dependent on the political branches for its powers in other vital respects. Its only irrevocable jurisdiction is original, and that reaches only cases affecting Ambassadors, public Ministers, or Consuls, or cases in which a state is a party. In all other cases it has appellate jurisdiction, but "with such exceptions and under such regulations as Congress shall make." One Congress, fearing a decision unfavorable to its post-Civil War enactments, ousted the court of jurisdiction in a case that had already been argued, and the Court submitted. The Court also is dependent upon the political branches for the execution of its mandates, for it has no physical force at its command. The story is traditional that President Jackson once withheld enforcement, saying, "John Marshall has made his decision:—*now let him enforce it!*" Also, the Court, of course, depends upon Congress for the appropriation of funds with which to operate. These all add up to a fairly formidable political power over the Supreme Court, if there were a disposition to exert it.

But perhaps the most significant and least comprehended limitation upon the judicial power is that this power extends only to cases and controversies. We know that this restriction was deliberate, for it was proposed in the Convention that the Supreme Court be made part of a Council of Revision with a kind of veto power, and this was rejected.

The result of the limitation is that the Court's only power is to decide lawsuits between adversary litigants with real interests at stake, and its only method of proceeding is by the conventional judicial, as distinguished from legislative or administrative, process. This precludes the rendering of advisory opinions even at the request of the nation's President and every form of pronouncement on abstract, contingent, or hypothetical issues. It prevents acceptance for judicial settlement of issues in which the interests and questions involved are political in character. It also precludes imposition on federal constitutional courts of nonjudicial duties. Recent trends to empower judges to grant or deny wiretapping rights to a prosecutor or to approve a waiver of prosecution in order to force a witness to give self-incriminating testimony raise interesting and dubious questions. A federal court can perform but one function—that of deciding litigations —and can proceed in no manner except by the judicial process.

In his pioneering studies, Judge Cardozo demonstrated that this is not the rigid and inflexible process some of our ancestors thought it to be. But its inherent methods make it unfit for solving some kinds of problems which elements of our society have from time to time expected the Supreme Court to settle.

While the President or the Congress can take up any subject at any time, a court in our Anglo-American system is a substantially passive instrument, to be moved only by the initiative of litigants. The Supreme Court cannot take most cases until at least one and generally two courts below have heard and decided them, which, with the present congestion of calendars, may be very long indeed. Also, as an appellate court, it properly can act only on the state of facts revealed by the record made in the court below, supplemented sometimes by general information of which it may take judicial notice. Hence a claim of right may be prejudiced by the incompetence, carelessness, or collusion of attorneys, as where they fail to make an adequate record to support the question sought to be raised. The decision of a case also may depend on its peculiarities of fact, for it is still true that hard cases make bad law. And when it is all over, the judicial decree, however broadly worded, actually binds, in most instances, only the parties to the case. As to others, it is merely a weather vane showing which way the judicial wind is blowing — a precedent that the Court in a similar case is likely to follow. Its real weight in subsequent cases, however, will depend on many factors, such as the quality of the prevailing opinion, the strength of any dissent, the acceptance or criticism by the profession, and the experience in application of the rule. Thus, the process of the courts is adapted to the intensive examination of particular legal grievances.

No conclusion as to what can be expected of the Court is valid which overlooks the measure of its incapacity to entertain and decide cases under its traditional working methods. With few exceptions, Congress has found it necessary to make review in the Supreme Court not the right of a litigant but a discretionary matter with the Court itself, in order to keep the volume of its business within its capacity. Last term, review was sought by appeal and certiorari in 1,452 cases, only 119 of which were allowed. It is not necessary to detail the considerations which move the Court to grant review beyond saying that the grant is not intended merely to give a litigant another chance, nor does it depend on the dollars involved or the private interests affected, but upon the importance of the case to a uniform and just system of federal law.

The routine during the Court term has been to hear arguments the first five days of each two weeks, followed by two weeks of recess for the writing of opinions and the study of the appeals and certiorari petitions, which must be disposed of periodically. The time allowed for each side to argue its case is normally one hour, and, in cases where the question seems not complex, it is half of that. In the early days of the Supreme Court, the volume of work permitted argument to extend over several days, as it still does in the House of Lords. Many cases argued before us today in two hours have taken days, weeks, and even months in the trial court or administrative body.

What really matters to the lawyer and the law is what happens between the argument and the decision. On each Saturday following argument or preceding a decision Monday, the Court holds its only regularly scheduled conference. It begins at 11 a.m. and rarely ends before 5:30 p.m. With a half-hour for lunch, this gives about 360 minutes in which to complete final consideration of forthcoming opinions, the noting of probable jurisdiction of appeals, the disposition of petitions for certiorari, petitions for rehearing and miscellaneous matters, and the decision of argued cases. The largest conference list during the October 1953 term contained 145 items, the shortest 24, the average 70. A little computation will show that the average list would permit, at the average conference, an average of five minutes of deliberation per item, or about 33 seconds of discussion per item by each of the nine Justices, assuming, of course, that each is an average Justice who does the average amount of talking.

All that saves the Court from being hopelessly bogged down is that many of these items are so frivolous on mere inspection that no one finds them worthy of discussion, and they are disposed of by unanimous consent. Even eliminating these, the time devoted at conference to argued cases is inadequate for detailed deliberation and results, more or less, in a canvass of impressions with the understanding that a vote on any case is tentative and on later consideration may be changed. And not infrequently the detailed study required to write an opinion, or the persuasiveness of an opinion or dissent, will lead to a change of a vote or even to a change of result. If there is further conferring, it is unofficial, usually between two or more Justices of like mind in the particular case.

The pressure of time may induce an attitude that discussion in conference is futile and thereby contributes to the multiplicity of individual opinions. It is often easier to write out one's own view than for nine men in such short time to explore their doubts and difficulties together, or to reach a reconciliation of viewpoints. The fact is that the Court functions less as one deliberative body than as nine, each Justice working largely in isolation except as he chooses to seek consultation with others. These working methods tend to cultivate a highly individualistic rather than a group viewpoint.

The individual study which any case receives before or after argument is the affair of each Justice. All receive the printed briefs and record, in some cases short, in others running to a great many volumes. Some records take five feet of shelf space. It is easily demonstrated that no Justice possibly could read more than a fraction of the printed matter filed with the Court each year. Nor is it necessary that he should. But as to his individual labors, with this mountain of papers, each Justice is the keeper of his own conscience.

In argued cases, conferences are followed by the preparation and circulation of opinions by Justices designated by the Chief Justice when he is with the prevailing view and, if not, by the senior Associate who is. But any Justice is free to write as he will, and there may be one or more opinions concurring in the result but reaching it by different reasons, and there may be a dissenting opinion or opinions. This occasions complaint by laymen and the bar that they are required to piece all these contributions together in order to make out where the Supreme Court really stands as an institution.

All of this is at odds with the practice of most courts of continental Europe, which make it a rule to announce the decision in one statement only and to issue no dissents or concurrences. Moreover, their work is institutionalized and depersonalized. The court's opinion bears the name of no author. Like our *per curiam* opinion, it may be the work of any member or of several in collaboration. This anonymity diminishes any temptation to exploit differences within the court, but it may also diminish the incentive for hard work on opinions. In any event, I am sure that not only Anglo-American tradition but judicial and professional opinion favors the identification of writers and the full disclosure of important differences within the Court. Mr. Jefferson would have required each Justice to write his reason in every case, as proof that he gave it consideration and did not merely follow a leader.

The dissenting opinion strives to undermine the Court's reasoning and discredit its result. At its best, the dissent, as Mr. Hughes said, is "an appeal to the brooding spirit of the law, to the intelligence of a future day. . . ." But Judge Cardozo has written:

". . . Comparatively speaking at least, the dissenter is irresponsible. The spokesman of the court is cautious, timid, fearful of the vivid word, the heightened phrase. He dreams of an unworthy brood of scions, the spawn of careless *dicta*, disowned by the *ratio decidendi*, to which all legitimate offspring must be able to trace their lineage. The result is to cramp and paralyze. One fears to say anything when the peril of misunderstanding puts a warning finger to the lips. Not so, however, the dissenter. . . . For the moment, he is the gladiator making a last stand against the lions. The poor man must be forgiven a freedom of expression, tinged at rare moments with a touch of bitterness, which magnanimity as well as caution would reject for one triumphant."

Dissent has a popular appeal, for it is an underdog judge pleading for an underdog litigant. Of course, one party or the other must always be underdog in a lawsuit, the purpose of which really is to determine which one it shall be. But the tradition of great dissents built around such names as Holmes, Brandeis, Cardozo, and Stone is not due to the frequency or multiplicity of their dissents, but to their quality and the importance of the few cases in which they carried their disagreement beyond the conference table. Also, quite contrary to the popular notion, relatively few of all the dissents recorded in the Supreme Court have later become law, although some of these are of great importance.

There has been much undiscriminating eulogy of dissenting opinions. It is said they clarify the issues. Often they do the exact opposite. The technique of the dissenter often is to exaggerate the holding of the Court beyond the meaning of the majority and then to blast away at the excess. So the poor lawyer with a similar case does not know whether the majority opinion meant what it seemed to say or what the minority said it meant. Then, too, dissenters frequently force the majority to take positions more extreme than was originally intended. The classic example is the *Dred Scott Case,* in which Chief Justice Taney's extreme statements were absent in his original draft and were inserted only after Mr. Justice McLean, then a more than passive candidate for the presidency, raised the issue in dissent.

The *right of dissent* is a valuable one. Wisely used on well-chosen occasions, it has been of great service to the profession and to the law. But there is nothing good, for either the Court or the dissenter, in dissenting per se. Each dissenting opinion is a confession of failure to convince the writer's colleagues, and the true test of a judge is his influence in leading, not in opposing, his court.

If the Supreme Court were any kind of institution except a court, it would be easy to suggest methods by which it could dispose of an increased volume of work. The objection to most such proposals is that they are incompatible with the personal and individual responsibility inherent in judicial office.

It has been suggested that a small committee of the Court could pass on certiorari applications. Some lawyers believe that this is done. That is not true. The Supreme Court does not function on any case by committee. Every qualified Justice acts on every petition expressly or by acquiescence.

It is often suggested that the Court could create a staff of assistants like those of administrative tribunals to take much of the drudgery of judicial work from the Justices. In fact, a suspicion has grown at the bar that the law clerks already constitute a kind of junior court which decides the fate of certiorari petitions. This idea of the law clerks' influence gave rise to a lawyer's waggish statement that the Senate no longer need bother about confirmation of Justices but ought to confirm the appointment of law clerks. Twice during the last term I was asked by prominent lawyers, once by letter and once orally, how they could get their petitions for certiorari past law clerks and to the consideration of the Justices themselves. The answer is that every petition is on the conference list, and its fate is decided by the vote or agreement without formal vote of every Justice who does not disqualify himself.

The extent and methods of utilizing law clerks' services naturally differ with the individual Justices. The law clerks regard themselves and are regarded not as aides to the Court, but as aides to the particular Justice who selects them. What a Justice delegates to his clerk will depend on the Justice's temperament and experience, but it is he who is responsible for his contribution to the Court's work. For myself, I believe that a court is one place where counsel should confront and address the very men who are to decide his case. I do not think judging can be a staff job, and I deplore whatever tendency there may be in the courts to make it such.

There have been suggestions that an increased work capacity could be obtained by enlarging the Court, which might then sit in sections or chambers as do some administrative bodies in this country and many courts abroad. The French Cour de Cassation and the Soviet Supreme Court both consist of sixty to seventy members who function, in fact, as several courts, each dealing with a specialized type of litigation; as, for example, commercial cases, other civil cases, criminal cases, military appeals, cases involving officials of the government, and admiralty cases. But our Constitution vests the judicial power in only "one supreme Court," and it has been the view of high authority that this precludes the Court from being split into chambers or sections; also, there has never been either political or professional sentiment in this country in favor of such a Supreme Court, and it would face very practical difficulties even if it were permissible under the Constitution.

The only way found practicable or acceptable in this country for keeping the volume of cases within the capacity of a court of last resort is to allow the intermediate courts of appeal finally to settle all cases that are of consequence only to parties. This reserves to the court of last resort only questions on which lower courts are in conflict or those of general importance to the law.

From what I have said it might almost be assumed that the Supreme Court could be ignored in the power equation of the American Government. But in living history this institution has profoundly influenced, for better or for worse, the course of the nation. Not only has it been the center of bitter debate itself, but its decisions have played some part in nearly every great political issue that has vexed our people.

What authority does the Court possess which generates this influence? The answer is its power to hold unconstitutional and judicially unenforceable an act of the President, of Congress, or of a constituent state of the Federation. That power is not expressly granted or hinted at in the Article defining judicial power, but rests on logical implication. It is an incident of jurisdiction to determine what really is the law governing a particular case or controversy. In the hierarchy of legal values, if the higher law of the Constitution prohibits what the lower law of the legislature attempts, the latter is a nullity; otherwise, the Constitution would exist only at the option of Congress. Thus it comes about that in a private litigation the Court may decide a question of power that will be of great moment to the nation or to a state.

The assertion of this power over the enactments of the states met with strong resistance, and its application to laws of Congress provoked bitter and persistent opposition. It is needless to trace the evolution of the power as now exercised. The Rooseveltian struggle with the Court did not impair the power, which is as positively asserted today as in pre-Roosevelt days. But neither did that struggle end the controversy over the proper use of the power, a controversy which lies just beneath the surface and is likely to break forth from time to time as long as the Republic shall last.

Public opinion, however, seems always to sustain the power of the Court, even against attack by popular executives and even though the public more than once has repudiated particular decisions. It is inescapable in our form of government that authority exist somewhere to interpret an instrument which sets up our whole structure and defines the powers of the Federal Government in about 4,000 words, to which a century and a half have added only about half as many amendatory words. The people have seemed to feel that the Supreme Court, whatever its defects, is still the most detached, dispassionate, and trustworthy custodian that our system affords for the translation of abstract into concrete constitutional commands.

The Constitution has gone through several cycles of interpretation, each of which is related to the political and economic condition of the period. Federal powers were consolidated and invigorated under Marshall. A reaction marked by conflict over the very nature and binding force of the compact embittered the time of Taney. There followed a period when attention turned to nationalism and to railroad building and industrial growth stimulated by a long period of almost uninterrupted peace. That came to an end in 1914, and we entered the period of international violence which now burdens and vexes us and puts our internal liberties under new strains.

That the Supreme Court, in some instances, can interpose judicial authority between political forces and those whose liberty they would override is a great distinction from those governments abroad which have been subverted by dictatorship. But I have tried to point out that while our judiciary is an effective instrument for applying to the case of an individual the just laws enacted by representatives of a freedom-respecting society, it has grave jurisdictional, procedural, and political shortcomings. These counsel against leaving the protection of liberty wholly to the judiciary, while heedlessly allowing the elected branches of the Government to be constituted without regard to their members' attitudes toward liberty.

Let us take the factor of delay. Since the Court may pronounce a judgment of unconstitutionality only in deciding a case or controversy, obviously it cannot take the initiative in checking what the Justices may know to be constitutional violations. It has no self-starting capacity and must await the action of some litigant so aggrieved as to have a justiciable case. Also, its pronouncement must await the decision in the lower courts. Often it is years after a statute is put on the books and begins to take effect before a decision on a constitutional question can be heard by the Supreme Court. The Smith Act of 1940 was held constitutional for the first time in 1951, and the Alien Registration Act, also of 1940, was passed on in 1952. The run of constitutional litigation, like that of all litigations, is slow and costly.

Such delays often mean that the damage is done before the remedy for invasion of civil liberties is available. For example: In 1951 the Court cast serious doubt upon the legality of the Attorney General's list of subversive organizations promulgated in 1947. But the list had long been widely circulated and accepted, and despite the Court's views it has never ceased to be used in the press, in the executive department, by and before congressional committees, and even in courts to prejudice individuals in their liberty, position, and good name.

Then, too, many of the most vital acts of government cannot be challenged at all by the case and controversy route, because the questions are political or involve the spending power, foreign affairs, or the war power. The Supreme Court is a tribunal of limited jurisdiction, narrow processes, and small capacity for handling mass litigation; it has no force to coerce obedience, and is subject to being stripped of jurisdiction or smothered with additional Justices any time such a disposition exists and is supported strongly enough by public opinion. I think the Court can never quite escape consciousness of its own infirmities, a psychology which may explain its apparent yielding to expediency, especially during war time.

If I may borrow a summation from my former self, I will repeat to you the conclusion of a lecture to the lawyers of the Ministry of Justice of France, delivered at their invitation in April 1946, when they were in the throes of writing a new constitution for France. After discussing the judicial vis-à-vis the political power in our system, I said:

"Opinion, of course, will differ as to the advantages and disadvantages of this constitutional and judicial system. The United States on the whole has been a prosperous country, with varied resources, making a favorable background for any experiment in government. Its inhabitants have not faced the strains that beset some less-favored nations. Even so, our history has not been free of sanguinary internal conflicts. It would not be realistic to contend that judicial power always has been used wisely. The Court has been sharply attacked by Presidents Jefferson, Jackson, Lincoln, and both Roosevelts. Yet no substantial sentiment exists for any curtailment of the Court's powers. Even President Roosevelt in the bitterest conflict with judicial power in our history suggested only change in the Court's composition, none in its constitutional prerogatives. The real strength of the position of the Court is probably in its indispensability to government under a written Constitution. It is difficult to see how the provisions of a 150-year-old written document can have much vitality if there is not some permanent institution to translate them into current commands and to see to their contemporary application. Courts will differ from time to time in the emphasis they will place on one or another of the Constitution's provisions, in part no doubt responsive to the atmosphere of the changes in public opinion. Interpretations will change from one generation to another, precedents will sometimes be overruled, innovations will be made that will not always be predictable. This always has been the history of the Supreme Court.

"The legal profession in all countries knows that there are only two real choices of government open to a people. It may be governed by law or it may be governed by the will of one or of a group of men. Law, as the expression of the ultimate will and wisdom of a people, has so far proven the safest guardian of liberty yet devised. I think our constitutional and judicial system has made a valuable and enduring contribution to the science of government under law. We commend it to your notice, not because we think it is perfect, but because it is an earnest effort to fulfill those aspirations for freedom and the general welfare which are a common heritage of your people and of mine."

The Court and Decision-Making

Interest in the Supreme Court extends well beyond the legal fraternity and constitutional scholars. Today members of many disciplines are using their respective intellectual tools in an attempt to better understand the behavior of the Court. Of particular interest to many scholars is the process whereby the Court reaches a decision. Samuel Krislov, in the following excerpt from his book, The Supreme Court in the Political Process, *seeks to view the Court as a small group which has established for itself forms of behavior designed to insure that the goals of the organization are achieved.*

Samuel Krislov

Perhaps the most striking fact about the Court is that its proceedings are almost completely collegial. There are no committees and no delegation of powers except for certain relatively minor responsibilities which each justice has for his own circuit. (In general, these are merely provisional powers.) It seems doubtful that a committee system could ever be established; in the course of the fight over the presidential "Court packing plan" of 1937, Chief Justice Hughes suggested in a letter than any action by a part of the Court would not meet the constitutional requirement of there being "one supreme Court." While this letter was purely informal, the reasoning behind it has not been seriously challenged, although of course there has been no occasion to do so.

The fact that all members participate in every single decision of the Court means that the time given to consideration of most matters must necessarily be short. In the early years the judges had little protection from unwarranted pleas; today of course they have considerable control of what comes before them.

Nonetheless, as Henry Hart has shown in an engaging discussion of Court work load, the justices must make about 8,000 decisions in a single conference or about one every four minutes. Further, he shows that if a judge spends an average of only five minutes on trivial applications for a writ and twenty minutes on more significant application, leaving two

Reprinted with permission of the Macmillan Company from *The Supreme Court in the Political Process* by Samuel Krislov, pages 59-68, copyright © by The Free Press, a Division of Macmillan Company, 1968.

hours for major cases including those in which he writes opinions, he will be fully occupied during an eight-hour, six-day week.[1] The Court, therefore, is always seeking more efficient methods of using each justice's time, preserving as much time for careful discussion as possible.

One such method is an increased utilization of law clerks. Today each justice is entitled to two clerks (Douglas chooses to have only one), and the Chief Justice three. The standard practice is for these to be chosen from recent honors graduates of top law schools, who serve as a clerk for one or a few years. Many of them, like Justice White, have themselves ultimately become judges. In recent years there has been some controversy over the alleged influence of these clerks. But the use of some staff seems unavoidable and the method appears well calculated to provide assistance of the highest quality. The short term of each clerk suggests the minimization of staff influence rather the opposite.

The first step in the decision process is for the judges to decide what cases they are going to hear. In the early stages of a decision the proceedings move on paper. Each justice has his own method of dealing with written briefs. Some attempt to master the great bulk of the written material themselves; others use their law clerks. They may devote a uniform amount of time to all cases or merely peruse those which are indicated to be of minor concern. In this regard the Chief Justice's action in preparing and sending out the "miscellaneous" docket — a title indicating relative triviality — is taken as a signal for a justice merely to skim through the case to see that his impression coincides with the judgment of the Chief Justice.

The Chief Justice can have great influence in the organization of the work. There are many things that he does automatically in his role as presiding officer over the Court to afford him initative that can be translated into effective power. These are minor matters of initiating and controlling the flow of cases. They do not guarantee that the Chief Justice will be the leader; they merely afford him a slight advantage. While many Chief Justices have controlled the Court — Marshall and Hughes — others have been ineffectual. In our own times Stone was unable to control the outpouring of personal bitterness and strong dissent on the Court. Some Chief Justices have been effective merely as presiding officers, while still other figures on the Court were regarded as the strong leaders on the bench as well. For example, Fuller was overshadowed by several members of the Court, though preserving the affection and respect of all and was regarded by Holmes as the best presiding officer he had known.

But the relationship is always a product of the respect held for the Chief as a personality rather than for the power of his office. When a messenger indicated to McReynolds that Chief Justice Hughes wished him to come to the conference, McReynolds curtly suggested the messenger inform the Chief Justice he, McReynolds, did not work for Hughes. In his handling of men, cases, the work load, and even the priority of items, the Chief Justice can sometimes but not always set a tone of harmony, conflict, leisure, or tautness.

The rules and traditions of the Court provide exact guidance for many if not most contingencies. Briefs are filed by the attorneys in prescribed manners and at prescribed times, with detailed regulations even as to the printing and style of the material in the briefs. The members of the Court then move to their first crucial question: deciding whether to decide. If the case comes up on certiorari, the Court must deny or grant the request for the writ; if the case is technically considered "on appeal," oral argument must be approved or dispensed with.

The heart of the Court process is the Friday conference, which begins at 11:00 A.M. and proceeds indefinitely, sometimes spilling over into Saturday. Each justice shakes hands around the table at the beginning of the conference — 36 operations in all. To assure secrecy, no outsider is ever allowed in the room during conference, and the junior justice in terms of length of service acts as messenger. Following a long tradition in such collegial bodies, the senior judge has the right to discuss cases first, while voting proceeds from the junior judge up. Since the voting pattern is pretty well deducible from the discussion, little advantage is gained by any justice through the voting arrangements, but it is obvious that such slight advantage as occurs inheres in seniority.

The Chief Justice presides over the conference and has the initial responsibility for classification of matters either as worthy of serious scrutiny or as relatively frivolous. A strong Chief like Charles Evans Hughes can use his power to summarize a case and pose solutions. If he is well informed and respected, his solutions may well control the discussion, whether it be on the jurisdictional question or on the merits of the controversy.

If the conference results in a decision to deal with the case further, the briefs are supplemented by oral argument. Cases are docketed—that is, listed on a calendar—and are normally reached in a few months, but sometimes even more than a year later. Oral argument has become increasingly less florid and dramatic and also less influential in recent years. The Court has severely limited the time allotted to the attorneys; Chief Justice Hughes is said to have cut off a counsel whose time had expired in the middle of a one-syllable word. The Court neither expects nor welcomes elaborate oratory, and the justices feel free to interrupt the argument in order to bring up points they wish clarified, usually within the attorney's time. Some clues to the final vote can often be deduced from the questioning, but it is also true that a justice may seek out an answer to a point that will help in developing his position rather than to embarrass the lawyer by presenting him with thorny problems. It is often difficult to ascertain which role the justice is playing, and erroneous conclusions are sometimes reached from the courtroom questioning.

After the oral argument a conference discussion takes place again, but now on the merits of the case rather than on the question of whether to spend more time on it. Again the Chief Justice has the initial advantage in suggesting disposition of the matter. Nevertheless, the fuller and freer discussion that usually takes place at this point, allows other members of the Court to assert their leadership. Thus Justice Black tended to set the tone of the majority of the court in the late years of the Stone tenure as Chief Justice, since Stone himself was out of step with the philosophy of most of his "wild horses."

The Chief Justice has one additional card up his sleeve — the power to assign opinions for the side he votes with in conference. If he should be in minority, then the senior justice assigns the opinion of the Court. Careful selection of the opinion writer can be influential in determining outcomes; a Chief Justice may choose to emphasize unity by selecting a moderate or to firmly establish a principle by entrusting a stalwart with the responsibility. There is even a patronage element to opinion assignment. Tradition, for example, allows a new justice to select his first important opinion wherever possible. In this way Chief Justice Hughes helped gain the continuing affection of Justice Black, whose membership in the Ku Klux Klan had been given nationwide publicity, by facilitating his announcement of a pro-civil rights decision soon after Black came to the Court.

Murphy has suggested that the Chief Justice is even in a position to moderate a majority he disagrees with by voting with them if he cannot prevent their success. Since he knows the outcome when he votes, he might well feel the assignment of a proper spokesman the most important result that could be retrieved from a bad situation.[2]

But there are limits to the internal politics of assignment, in that a Chief must bear in mind the law specialties of the justices, their relative ability to handle and write opinions for a heavy load of cases, and the realities of external politics as well. Justice Reed, for example, handled Commerce Clause cases, and Douglas taxation matters. Van Devanter had great difficulty in completing even a moderate number of assignments, while Holmes was, and Douglas is, a facile writer. One of the most interesting examples of case assignment showed the effects of external politics. This occurred when Reed, a border state Democrat of impeccable credentials, was, at Jackson's suggestion, substituted as Court spokesman in *Smith* v. *Allwright* (outlawing the white primary system) in place of Frankfurter, a Massachusetts Republican and himself a member of a minority group.

INTERRELATIONS ON THE BENCH

Apparently the Chief Justice and senior justices do assign opinions to achieve certain results. Evidence seems to vindicate the impression that Hughes gave himself or Roberts, the other swing man on the Court in the 1930s, major assignments in order to maximize the appearance of unity on a badly divided Court. Black, as senior justice for a minority position on many issues, tends to choose writers with a strong and unequivocal view. Warren has used both strategies. Danelski has sought to demonstrate that which seems obvious but which is in fact difficult to prove—that assignments are based also upon the Chief Justice's perception of the ability of a particular judge. Danelski's method of demonstration — the number of cases written by justices that are subsequently cited in the law books, correlated with the perceptions of the Chief Justices deducted from their memoirs and correspondence as to the ability of their associates — is subject to the criticism of circularity; the results may merely indicate that the perceptions of the Chief Justices were in fact quite correct and that good men turn routine cases into important ones which are cited in the future.

Nominally only the result in a case is presumed to be binding and a future precedent ("stare decisis"). In fact, however, the wording of an opinion is scrutinized very closely, the arguments evaluated, and the cues thus culled incorporated in the trends of later decisions by both attorneys and lower court judges. Walter Murphy has demonstrated this rather neatly[3] by studying an extreme example, the Japanese Exclusion Cases. *Korematsu* has been cited quite frequently through the years but hardly for its concrete result — the internment of an entire minority group — but rather for its somewhat disingenuous verbal assurances that racial categories "are immediately suspect." This statement—technically dictum, or mere verbiage, obviously opposite in its intent to the overt result effected by the decision — is the real heritage of that case.

Since wording constitutes in all instances a major component of any judicial policy, great care is exercised in writing opinions, and considerable bargaining goes on behind the scenes over the final product. The justice chosen to write the opinion is therefore in a strategic position; it is this that makes his choice significant. The opinion writer often balances the marginal utility of possible additional votes and further assent by other justices against the price of changes in the opinion and alteration of wording needed in order to secure such adherence. An opinion may be broad or narrow, technical or sweeping, emphatic or tentative. Any number of statutory or constitutional provisions or judicial doctrines may be used. All of this is subject to negotiation.

This process of setting forth approaches and arriving not only at the disposition of the case but the actual wording in the opinion — analogous to the function of drafting of statutes in the legislative process — requires a high order of skill. Because of the publicity value of individual dissent and the advantage of coherency and internal logic that single opinions at least theoretically can have, it might well be that even the legal public overvalues opinion writing in the collegial Court and fails to appreciate the behind-the-scenes contribution of the justice who devotes himself to institutional needs rather than solo performance. The reputation of Justice Van Devanter, for example, has risen in recent years as memoirs and letters of his colleagues begin to suggest an influence barely discernible from the outside of the Court.

This process of internal bargaining is intensely personal and depends not merely on legal prowess but upon all of the facilities of human interaction, including gregariousness and personal attractiveness. Even friendship plays an important role in shaping attitudes although the opposite is probably even truer — that common attitudes help to develop friendships. Social relationships have indeed had great influence; Brandeis seemingly altered Holmes's civil liberties stand, while Stone, who initially was close to Taft and his cohorts, was drawn socially and later ideologically to Holmes and Brandeis. Like attitudes, however, are not a guarantee of mutual respect and friendship. Rutledge embraced Stone's commerce views and was reasonably close though "more liberal" on most other matters, yet Stone regarded him as a "weak sister."

Danelski and Murphy have attempted to analyze further the dynamics of personal relations on the Court in terms of the Bales-Slater notions of leadership.[4] Bales and Slater, social psychologists studying small groups, had earlier suggested two types of leaderships: "task" leadership — leadership in the achievement of group goals—and "affect" leadership — leadership in the maintenance of group cohesiveness through good social relations and the definition of moral standards of the group. They found in their study of young children organized in small groups that it was rare for these two types of function to be in the hands of a single person. Broader organizational and societal studies have also suggested that these two dimensions are usually separate. Indeed, some studies have intriguingly suggested that attempts by social-moral leaders to influence practical policies usually cause a loss of their effectiveness.

Much the same thing, Danelski and Murphy suggest, exists on the Court. The Chief Justice normally has an opportunity to establish both types of leadership, at least indirectly. If he succeeds, like Marshall and Hughes, his influence can be pervasive. If he is a social leader and can work effectively with his task leader, as Taft did with Van Devanter, the Court may be harmonious and effective. Rivalry with potential task leaders — for example, Stone with Black and with Frankfurter — is disruptive.

Eloise Snyder has also given us a fascinating picture of the dynamics of small-group interaction on the Court. Though there are, as with most studies, problems with some of her methods and data, the general picture seems to conform with our knowledge of the Court. She suggests that most incoming justices spend a term or two marking time in a relatively neutral manner, poised above internal disagreements, absorbing information; finally the justices make a commitment on the basic issues that divide the Court. Once that commitment is made, the justices show great stability in their positions on the broad issues. There seems to be independent if imprecise information in the "gossip" literature on the Court to suggest that ideological and social commitments tend to be made together and to remain largely stable.[5] (However the experience of Justices Brennan and Goldberg, who instantly identified their positions suggests that in a highly structured situation affiliation might take place sooner.)

That the justices recognize the importance of their social relationships is suggested by the resignations of Clarke, generally attributed to unpleasantness with McReynolds, and Curtis, expressly with the conduct of Chief Justice Taney in the Dred Scott case. By covertly altering the printed opinion to exclude statements made in the announcement of the decision which Curtis had criticized in his dissent Taney lost the confidence of the associate justice. Similarly, when Mr. Justice McLean dissented in open court without giving prior notice, in violation of regular practice, he created animosity that interfered with Court effectiveness for quite a period of time. A good method of promoting task effectiveness is to create social cohesion within the working group. Marshall was the most successful exponent of this method. In more recent years, Taft held informal Saturday evening gatherings to supplement the natural affinity of a crew of men so many of whom he had appointed or sponsored. Murphy calls this the development of a "rump" Court, completely devoid of any "task" elements, at least on the surface. The Taft Saturday evenings were avowedly aimed at controlling the Court.

The division of the Court into such "rumps" or blocs — whether merely voting coalitions or enforced by personal solidarity as well — is an important factor in Court decisions. Similar points of view in a small group are mutually reenforcing and disagreement painful. Some justices have been noted for their persistently individualistic view of legal matters; others conform more easily. A division of opinion in the Court, usually fairly predictable and along fairly stable lines, creates the framework in which issues are discussed and joined.

If the same group of like-minded justices consistently prevails in the majority, the opponents in minority must shape their strategy to "appeal to the bar of history," expecting to prevail at some future time. If the minority drops below four, it ceases to have any force in consideration of a case on certiorari and thus loses footing. If a minority is large enough, on the other hand, it may hope to gain further adherents.

In the more usual situation of no fixed majority coalition, numerous patterns can prevail. Two writers, Shapley and Shubik, have introduced a "power index" to measure the effects of such combinations.[6] The index is built on the notion that the person who casts the deciding vote can be said to have had the power of decision. On the Supreme Court this would be the person who casts the fifth vote, assuming all participate. Normally, we do not know who was actually the pivotal fifth voter, so Shapley and Shubik suggest we assign the likelihood to the participants in the majority. This would mean, for example, that if six men voted for a decision, each majority justice would be credited one sixth of the pivotal power — the probability of his having cast the fifth vote. If we know the pattern of the division of votes, we can also figure out in advance the probable share of pivotal power held by each voting group. The voting pattern possibilities on the Court are relatively limited; some of them are indicated below, together with the expected power of each.

Division on the Court	Share of Power of Voting Groups
4,4,1	.33, .33, .33
3,3,3	.33, .33, .33
4,3,2	.33, .33, .33
4,3,1,1	.500, .167, .167, .167
4,2,2,1	.500, .167, .167, .167
4,2,1,1,1	.600, .100, .100, .100, .100
3,2,2,2	.500, .167, .167, .167, .167

It can be seen that power is not strictly proportional to voting strength. Rather, it is determined by the total pattern of division. One man in a four-to-four situation has the power of a group of four— or of any three in three-three-three division. Groups gain rapidly in power by coalition. A two-man group would have one fourth of the total power in the Court rather than an expected two ninths. A five-man group always voting together would, of course, have not five ninths but nine ninths of the power; even a four-man coalition in an otherwise completely divided Court would have two thirds of the power and would be pivotal in a large number of situations.

It seems likely that Supreme Court blocs with four or five members find it desirable to maintain the coalition and that, working within limits imposed by their judicial obligations, they make concessions designed to maintain agreement. In a group of more than five the impetus to accommodation probably diminishes. As a minority grows smaller than four or five and thus becomes less likely to serve as the nucleus for a majority, the inclination toward personal expression becomes greater than the motivation to work out joint positions.

Notes

[1] Henry Hart, Jr., "The Time Chart of the Justices," 73 *Harvard Law Review* (1959), pp. 84-101. For some skeptical appraisals see Thurmond Arnold, "Professor Hart's Theology," 73 *Harvard Law Review* (1960), p. 1,298.

[2] Walter Murphy, "Marshalling the Court: Leadership, Bargaining, and the Judicial Process," *University of Chicago Law Review* (1960), pp. 640-72, esp. p. 664.

[3] Walter Murphy, "Civil Liberties and the Japanese-American Cases: A Study in the Uses of Stare Decisis," 11 *Western Political Quarterly* (1958), p. 3.

[4] Walter Murphy, "Marshalling the Court: Leadership, Bargaining, and the Judicial Process," *University of Chicago Law Review* (1960); David Danelski, "The Influence of the Chief Justice in the Decisional Process of the Supreme Court," unpublished paper given at the American Political Science Meeting, September 1960.

[5] Eloise Snyder, "The Supreme Court as a Small Group," 36 *Social Forces* (1958), pp. 232-38.

[6] L. S. Shapley and M. Shubik, "A Method for Evaluating the Distribution of Power in a Committee System," 48 *American Political Science Review* (1954), p. 787.

Chief Justice Taft and Judicial Administration

Walter F. Murphy

Chief Justice William Howard Taft (1857-1930) is generally pictured as a jovial man of more than average weight. He was also an inveterate politician with strong views on questions of public policy and judicial administration. The essay by Walter Murphy discusses Taft in his role as administrator of a highly fragmented judicial system. Fortunately for us, Taft was also a diligent and candid letter writer and his correspondence has provided us with a wealth of insight into the workings of the Court. The Supreme Court is frequently viewed as an institution apart from the political process. It dispenses justice and wisdom undefiled by the mundane realities of political life. The degree to which this mechanistic view is erroneous is made evident in this essay. By the same token, it is not warranted to go to the other extreme, as some "legal realists" have, and say that justice is whatever the judge had for breakfast that morning. Juristic theory and the role of stare decisis *are still important elements in any explanation of American jurisprudence. Taft is remembered not so much for the cogency of his opinions as for his role as law reformer and judicial administrator. He campaigned vigorously and publicly for passage of the Judiciary Act of 1925 which permitted the Court to gain control over its agenda and hence prepared the way for the Court to deal with the complex problems of the coming decades.*

One of the most important but least discussed limitations on Supreme Court power is that imposed by the "bureaucracy" of the lower courts. Except in rare disputes the Supreme Court does not render either the initial or the final decision in a case. The Justices typically formulate general policy, leaving specific application to judges of inferior state and Federal courts. Lower court judges have different backgrounds, ambitions, loyalties, and perspectives than do Supreme Court Justices. Furthermore, legal technicalities and the often necessarily broad nature of Supreme Court mandates combine to allow these judges a degree of

Reprinted by permission of the author and publisher from Walter F. Murphy, "Chief Justice Taft and the Lower Court Bureaucracy: A Study in Judicial Administration," *Journal of Politics,* 24 (August 1962), 453-476. Abridged by the Editors.

discretion sufficient to modify policies apparently approved by the High Bench.[1]

A politically sophisticated Justice who wishes to see a particular controversial doctrine become accepted as "ruling law" must come to grips with this bureaucratic check. The purpose of this paper is to suggest, through an analysis of the efforts of Chief Justice William Howard Taft to bring about smoother relations within the judicial system, some of the means which a Justice can employ to lessen friction with lower court judges.

DIPLOMACY IN ADMINISTRATION

"I am the head of the judicial branch of Government," Taft said when he became Chief Justice, and from his own unhappy experiences as head of another branch of government he had learned the dangers of an unruly bureaucracy. Accordingly, one of the first tasks which he saw confronting him was the neutralization of this hazard in the court system. He told his brother that he was going to try to "come into touch with the Federal Judges of the country, so that we may feel more allegiance to a team and do more teamwork."[2] Teamwork became the Chief Justice's favorite slogan, and he immediately translated the slogan into action by sending a cordial personal letter to every district judge asking for suggestions on needed reforms in court procedure. He also wrote to every senior circuit judge requesting advice and information on problems with overcrowded dockets. "I am very anxious," Taft told his fellow judges, "to introduce teamwork among the Federal Judges of the country, and I call on you to help me in this matter." Every reply was carefully and promptly acknowledged and individual suggestions were frequently discussed.

Taft was also solicitous of the state bench. He wrote to the Chief Justice of each state, noting that he had instructed the clerk to send to every state supreme court the opinions of the U.S. Supreme Court. In return, he requested that the reports of state decisions be fowarded to Washington. "I feel," Taft explained, "as if the Judges in the Courts of last resort in this country should be brought more closely together, and that [an exchange of opinions] would facilitate a mutual understanding."

Federal and state judges were undoubtedly flattered to have the Chief Justice of the United States seek their advice. One incident which occurred in 1921, though probably intended by Taft as nothing more than an act of personal kindness as well as administrative efficiency, must certainly have increased this rapport, at least among judges who knew what the Chief Justice was trying to do. Judge Walter I. Smith of the Eighth Circuit, whom Taft had appointed to the bench, had been stricken with paralysis in 1916 and despite his attempts to continue work had been almost completely unable to discharge his duties. Unfortunately, Smith was only sixty years old, ten years too young to retire with pay. The Chief Justice, however, took the matter up with some of his friends in Congress and secured Senate passage of a special act allowing the judge to resign and still receive full retirement benefits. The House Judiciary Committee—again at Taft's urging — favorably reported the measure, but Smith died before the House could act.

These early moves were most diplomatic and helped create an atmosphere conducive to closer cooperation among judges; but the Chief Justice wanted a degree of teamwork which demanded central control. And central control was precisely what was lacking in the judicial system. Congress, as Frankfurter and Landis commented, "had created a hierarchy of courts, not of judges."[3] There was no agency or person to whom a Federal judge had to answer for delays in deciding cases. Nor did the Chief Justice possess plenary authority to assign judges with light caseloads to temporary duty in districts which were heavily overburdened. Temporary assignment was possible, but generally speaking only within and not across circuit lines.

By 1921 there was urgent need for Federal judicial reform. To recommend legislation to meet this situation, Harry Daugherty, Harding's Attorney General, established a special committee composed of three Federal judges and two United States Attorneys. The committee's work was completed at about the same time that Taft was appointed to the bench, and Daugherty asked the Chief Justice's assistance. Always willing to advise, Taft agreed and met in mid-July in Washington with the Attorney General and the committee members. Later in the month Daugherty sent Taft a copy of the committee's final report as well as drafts of bills designed to carry out its recommendations.

The report made three specific suggestions. The first was that Congress create in each of the nine numbered circuits a district judge "at large," who could be assigned to trouble spots within the circuit by the senior circuit judge, or anywhere in the country by the Chief Justice if his services were not needed at the time within the circuit. Second, the committee proposed establishment of a judicial conference composed of the Chief Justice, the Attorney General, and the senior circuit judge from each circuit. At its annual meeting the conference would try to solve the more pressing problems of judicial administration, and would also have the duty of recommending any needed legislation to Congress. The third committee suggestion was that the Chief Justice be given broader authority to assign district judges across circuit lines.

Daugherty asked the Chief Justice to comment on the report and to "draw up a tentative bill" for a judicial conference. The Chief Justice replied that he had found the committee's report "admirable," and had only a few changes to offer. The major one was that there be a provision for two district judges at large in each circuit rather than only one — a total of eighteen, rather than nine new judges. Taft said that he had talked to Senator Frank Kellogg about this increase and that Kellogg had thought that the chances of passage were excellent.

As for the judicial conference proposal, Taft had no basic criticism of the draft which Daugherty had sent him. He did, however, suggest inclusion of a section requiring each district judge to file annually with his senior circuit judge a report of the business disposed of and that still remaining on the docket of his court.

Daugherty answered that he had very carefully considered doubling the request for new judges, but was afraid that an increase would not be accepted by Congress. He promised, however, to talk it over with members of the special committee. The Attorney General was apparently convinced, for when he forwarded the committee's report to the Chairman of the House Judiciary Committee on August 18, 1921 (the report was back-dated to July 21, 1921), it recommended eighteen judges-at-large.

On August 22, Daugherty sent the Chief Justice a copy of two bills embodying the committee's report. Taft was delighted to see the bills in shape, but he could not pass up the opportunity to offer the Attorney General some practical political advice: "I hope you will smooth the passage . . . by seeing the two Democratic leaders and intimating to them that in the Southern Circuits you can give them one Democrat in each Circuit. . . ."

Not content with merely working behind the scenes, the Chief Justice began to beat the bushes to build up interest in and support for the reform measures. In August he addressed the Judicial Section of the American Bar Association and praised the pending legislation as introducing into the judicial system "an executive principle to secure effective teamwork." Later in the fall he testified at length in favor of the bills before both the Senate and House Judiciary Committees; then in December he spoke in defense of the proposals to the Chicago

Bar Association. In February, 1922, he made a similar speech to the New York County Lawyers Association, and another to the American Bar Association the following August, just as the measures were entering the final stage of the legislative process.

Prodded by Taft and the Harding Administration, and perhaps also by anticipation of new patronage, Congress reacted favorably to the suggestion of additional judges and administrative reform, though this reaction was effected neither with particular speed nor with any marked degree of unanimity. The House Judiciary Committee consolidated and amended the proposals drafted by the Attorney General's committee, and this bill, H. R. 9103, passed the House in December, 1921. The Senate approved its own and somewhat different version the following April; and it took two separate conference committees over four months to iron out these differences. The bill did not become law until September 14, 1922.

The final statute differed in several important respects from the report of the Attorney General's committee. The idea of "judges-at-large" threatened to upset established patronage arrangements. The provision for these "carpet bag judges," as Representative Stevenson of South Carolina called them, was eliminated in the House Committee, and no real effort was made to reinstate it on the floor either in the House or Senate. Instead, both houses agreed—after considerable bargaining—to the creation of twenty-four additional but regular district judgeships.

Nor did the idea of a judicial conference appeal to all legislators as a salutary device. Echoing similar arguments voiced in the House, Senator Shields of Tennessee protested that such a meeting would make the Chief Justice the political head of the Federal court system and establish him as "Commander in Chief" of the judiciary. Despite such objections — whose validity Taft officially denied —both houses approved the judicial conference proposal.

The provision granting the Chief Justice broad authority to assign district judges to temporary duty had an even rougher road. It passed the House over the same sort of argument made against judges-at-large and the judicial conference, but it was stricken in the Senate Judiciary Committee. The Committee, however, later reversed itself and restored the provision subject to two specific limitations. The senior circuit judge of the circuit which had requested the additional judge had to sign a certificate of need, and the senior circuit judge of the circuit in which the judge was permanently assigned had to consent to the temporary transfer.

While this statute increased the Chief Justice's control over the judicial system, he was still by no means a commander-in-chief of Federal judges. The Conference of Senior Circuit Judges was an important step toward real coordination of court administration, but it provided an instrument of persuasion rather than of command. Although Federal judges probably gained a more acute sense of belonging to a group of professional men who shared common responsibility and common problems, their courts remained largely independent.

The Chief Justice understood the close limits of his new authority. In answer to a complaint from the Chairman of the National Committee on Law Enforcement that Federal judges in Arizona were less than diligent in some phases of their work, Taft promised to write to the judges. But, he added, "the fate of a Chief Justice in attempting to make District and Circuit Judges do what they are not disposed to do is a difficult one." In 1927 Taft wrote to a district judge in Oregon to urge him to decide a certain patent case which had been argued some four years earlier. "Of course," the Chief Justice candidly admitted, "I write this letter with no assumption that I may exercise direct authority over you in the discharge of your duties, but as the head of the Federal Judiciary I feel I do have to appeal to you, in its interest and in the interest of the public whom it is created to serve, to end this indefinite situation."

JUDICIAL APPOINTMENTS

Being able to choose the team is one of the most obvious ways of promoting teamwork. Taft had a running start in this regard since, when President, he had appointed almost 30 per cent of Federal judges, and a large number of these men were still on the bench. Keeping the bench staffed with "sound" judges was more difficult, since judicial participation in the politics of appointment raises serious problems, both ethical and practical. The Chief Justice easily shrugged off any ethical doubts. "I presume," he told a friend, "I have a legitimate right to possess the President of such information as I think useful, if he desires to receive it."[4] Soon Taft would forget his qualification and would be pressing recommendations when he knew the President did not care to receive them.

The practical problems presented more complex obstacles. Nevertheless, when he first took over the chief justiceship, Taft apparently had real influence with the Harding Administration. In the summer of 1921, shortly after his appointment to the bench, Taft told an old classmate that he thought he had "established a very pleasant relationship with the Attorney General and with the President. The Attorney General assures me that he expects to talk with me all the time about the selection of Judges, and I am very sure of what he says. . . ." The Chief Justice was soon writing Daugherty on a "Dear Harry" basis, as he literally bombarded the Executive Department with suggestions for court appointments.

Before making his recommendations Taft often solicited the advice of lawyers, politicians, newspapermen, family, and friends. While his own candidates did not always get the nomination, he was usually able to block appointment of people to whom he objected. The Chief Justice ascribed his success more to Daugherty than to Harding. Even when the scandals in the Justice and Interior Departments were being exposed, Taft defended the Attorney General because "he has stood up in the matter of Judges and their appointment . . . against the vicious system of Senatorial selection of candidates for political purposes. . . ."

Inevitably, the Chief Justice's standards differed from those of Senators, and the President had to choose between the two. Furthermore, as Taft himself realized, his persistence in injecting himself into the appointing process (often without invitation despite the original understanding with Daugherty) irritated the President. This irritation was undoubtedly aggravated by newspaper reports that Harding had delegated authority to select judges to the Chief Justice. "I think," Taft fretted in early 1923, that the President "has grown a little sensitive about the constant reports that the matter is in a way delegated to me."

During Harding's last months in office, Taft was aware that his influence was waning and when Coolidge became President Taft tried to reestablish his influence. He went to Harding's funeral with Coolidge, and on the funeral train he discussed an appointment problem with the new Chief Executive. After returning to Washington the Chief Justice called on Coolidge at his hotel to complete the conversation. "I hope," Taft wrote the President a few days later, "that you will permit me to write you on questions of this sort, where I may have any means of information, because of my intense interest in securing a good judiciary, and my earnest desire to help you in your manifold labors when I can be of assistance in a field like this one."

Coolidge did not reply to this letter, but in answer to another note, the President apologized for his oversight. "When your notes come to me, sometimes I put them aside in my desk for my private information, so that I am afraid they do not get the proper acknowledgement. You will know, of course, that they are all the more welcome for being of that nature."

TWO CASE STUDIES

Two case studies can illustrate the role Taft attempted to play in the appointing process. One of these cases involved both the Hoover and Coolidge Administrations, the other only that of Coolidge. While it is impossible to characterize either as typical of the appointing process itself, each is quite typical of the sort of activity in which Taft was constantly engaged.

The Problem in St. Louis

The Judiciary Act of 1922 established a new district judgeship in St. Louis and the filling of this vacancy created a thorny problem. Senator Selden P. Spencer, Republican from Missouri, began to push as his candidate a state circuit judge named Vital Garesche. Taft, however, distrusted Garesche. Moreover, he had his own candidate for the position: he had promised President Lowell of Harvard that he would support George Hitchcock. "I am not infrequently consulted," Taft had written, "and if I am, I can put in a very strong word for him, as I shall be delighted to do."

When the Chief Justice heard of Spencer's candidate, he took immediate action. On January 6, 1923 he sent Harding a letter warning him that there was a complex piece of bankruptcy litigation pending in St. Louis and that the next district judge would have to appoint a receiver who would handle very large sums of money. "I have observed," Taft cautioned, "great activity on the part of men, who are interested in that litigation, to secure Garesche's appointment." The Chief Justice enclosed a clipping from the *St. Louis Star* and communications from several people in St. Louis, including a letter from U.S. Circuit Judge William S. Kenyon, who stated that Garesche was "a political judge, he is a man who uses his influence on the Bench to secure support, and he is a man to punish his enemies." Taft ended his own letter with an apology for intrusion into the affairs of the Executive Department: "Of course, you have more evidence on the subject than I have, but I venture to think that some people tell me more frankly the situation than perhaps they do you, and I have thought it my duty to bring this matter to your attention."

Two weeks later the Chief Justice wrote a similar though shorter letter to the Attorney General. For some reason, perhaps Taft's intervention, Spencer's pressure was checked; but when Harding died the vacancy was still unfilled.

Spencer lost no time with the new President. He went on the funeral train with Coolidge and re-opened the possibility of an appointment for Garesche. Unfortunately for Spencer, Taft was riding on the same car, and he took Coolidge aside and stated his case against Spencer's man. It was to press his argument against Garesche that Taft visited Coolidge at the Willard Hotel on their return to Washington. When the interview was over the Chief Justice was certain that Garesche would not get the nomination.

Spencer, however, was busily claiming that Garesche would be the new Federal judge; and Casper Yost, editor of the *St. Louis Globe-Democrat*, wrote Taft a worried letter on September 15, 1923. In his reply the Chief Justice tried to reassure Yost by giving a full account of his conversations with the President. Taft also noted with approval that Yost had personally written Coolidge: "I think the more people that you send him to protest against the appointment, with a full explanation of the character of the candidate, the better it will be."

Meanwhile, Taft had written a number of his other friends about Garesche, and he forwarded their replies to Warren F. Martin, Special Assistant to the Attorney General. But the Chief Justice knew that to attack Garesche was not sufficient. He had to press his own candidate. He had already spoken to Coolidge about Hitchcock, and on October 6, 1923 he forwarded the President an endorsement of Hitchcock by Federal

Judge Walter Sanborn of the Eighth Circuit, whom Taft described as "the Senior Circuit Judge of the country, and one of the best Judges we have had."

There the matter stood for another three weeks. Then Daugherty got in touch with Taft to ask his views on a man named Hogan. Taft, in turn, wrote to Yost and to U.S. District Judge Charles B. Faris requesting advice about the new candidate. Yost quickly replied that, in his opinion, Hogan was "morally better than Garesche [but] he is even less competent." Yost also reported that he had heard that Spencer was saying that Hitchcock was "personally offensive." Since this objection from a member of the President's party would block senatorial confirmation, it made, if true, any additional efforts to secure Hitchcock's nomination futile. As other possibilities, Yost included the names of four local lawyers, Davis, Grimm, Hamilton, and Hill, whom he thought highly qualified for the judgeship.

The Chief Justice told Yost that he had sent this information "to a place where it would do the most good," probably to the Attorney General, for on the same day Taft gave Daugherty some confidential material on Hogan, concluding that "he is even worse than Garesche." Taft also included some comments about three "good" candidates, Davis, Hamilton, and Grimm. Taft must have had some source of information other than Yost about these lawyers because on the day before he received Yost's comments on them he had written to Yost, to Judge Faris, and to T. J. Akins, also of St. Louis, asking their opinions of the three men. A short time thereafter, Taft corresponded with former Governor Herbert S. Hadley — who had been one of Roosevelt's floor managers at the 1912 Convention and was now Chancellor of Washington University at St. Louis — regarding Hitchcock and the four Yost had mentioned.

On November 16, Taft wrote again to Faris and Yost and told them of a conversation he had just had with the Attorney General. It now seemed that the President would appoint neither Garesche nor Hitchcock. Daugherty had mentioned as a fresh possibility Forrest Donnell, who had been Spencer's partner. The closeness of this relationship worried the Chief Justice. Yost, however, was most reassuring, stating that Donnell had "a reputation for integrity and ability. . . . I do not believe that Donnell could be used by Spencer or any one else."

In spite of Taft's frequent statements that he was certain the President would not name Garesche, the Chief Justice kept reminding Coolidge of Garesche's lack of fitness. In November Taft sent the President an editorial from the *St. Louis Post-Dispatch* attacking Spencer's candidate, and in December the Chief Justice forwarded a letter which Harding had written explaining why he had decided against Garesche.

Just after Christmas, Congressman C. A. Newton of Missouri confided to Taft that Senator Spencer had "stated that he can not agree to the appointment of any man whose name has been mentioned because he wants the man who gets the appointment to feel that he owes the appointment to him. . . ." Taft could only answer stoically: "there is nothing left for me to do now but to wait and pray." In the privacy of his family, the Chief Justice was less restrained. He exploded to Horace Taft that Spencer was "full of pious unction, unscrupulous, a liar, immoral . . . but earnest and desperate in demanding the appointment of a United States Judge whom he can control in St. Louis. . . ." Drawing on his own unhappy experiences in the White House, Taft added despondently that "every President finds it necessary, to accomplish the greater thing, to yield to the blackmailing of unscrupulous Senators."

The Chief Justice was overly pessimistic. Judicial virtue was not to be trampled underfoot, at least not in this instance. Spencer could block Hitchcock's appointment, but he was not able to get Garesche nominated. Instead, Charles Davis, a state circuit judge and one of the men Yost had suggested as highly qualified, became the compromise appointee.

Eastern District of North Carolina

In 1924-25 Taft played an even more positive part in selecting a new judge for the Eastern District of North Carolina. The incumbent, H. G. Connor, planned to retire in 1925; and in late 1924 Colonel Isaac M. Meekins, then counsel for the Alien Property Custodian and a former U.S. Attorney in the Taft Administration, wrote the Chief Justice to request his assistance in securing the appointment. Taft remembered — or at least was reminded by Charles D. Hilles, his former White House Secretary who was now Chairman of the Finance Committee of the Republican National Committee — that at the 1912 Republican Convention, Meekins had been one of the uninstructed delegates whom the Roosevelt forces had tried to capture. Meekins, however, had stood firmly for Taft despite all sorts of promises and threats.

As did every vacancy on the Federal bench, this one caused a scramble, but here the Justice Department had a freer hand since neither North Carolina Senator was a Republican. As Meekins visualized the situation, there were three candidates besides himself: George E. Butler, a local attorney; H. F. Seawell, former U.S. Attorney; and I. B. Tucker, the current U.S. Attorney. The Colonel sent Taft a concise evaluation of each of his rivals. Seawell was a populist; Butler had been a Roosevelt supporter; and Tucker was sound, but lacked experience.

The Chief Justice quickly endorsed Meekins. He wrote Attorney General Stone on November 23, 1924: "My own judgment about North Carolina is that the best man to appoint is Colonel Meekins." A week later Taft reported to Meekins that he had talked with the Attorney General twice about the appointment and there did not appear to be too much agitation. The Chief Justice also stated that he had contacted Hilles "and asked him to write the President. . . . I am going to see the President tomorrow morning, and shall talk with him about it."

On the same day that Taft reported to Meekins, Hilles told the Chief Justice that a letter from George Wickersham, who had been Taft's Attorney General during Meekins' tenure as U.S. Attorney, would help, and suggested that Taft arrange this. Hilles also said that he had been in touch with Congressman Bertrand Snell, Chairman of the House Rules Committee and an Amherst classmate of Harlan Stone. "I think," Hilles wrote, "that Snell will help us."

Back in North Carolina, U.S. Attorney Tucker was shaping up as the most formidable opponent. Assistant U.S. Attorney General Rush Holland was backing Tucker, as were state circuit judge Henry Grady and several influential political leaders including North Carolina National Republican Committeeman John J. Parker — though Meekins had obtained a statement from Parker expressing no objection to his candidacy.

Judge Grady and Sophia Burber, who had been Judge Connor's private secretary for twenty-one years, each wrote Taft endorsing Tucker's candidacy and asking the Chief Justice's assistance. Taft candidly replied to both that he had already recommended Meekins. To Grady the Chief Justice added the righteous reminder that "these appointments are made by the President and recommended by the Attorney General. I can only indicate my judgment when called upon."

After finishing this letter to Grady, the Chief Justice dictated another to George Wickersham asking him to write Coolidge in support of Meekins. A few days later, Taft, at Meekins' request, called Warren F. Martin and got him to arrange a meeting between the candidate and Senator F. M. Simmons of North Carolina. The Chief Justice also told Meekins to go see Wickersham so that the former Attorney General might refresh his memory and compose a stronger letter to the President. Meekins and Wickersham had their conference, and Wickersham sent a laudatory endorsement to Coolidge.

Around New Year's, Taft again saw Stone about the appointment and put the Attorney General in touch with Wickersham, who straightened out several questions about Meekins' service during the Taft Administration. In early January, 1925, Meekins was nominated for the judgeship, and, with the endorsement of North Carolina's Senator Lee Overman, was swiftly confirmed by the Senate.

On December 7, 1924, *The Charlotte Observer* had carried a page one story that Taft was trying to get Meekins appointed. After the nomination was announced, H. F. Seawell wrote to the Chief Justice taking him to task for his opposition, and asking if Taft would oppose him again in the future. Taft answered that Seawell was mistaken. He had not opposed anyone in North Carolina; he had simply supported the man whom he had thought best for the job. If another vacancy occurred, the Chief Justice promised, "you could become a candidate without any adverse recommendations from me, should I be consulted...."

TAFT, COOLIDGE, AND HOOVER

As with the Harding Administration, Taft's influence with Coolidge did not remain at a high level. In March, 1925, the Chief Justice complained to his son, Robert, that "the President thinks that I am too insistent of having good men and not sufficiently sympathetic with his trials with Senators, and I am going to keep out of judicial selections hereafter." In 1926, he told Hilles that he had not been consulted about a vacancy on the district bench in Georgia: "this present Administration makes its selection in a very curious way, and I have very little to do with it."

Taft's activity, if not his interest, did drop off markedly, but the decline was only temporary. In 1927 Congress created a new judgeship in Connecticut, and Horace Taft tried to persuade his brother to use his influence to block the machinations of the local Republican bosses. Although for a time the Chief Justice resisted temptation, eventually he plunged into the dispute with his usual gusto. Encouraged by his success in getting a good man for Connecticut, Taft was soon back in full swing, freely offering advice both to the President and the Attorney General on vacancies everywhere in the country. But Taft knew his advice was frequently unwanted and unheeded. As he told Judge Arthur Denison, "It seems now that we have got to rejoice if we don't have a bad appointment. We can not aspire to good ones." This comment was not altogether fair to the Coolidge Administration, nor was it altogether accurate in terms of the success of the Chief Justice's own recommendations. Taft had, for instance, urged that Augustus Hand and Thomas Swan, Dean of the Yale Law School, be appointed to the circuit bench.

Taft had become aware of his loss of influence with Coolidge just after Harlan Stone's appointment to the Court and the succession of John S. Sargent as Attorney General. These two events occurred as Coolidge began to serve as a President elected in his own right, but Taft put the blame on Sargent rather than on Coolidge's jealousy of presidential prerogative. Six weeks after Sargent had taken over the Justice Department, Taft complained that "the President has not consulted me nearly so much about Judges as he did. When Stone was Attorney General he was anxious to know what I knew." Nine months later Taft wrote that Sargent was "a good man, but he is stupid and slow and utterly lacking in methods which will secure good appointees...."

Sargent may have consulted the wrong people — or failed to consult the right ones — and Coolidge may have exercised poor judgment, yet Taft saw the roots of the problem running back to his ancient enemies on Capitol Hill — "the vicious disposition of Senators to use appointments to the Bench for their own political purposes...." "Presidents," he explained to Horace Taft, "come in determined to maintain a high standard of Judges, but Republican Senators exercise a vicious influence to lower it."

Despite his bitter feelings toward the Senate and his disappointment with Coolidge's judgment, the Chief Justice did not completely lose his sense of humor. Shortly before Hoover's inauguration Taft wrote his son that a rumor was going around Washington that the new President would appoint Coolidge to the Supreme Court. "There is one difficulty about it," the Chief Justice remarked drily, "and that is that there is no vacancy on the Bench, and the second is that I don't think he would regard himself as quite prepared for that place, though he certainly would make as good a Judge as some whom he has appointed."

Since Taft put much of the blame for what he considered poor judicial appointments on Sargent, he was quite interested in Hoover's selection of an Attorney General. The Chief Justice was concerned lest the post should be given to William Donovan, a lawyer for whom he professed little professional respect ("a short horse," Taft called him), and a man, no doubt, with whom Taft did not expect to be able to work closely. For a few weeks after the 1928 election, the Chief Justice tried to drum up support for George Wickersham, but by late November he had decided that the current Solicitor General, William Mitchell, would be the best of the available candidates. Mitchell, like his old friend Pierce Butler, was a nominal Democrat; but Taft had had such great faith in their fundamental conservatism that he had strongly supported Butler's appointment to the Court and Mitchell's selection as Solicitor General.

Soon after deciding on Mitchell, Taft asked his son, Robert, to try to talk to Hoover about the appointment. Stepping up his campaign, the Chief Justice wrote Robert McDougal of Chicago that Mitchell was "a wonderful man" whose appointment as Attorney General would be Hoover's "greatest opportunity." To Henry Chandler, owner of the *Los Angeles Times*, Taft coyly confided that he had an important suggestion for the new President's cabinet which he would like to make to Chandler, providing he could relay it to Hoover. Chandler replied that he would be happy to pass the name on to the President-elect.

On Christmas Eve, the Chief Justice wrote Chandler a long letter extolling Mitchell's ability. "The Court has such confidence in him that it reads his briefs first in order to know what there is in the case." Taft admitted his obvious personal enthusiasm but claimed that in this regard "I represent the feeling of the entire Court...."[5] In closing the Chief Justice added: "Now I mean myself to go to speak with Mr. Hoover, but what I would like to do is to stimulate you, who will advise Mr. Hoover, to inquire into the very exceptional qualities of Mr. Mitchell." A week later Chandler answered that he would do what he could to help.

Meanwhile, Taft had also written George Wickersham and asked if he could not "do something to get to Hoover this conception?" Wickersham replied that he would do all he could, but doubted that Hoover even knew Mitchell. It seemed to Wickersham that Donovan was still the most likely choice.

During much of this period Hoover was out of the country on a good will tour of Latin America; but, the Chief Justice knew, the President-elect had been in frequent contact with Justice Stone about appointments, and Taft was hoping that he, too, might get in on the consultations. He was finally able to do so on January 11, 1929. Two days later, the Chief Justice wrote his daughter a succinct account of the visit:

I went over to see Hoover Friday night to advise him about his Attorney General, but I am afraid he was not disposed to take, with the confidence that I think he ought, my recommendation. He has some rather grandiose views . . . and unless he changes his view he will find himself with a very poor Attorney General, with nothing like the capacity of the man he is looking for.

Taft's gloom was deepened later in the week when he received a letter from Chandler stating that he had now concluded that Mitchell did not have a chance. Nevertheless, Chandler promised to try "through a very close friend and influential individual to have your suggestion urgently supported. . . ."

The Chief Justice believed that Mitchell's main competitor was not Donovan but Justice Stone. Stone, however, had no intention of leaving the Court for a cabinet post and in late February Taft's hopes for Mitchell were boosted when he heard that Brandeis and Senator Borah were supporting the Solicitor General and that many of the people who had been backing Stone were coming over to Mitchell as it became clear that the Justice would not leave the bench.

Whatever the forces working behind the scenes, Hoover selected Mitchell later in February. The Chief Justice was delighted and hopeful that the problems of lower court appointments could be greatly lessened. As he explained to Charles P. Taft, II: "Congress has created a good many new Judges, and I am glad of it, if we can be sure that they will be good Judges. I think they are going to be in the hands of an Attorney General who will insist on having good ones and will find Hoover behind him in making the same contention."

Six weeks after Hoover took office, the Chief Justice expressed qualified approval of the new Administration's record. "The President," he wrote his son, "has made some very good judicial appointments. There are two or three that could be improved, but I think he has done especially well in New York. That is because he has had a first class Attorney General." In the summer of 1929, while he was vacationing at Murray Bay, Canada, Taft wrote to Pierce Butler that he had heard that Mitchell "is working out satisfactory results, and Hoover is ready to stand by him. I hope this is correctly reported to me." In reply to an inquiry from Van Devanter Taft said, "In conversations with [Mitchell] I have obtained the impression that he is getting on well. He gave me some of the details. They disclose that he is on the right road—persistently so—and I think he will come out all right and overcome such obstacles as present themselves."

The Chief Justice did not attempt to continue the role of uninvited overseer which he had played during Coolidge's second administration or that of censor which he had played during Harding's presidency. Occasionally he became involved in ranking judicial candidates, but to a considerably smaller degree than in previous years. In part, this decline in activity may have been due to his initial confidence in Mitchell. In part it may also have been due to Taft's rapidly failing health.

Despite this relative inactivity, the Chief Justice's honeymoon with the Hoover Administration came to an abrupt end in the fall of 1929. In October Taft complained to his daughter that he was "intensely disappointed" at the nomination of "two or three utterly incompetent Judges." Once again he placed the primary blame on Republican Senators, but he added: "I am very much disappointed at the Attorney General, upon whom I counted with a great deal of confidence, but he has been overcome by the political situation, and it isn't too much to say that it is a disgraceful surrender."

CONCLUSION

The preceding narrative throws some light on the possible means which a Supreme Court Justice might use to lessen friction with lower court judges. At least in the Federal system, influencing appointments is clearly the most promising tactic. Gratitude may play some role, providing the judge knows to whom he should be grateful; but gratitude, as Presidents have often been made painfully aware, is neither a predictable nor a stable emotion. What is more important is that the helping Justice can select men who he is relatively sure will agree with him on controversial public policy issues. Again there is no certainty that the new judge will behave as desired, but at least the helping Justice has had some reasonable basis for prediction.

Taft's experiences supply a set of examples showing that a Justice not only theoretically can, but actually has been able to exert significant influence in the selection of lower court judges. Moreover, Taft's experiences indicate that a more astute member of the Court might have had more lasting success had he been content with advising in fewer situations, possibly restricting himself to circuit court appointments or to district court situations where no Senator from the President's party was involved, or where the Senator was undecided, or where two Senators were at odds.

In the St. Louis case, Taft based his recommendations mainly on the competence and integrity of the candidates. In the North Carolina case, a personal political debt was probably an important factor. There is no reason why the helping Justice could not also take ideology into account. In trying to influence Supreme Court appointments, Taft in fact did quite frankly advise Harding on candidates' political views. Indeed, when their own deeply felt values are at stake, it is difficult for most men to distinguish clearly between competence and ideology.

In some respects Taft had unique advantages in influencing appointments. No other member of the Court has ever been President. In addition, the Republican party controlled the White House and both houses of Congress during Taft's entire tenure as Chief Justice, and Taft could count many old friends on Capitol Hill. Yet Taft's position was not without its disadvantages. The advice of a former President is not always welcomed by the incumbent, as Taft's own relations with his predecessor should have taught him. And Taft had friends as well as foes in Congress, with most of the latter in his own party.

Even if Taft's unique advantages were judged to have outweighed his disadvantages, other Justices could build on his experiences. The overwhelming majority of Supreme Court Justices have had considerable political experience before coming to the High Bench, and many Justices have commanded influence in the ranks of the party which was in power during much of their terms of office — Jay, Taney, Chase, Miller, Waite, White, Brandeis, Sutherland, Stone, Murphy, and Vinson, to cite only the more obvious examples of the past. Nor need a Justice's influence be restricted to his own party. There is no reason why a President might not adopt the same sort of sophisticated attitude which Taft himself took both as Chief Executive and as Chief Justice, and subordinate party label to fundamental political philosophy.

The limited effectiveness of pure reason as a means of persuading men to act makes diplomacy in administration a necessity for smooth functioning of any governmental system. Here Taft left an enviable record. While he was often overeager to advise Presidents and Attorneys General, he displayed a keen sense of propriety and forbearance in dealing with judges. Several examples have already been offered of his early efforts to solicit advice and cooperation from both Federal and state judges, and Taft apparently never lost his graceful touch. On November 16, 1928, for instance, he wrote to welcome Judge Bascomb S. Deaver to the district bench. Later in the letter the Chief Justice said he was being consulted about candidates for United States Attorney in Georgia, and he asked Deaver for his impressions of the current Assistant Attorney in the district. Taft may or may not have truly needed this information, but in either case seeking Deaver's opinion was certainly a means of establishing immediate rapport.

The Judicial Conference, for which Taft deserves much of the credit, is the most obvious institutional means which can be used to build up rapprochement between the Supreme Court and lower Federal courts — though its full utilization is to a great extent restricted to the Chief Justice.[6] Meeting with representatives of the various circuits gives a Chief Justice a fruitful opportunity to build up good will, providing he is informed about the business of the courts, trained in legal niceties, and tactful in personal relations. Real as opposed to merely formal consultation would undoubtedly flatter inferior judges' egos and increase cooperation, though it might also entail trimming public policies which the Chief Justice desired. The Conference, of course, does not automatically create harmony. The Chief Justice must be statesman enough to perceive his opportunities, and politician enough to exploit them.

None of the tactics discussed in this paper can be substituted for technical competence in handling judicial business, literary skill in writing opinions, or the capacity for wise judgment. Nor is it likely that any combination of these or other means can completely eliminate friction with the court system. But influencing appointments, consultation with individual judges, tactful solicitation of cooperation in an effort to build a sense of teamwork and *esprit* among judges, can each be an important factor in predisposing lower court judges to accept freely and wholeheartedly Supreme Court decisions on controversial public policy issues. A Justice, ambitious for himself or for the policies in which he ardently believes, cannot rationally overlook either the bureaucratic check on his own power or the means to weaken the effect of that check.

Notes

[1] See my "Lower Court Checks on Supreme Court Power," *American Political Science Review*, LIII (Dec., 1959), 1017-1031.

[2] William Howard Taft to Horace Taft, Dec. 30, 1921, the Taft Papers, the Library of Congress. Unless otherwise noted all correspondence cited is from the Taft Papers.

[3] Felix Frankfurter and James M. Landis, *The Business of the Supreme Court* (New York: Macmillan, 1928), p. 218.

[4] WHT to Charles D. Hilles, Jan. 14, 1923. Taft's efforts to influence Supreme Court appointments are analyzed in my "In His Own Image," *1961 Supreme Court Review*, pp. 159-193.

[5] Whether Taft could in fact speak for the Court can, of course, never be proved, but Justice Stone's opinion of Mitchell was very similar to that of the Chief Justice. On March 22, 1928, Stone wrote to John Foster Dulles: "I would say, all in all, no man who appears in our Court makes as satisfactory arguments as does he, or aids the Court so much. He is a prodigious worker and has done great things in the Solicitor General's office.... He has a striking quality of intellectual integrity and straightforwardness which has won the confidence of the Court to a remarkable degree."

[6] The Chief Justice does not have exclusive power here. Associate Justices are normally invited to conference dinners, and they will have other opportunities to consult informally with lower Federal judges. Furthermore, as circuit judges, Associate Justices may attend and perhaps even preside over judicial conferences in their circuits. Eight of the nine Justices answered a written inquiry about their attendance at circuit conferences. Seven of the eight said they regularly attended, and while none of the seven presided over the conferences two have been asked to do so.

The Anatomy of Bureaucracy

Charles E. Jacob

Bureaucracy is characteristic of large organizations. While the existence of bureaucracies can be traced to ancient times, the power and pervasiveness of bureaucratic structures, both public and private, has increased so greatly in this century that leaders from many sectors of society have expressed concern. Of the public bureaucracy they ask: To whom are you responsible? In America the President is considered to be, by most people, the leader and overseer of the national bureaucracy. In fact, however, the President is only one of many political actors in the system seeking to influence the decision-making of the bureaucracy. One of the more important developments of recent decades has been the growth of self-conscious power within the bureaucracy itself. The increasing autonomy of the bureaucracies, particularly in personnel matters, has been coupled with a growing interest in influencing governmental policy. The crucial struggle today is not between the President and Congress, but between the bureaucracy and the politicians, the latter representing the popular interests. The following excerpt from Charles Jacob's Policy and Bureaucracy *discusses the theoretical framework for explaining the nature of modern bureaucracy postulated by the German sociologist, Max Weber. Jacob continues by suggesting limitations in Weber's model in light of contemporary American experience.*

Bureaucracy may be thought of as a complex system of men, offices, methods, and authority which large organizations employ in order to achieve their goals. Since bureaucracy is characteristic of large organizations, much of what follows will be as true of private bureaucracies like the modern corporation and the university as it is of public bureaucracy found in government. And while our primary concern is to understand the nature of governmental administration, examples drawn from private bureaucracy are relevant in elucidating the operation of public bureaucracy. Bureau-

Reproduced from *Policy and Bureaucracy,* by Charles E. Jacob, ed., by permission of Van Nostrand Reinhold Company, a division of Litton Educational Publishing, Inc., Litton Industries, Princeton, N. J., 1966.

cratic patterns of organization did not suddenly spring forth, full-blown, in the last century. There are records of ancient bureaucracy that have long fascinated the historian and sociologist. It is the elaboration and predominance of bureaucracy in modern society and government that make its consideration so vital to the contemporary political scientist. The first major attempt to theorize extensively about the nature and significance of bureaucracy was made by the eminent German sociologist, Max Weber (1864-1920). Our debt to Weber's pioneering efforts is immense, and it must be with his careful formulation of an ideal type that we make our point of departure on the way to understanding modern bureaucracy. For convenience, Weber's construct may be set down in terms of the four systematic elements of our definition: (1) men, (2) offices, (3) methods, and (4) authority.

(1) The bureaucrats, or men who hold office in a bureaucracy, are vocationally oriented. They have reached office by route of a particular course of training in a specialized field. The division of labor required by the large organization demands specialized technical qualifications from its officials. In general, the job of the bureaucrat is one of management — either of persons or things—a service which he contributes to the organization in return for his livelihood. In addition, according to Weber, appointment to office rather than election is characteristic of the professional bureaucrat. The official as a rule enjoys high status in society. His status, or social esteem, results from educational and technical or professional accomplishments which are usually symbolized in certificates, university degrees, or other records of achievement. Additional status is lent by the institution or office in which the bureaucrat works. Officeholding is actually more than a vocation; it is a career. The official is promoted in a series of ascending steps throughout his career. He normally holds claim to tenure in his office and is removable only for cause. Likewise, he is paid a fixed salary which is dependent not upon how much work he performs but rather on the position of his office in the total organization. Salary increases follow promotion to the next, higher level, and it is characteristic of the compensation system to include a pension after retirement. In sum, the career of the official is characterized by his relationship primarily to the organization office (bureau) rather than to another *person*. Duties, obligations, and loyalties are directed toward the institution itself.

(2) The bureaucratic office is characterized by a special area of competence. It is one, perhaps small but indispensable, part of the total organizational matrix. Its relationship to the other offices of the organization is determined by the principle of hierarchy. It is subordinate and accountable to offices above it and receives subordination and accountability from those offices resting beneath it. Matters of direction, control, and discipline flow from the top down in step fashion. As Weber has noted, although control is exercised formally through the hierarchy, ideally the essence of this control is control by knowledge. Knowledge in an administrative system is of two kinds. Specialized, technical knowledge is one source of power; in pratice, experience and an acquaintance with office methods, practices, and conventions are other sources of superior knowledge and power. In the typical bureaucratic unit there is a total separation between the use and ownership of the means of production or administration. As *employees*, officials use the furniture, machinery, libraries, laboratories, or other resources of the organization during their regular working hours. Thus all the appurtenances of the position are borrowed by the official, and he is accountable for their use to the organization. This contributes to a final characteristic of the bureaucratic system—its formalistic impersonality. Neutral norms and procedures,

applying to all, excepting none, and creating an atmosphere of impersonal equity are hallmarks of ideal bureaucracy.

(3) The methods by which bureaucracy operates are basically an outgrowth of the system of offices which characterizes it. Within the hierarchy each office operates according to established rules and norms. The object of such an atmosphere is to enhance the efficiency of the office and the psychic well-being of the official. The bureaucrat can calculate an appropriate course of action within the rules and be assured that his acts are justified or "safe." This mode of behavior explains in part the heavy reliance upon records and files which is typical of bureaucracy. All communications must be prepared in multiple copies and records of all conversations, orders, and transactions must be systematically filed away for future reference. The system of recorded precedents promotes efficiency and uniformity within the office and supports individual official acts with predictability.

(4) The system of authority which Weber found most appropriate to the modern bureaucratic organization was one based upon rational-legal grounds. The reason Weber regarded this basis of authority as superior to alternative sources was not merely because it was becoming more common in his own times, but because he felt it was by far the most efficient. As Peter Blau has noted, Weber's analysis of bureaucracy is a *functional* one. His foremost concern was to find what system of authority would produce the highest degree of goal achievement for the organization. A system of authority deriving from impersonal, abstract legal norms based upon rational calculations by legislators, constitution makers, or entrepreneurs and applying equally to all members of the organization constituted, for Weber, the maximum of efficiency. Law was deemed corporate in nature, and obedience to the law was given by the official in his capacity as a member of a corporate group. In practice, the official obeys a superior person, but obedience is not really given to the person but to the office which is a legitimate personification of the rational-legal order.

Weber admitted two other types of legitimate authority to his analysis—traditional and charismatic. Authority finding its source in traditional grounds has been widely exercised throughout history. What makes such authority legitimate is its appeal to the sanctity of long-established practices and conventions. In turn, the sanctity of the traditions vests with status those who interpret and apply them. A tradition-based authority system can be bureaucratic, employ a large administrative staff, and yet violate the ideal bureaucratic canon of formalistic impersonality since officials in such a system give loyalty to persons directly and primarily rather than to legal norms. The third type of legitimate authority Weber analyzed is charismatic. Whereas under traditional systems, authority becomes personalized (and, thereby, less efficient), under charismatic rule all authority is totally personal, drawing legitimacy from no other source than the command of a superhuman, otherworldly leader. Such leadership is inspirational in nature, and, as long as charisma persists, the godlike determinations of the charismatic leader are accepted as legitimate and absolute by his followers. Pure charisma is decidedly nonbureaucratic in that such authority, depending on the whim of the leader, totally rejects routine. However, Weber concluded that over a period of time, with the establishment of a system of succession, charisma could become routinized. In this instance, charisma could function authoritatively within a bureaucratic framework. Weber realized that the three types of authority he described seldom exist in pure form and that any given administrative system can be based upon elements of two, or even all three, forms of legitimacy. Yet the ideal Weberian type — and the one with which we are most closely familiar—is the rational-legal bureaucratic system.

BEYOND WEBER

Many of the characteristics of bureaucracy that Weber has outlined for us would be familiar to the contemporary citizen on the basis of his experience. Such concepts as hierarchy, routine, formality, standardization, "paper work," and regulations all seem to accord accurately with our image of modern administration in the big organization. Yet when we look more closely at bureaucracy in operation we are bound to conclude that practice diverges rather widely at many points from the Weberian ideal type. This is true for two reasons. First, Weber's construct is partially limited in its applicability to the social and political context in which he lived. Second, the construct is, within its own terms, a one-sided statement of reality. That is, Weber was so concerned to point out the functional utility of a rational-legal bureaucratic system that he failed to pay sufficient attention to internal characteristics that *inhibit* the rational goal achievement he seeks.

The social and political environment of Western Europe, and particularly of Germany, in Weber's time provided a more commodious setting for the smooth operation of a rigid bureaucratic system than does contemporary America. In our times a plurality of competing groups contend for social recognition and political power and find justification in an egalitarian ethic. Essentially, because of democratic expectations which thrive and strive in this society, administrative bureaucracy is not immune to pressures from a variety of diverse sources. Bureaucracy must live within a fluid class system rather than the highly stratified one to which Weber was attuned. Politically, the separation of powers ... has made bureaucracy subject to undulating institutional pressures that it cannot anticipate or gauge with precision. An example or two may give substance to these generalizations. One branch of the American bureaucracy is charged with the regulation of various aspects of economic life. The Federal Communications Commission, for example, in granting franchises for new television channels finds itself subject to the importunities of the television industry; the Federal Power Commission in regulating rates rarely acts totally oblivious to the claims of private power industries; nor can the Secretary of Agriculture (or the President) make farm policy disregarding the opinions of clientele farm organizations. Furthermore, in any of these cases, should a fearless bureaucrat attempt to follow what he considers the most rational course of action independently, he would find himself blocked not only by private clientele groups but also by their allies and spokesmen in Congress.

Bureaucracy is also challenged in the American institutional context by sporadic interference from the legislative branch. An extreme example of the havoc that one man can create over a whole department is the wide range of techniques used by the late Senator Joseph McCarthy in his battles with the Department of State. Officials were publicly denounced, policy objectives distorted, and personal agents employed within the department by the Senator in order to bring into disrepute the entire establishment. On such occasions the remarks of Max Weber about the security of officials in a bureaucratic system seem chimerical. Less extreme examples of congressional interference—for laudable motives and base — are limitless. Many a congressman denounces bureaucrats for short-sighted, irresponsible behavior; many another congressman denounces the bureaucrats out of jealousy of their expertise or their prerogatives.

Since in modern America public officials are drawn from a rather wide range of regional, class, and ethnic backgrounds, administration is not the preserve of any one group or stratum of society. While this is considered laudable in an ideological sense, it has resulted in a bureaucracy that has no particular claim to high status. The third assistant secretary is not nearly the object of esteem in the United States that he is in Great Britain or Germany. This is merely a function of a less stratified society, possibly augmented by occasional waves of anti-intellectualism. Finally, the existence of great occupational mobility coupled with the availability of higher financial rewards outside government service have made the public bureaucracy less stable and more subject to circulation among the officials than Weber anticipated. It is not uncommon for the young law graduate to gain a few years' experience in the Securities Exchange Commission and then move on to a more lucrative career in a corporation law firm.

Additional qualifications of Weber's ideal type are not related to any particular social or political context but are produced out of the bureaucratic syndrome itself. Fundamentally, a bureaucratic system is a social system, a system in which interpersonal relations cannot be ignored or overcome by an impersonal reign of office routine as Weber suggested. Indeed, it has been shown on numerous occasions that attempts to impose what appear to be highly rational organizational schemes on a given set of bureaucratic employees meet with frustration and produce consequences in opposition to the goals sought (dysfunction). A reason for such administrative failure is that unfortunately (or otherwise) human beings do not always function rationally. Understanding this, social scientists have recently come to the conclusion that a rewarding source of insight into the bureaucratic process is to be found in the study of personality. Thus Robert Presthus in his study of *The Organizational Society* has fruitfully applied some of the theories of the psychiatrist, Harry Stack Sullivan. Sullivan, having addressed himself to the question of the degree to which personality is a result of social interaction, suggests that one way to interpret irrational and sometimes dysfunctional official behavior within bureaucracy is to determine whether *situations* are anxiety producing or anxiety relieving. The manner in which employees attune themselves to situations arising in a bureaucratic context may be more dependent upon individual personality traits or drives and reactions to other personalities than upon the impersonal factors of an office environment. In a provocative attempt to theorize about different patterns of accommodation to bureaucracy, Presthus has suggested three types. "Upward-mobiles" react to the bureaucratic situation with zest, loyally accepting authority, operating efficiently — keenly aware of status differentials, and taking pleasure in their service to the organization. "Indifferents," on the other hand, fail to identify with the aims and conventions of their employer organizations. Though functional, their bureaucratic position is seen as a means of making a living. Beyond that, they are alienated from their work, taking refuge in outside, psychically "meaningful" preoccupations. The third type of accommodation that Presthus percieves is that of the "ambivalent," the least fortunate of the three types, both from his own and the orgaization's point of view. He is caught between a craving for the rewards offered by the big organization and his contempt for the bureaucratic methods that are the price of these rewards. Personally, he is unhappy and frustrated; organizationally, he is dysfunctional.

A further critique of Weber's ideal type must deal not only with acts of omission, such as his inability to apply personality theory, but also with the frequent inapplicability of some of his choice canons of bureaucracy. A useful, but by no means exhaustive, consideration of three principles of bureaucracy—formality, predictability, authority—will indicate that they are far less rigid in application than Weber imagined. Bureaucratic formality, for example, can be a highly functional trait of organizations. It may provide an atmosphere wherein personally antagonistic employees can cooperate effectively in furthering organizational goals because communication and the official integrity of each is maintained under the protective cover of bureaucratic protocol. On the other hand, it is a deficient view of bureaucracy that fails to take into account the importance of *informal* organizations. Informal organizations are so much a part of bureaucracy (formal organization) that one writer has concluded the latter could not operate without the existence of the former. One purpose of informal organization is to act as an escape valve for the expression of personal desires, motives, and needs for which there is no place in the formal organization. For example, companionship has no place in bureaucracy, but an informal creation of friendships among highly compatible persons may enhance morale and increase productivity. Alternatively, it is possible that if friendship groups harden into prepossessing cliques, intergroup or interpersonal antagonisms may result in bad morale and dysfunction. In either case, informal organization is vitally important to the efficiency of bureaucracy. Peter Blau discusses an instructive case study of cohesiveness and efficiency which resulted from informal organization in a federal law enforcement agency. Officials of the agency made frequent investigations, the interpretations and results of which required skill and care in the use of principles of auditing, accounting, and legal reasoning. Occasionally, some officials would be uncertain of their methods but avoided questioning their superior since they felt this would reflect unfavorably on their own capabilities. Instead, they regularly violated an agency rule prohibiting contacts among agents working on different cases. The contacts were usually among close friends and were often carried on under a disguise accepted by both parties which gave the consultations a character of casual conversations not directly related to a specific case. The advice-giver received satisfaction in the status he felt as a consultant to a colleague, or simply because he was able to help a friend. The advice-receiver was enabled to do his job satisfactorily and to avoid the official onus of incapacity. Morale was high because of the cohesive atmosphere of the office, and total efficiency was improved.

Predictability has long been considered a desirable attribute, within and without the bureaucratic context. Elementary common sense teaches that an individual will be more at ease and more effective in his work if the consequences of his actions are carefully laid out in specific rules and regulations. Yet this commonplace, like so many others, depends for its validity on the situation and the position of the individuals concerned. A study of industrial bureaucracy convinced Alvin Gouldner that precise predictability in employee relations was by no means always desirable or productive of efficiency from the point of view of organization leaders. Particularly at the lower levels of the organization, matters concerning promotion, wage increases, or conditions of dismissal were purposely made as unpredictable as possible. The rationale behind this approach dictated that insecurity and anxiety would produce greater motivation, perhaps interpersonal competition, and higher productivity. This situation, of course, has been a key motivation to unionization and the establishment by means of labor contracts of norms governing conditions intimately affecting workers. Nonetheless, from the point of view of a superior, there is good reason to avoid a careful structuring of the work environment of his subordinates. An overprecise delineation of workers' rights and duties may make it extremely difficult to exact performance beyond the strict norm when the organization is confronted with pressing needs. In such a situation, a manager must resort to authoritative sanctions or draw for persuasion upon a fund of good will. Every organization needs a "Catch-22."[1]

This brings us to the heart of a final qualification of bureaucratic rules: the complexity of authority. "Legality" may well be the fundamental basis of bureaucratic authority; the securing of constant compliance with all the laws of the organization, however, discloses a source of challenges to the modern bureaucratic official. Weber thought largely in terms of sanctions where rules were violated. Yet a strict and frequent application of sanctions may have the unintended consequence of reducing morale and efficiency in any organization. We are all familiar with rules that are honored in the breach. It is often the better part of wisdom for an official to be permissive about his subordinate's adherence to certain book rules. Even so authoritarian an organization as an army finds it useful at times to wink at its own rules. This is particularly true in crises and combat situations when the normal stiff formality of military address and salute between officers and enlisted men give way to a preference of informality and camaraderie which are productive of much greater efficiency. In any organization an official endowed with manipulative skills may well be able to dispense almost entirely with coercive sanctions and secure compliance with organizational objectives by creating social obligations. The very act of disregarding specific rules that matter little can create a bond of friendship between superior and subordinate that will permit the former to exact higher efficiency from the latter as a matter of social reciprocity. To identify just one more source of authority not related to coercive sanctions, consider the position of a Nobel Prize winner in a large scientific institute or government agency. Such a person's advice, opinions, or directives are likely to be accepted unquestioningly by his subordinates out of motives of respect or even adulation. The prerogatives of professionalism and expertise and the intraorganization status they create are of greater significance in modern bureaucracy than Weber imagined.

THE POLICY ROLE OF THE PUBLIC BUREAUCRACY

In modern government, bureaucracy has come to be equated with administration, and, for practical purposes, this is not an erroneous equation. For as we have seen, the vast majority of government bureaucrats is employed in the administrative arm of government. To be sure, an organizational pattern that is bureaucratic in nature exists in the legislative branch with its elaborate system of committees, hierarchies, and sharply articulated formal and informal rules. At a later stage, we shall consider the implications of bureaucracy in the area of legislative policy making. For the present, however, public bureaucracy may be taken to mean administration. Traditionally, the function of administration has been assumed to be the implementation of public policy; the making of policy was the prerogative of the sovereign representatives of the people. The very term applied to administrators — civil *servants* — indicates their traditional status of subordination in government. Hence, to speak of the "policy role" of the public bureaucracy is to fly in the face of constitutional norms and ideological prescriptions. But fly we must if we are to gain a realistic understanding of the multifaceted nature of policy making in American government today.

The initial point of access by bureaucrats to the regions of policy making is discovered in the exercise of the legitimate function of implementation. In theory, Congress (or Congress *and* the President, if a friendly atmosphere prevails) decides policy needs and sets forth its determinations in public law. Administrative handmaidens then translate statute book provisions into governmental activity. An example is in order. In 1934 Congress passed a Securities and Exchange Act by which it established a Securities and Exchange Commission. The job of the Commission is to protect the interests of the public and of investors against malpractices in the financial and securities market. It does this largely through its licensing authority under which it may approve or deny, revoke or suspend operating licenses to stock exchanges and brokers. It may permit or withhold the registration of securities for trading on the market. Its membership of five commissioners and staff of 800 have nearly unlimited discretion in regulating securities according to their view of the public interest. Its example is repeated many times in other agencies that have been delegated broad powers to regulate, according to the common rubric, in the "public interest, convenience, and necessity." No meaningful definition of policy making could be conjured to exclude the activities of such administrative agencies.

A more direct instance of bureaucratic participation in the policy making process is the exercise of the rule making authority granted to many agencies by Congress or simply assumed in practice through custom and usage. A railroad wishing to increase its fares, or discontinue service on one of its lines, must consult rules established by the Interstate Commerce Commission and not congressional lawmakers directly. Directives, orders, and commands issue daily from the offices of federal agencies, departments, bureaus, and commissions. Each of these makes or states policy affecting the rights of individuals, the character of economic life, and the destiny of the nation. An example of one such order that aroused a certain amount of congressional criticism was a 1963 directive from the Pentagon authorizing military commanders to declare "off limits" areas close to their bases where "relentless segregation" was being practiced.

Less tangible means of administrative policy making than rule making or discretionary implementation are to be found in the use and even dependence upon administrative advice by Congress and the executive in their policy making labors. The same causes that fostered the growth of bureaucracy necessitate the use of bureaucratic expertise in reaching policy decisions. Rational courses of action can only be taken on the basis of consultation with expert, specialized intelligence. A presidential decision to invade Cuba, raise the tariff on bicycle imports, or outlaw discrimination in public housing can only be reached after careful consultations with experts in foreign policy, economics, and law. Congress is equally dependent on the information and advice offered by the downtown bureaucrats. To be sure, congressional committees are organized functionally to deal with a limited segment of the legislative terrain, such as taxes, commerce, agriculture, or labor. Problems in each of these major areas, however, are bound to be so complex that the most experienced legislator would find it impossible to depend upon his own resources in formulating policy. In some cases legislators become lost in the maze of information offered by bureaucratic specialists. The following colloquy from a committee hearing, in which a legislator attempts to reach a rational conclusion about the selection of various naval craft by the Defense Department, is suggestive:

SECRETARY MCNAMARA: It is a question of antisubmarine emphasis versus antiaircraft plus antisubmarines. The three DE's are almost exclusively for antisubmarine warfare. The two DEG's had some desirable capability beyond antisubmarine warfare.

Our chief problem is antisubmarine warfare, and it seemed to me wise to consider putting in three antisubmarine warfare ships instead of two that had some antiaircraft capability.

MR. HARDY: I can't disagree with any of these things—they are completely over my head — but I am trying to explore how we arrive at the specific things we have.

Beyond all these means of participation in the policy process, bureaucracy has an additional persuasive technique which it sometimes employs in the shaping of policy. As spokesmen for particular problem areas of economic and social life, bureaucrats represent natural constituencies or clientele groups in society. For example, farmers are keenly interested in the work of the Department of Agriculture; the military is immediately affected by Defense Department policy; organized labor concerns itself with the Department of Labor and the National Labor Relations Board. Consequently, in the process of attempting to influence policy, it is not uncommon for any of these or other agencies to enlist the support of their clientele organizations. (On the other hand, it is just as common for clientele agencies to pressure the bureaucrats for policies favoring their clients.) In any case, effective working alliances are developed between private interest groups and public bureaucrats in favor of common policy goals. Hence, in a situation where the Department of Defense and the military services are united in support of particular policies, it is exceedingly difficult for either the President or Congress to oppose them effectively. Occasionally, differences on policy matters develop between administrator and clientele. In such a situation the elements of conflict, bargaining, and shifting coalitions—which are the substance of politics—come into play. The bureaucrat does not always win out in the policy struggle; the point worth emphasizing is that he nearly always does participate in it.

BUREAUCRACY UNDER FIRE

Even a brief discussion of the role of the public bureaucracy would be deficient if it failed to take account of the wide range of criticisms of the system. Ironically, one category of complaints often heard denounces the alleged inefficiency of bureaucracy. Although the basic motive of a bureaucratic system is the rational and efficient achievement of goals, it is undeniable that bureaucracy carries within it the seeds of its own inefficiency. The heavy reliance on rules, regulations, and canons of procedure can, and sometimes does, have the consequence that the bureaucrat is so preoccupied with procedural niceties as to lose sight of substantive goals. As the sociologists phrase it, a "displacement of goals"—in which means become ends — is an occupational hazard of bureaucracy. Occasionally, a state of trained incapacity develops where a bureaucratic technician is so adept at a very specialized skill applicable in a specific context that a change of context renders him incapable. A similar criticism of bureaucratic procedure is the inordinate amount of routine paper work that characterizes any sizable office. What the French call *La paperasserie*, the Germans, *vielschreiberei*, and Americans, "red tape," is a universal bureaucratic component of inefficiency. An amusing story making the conversational circuit in Washington was reported in *The New York Times* in 1963. It tells of a government clerk who received dozens of papers daily which he read, initialed, and deposited in his "out" basket. One day a report meant for another office found its way to his desk, and he followed the usual reading, initialing, and dispatching routine. Two days later the report was returned with this memorandum attached: "This document was not designed for you to handle. Please erase your initials and initial the erasure."

Such elements exist in all bureaucracy, but it is wise to place them in perspective. Bureaucracy as a system should not be considered hopelessly inefficient as a whole merely because we can point to specific examples of inefficiency. Curiously, our attitudes about bureaucratic inefficiency and red tape vary, depending upon *which* bureaucracy we are talking about. One sees much hand-wringing about governmental bureaucratic waste. I have yet to hear horror stories about an inefficient General Motors Corporation or an inefficient American Telephone and Telegraph Company. Presumably, however, these large organizations are not miraculously immune to bureaucratic deficiencies.

A more serious criticism of public bureaucracy addresses itself to the obviously great power exercised by administrators and questions whether administrative discretion can possibly be made clearly responsive and accountable to elective officials and, in turn, to the public. It is difficult to deal with this question satisfactorily. For, on the one hand, one may say with confidence that extreme fears of a despotism conducted by power-crazed bureaucrats are not rationally based upon anything we know about administrators as individuals or bureaucracy as a dynamic force. On the other hand, only the most sanguine observer would ignore the implications of a vast and complex establishment of appointed officials exercising wide discretionary use of delegated legal powers. It would seem that the most the citizen can ask is that the administrator be a man of integrity and good judgment and that he conduct his office with a regard to the professional criteria of excellence which apply to his specialized area of operations. Moreover, the other branches of government are not helpless before the specter of bureaucratic power. Frequently Presidents issue executive orders governing various aspects of the administrative process, shifting personnel, changing functions, reorganizing agencies, and so on. An outstanding example is President F. D. Roosevelt's issuance of Executive Order 8248 in 1939 which created, with a single stroke, the Executive Office of the President. His successors have liberally altered the composition of the executive office to meet their own needs and the requirements of changing governmental relationships. Likewise, Congress plays a part in the governing of administration through committee checks, reorganization plans, and the setting of procedural standards. Thus in 1946 Congress passed the Administrative Procedure Act which applied specified judicial standards to administrative conduct.

A corollary of the concern about the discretionary authority of administrators is the twofold charge that they either exercise too much policy initiative in pressing for schemes of economic or social change, or that they act as a collective drag on progress in government because of bureaucratic inertia. Again, both charges can be documented with appropriate case studies. Certainly it cannot be gainsaid that administrators are capable of bringing about profound shifts in economic and social relationships. In the first Kennedy administration the persistent application of administrative pressures by such agencies as the Civil Rights Division of the Justice Department, the Interstate Commerce Commission, and other agencies and departments quietly brought about an increased enjoyment of basic civil rights by Negroes. On the other hand, Philip Selznick shows in a careful study how the administrators who manage the Tennessee Valley Authority have altered the goals of the original plan. Initially they played an important part in lifting the standard of life in the Valley area; in the long-term course of development, however, the bureaucratic face hardened, and conservative pressures inhibited the fruition of some advocates' goals for the program. It is in the nature of bureaucracy to be capable of both spirited action and stubborn delay. Thus the bureaucrat must harden himself to the ambivalent criticism of getting nothing done and doing it in an irresponsible way.

CONCLUSION

The development of new economic and technological forces during the last seventy-five years has produced a revolution in the organizational life of American society. Thus transformation has been characterized by size, concentration, and standardization in public and private life. Bureaucracy has been perfected as the system for organizing the new forces at work. The co-ordination of highly specialized talents and activities on the principle of hierarchical divisions whose relationships are governed by rules and regulations — both formal and informal —constitutes the genius of bureaucracy. The system is not perfect largely because the human beings who operate it and operate within it are not perfect.

The reason bureaucracy is so important in a public sense is that it has come to share an important position of leadership in policy making. This new role is so prominently exercised as to be responsible for the assignment of the descriptive title, "Administrative State" to contemporary American government.

Notes

[1] In a grimly humorous satirical novel about military life and military bureaucracy, Joseph Heller has bombardier Yossarian desperately anxious to take leave of his plight as an air force bombardier after forty-four missions. Yossarian hits upon the idea of pleading insanity. He is assured by the air force doctor that, while insanity is a legitimate cause for grounding airmen, his quest is in vain:

"You mean there's a catch?" [Yossarian asked.]

"Sure there's a catch," Doc Daneeka replied. "Catch-22. Anyone who wants to get out of combat duty isn't really crazy." (Joseph Heller, *Catch-22* [New York: Simon and Schuster, 1961], p. 45).

Intergovernmental Relations in the Twentieth Century

Federalism is the political system whereby citizens simultaneously live under two separate layers of authority, a central or national government on the one hand, and constituent or state government on the other. The Constitution allots functions and powers to each of the layers of the government. Some of the functions are assigned exclusively to one or the other jurisdictions, while others are performed by both, e.g., the collection of taxes. The thrust of the literature on federalism, at least until recent years, has been to emphasize the "separateness" of the national and state governments. Daniel Elazar, in the essay which follows, challenges the view that "separateness" is the major characteristic of our federal system and suggests that co-operative federalism—the patterned sharing of governmental activities by all levels of government—has been the accepted mode of operating since the system was established in 1789. This co-operative federalism is not really decentralization so much as it is noncentralization, "predicated on broad national legislative and fiscal powers joined with a traditional penchant for maintaining maximum local control over governmental activities." Elazar suggests that intergovernmental relations in the twentieth century have evolved through five periods, each with its peculiar characteristics. With the programs proposed by the administration of Richard Nixon, have we entered a sixth period with its own peculiar characteristics?

Daniel J. Elazar

One very practical manifestation of the political changes that have characterized the twentieth century has been the great increase in government activity, much of it in the form of new intergovernmental programs. Despite popular views to the contrary, intergovernmental collaboration is not a new phenomenon. Co-operative federalism — the patterned sharing of governmental activities by all levels of government — has been characteristic of the American federal system since its establishment. American governments have traditionally assumed responsibili-

Reprinted, by permission of the author and publisher, from Daniel J. Elazar, "Intergovernmental Relations in the Twentieth Century," *Annals of the American Academy of Political and Social Sciences,* 359 (May 1965), 11-22. Abridged by the editors.

ties only in response to public demands but, where governments have acted, federal, state, and local governments usually have acted in concert. Whether this "co-operative federalism" was intended by the founders of the Union or not, it was quickly demonstrated to be necessary. Governments operating in the same territory, serving the same people, generally sharing the same goals, and faced with the same demands could not maintain a posture of "dual federalism" (the separation of functions by levels of government).[1]

THE AMERICAN PARTNERSHIP

By the mid-twentieth century, certain basic principles and mechanisms for intergovernmental collaboration have become part of the American governmental tradition, most of which came into existence a century ago and persist to color the character of American federalism today. Among the principles are: national supremacy, broad national legislative and appropriation powers, noncentralized government, and maximum local control. Among the mechanisms are: a nondisciplined, noncentralized party system; routinized legislative "interference" in administration; regular intergovernmental consultation; and a system of grants-in-aid from higher to lower levels of government.

From the very first, Congress has acquired the authority to legislate very broadly under the Constitution. Although this authority was frequently diluted by the Supreme Court and by Congress itself until the 1930's, it was nonetheless apparent in the general expansion of federal activities in the intervening years. Also demonstrated from the first was the inherent superiority of the federal government as a raiser of revenue because of the tax sources available to it and the reluctance of the people to allow equally substantial state and local tax levies. For these reasons, federal funds provided the stimulus for new programs in a majority of the states throughout the nineteenth century.[2]

These two trends, coupled with the great political decisions of the nineteenth century, firmly established the principle of national supremacy. Along with it, however, the equally important principle of noncentralized government was also established. If the general government was early cast in the role of stimulator and partial supporter of such major governmental functions as education, internal improvements, and public welfare, the states — either directly or through their local subdivisions — were simultaneously cast in the role of managers and administrators of these functions. Policy-making for these programs became a joint state-federal activity.

This arrangement is often mislabeled decentralization. Decentralization implies the existence of a central authority having a legitimate monopoly of governmental power which can concentrate, devolve, or reconcentrate functions more or less as it pleases. Noncentralization — on the other hand, the keystone of every true federal system—implies the constitutional coexistence of a general government and governments with more particularized authority which share governmental power. In the American case, the basic authority of the states is delineated in the Constitution and cannot be withdrawn except with their consent thus making dynamic federal action possible without concomitant reduction of local self-government by protecting the less formal institutions that deconcentrate power.

The American commitment to noncentralization has forced federal authorities to seek ways to develop nationwide programs with minimum national requirements within the framework of the co-operative system and has enabled the states to secure federal assistance without fearing any real loss of their integrity.

Thus it has always been the prerogative of the states to decide whether or not to accept any federal aid proffered under formal grant programs. And, despite the prevalent idea that no state can resist federal subsidies, few, if any, states have ever taken advantage of every grant offered them. The strong record of state participation, particularly in the major programs in any given period, is really a reflection of the nationwide consensus as to their value and necessity. Such programs represent only a few of the over a hundred available to the states and localities today. Moreover, many states do not take advantage of all the funds available to them under grants they have accepted. In both cases, state policy-decisions rule.

Even more important, noncentralization means that the states, as of right, share in the initial development of most co-operative programs before they are written into law. They share in the shaping of policies from the first and throughout the existence of each program, and develop their own patterns of program implementation within the framework of agreed-upon guidelines.[3]

The sharing process has worked both ways. The states have become involved in the fields of foreign affairs, interstate commerce, defense, and monetary policy just as the federal government has become involved in the fields of education, health and welfare, agriculture, and urban development.[4]

Moreover, local governments, public nongovernmental agencies, and private interests have acquired roles of their own as partners in the process because they have made an effort to become involved and have found ways to "pay the ante" required to sit in on the great game of government in the United States.

THE FORMS OF THE PARTNERSHIP

Intergovernmental co-operation has taken on a variety of forms, all of which have histories as old as the sharing system itself. Among the most common and recurring are those of *informal cooperation* through conferences, the provision of advisory and training services, the lending of equipment and personnel, and the performance of services by one government in place of another. Such collaboration is barely visible to the general public except when a conference is sponsored by the White House or when a public-health team moves into a community on the heels of an epidemic. The informal luncheon meeting, no matter how important, attracts no attention whatsoever.

Formal co-operation activities, on the other hand, are based on *contracts and compacts for co-operative action*. In the largest sense, contractual relationships are basic to a federal system which is founded upon a fundamental compact to begin with. In essence, it is the contractual relationship that makes possible large-scale intergovernmental co-operation to achieve common ends. Every formal co-operative relationship involves some form of contractual tie. The flexibility of the contract as a device enhances its usefulness and allows it to be adapted for many purposes. There are contractual relationships for co-operative research, for the division of costs of support shared activities, for provision or exchange of services, to prevent conflict or misunderstanding, for exchange of personnel, for joint enforcement of laws, for sharing revenues, and for lending agreements.

Recurring informal contracts are often formalized to the point of receiving statutory recognition and contractual ratification, through *contracts for simple sharing*. These are relationships that involve nothing more than a formal agreement to share resources without formal transfers of funds or personnel from one government to another. They are often used to prevent needless duplication of time, money, and effort or to enhance the possibilities for more comprehensive execution of particular programs. State-federal crop reports, Bureau of Labor Statistics calculations, state regulation of nuclear installations, formal agreements for the exchange of tax information or co-operative inspections of public utilities are examples of this type of relationship.

Another form of co-operation involves the interchange of *personnel*. This includes the provision of "services-in-aid," that is, arrangements by one government to lend its personnel to assist another; jointly paid agents; joint inspections by personnel of more than one government; and the deputization of personnel of one government by another for co-operative purposes. Under this type of co-operative activity, federal engineers are lent to states and localities to plan projects; county sanitarians are paid with federal, state, and local funds and have special obligations to all three governments; banks are jointly inspected by state and federal officers; and state hospital guards are deputized by the local police.

The pervasiveness of the partnership has led to the development of *interdependent activities* in which one government depends upon another (or both depend upon each other) for the enforcement of laws or the administration of programs otherwise not apparently "shared." The administration of elections is one good example of this. The election of national officials is contingent upon state implementation of the constitutional requirements. In this case, there is federal dependence upon state action. States, on the other hand, may depend upon federal authorities to exclude the transportation of prohibited goods (liquor, oleo, firecrackers) across their boundaries.

First in importance among the forms of intergovernmental co-operation are the grants-in-aid: federal transfers of funds to the states and federal or state transfers to local governments for specified purposes usually subject to a measure of supervision and review by the granting government. They are particularly distinctive because they involve the transfer of funds from one government to another in order to attain certain agreed-upon ends. The first grants-in-aid were generally transfers of land to be sold to finance specific programs. Supervision of these grants was relatively loose by today's standards but still significant; conditions attached to them governed disposition of the lands and use of the proceeds earned.

Cash grants-in-aid, like land grants, date from the nineteenth century—six were established before 1900—but did not flower until the twentieth. Since 1911 some sixty-five new federal grant-in-aid programs have been established, fourteen of which have since been discontinued. In general, they have been more rigorously administered by all governments concerned.

Grants-in-aid are of three kinds: (1) flat grants, which provide each recipient government with an equal sum regardless of local conditions or deviations from the national means, and without requiring formal matching of funds by the recipient governments—although recipients may have to shoulder administrative costs; (2) proportionate grants, as with road-building, made to recipient governments in proportion to their own contributions to the program or project in question, and often allocated on the basis of preset formulas which take the need and capabilities of the recipient into account; and (3) percentage grants, allocated like proportionate grants but with the granter's contribution fixed as a set percentage of the cost to the grantee for maintaining a particular program. Among the best known of these are the federal public welfare grants and some state grants to local school districts. Grants-in-aid may also include grants in kind, which generally resemble flat grants and are rarely subject to extensive supervision.

Other forms of intergovernmental sharing include tax offsets (used when nationwide compliance is necessary as in the unemployment compensation program), shared revenues (such as timber and mineral royalties and shared license fees), and grants or contracts awarded on similar terms to public and private applicants (such as federal research grants to universities). These all represent variations of the grant-in-aid principle, developed to meet conditions which would frustrate simpler grant mechanisms.

Supplementing the regular channels of co-operative control, the sharing system is strengthened through the maintenance of a nondisciplined, noncentralized party system which encourages elected representatives to follow the interest of their districts—from wards through states — rather than maintain party responsibility. This system encourages them to frame programs in such a way as to guarantee the maintenance of local control, thereby increasing their own power. One of the consequences of this has been the development of routinized mechanisms for continuous legislative "interference" (used in the neutral sense) in the administration of government programs, further enhancing local control over program execution as well as policy-making.

THE COURSE OF THE TWENTIETH-CENTURY PARTNERSHIP

The record of the partnership since approximately 1913 has been one of maintaining and appropriately modifying the patterns established earlier, in the face of a continually increasing "velocity of government"—the amount of total government activity in relation to the total activity of society—through the formal institutionalization of the co-operative system.[5]

This has meant (1) the development of more complex and sophisticated techniques for administering co-operative programs to secure better financial control by the granting government, (2) improved sharing of policy formation by all participants, including the panoply of interest groups that contribute so much to policy-making in the United States, (3) expansion of the range and variety of shared activities so that today one is hard-pressed to find any area of public concern that does not somehow involve government and in turn, federal-state-local collaboration, and (4) the adjustment of the theories and mechanisms of federalism to meet new times, situations, and demands. This, in turn, has led to growing public recognition of the co-operative system for what it is and an increased interest on the part of public official and scholars in understanding how American federalism really functions.

The course of intergovernmental relations in this century can be traced through four periods and into a fifth. Understandably, the trends in intergovernmental relations are closely tied to the larger political and economic movements on the American political scene.

By 1913 the era of virtually unregulated enterprise capitalism was coming to an end. During the next generation, government regulations was progressively extended over an even more complex corporate economy while an ideological battle over the legitimacy of government's new role was being fought.

The first period may be characterized as one of *progressive agrarianism*. It was actually inaugurated when the Republican party, whose national majority status had been consolidated in the critical elections of 1892 and 1896, briefly gave way to a progressive and activist Democratic administration in 1913.[6] It reflected the first concerted national response to the Populist-Progressive-Liberal agitation for positive government action to meet the problems of an industrialized society, and laid the foundations for co-operation in the subsequent periods. Growing government activism, begun in part under Theodore Roosevelt, brought with it revival of large scale co-operative activity. The magnitude of this revival is seen in the more than sixfold increase in federal

TABLE 1. Twentieth-Century Patterns of American Federalism

Year	Period	Economic Era	Political Condition	State of Intergovernmental Relations
1900 1910	Transition (1895-1911)[2]	Concentrated Enterprise Capitalism (1877-1913)[2]	GOP majority party	Passing of nineteenth-century co-operative programs. New experiments in collaboration under T. Roosevelt. Widespread state experimentation has important influence on public.
1920	Progressive Agrarianism (1911-1921)[2]	Transition Era (1913-1933)[2]	(Democratic Administration, 1913-1921)[2]	Wilson's "New Freedom" lays foundation for twentieth-century co-operative federalism.
1930	Normalized Entrenchment (1921-1931)[2]		1928 Critical Elections 1932	GOP restoration starts second period. Existing co-operative programs continued and improved but no significant new federal starts. State experimentation again significant.
1940	Crisis-oriented Centralism (1931-1945)[2]		Democrats forge majority coalition, become majority party.	New Deal "explosion" in federal-state co-operation, heading off centralization through temporary concentration of power in Washington. Expansion of federal-local and unilateral federal programs along with co-operative ones.
1950 1960	Noncentralist Restoration (1946-1961)[2]	Regulated Capitalism (1946-)[2]	(GOP Administration, 1953-1961)[2] 1956 Critical Elections 1960	Fourth period brings great expansion of small co-operative programs, great expansion of state government expenditures, and increased concern with states' role.
	Concentrated Co-operation (1961-)[2]		Democratic Majority coalition reforged	Fifth period brings new emphasis on federal stimulatory action and new threat of centralization from outside of the co-operative system.

[2]Dating of periods is approximate.

grant expenditures and the near doubling of the number of formal grant programs between 1912 and 1920 (see tables)[7] and the development of "many other forms of formal and informal co-operative activities as government at all levels took on expanded roles in American life."

This period saw three important developments that were to influence the course of intergovernmental relations thereafter: (1) the beginning of clear public recognition of the possibilities inherent in an intergovernmental partnership to meet the nation's new governmental needs, (2) the inauguration of modernized forms of federal-state collaboration particularly through the grant-in-aid system, and (3) the first efforts to develop a more sophisticated understanding of the functioning of the American federal system. Woodrow Wilson set the tone for all three. Concerned simultaneously with expanding the federal role and with preserving the federal-state relationship, his public expressions and the programs enacted during his administration reflected the idea that the federal government was to assist the states in developing and maintaining programs already approved or requested by a substantial number of them. The agricultural-extension, highway-construction, and vocational-education grant programs — the major ones inaugurated in Wilson's administration — all reflect this. In the case of the first two, and of the forest-protection program expanded under Wilson, formal co-operative relationships were actually established to replace or prevent unilateral federal action.These new grant programs betrayed the agrarian bent of Wilsonian Progressivism, being specifically designed to benefit the declining rural American majority.

TABLE 2. Federal Grants to State and Local Governments, 1902-1964 (Selected Years)[a]

Year	Total in $ '000s	Number of Grant Programs in Operation
1902	3,001	5[b]
1912	5,255	7[b]
1920	33,886	11
1925	113,746	12
1933	192,966	12
1937	2,663,828	26
1942	1,819,574	27
1946	894,625	28
1953	2,762,912	38
1957	3,816,404	45
1961	7,103,983	46
1964	9,864,000	51

[a]Sources: Advisory Commission on Intergovernmental Relations, Statistical Abstract of the United States, 1964.
[b]Exclusive of fifteen land grant programs.

As both federal and state governments became involved in the same general areas of activity, it became profitable for them to work out appropriate co-operative relations, even for apparently unilateral programs. This was particularly true in matters involving government regulation. Bank regulation had been a co-operative activity since 1865; regulation of railroads became increasingly co-operative as it became more meaningful. There was even some co-operation in the administration of anti-trust legislation. Law enforcement had always led to a great deal of co-operative activity which was intensified after passage of the spate of federal criminal legislation to assist in handling interstate crimes, in this period. Perhaps the foremost "temporary" co-operative program of the period was selective service for World War I. In some cases federal-state collaboration was explicitly authorized by law. In others, collaboration just grew informally because it was mutually advantageous.

The second period was one of *normalized entrenchment*. It began when the Republicans resumed power in Washington in 1921, and was characterized by a general reluctance to increase the role of government coupled with a negative attitude toward intergovernmental collaboration. Despite the hostile political climate, this period saw the expansion of existing programs and refinements in their co-operative administration. Actual expenditures for co-operative programs increased six-and-a-half times between 1920 and 1932. After an initial period of intensive federal supervisory activity to get the new programs under way, administrative arrangements began to take on a significantly noncentralized character.

At the same time, the number and scope of administrative decisions required to implement complex grant programs gave those who made the programs work substantial influence in shaping the character of intergovernmental co-operation. The professional associations of state and federal officials engaged in the same tasks, and national associations of state officials, such as the American Association of State Highway Officials and the Association of Land Grant Colleges and Universities, whose memberships cut across all levels of government and all jurisdictions, began to assume important policy-making duties. These developments further limited the potential role of the federal bureaus to set policy unilaterally.

The second period was one of considerable activity in the states, activity that would later win the period designation as the "seedtime of reform." Whereas federal expenditures rose by only $503 million between 1922 and 1932, state-local expenditures rose by $2,752 million. The expansion of state activity invariably meant an increase in state involvement in previously "local" problems. The expenditure figures are revealing. State transfers of payments to localities rose from $312 million in 1922 to $801 million in 1932, exceeding the growth of all federal transfers in the same period both proportionately and absolutely. Increases in established federal-aid programs in the 1920's and new state-initiated programs in the welfare field precipitated this growth.

The third period, characterized by *crisis-oriented centralism*, coincided with Democratic achievement of majority party status. Their inauguration of the New Deal as a governmental response to the massive depression problems of a society by then over 56 per cent urban, and later a global war, brought great expansion of new federal programs, co-operative and otherwise. Some of these were in response to state and local pressures; others were developed by reformers eager to stimulate state and local action. The great acceleration of the velocity of government made co-operative federalism all-pervasive. The crisis broke down much of the resistance to federal aid. As a result, existing co-operative programs were made more national in scope, and new ones were broadly oriented from the first.

The co-operative system was subtly reoriented toward Washington, as that city became the nation's unrivaled center of political excitement, if not of governmental inventiveness. "Bright young men" of all ages were brought into the federal government to plan new schemes to meet the problems of the day, many of whom had no particular attachment to the principles of federalism, *per se*. The sheer fact of state and local dependence on federal aid meant that they were willing to tolerate pressures from Washington which they might have rejected forcefully in other times.

Yet the most significant fact that stands out in all this is the way in which the application of accepted techniques and principles of co-operative federalism prevented the tremendous growth in national government activity from becoming an excuse for an equivalent centralization of power. Regardless of the growth of federal influence, the unwillingness of some New Deal planners to develop co-operative programs rather than unilateral ones, and the notions of some political theorists popular in that day that federalism was obsolete, the entrenched forces of American politics directed most new federal programs into co-operative channels. Thus, all but one of the great public welfare programs originally designed by Roosevelt's "brain trust" to be directly administered by federal officials, were reshaped by other administration leaders and by Congress into shared programs in which state and local roles were central. So it was with virtually all the other programs inaugurated in this period that did not absolutely have to be centrally administered.

Indeed, while the New Deal brought formerly unilateral state programs into the sharing system, it also brought in several initially unilateral federal programs as well. Often, experienced public servants (among them FDR himself) were plucked from successful agencies in progressive states and brought to Washington to manage new programs. Their understanding of state and local needs helped maintain the sharing system. Within the states themselves, new co-operative programs were generally subject to modification to meet special local needs. In many cases of erstwhile "centralization," first appearances are deceiving. Consider the Hatch Act requiring states to establish merit systems for federal-aided programs. While this law was greeted by many as a serious limitation of state autonomy, its requirement that states adopt a single merit system of their own design in lieu of federally-imposed program-by-program controls (common in earlier grants-in-aid) helped maintain their integrity as political systems.

The third period featured an expansion of direct federal-local relationships. Partly through urban assistance programs, partly through emergency relief activities, and partly through expanded agricultural programs, the federal government undertook formally to assist local communities in the same spirit of partnership that had animated other forms of intergovernmental relations. This, of course, exacerbated the already complex problems of the states' co-ordination in their internal affairs, even while bringing local relief in a time of crisis.

The growing institutionalization of the intergovernmental partnership was reflected in the development of new institutions to enhance the ability of the states and localities to participate in the development of policy and the improvement of administrative procedures. The Council of State Governments and the complex of "conferences" of state officials connected with it came into being. Headquartered in Chicago, they provided the states with an able instrument to use in negotiating with Washington and a means to further interstate co-operation, providing a measure of "federalism-without-Washington." Local officials, similarly organized, were also called upon to help shape the co-operative programs of the new era.

By the end of the third period, the role of government in a mixed economy had been firmly established and generally accepted. With the beginning of the fourth period a new generation of regulated capitalism, in which government played a positive role in the economy, began. But the fourth and fifth periods reflect this new generation. A Republican interlude during most of the fourth period served to consolidate and assimilate the changes of the New Deal; then it gave way to a restoration of the Democratic majority coalition through the critical elections of 1956 and 1960. The Democrats' return to office in 1961 inaugurated the fifth period in a burst of renewed federal activism.

The fourth period was one of *noncentralist restoration*, marked by a resurgence of the states as spenders and policy-makers and great expansion of local government. Its public image was set by Dwight D. Eisenhower, who repeatedly called for increased reliance on state efforts in place of federal "intervention." However, its real tone was not one of federal "retrenchment" or unilateral state assumption of previously shared responsibilities, as the President and his advisors suggested, but of continued expansion of intergovernmental collaboration — some twenty-one new grant programs were established between 1946 and 1960 — with the states and localities assuming a stronger position in the federal system.

This took four forms. There was a substantial shift in the balance of government expenditures for domestic purposes, with the states and localities coming to outspend the federal government by a two-to-one margin. There was also a marked relaxation in detailed federal supervision of state handling of established grant programs, a reflection of the increased professionalization of state and local program administrators and the growing willingness of their federal counterparts to trust their judgment. The states and localities, through their representatives in Congress, were responsible for the initiation of most of the new programs, which generally involved small grants to give them greater leverage in expanding their services. Finally, the states and localities again became centers of experimentation, developing "pilot projects" of all sorts, often aided with foundation grants or small doses of federal funds.

The states also began to concern themselves with acquiring some control over the unilateral federal programs carried on within their boundaries and, in some very important cases, a role in the federal-local programs. In some cases, this was a matter of informal intervention to co-ordinate programs or to render supplementary services. In others, it involved the acquisition of very real power over the implementation of programs within the state.

An added impetus to the resurgence of the states was the increased interest in studying the federal system and its functioning by government commissions for the first time in American history and by academic scholars who continued the tradition begun in the Progressive period. The official studies sponsored by the President suffered somewhat from the disability of starting with the mistaken assumption that the ideal federal system demanded maximum separation of government functions by level. Those sponsored by Congress, on the other hand, were directed toward understanding how the existing co-operative system worked without questioning its legitimacy. The most important direct products of these studies were the relatively small but continuing efforts by the federal administration and Congress to smooth over the rough edges of intergovernmental relations, as evidenced by the establishment of the Advisory Commission on Intergovernmental Relations. As the period ended, public discussion turned to consider the problems of co-ordinating diverse federal assistance programs within the state and metropolitan areas so as to allow both to better maintain their governmental and social integrity.

With the return of the Democrats to power in 1961, a fifth period of *concentrated co-operation* was inaugurated. Increased federal activity in a number of fields was coupled with an intensification of the debate over "states rights" on one hand and widespread acknowledgment of intergovernmental collaboration on the other. While this period is not yet sufficiently advanced to be fully characterized, it seems clear that it will be one of considerable governmental expansion, particularly at the federal level, to deal with the problems of a metropolitan society. Part of this represents federal "picking up the slack" after the fourth period and part, the extension of government in new ways.

Most of the new federal domestic programs have been resurrected from New Deal days, but recently some potentially new departures have been proposed. They are of two different kinds. There is a movement underway to raise federal minimum requirements in some programs unilaterally in a way that would seriously limit state discretion to adjust them to local needs. At the same time, serious proposals have been made to provide some federal aid through block grants and shared revenues to be used as needed at the states' discretion, thus widening their policy-making powers. However, most of the new programs enacted as of this writing, including the two most revolutionary ones (the Civil Rights Act of 1964 and the antipoverty program) are being implemented so as to continue the established traditions of intergovernmental collaboration. Both provide for substantial state and local participation and maximum possible local control. The antipoverty program, for example, is designed to provide federal money for locally sponsored projects and gives the states veto power over most projects proposed for within their limits.

THE MAINTENANCE OF THE PARTNERSHIP

The foregoing description of the successful maintenance of the traditional system of noncentralized co-operation to date should not obscure the great centralizing pressures operating within the American political system today which may have a decisive impact before the century's end. Nor should it obscure the rough edges within the co-operative system itself that could contribute to a drastic change in the character of the American partnership. The need for managing a national economy, meeting foreign pressures, and securing the constitutional rights of all citizens, as well as the pressures toward elimination of diversity within the country — all these operate to centralize governmental power even when steps to prevent centralization are taken within specific programs. With the constitutional barriers to centralization lowered, the pressures of reformers to secure their reforms and of politicians to secure their rewards wherever it is easiest, without regard for the principles of federalism, further complicate the situation. Finally, the great growth of direct federal relations with private parties through defense and veterans' expenditures, agricultural subsidies, and loan guarantees, none of which are susceptible to organization along traditional co-operative lines, cut into the old patterns even when they are brought into the co-operative system by the back door.

Within the co-operative system, there are problems — for example, weak state and local governments unwilling or unable to uphold their share of the partnership and proliferating "red tape" required by federal administrators to meet federal requirements. There is another problem in that the public information system, as it is presently constituted, tends to focus public attention on Washington to the exclusion of the states and localities.

Logic tells us that noncentralized co-operative federalism is not an easy system to maintain, particularly in a nation that prides itself on being pragmatic — less concerned with form than with function and willing to try anything if it "works." Yet the system has been maintained despite the pressures and in the face of all logic because it has continued to satisfy most of the particular interests in this country more often than not. If not one of them gets everything he wants, each gets something, re-enforcing their attachments to a system they feel they can hope to influence.

Notes

[1] For a discussion of federal-state co-operation before 1913, see Daniel J. Elazar, *The American Partnership* (Chicago: University of Chicago Press, 1962).

[2] Adequate statistical data for most of the nineteenth century is lacking, but the author's sampling based on the available data confirms this. The figures usually cited show state-local expenditures as exceeding federal expenditures by an approximately two-to-one margin until 1933. However, when the value of federal land grants to states, localities, corporations, and individuals is included in the calculations of federal expenditures and the share of state and local expenditures derived from federal endowments is eliminated, the result is quite different.

[3] For a brief, yet thorough discussion of this aspect of American federalism, see Morton Grodzins, "Centralization and Decentralization in the American Federal System," *A Nation of States,* ed. Robert A. Goldwin (Chicago: Rand, McNally, 1963).

[4] See, for example, Dennis J. Palumbo, "The States and American Foreign Relations" (Unpublished doctoral dissertation, Department of Political Science, University of Chicago, 1960); Morton Grodzins, "The Federal System," *Goals for Americans,* ed., President's Commission on National Goals (Englewood Cliffs, N.J.: Prentice-Hall, 1960); and Edward C. Banfield (ed.), *Urban Government* (New York: Free Press of Glencoe, 1961).

[5] While no single date for the real beginning of the "twentieth century" is precisely accurate, 1913 is chosen as the most appropriate, since it was the first year of Woodrow Wilson's "New Freedom," which represented the first great and co-ordinated nationwide response to the problems of the new century and the beginning of a five-year period of great changes in American life.

[6] A "critical election" has been defined as one in which substantial shifts occur in the voting behavior of major electoral blocs, shifts which become sufficiently "permanent" to set the voting patterns for a generation. The United States has experienced critical elections at the national level in pairs every twenty-four to thirty-two years. Every two generations, they have reflected a shift of the voting majority from one political party to the other.

[7] The figures cited here and subsequently—unless otherwise indicated—are from the report of the Advisory Commission on Inter-governmental Relations, "Periodic Congressional Assessment of Federal Grants-in-Aid to State and Local Government" (June 1961).

The Bureaucracy in Pressure Politics

J. Leiper Freeman

In the decade preceding World War I it was widely accepted that the field of politics and the field of administration were separate spheres of public life and that evil consequences resulted from the influence of politics on the business of government. Such a view was congenial to the philosophy of the Progressives who were basically anti-political. They sought to pattern our civil service after what they believed was the experience of the British government. In more recent decades this view has been largely discarded and replaced by the theory that administration is inevitably bound up with policy, and through policy with politics. From the earliest days of the Republic federal agencies have advocated programs and advised Congress on policy. In the following essay, J. Leiper Freeman suggests that we look upon administrative agencies as deeply committed political actors. They administer the laws, to be sure, but they also attempt to influence public opinion and legislative action thereby promoting the interests of their members and of related groups. In short, administrative agencies in many ways resemble and behave like pressure groups.

It is not a novel statement that we live in a society of "organization men," but we have yet to comprehend adequately the implications of this fact. Today's bureaucratic world is a reality within which the vast majority of Americans are enmeshed. Large, complex, specialized, hierarchical organizations are means of achieving the mass production, communications, services, regulation, and destruction possible in modern society. These bureaucracies are both public and private, large and small, demanding and lenient; but in any case they are the dominating form of social organization in America today.

Although bureaucracies are primarily regarded as organizations which execute policies assigned to them by society, they must also be reckoned with as sources of influence upon social policies. The nature of this influence is basically

Reprinted, by permission of the author and publisher, from J. Leiper Freeman, "The Bureaucracy in Pressure Politics," *Annals of the American Academy of Political and Social Sciences,* 319 (September 1958), 11-19. Abridged by the editors.

twofold. First, members of bureaucracies can give shape to stated policies through the exercise of choice and judgment in administering them. Second, in attempting to affect the objectives and working conditions which society will authorize for their organizations, members of bureaucracies necessarily engage in pressure politics.

It is with this second aspect of bureaucratic behavior that this article is chiefly concerned. Furthermore, it is confined to pressure politics engaged in by governmental, as opposed to private, bureaucracies and to pressure politics aimed at influencing official governmental policies.

Public bureaucracies—national, state, and local — today employ about one-eighth of the labor force of the United States. About 3 million of these members of public bureaucracies are in the armed forces; slightly more than 2.2 million are civilian employees of the federal government; more than 1.1 million are classroom teachers in the public schools; about 3.5 million are otherwise employed by the state and local governments. If these bureaucrats, numbering between 9 and 10 million, formed one large group sharing a common identity, they would constitute a force in pressure politics to defy the imagination. But public bureaucrats are divided into many bureaucracies by levels of government, by special functions, by special technologies, by differing clienteles, and by territories. The result is a patchwork of official organizations devoted to limited, specialized interests.

BUREAUCRACIES AS PRESSURE GROUPS

Since a public bureaucracy is concerned with special and limited aspects of public policy, to a degree it resembles the ordinary private pressure group. It is a congregating place for individuals concerned with the same subjects. Some of these interested individuals become members of the administrative agency while others join groups which look to that organization as a rallying point, and the agency takes a leading part in representing their interests. In this representative process perhaps the bureaucracy's most important function is to promote the idea that its special area of concern is important — be it education, air power, or mental health. The bureaucracy also promotes special solutions to policy problems in its area. Finally, it promotes objectives which are of particular interest to its members *as bureaucrats*. These are matters such as their working conditions, status, and compensation, as well as the maintenance and survival of their organization.

A public bureaucracy, as part of the official government, is subject to some controls over its pressure politics which do not apply to private groups. There are laws at the federal level to restrict the public relations and legislative activities of bureaucrats. Federal agencies are forbidden by an act passed in 1913 to use public funds to compensate "any publicity expert unless explicitly appropriated for that purpose." Another act, passed in 1919, provides that appropriations shall not be used, unless explicitly authorized by Congress, "directly or indirectly to pay for any personal service, advertisement, telegram, telephone, letter, printed or written matter, or other device, intended or designed to influence in any manner a Member of Congress, to favor or oppose, by vote or otherwise, any legislation or appropriation by Congress, whether before or after the introduction of any bill or resolution proposing such legislation or appropriation...."

These general restrictions, however, have served mainly as policy statements to be used as threats against agency officials rather than as bases for actual cases. "Publicity experts" have not been hired, but "information," "education," and "publication" officers have been employed in good quantity. Although these publicists have often been flayed in the halls of Congress, no cases have arisen in which they have been held as violators of the law. Furthermore, despite the prohibitions against spending public funds to influence a member of Congress, there has remained a great latitude for legislative activity by public administrators. The expectations of Congressmen in this regard were well summarized by Representative Frank Buchanan in his committee's investigation of bureaucratic lobbying in 1950:

> ... It is equally necessary for the executive branch of Government to be able to make its views known to Congress on all matters in which it has responsibilities, duties, and opinions. The executive agencies have a definite requirement to express views to Congress, to make suggestions, to request needed legislation, to draft proposed bills or amendments, and so on. And there is, of course, the power centered in the executive branch to overrule by veto any action of Congress which is not supported by a clear two-thirds majority of both Houses.[1]

CHIEF EXECUTIVE CONTROLS

It is safe to conclude that such statutory restrictions are not important limitations upon administrative propagandizing and lobbying in the federal government, and they are even less so in state and local governments where laws governing political activities of bureaucrats are generally less numerous and less stringent. Instead, more meaningful controls over bureaucratic pressure politics are to be found in the powers of the Chief Executive.

At all levels of government today there is a tendency toward giving the Chief Executive more effective authority over finance, organization, and personnel to help him control the actions of administrative agencies. These sanctions do not necessarily remove bureaucrats from the arena of pressure politics, but they tend to channel their activities along lines amenable to the Chief Executive. The stronger these sanctions are — as in the case of the city manager or strong mayor form of municipal executive, or the strong governorship, or the Presidency — the smaller the relative autonomy allowed bureaucrats in legislative and public relations.

In the federal government, the Bureau of the Budget and the provisions of the Budgeting and Accounting Act of 1921 aid the President in establishing central control over tendencies toward agency autonomy in seeking appropriations. Executive departments and bureaus are prohibited from seeking amounts larger than those requested for them in the President's budget when they appear before appropriations committees of Congress. Nevertheless, there have been instances in which questioning by committee members has brought into the record a bureau's original requests which perhaps the Budget Bureau had eliminated or curtailed. This device for circumventing the prescribed budget procedure is probably welcomed by an administrator, with friendly committee members and sympathetic interest groups doing the prodding. Yet, on the whole, the executive budget is a significant means of co-ordinating administrative requests for funds.

In proposals for legislation, the Bureau of the Budget is also of some help to the President since it has the power to require that agencies' legislative requests should be submitted to it to determine whether they are "in accord with the program of the President." This does not prevent an agency from submitting proposals to Congress which are not "in accord," but it is supposed to enable Congress to know whether measures are consonant with the President's program when it takes action on them. There is no clear agreement among persons who have studied the effectiveness of this procedure, but the most recent evaluation indicates that in recent years it has become somewhat more effective in curbing autonomous action by the various agencies.[2]

The organizational status of a bureaucracy in the executive hierarchy determines to some degree the autonomy its members will have in their public and legislative relations. The more independently an agency is located in the structure of executive authority, the less formal power the Chief Executive can exercise over its political activities as well as on its administration of the laws. Thus, independent commissions and government corporations may enjoy some measure of independence from central direction of their political entrepreneurship which is not available to regular departments.

Personnel and Schedule C

Under the kind of government most often found in the United States, with a popularly elected Chief Executive having constitutional authority separate from the legislative branch, the President needs and usually has a coterie of political appointees. They serve both as political directors of the agencies and as leaders of the bureaucracies in their attempts to promote policies in their special spheres of interest.

The federal government under the Eisenhower administration enlarged the number of offices in this category by creating the so-called Schedule C positions for policy-making personnel in order to give the Republicans a larger crew of high-echelon officials. The major rationale for this enlargement was that the huge bureaucracies inherited from the previous administration, largely protected by Civil Service status, would otherwise be so intractable that the new administration would not be able to curb their autonomous tendencies. The results of this measure are not yet clear, although it has led to the removal of certain posts at the bureau-chief level from merit system status and to the creation of a number of new assistant secretaries and administrative assistants, who are patronage appointees. They compose an enlarged group of party representatives engaged in legislative liaison, public relations, and policy development at higher levels of the administration. They may have also reduced the political leeway of officials at lower levels.

BUREAUCRATIC AUTONOMY

Despite the restrictions which may be placed upon bureaucracies because they are part of the government, they still have considerable autonomy within the executive structure to engage in pressure politics. They enjoy certain advantages by being in the official family which help to offset the restrictions placed upon them. One advantage is the fact that they are expected by legislators to make recommendations to the legislative body on a continuing, legitimate basis. Furthermore, they may have the blessings of the Chief Executive in their legislative operations and consequently can speak with considerable force as the administration's specialists.

When Representative Buchanan voiced the thought that bureaucrats should "make their views known" to Congress, he was speaking with restraint. Virtually no piece of legislation of any consequence reaches any advanced stage of the legislative process without at least one administrative agency making some statement concerning it. On many bills, the chances are great that the proposal originated in an executive agency. Furthermore, in the highly decisive stage of the legislative process—committee hearings—officials from the administration are invariably among the most regular and most crucial witnesses. Legislators at all levels of government, despite their defensiveness toward bureaucracy, like to hear from the bureaucrats most intimately concerned when making up their minds about proposed legislation, and the bureaucrats oblige them energetically.

The various bureaucracies are also expected by the Chief Executive and top leaders of the administration to carry a good deal of the burden of legislative leadership for the executive branch in their own special areas. This aspect of lobbying by administrative agencies is sometimes overlooked or unduly subordinated by students of the subject because of a preoccupation with the desirability of integrated executive leadership. In reality the Chief Executive cannot personally get involved in every legislative skirmish without tending to reduce his effectiveness and dissipating his resources for political leadership. On lesser matters and indeed on many that are of considerable importance, the bureaucracies are depended upon by the top level of the executive branch to work out the proposals, to secure their introduction, to mobilize support from the public and elsewhere, and to negotiate with the committees and the leaders of the legislative branch to secure favorable action.

GENERAL LEGISLATIVE LIAISON

Administrative agencies do not wait until a specific proposal is to be urged upon the legislature to cultivate harmonious relations with legislators. A continuous process of legislative liaison is maintained. This may be found at all levels of government and at all tiers of administration within these levels, although it is most marked at the higher echelons of federal administration. In the federal government, the growth of this process is reflected in recent institutional developments in which the major agencies have appointed high ranking officials with sizeable staffs to spend their full time on it. Every bureau is also equipped to consider requests from Congressmen and to furnish them information speedily. In the field offices, major headquarters follow the same pattern.

Accommodating legislative requests and inquiries where legitimately possible serves to keep agencies in the good graces of legislators and opens the way for suggestions and requests from administrators in return. Field officials usually work with Representatives and Senators from their own area. In Washington, where the liaison machinery is more elaborate and more concerned with agency-wide problems, particular attention is focused upon Congressional leaders and members of key committees.

While a good part of this activity is precautionary in that it is intended to keep legislators from becoming annoyed with an agency, it is also part of the agency's attempt to "cast bread upon the waters," to maintain a reservoir of good will, and to keep the solons aware of the important work the agency is doing.

At the state and local levels, legislative liaison has not become as highly organized and institutionalized as it has at the national level, but the essential ingredients are the same.

STRATEGY WITH COMMITTEES

Because so much of the meaningful work of legislative bodies is done in committees rather than in the full assemblies, the relations of spokesmen for the bureaucracies with committee members specializing in given policy areas are crucial aspects of administrative pressure politics. Committee members and agency officials who work together on common problems can build up the kind of understanding which maximizes the effect of agency opinions upon committee decisions. Committee recommendations in turn have a primary effect upon the content of laws passed by the parent body. Committee hearings therefore are not merely means by which legislative groups exert control over bureaucracies, they are also critical opportunities for bureaucrats to influence legislation.

In general, committee members need information on policy questions, and administrative officials are in a position to have a vast store of it to present. This information, derived from the elaborate network of a bureaucracy, is a source of power. By presenting it strategically, leaders from the bureaucracy can use hearings to good advantage. Since hearings are usually covered by the press, the information presented may not only make a direct impression upon the committee members but also furnish ammunition to the agency's friends among the public.

Using higher-echelon support

Leaders of a bureaucracy who appear before legislators to advocate any new laws or changes in policy which their agency desires usually try to enlist the support of others. In many instances one of the most helpful sources of support is the Chief Executive or others in the higher echelons of the administration. Many things that an agency desires are not regarded as being of vital importance to the top leaders of the administration, even though the Chief Executive and his advisors may have nothing against their passage. If, however, the bureau chief and department officials seeking the legislation can secure from the Chief Executive a statement to the legislative committee, or a comment to the press, or a paragraph in a speech favorable to their proposal, they may very well enhance its possibilities of adoption.

The effectiveness of this action is, of course, related to the state of the Chief Executive's popularity and prestige with the legislators. If the bureaucrats decide that the Chief Executive would in a given instance be more of an albatross than a guardian angel, they will naturally hope that he will not associate himself with their legislative project in any way.

The use of higher-echelon support is also available to bureaucrats as a defense against unwanted legislation. Their advice is given much weight in questions regarding the use of the Chief Executive's veto power on legislation falling within their special spheres of competence.

Mobilizing employee support

One of the great reservoirs of political strength available to agency leaders in certain kinds of legislative activities lies in their organization's employees. This is naturally more true of the larger organizations since elected officials tend to be impressed by numbers. In the federal government, the Post Office Department (with over 500,000 employees) is a good example of an agency which tends to profit appreciably from employee support.

There is no particular evidence, however, that employees are necessarily helpful to their agency leaders on *all* legislative matters. Detailed studies of municipal department heads' legislative strategies show that they are not inclined to view their employees as important sources of support in dealing with the city council except on matters such as salaries, job conditions, and the like. The reason is that public employee organizations tend to concentrate their efforts on their interests as bureaucrats, often relegating larger policy questions to a secondary position. For this reason, agency leaders are often faced with the problem of tying employee benefits to other policy objectives and thereby evoking a maximum effort by the mass of the bureaucrats in their organizations to influence the legislative body.

At the federal level, a recent example of the linking of employee interests with broader policy objectives was seen in the fight waged by the Post Office Department to secure a modernization of the postal service and the most comprehensive revision of postage rates in over twenty years. Within the postal service, postmasters and postal employees were convinced that new buildings and equipment and increases in salaries were not to be obtained without the revision, and they contributed to the effort to obtain it. Legislative representatives from state and national organizations of postmasters conferred with the legislators. Organizations of postal employees lobbied and propagandized for it heavily.

The employees of the Brooklyn Post Office paid for a full-page advertisement in the *New York Times* to reprint an article by Senator Olin D. Johnston,

Chairman of the Senate Committee on Post Office and Civil Service, which in general advocated modernization of the service and increasing the postage rates. Readers were urged to clip the article and mail it to their Senators.

Mobilizing clientele support

Employees are, after all, not always the most appropriate pleaders in behalf of a bureaucracy in the legislative arena. Legislators are inclined to regard employees as pleading their own cases and therefore may discount their contentions. Consequently, administrative leaders seek to have their proposals endorsed by private groups who carry weight with legislators.

The easiest groups of this type for most agencies to mobilize are the so-called clientele groups. In many instances they are highly organized and easily identified. The Veterans Administration counts heavily on the American Legion and to a lesser extent on other veterans organizations to support its recommendations to Congress. In fact, it seldom tends to make a recommendation to Congress that is not reasonably acceptable to these organizations, so strong is their partnership in all pressure politics dealing with veterans affairs.

The pattern is similar with many other agencies and their clienteles such as the Commerce Department and business organizations; the Labor Department and the unions; and the Agriculture Department and the Farm Bureau, the Grange, and other farmer organizations. These other groups do not, however, always show the same degree of collaboration as that evinced by the Veterans Administration and its customers.

In fact, many of the difficulties attending Secretary Ezra Benson's efforts to convince Congress that his department's recommendations are the answer to the farm problems of the United States are related to an estrangement between the present leadership of the Department of Agriculture and significant portions of its clientele. Agency leaders who fail to maintain the confidence of their patrons are apt to lose the most crucial element of their support in legislative relations. Groups that are not in the clientele of an agency are more difficult to encourage to take as much interest and exert as much effort in the agency's behalf.

Other group support

Bureaucracies welcome and at times aid the organization of groups to serve as their sponsors. These groups are not necessarily composed of steady customers of an agency, but they are made up of people who for various reasons are interested in its aims and its existence. Some of these groups are completely unofficial in nature; but many are given some official recognition in the agency's operations, rendering them quasi-public in character. By elaborating their administrative structure, public bureaucracies at all levels of American government have enlisted the participation of interested and often influential citizens in their business to give them advice and sometimes even to help them set and administer policies. In turn, the bureaucracies expect and usually receive support for their legislative objectives.

Among the many groups of this type to be found at the federal level are, for example, the various reserve officer associations of the military branches, or the very exclusive advisory committee of the Commerce Department, or any of the many other advisory committees in other units. Over the years the Agriculture Department has built up one of the most complex systems of citizen participation in administration at the local level that could be imagined. Some of its major programs are handled at the county level by committees elected by farmers and working in conjunction with full-time paid employees of the Department. In this way, for example, the Agricultural Stabilization and Conservation Service enlists sponsors composed of local farm leaders in county after county across the nation.

In local governments, outstanding examples of sponsor groups are to be found in Parent-Teacher Associations or in "Friends of the Library." And at a more official and formal level they may be found in the plethora of boards and commissions which are officially charged with setting policies for various municipal agencies.

The way in which board sponsorship works to an administrator's advantage was observed a few years ago in a New England city. The head of the library board was the woman with the most prestige in town, and the librarian was regarded as her protegée. These two ladies got the board chairman's husband to agree to buy a bookmobile for the public library if the city would agree to maintain it. Then the City Council was presented with this proposition at a meeting in which the library board was well represented and virtually able to make the matter one in which the Council would appear cheap if it refused. The Council, seeing that it had little choice, voted the funds to maintain the bookmobile and, of course, to furnish a driver.

Pressure by administrative decision

Bureaucrats can often generate pressure upon legislators through the exercise of their legitimate discretion in the course of conducting the public's business. One of the most recent and most widely argued examples was furnished by Postmaster General Arthur Summerfield. He gave orders to curtail mail deliveries one day a week last year when Congress was showing reluctance to appropriate some funds which Mr. Summerfield said were necessary to prevent deficiencies in his agency. Despite outraged cries, Congress gave Mr. Summerfield the money. After all, people wanted their mail on Saturdays.

Looking again at the municipal level, the Water Commissioner of a New England city used his administrative powers to help arouse public support and pressure upon the Council for a bond issue to expand the water supply — a measure which certain industries in the city favored. Although it was a hot and dry summer, the Commissioner helped the drought along for some people by diverting water to the country club from a main which served many residences in a high part of the city. When the residents on this main could not draw bath water, not knowing that their water was being siphoned off to the golfers' showers, they were even more emphatic than the Water Commissioner and his industrialist supporters that the water supply needed expansion. Eventually the Council voted the bonds.

GENERAL PUBLICITY ACTIVITIES

The ultimate aim of bureaucratic publicity is in large measure to create a climate of opinion which will be favorable to its objectives. Some of an agency's publicity is necessary to the administrative process of making more acceptable to the public the things it has already been assigned to do. But the cultivation of favorable public images also may serve to build up support for legislation which the agency desires but does not have, and it is difficult to separate one function of bureaucratic publicity from the other.

The many books and articles written about the exploits of the Federal Bureau of Investigation agents, the continuous, favorable publicity accorded to Mr. J. Edgar Hoover, and the speeches and writings of Mr. Hoover himself all help to make the jobs which are assigned to the FBI easier to accomplish. Yet this publicity also makes the agency more successful in its relations with Congress, for Congressmen are sensitive to the image maintained among the public at large.

Of course, the FBI is unusually fortunate in comparison with other federal bureaus in the nature and extent of its publicity, but many administrative units get a good deal of coverage on a fairly steady basis. There are abundant opportunities for members of the higher echelons of the bureaucracy not only to release news through regular channels and to talk to reporters, but also to make addresses, write articles, and in other ways create publicity for their organizations. Furthermore, in the field offices, regional press coverage is generally well maintained, especially for the larger agencies, and this substantially supplements the publicity emanating from Washington. Since nine-tenths of federal employees are not in Washington, there is immense opportunity for publicity to be generated at local levels, where it can often affect the constituents of Congressmen most directly.

There is also usually a network of friendly media especially interested in the subjects dealt with by an agency and willing to help carry the propaganda battle. Some of these are "trade" publications, which, combined with official publications and reports, give bureaucracies ample outlets to reach the most interested audiences. Due to the limited nature of general public interest in most public problems, it is frequently more important to reach the highly concerned portion of the public than to try to publicize in general.

Bureaucrats can become victims of their own overzealous publicity tactics. Legislators are capable of being very sensitive to what they regard as improper administrative propagandizing, especially if it encroaches on their domains. It does not help administrative leaders and the agencies they represent to become branded as propagandists. The kinds of retribution they suffer in such instances vary from oratorical chastisement in the legislative halls to denial of the very objects which they seek to have the legislators bestow — funds and authority.

Notes

[1] United States Congress, House, Select Committee on Lobbying Activities, *Legislative Activities of Executive Agencies,* Hearings, 81st Congress, 2d Session, Part 10 (Washington, 1950).

[2] Richard E. Neustadt, "Presidency and Legislation: The Growth of Central Clearance," *American Political Science Review,* Vol. 48 (September 1954), pp. 641 ff. For a different point of view, see Arthur A. Maass, "In Accord with the Program of the President?" in Carl J. Friedrich and J. K. Galbraith (Eds.), *Public Policy* (Cambridge, Mass.: Graduate School of Public Administration, Harvard University, 1953), pp. 77-93.

Some Lessons of Experience

Marver Bernstein

The simple fact is that the career civil service has great policy-making powers today and this power is more likely to increase than decrease in the future. The dilemma for democracy is how to maintain a competent civil service while at the same time making it responsive to the people. Concepts of efficiency, expertise, and professionalism tend to run counter to the traditional norm of political responsibility. There is a tendency for administrators to want to keep "politics" out of their agency's affairs. By "politics" they generally mean that they want the President and Congress to leave them alone. But the President and Congress have been elected by the people to run the government and keep it responsive to the needs of the electorate. Hence, there is a conflict between politicians and bureaucrats. The President is required to appoint some two thousand "political executives" to help him manage the agencies. A political executive is an official who performs policy-making functions and who is not under the civil service requirements. Many groups, including the bureaucracy, want to "assist" the President in naming these political executives. If the President is to have any influence over the agencies, he must have his choices in key positions throughout the bureaucracy. This is easier said than done. He finds he must fight for his choice against many groups and even against his own subordinates. These political executives are an important and fascinating group. Many of them are brought into government from the private sector and the contrast in life styles is striking. The Brookings Institution, a private foundation, sponsored a series of round-table discussions in 1958 in which the political executive participants expressed their views on what differences they perceived between private and public executive positions and their personal assessments of their experience in government.

Each president of the United States faces the never-ending task of creating

Reprinted by permission of the Brookings Institution from *The Job of the Political Executive* by Marver Bernstein, © Brookings Institution, Washington, D.C., 1958, pages 200-219.

and replenishing a corps of officials to fill executive posts in more than three-score federal departments, agencies, boards, commissions, and corporations. As the Round Table participants recognized, the recruiting process must be based on a recognition that skills of business management are not readily transferable to government and qualities of high competence in business are not necessarily those that earmark the able government executive.

GOVERNMENT IS DIFFERENT

Early in the Eisenhower administration, it was clear to the new appointees that the environment of government differs markedly from that of private business, and that government makes exceptional demands upon executives. As George M. Humphrey, the first Republican Secretary of the Treasury in twenty years acknowledged:

> When I came to Washington in January [1953], I did not realize so clearly as I do now how different government is from business, and how much more difficult it is to get things done. The job of making changes looked a lot easier from the outside.

Factors that differentiate government from business apply to other aspects of American society as well. As the under secretary of agriculture in an earlier Democratic administration commented:

> It is exceedingly difficult clearly to identify the factors which make government different from every other activity in society. Yet this difference is a fact and I believe it to be so big a difference that the dissimilarity between government and all other forms of social action is greater than any disimilarity among those other forms themselves. Without a willingness to recognize this fact, no one can even begin to discuss public affairs to any good profit or serious purpose.

Public Nature of the Government's Business

Above all else, government is differentiated from other activities by its public nature, which represents both its exposure to public scrutiny and its concern with the public interest. While the "public interest" perhaps has not been satisfactorily defined, it suggests that there are widely-shared interests in society that transcend those of an industry or a special group and that government exists in large part to promote and protect the interests of all the people. As the promoter of the public interest, government must be led and operated by men whose breadth of view and perspective are broader than those of a private individual intent on gaining personal profit. Understanding of the differences between government and other activities and institutions requires recognition that no nongovernmental institution in society has such central and deep concern for everyone, is so closely connected to and dependent upon everyone, and carries on activities which are based so vitally on prevailing social values and reflect popular needs and aspirations.

Virtually nothing that government does is immune from public debate, scrutiny, and inquiry. Matters of administrative detail that are private matters in business are often the subject of investigation and criticism.

> Each employee hired, each one demoted, transferred, or discharged, every efficiency rating, every assignment of responsibility, each change in administrative structure, each conversation, each letter, has to be thought about in terms of possible public agitation, investigation, or judgment. Everything has to be considered in terms of what any employee anywhere may make of it, for any employee may be building a file of things that could be made publicly embarrassing. Any employee who later may be discharged is a potentially powerful enemy, for he can reach the press and Congress with whatever charges his knothole perspective may have invited.

Secretary Humphrey characterized the governmental situation similarly:

> In business it is usually easy to reply to incoming letters, and the replies can be

pretty rough if the situation justifies. But in government! Any letter a Cabinet officer writes may at any time show up in the press, on the floors of Congress or in court. A government man must be certain his letter will stand up under the law, under public scrutiny and in the political forums. Every citizen who writes in is a constituent of two Senators and one Representative; practical politics requires them to act as his advocates, at least up to a point.

The public nature of the government's business is characterized also by public accountability. Both in democratic theory and in practice, officials must be held accountable by law for the decisions they make, the things they do, and the money they spend. In the United States the objectives of maintaining close, continuous control over officials who exercise public power has ordinarily been achieved not by pinpointing responsibility for particular programs but principally by establishing limits to executive discretion and freedom of operation. Congress normally has surrounded executives with detailed rules governing the organizational structure of government offices, the hiring and firing of employees, the spending of money and accounting for its use, the purchase of office supplies, and the procedures and methods of public administration.

Restrictions on Executive Power

While the public may, from time to time, express its fear that government officials are too powerful, officials are likely to be impressed with the restrictions on their power. It may be a solace to embattled Republican executives in the Eisenhower administration that the following comment was made in 1945:

Indeed, this sense of a lack of power is what drives people out of Washington. To have to "think of everything in terms of everything else" causes many men to think that they are so hedged about by restrictions that they "can't do anything," with the result that, after a while, they simply give up with a feeling that they might as well go back home. The orders and statutes in our big democracy do not invest persons with power; they invest organizations with responsibility.

Scope of Governmental Programs

Another characteristic that differentiates government from all other institutions and activities is the breadth of its activities and their pervasive impact on individuals and groups. American government helps to support the destitute, the blind, and the dependent. It sponsors youth clubs to eliminate juvenile delinquency and promotes agricultural development. It inspects meat and insures home loans, bank deposits, and human lives. It operates railroads, plans and constructs highways, generates and sells electric power, and subsidizes ships, airlines, and the newspaper industry. It mediates disputes between labor and management, runs employment offices, and guarantees workers the right to join a union of their own choosing. It clears slums and subsidizes low-cost housing. It makes payments to farmers for soil-conserving practices and warehouses surplus food. It provides tariff aid to domestic industry, free medical care for veterans, economic data for businessmen, and navigation aids for shippers.

Since the basic change in international affairs and the resulting reorientation of American foreign policy in the 1940's, national security and international politics have become more and more significant in public affairs. Military and defense activities and the conduct of foreign affairs account for more than half of the expenditures of the federal government. Today national security involves not only the training of combat soldiers, but also the education of the nation's youth, and the continued development of scientific facilities for research in atomic energy, cosmic rays, ballistic missiles, jet aircraft, and other subjects. In emergency periods, national security may require mobilization of the nation's economy and manpower for concentration on the tasks of war or defense.

Since the depression of the 1930's, the facts of economic life and the political realities of the modern industrial world have compelled government to accept primary responsibility for the satisfactory operation of the domestic economy. Public opinion no longer tolerates severe economic depressions, and in an economic crisis no administration can avoid remedial governmental action. As President Eisenhower said in 1956:

> Experience ... over many years has gradually led the American people to broaden their concept of government. Today we believe as strongly in economic progress through free and competitive enterprise as our fathers did, and we resent as they did any unnecessary intrusion of government into private affairs. But we have also come to believe that progress need not proceed as irregularly as in the past, and that the Federal Government has the capacity to moderate economic fluctuations without becoming a dominant factor in our economy.

Size and Complexity

The federal government is the largest employer and most complex enterprise in the country. In January 1958, about 2.4 million civilians were employed full-time while personnel on active military duty numbered about 2.8 million. In contrast, the American Telephone and Telegraph Company, the nation's largest private employer, had 800,000 employees, and only four other American corporations had as many as 200,000 workers: General Motors, with about 600,000; General Electric, with about 280,000; United States Steel, with about 260,000; and the Great Atlantic and Pacific Tea Company, with about 200,000.

Many federal departments and agencies are as large as most big corporations. In June 1958, civilian employment exceeded 50,000 in ten departments and agencies: Post Office, 538,000; Army, 416,000; Navy, 364,000; Air Force, 316,000; Veterans Administration, 172,000; Agriculture, 101,000; Treasury, 77,000; Commerce, 57,000; Interior, 56,000; and Health, Education, and Welfare, 55,000. According to the Hoover Commission Task Force on Personnel and Civil Service, in 1954 there were about 350 major operating bureaus below the departmental and agency level, and 65 separate departments, agencies, boards, commissions, and corporations. The median size bureau among the 266 bureaus studied in detail by the Task Force was 1,800 people. Forty-four had more than 5,000.

The size of the governmental establishment has contributed to its extraordinary complexity. Government activities have grown in piecemeal fashion in response to the demands of a dynamic society, and administrative authority has been dispersed widely and at times chaotically through several layers of administration. Important matters are rarely the exclusive concern of a single bureau or agency. The decisions of one agency affect, and are affected by the decisions and programs of other agencies. This interpenetration of governmental activities makes it necessary for an executive to share powers of decision with others. He rarely has final authority, and his authority is rarely commensurate with his responsibility. It is not possible to organize the executive branch so that each department, bureau, or agency has a full measure of independence and autonomy. Thus the need to provide co-ordinating devices is continuing and inescapable.

Interpenetration of Government Activities

Former Secretary Humphrey found the interpenetration of government activities to be the distinctive characteristic of government administration:

> Government is vast and diverse, like a hundred businesses all grouped under one name, but the various businesses of government are not integrated nor even directly related in fields of activity; and in government the executive management must operate under a system of divided authority ...

when a government executive decides on a course of action not already established under law, he must first check with other agencies to make certain his proposal does not conflict with or duplicate something being done by somebody else. It is common in government, much too common, for several agencies to be working on different facets of the same activity. The avoidance of overlapping or conflict calls for numerous conferences, for painstaking study of laws and directives, for working out plans in tedious detail so that what one Cabinet officer does will not bump into what another is doing— or run counter to our interests and activities abroad. . . .

Before coming to Washington, I had not understood why there were so many conferences in government, and so much delay. Now I do. Everything is more complex. . . .

These factors impose a heavy burden on executives. As the Hoover Commission Task Force on Personnel and Civil Service asserted: "Because of the size, complexity, tempo, and interrelations of the Government's operations, the demand for competent managers has run ahead of the supply."

Salary Differentials

Government executives are employed at salary levels well below those in private industry in roughly comparable positions. In all likelihood, government will never be able to reward its executives with salaries as high as those available in industry, and perhaps it never should. Nevertheless, existing wide discrepancies in executive salary levels deter promising men and women from pursuing careers in governments, make it more difficult to keep able executives in government, and obstruct the interchange of executive personnel between private life and public service. Salary differentials would, however, be less significant if the prestige of government employment was greater. Not only must the government executive anticipate financial sacrifices, but he must also expect low prestige and considerable abuse and harassment from Congress and the public, who will occasionally question his integrity, the sincerity of his convictions, and his suitability for public employment.

INSECURITY AND INSTABILITY IN GOVERNMENT

The design of the American government tends to produce conflict, friction, and tension. Political power has been widely diffused on a geographical basis between the federal government and the states and within the federal government itself among the legislative, executive, and judicial branches. What distinguishes the U.S. government from most other national governments is not the separation of powers but rather the degree to which that constitutional principle has been modified drastically by devices of checks and balances.

. . . everybody who has observed American government in action knows that much of the tumult and the shouting derives from the fact that virtually all *power is shared* between rival units of government driven by different interests. What the founding fathers designed was a system of relatively discrete areas of responsibility—the President as the executive and the Congress as the legislature, each politically independent of the other. But there is in reality no completely clean division between execution and legislation and the so-called "checks" furnished by the Constitution are, in fact, forms of shared power.

Fragmentation of Political Power

The fragmentation of political power by the proliferation of checks and balances has made legislative-executive relations a source of built-in conflict in the federal government. Just as the sprawling executive branch was put together by bits and pieces, so Congress is composed of a series of small legislatures—the committees—where the real legislative power is exercised. The party system, in turn, is anchored in state and local political organizations whose concern for local and sectional interests takes precedence, normally, over national issues of public policy. Interest groups, in turn, try to perpetuate the dispersion of political power because the lack of some central control within the federal government increases their capacity to influence operations. In such a setting, a high premium has been placed on the unifying influence of the President.

The survival of individual agencies as effective administrative organizations in this environment depends substantially on the ability of executives to operate in an atmosphere of friction and tension and to stabilize that environment by collaborating with congressional committees, interest groups, and other sources of political support. At the same time, however, the building of defensive alliances in the departments and agencies strengthens the drive for operating autonomy and makes the presidential task of political and administrative integration more difficult. As one member of the Round Table stated:

> The instability of the political environment in Washington is a direct function of the presidential system. It is set up to produce conflicts. While the conflicts may not necessarily touch an executive directly, they certainly determine the environment in which he works. Even in days when the administration seemed most completely in control of Congress, there was a great deal of backbiting and pulling and hauling. The place was far from tranquil even in those days. Executives in Britain have their trials and tribulations, but everything there is better cushioned and more neatly ordered. The trials are just as great, but the corners are not as sharp. The executive is more apt to be bruised than cut to pieces.

In the American political system, powerful centrifugal forces and tendencies infinitely complicate the art and process of governing. For better or worse, the splintering of authority and responsibility in the federal government has established limits to effective administration that can be overcome only by political leadership and popular approval. As the experience of former Secretary of the Army Robert Stevens indicates: "The security of a family textile business is not good training for an alley fight."

Consequences of Democracy

Apart from the constitutional and structural factors that contribute to the instability of the federal environment, other institutional arrangements, values, and attitudes, more or less indigenous to democratic government, produce a sense of insecurity in government executives. According to one Round Table participant: "A democratic society has a thousand ways of making its rulers insecure, and we presumably don't want to change very many of them. Even the elected official runs scared, and that is the way we want him to run."

The imperatives of democratic government call for a multitude of rules governing routine administrative operations as well as some devices designed to limit the discretionary authority of executives in making large decisions. For the sake of public accountability, executives in government are required to live in a goldfish bowl, with Congress, the interest groups, and the press watching all the time.

Although it is difficult to account for precisely, a sense of personal insecurity seems to be a characteristic of executive jobs in Washington. The environment in which public business takes place seems to raise the issue of whether an executive is doing anything useful in his job or whether he is wanted or needed. One executive described it as:

> ... the sort of feeling all the time that you have to stop to reassess your relationship to the job and your contribution. You ask yourself: Are you really needed? Are you really wanted? There is a sense also of responsibility to the job and a questioning whether you are measuring up to it. This is a terribly pervasive feeling. It motivates a great deal of what most of us do.

Business executives probably suffer from tensions that may not be distinguishable from those of government executives. But according to one participant with extensive executive experience in both government and private business:

> This operation in a goldfish bowl does seem to make the tensions of the public service much greater than those I see in business. In business you can delegate to a greater degree and hold people down the line responsible. In government the focus of responsibility on the top executives is much greater than in the corporations I have worked with.

The diffusion and sharing of power in American politics tend to make every government organization pluralistic in its interests, while most business corporations are monolithic in their organization. Consequently, the executive in government is limited in the possibilities of large-scale delegation of authority.

While tensions may be acute in business, they tend to concern matters that are less fundamental than those that preoccupy many executives in government. One participant observed:

> The man who makes a mistake in the shoe manufacturing business by picking the wrong styles can measure his judgment in terms of the volume of sales. He may be able to recover his financial losses next year. In any case, after all, it is his money, and you can't take that with you. But the fellow in a bureau of the Atomic Energy Commission deals with the survival of the country and even the fate of mankind. His job accomplishments cannot be calculated neatly and objectively. He feels a kind of wearing responsibility that few business executives feel. The consequences of error are so catastrophic and irreparable that sober and serious fellows would feel worse in administering that responsibility than they would in making financial decisions.

The Round Table concurred with the conclusion of the Hoover Task Force on Personnel and Civil Service that the heart of the federal personnel problem lies in increasing the supply of executives available within the government on a stable basis. The problem has been difficult to solve because the capacities which are so essential in government executives are nowhere systematically developed in American life. As the Task Force stated: "To lead the life of a political executive of high rank amidst the asperities of American politics is a test of toughness, of intelligence, and of devotion to the public interest."

Although the Task Force referred only to politically appointed executives in the passage quoted, the observations are applicable to high ranking civil service executives as well.

SATISFACTIONS DERIVED FROM THE JOB

In its discussions of the jobs of federal executives, the Round Table talked frankly and spontaneously about such matters as the political setting of executive work, the executive's relationship to Congress, the jobs and skills of career executives contrasted with those of political executives, and the limitations on executive discretion in the federal government. Throughout its talks, the Round Table tended to emphasize the problems faced by federal executives. It hoped that thoughtful discussion of the factors that make it difficult "to get things done" in Washington might encourage other executives to face up to complicated and difficult issues in the management of various programs and activities of the federal government.

When members of the Round Table were given an opportunity to review their extended comments about federal executives, a question was raised whether the discussions stressed too much the frustrations of the job. The consensus of the Round Table was that pessimism was not the quality that earmarked their discussions.

> What we have been doing is trying to face up realistically to some difficult problems. We have tried to describe an extremely dif-

ficult, complex, and, at times, frustrating job. But every important job is frustrating at times. If, for a fleeting moment, we wonder if we have exaggerated certain aspects of our jobs, it helps to recall that all important jobs have elements of complexity and frustration.

The Round Table hoped that a report of its conversations might be helpful to a new executive if it could account for the disappointments he would encounter in his government service. As one member stated: "There are going to be some things that he can't do anything about. But if he understands that other people are having the same troubles, it will be immensely easier for him to bear up under it. And if he is forewarned, he will be better prepared."

A member who subsequently retired from government service expressed the Round Table's views clearly:

We must be careful to maintain a realistic outlook toward our jobs. Government employment today should be painted as it is without gloss. All of us who are in government as teachers, civil servants, and policy people have a liking for affairs of state. We are people of generally good intentions who want to do good through the state and promote the well being of society. Therefore, after taking a realistic look at the employment situation in government, our inherent idealism comes to the fore, and we want to brighten up the picture a little. This picture could certainly be a happier one, but let us be sure to make it so by plumbing the present deficiencies and overcoming them rather than by concealing any factors that may make government services less appealing.

While the Round Table resisted the temptation to sugar-coat the job of the federal executive, it did try to indicate why its members stayed on the job, despite the complexities and obstacles encountered in Washington. One member asked: "Are there any of us who can think of something we would rather do because it would be more satisfying than what we do now?" A participant with many years of experience as a business executive prior to his government service said:

I look over my long experience in business before I came to Washington and contrast it with my government service. I conclude that this is one of the most satisfying experiences I have had. Even though there are frustrations and disappointments in dealing with other executive agencies and with Congress, I still wouldn't trade my present job for one in business. I would not trade because in the end, through our methods of give and take, we arrive at something that may not be perfection but it usually does get us on the road toward a better way of life. Compromise is something I didn't know before I came here, at least in the same degree. I learned that compromise is vitally important in government and society. This is a lesson that more Americans need to learn. Many of us come into government with a fixed and simple picture of government operations only to learn, if we stay for more than a few months, that things can't be done here as they are handled in a single company by a president and his board of directors.

A former government executive added:

When I went back to the clubs I was going to before, I found that people were talking about the same things they were when I left four years before. They seemed to have no conception of what the government was or how it worked. I felt like I was back in a little boy's game, despite the fact that I was making five times as much money as I did in Washington.

One participant was emphatic in his strong endorsement of executive work in government:

The privilege of executive experience in the federal government is strongly affirmative. The daily involvement in critical programs affecting large numbers of people offers a stimulation that cannot be equalled in other types of executive positions. Even the conflicts and pressures in the job offer an exciting "gamesmanship" experience for every executive. The association with other Americans from all segments of the community in a common program contributes significantly to personal development and understanding. Success, even in a limited area, becomes more meaningful because of the process through which it has been achieved and because of the broad impact of its consequences. Although demanding, such an experience is also rewarding. Few men or women are able to duplicate the positive quality of such an experience outside the government.

The Round Table's views on the rewards of federal executive life were substantiated by a number of former executives who had served in subcabinet and similar positions in recent years. One wrote:

I have been out of government service three years, and it is difficult to generalize because there are so many contradictions, but here goes:
1. It was the most interesting and satisfactory working experience I have had. I enjoyed the feeling of contributing to big things and to some extent of having made a useful personal contribution.
2. Personal associations within the government, being much less competitive, are more friendly and enjoyable. I felt a community of purpose with people I liked very much.
3. I stayed about long enough. Disposing of other people's money, necessary though it is, is not the same as earning it.
4. My personal affairs are now nearly back to where they were before I went to Washington.
5. I would do it again.

Another former executive wrote:

I consider the time I spent in Washington as the most stimulating assignment I have ever had. Having been quite critical of certain government trends in Washington while in business, I was challenged to find myself unexpectedly in a position where I could do something about the very things I had criticized. It was a sobering experience. To exchange views with other government officials and to have one's convictions either sharpened or dulled proved to be a real policy-making test. I don't begrudge for a moment the financial sacrifices I made. Working as a high government official was an honor I deeply appreciate.

A former assistant secretary now serving another branch of the government reflected soberly on his tour of duty in Washington:

A federal executive in Washington has rewarding but exasperating experiences. In the first place, he is called upon to work harder than he had imagined. One doesn't mind working from early in the morning to 7 or 7:30 p.m. six days a week for a period of several months or even a year or two. But after that time, I found myself longing for sunshine, a fishing pole, or a swimming pool. Another vexation is the inability to replace incompetent help because of seniority, "bumping rights," or veterans' preference. It should be easier to reward exceptional competence and easier to get rid of exceptional incompetence. Despite the gloomy tenor of these remarks, however, a tour of duty in Washington is a thrilling experience. One would not trade close association with present and past history for all the money in the world, nor would one want to do it permanently for the same compensation. The mere opportunity for contact, even though perhaps usually casual, with the country's leadership is satisfying to one's self-respect and constitutes adequate compensation to any man who wants above all else to be of some service to his country.

In thinking about the knowledge and understanding that new executives require and the political setting in which they work, the Round Table did not overlook those aspects that make government a unique human enterprise. Nor did it make light of the untidy, sprawling nature of the executive branch and the problems and pitfalls in attempting the essential task of bridging the constitutional gulf between the executive and legislative branches. Moreover, it had a fresh and realistic grasp of the environmental factors that make for instability in political life and provide wide-range opportunities to block, thwart, or dilute the decisions and policies of federal executives. Without sentimentality or superficial emotion, it was deeply convinced that service in an executive post in government can be immensely rewarding and satisfying.

The Evolution of Nominating Machinery in America

Austin Ranney
Willmoore Kendall

Political parties are distinguishable from other organizations in America because they alone can legally offer candidates to contest in general elections. Also, unlike other organizations interested in politics, parties are public organizations open to all with most of the leadership chosen, in one form or another, by the electorate. The history of parties in the United States has been closely related to the trend toward wider suffrage and increased participation by the electorate. Ranney and Kendall, in a dated yet perceptive analysis of our parties, trace the evolution of our nominating process for office. Only in the United States is the crucial nominating process within parties extended beyond the bounds of a small activist group. The idea that the total membership of a party, or of the electorate, ought to participate in the nomination of party candidates is shocking to most foreign observers. They ask: How can your parties remain united, disciplined, and programmatic if you periodically open the flood gates to all? The short answer is, of course, that our parties are neither united, disciplined, or programmatic. As the participation in the nomination process for candidates has increased, the ability of party organizations to control the use of their most valued asset, their label, has correspondingly decreased. The theoretical question is: Are the goals of wide participation in the nomination process and party cohesiveness and responsibility logically compatible?

The evolution of nominating machinery in America is closely related to the general institutional development of political parties. In tracing it, we may usefully break it down into the following five major phases:

(1) From early colonial times until about the time of the Revolution. Most nominations for elective offices in the colonial governments were made by one or the other or both of two methods: those who wished to hold office simply made public announcement of their candidacies, or announcement was made on

From *Democracy and the American Party System* by Austin Ranney and Willmoore Kendall, pages 274-286, copyright, 1956, by Harcourt, Brace & World, Inc., and reprinted with their permission. Abridged by the editors.

their behalf by primitive versions of the "caucus"—i.e., by small, informal, irregular, and secret gatherings of some of the community's leading citizens, brought together on a basis of straight co-optation. Gradually, however, as lines were drawn in colonial politics between the Whig-Patriot and Tory-Loyalist "parties" and the struggle between them grew more and more intense, both developed continuing organizations of a less irregular and more formal character: correspondence committees, patriotic societies, and, most important of all, so-called "parlor caucuses"—that is, self-constituted, usually secret gatherings of "party" leaders, some of which, by the time of the Revolution, had a continuing membership and highly regularized procedures. The most famous of them was the "Boston Caucus Club...."

(2) From the Revolution to the launching of the new national government in 1789. During this period, nominations for elective offices in the new state governments and for members of the national Congress were made by various methods: correspondence among "party" leaders, mass meetings of local "party" members, recommendations by prominent citizens, and, most commonly, by caucuses, which assumed during this period the form in which we know them today. Before the end of the period, however, there had emerged, in a few states, a new method of making nominations for statewide and county offices, namely, conventions of delegates elected *ad hoc* by local "party" groups. These conventions, to be sure, did not have the settled status and the rules governing procedure and membership that we now associate with the delegate convention; and they met irregularly and infrequently. But it is worth noting that these were the years during which the convention became available as an alternative.

(3) From about 1789 to about 1830. In the 1790's the conflict between the Federalists and the Jeffersonian Republicans crystallized all over the nation, and each group developed into something closely resembling a modern political party. Each party soon included among its prime objectives the election of its adherents to offices selected by statewide and national constituencies; and since the caucuses and conventions mentioned above were mostly local affairs, designed for nominating candidates for local offices, the parties found themselves obliged to develop new machinery, designed with an eye to the larger constituencies. The Jeffersonians, who were the first to recognize this necessity, solved the problem temporarily, in many of the states, by setting up the so-called "legislative caucus," which brought together the Jeffersonian members of the state legislature for the purpose of picking a gubernatorial candidate. The Federalists soon imitated the Jeffersonian legislative caucus, and for the next thirty-odd years both parties used it continuously for making nominations for statewide offices. On the national level, the Federalist party took the lead: beginning in 1800, its representatives and senators met in secret caucus and agreed upon candidates for president and vice-president. The Republican party promptly provided themselves with the equivalent of the Federalist "Congressional Caucus," and used it for nominating presidential candidates until 1824. From an early date, however, the Republicans held open sessions.

Almost from the moment of their establishment, the legislative and congressional caucuses drew a heavy barrage of unfavorable criticism, mainly from the Jacksonian Democrats within the Republican party, who denounced the caucuses as aristocratic, immoral, and oversusceptible to manipulation by the "wire pullers." Through the final years of the period here in question some of the legislative caucuses were abolished under Jacksonian pressure, and some were "diluted" (by the addition of delegates elected by party groups outside the legislature) in an attempt to meet Jacksonians' criticisms. On the national level, the Congressional Caucus kept on going, though under increasing fire, until 1820, but by 1824 it had fallen so low in public estimation that less than a third of the eligible Republican participants bothered to attend (by this time the Federalist party had passed out of existence, and the Republicans had the national field to themselves); and those who did attend brought further ridicule and condemnation upon the whole institution by passing up Jackson and nominating the near-nonentity, William H. Crawford.

(4) From about 1830 to about 1900. As we have already noted, some nominations were being made by conventions as early as the 1780's, and the incidence — as well as the respectability — of such nominations gradually increased over the ensuing years until, by 1830, conventions had entirely displaced the legislative caucuses in most of the states. The first national nominating conventions met to name candidates for president and vice-president in 1831 (the newly formed Anti-Masonic party) and 1832 (the Jacksonian Democratic party). From then until the end of the century the delegate convention was the most common method of making nominations, though we must note that the local caucus continued to be used for naming candidates for *local* offices in many areas. The period 1830-1900, accordingly, witnessed the emergence of the state and local party committees that have been, ever since, a characteristic feature of our party system. (They came into existence because the conventions, which named them, had to make provision for carrying on party work in the intervals between conventions.) Like the legislative-caucus system it replaced, however, the convention system came under increasingly heavy attack as the years passed — and the criticisms sounded very much like those which had previously been directed at the caucus. Conventions, their opponents argued, are undemocratic, not truly representative of the party rank and file, subject to manipulation, bribery, and corruption, and caught in the iron grip of the "bosses." And by the turn of the century or thereabouts, the critics had mustered strength enough to overthrow the convention system in most areas and replace it with our present system of making nominations.

(5) From about 1900 to the present. On September 9, 1842, the Democrats of Crawford County, Pennsylvania, nominated a candidate for public office by direct primary, and thus became the originators of a new fashion in nominating machinery that — tailored as it is to avoid the kind of charges then directed against the caucus and the convention — has since shown itself to have a well-nigh irresistible appeal for those who determine the nature of our electoral system. Through most of the nineteenth century, as it spread first to other localities in and around Pennsylvania and then to more distant places, it continued to be called the "Crawford County System." It did not, to be sure, gain its first legal foothold until the end of the century, when several states in the South and West adopted laws making its use optional for local and state nominations; and not until 1903 did the first state (Wisconsin) enact a law requiring its use for most nominations. But over the next decade and a half events moved swiftly in its favor, so that by 1917 all but four states had adopted the compulsory direct primary for some or all statewide offices, and by 1956 all the states had done so.[1]

AMERICAN NOMINATING MACHINERY TODAY

The Legal Regulation of Nominations

Until 1866, the parties' caucus and convention nominating procedures were entirely unregulated by and "outside of" the law. The first steps toward legal regulation of nominations were taken by California (March, 1866) and New York (April 1866). The California law, directed at various forms of corruption and bribery, was "optional" in character, i.e., its sanctions applied only to those political parties or other organizations that voluntarily invoked them. The New York law, though mandatory for all political organizations, went no further than to prohibit improper attempts to influence the vote of primary electors. From 1866 to 1900, a number of other states adopted laws, some optional and some mandatory, prohibiting various types of fraud in caucuses, conventions, and direct primaries. And since 1900, all the states have enacted laws regulating primary elections, with the result that the legal provisions governing primary elections are now at least as elaborate as those governing general elections.

The great bulk of the laws regulating nominating procedures, like those regulating party organization and membership, are *state* laws. In general, they deal with such matters as eligibility for a party's nomination, eligibility for voting in a party's primaries, the conditions under which party primaries are to be held and the votes to be counted, and the methods of nomination to be required or authorized for this office or that one. As matters now stand, thirty-three states require that all nominations for all offices be made by direct primary. And fifteen states require nominations for some offices to be made by direct primary, and those for other offices to be made by caucuses, by conventions, or by a combination of the two.

The Nature of the Various Nominating Methods

Caucuses. Strictly speaking, a "caucus" is any face-to-face assembly of the members of a party or faction that is held for the purpose of determining its candidates and policies. Thus a meeting at which Democratic members of the U.S. Senate select a floor leader or decide upon parliamentary strategy is a "caucus"; and a strategy conference held in a "smoke-filled room" by the supporters of one of the aspirants to a particular party's presidential nomination is also a "caucus." But when we speak of the caucus as a nominating device, we normally assign to the term a somewhat narrower meaning, namely, that of face-to-face assembly of *party members* as contrasted with *delegates of party members*. A few states still permit caucuses to be used for the nomination of candidates for local offices and for the selection of delegates to nominating conventions for larger constituencies. In the (relatively few) situations where the caucus is still used, however, it only faintly resembles the caucuses of the eighteenth and early nineteenth centuries. In the latter the party leaders exercised strict, though informal (i.e., non-legal) control over admission, and voting was conducted according to *party* rules and procedures; while in the present-day caucus, state laws, not party rules, determine who can attend and what procedures must be followed. State laws, however, do not always use the term in the narrow sense we have just explained. In some states, for example, it is applied to a procedure whereby the polls are kept open at a certain place for a specified number of hours on a prescribed day, and legally qualified party members can come in at any time and vote by secret, state-supervised ballot, a procedure hardly distinguishable from what is generally called a "direct primary." And some states provide for "nonpartisan caucuses," in which party names and membership requirements are not permitted to intrude! But the main point to grasp is that caucuses have been reduced to a minor—and highly inconspicuous—role in our total machinery for making nominations.

Conventions. A nominating convention is an assembly of *delegates*, selected in whatever manner by the members of a party, whose purpose is to determine its official candidates and policies. As we have already observed, this was the prevailing nominating procedure in the United States through most of the nineteenth century, though it lost ground rapidly after 1900. Today only a few states, including, however, New York and Indiana, use it for some or all statewide offices. (A somewhat larger number of states, as noted above, still use it for making nominations for certain local offices.) Like the caucus, the convention used to be governed entirely by party rules. Today, however, state and local conventions are more or less closely regulated by state law; and only the national nominating conventions continue to be governed largely (but not entirely) by party rules.

By far the best-known nominating conventions are, of course, those held by the national parties every presidential year for the purpose of naming candidates for the presidency and vice-presidency.

Petitions. In some states, would-be candidates for some offices can get their names on the general-election ballot by filing a petition signed by a specified number of voters. Nomination by petition is the sole formal method of nomination in most of the world's democracies. In Great Britain, for example, becoming an official candidate for a seat in the House of Commons is simply a matter of filing with the "returning officer" a statement of one's name, address, and business, together with the names of ten registered voters who support one's candidacy—a "proposer," a "seconder," and eight "assenters." In the United States, nomination by petition is used for all candidates in many nonpartisan municipal and judicial elections; and in some states, filing a petition is the only way that third-party and "independent" candidates can get their names on the general-election ballot.

Most nominations for most elective offices in the United States today, however, are made by direct primary.

The Direct Primary

In General. Under the direct primary, nominations are made *directly* by the party "members" themselves, not *indirectly* by the latter's "representatives" (as in conventions), and by secret ballot, not open voting (as in most caucuses). There are several varieties of direct primaries, each of which we shall presently describe; but they are all based upon the notion that *primary* elections (i.e., elections in which members of a particular party determine who shall be its nominees) should be conducted as nearly as possible in the same manner as *general* elections (i.e., those in which the voters decide which nominees shall be elected to public office). Thus all variants of the direct primary have at least these three features in common with the typical general election in the United States: (1) they are regulated for the most part by law, not party rules; (2) they are conducted by public officials, not party officials; and (3) any citizen who satisfies certain legal requirements can participate without the party leaders' having any say in the matter, one way or the other.

In general, direct primaries involve the following procedures: The aspirant to a party's nomination for office gets his name on the primary ballot — either (a) by filing a petition signed by a specified number of party members in his constituency, or (b) by announcing his candidacy and paying a fee into the state treasury. In about half the states, anyone, including a member of another party, is legally free to run in any party's primary; in California, indeed, the law expressly permits such "cross-filing," and it is common practice. In most of these states, the candidate who wins the nominations of both parties can accept only one of the two; but in California the law permits him to accept both, provided only that he has carried the primary of his own party.[2]

After the filing period has elapsed, the state prints the ballots and determines what persons are eligible to vote in each party's primary. It then conducts the election almost exactly as it conducts general elections, counts the votes, declares the results, presides over the review of contested elections, and prints the names of the winners on the general-election ballot.

The direct-primary system differs from state to state on only one major point: the mode of determining *who can vote* in the primary of each party. In this connection there are three main types of primaries: "closed," "open," and "blanket."

Closed Primaries. A "closed primary" is one in which a voter who wishes to vote in a party's primary must first pass a "test" of affiliation, the purpose being to make sure that only the "members" of that party shall have a voice in determining its nominees. The main advantage the closed primary's proponents claim for it is that it tends to discourage "raiding" and "colonizing" by members of the opposition, and thus to promote the integrity, unity, and responsibility of the parties. At present, thirty-eight states employ the closed primary in one form or another.

Open primaries. An "open primary" is one in which a voter who wishes to vote in a party's primary may do so without having to pass any test of affiliation whatever. In some states, the voter gets the ballots of all parties, marks one, and deposits the others in a special box for unused ballots. In other states, he receives a ballot with the names of the candidates for nomination in all parties printed on it in separate columns for each party. He is instructed to make choices in the column of one party only, and warned that if he votes in the columns of more than one party his ballot will be thrown out. The main advantage claimed for the open primary is that it tends to preserve the secrecy of the voter's party affiliation and this to protect him from any sort of punishment or retaliation for his choice among the parties. Nine states now use this system.

The Washington "Blanket Primary." Since 1936, the voter in the state of Washington has marked a primary ballot on which the names and party affiliations of all candidates of all parties for a given office are printed under a distinct heading for that office. He votes for one candidate under each heading, and is not restricted to the candidates of any one party for all offices. Washington's is the only primary system in which the voter can "split" his vote among the parties, and several political scientists have condemned it on the ground that it "corrupts the meaning of party" and is "a barrier to the development of a program-conscious attitude among party members." Ogden's study or the actual operation of the system, however, indicates that there is only a little more ballot splitting in the primaries than in the general elections, and that the blanket primary has not significantly harmed party organization or "regularity."[3]

The Impact of the Direct Primary Upon the Parties

Has It "Democratized" Them? The early-day advocates of the direct primary believed that it would "democratize" the parties' internal structure because it would take the nominating power away from the "bosses" and give it to the "members." Its opponents believed that the direct primary, by destroying the power of party leaders over nominations, would cause the parties to "disintegrate" by reducing them to congeries of confused and confusing factional disputes.

Most present-day commentators agree that the direct primary has fulfilled neither set of expectations — not even the forecast, common to both, that it would destroy the party leaders' power over the nominating process. Most primary elections, they contend, are won by "organization" candidates, as likely as not the same candidates who would have won had the direct primary never been invented, so that the "machines" are about as much in control of nominations as they ever were; and there is no evidence that the cohesiveness and "responsibility" of the parties have been affected one way or the other by the displacement of the caucus and the convention. Most of these commentators, however, would oppose abolition of the direct primary, on the grounds not that it has broken the power of many "bosses," but that it does oblige the party leaders to put up candidates who can survive the give-and-take of a primary-election struggle, and also provides the party members with a last-resort "shotgun-behind-the-door," which they can use whenever the leaders try to put over something outrageous.

Has It Hastened the Trend to One-Partyism? Earlier in the present chapter we presented data pointing to an increase in the incidence of one-party areas, and to the coincidence of the increase with the heyday of the direct primary. We must now pause to inquire — since the fact that two events happen simultaneously does not prove that one of them "causes" the other — whether there is any reason to suppose that the coincidence is other than accidental. This question could be answered empirically only if we were in a position to set up a controlled experiment (for instance, by taking two similar modified one-party counties side by side, one with and the other without the direct primary, and observing what happens)—which we are not. And no amount of data confirming the coincidence would bring us any closer to proof of a causal connection. Our inquiry, therefore, must be raised to the level of theory. Let us *assume* two similar modified one-party counties side by side, one with and the other without the direct primary, and let us ask whether the former, in the nature of the case and by contrast with the latter, would be likely to develop toward one-partyism. The present writers think it would, and for two reasons. First, just to the extent that one party is dominant over the other, voters can "make their votes count" by voting in the dominant party's primaries, which they can do only if there are such primaries, and which they will learn to do increasingly as time passes. And second, just to the extent that one party is dominant over the other, promising young men with political ambitions will offer themselves as candidates in the dominant party's primary, which again they can do only if there are such primaries. And the effect in both cases is to weaken progressively the second party by draining off interest in what it is doing by comparison with what the dominant party is doing, and by starving its leadership of bright young men who mean business about politics. Or, to put it the other way around, the second party's chances of holding the interest of the rank and file, and of attracting capable potential leaders among the young, are enormously greater in the county which has no direct primary.

Has It Affected the Control of Nominations? The direct primary has undoubtedly increased the volume and added to the complexity of the tasks that party leaders and workers have to perform: it has nearly doubled the number of elections for which they must organize, work, and gather funds. It seems probable that it has also altered, to some extent, the character of the contests within each party for control of the nominating process. Before its adoption, these contests were fought out among party leaders and party workers, i.e., among persons belonging to the party's innermost circles. Under the direct-primary system, by contrast, persons outside these circles — those who vote in the party's primary but are not party leaders or party workers — take part in the contests, and in a sense have the last word as to their outcome. This, of course, is all to the good as far as the partisans of the direct primary are concerned: what they want is genuine "intraparty democracy," and precisely what they mean by this is control of the nominating process by the rank-and-file "members," not the "bosses." Any assessment of the effects of the direct primary or of the thinking underlying it must, therefore, turn finally upon answers to the question, Where *does* control of the nominating process now reside in American parties?

CONTROL OF NOMINATIONS IN AMERICAN PARTIES

Those who have studied the control of nominations in American parties seem to agree on two propositions: (1) Most nominations are *leader-controlled*, i.e., *not* controlled by the rank-and-file party members (who rarely rise up, take the "shotgun" out from "behind the door," and pass over organization candidates in favor of candidates opposed by the party leaders). And (2) the nominating process is *decentralized*, in the sense that nominations for national public offices are more often controlled by state and local party leaders than by national leaders. Let us examine the evidence on each of these two points.

Leader Control

The Evidence. Few attempts have been made to measure precisely what effects the direct primary has actually had on the control of nominations. What evidence we have on this point consists of statements made by students of the subject on the basis of personal observation of the general workings of the system over a number of years. But certainly the consensus among these students is that the party organizations or "machines" usually put forward slates of carefully selected candidates, back them in the primaries, and elect them, often with little or no opposition. Ewing's and Turner's studies of the effects of incumbency on primary elections tend to bear this out, since they show that incumbents who seek renomination win about 90 per cent of the time and are unopposed about half the time.

Key's recent study of nominations for state legislative posts suggests, however, that the organization's power over nominations varies according to the type of party system. In the primaries of the dominant parties in the one-party and modified one-party areas, his figures indicate, competition is keener than in the primaries of either party in the two-party areas, and the keener competition tends to weaken organization control.[4] This, to be sure, is what we should expect in the light of our earlier discussion . . . where we saw that the organiza-

TABLE 1. Relative Participation in the Primary and General Elections of 1942[5]

(The figures indicate the vote in the primaries as a percentage of the vote in the general elections.)

Percentages	Number of States	Identity of the States
Under 35	4	Colorado, Maine, Massachusetts, Utah
35-44.9	8	Indiana, Iowa, Michigan, New Hampshire, New Jersey, Ohio, Wisconsin, Idaho
45-54.9	4	Kansas, Maryland, Nebraska, Nevada
55-64.9	6	Illinois, Kentucky, Missouri, Pennsylvania, Vermont, Washington
65-74.9	6	Minnesota, Montana, New Mexico, South Dakota, West Virginia, Wyoming
75-84.9	3	California, North Dakota, Oregon
85-99.9	1	North Carolina
Over 100	11	Alabama, Arizona, Arkansas, Florida, Georgia, Louisiana, Mississippi, Oklahoma, South Carolina, Tennessee, Texas

(Data not available on the other states)

tions of the dominant parties in the one-party areas play little or no role in the making of nominations. In the "multifactional" one-party areas especially, the direct primary has undoubtedly lessened the power of the few leaders at the top of the party hierarchy to make nominations; so that the Democratic primaries in such states as Arkansas, Florida, and Mississippi probably resemble more closely the utopia of the partisans of the direct primary than those in the two-party states or the bifactional one-party states.

One other point in connection with leader control of direct-primary elections merits notice: In most areas notably fewer persons vote in the primaries than in the general elections. The absence of centrally gathered statistics for primary elections in all the states makes it difficult to document this point for the whole nation over any specific period of time. But the Bureau of the Census did gather such statistics for the 1942 primary and general elections, and its results are shown in Table 1.

As we have already pointed out, winning primaries is high-priority business for party leaders and workers. They see to it, therefore, that *their* voters get to the polls, in good or bad weather and however dull the contests may appear to the casual observer. Consequently, "organization" votes are likely to be the hard core of the total vote in any direct primary election; and the smaller the total vote, the more likely it is that the nominations will be controlled by the leaders rather than the rank and file. If this line of reasoning is correct, however, the low level of participation in the primaries reflected in Table 1 suggests that in most areas most nominations are indeed controlled by party leaders.[6]

The Pre-Primary Convention. The party organization, say some political scientists, is charged with the responsibility for conducting campaigns for the party's nominees; and its choices as to who those nominees shall be should, therefore, have some kind of inside run in the primary, just as the rank and file should be in a position to reject organization candidates when they wish. Nor, they add, is there any reason why one of these "should's" must be sacrificed to the other: let the law require a "pre-primary convention" of party leaders for the purpose of naming *their* slate of candidates for the primary; let the organization candidates be designated as such on the primary ballot; and then let anti-organization candidates get themselves on the ballot by petition. Formalizing the organization's position in this way, they contend, will bring about the proper balance between the power that should accompany the organization's responsibility, and the rank and file's indisputable claim to the last word. New Mexico, Utah, Colorado, Rhode Island, Nebraska, and Massachusetts now employ one or another version of the pre-primary convention.

Notes

[1]For many years Connecticut was the only state which did not use the direct primary. In 1955, however, Connecticut adopted a system which is a peculiar combination of a pre-primary convention, a referendum, and a closed primary. The new system works as follows. Party delegate conventions meet and select a nominee for each office, and these nominees are certified to the public authorities as "party-endorsed" candidates. During a period of fourteen days after the convention, any candidate who received at least 20 per cent of the votes in the convention for the nomination to any office may, by petition, file or have filed on his behalf a "candidacy" for that nomination. If one or more such candidacies are filed, a regular closed primary is held to choose the nominee from among the "party-endorsed" and the petitioning candidates; and

whichever receives the largest number of votes is decared the party's official nominee for the office. If no candidate petitions for a primary within the designated period, the "party-endorsed" candidate is automatically declared the official nominee.

[2] On "cross-filing" and its effects, see Robert W. Binkley, Jr., *Double Filing in Primary Elections* (Berkeley: University of California, Bureau of Public Administration, 1945); and Evelyn Hazen, *Cross Filing in Primary Elections* (Berkeley: University of California, Bureau of Public Administration, 1951). The relevant California statutes were recently amended, however, and now provide that every candidate in a primary must have his party affiliation printed alongside his name, thereby telling the voter whether the candidate is "native" or "foreign" to the party whose nomination he is seeking. Most observers believe this new provision will lessen the likelihood of a Republican's winning a Democratic nomination and vice versa. [Editors note: Cross-filing was abolished by the California Legislature in 1958.]

[3] Daniel M. Ogden, Jr., "The Blanket Primary and Party Regularity in Washington," *Pacific Northwest Quarterly,* Vol. XXXIX (January, 1948), pp. 33-38. See also Claudius O. Johnson, "The Washington Blanket Primary," *Pacific Northwest Quarterly,* Vol. XXXIII (January, 1942), pp. 27-39.

[4] V. O. Key, Jr., "The Direct Primary and Party Structure: A study of State Legislative Nominations," *American Political Science Review,* 8 (March 1954), 14-16.

[5] This table is a revised presentation of the data given in Charles E. Merriam and Harold F. Gosnell, *The American Party System,* 4th ed. (New York: The Macmillan Company, 1949), Figure 10 on p. 311.

[6] Note that of the eleven states with a larger vote in the primaries than in the general election, ten are either one-party or modified one-party states. This is what we should expect from our analysis of the role of the primary in such states.

The Changing Pattern of Urban Party Politics

As America encountered the first pangs of urban growth in the latter decades of the nineteenth century, it became apparent that the cities were administratively unable to meet the increased demand for services. Into this void came the political parties. The urban "machine" sought to provide services, leadership, and a social base for the city folk, particularly the newly-arrived immigrants. These urban parties have long been the target of attack by reformers. Today the remains of those once powerful, uniquely American, organizations are to be found in only a few cities. What has accounted for their decline? What kind of politics and organizations have taken their place? Fred Greenstein provides some insight into the social and political changes which sapped the resources of old style parties and offers some opinions on the directions urban parties are likely to follow in the future.

Fred I. Greenstein

Highly organized urban political parties are generally conceded to be one of America's distinctive contributions to mankind's repertory of political forms. Just as the two major national parties in the United States are almost universally described in terms of their disorganization—their lack of an authoritative command structure — the municipal parties have, until recently, been characterized by most observers in terms of their hierarchical strength. E. E. Schattschneider once summarized this state of affairs in the memorable image of a truncated pyramid: a party system which is weak and ghostlike at the top and solid at the bottom.[1]

This essay deals with the disciplined, largely autonomous local political parties which sprang up in many American cities in the nineteenth century. Much of the literature on these political configurations is heavily pejorative, concerned more with excoriation than explanation. Even the basic nomenclature, "boss" and "machine," is laden with negative connotations, although recently there has been a turn toward nostalgic roman-

Reprinted by permission of the author and publisher from Fred I. Greenstein, "The Changing Pattern of Urban Party Politics," *Annals of the American Academy of Political and Social Sciences,* 353 (May, 1964), 2-13.

ticization of the "vanishing breed" of city bosses.[2]

Here, for reasons which I shall indicate, the attempt shall be to delineate rather than to pass moral judgment: What was the nature of old-style urban party organization? Why did this political pattern develop and how did it operate? What contributed to its short-run persistence in the face of reform campaigns? Under what circumstances have such organizations disappeared and under what circumstances have they continued into the present day — or even undergone renaissances? What are the present-day descendents of old-style urban party organizations?

Analytic delineation invariably involves oversimplification. This is doubly necessary in the present case, because our knowledge of the distribution of types of local party organization is scant. We have no census of local political parties, either for today or for the putative heyday of bosses and machines. And there is reason to believe that observers have exaggerated the ubiquity of tightly organized urban political parties in past generations, as well as underestimated somewhat their contemporary prevalence.

OLD-STYLE PARTY ORGANIZATION: DEFINITIONAL CHARACTERISTICS

Ranney and Kendall have persuasively argued that the imprecision and negative connotations of terms like "boss" destroy their usefulness. What, beyond semantic confusion, they ask, can come from classifying politicians into "bosses" versus "leaders"? Such a distinction leads to fruitless preoccupation with the purity of politicians' motives rather than the actuality of their behavior; it overestimates the degree to which figures of the past such as Richard Croker, William Tweed, and Frank Hague were free of public constraints; and it obscures the fact that *all* effective political leaders, whether or not they are popularly labeled as bosses, use quite similar techniques and resources.[3]

Granting these points, it still seems that a recognizable and noteworthy historical phenomenon is hinted at by the venerable terms "boss" and "machine." If the overtones of these terms make us reluctant to use them, we might simply speak of an "old style" of party organization with the following characteristics:

(1) There is a disciplined party hierarchy led by a single executive or a unified board of directors.

(2) The party exercises effective control over nomination to public office, and, through this, it controls the public officials of the municipality.

(3) The party leadership — which quite often is of lower-class social origins—usually does not hold public office and sometimes does not even hold formal party office. At any rate, official position is not the primary source of the leadership's strength.

(4) Rather, a cadre of loyal party officials and workers, as well as a core of voters, is maintained by a mixture of material rewards and *nonideological* psychic rewards — such as personal and ethnic recognition, camaraderie, and the like.[4]

THE RISE OF OLD-STYLE PARTY ORGANIZATION

This pattern of politics, Schattschneider comments, "is as American as the jazz band . . . China, Mexico, South America, and southern Italy at various times have produced figures who played roles remotely like that of the American boss, but England, France, Germany, and the lesser democracies of Europe have exhibited no tendency to develop this form of political organization in modern times."[5] What then accounted for the development of old-style party organization in the United States?

The Crokers, Tweeds, and Hagues and their organizations probably could not have arisen if certain broad preconditions had not existed in American society and culture. These include the tradition of freewheeling individualism and pragmatic opportunism, which developed in a prosperous, sprawling new society unrestrained by feudalism, aristocracy, monarchy, an established church, and other traditional authorities. This is the state of affairs which has been commented on by countless observers, even before de Tocqueville, and which has been used to explain such disparate phenomena as the failure of socialism to take hold in the United States, the recurrence of popularly based assaults on civil liberties, and even the peculiarly corrosive form which was taken by American slavery.[6]

It also is possible to identify five more direct determinants of the form that urban party organization took in the nineteenth century, three of them consequences of the Industrial Revolution and two of them results of political institutions and traditions which preceded industrialization.

Massive urban expansion

Over a relatively brief span of years, beginning in the mid-nineteenth century, industrial and commercial growth led to a spectacular rise in the number and proportion of Americans concentrated in cities. A thumbnail sketch of urban expansion may be had by simply noting the population of urban and rural areas for each of the twenty-year periods from 1840 to 1920:

	URBAN POPULATION	RURAL POPULATION
	(in millions)	
1840	1.8	15.2
1860	6.2	25.2
1880	14.1	36.0
1900	30.1	45.8
1920	54.2	51.6

These statistics follow the old Census Bureau classification of areas exceeding 2,500 in population as urban. Growth of larger metropolitan units was even more striking. In 1840 slightly over 300,000 Americans lived in cities — or, rather, a single city, New York — with more than a quarter of a million residents; by 1920 there were twenty-four cities of this size, containing approximately 21 million Americans.

The sheer mechanics of supporting urban populations of this magnitude are, of course, radically different from the requirements of rural life. There must be extensive transportation arrangements; urban dwellers are as dependent upon a constant inflow of food and other commodities as an infant is on the ministrations of adults. A host of new administrative functions must be performed as the population becomes urbanized: street construction and maintenance, bridges, lighting, inter-urban transportation, sanitary arrangements, fire-fighting, police protection, and so forth. Overwhelming demands suddenly are placed on governments which, hitherto, were able to operate with a minimum of effort and activity.

Disorganized forms of urban government

The forms of government which had evolved in nineteenth-century America were scarcely suitable for meeting the demands of mushrooming cities. Governmental structures reflected a mixture of Jacksonian direct democracy and Madisonian checks and balances. Cities had a multitude of elected officials (sometimes they were elected annually), weak executives, large and unwieldy councils and boards. The formal organization of the cities placed officials in a position permitting and, in fact, encouraging them to checkmate each other's efforts to make and execute policies. Since each official was elected by appealing to his own peculiar constituency and had little incentive to co-operate with his associates, the difficulties caused by the formal limitations of government were exacerbated. In a period when the requirements for governmental action were increasing geometrically, this was a prescription for chaos.

Needs of businessmen

A third aspect of mid-nineteenth-century American society which contributed to the formation of old-style party organizations was the needs of businessmen. There was an increasing number of merchants, industrialists, and other businessmen, licit and illicit, who needed — and were willing to pay for — the appropriate responses from city governments. Some businessmen wanted to operate unrestrained by municipal authority. Others desired street-railway franchises, paving contracts, construction work, and other transactions connected with the very growth of the cities themselves.

Needs of dependent populations

The needs of the bulk of the nineteenth-century urban population were not for profits but for the simple wherewithal to survive and maintain a modicum of dignity. It is difficult in the relatively affluent society of our day to appreciate the vicissitudes of urban life several generations ago: the low wages, long hours, tedious and hazardous working conditions, and lack of security which were the lot of most citizens. Even for native-born Americans, life often was nasty and brutish. But many urbanites were first- and second-generation immigrants who, in addition to their other difficulties, had to face an alien culture and language. Between the Civil War and the First World War, the United States managed somehow to absorb 25 million foreigners.

Unrestricted suffrage

Urban dwellers were not totally without resources for their own advancement. The American tradition of unrestricted male franchise was, in the long run, to work to their advantage. Although it doubtless is true that few city dwellers of the day were aware of the importance of their right to vote, politicians *were* aware of this. Because even the lowliest of citizens was, or could become, a voter, a class of politicians developed building upon the four conditions referred to above: the requirements of organizing urban life, the inability of existing governments to meet these requirements, and the presence of businessmen willing to pay for governmental services and of dependent voting populations in need of security from the uncertainties of their existence.

The old-style urban party leader was as much a product of his time and social setting as was the rising capitalist of the Gilded Age. Building on the conditions and needs of the day, the politician had mainly to supply his own ingenuity and co-ordinating ability in order to tie together the machinery of urban government. If a cohesive party organization could control nominations and elect its own agents to office, the formal fragmentation of government no longer would stand in the way of municipal activity. The votes of large blocs of dependent citizens were sufficient to control nominations and win elections. And the financial support of those who sought to transact business with the city, as well as the revenues and resources of the city government, made it possible to win votes. The enterprising politician who could succeed in governing a city on this basis was a broker *par excellence;* generous brokers' commissions were the rule of the day.

The importance of out-and-out vote-buying on election day as a source of voter support can easily be overestimated. Party organizations curried the favor of voters on a year-long basis. In a day when "better" citizens espoused philosophical variants of Social Darwinism, urban politicians thought in terms of an old-fashioned conception of the welfare state. In the familiar words of Tammany sachem George Washington Plunkitt:

What holds your grip on your district is to go right down among the poor families and help them in the different ways they need help. I've got a regular system for this. If there's a fire in Ninth, Tenth or Eleventh Avenue, for example, any hour of the day or night, I'm usually there with some of my election district captains as soon as the fire engines. If a family is burned out I don't ask whether they are Republicans or Democrats, and I don't refer them to the Charity Organization Society, which would investigate their case in a month or two and decide they were worthy of help about the time they are dead from starvation. I just get quarters for them, buy clothes for them if their clothes were burned up, and fix them up til they get things runnin' again. It's philanthropy, but it's politics, too — mighty good politics. Who can tell how many votes one of these fires bring me? The poor are the most grateful people in the world, and, let me tell you, they have more friends in their neighborhoods than the rich have in theirs.[7]

With numerous patronage appointees (holders not only of city jobs but also of jobs with concerns doing business with the city), party organizations could readily administer this sort of an informal relief program. And, unlike many latter-day charitable and governmental relief programs, the party's activities did not stop with the provision of mere physical assistance.

I know every man, woman and child in the Fifteenth District, except them that's been born this summer — and I know some of them, too. I know what they like and what they don't like, what they are strong at and what they are weak in, and I reach them by approachin' at the right side.

For instance, here's how I gather in the young men. I hear of a young feller that's proud of his voice, thinks that he can sing fine. I ask him to come around to Washington Hall and join our Glee Club. He comes and sings, and he's a follower of Plunkitt for life. Another young feller gains a reputation as a baseball player in a vacant lot. I bring him into our baseball club. That fixes him. You'll find him workin' for my ticket at the polls next election day. Then there's the feller that likes rowin' on the river, the young feller that makes a name as a waltzer on his block, the young feller that's handy with his dukes — I rope them all in by givin' them opportunities to show themselves off. I don't trouble them with political arguments. I just study human nature and act accordin'.[8]

This passage reflects some of the ways in which party activities might be geared to the *individual* interests of voters. *Group* interests were at least as important. As each new nationality arrived in the city, politicians rather rapidly accommodated to it and brought it into the mainstream of political participation. Parties were concerned with the votes of immigrants virtually from the time of their arrival. Dockside naturalization and voter enrollment was not unknown.

But if the purpose of the politicians was to use the immigrants, it soon became clear that the tables could be turned. In Providence, Rhode Island, for example, a careful study of the assimilation of immigrant groups into local politics shows that, within thirty years after the arrival of the first representative of a group in the city, it began to be represented in the councils of one or both parties. Eventually, both of the local parties came to be dominated by representatives of the newer stocks. Thus, in 1864 no Irish names appear on the lists of Democratic committeemen in Providence; by 1876 about a third of the names were Irish; by the turn of the century, three-quarters were Irish. In time, the Republican party became the domain of politicians of Italian ancestry.[9] Perhaps the most dramatic example to date of urban party politics as an avenue of upward social mobility was in the antecedents of President Kennedy, whose great-grandfather was an impoverished refugee of the Irish potato famine, his grandfather a saloon keeper and a classical old-time urban political leader, his father a multimillionnaire businessman, presidential advisor, and ambassador to the Court of St. James.

When the range of consequences of old-time party organizations is seen, it becomes apparent why moral judgments of "the boss and the machine" are likely to be inadequate. These organizations often were responsible for incredible corruption, but they also — sometimes through the very same activities — helped incorporate new groups into American society and aided them up the social ladder. The parties frequently mismanaged urban growth on a grand scale, but they *did* manage urban growth at a time when other instrumentalities for governing the cities were inadequate. They plied voters, who might otherwise have organized more aggressively to advance their interests, with Thanksgiving Day turkeys and buckets of coal. But, by siphoning off discontent and softening the law, they probably contributed to the generally pacific tenor of American politics. It seems fruitless to attempt to capture this complexity in a single moral judgment. One can scarcely weigh the incorporation of immigrant groups against the proliferation of corruption and strike an over-all balance.

WHY REFORMERS WERE "MORNIN' GLORIES"

Stimulated by high taxes and reports of corruption and mismanagement on a grand scale, antiboss reform movements, led by the more prosperous elements of the cities, became increasingly common late in the nineteenth century. Compared with the regular party politicians of their day, reformers were mere fly-by-night dilettantes—"mornin' glories."[10] They lacked the discipline and the staying power to mount a year-long program of activities. Perhaps more important, the values of the reformers were remote from — in fact, inconsistent with — the values of the citizens whose support would be needed to keep reform administrations in office.

Reformers ordinarily saw low taxes and business-like management of the cities as the exclusive aim of government. To the sweatshop worker, grinding out a marginal existence, these aims were at best meaningless, at worst direct attacks on the one agency of society which seemed to have his interests at heart.

THE DECLINE OF OLD-STYLE PARTY ORGANIZATION

Although in the short run old-style party organizations were marvelously immune to the attacks of reformers, in recent decades the demise of this political form has been widely acclaimed. Because of the absence of reliable trend data, we cannot document "the decline of the machine" with precision. The decline does seem to have taken place, although only partly as a direct consequence of attempts to reform urban politics. Events have conspired to sap the traditional resources used to build voter support and to make voters less interested in these resources which the parties still command.

Decline in the resources of old-style urban politicians

Most obviously, job patronage is no longer available in as great a quantity as it once was. At the federal level and in a good many of the states (as well as numerous cities), the bulk of jobs are filled by civil service procedures. Under these circumstances, the most a party politician may be able to do is seek some minor form of preferment for an otherwise qualified job applicant. Furthermore, the technical requirements of many appointive positions are sufficiently complex to make it inexpedient to fill them with unqualified personnel.[11] And private concerns doing business with the cities are not as likely to be sources of patronage in a day when the franchises have been given out and the concessions granted.

Beyond this, many modern governmental techniques—accounting and auditing requirements, procedures for letting bids, purchasing procedures, even the existence of a federal income tax — restrict the opportunities for dishonest and "honest" graft. Some of these procedures were not instituted with the explicit purpose of hampering the parties. Legislation designed deliberately to weaken parties *has*, however, been enacted — for example, nomination by direct primary and non-partisan local elections, in which party labels are not indicated on the ballot. Where other conditions are consistent with tight party organization, techniques of this sort seem not to have been especially effective; old-style parties are perfectly capable of controlling nominations in primaries, or of persisting in formally nonpartisan jurisdictions. But, together with the other party weakening factors, explicit anti-party legislation seems to have taken its toll.

Decline of voter interest in rewards available to the parties

Even today it is estimated that the mayor of Chicago has at his disposal 6,000 to 10,000 city patronage jobs. And there are many ways of circumventing good government, antiparty legislation. An additional element in the decline of old-style organization is the increasing disinterest of many citizens in the rewards at the disposal of party politicians. Once upon a time, for example, the decennial federal census was a boon to those local politicians whose party happened to be in control of the White House at census time. The temporary job of door-to-door federal census enumerator was quite a satisfactory reward for the party faithful. In 1960 in many localities, party politicians found census patronage more bother than boon; the wages for this task compared poorly with private wages, and few voters were willing to put in the time and leg work. Other traditional patronage jobs — custodial work in city buildings, employment with departments of sanitation, street repair jobs — were becoming equally undesirable, due to rising levels of income, education, and job security.

An important watershed seems to have been the New Deal, which provided the impetus, at state and local levels as well as the federal level, for increased governmental preoccupation with citizen welfare. The welfare programs of party organizations were undercut by direct and indirect effects of social security, minimum wage legislation, relief programs, and collective bargaining. And, as often has been noted, the parties themselves, by contributing to the social rise of underprivileged groups, helped to develop the values and aspirations which were to make these citizens skeptical of the more blatant manifestations of machine politics.

VARIETIES OF CONTEMPORARY URBAN POLITICS

Nationally in 1956, the Survey Research Center found that only 10 percent of a cross section of citizens reported being contacted personally by political party workers during that year's presidential campaign. Even if we consider only non-southern cities of over 100,000 population, the percentage is still a good bit less than 20.[12] This is a far cry from the situation which would obtain if party organizations were well developed and assiduous. But national statistics conceal a good bit of local variation. A survey of Detroit voters found that only 6 per cent of the public remembered having been approached by political party workers; in fact, less than a fifth of those interviewed even knew that there *were* party precinct officials in their district.[13] Reports from a number of other cities—for example, Seattle and Minneapolis—show a similar vacuum in party activity.[14]

In New Haven, Connecticut, in contrast, 60 per cent of the voters interviewed in a 1959 survey reported having been contacted by party workers.[15] The continuing importance of parties in the politics of this municipality has been documented at length by Robert A. Dahl and his associates.[16] New Haven's Mayor Richard C. Lee was able to obtain support for a massive urban redevelopment program, in spite of the many obstacles in the way of favorable action on such programs elsewhere, in large part because of the capacity of an old-style party organization to weld together the government of a city with an extremely "weak" formal charter. Lee commanded a substantial majority on the board of aldermen and, during the crucial period for ratification of the program, was as confident of the votes of Democratic aldermen as a British Prime Minister is of his parliamentary majority. Lee was far from being a mere creative creature of the party organization which was so helpful to him, but he also was effectively vetoed by the party when he attempted to bring about governmental reforms which would have made the mayor less dependent upon the organization to obtain positive action.[17]

Further evidence of the persistence of old-style party activities came from a number of other studies conducted in the late 1950's. For example, in 1957 party leaders from eight New Jersey counties reported performing a wide range of traditional party services, in response to an ingeniously worded questionnaire administered by Professor Richard T. Frost.[18]

There was even some evidence in the 1950's of a rebirth of old-style urban party activities — for example, in the once Republican-dominated city of Philadelphia, where an effective Democratic old-style organization was put together. Often old-style organizations seem to exist in portions of contemporary cities, especially the low-income sections. These, like the reform groups to be described below, serve as factions in city-wide politics.[19]

Why old-style politics persists in some settings but not others is not fully clear. An impressionistic survey of the scattered evidence suggests, as might be expected, that the older pattern continues in those localities which most resemble the situations which originally spawned strong local parties in the nineteenth century. Eastern industrial cities, such as New Haven, Philadelphia, and many of the New Jersey cities, have sizable low-income groups in need of traditional party services. In many of these areas, the legal impediments to party activity also are minimal: Connecticut, for example, was the last state in the union to adopt direct primary legislation, and nonpartisan local election systems are, in general, less common in industrial cities than in cities without much manufacturing activity.[20] Cities in which weak, disorganized parties are reported—like Seattle, Minneapolis, and even Detroit (which, of course, *is* a manufacturing center of some importance) — are quite often cities in which nonpartisan institutions have been adopted.

Services Performed by New Jersey Politicians

The Service	Percentage Performing It "Often"
Helping deserving people get public jobs	72
Showing people how to get their social security benefits, welfare, unemployment compensation, etc.	54
Helping citizens who are in difficulty with the law. Do you help get them straightened out?	62

SOME NEW-STYLE URBAN POLITICAL PATTERNS

In conclusion, we may note two of the styles of politics which have been reported in contemporary localities where old-style organizations have become weak or nonexistent: the politics of nonpartisanship and the new "reform" factions within some urban Democratic parties. Both patterns are of considerable intrinsic interest to students of local government. And, as contrasting political forms, they provide us with further perspective on the strengths and weaknesses of old-style urban politics.

The politics of nonpartisanship

The nonpartisan ballot now is in force in 66 per cent of American cities over 25,000 in population. Numerous styles of politics seem to take place beneath the facade of nonpartisanship. In some communities, when party labels are eliminated from the ballot, the old parties continue to operate much as they have in the past; in other communities, new local parties spring up to contest the nonpartisan elections. Finally, nonpartisanship often takes the form intended by its founders: no organized groups contest elections; voters choose from a more or less self-selected array of candidates.

In the last of these cases, although nonpartisanship has its intended effect, it also seems to have had — a recent body of literature suggests[21]—a number of unintended side effects. One of these is voter confusion. Without the familiar device of party labels to aid in selecting candidates, voters may find it difficult to select from among the sometimes substantial list of names on the ballot. Under these circumstances, a bonus in votes often goes to candidates with a familiar sounding name — incumbents are likely to be re-elected, for example — or even candidates with a favorable position on the ballot. In addition, campaigning and other personal contacts with voters become less common, because candidates no longer have the financial resources and personnel of a party organization at their disposal and therefore are dependent upon personal financing or backing from interest groups in the community.

Nonpartisan electoral practices, where effective, also seem to increase the influence of the mass media on voters; in the absence of campaigning, party canvassing, and party labels, voters become highly dependent for information as well as advice on the press, radio, and television. Normally, mass communications have rather limited effects on people's behavior compared with face-to-face communication such as canvassing by party workers.[22] Under nonpartisan circumstances, however, he who controls the press is likely to have much more direct and substantial effect on the public.

Ironically, the "theory" of nonpartisanship argues that by eliminating parties a barrier between citizens and their officials will be removed. In fact, nonpartisanship often attenuates the citizen's connections with the political system.

The reform Democrats

The doctrine of nonpartisanship is mostly a product of the Progressive era. While nonpartisan local political systems continue to be adopted and, in fact, have become more common in recent decades, most of the impetus for this development results from the desire of communities to adopt city-manager systems. Nonpartisanship simply is part of the package which normally goes along with the popular city-manager system.

A newer phenomenon on the urban political scene is the development, especially since the 1952 presidential campaign, of ideologically motivated grass-roots party organizations within the Democratic party.[23] The ideology in question is liberalism: most of the reform organizations are led and staffed by college-educated intellectuals, many of whom were activated politically by the candidacy of Adlai Stevenson. In a few localities, there also have been grass-roots Republican organizations motivated by ideological considerations: in the Republican case, Goldwater conservatism.

New-style reformers differ in two major ways from old-style reformers: their ideological concerns extend beyond a preoccupation with governmental efficiency alone (they favor racial integration and improved housing and sometimes devote much of their energy to advocating "liberal" causes at the national level); secondly, their strategy is to work within and take control of the parties, rather than to reject the legitimacy of parties. They do resemble old-style reformers in their preoccupation with the evils of "bossism" and machine politics.

There also is an important resemblance between the new reform politician and the old-style organization man the reformer seeks to replace. In both cases, very much unlike the situation which seems to be stimulated by nonpartisanship, the politician emphasizes extensive face-to-face contact with voters. Where reformers have been successful, it often has been by beating the boss at his own game of canvassing the election district, registering and keeping track of voters, and getting them to the polls.[24]

But much of the day-to-day style of the traditional urban politician is clearly distasteful to the new reformers: they have generally eschewed the use of patronage and, with the exceptions of campaigns for housing code enforcement, they have avoided the extensive service operations to voters and interest groups which were central to old-style party organizations. For example, when election district captains and other officials of the Greenwich Village Independent Democrats, the reform group which deposed New York Democrat County Leader Carmine DeSapio in his own election district, were asked the same set of questions about their activities used in the New Jersey study, strikingly different responses were made.

The successes of this class of new-style urban party politician have vindicated a portion of the classical strategy of urban party politics, the extensive reliance upon canvassing and other personal relations, and also have shown that under some circumstances it is possible to organize such activities with virtually no reliance on patronage and other material rewards. The reformers have tapped a pool of political activists used by parties elsewhere in the world — for example, in Great Britain — but not a normal part of the American scene. One might say that the reformers have "discovered" the British Labor constituency parties.

It is where material resources available to the parties are limited, for example, California, and where voter interest in these resources is low, that the new reformers are successful. In practice, however, the latter condition has confined the effectiveness of the reform Democrats largely to the more prosperous sections of cities; neither their style nor their programs seem to be successful in lower-class districts.[26] The areas of reform Democratic strength are generally *not* the areas which contribute greatly to Democratic pluralities in the cities. And, in many cities, the reformers' clientele is progressively diminishing as higher-income citizens move outward to the suburbs. Therefore, though fascinating and illuminating, the new reform movement must at least for the moment be considered as little more than a single manifestation in a panorama of urban political practices.[27]

SERVICES PERFORMED BY NEW YORK REFORM DEMOCRATS[25]

The Service	Percentage Performing It "Often"
Helping deserving people get public jobs	0
Showing people how to get their social security benefits, welfare, unemployment compensation, etc.	5
Helping citizens who are in difficulty with the law. Do you help get them straightened out?	6

CONCLUSION

The degree to which *old-style* urban party organizations will continue to be a part of this panorama is uncertain. Changes in the social composition of the cities promise to be a major factor in the future of urban politics. If, as seems possible, many cities become lower-class, nonwhite enclaves, we can be confident that there will be a continuing market for the services of the service-oriented old-style politician. Whether or not this is the case, many lessons can be culled from the history of party politics during the years of growth of the American cities — lessons which are relevant, for example, to studying the politics of urbanization elsewhere in the world. In the nineteenth century, after all, the United States was an "emerging," "modernizing" nation, facing the problems of stability and democracy which are now being faced by countless newer nations.

Notes

[1] E. E. Schattschneider, *Party Government* (New York, 1942) pp. 162-169.

[2] Among the better known accounts are Frank R. Kent, *The Great Game of Politics* (Garden City, N. Y., 1923, rev. ed., 1930); Sonya Forthall, *Cogwheels of Democracy* (New York, 1946); Harold F. Gosnell, *Machine Politics* (Chicago, 1937); and the many case studies of individual bosses. For a recent romanticization, see Edwin O'Connor's novel, *The Last Hurrah* (Boston, 1956).

[3] Austin Ranney and Willmoore Kendall, *Democracy and the American Party System* (New York, 1956), pp. 249-252.

[4] This last definition criterion explicitly departs from the characterization of a "machine" in James Q. Wilson's interesting discussion of "The Economy of Patronage," *The Journal of Political Economy,* Vol. 59 (August 1961), p. 370n., "as that kind of political party which sustains its members through the distribution of material incentives (patronage) rather than nonmaterial incentives (appeals to principle, the fun of the game, sociability, etc.)." There is ample evidence that for many old-style party workers incentives such as "the fun of the game," "sociability," and even "service" are of central importance. See, for example, Edward J. Flynn, *You're the Boss* (New York, 1947), p. 22; James A. Farley, *Behind the Ballots* (New York, 1938), p. 237; and the passage cited in note 8 below. The distinction between "material" and "non-material" incentives would probably have to be discarded in a more refined discussion of the motivations underlying political participation. So-called material rewards, at base, are non-material in the sense that they are valued for the status they confer and for other culturally defined reasons.

[5] *Op. cit.,* p. 106.

[6] See, for example, Edward A. Shils, *The Torment of Secrecy* (Glencoe, Ill., 1956) and Stanley M. Elkins, *Slavery* (Chicago, 1959, reprinted with an introduction by Nathan Glazer, New York, 1963).

[7] William L. Riordon, *Plunkitt of Tammany Hall* (originally published in 1905; republished New York, 1948 and New York, 1963; quotations are from the 1963 edition), pp. 27-28.

[8] *Ibid.,* pp. 25-26.

[9] Elmer E. Cornwell, Jr., "Party Absorption of Ethnic Groups: The Case of Providence, Rhode Island," *Social Forces,* Vol. 38 (March 1960), pp. 205-210.

[10] Riordon, *op. cit.,* pp. 17-20.

[11] Frank J. Sorauf, "State Patronage in a Rural County," *American Political Science Review,* Vol. 50 (December 1956), pp. 1046-1056.

[12] Angus Campbell, Philip E. Converse, Warren E. Miller, and Donald E. Stokes, *The American Voter* (New York, 1960), pp. 426-427. The statistic for nonsouthern cities was supplied to me by the authors.

[13] Daniel Katz and Samuel J. Eldersveld, "The Impact of Local Party Activity on the Electorate," *Public Opinion Quarterly,* Vol. 25 (Spring 1961), pp. 16-17.

[14] Hugh A. Bone, *Grass Roots Party Leadership* (Seattle, 1952); Robert L. Morlan, "City politics: Free Style," *National Municipal Review,* Vol. 38 (November 1949), pp. 485-491.

[15] Robert A. Dahl, *Who Governs?* (New Haven, 1961), p. 278.

[16] *Ibid.;* Nelson W. Polsby, *Community Power and Political Theory* (New Haven, 1963); Raymond E. Wolfinger, *The Politics of Progress* (forthcoming).

[17] Raymond E. Wolfinger, "The Influence of Precinct Work on Voting Behavior," *Public Opinion Quarterly,* Vol. 27 (Fall 1963), pp. 387-398.

[18] Frost deliberately worded his questionnaire descriptions of these services favorably in order to avoid implying that respondents were to be censured for indulging in "machine tactics." Richard T. Frost, "Stability and Change in Local Politics," *Public Opinion Quarterly,* Vol. 25 (Summer 1961), pp. 231-232.

[19] James Q. Wilson, "Politics and Reform in American Cities," *American Government Annual, 1962-63* (New York, 1962), pp. 37-52.

[20] Phillips Cutright, "Nonpartisan Electoral Systems in American Cities," *Comparative Studies in Society and History,* Vol. 5 (January 1963), pp. 219-221.

[21] For a brief review of the relevant literature, see Fred I. Greenstein, *The American Party System and the American People* (Englewood Cliffs, N. J., 1963), pp. 57-60.

[22] Joseph T. Klapper, *The Effects of Mass Communication* (New York, 1960).

[23] James Q. Wilson, *The Amateur Democrat* (Chicago, 1962).

[24] There is another interesting point of resemblance between old- and new-style urban party politics. In both, an important aspect of the motivation for participation seems to be the rewards of sociability. Tammany picnics and New York Committee for Democratic Voters (CDV) coffee hours probably differ more in decor than in the functions they serve. An amusing indication of this is provided by the committee structure of the Greenwich Village club of the CDV; in addition to the committees dealing with the club newsletter, with housing, and with community action, there is a social committee and a Flight Committee, the latter being concerned with arranging charter flights to Europe for club members. See Vernon M. Goetcheus, *The Village Independent Democrats: A Study in the Politics of the New Reformers* (unpublished senior distinction thesis, Honors College, Wesleyan University, 1963), pp. 65-66. On similar activities by the California Democratic Clubs, see Robert E. Lane, James D. Barber, and Fred I. Greenstein, *Introduction to Political Analysis* (Englewood Cliffs, N. J., 1962), pp. 55-57.

[25] Goetcheus, *op. cit.,* p. 138.

[26] DeSapio, for example, was generally able to hold on to his lower-class Italian voting support in Greenwich Village; his opponents succeeded largely by activating the many middle- and upper-class voters who had moved into new high-rent housing in the district.

[27] Probably because of their emphasis on ideology, the new reform groups also seem to be quite prone to internal conflicts which impede their effectiveness. One is reminded of Robert Michels' remarks about the intransigence of intellectuals in European socialist parties. *Political Parties* (New York, 1962, originally published in 1915), Part 4, Chap. 6.

The Need for Party Government

A chronic complaint heard from reformers and academicians is that the American parties are deficient because they do not govern. The image to which they compare our parties is that of Great Britain, where they believe that parties do rule. The general theory reformers advocate what may be called "policy government." The advocates of policy government accept the belief that a strong, positive government is essential to the solving of complex social and political problems. They also believe that the separation of powers doctrine is inadequate for the twentieth century since it limits the power of the President, who, they assert, is the natural and proper leader for contemporary times. The way to invigorate our government institutions is by establishing strong parties with centralized control over nominations for office and the power to discipline mavericks. The party leadership must take firm stands on issues and implement these policies in office. The parties should be strikingly different in perspective so that "liberals" would all be in one party while "conservatives" all in the other. In short, the parties ought to be based on conflict and ideology. The following selection by James M. Burns, a long-time reform advocate, is a concise presentation of the "policy government" position.

James M. Burns

The story goes that Daniel Webster's father Ebenezer, near death in a town given to anti-Federalist sentiments, begged to be carried back to New Hampshire, saying, "I was born a Federalist, I have lived a Federalist, and I won't die in a Democratic town." Later generations are inclined to scoff at such a show of party spirit. Many of us switch from party to party as blithely as we change fashions in clothes. We laud the statesmen who rise above party allegiances and we sneer at the faithful party hack. We pride ourselves on being "independents." The average American feels more loyal to the Elks or to the Legion than to his political party.

The argument [here] is that only by vitalizing our two-party system, by play-

Reprinted by permission of the publishers from James MacGregor Burns, *Congress on Trial,* copyright 1949 by Harper and Row, Publishers, Inc., pages 193-202.

ing national party politics more zealously, and by centralizing control of our parties, will Americans be able to stabilize presidential leadership and foster teamwork in the federal government. The question, in short, is the prospect of party government in America—meaning by party government a condition where centralized and disciplined parties formulate national policy on key issues and use governmental machinery to carry out that policy. This term is used in contradistinction to presidential government, congressional government, and cabinet government, not one of which, it has been suggested above, can safely and effectively master the problems arising in an era of chronic crisis.

THE NEED FOR EXTRA-CONSTITUTIONAL REFORM

Ideally, party government works as follows: As a result of winning a majority of the votes, one of two rival political parties wins power. Its platform is attuned to national needs. Its leaders are responsible to a majority of the people. The head of the party becomes President, and other high-ranking party officials assume key positions in Congress, in the Cabinet, and in state governments. A group of national politicians tries to translate majority will into majority rule, and in doing so puts the general interest above special interest.

Since power is centered in the party leadership, there can be no shirking or concealing of responsibility. If affairs go badly, the voters know whom to blame. The opposition party, which has not shared power and which therefore has no responsibility for any unhappy turn of events, is waiting to take over the government if the next election gives it a majority of the votes.

Such a system has obvious advantages. It allows leadership. It fixes responsibility. It harmonizes the various branches of government. It is simple in theory and in practice. Above all, it stresses national action to meet national needs.

Party government has special meaning for Americans because of our urgent need of a way to stabilize the power of the Chief Executive without stunting him. If presidential power is now "dangerously personalized," the President must be made to share his authority with others. But he cannot share it with congressional leaders, cabinet members, or even the Vice-President when these officials are blinded by particularist concerns of one kind or another, as they often are. He can, however, share that power with other party leaders who are as eager and able to take a national view of national problems as the President himself. He can do so without losing the flexibility of action that must remain in the White House. For the party leaders cannot check the President legally or constitutionally, but they can erect a "Stop" sign or at least a "Go Slow" sign that will have some chance of thwarting rash adventures.

And even more. By keeping in contact with his party, the President can more easily stay abreast of majority feeling during the years between elections. The party, with its tens of thousands of committees reaching into every corner of the land, has the potential machinery for grasping and analyzing shifts in public opinion across the nation. The party mobilizes and organizes political sentiment; the President influences majority opinion but he is also deeply influenced by it. In this sense the party is the institutionalization of majority action.

The best hope for the future of American politics and government lies in a fruitful union between presidential power and party government. The President needs the discipline involved in working with other national party politicians. He also needs their aid and *expertise*, especially as new problems emerge between elections. The party in turn requires presidential leadership to keep it alive to national needs, and it benefits from the capacity of the great President to draw the various elements of the party into some kind of harmony. In short, successful party government must have a sizable admixture of presidential government.

Although they have never seen it in action, American thinkers have often dreamed of party government. Thus Henry Jones Ford wrote many years ago of the "cardinal principle of American politics" that "party organization continues to be the sole efficient means of administrative union between the executive and legislative branches of government, and . . . whatever tends to maintain and perfect that union makes for orderly politics and constitutional progress; while whatever tends to impair that union, disturbs the constitutional poise of the government, obstructs its functions, and introduces an anarchic condition of affairs full of danger to all social interests."

More recently Finletter has written: "The national parties should be the force in this country which holds down the organized groups to their proper functions. They should be the link between the Executive and Congress which enables the government to work in the national interest and against the pressures of local interests, organized or not."

The central issue of American politics today is whether our parties can sustain party government in the above sense. Certainly they cannot do so in their present form. Party government assumes the existence of centralized, cohesive parties like the British ones. Ours are quite the reverse. As noted in previous chapters, they cannot hold their lines in Congress on public policy. They cannot keep organized minorities in line. Led by state and local bosses, they lack central organization. They give little help to their candidates at election time and they cannot discipline office-holders after election.

Our parties show many baffling traits. They form a web over the entire country, touching almost every town and hamlet; yet they are so weak at the top as to be virtually headless. They are many decades old and their names are on everyone's lips; yet as organizations they operate in a shadowland. It is safe to say that nine out of ten voters do not have a clear notion of the make-up of their local, state, and national party organizations; how party officials are appointed or elected; how the electoral machinery works. The major parties probably have more members than any other organization in the country; yet on important national policies they knuckle under to organized groups a third their size. Like the brontosaurus of old, the major party looms large on the landscape through sheer bulk, but it is often at the mercy of the more agile creatures around it.

Nevertheless, the American party system can be strengthened. It is raw material that can be worked with. Why?

In the first place, no impassable constitutional barrier stands in the way. It is true that our parties have had to adjust to the division of power between the nation and the states, and to the separation of power among President, Congress, and Judiciary. But our governmental forms have also had to conform to our party system. The American people through their parties have established a different order from that contemplated by the spirit or the letter of the Constitution. The parties have tremendous advantages in this sense. Since they are not constitutional organs, they can be changed without amendment. At the same time, they can influence what government is, as well as what government does.

Whether one is dealing with the one-party system of Soviet Russia, with the multi-party system of France or Italy, with the tightly knit two-party system of Great Britain, or with the decentralized two-party system of the United States, he finds that the nature of the parties is the key to the nature of the government. The parties are what we make them; the government, in part, is what we make the parties.

Another hopeful factor is the stamina and adaptability of our political forms. Our parties have had to make their own way from the beginning. The Constitution left no place for them. Most of the Framers feared the effects of "faction," and they set up machinery to dampen down those effects. Even Andy Jackson, some years before he became President, warned Monroe against "the monster called 'party spirit.'"

The people and the politicians, acting outside the Constitution, forged their own political arrangements out of their own needs and aspirations. Their job is not finished; we have reached a condition of equipoise where a jerry-built party structure has linked arms with a faulty system of government. To strengthen the party system involves an act of will on the part of politicians and voters today rivaling the earlier efforts of our forefathers.

An important consolidating force in the party is the President. His part in giving direction and meaning to the party in power, and indirectly to the opposition, can hardly be exaggerated. He serves as a polarizing element in national politics. As *de facto* leader of the party, he directs it through the national chairman. Planks of the national platform that otherwise would be obscure, he defines and projects before the public eye. He partially offsets the divisive effects of control of the party by scores of state and local organizations.

In trying to elect him the party gathers its far-flung forces every four years in a massive effort that does something to knit the party together, if only temporarily. President and party are essential to each other; because he must keep his party's support he is subject to a measure of party discipline; because the party needs his leadership it submits to a measure of national control.

Party government can be had. The question is whether the American people are willing to take the drastic steps necessary to create it.

THE PRICE OF PARTY GOVERNMENT

The price of party government is the wholesale reconstruction of our obsolete and ramshackle party system. The major parties cannot be the means of strengthening and stabilizing national government until they first are reinforced at the top. Power must be shifted from state and local organizations to the national level. Such an effort requires:

(1) A national party leadership responsive directly to the party membership but free to act with boldness and imagination. At present the Republican and Democratic national committees consist mainly of nonentities, except for a few bosses with national reputations. States are represented equally on the committees regardless of party strength. Such an arrangement is clumsy and undemocratic. To be sure, the committees' unrepresentative make-up is no cause for concern because they do little except make arrangements for the national conventions and exercise some control over party funds. Under a centralized system, however, the committees would run the whole party organization, and they would have to be directly accountable to the rank and file.

(2) A small executive council for each major party, composed of officials with national reputations. Except for occasional chiefs such as Mark Hanna and James A. Farley, our major parties have been notoriously wanting in leaders who could think in terms of national politics and the general interest rather than in terms of state and local advantage. The council would fix major policy for the party. Its members would hold controlling positions in the government — in both Administration and Congress — once the party took power, and it would work closely with the majority policy committees in Congress and with a joint cabinet.

(3) A national party leader who would speak and act for the membership. Generally the party in power has such a leader in the President. The party defeated in the previous presidential election has no head. Necessarily it suffers as an organized opposition to the group in power.

(4) Annual conventions acting directly for the party rank and file. At present conventions are held every four years in order to select the national tickets and draw up the party platforms. Since the formation of public policy is a continuous affair, the party platforms should be revised at least annually to keep abreast of new developments in the nation and abroad. These annual conventions would choose the national party leader who would presumably be the President in the case of the party that won the last presidential election. At intervals during the year the national committee or the executive council would rather have the right to announce party policy within the framework of the national program.

(5) The right of veto by the national party leadership of any policies of state and local organizations that were inconsistent with the national platform.

(6) Enlarged staff for the central party office. At present the national headquarters languish between presidential elections, blossoming in furious activity only for a few months every four years. Rejuvenated parties would carry on research, publicity, and organizing activities around the year every year. They would command the services of some of the country's ablest political strategists, writers, speakers, and organizers.

All these are among the structural changes necessary to vitalize the party system in the United States. But such a reorganization cannot do the job alone. It can serve its purpose only as part of a strenuous and persistent effort to transfer control of the parties from state and local organizations to the national leadership. All power need not be at the top, but most of it should be. Otherwise the elaborate structure proposed above might have no effect.

Essentially the problem is one of party discipline. National leadership will be a will-o'-the-wisp unless the central officials can read out of the party those who, after using the party label and machinery to gain office, then proceed to ignore the party platform. The "purge" should be used freely against those disloyal to the party on vital public policy. Such discipline need not be administered by public appeals, as in the case of President Roosevelt's attempted purge of 1938, but it can be made effective if the party machinery is properly set up and operated. Control, in short, must be exercised by the leadership through the party organization itself.

What are potential sources of such control? One is financial. Placing command over party funds in the central office would give the national leaders more influence over state and local party decisions, including the selection of candidates.

A second potential source of control is the patronage power. As a matter of settled policy, patronage should be withheld from party members in office who disregard party pledges. It is bad politics and bad government to allow rebels to deal out jobs—bad politics because the rebels thereby acquire additional power at the expense of the national leadership, and bad government because the rebels will give the jobs to persons whose loyalty to the program will be doubtful.

A third source of control might be a moral sanction—"constitutional" arrangements within the party that require approval by the national headquarters of the choice of all candidates for national office and of all planks relating to national issues.

The first two of these reforms might not stir up much fuss, but the third has explosive elements. The idea of handing the national leaders veto power over senatorial and congressional candidates smacks of arbitrary meddling in local affairs. In fact, however, such an arrangement is democratic and responsible, because it means that the party is insisting that its candidates stand behind its promises. It means that the choice within the state of candidates for Senate or House is a matter of national concern—as it surely is. Nothing is more likely to debase American politics than the spectacle of a party's nominees for Congress taking every position across the political spectrum.

Party reform along these lines might do more harm than good, however, unless it was coupled with participation in everyday politics by average citizens on an unprecedented scale. Concentrating power in the central leadership would be dangerous if the result was simply to replace local and state machines with a national machine.

The first step is political education. Most Americans—even those who vote a straight party ticket year after year—do not know how their local, state, and national organizations are run, or who runs them. They do not know why it is that the "party insiders" present the ordinary party member with a choice between evils at the primaries, if indeed there is any choice at all. Naturally our parties have often failed in their primary task—the promotion of wise public policy—when the party chiefs have been concerned chiefly with the private spoils of office.

After education comes popular action. Voters whose main stake is in the handling of the great issues of our time, whose interest is not in getting special favors from government, must meet and master the spoilsmen in the citadels where the spoilsmen hold command—i.e., in the party councils. That means doing the work that the insiders have done for generations, only doing it better: registering voters and getting them to the polls, gaining seats on local party committees and ultimately in the higher governing bodies, carrying the party gospel to the people through house-to-house canvassing, handling publicity, raising money, organizing committees, and the like.

Those who undertake such tasks in this spirit would find no reward except the greatest reward of all—heightened personal influence over the handling of the great issues that will determine the nature of the world we live in.

Party politics, like war, is too important to be left to the professionals.

On the Superiority of National Conventions

Aaron B. Wildavsky

What is the purpose of a political party in America? There are two basic competing views on this question. The first view, discussed in the previous selection, stresses ideology, discipline, and centralization as the proper basis for parties. In contrast to this "policy government" position is what may be labeled the "consensus government" school of thought. Those who oppose ideological parties emphasize the point that parties should be mechanisms for compromise and reconciliation. The goal of the political system, and hence of the parties, ought to be to minimize conflict between groups, not exacerbate it. As an instrument to formulate public policy, parties are congenitally inadequate. It is the office holders who should be judged by the electorate on their policies, not parties offering abstract solutions from the sanctuary of non-incumbency. Parties in America are primarily useful as mechanisms whereby prospective leaders can compete for public approval. If America seeks to maintain its federal system, its parties must remain inclusive and decentralized. The reformers, so the supporters of "consensus government" argue, are asking for a radical shift in our basic theory of government without accepting responsibility for the probable consequences of such change. The goal of American parties is, and ought to be, to win elections, not promote the true faith. Aaron Wildavsky is attempting to describe the function of our National Conventions within the general framework of this "consensus government" philosophy.

The appraisal of national conventions as mechanisms for nominating presidents involves many problems of political theory. Who should be entrusted with the task of nomination? Can we reconcile the desirability of popular participation with the need for maintaining a strong party leadership? To what extent does the nominating convention contribute to the maintenance of the political system in which it is imbedded? Does the apparent lack of decorum in this high

Reprinted by permission of the publisher from Aaron B. Wildavsky, "On the Superiority of National Conventions," *Review of Politics*, 24 (July 1962), 307-319.

political body adversely affect the kinds of decisions it makes? What are the implications of increasing the visibility of convention nominations? Any attempt to deal with these and similar questions necessarily involves an admixture of normative and descriptive theory. Postulation of what ought to be can hardly be separated from consideration of the actual or likely consequences of alternative courses of action. The merits of existing party platforms, for example, cannot be fruitfully discussed apart from knowledge of the relevance of issues to voters. In this context, I propose to evaluate national conventions and the various proposals for altering or abolishing them in the light of the degree to which they meet widely shared goals for the American political system.

No one will deny that presidential nominating conventions are peculiar.[1] After all, they perform a peculiar function. The task of the convention is to unite a party which is not inherently united, behind a popular candidate who is unpopular with many delegates, in order to speak for all the people after battling half of them in an election. It would be surprising if a political institution which must accomplish these goals did not reflect some of the contradictions it is designed to embody.

The critics of national conventions[2] find them gay when they should be solemn, vulgar when they should be genteel. In a word, they find the conventions somehow too American. The reforms proposed by these critics suggest that grave decisions should be made at a solemn convention or that the convention system should be abolished entirely. Yet we shall see that every major change suggested has the unfortunate result of leading to consequences much worse than the evils they are supposed to remedy.

In order to evaluate national conventions, and the alternatives to them, we need a set of goals which most Americans would accept as desirable and important. The following six standards appear to meet this test: any method for nominating presidents should: 1. aid in preserving the two-party system; 2. help secure vigorous competition between the parties; 3. maintain some degree of cohesion and agreement within the parties; 4. produce candidates who have some likelihood of winning voter support; 5. lead to the choice of good men; 6. result in the acceptance of candidates as legitimate.

Let us first evaluate the alternatives to national conventions to see if they are superior to the existing system.

A national primary has often been suggested. This, however, would have serious disadvantages. It is quite probable that as many as ten candidates might obtain enough signatures on nominating petitions to get on the ballot. Nor would it be surprising if they divided the vote equally. The victor would then have to be chosen in a special run-off primary. By following this procedure the United States might have to restrict its presidential candidates to wealthy athletes: no poor man could ever raise the millions required for the nominating platform petition, the first primary, the run-off primary, and the national election; and no one who was not superbly conditioned could survive the pace of all these campaigns.

National primaries might also lead to the collapse of the party system as we know it. It is not unusual for a party to remain in office for a long period of time. If state experience with primaries is any guide, this would result in a movement of interested voters into the primary of the winning party where their votes would count more. As voters deserted the losing party, it would be largely the die-hards who were left. They would nominate candidates who pleased them but who could not win the election because they were unrepresentative of a majority of the nation. Eventually, the losing party would atrophy, thus seriously weakening the two-party system and the prospects of competition among the parties. The winning party would soon show signs of internal weakness as a consequence of the lack of opposition necessary to keep it unified.

A national primary is also likely to lead to the appearance of extremist candidates and demagogues who, unrestrained by allegiance to any permanent party organization, have little to lose by stirring up mass hatreds or making absurd promises. A Huey Long or a Joe McCarthy would have found a fertile field in a national primary, an opportunity sufficient to raise the temperature of American politics to explosive levels even if he did not win. The convention system rules out these extremists by placing responsibility in the hands of party leaders who have a permanent stake in maintaining the good name and integrity of their organization. Some insight into this problem may be had by looking at the situation in several southern states where most voters have moved to the democratic primary and where victory in that primary is tantamount to election. The result is a chaotic factional politics in which there are few or no permanent party leaders, the distinction between the "ins" and "outs" becomes blurred, it is difficult to hold anyone responsible, and demagogues arise who make use of this situation by strident appeals, usually of a racist variety. This functional theory of demagoguery (in which extreme personality takes the place of party in giving even a minimal structure to state politics) should give pause to the advocates of a national primary.

The remaining radical alternative is nomination by one of the branches of Congress This, though, would be out of the question. The caucus system of nomination was rejected in Andrew Jackson's time because it did not give sufficient representation to the large population groups whose votes were decisive in the election. Furthermore, the large fluctuations of party membership in Congress lead to serious difficulties. If a party happened to do very poorly for a few years in several sections of the country, the representation in Congress from those areas would be small and they would, in effect, be deprived of a voice in nominating a president. Thus, if northern Democrats suffered a serious reverse one year, the southern members of that party would be in complete control. This nominating procedure would advertise itself as being national in scope, but it would be far more likely than the present system to produce candidates with a limited, sectional appeal. The attempts of leaders in areas where the party is weak to strengthen themselves by nominating a candidate who might help increase their vote would be stymied.

Perhaps, it may be argued, what is required is not some radically new method of nominating candidates, but reform of some of the more obnoxious practices of the present system. High on the list of objectionable practices would be the secret gathering of party leaders in the smoke-filled room. Some liken this to a political opium den where a few irresponsible men, hidden from public view, stealthily determine the destiny of the nation.[3] Yet it is difficult to see who, other than the party's influential leaders, should be entrusted with the delicate task of finding a candidate to meet the majority preference. Since the head-on clash of strength on the convention floor has not resolved the question, the only alternatives would be continued deadlock, anarchy among scores of leaderless delegates, splitting the party into rival factions, or some process of accommodation.

Let us suppose that the smoke-filled room were abolished and with it all behind-the-scenes negotiations. All parleys would then be held in public, before the delegates and millions of television viewers. As a result, the participants would spend their time scoring points against each other in order to impress the folks back home. The claim that bargaining was going on would be a sham, since the participants would not really be communicating with each other. No compromises would be possible, lest the leaders be accused by their followers of selling out to the other side. Once a stalemate existed, it would be practically impossible to break and the party would probably disintegrate into warring factions.

An extensive system of state primaries in which delegates were legally compelled to vote for the victorious candidate would lead to the disappearance of the smoke-filled room without any formal action. As the delegates could not change their position, there would be little point in bringing their leaders together for private consultations. Sharply increasing the number of pledged delegates would introduce such rigidity into the convention that it would perpetually be faced with stalemates which could not be overcome because no one would be in a position to switch his support.

While candidates are being nominated and during the balloting at national conventions, demonstrations, partly spontaneous, largely prearranged, take place on the floor. Much criticism has been leveled at this raucous display. But criticisms of demonstrations as unseemly and vulgar seem to me to be trivial.

There is no evidence which would substantiate a claim that the final decision is in some way worse than if demonstrations were banned. Lincoln, Bryan, and Willkie are the prime examples of men aided in their nomination by the exuberance of their supporters.

The criticism neglects the important communicating function of demonstrations. Imagine the scene if a candidate were nominated or scored an advance in the balloting and this was accompanied by a brief, polite moment of applause. Surely, no one would believe that a candidate who worked up so little response could stir any enthusiasm among the people. It is possible that this criticism of demonstrations comes from individuals who prefer rule by the genteel. A sedate convention might be more appropriate for a sedate country.

In still another way the demonstrations help meet the need of many delegates for an active function which they can perform and tell about when they get home. As in almost any large political gathering (the number of delegates and alternates is in the thousands) only a small number actively participate in planning strategy or in trying to influence other people. The rest often find that they have no well-defined political role other than casting one vote out of many and may feel at a loss to explain their lack of activity to themselves as well as to the people back home. The demonstrations provide an opportunity for the delegate to enhance his feelings of importance by active participation in a colorful event which he can recount when he returns. Since one of the advantages of the convention is to gather the party faithful and imbue them with a sense of belonging to a national party, a mechanism which increases the delegate's sense of satisfaction is by no means unimportant.

Undoubtedly, demonstrations have been overdone and might be cut short. This task can safely be left to the requirements of television. As the 1960 conventions showed, televising dictates briefer demonstrations to retain the attention of the vast audience which the party would like very much to influence in its favor.

The members of each party may love it on a sentimental basis; they certainly love the idea of getting into office; but do they love each other? The convention provides the acid test of party unity by determining whether the disparate elements which make up each party can agree on one man to represent them—a man who cannot possibly be equally attractive to all of them. The much maligned party platform is exceedingly important in this regard not so much for what it says but for the fact that it is written at all. The platform tests the ability of the many party factions to agree on something even if, on crucial points, the differences have to be papered over.[4]

The problem of the platform does not lie in evil, scheming politicians who want to confuse the public, but rather in the nature of the American people and their extraordinary diversity. In order to gain a majority of electoral votes, a party must appeal to all major population groups. Since all these interests do not want the same thing in all cases, it is necessary to compromise and, sometimes, to evade issues which would split the party and lead to drastic loss of support. A perfectly clear, unequivocal, consistent platform on all major issues presupposes an electorate which divides along such lines, and that is not the case in this country.

The concern of reformers with party platforms stems primarily from two assumptions: first, that there is a significant demand in the electorate for more clear-cut differences on policy; second, that such elections are likely to be a significant source of guidance on individual issues to policy makers. Yet both these assumptions are either false or highly dubious. Herbert McCloskey and his associates have shown that on a wide range of issues leaders in both parties are much further apart than are ordinary members who, in fact, are separated by rather small differences.[5] To the degree that party platforms do spell out clear and important differences on policy — and these were considerable in 1960 — this probably results far more from a desire of party leaders to please themselves or from misinformation about what the voters desire than from any supposed demand from the electorate. Moreover, as Robert A. Dahl has demonstrated so well, it is exceedingly difficult (if not sometimes impossible) to discover just what an election means in terms of the policy preferences of a majority. Given a reasonable difference in the salience of issues for voters, it is quite possible for a candidate to win 75 per cent of the vote although 75 per cent of the voters opposed each of his policies. Finally, the Michigan Survey Research Center points out that the number of people who (a) know about most issues, (b) differentiate between the positions of the candidates, (c) care about the issues, is very small. And these are likely to be the most interested and involved section of the population whose allegiance to party is strongest and who are least likely to change their votes on the basis of one or a few issues.[6] About all that one can expect from an election is an indication of the general direction in which a candidate and the dominant factions in his party intend to go, and the party platforms do reasonably well in this respect.

Some critics object to the convention's stress on picking a winner rather than "the best man" regardless of his popularity. Now this is a rather strange doctrine in a democracy where it is presumed that it is the people who should decide who is best for them and communicate this decision in an election. Only in dictatorial countries do a set of leaders arrogate unto themselves the right to determine who is best, independently of the popular preference. An unpopular man can hardly win a free election. An unpopular President can hardly secure the support he needs to accomplish his goals. We deceive ourselves when we treat popularity as an evil condition instead of a necessary element for obtaining consent in democratic politics.[7]

Although popularity is obviously a necessary condition for nomination, it should not be the only condition. The guideline for purposes of nomination should be to nominate the best of the popular candidates. But "best" is a slippery word. A great deal of what we mean by best in politics is "best for us" or "best represents our policy preferences." And this can hardly be held up as an objective criterion. What is meant by "best" in this context are certain personal qualities such as experience, intelligence, and decisiveness. Nevertheless, it is doubtful whether an extreme conservative would prefer a highly intelligent radical to a moderately intelligent candidate who shared the conservative's policy preferences. Personal qualities are clearly subject to discount based on the compatibility of interests between the voter and the candidate.

Insofar as the "best man" criterion has a residue of meaning, I believe that it has been followed in recent times. Looking at the candidates of both parties since 1940 — Roosevelt, Truman, Stevenson, Kennedy for the Democrats, and Willkie, Dewey, Eisenhower, Nixon for the Republicans — there is not one man among them who could not be said to have some outstanding qualities or experience for the White House. Without bothering to make a formal declaration of the fact, American political leaders and their followers have apparently agreed to alter the requirements of availability. They have restricted their choice to those popular candidates who give promise of measuring up to the formidable task of the President as preserver of the nation and maintainer of prosperity. The nominee whose sole virtue is his innocuousness or pleasant smile seems to have disappeared.

It has been alleged, however, that this criterion has been violated because nominations have come to be determined by popularity, that is, by expressions of mass preferences as reported in polls and state primaries. Merely defining the candidate who won the nomination as most popular is not sufficient to prove the thesis; it must be shown that the voters agreed who was the most popular candidate, that this was communicated to the delegates, and that they nominated him. It would be hard to say that William Howard Taft, Warren Harding, Alfred Landon, Wendell Willkie and Thomas Dewey, to name a few, were indisputably the most popular Republican candidates. Dwight Eisenhower might fit in this category (though he had to fight for the nomination) but he represents just one case and is counterbalanced by Theodore Roosevelt's failure to obtain the nomination in 1912. There is no evidence to suggest that, among Democratic candidates, Woodrow Wilson was more popular than Champ Clark in 1912, that James M. Cox and John Davis fit the most popular category, or that Franklin Roosevelt could have been placed there with certainty before his first nomination. If anyone was most popular in 1952 it was Estes Kefauver and not Adlai Stevenson.

A surface view of the situation in 1960 might suggest that John F. Kennedy's nomination was due to an irresistible current of public opinion. Obviously, Kennedy's excellent organization[8] and the difficulty of refusing the nomination to a Catholic who had won important primaries[9] must be taken into account. Furthermore, the Republican experience suggests another important factor. We never discovered whether or not Nelson Rockefeller was more popular with the voting public than Richard Nixon because the latter had such strong support among party professionals that the former decided it was not worth running. A crucial difference between the two conventions was that there was no Demcrat to oppose Kennedy who could claim a widespread preference among party leaders as was the case with Nixon in the Republican Party.

To be sure, popularity as evidenced through victory in primaries is important. But the unpledged delegates, comprising some two-thirds of the total, may use their judgment to disregard this factor as they did in nominating Willkie and Stevenson who entered no primaries. The significance of primaries derives not nearly so much from the delegates they bring to an aspirant's side as from the indication they give that he is likely to win the election. The candidate who feels that he already has considerable delegate strength would be foolish to enter a primary unless he was quite certain he could win. All he can gain is a few additional votes but he can lose his existing support by a bad showing that would be interpreted to mean he could not win the election. Naturally, primaries are the vehicles of candidates who must make positive demonstrations of support in order to be considered and are hardly worse off by losing than if they had not entered at all. Candidates who are strong at the outset can pick and choose the one or two primaries they wish to enter and can use the most favorable circumstances to defeat their opponents. It does not seem too great an emphasis on popularity to ask that an aspirant be able to win at least one or two primaries. Alternately, it does not seem too shocking that the candidate who wins all the contested primaries, as Kennedy did, should be given prime consideration.

No doubt the primaries, though held in different sections of the country and in different kinds of states (Wisconsin, California, West Virginia) are by no means a perfect representation of the electorate. Yet this is a rather peculiar argument coming from those who wish to downgrade the importance of primaries; for if primaries were truly representative of the nation their importance would be enormously enhanced. How could the nomination be denied to a candidate who had apparently proved that he had the support of a majority of a very large and accurate sample of the voting population?

The conclusion I would draw is that the primaries, together with other methods of delegate selection which give predominance to party activists, provide a desirable balance between popularity and other considerations which party leaders deem important.[10] Without denying an element of popular participation, the decision is ultimately thrown into the hands of the men who ought to make it if we want a strong party system — the party leaders.

For some critics the defects of conventions lie not only in their poor performance in nominating candidates but also in their failure to become a sort of superlegislature enforcing the policy views in the platform upon party members in the Executive Branch and Congress. This is not the place to become embroiled in the seemingly endless debate over "party government." But it is in order to suggest that such a role for the conventions implies a radical change in our entire political system and might well result in a breakdown of the existing nominating structure by saddling it with unbearable burdens. To make the convention's policy decisions truly effective — that is, binding on the President and Congress — would mean a radical shift in power from the constitutionally delegated authorities, and from the people who elect them, to the delegates and those who elect and control them. There is no evidence that anyone will either try to do this or, indeed, has any chance whatsoever of proving successful at it. There is certainly no reason to believe that such a change would meet with the preferences of more than an insignificant minority of citizens.

Let us suppose, nevertheless, for the purposes of argument, that the conventions would somehow become much more influential on matters of national policy? How could either party retain a semblance of unity if the stakes of convention deliberations were vastly increased by converting the platform into national policy? If one believes that heated discussion necessarily increases agreement, then the problem solves itself. Experience warns us, however, that the airing of sharp differences, particularly when the stakes are high, is likely to decrease agreement. Today, the choice of nominees at the convention is accepted as legitimate by all but a few delegates. The fact that platforms are not binding permits the degree of unity necessary for the delegates to stay long enough to agree on a nominee. By vastly increasing the number of delegates who would bitterly oppose platform decisions, and who would probably leave the convention, the proposed change would jeopardize the legitimacy of its nominating function. Paradoxically, the temptation to make the platform utterly innocuous so as to give offense to no one would be difficult to resist.

There are also good reasons for opposing the desires of those who love the conventions so well that they would like to see them convene once every year or two years. If the purpose of these meetings is to give free advice there would seem to be little point to them. Congressmen are likely to pay as little attention to convention talk as they did to the pronouncements of the Democratic Advisory Committee. After all, Congressmen are subject to different risks and sanctions than are most delegates, get no great help from the national party in securing nomination and election, and have no reason to be beholden to it for suggesting policies which may get them into trouble. As they have uniformly decided in the past, Congressional leaders will likely refuse to participate in organizations in which they cannot control the result but are committed to support the proposals. The differences between the convention and Congressional constituencies are such that in a convention the legislative leaders are bound to suffer many defeats which could well render them ineffective. The notion of getting delegates together under circumstances where their disagreements are certain to come out into the open, merely for the purpose of making recommendations, does not seem promising. It is doubtful whether most delegates, who could not be expected to take an active part in formulating proposals, would feel it worthwhile to participate in a convention which lacked its major rationale and interest—the choice of a presidential nominee.

Although I hope to have avoided the error of assuming that whatever is is right, the superiority of national conventions to the available alternatives is clearly demonstrable. Only the convention permits us to realize in large measure all the six goals — the two-party system, party competition, some degree of internal cohesion, candidates attractive to voters, good men, and acceptance of nominees as legitimate — which we postulated earlier would commonly be accepted as desirable. We get good candidates but not extremists who would threaten our liberties or convert our parties into exclusive clubs for party ideologists. Leaders are motivated to choose popular candidates who will help maintain vigorous competition between the parties but who are unlikely to split them into warring factions.[11] The element of popular participation is strong enough to impress itself upon party leaders but not sufficiently powerful to take the choice out of their hands. The convention is sufficiently open to excite great national interest but it is not led into perpetual stalemate by pseudo-bargaining in public. Voters have a choice between conservative and liberal tendencies—a choice which is not absolute because a two-party system can be maintained only if both parties moderate their views in order to appeal to the large population groups in the country. In all these ways, national conventions make an essential contribution to the maintenance of the peculiarly American political system, a contribution which could not be made by any competitive mechanism now on the horizon. It would be interesting to speculate on the reasons why a political institution, which no one consciously set out to create in its present form, should have evolved in such a way that the delicate balance between its parts serves us so well.

Notes

[1] One of the earliest and still one of the best discussions of conventions is found in M. Ostrogorski, *Democracy and the Organization of Political Parties* (New York, 1911). A brief but important paper which summarizes a great deal of existing knowledge in short compass and relates

it to other knowledge about politics is Nelson Polsby's, "Decision-Making at the National Conventions," *Western Political Quarterly,* Vol. XII (September, 1960), 606-617. For a comprehensive survey of a single convention see Paul David, Malcolm Moos, and Ralph Goldman, *Presidential Nominating Politics in 1952,* Vols. I through V. A vast amount of data about conventions is presented in Paul David, Ralph Goldman, Richard Bain, *The Politics of National Party Conventions* (Washington, D.C., 1959).

[2] Conventions have been subject to criticism for many years and in many places. A brief introduction to this literature might include James (Lord) Bryce, *The American Commonwealth* (New York, 1891); M. Ostrogorski, *op. cit.;* Louise Overacker, *The Presidential Primary* (New York, 1926); E. E. Schattschneider, *Party Government* (New York, 1942); American Political Science Association, Committee on Political Parties, *Toward a More Responsible Two-Party System* (1950); Estes Kefauver, "Indictment of the Political Convention," *New York Times Magazine,* March 16, 1954; Stephen K. Bailey, *The Condition of Our National Parties* (New York, 1959).

[3] The party leaders — governors, state chairmen, national committeemen, county officials, mayors, elder statesmen — are often men of independent influence and somewhat different interests and there may be only a limited range of agreement among them. In addition, they are severely limited in their choice by their estimate of what other delegates will stand for and what the voters will acept at the polls. David, Moos, Goldman, *op. cit.,* "The National Story," p. 191, state: "There were not many delegations at Chicago in 1952 in which a single leader could make the decisions and vote the delegation without even asking his colleagues' views; it would be difficult to name even one where this was completely the case."

[4] See Pendelton Herring, "The Uses for National Conventions," in *The Politics of Democracy* (New York, 1940), 225-239.

[5] Herbert McCloskey, Paul J. Hoffman, and Rosemary O'Hara, "Issue Conflict and Consensus Among Party Leaders and Followers," *American Political Science Review,* Vol. LIV (June, 1960), 406-427. This study is especially relevant for our concerns because the authors turned to the Democratic and Republican national conventions for their samples of party leaders.

[6] Angus Campbell, Phillip Converse, Warren Miller, Donald Stokes, *The American Voters* (New York, 1960), especially pp. 168-265.

[7] Only if one assumes that it is the characteristic behavior of parties in a two-party system to disregard its chances for election, does it make sense to speak of popularity in a derogatory way. Glancing at the recent history of such nations as England, Canada, Australia, and New Zealand, it appears that party leaders who continually lose elections either lose their posts or are subject to severe attack from within their own party. On the theoretical aspect of this problem see Charles Lindblom, "In Praise of Political Science," *World Politics,* Vol. 9 (January, 1957), 240-253. See also Gerhard Lowenberg, "The Transformation of British Labour Party Policy Since 1945," *The Journal of Politics,* Vol. 21 (May, 1959), 234-257.

[8] One of the limitations imposed on Kennedy's opponents by his religion came out clearly when (as an observer attached to the Ohio delegation) I discovered that the Johnson staff men did not use the traditional tactic of claiming that Kennedy could not win the election. "That," in the words of a Johnson man, "would have been interpreted to mean a reference to the religious issue."

[9] By contrast, the ineptness of the Stevenson people is illustrated by a scene I witnessed early on the morning of the day the voting was to take

place. Although no staff person supporting Stevenson had previously showed up at the Ohio delegation's hotel, one arrived around 8 a.m., tapped me on the shoulder and inquired: "Do you know who's supporting Stevenson here?" Discovering that I was not a delegate and the near-by representative of the city police vice-squad (sent to watch for pickpockets and prostitutes) could not help him either, he went in search of aid. An hour later he returned full of confidence and figures indicating support for his man; but Stevenson received not one vote.

[10] A common criticism of primaries is that they are held at widely separated intervals so that some candidates do not declare themselves in time to enter and others are exhausted by a grueling series of campaigns. Unfortunately, this is not always the best of all possible worlds and we cannot have everything we want. If primaries were all held at the same time they would take on the aspect of a national primary with all its disadvantages and without the one great advantage of being open to all interested voters in the nation. Candidates like Hubert Humphrey and Estes Kefauver and possibly even Robert A. Taft could not have afforded the enormous expenditures required to put their views before the public in so many places at once.

[11] The two major party splits in this century occurred while an incumbent was securing his own nomination. Nelson Polsby, *op. cit.,* suggests that the Progressive split in the Republican Party led against President Taft in 1912 and the Dixiecrat revolt led against President Truman in 1948 indicate that incumbent Presidents, as hierarchical leaders, are particularly prone to underestimate the costs of their actions to party unity.

Our Two-Party System and the Electoral College

Ronald C. Moe

If we accept the "consensus government" theory as appropriately explaining our contemporary party system, the next question becomes: Why do we have only two major parties? As the following essay suggests, there are several schools of thought on that question. Whatever the cause of our two-party system, the result has been that our parties have been able, at least since the Civil War, to keep conflict within reasonable bounds. We have not been required to assemble coalition governments nor have Administrations been subjected to divided partisan control of the Executive. The politics has been, by and large, pluralistic, moderate, and progressive without violent oscillation in public policy. Ronald Moe suggests that our generally moderate politics is no accident, but rather is largely a consequence of our electoral institutions and that these institutions are under attack today.

I

Despite momentary romances with third parties, the American people have entertained a long love affair with our two-party system. While the degree of partisan competitiveness does vary from one area to another and while there remain instances of one-partyism, the two major parties have been able to keep major political conflict largely within the family. Since the Civil War no third party has seriously contested their hegemony.

Our two-party system has attracted considerable scholarly attention over the decades. Why should America, the most heterogeneous of lands, enjoy the stability and moderation generally associated with a two-party system? Scholars, foreign and domestic, have not been entirely persuasive in their attempts to answer this question. Some have argued that a single "cause" has led to the establishment and maintenance of only two parties while others have assumed that several factors working together have accounted for our dualistic politics. In approaching this

A slightly altered version of this essay appeared as "Let's Keep the Electoral College," *National Review,* April 7, 1970, pp. 356-359.

question it is useful to classify the explanations into three groups: dualistic theories; consensus theories; and institutional theories.

II

Those who espouse dualist theories generally seek to trace the origins of our present party system back to the conflicts which engaged our Founding Fathers. The path is sometimes tortuous. Initially, the battle was between the Federalists and anti-Federalists over the Constitution. Later the lines shifted so that the conflict became sectional, first between the financial interests in the East and the agrarian interests of the West, and subsequently between the North and the South over the question of slavery. Today, many dualists believe, the battle is largely between urban and non-urban interests.

A variation on this historical theme is offered by some social scientists who see our dualist politics as the offspring of our national character. Americans somehow like to think in dualistic "either-or" terms. They purposely shun shades of difference in favor of clear-cut contests between two groups. This tendency towards ideological dualisms provides an environment conducive to the maintenance of a two-party system. Critics of this view offer the rejoinder that just the opposite is true. Americans, they contend, are able to find many different positions on a single issue and establish interest groups to promote each view. Whether Americans are more or less sophisticated than other peoples in their political decision-making has long been debated and is not near resolution.

A second category of theories revolves around the notions of social consensus. Many scholars attempt to explain our party system in terms of widely held social and political norms. Despite our heterogeneous cultural heritage and society, Americans, so numerous studies have informed us, share a consensus over fundamentals which divide many other societies. Virtually all Americans accept the prevailing social, economic, and political institutions; they accept the Constitution and its governmental apparatus, the regulated, free enterprise economy, and the social class pattern. This consensus is lacking in many other countries where basic institutions are often questioned as to their legitimacy In such countries, multiple party systems tend to thrive.

It should be noted that the social consensus theories, so popular in the 1950's and early 1960's, are having a rough time of it today. There is not as much consensus today as there was in the past. Critics also note that these theories settle little as it is difficult to determine whether consensus permitted the two-party system to thrive or whether the two-party system provided the basic climate in which consensus might exist. Causal propositions in this regard are difficult to make with any certainty.

Finally, we come to the various institutional theories which find support. This school argues that America's heterogeneous society would spawn many parties, not few, if no artificial checks were in operation. In other words, our two-party system is not a natural outgrowth of American character or history, nor is it a product of some ephemeral consensus. It is the result of our electoral system and our constitutional institutions. The corollary to this argument is that if we were to substantially alter our electoral system we would substantially alter our political party system. They are inseparable.

While it is in fashion to attribute approximately equal credit to each of these three categories of explanation, this author does not find that such equal credit is warranted by the evidence. No doubt there are some supporting factors to be found in the arguments of the dualist and consensus schools, but these probably are not determinative. The evidence appears to support the idea that political party systems are electoral artifacts which can be altered by changing the rules of the game notwithstanding cultural factors which might tend to militate against change.

The thesis of this article narrows the above generalization by suggesting that certain electoral institutions are primarily responsible for our present dual party system. The electoral institutions in question are the state laws regulating parties; the single-member district concept for Congress; and the Electoral College. These are the three institutional pillars largely responsible for sustaining our two-party system.

III

Our national parties have been aptly described as loose alliances of state parties. E. E. Schattschneider notes: "Decentralization of power is by all odds the most important single characteristic of the American major party; more than anything else this trait distinguishes it from all others. Indeed, once this truth is understood, nearly everything else about American parties is greatly illuminated...." The Massachusetts and Alabama Democratic parties, for example, bear little family resemblance. The state party systems are, for the most part, products of the various state electoral laws.

In the 19th century, states tended to view parties as private groups and made few laws to supervise their activities. Coincident with the Progressive Movement and its interest in direct primaries, state legislatures began to pass laws regulating parties and elections.

The situation became acute in many states during the 1912 election when secessionist Republicans formed the Bull Moose Party after the Convention and attempted to wrest control of the party apparatus in many states. In most states it was relatively easy to get on the ballot so Theodore Roosevelt was able to run a strong race against the regular party. The state parties became alarmed and passed much electoral legislation, the most important having to do with definitions of what constituted a legitimate party.

California provides an excellent example of how state laws encourage the two-party system and discourage the formation of splinter parties. If a group wants to run a candidate for President, it must first constitute itself a party. This means that they must have an enrolled membership of one percent of the total registered voters by January 1 of the year they seek to hold a primary and run a presidential candidate. Thus, a new party cannot be established after the political conventions. This also means that the group has to work hard, well in advance, in order to run a candidate in November.

While the regulations appear rigorous, they are fair and surmountable as attested to by the success of the Peace and Freedom Party and the American Independent Party in 1968. The rules discourage secessionist movements and millionaires trying to buy their way on to the ballot.

IV

The second institutional pillar of our two-party system is the single-member district concept as it is applied to congressional elections. The single-member district concept refers to the method by which many countries elect members to their legislature. It might be more accurately described as the first-past-the-post system. If a national decides to have territorial units represented in its legislature it must devise a method for apportioning these districts and this, in turn, affects the nominating process of the parties.

In a majority of instances where the single-member district concept prevails, plurality elections are followed. That is, the candidate who receives more votes than any other candidate wins the single seat at stake, even if his vote falls short of a majority.

It is well known that this system produces inaccurate results. A party may receive, for instance, a majority of seats without having received a majority vote from the electorate. Theoretically, at least, the Democrats could receive only 435 more votes than the Republicans nationwide, a minute fraction of one percent, and enjoy complete control over the House, 435-0, if the votes were distributed perfectly among the districts. Realistically, of course, the problem is one of distortion. In 1968, for example, the Republicans, nationally, received 48.9 percent of the votes cast for all representatives, yet received only 44 percent of the seats in the House. In fact, since 1932, the Republicans have been under-represented in every Congress except the Eightieth (1947-49).

The theory underlying the single-member district concept is best understood when compared with the opposite theory; proportional representation. Under pure proportional representation all votes in the country are tabulated together and the parties are awarded seats according to the percentage of votes received nationally. If the country had 25 or so parties, as was the situation in Fourth Republic France (pre-de Gaulle), each party would submit a list of candidates in order of preference and then an agency of the national government would distribute the seats among them according to their relative strength. In a 600 member assembly, for example, if an extreme party received only three percent of the votes spread over all the districts, it would still be assured of 18 seats in the assembly. A party receiving only three percent of the votes nationally in a country operating under the single-member district concept coupled with plurality elections would, in all likelihood, have won no seats in the legislature.

The point is obvious — proportional representation, or the application of the one-man, one-vote principle to general legislative elections, increases the probability of legislatures composed of many small parties with coalition government required to rule. The weakness of Fourth Republic France was attributed, in the main, to the plethora of parties and their inability to establish a stable government.

De Gaulle, upon ascension to power, eliminated proportional representation and instituted a single-member district system without, however, including a plurality election clause. Even with run-off elections required (a gimmick to weaken the Communists), most of the minor parties were driven from the scene and the elections came to resemble rather closely their American and British counterparts.

The fact is that it is simply impossible to have an absolute parity of voting power—that is, every man's vote counting equal in the *final* distribution of seats in the legislature—if a nation wants its legislature to represent territorial units. It is equally impossible to have absolute parity of voting power except under a system of national proportional representation and such a system virtually assures a multiparty political system.

The goals of voting parity and the maintenance of a two-party system are, for all practical purposes, incompatible.

V

The final institutional pillar of our two-party system is the Electoral College. The concept underlying the Electoral College is similar to that of the single-member district system except that it applies to the presidency. In effect, just as a congressman cannot be split in half because the opposition party received only a few votes short of the necessary plurality, a state is similarly viewed as indivisible. The unit rule means that all of the state's electoral votes will be cast for the one candidate, and his party, who garnered the greatest number of votes.[1]

Occasionally, critics will claim that the unit rule serves to disenfranchise the minority. This is false. First, they had an opportunity to vote and to win. They did not win, but it does not follow that they were disenfranchised. To lose is not to be disenfranchised.

The race for President is not just another election race. This contest sets the tone for the whole political system. The fact that a party and its presidential candidate must win more votes than any other candidate in a given state in order to receive any electoral votes means that a high premium is placed on remaining a unified party.

If a party permits its ranks to be split, it loses not just the amount of votes that the dissenters can subtract from the total, but any chance at all for the votes cast by the electors of the state.

Consequently, the stakes are high. Traditionally, the parties have been moderate and pluralistic for they found they lost when they indulged in exclusive ideologies. Both major parties were required to be inclusive in character. "True believers" and congenital reformers, eager to emulate European parties, are constantly annoyed at the non-doctrinnaire approach to politics followed by the two parties.

Not only are the two parties required to be moderate and non-doctrinnaire, they also are required to be national in orientation and organization. If a party confined its appeal to one section of the country, it might be able to build a majority in the popular vote and still lose in the Electoral College. Parties early found that it really did no good to build up a substantial lead in New York, say, if it meant that Minnesota and smaller western states were ignored. They count too.

A presidential candidate needs only one more vote than any other party to win New York, then the battle has to be shifted to other states. Building a massive plurality in one state, at the expense of attention to other problems and other areas of the country is not smart politics. The big states, while crucial, do not hold the entire key to the election. Mr. Nixon proved this rather conclusively in 1968.[2]

The Electoral college, then, provides certain statistical imperatives which steer presidential politics towards a two-party pattern and moderate, national leaders.

VI

All of this is to suggest that our two-party system is no accident, it is not peculiarly a product of American "culture" or of some other sociological phenomenon. It is an institutional artifact which we have the option of preserving or destroying.

Today, one of the pillars of our two-party system, the Electoral College, is under concerted attack by reformers of all stripes.

The debate has been quite one-sided so far—that is, only the critics have been heard. This is, in part, understandable since virtually everyone today fashions himself a critic of one type or another. The Electoral College, so the argument goes, is an anachronism and ought to be abolished before it causes chaos. This is one thing Barry Goldwater, Hubert Humphrey, Gore Vidal and Richard Nixon can agree upon. If ever there was consensus on an issue, this is it.

The first step toward wisdom in matters of electoral structure is to recognize that no electoral system will ever be able to eliminate in advance all chance of confusion and crisis. When we are talking about elections, we are talking about one of the oldest problems known to man, succession to power. One of the traditional attractions of republics as a polity has been its answer to the question of succession. Somehow elections seem a less expensive way to transfer power from one group to another than to resort to a clash of arms or intermidable palace intrigues.

Recognizing the immensity of the problem, possibly our goal ought to be to devise a system in which the odds against crisis are minimized and the odds of a majority executive maximized. This was the goal of the Founding Father, not the creation of a perfect system with all risks eliminated. They were never utopian.

The unfortunate aspect to our inordinate affection for the present is that it makes it more difficult to raise meaningful questions about our political institutions. The relevant question with regard to the Electoral College, for example, is whether or not the Electoral College performs a useful function toward maintaining the two-party system today. Not, what were the original purposes of the institution or what might have happened in a particular election a century ago if no candidate had received a majority. These kinds of questions are of interest to historians, but essentially irrelevant to the contemporary problem of succession to power.

Those who criticize the Electoral College cannot be charged with failure to offer an alternative. In fact, there are many alternative plans being circulated which run from pure proportional representation to electoral voting according to congressional district to simple direct election.

The proposal enjoying the most support at present is to eliminate the Electoral College altogether and substitute simple direct election. Modifications have been added, however, in recent months. A provision was generally accepted that if no candidate received 50 percent of the popular vote in the general election a second, run-off election, would be held between the two candidates who received the most votes. This proposal has subsequently been further modified so that if no candidate receives 40 percent of the vote, a run-off election will be held. These modifications are designed to placate those who see problems of a minority President and multiple parties becoming critical. The above described proposal, herein greatly simplified, is essentially that which both Senator Birch Bayh, chairman of the Senate Constitutional Amendments Subcommittee, and the American Bar Association have vigorously campaigned for.

Their political goal, in philosophical terms, is to "have every vote count equally in the final counting process." Is there a price that must be paid in order to achieve this deceptively appealing end? The sponsors answer in the negative. I suggest, to the contrary, that there will be a very high price paid to achieve this end. We had best be aware of it in advance.

VII

The direct election plan is ironic in the sense that it proposes to institutionalize a weakness which it alleges the Electoral College possesses, but which, in reality, it has not exhibited since 1824. The flaw of that year, according to political folklore, was that a third candidate, Henry Clay, was able to jockey for personal advantage in determining to whom he would shift his support. The great contemporary fear is that no presidential candidate will get a majority of the electoral votes and hence the election will go to the House with the third party candidate holding the critical balance of power. This fear was spelled out in great detail in the newspapers during the recent election as they conjured up horror stories about what would happen if the vote were thrown into the House.

Let us look briefly, then, at the cause of this fear, Mr. Wallace and his American Independent Party. It should be noted, at the outset, that it is impossible to ignore any candidate who receives 10, 15, or 20 percent of the popular vote. He has a right to be heard. The question is: Under what conditions can the influence of a third party be kept minimal while still permitting all votes to somehow count? The fear was that under the current Electoral College system, Mr. Wallace would play a maximum role in terms of his voting strength rather than a minimal role.

The reasoning of those who believed such an argument, I submit, was faulty. The Electoral College, far from exaggerating the strength of third parties, minimizes their strength. Also, the Electoral College virtually assures, if we use history as a guide, a majority vote, in terms of electoral votes, to a major party candidate, thus eliminating the uncertainty which follows any run-off election whether popular or in the House.

Under the present system with its unit rule the probability of a majority President, that is, one cloaked with the legitimacy of over 50 percent of the popular as well as electoral vote, is very high. If ever the system was to fail us, it should have been in 1968. The two major parties were evenly split with a strong third party having a national base challenging their hegemony. Why was the Wallace effort so unsuccessful?

It was unsuccessful because, and not in spite of, the unit rule of the Electoral College. The functioning of the unit rule exhibits many subtle manifestations. It is not merely a mechanical process applied by the commentators on election night. It also influences how people will vote in the first place. Mr. Wallace's vote would no doubt have been substantially greater under direct election for then the votes would have been cumulated nationally. Many people realized that to vote for Wallace, this being their first choice, was in most states to waste a vote since he would not gain a plurality in the state. Hence, they voted for one of the two major candidates. The unit rule, therefore, has anticipatory impact on the voting decision of the individual citizen.

The Electoral College assures that in virtually every instance a majority President, a majority of the Electoral votes of the states, is elected in the first instance thus permitting the President to begin his job without a question being raised as to his legitimacy. Is not the strength of our political system explained largely in terms of the stability of our succession process? The Electoral College permits us to settle the problem of presidential selection quickly and bestow legitimacy on the man who captured enough states to win a majority of electoral votes.

The Electoral College is "undemocratic" only if we are willing to brand all forms of indirect selection of officials or distortions of the one-man, one-vote principle by definition as "undemocratic." Our Founding Fathers offered no such definition. They contended that they had established a "popular government," with "republics" and "democracies," as understood in terms of the participants, being equally valid species of this genus. A republic, or rule by indirect participation, is a valid form of popular government. The Electoral College, while not democratic in the narrow sense, is surely within the intellectual framework of popular government and its subtype, the republic. The Electoral College, with its traditional unit rule, is a subtle, yet effective method of keeping the politics of the presidency, and hence, to a large degree, of our parties, within manageable proportions.

The indirect selection process of the Electoral College insures that the splinter third parties will have great difficulty in gaining sufficient strength to be decisive in the final outcome. Under any of the proposals, whether for direct election, proportional representation of electors, or the host of variations on these two themes, the third party, in this last election the American Independent Party, would have been permitted to exercise maximum leverage.

Under direct election, Mr. Wallace's strength would no doubt have reached that which the polls indicated he enjoyed prior to the election day. If this assumption is correct, even with the 40 percent requirement, a run-off election would have had to have been held with Wallace and his party providing the crucial swing factor.

In other words, the reformers want to rid us of a system which discourages splinter parties and minimizes the odds of non-majority presidents and substitute in its place a system whereby splinter parties and candidates will have maximum influence. We will change from a situation where crisis is possible, but unlikely, to a situation where it may be chronic.

VIII

Few words cause more intellectual confusion than the word "reform." When someone says they want to "reform" some institution, they have generally begun their intellectual deliberations with a conclusion and worked backward. Almost by definition the status quo is judged "bad" and it then becomes necessary to rewrite the rules governing that institution in order to provide advantages to a particular group promoting a particular set of policies. Change, a more neutral word than reform, is almost always justified in terms of the general welfare when, in fact, changes in rules and institutions invariably aid one group at the expense of another. Change, then, is not inherently good. There are good changes and bad changes and the criteria for good and bad is to be measured according to the general theory of politics one accepts.

Throughout this essay a theory of popular government has underlain the substantive arguments. The theory is that democracy, as generally defined today, functions best when there are only two major parties, as opposed to a multiparty system. These parties ought to be relatively non-doctrinnaire and national in their organization and appeal. They ought to conceive of themselves as the "ins" and the "outs" with both parties being committed to the fundamental values of the regime. Two-party politics suggests that both parties ought to contain a portion of most groups in the society and that neither ought to become exclusive or ideological. While such a politics may lack the momentary excitement of the righteous cause victorious, it is a politics which permits all groups to share in power and hence provides the environment necessary for the society to face the real problems and make measured social progress.

The Electoral College, with its traditional unit rule, is a critical factor in the maintenance of our two-party politics. While it is conceivable that our politics would remain largely non-ideological and within the two major parties without the Electoral College, it is unlikely. The Electoral College does serve an important function today. One can, of course, be opposed to the two-party model of politics or one can desire to have ideologically oriented parties, as does the New Left today. If this is the political theory you support, then the elimination of the Electoral College should be high on your list of priorities. What the facts do not support, however, is the argument that the demise of the Electoral College will actually strengthen the two major parties and curtail the potential dangers of third parties.

Our two-party system is capable of being maintained only if the three pillars described previously are maintained in good order. To destroy any one of them would be to endanger the entire structure. At the very least, we owe it to those who are to follow not to scuttle our electoral system, which has served us so well for nearly two centuries, without first attempting to understand the system. We must not permit ourselves to fall into the trap of substituting emotion and slogans for reasoned analysis.

Notes

[1] The unit rule for voting in the Electroal College is a tradition, not a Constitutional requirement. Recently, the legislature of Maine voted to eliminate the unit rule and replace it with a modified congressional district elector plan.

[2] Some liberal groups have recently decided that the Electoral College with its unit rule ought to be maintained. Their reasoning is that it benefits the large industrial states wherein certain minority groups can exert maximum influence. Statistically, of course, this is a questionable argument. Because of the present system which provides for a base of three

votes per state, every state with a population below the median gains political influence in relation to those states above the median in population. Using the 1960 census and the two most extreme states, Alaska and New York, each elector from Alaska represented 75,389 citizens while each elector from New York represented 390,286 citizens. The unit rule does not change the impact of these statistics. The real significance of the "malapportionment" of electors is that it forces the parties to think and operate in national terms. The greater the spread in appeal of the party, the greater the chance of victory. The election of 1968 is a classic example of where distribution of votes counted for more than sheer numbers. While Nixon and Humphrey were close in the popular vote, Nixon's appeal was more national than Humphrey's so he was able to win one elector per 105,594 votes while Humphrey, whose appeal was largely in a few industrial states, required 163,696 votes to win one elector. Wallace was hampered even more by the limitations imposed by his sectional strength and needed 215,185 votes to receive one electoral vote.

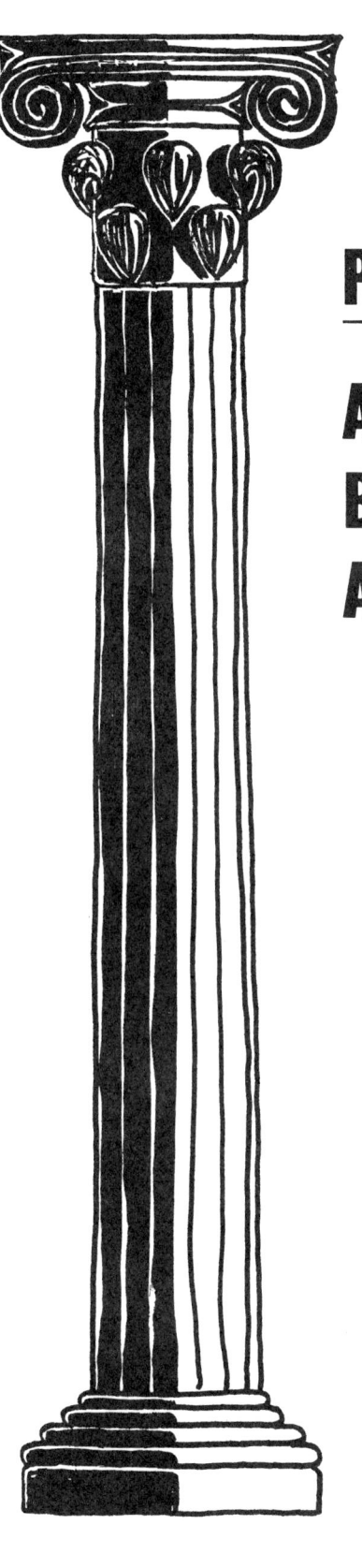

Part Three

American Political Behavior and American Democracy

Learning Democratic Norms

Robert E. Lane
David O. Sears

There has never been complete agreement among Americans generally nor political scientists particularly as to what constitutes a "democratic" process. Most of us are content with some vague statement of an ideal, like the phrase from the Gettysburg Address, "government of the people, by the people, and for the people." But that ideal leaves much unstated. For example, how directly involved do we expect individual citizens to be? Some would argue that the American ideal is full participation, even in particular policy decisions, by individual citizens; others insist that ours is a Republican form which calls upon citizens to vote for officials and then, for the most part, stand back and let them make policy. Still others observe that we have, and perhaps ought to have what Peter Bachrach calls in a later reading "elitist democracy." Instead of joining this argument at the philosophical level, most students of political behavior have preferred to begin by seeking to describe with care *the level of actual political participation. They would hold in abeyance their conclusions as to whether the process they describe is, in fact, democratic. One of the first questions that may be asked in seeking to describe accurately the nature of political participation in America is: How are political values, beliefs, and attitudes learned? Within that basic query others arise: When do we learn about politics and political figures? Do we generally learn approving or disapproving attitudes? What roles do institutions like the family, school, and church play in shaping political attitudes? What forces lead to change in political orientations? Though definitive answers to these questions are scarce, the research to date has produced provocative results. This selection from Robert Lane and David Sears' book,* Public Opinion, *summarizes the major conclusions of these socialization studies and indicates the directions they are pointing.*

Robert E. Lane and David O. Sears, *Public Opinion,* ©1964. Reprinted by permission of Prentice-Hall, Inc., Englewood Cliffs, New Jersey. Abridged by the editors.

THE POLITICAL ACCULTURATION OF THE AMERICAN CHILD

The child's opinions about politics, like his opinions on religion, are close reflections of his parents' views. The first and basic training he receives is in the family. Here he learns attitudes toward authority, toward others, toward himself, toward a vague outside community and nation. He learns habits of thought and behavior: independence, conscientiousness, trust. Let us examine, as a kind of baseline, the political orientations of these broad kinds discovered in several studies in the United States.

First, with respect to the most general orientation, an attitude toward the society outside the home, the political community and nation, Easton and Hess report an early positive sense of trust and support. On the basis of an examination of the responses of some 700 school children in the Middle West, they say, "The sentiments of most children with respect to their political community are uniformly warm and positive throughout all grades, with scarcely a hint of criticism or note of dissatisfaction."[1] "America" as a symbol and as a designation of their own country becomes suffused with this positive emotion. More than that, it becomes confused with religion for "not only do many children associate the sanctity and awe of religion with the political community, but to ages 9 or 10 they sometimes have considerable difficulty in disentangling God and country."[2] As these authors note, such a strong affective tie to country creates a bond which is likely to last a lifetime. They might also have observed that it lays the groundwork for a more dangerous view: "my country right or wrong." The Easton and Hess findings thus suggest the reason for Litt's findings that from a fifth to a third of some Boston area high school students could be classified as "very" chauvinistic.[3]

Attitudes toward authority represent another basic common orientation. Greenstein's study of some 659 preadolescent school children in New Haven reveals in this respect, too, a positive, supportive, uncritical view of political life. These views are developed in the earliest years not on information about what the President or the Mayor does, but on purely emotional grounds; later, of course, these opinions become somewhat more informed and critical but they retain this positive tone.[4] For example, Hess and Easton find that the President retains, with older school children, his favorable image in his job-related qualities, but he tends to lose his overwhelming advantage as a moral or sociable person.[5] The results of both studies indicate that the positive affective or emotional components of these opinions develop prior to cognitive elaboration about their objects; put another way, information follows evaluation, rather than preceding it, in the course of the child's development.

Like the findings on love of country, these overwhelmingly trusting views of the President (and the Mayor too) might cause political theorists to worry. Such trust forms an ideological bridge for loyal citizenship, but might it not also foster overly dependent and uncritical attitudes toward authority? Apparently not. Not only does the American (adult) have a generally restrained and balanced view of political authority,[6] but when American students are compared with German and Filipino students, they are actually considerably more critical of authority. These comparisons, based on comparable samples of older adolescents, are shown in Table 1.

On the face of it, this is strong evidence that the youthful American's investiture of civic and political authority with the qualities of the benevolent leader does not, even in adolescence, prevent a certain autonomy, capacity to criticize, or even disobedience of paternal and political authority. Apparently as the American child grows to maturity, he learns other opinions which counterbalance, to some degree, the earlier *blind* faith and trust in authority. Even so, it is clear that most American children learn from the early grammar school years to trust political authority, to respect it, and to love their country. This positive feeling for political authority, at least, most children share.

THE BEGINNINGS OF PARTISANSHIP

This happy consensus of opinion is disrupted, to some extent, by the fact that these children also begin rather early to identify with certain groups having conflicting political beliefs — such as religious, ethnic, and racial groups, socioeconomic classes, and political parties. Identification with these last two, as we shall see, forms for many purposes the basic touchstones for political partisanship. Let us look first at party identification.

TABLE 1. RESPONSES TO QUESTIONS ON AUTHORITY BY YOUTH IN THE UNITED STATES, GERMANY AND THE PHILIPPINES

Worse to be a bully than to disobey superiors:

	Yes
Philippine sample	41%
German sample (Bad Homburg)	41
American sample (Oak Park)	85

Right for a soldier to refuse to obey an order to shoot an innocent military prisoner:

	Yes
Philippine sample	66%
German sample	50
American sample	84

Right for a boy to run away from home if father is cruel and brutal:

	Yes
Philippine sample	46%
German sample	45
American sample	80

Should people who unjustly criticize the government of a country be thrown in jail:

	Yes
Philippine sample	31%
German sample	36
American sample	21

Source: Bartlett H. Stoodley, "Normative Attitudes of Filipino Youth Compared with German and American Youth," *American Sociological Review*, Vol. 22 (1957), pp. 557-559.

Party Identification

Research on youthful political beliefs indicates that children learn to identify with political parties during the grammar school years. For example, Easton and Hess say, about their sample of 700, "A strong majority in each grade from two (age 7-8) through eight (age 13-14) state that if they could vote they would align themselves with (one) of the two major parties in the United States ... the children may be adopting party identification in much the same way they appropriate the family's religious beliefs, family name, neighborhood location or other basic characteristics of life."[7] Hyman says, "The adult (political) pattern that seems established in most complete form in earlier life is that of *party affiliation*."[8]

Not only does party preference develop early in life, but it generally follows the preferences expressed by the parents. The dominant trend in American society seems to be for parents to agree on a party preference, and for the children to adopt that preference. The stability of these early preferences is illustrated by the data from the Survey Research Center's 1952 election survey on adult preferences. As shown in Table 2, this was the dominant trend in their nationwide sample.

Clearly if the child's parents agree upon a consistent party preference, the child is extremely likely to adopt that preference. If neither parent can form a consistent preference, the child is much more likely to be independent in his preference. Since the majority of the respondents in this survey had parents who agreed upon a preferred party, and since most of the children followed their parent's choice, it is possible to say that this is the dominant trend in America.

That this transmission of political party loyalties does not occur in all countries, nor even in all Western coun-

TABLE 2. Party Preference as a Function of Parental Party Preference

Child's Preference	Both Parents Democrats	Both Parents Republicans	Both Shifted
Democratic	82%	22%	47%
Republican	15	73	37
Other	3	5	16
% of total sample	41	24	6

Source: Angus Campbell, Gerald Gurin, and Warren E. Miller, *The Voter Decides* (New York: Harper, 1954), p. 99.

tries, is illustrated by evidence from Europe. In France most adults do not know what their father's political party or *groupement* was when they were growing up,[9] and in Sweden the age 11-12 group shows 73 per cent "undecided as to best party," the 13-15 group, 66 per cent undecided. Not until age 19 do a majority take the positive party alignment which, in America, was established at age 7 or 8.[10]

Class Identification

We do not have comparable figures on the development of class identification or the use of social class as a guide for political opinions, but there seems to be much more confusion on this point than on party position. For example, among the *high* income group in high schools, the proportion of youth considering themselves members of the working class nearly doubles from 9th to 12th grade (from 14.1 per cent to 25.7 per cent)—a direction which seems the reverse of what one would predict for the relatively better off.[11] On the other hand, this should not be too surprising in view of the fact that even among adults (presumably these students' parents) there is often a reluctance to make class self-identifications. As many as a third of a nationwide sample were unable or unwilling to identify themselves as members of any social class.[12] Furthermore, in Europe socio-economic classes are more likely to guide political orientations (with alliances between the working class and the socialists and communists, and between the middle class and the more conservative parties), while in the United States party identification is more likely to guide political opinions.[13]

In spite of these confusions on social class, American youth tend to adopt stances on class-related ideological issues fairly early (in the 1940's working-class youth age 16 or younger were twice as "pro-labor" in their issue orientation as middle-class youth at this age level), and these differences increase as they grow older.[14] A concomitant change, partly accounting for this difference, is the increased interest, and the informational support and organization of their ideas: greater organization of opinions is a function of age and education. As a result, by the time adolescents have reached the twelfth grade only 9 to 16 per cent give "undecided" responses to questions on nationalization of railroads, class conflict, the right to strike, and so forth. Their basic political orientations, already fairly firm by the ninth grade, are pretty well settled by the twelfth.[15] And as one might expect, these relatively late advances in interest and orientation occur most often among youth whose family backgrounds gave them the least interest and orientation at the beginning of high school—that is, from homes where the parents were poorest and had the least education.

Implications of Youthful Partisanship

In summary, before the average child reaches high school, he has adopted a partisan attitude toward the two political parties, as well as partisan stances on the major ideological issues. Only a small proportion of students leave high school without some ideological position. These opinions in general are replicas of those held by the child's parents, particularly if the parents agree on the issues and if they express their opinions to the child.

There are two important implications of this dominant pattern. First, if political opinions are in general formed largely as imitations of parental models, clearly a "traditional drag" upon innovation and change will be created. It is important to note, however, that the research on opinion development has focused too narrowly upon party affiliation and candidate preference. It would be highly misleading, for example, to say that no change has ensued between a man's adopting his father's Democratic political preference and voting for Al Smith in 1928, and *his* child's maintaining the familial tradition in voting for John F. Kennedy in 1960. A great many changes in political thinking may have occurred over those two generations, although obscured by the continuity of votes for the Democratic candidate. Hence one of the themes of the subsequent discussion concerns changes in political thinking occurring within what may be a relatively invariant pattern of party preferences.

The second point is that in the course of the development of political consciousness, the child becomes opinionated considerably before he becomes knowledgeable, due largely to imitation of parental preferences in party, candidate, and ideology....

Before turning to these issues, however, it is necessary to consider the stability of these early, parentally-influenced opinions. Although most children have learned, by the end of adolescence, to parrot their parents' preferences, many influences are at work subsequently to encourage defections from this early learning. Hence it is to the stability of the parental influence that we turn next.

GROWING AUTONOMY: THE IMPACT OF SCHOOL AND OF YOUNG ADULTHOOD

We have been outlining in a rather sketchy way the childish and adolescent political world; by the time a youth is in high school, this world picture represents, in the first place, the reflection of the parental orientation, second, the effect of maturation processes, including a growing set of capabilities, and third, the influence of the school in developing and changing the politics of the youth in its care. In some ways, then, under these various influences, youth are growing into adults like their parents, and in some ways they are, even as adolescents, departing from the parental pattern. We cannot easily sort out these several influences, but new research has suggested certain ways in which the opinion pattern changes. Among the influences which produce departures from the parental traditions during school years are (a) rebellion against parents and their beliefs, (b) the general educational process, and specifically, civic education in school, and (c) peer-group influence in and out of school, including the prevailing "climate of opinion" among the community of youth. Briefly let us examine these various factors modifying the original political endowment.

Rebellion

The parental model, of course, is so integral a part of many persons that "rebellion" or even deviance may not take place until well into adulthood. Renneker reports the case of a 47-year-old university professor who had "a 'strange' association which flitted across his mind during his father's funeral. He felt a sense of sad relief and was suddenly conscious of the thought that now he could vote for any candidate. This remained puzzling until it was recalled in therapy; it had never occurred to him that he wasn't free to vote for whomever he selected."[16] But our main focus of interest is an adolescent "rebellion," or the rebellion of the young adult still under the influence of his parents.

The minimal extent of this rebellion in party affiliation is suggested by the Survey Research Center data given in Table 2, showing the relationship of parental voting patterns to those of their progeny. Those data indicate that rebellion in party affiliation is relatively infrequent, to say the least. Yet it does happen.

On the whole, the evidence suggests that "political rebellion" — that is, differing from the parents on political matters — when it occurs, has a rather complex set of sources. Middleton and Putney, in a study of 1,440 college students, show that generalized adolescent rebellion (defined by such questions as, "When you were in high school, how often did you defy your parents and do things contrary to their instructions or wishes?") bore little relationship to political rebellion of this particular kind (at least this was true of college students, who are generally of a relatively high socio-economic level).

Nor, for this group, was strictness of parental discipline very important in directly causing political rebellion, but there was a curious roundabout relationship, which was important. Over-strict discipline or over-lenient discipline (probably indifference) tended to reduce the closeness of relationship between child and parents. Then — and this is the important point — the less close a person felt toward his parents, the more likely he was to rebel politically.[17] Here, Middleton's and Putney's work is supplemented by a study by Maccoby, Matthews, and Morton showing that those people in the *lower* socio-economic groups who felt they had suffered from over-strict discipline from their parents *are* likely to rebel politically.[18] Over-strict discipline, then, and to some extent lack of discipline, are, in one way or another, likely to encourage both upper- and lower-class youth to take on political opinions different from those of their parents. Moreover, both studies find that this political rebellion is greater when the parents are interested in politics than when they are not. If they are not interested, as Lane suggested on the basis of his study of working-class father-son relationships, there is not much point in political rebellion. Rather, this study suggests, the political outcome of damaged father-son relationships is apathy and despair over the future of the political order.[19]

It is important to point out, moreover, that rebellion goes in both political directions: the child of a conservative will, under these circumstances, become more radical, and the "rebelling" child of a liberal Democrat becomes more conservative. Rebellion and radicalism have no particular affinity in this country. And, too, it should be noted that here rebellion is a rather mild differentiation, not an adoption of violent change.

In summary, rebellion against parental beliefs does not play a large role in determining the political opinions of American voters. Under special circumstances, some rebellion does occur, however. It does not have a unidirectional effect; in America, radical ideologies are not the inevitable effect of rebellion against the parents. Finally, it is clear that political rebellion is not an integral part of that constellation we think of as "adolescent rebellion." The rebelling adolescent is much more likely to rebel in terms which are more important to his parents, such as in his dress, his driving, his drinking, his obedience of the law, his sexual behavior, and so forth. Only in rather rare instances does it have political effects as well.

Education

In an obvious sense, education helps young people to achieve opinions which are different from those of their parents if the parents had less education. But even if the parents had "as much" education it was certainly a different variety since it would be marked by the needs and ideas of a period some twenty-five years earlier. In either event an education helps provide the informational basis and variety of views which make deviance possible. In one sense children are like the people of traditional societies — they have the beliefs and prejudices of a single culture, passed on from father to son. Education modifies this. A study by Pressey illuminates how the changes in the moral and religious norms of society altered the ideas of *college* students over the 1923-1943 period, but did not alter the ideas of high school students.[20] The home and, to some extent, early formal education, encapsulate the past; higher education subjects it to scrutiny in the light of different ideas. Thus, if a young person is ready, for whatever reason, to change from the parental model, school and especially college, facilitate this.

A study of young adults in Cambridge, Massachusetts, reveals these factors in operation at each educational level — though, again, focusing too narrowly on party affiliation and candidate preference (the components of what is called in this study "the Index of Political Change"). The results of this study on education and political change are reported in Table 3. These data show that the degree of change, or deviation from parental beliefs, increases, with only one exception, as the amount of education increases. This is the main point we are making here. There is no reliable trend toward one party or the other as education increases.[21]

As well as increasing deviation from parental beliefs, the general effect of education is to increase a person's tolerance of heterodoxy, support of civil liberties and civil rights, to reduce his authoritarianism and prejudice, to increase his sense of political effectiveness and rates of participation, and generally to shape a political being who corresponds more closely to the model of the liberal, democratic, informed participant. In every case, however, these attitudes are jointly the product of home and school: students from poorer homes and poorer neighborhoods are less adequate in these respects than those in the equivalent grade from better homes and neighborhoods.

What happens when the school makes a deliberate effort to provide civic and political education for a democratic society? That is, what happens when the school gives special attention to these very goals? In an ingenious study of these programs in three schools serving different socio-economic groups, Edgar Litt examined the effects of civic education programs upon the political attitudes of adolescent high school students. He focused on four sets of attitudes:

TABLE 3. RELATIONSHIP BETWEEN EDUCATION AND THE "INDEX OF POLITICAL CHANGE"

Index of Political Change	College Graduates	Some College	High School plus Business or Vocational	High School Graduates	Some High School
More Republican than parents	24%	32%	17%	27%	23%
No change	42	52	61	58	72
More Democratic than parents	34	16	22	15	5
Total	100%	100%	100%	100%	100%
Number of subjects	55	25	41	88	75

Source: Eleanor E. Maccoby, Richard E. Matthews, and Anton S. Morton, "Youth and Political Change," *Public Opinion Quarterly,* Vol. 18 (1954), p. 37.

(a) elements of the democratic creed ("Every citizen should have an equal chance to influence governmental policy," etc.); (b) political chauvinism ("The American political system is a model that foreigners would do well to copy," etc.); (c) political activity ("It is not very important to vote in local elections," etc); (d) understanding the political process as conflict adjustment ("Politics should settle social and other disagreements as its major function," etc.).

On each of these four dimensions, students in the upper-class school showed the highest degree of initial agreement with the attitudes being taught. The students in the lower-class school showed the least initial agreement, suggesting that the civic education programs might produce the most change in this group. However, the effects were not uniform with respect to attitude dimensions or in the different schools. In all three schools, the civics programs markedly increased support for the democratic creed, and markedly decreased political chauvinism. No matter what the students' backgrounds or the nature of their schools, they became better citizens in these respects. Presumably, if their initial opinions reflected those of their parents, they became different and better citizens than their parents, as well.

However, education on the last two dimensions (attitudes toward political activity and understanding political conflict) was effective only in the upper-class school. In the middle- and lower-class schools, these parts of the program had little effect. This failure may have been due to the parental cynicism about the political process so prevalent in lower-class homes. However, there was also considerable evidence that the teachers were, in effect, telling the lower-status boys and girls to obey political leaders and conform to these leaders' beliefs, rather than encouraging the children to think they themselves could change things by assuming active political leadership. The Platonic code (only the "guardians" to be educated for leadership) here, in fact, had its modern incarnation.[22]

Peer-Group Influence and School Climate of Opinion

One thing that happens to a child as he grows up is that he talks to more people outside his immediate family. The data from some 2,500 high school students in New Jersey, shown in Table 4, indicate that a considerable increase in the discussion of politics with friends occurs during the high school years, although discussion within the family also increases somewhat during this period. The possibility of conflict with parental beliefs thus increases as the child grows older, since his friends may well not hold the same opinions as his parents. For those who are looking for an alternative to family norms and opinions, the peer group may be a potent source of influence.

The peer group, however, is only a part of the school community, and the school only part of a wider community. A recent study of the schools teaching

TABLE 4. RELATIONSHIP OF AGE TO PARTNERS IN POLITICAL DISCUSSION[a]

Partner in Political Discussion	9th and 10th Grades (1952)	11th and 12th Grades (1954)	Change
Father	66%	66%	0
Mother	39	46	7%
Friend in own grade	23	42	19%

[a]Percentage of students in each grade reporting political discussion with father, mother, and friend.
Compiled from data in Herbert Hyman, *Political Socialization* (New York: The Free Press of Glencoe, 1959), p. 101.

some of the same students reported in Table 4 showed that the "climate of opinion" in the schools themselves made a difference. This climate did not refer to anything the teachers did in the classroom, but rather to the relative proportions of students from Republican and from Democratic families. The rates of defection from parental political opinions were higher for a Democrat in a school with more Republicans, than for a Republican in such a school, and vice versa. Moreover this was more true of boys than girls, probably because they discuss politics more, and because the relative strength of attachments to peer groups and family groups favored the peer groups for these males seeking adolescent independence.[23] Berelson and others refer to this community influence as the "breakage effect" — an analogy from a gambling situation where "the house" wins in a tied conflict. Here the idea is that the community is like "the house" and a community majority will pick up the "votes" or loyalties of people who are conflicted in their opinions. These people will yield their opinions to the majority view.[24] Thus peer groups as friends, and as a community of associates, help, during youth — and, of course, adulthood — to wean a person from the opinions on which his parents nurtured him.

DEFECTIONS DURING ADULTHOOD

In an "open society" such as our own, with great geographical and vocational fluidity, the family soon ceases to have the importance in an American's life that it does in more static societies. When the child leaves high school or college, he ordinarily leaves the household of his parents, and often leaves the vicinity altogether. Most young men do not pursue the vocation of their fathers. With decreasing contact with the social environment of his childhood, then, the young adult is subjected to new kinds of influences as he carves out his own niche in society. Often he moves into a distinctively different group of vocational associates; he may marry someone from a background quite dissimilar from his own; his friends and acquaintances may have a political orientation quite different from that held by his friends in his boyhood community. Some of these movements in early adulthood are predominantly in one direction, such as the general movement from rural to urban areas, the emigration of Negroes from the South to industrial areas of the North, and so forth. But others represent an exchange of persons, a two-way movement, with more complicated political consequences.

Social Mobility

Perhaps the most notable example is social mobility, or moving into a social class different from that of one's parents. The socially mobile young adult might well be tempted to become an Independent, as a way of avoiding the conflict between parental beliefs and the predominant political opinions of his new social environment. Apparently this does not occur to any great extent. What does happen is rather interesting.

According to Maccoby, Matthews, and Morton, young adults who move up in the social scale adopt the political party of the new, higher class to which they aspire (usually the Republican party), but often retain the lower-class ideology, at least temporarily. On the other hand, those who move down tend to retain the Republican party identification of the middle class, but tend to accept much of the social welfare ideology of the working class.[25] Thus, either kind of mobility creates an inconsistency between ideology and party label —a circumstance which probably makes their political choices less certain for a number of years. Thus the parental tradition persists, in one form or another,

TABLE 5. AGE AND POLITICAL AGREEMENT OF FRIENDSHIP GROUPS

Age	Percentage of Three Best Friends Who Vote the Same as Respondent
21–25	53%
26–34	69
35–44	75
over 45	77

Source: Bernard R. Berelson, Paul F. Lazarsfeld, and William N. McPhee, *Voting* (Chicago: University of Chicago Press, 1954), p. 97.

into the new situation and creates conflicts with the new belief patterns which emerge in these mobile situations.

Part of the conflict is due to the fact that the young adult is often a kind of marginal man, having firm contacts both with the parental order he is leaving behind and the new circumstances of the life he is moving into. The young adult also frequently lives among friends and co-workers who have not themselves established their life patterns.

However, the stability and homogeneity of one's social environment increases as one grows older; one's friends come to resemble one another (and oneself) more and more closely. In their Elmira sample, for example, Berelson and associates found the ... relationship between age and the political agreement of one's three best friends (see Table 5). The instability and conflict of the young adult's life seems to diminish sharply in his late twenties; there is a rather marked increase in deviation from parental political norms at that point,[26] and, as may be seen in Table 5, a settling down into a homogenous opinion environment which does not change greatly after that.

When a young person marries he (or she) creates a small group which fuses different parental traditions and moves on to create a new order. In general, women tend to leave the political tradition of their parents and to join in the tradition of their husbands: the wife-husband tendency to agree is greater than any other adult family pair. Where this has meant "conversion" it has been preceded by intense political discussion in the home — greater than any discussion among friends or co-workers.[27] If this should fail and a divided family persist, then it appears that the progeny will either tend to be apathetic or some one of the many varieties of independents.

There is considerable lore on the effect of aging on political ideas, most of it suggesting the increasing conservatism of the older generations. In order to test this hypothesis Crittendon reviewed the American Institute of Public Opinion poll for the 1946 to 1959 period, and analyzed the change of opinion of a series of four year "generations," of which the oldest was a group born between 1878 and 1881, and the youngest was a group born between 1934 and 1937. By comparing the shifts of each of these "generations" to the shifts of all the others he was able to show conclusively that, at least during this historical period, there was a tendency for an increased Republicanism with age, relative to the trend for the entire nation to become more Democratic.[28] Up to the point of retirement older people are usually better off — no doubt that had something to do with it. But for other reasons it is probably also true that older people are less ready for change; that is, they are more conservative. It seems to be established that the longer one associates with a party, or a union, the more intensely loyal one is. Perhaps the same is true of a social order, a set of customs, a cultural pattern — the more one has lived in it, the more one wants it to continue as one has known it over the years.

Notes

[1] David Easton and Robert D. Hess, "The Child's Political World," *Midwest Journal of Political Science,* Vol. 6 (1962), pp. 236-237.

[2] *Ibid.,* p. 238.

[3] Edgar Litt, "Civic Education, Community Norms, and Political Indoctrination," *American Sociological Review,* Vol. 28 (1963), p. 73.

[4] Fred I. Greenstein, "The Benevolent Leader: Children's Images of Political Authority," *American Political Science Review,* Vol. 54 (1960), pp. 934–943.

[5] Robert D. Hess and David Easton, "The Child's Changing Image of the President," *Public Opinion Quarterly,* Vol. 24 (1960), pp. 632–644.

[6] See Robert E. Lane, *Political Followership,* forthcoming.

[7] Easton and Hess, "The Child's Political World,"*op. cit.,* p. 245.

[8] Herbert Hyman, *Political Socialization* (New York: The Free Press of Glencoe, 1959), p. 46. Hyman's emphasis.

[9] Philip E. Converse and Georges Dupeux, "Politicization of the Electorate in France and the United States," *Public Opinion Quarterly,* Vol. 26 (1962), pp. 1–23.

[10] Hyman, *op. cit.,* p. 62.

[11] *Ibid.,* p. 64.

[12] See Angus Campbell, Philip E. Converse, Warren E. Miller, and Donald E. Stokes, *The American Voter* (New York: Wiley, 1960), pp. 342–368.

[13] Angus Campbell and Henry Valen, "Party Identification in Norway and the United States," *Public Opinion Quarterly,* Vol. 25 (1961), pp. 505–525.

[14] Hyman, *op. cit.,* p. 65.

[15] *Ibid.,* p. 59.

[16] Richard E. Renneker, "Some Psychodynamic Aspects of Voting Behavior," in Eugene Burdick and Arthur J. Brodbeck, *American Voting Behavior* (New York: The Free Press of Glencoe, 1959), p. 402.

[17] Russell Middleton and Snell Putney, "Political Expression of Adolescent Rebellion," *American Journal of Sociology,* Vol. 68 (1963), pp. 527–535.

[18] Eleanor E. Maccoby, Richard E. Matthews, and Anton S. Morton, "Youth and Political Change," *Public Opinion Quarterly,* Vol. 18 (1954), pp. 23–29.

[19] Robert E. Lane, "Fathers and Sons: Foundations of Political Belief," *American Sociological Review,* Vol. 24 (1959), pp. 502–511.

[20] S. Pressey, "Changes from 1923 to 1943 in the Attitudes of Public School and University Students," *Journal of Psychology,* Vol. 21 (1946), pp. 173–188.

[21] Maccoby and associates, *op. cit.,* pp. 36–39. There is some reason to view with caution this association of education with a tendency toward political change. National figures do not show a marked discrepancy between the rate of defection among college trained adults compared with others. On the other hand, almost all studies examining ideological change report the marked effect of college education. Probably the association is as indicated, but varies more with the historical period under review than the Maccoby and associates study suggests.

[22] Litt, *op cit.*

[23] Martin L. Levin, "Social Climates and Political Socialization," *Public Opinion Quarterly,* Vol. 25 (1961), pp. 596–606.

[24] Bernard R. Berelson, Paul F. Lazarsfeld, and William N. McPhee, *Voting* (Chicago: University of Chicago Press, 1954), p. 100.

[25] Maccoby and associates, *op. cit.,* p. 33-36.

[26] Berelson and associates, *op. cit.,* p. 89.

[27] Maccoby and associates, *op. cit.,* p. 33.

[28] John Crittenden, "Aging and Party Affiliation," *Public Opinion Quarterly,* Vol. 26 (1962), pp. 648–657.

Another of the questions that arises in the studies of political socialization is: Does socialization vary with class, group, or geography? Several of the studies cited in the preceding article by Lane and Sears suggest an affirmative answer. This article by Dean Janos, Herbert Hirsch, and Fredric Fleron reports their study of a sample of Appalachian children. Not surprisingly, they discovered quite a different image of political authority than has been reported elsewhere.

The Malevolent Leader: Political Socialization in an American Subculture

Dean Jaros
Herbert Hirsch
Fredric Fleron, Jr.

Perhaps the most dramatic finding of recent research on the political socialization of children is that youngsters appear to be overwhelmingly favorably disposed toward political objects which cross their vision. Officers and institutions of government are regarded as benevolent, worthy, competent, serving and powerful.[1] The implications of such findings are striking indeed. Childhood political dispositions may represent the roots of later patriotism; we may be observing the building of basic regime-level supportive values at a very young age.[2]

These findings are by no means new; in fact, they might be classified as part of the conventional wisdom of the discipline. Moreover, they are extremely well documented, and the study of childhood political socialization has advanced to consider far more than basic regime-level norms. Despite all this, however, there are still many empirical questions to be asked about such norms. Perhaps the recent assertion that the political scientist's model of socialization is "static and homogeneous"[3] is particularly apropos here. Consider two closely related characteristics of the appropriate literature: 1) the "positive image" which children have about politics and political figures has been synthesized from data gathered largely in the United States and to some extent in urban, industrialized communities within the United States;[4] and 2) empirical explanation of the favorable disposition which children manifest has not progressed

Reprinted by permission of the authors and publisher from Dean Jaros, Herbert Hirsch and Fredric Fleron, Jr., "The Malevolent Leader: Political Socialization in An American Subculture," *American Political Science Review*, 62 (June, 1968), 564-575. Abridged by the editors.

very far. Though there may be hypotheses about how children get this way, there has been little systematic testing of the relationships between variables.

There is some danger that the major findings may be essentially "culture bound." There are few data on the political values of children in other countries or even in rural, racial, or ethnic subcultures within the United States. Moreover, what evidence there is hints at important cross-cultural variations in political learning;[5] less positive images may characterize other cultures. Political socialization is the process by which the child learns about the political culture in which he lives.[6] The content of what is socialized may well differ from culture to culture or from sub-culture to sub-culture.

The failure to explain children's positive orientations toward politics may be a function of the cultural problem. If the great majority of children in one culture manifest a glowing image, variance in disposition is not prominent, and empirical explanation in terms of accounting for variance may not suggest itself as a crucial task; also it may be quite difficult. In order to explain children's political images, one has to have a distribution of affect; there have to be some relatively negative images to come by. Research into children's political views in other cultures or sub-cultures may provide us with such negative images. But even if it does not generate the necessary data to conduct explanatory analysis, it would lessen the culture bound nature of findings in political socialization.[7]

This paper attempts to realize these desiderata through a study of childhood socialization in the Appalachian region of eastern Kentucky. Appalachia may be classified as a sub-culture within the United States for at least two reasons. First, the poverty and isolation of the region impose characteristics that differentiate it from most other areas in the country. Secondly and relatedly, many cultural norms of Appalachia differ radically from those considered to be standard middle-class imperatives.[8]

I. TWO EXPLANATIONS OF CHILDREN'S POLITICAL AUTHORITY ORIENTATIONS

There are several relatively untested hypotheses about the sources of the positive notions children are observed to hold toward the political. Many of them prominently involve the family as a socializing agent. Because of the intriguing nature of family-related variables in Appalachia, the region provides an excellent context in which to investigate these assertions.

Among these explanations is the view that the family directly transmits positive values about government and politics to the child while shielding him from stimuli which have negative connotations, such as stories of political corruption, expedient bargaining, etc.[9] In short, the family directly indoctrinates the child as to the benevolent nature of political authority, to view the political world in essentially the same terms as characterize the parents' generally supportive outlook on the political regime.[10] In Appalachia, in contrast to most of the rest of the United States, there is a great deal of overt, anti-government sentiment in the adult population. Rejection of and hostility toward political authority, especially federal authority, has long characterized the region.[11] It is very difficult to believe that here parents could transmit positive images of regime symbols to their children. In fact, "... the civic instruction which goes on incidental to normal activities in the family,"[12] suggested as a likely cause of children's favorable affect, would in Appalachia be a source of political cynicism.

Secondly, we might take the thesis that the family is an important socializing agent because the child's experiences with his immediate authority figures (parents) are somehow projected to include more remote agencies, including the political. The father, perceived as providing and benevolent, supposedly becomes the prototypical authority figure.[13] For the child, the regime becomes "the family writ large,"[14] especially sacred as its image benefits from the emotional kind of bond that exists between parent and child. In Appalachia, there is a high degree of family disruption. The father may well not live at home. Far from providing a glowing prototype of authority, he may be a pitifully inadequate figure, unemployed or absent, not providing for his family, deserving of (and receiving) scorn.[15] If the Appalachian child generalizes the father figure or the family authority structure to the political, he is not very likely to be generalizing a positive configuration.[16]

II. METHOD

Data were gathered from a nearly complete enumeration (N = 2,432) of rural public school children in grades 5-12 in Knox County, Kentucky during March, 1967. Paper-and-pencil questionnaires were administered in classrooms in connection with an evaluation of a Community Action Program of the Office of Economic Opportunity. This paper is based on the responses of a random sample of 305 of these subjects.[17]

Affect toward political authority was measured in two ways; through reports of images of the President,[18] and through "political cynicism" scale scores.[19] Images of the President were used because this figure apparently occupies a key position in the development of both cognitions of and affect toward the regime.[20] The Presidency provides an introduction; notions first held toward this role are probably subsequently generalized to other political institutions and to the entity of government itself.[21] The specific instrumentation is that developed by Hess and Easton.[22]

By contrast, political cynicism, "rather than referring to specific political issues and actors ... is a basic orientation toward political actors and activity. It presumably pervades all encounters with political objects."[23] In short, political cynicism relates to a basic general evaluative posture toward politics. Though perhaps a developmental descendant of images of the President, this variable represents far less specifically focussed regime-level affect. The specific instrumentation is the political cynicism scale developed by Jennings and Niemi.[24]

In addition to desiring variables important in the introduction of children to politics and ones which seem to encapsulate a more generalized and developed kind of regime-level affect, we chose these measures because of the fact that they have generated reliable data. We wished to take advantage of direct replicative possibilities.

Unfortunately, no direct information about the political values of the parents of our sample is presently available.[25] Though the aggregate view of political institutions and personalities held by Appalachian adults is reportedly less positive than those of other Americans, the only personal level data available are child-reported. Our indicators of parental affect toward political authority consist of two family-related items from Easton and Dennis' scale of political efficacy.[26] Two problems arise in using these items as indicators of parental values. First, the index in question was designed to measure a variable in children, not adults. However, the items "inquire about the relationship between government and the child's family...." The index is not regarded as a direct reflector of children's efficacy *per se*. In fact, it shows how a child has come to "view expected relationships between adult members of the system and the authorities" as well as tapping a "nascent attitude" of the child himself.[27] Youngsters tend to evaluate political objects in child-related terms.[28] Clearly this index does not measure that kind of dynamic. The items can be interpreted as a report on family (adult) orientations to political authorities. Indeed, such a report, involving the perception of children, may be a more significant independent variable than the actual values of the parents. A person's values, of course, can have no direct impact on the behavior of another individual. Any effect must be mediated through the influencee's cognitive and evaluative processes.

Secondly, given this, can items which tap efficacy be said to reveal anything about "positive" or supportive regime-level attitudes among adults? Though it is easy to imagine people highly enthusiastic about their political authority without possessing "citizen competence,"[29] it is probable that in democratic societies sense of efficacy is in fact related to general affect toward political authority. Inefficacious feelings are related to alienation and what has been called "political negativism."[30] These are the very antithesis of supportive dispositions. Moreover, recent scholarship has specifically considered efficacy to be a crucial variable in regime-level supports.[31]

The nature of the family authority structure is measured by 1) "father image" items analogous to Hess and Easton's Presidential image items[32] and 2) noting whether the father in fact lives at home.[33]

III. THE APPALACHIAN CHILD'S AFFECT TOWARD THE POLITICAL

Our subjects' evaluation of political authority have a very prominent feature: they are dramatically less positive than those rendered by children in previously reported research.

Table 1 describes the affective responses of the Appalachian children to the President and directly compares them to Hess and Easton's findings on Chicago-area children. Though our sample includes children from fifth through twelfth grades and Hess and Easton's from second through eighth, it is possible to make comparisons using only the fifth through eighth grade portions of both. It is clear that for all five President-evaluation items, the distribution of responses of the Knox County youngsters is significantly less favorable than that of the Hess and Easton sample. In fact, when compared against "most men," the President does not do particularly well. In aggregate, he is not a paramount figure, and there are a fair number of youngsters (about a fourth) that express overtly unfavorable reactions to him.

Hess and Easton, it will be recalled, note that age greatly affects the nature of their sample's responses. Generally, they showed that the very favorable view that the very young have of the President's personal qualities (Items 2, 3, and 5) declines with increasing age, while high regard for his performance capabilities is maintained or even increased as the child grows older.[34] The diminution of "personal" portions of the image is not interpreted as a disillusionment with authority, but as increasing realism. The maintenance of the role-filling portions is regarded as most relevant to future adult behavior, translating into respect for political institutions.[35] In short, the changes of children's images of the President with age present a very fortunate configuration considered from the standpoint of loyalty and support for the regime. The Knox County data, bleak to begin with, show few such encouraging tendencies when controls are imposed for age. Even extending the analysis to the older portions of the sample does little to effect change. To be sure, the personal portions of the image appear slightly less positive than those of younger children. Only 31% of the high-school seniors think the President likes almost everybody, while 31% think he likes fewer people than most men; no twelfth graders think the President is the best person in the world, while 31% think he is not a good person. But overall, the picture is static. *Tau* correlations between age and

TABLE 1. FIFTH-EIGHTH GRADE CHILDREN'S EVALUATIONS OF THE PRESIDENT

	Response	Knox County data*	Chicago area data†	Smirnov two-sample test
1) View of how hard the President works compared with most men.	harder	35%	77%	
	as hard	24	21	$D = .42, p < .001$
	less hard	41	3	
	Total	100% (N = 128)	101% (N = 214)	
2) View of the honesty of the President compared with most men.	more honest	23%	57%	
	as honest	50	42	$D = .34, p < .001$
	less honest	27	1	
	Total	100% (N = 133)	100% (N = 214)	
3) View of the President's liking for people as compared with most men.	like most everybody	50%	61%	
	likes as many as most	28	37	$D = .20, p < .01$
	doesn't like as many	22	2	
	Total	100% (N = 125)	100% (N = 214)	
4) View of the President's knowledge compared with most men.	knows more	45%	82%	
	knows about the same	33	16	$D = .37, p < .001$
	knows less	22	2	
	Total	100% (N = 124)	100% (N = 212)	
5) View of the President as a person.	best in world	6%	11%	
	a good person	68	82	$D = .19, p < .01$
	not a good person	26	8	
	Total	100% (N = 139)	101% (N = 211)	

*The Knox County subjects were provided with a "don't know" option apparently not available to their Chicago-area counterparts. This was done to avoid forcing the subjects, who are relatively undeveloped intellectually, to choose among possibly meaningless options. As expected, choice of the don't know alternative was very frequent. For each of the five items above, approximately 30% responded that they did not know. In the interest of comparability, the data do not include these responses. Reported non-responses (about 1%) to items 4 and 5 are likewise excluded from the Chicago-area data.

†These data are compiled from those reported in Hess and Easton, op. cit., pp. 636-637.

positive responses to the three personal image items range between .02 and .04 and are not significant.

In those portions of the image supposedly more crucial to adult regime-level behavior, there is no increase in favorable response to the President. However, a decline in the proportion of overtly unfavorable reactions does produce a significant relationship between age and positiveness on the item dealing with how hard the President works ($\tau_c = .14$, $p<.05$) and a perceptible though not significant relationship between age and positiveness on the item dealing with the President's knowledge ($\tau_c = .09, p > .05$). At best, these are modest trends. There is relatively little ground for saying, "The President is increasingly seen as a person whose abilities are appropriate to the demands of his office...."[36]

Furthermore, the very high incidence of "don't knows" does not decline significantly with age (see note to Table 1). Such a high rate was to be expected of a deprived, unsophisticated population. But the fact that it remains high even among high-school seniors (mean non-response rate is 27%) provides further evidence that, politically speaking, nothing is happening to these Appalachian youth as they mature. They certainly do not appear to be developing into adults devoted to symbols of extant political authority.

Finally, the stark contrast of these data to those on other American children is heightened when the consideration of social class is introduced. It has often been observed that lower class children have a greater propensity to idealize political figures.[37] This may well be due to the fact that such children are less politicized than their middle-class counterparts. Being less developed and less knowledgeable, they have developed fewer critical faculties and continue to exhibit the "immature" response of excessive deference. It is impossible to determine whether the same class phenomenon operates within Appalachia, for the sample as a whole is overwhelmingly lower class.[38] But because of their lower class position relative to the rest of the country, Knox County youngsters generally should be highly idealizing. The data, of course, reveal the diametric opposite. It is clear that Appalachia constitutes a distinct sub-culture, one in which there are operative variables sufficiently powerful to prevent the occurrence of what is by now expected as a matter of course.

Table 2 describes the more generalized affect manifested in political cyni-

TABLE 2. POLITICAL CYNICISM SCORES*

		Knox County data (whole sample)	Knox County data (high school only)	SRC national sample	Smirnov two sample test
most cynical	6	8%	26%	5%	Knox County data (whole sample)
	5	11	22	3	and SRC national sample,
	4	19	11	13	$D = .16, p < .001$
	3	19	20	37	Knox County data (High school
	2	23	15	25	only) and SRC national sample,
least cynical	1	21	6	17	$D = .40, p < .001$
Total		101% N = 305	100% N = 54	100% N = 1869	

*It has been assumed that the Political Cynicism Scale generated Guttman scalar patterns in the Knox County Data as it did in the SRC National Sample. To compensate for the possible invalidity of this assumption, the items were conservatively dichotomized and conservatively scored. Only choice of the most cynical available alternative was considered a cynical response. Failure of a respondent to choose the most cynical alternative *for whatever reason*, included non-response, resulted in the recording of a non-cynical item score.

cism. The scores of the Knox County youngsters are compared to those of the Survey Research Center's nation-wide sample of high school seniors.[39]

The greater cynicism of the sub-culture sample is evident. Since the Survey Research Center deals only with high school students, perhaps comparisons should be made only with the high school portion (grades 10-12) of the Knox County sample. Though this portion is significantly more cynical, the small number of subjects in it perhaps recommends use of the entire sample. One might think that the introduction of younger respondents would depress cynicism scores (age and cynicism are reportedly positively related in children),[40] but this does not happen to any great degree. In any event, even the entire 5-12 grade Knox County sample is significantly more cynical than the SRC twelfth graders. The implication of this, of course, is that in Appalachia, unlike the rest of the United States, there is relatively little change in cynicism with maturation. That this is the case is revealed by the nonsignificant $\tau_c = -.02$ between school grade and political cynicism score. Early in life these children appear to become relatively cynical and they stay that way.

Thus, though at this point it remains unexplained, there is no doubt that Appalachian children manifest far less favorable political affect than do their counterparts elsewhere in the United States. Regardless of the index in ques-

TABLE 3. RELATIONSHIP BETWEEN FAMILY POLITICAL ORIENTATION AND CHILD'S POLITICAL AFFECT

Family political orientation item	Child's political affect measure	τ_c	Significance
"I don't think people in the government care much what people like my family think"	view of how hard President works	.23	$p < .001$
	view of the honesty of the President	.06	$p > .05$
	view of the President's liking for People	.18	$p < .001$
	view of the President's knowledge	.01	$p > .05$
	view of the President as a person	.05	$p > .05$
	political cynicism scale	−.20	$p < .001$
"My family doesn't have any say about what the government does."	view of how hard President works	.10	$p > .05$
	view of the honesty of the President	.06	$p > .05$
	view of the President's liking for people	.07	$p > .05$
	view of the President's knowledge	.13	$p < .01$
	view of the President as a person	.06	$p > .05$
	political cynicism scale	−.13	$p < .01$

*Disagreement scored as positive value.

tion, the responses of our sample stand in sharp contrast to other research. Just as supportive dispositions in citizens have been asserted to have early roots, so may the Appalachians' often-noted rejection of political authority germinate during early years. Moreover, also in some contrast to findings of other research, the affective orientations of these subjects does not change greatly with increasing age. These negative images are relatively static. This nonvariant affect suggests the operation of a pervasive socialization agent early in the lives of these children.[41] This in turn suggests the desirability of examining the casual efficacy of variables related to an early agent frequently assumed to be an important socializer: the family. It is to this task that we now turn.

IV. THE FAMILY AS TRANSMITTER OF SPECIFIC POLITICAL VALUES

What kinds of general explanatory propositions about the socialization process are consistent with these data? If parents typically transmit the substantive content of their values about government to their children, then the very negative political affect observed among Appalachian youngsters should be related to similar assessments on the part of their mothers and fathers.[42] Evidence on this can be gained by examining the nature of the relationship between our family political orientation items and childrens' political affect (Table 3).

Since responses to family political orientation items were recorded in terms of degree of agreement (from disagree very much to agree very much), they constitute ordinal variables as do the presidential image and cynicism measures. The evidence on the amount of impact they have on these child political affect variables, however, is mixed. Some fairly substantial *taus* are accompanied by others approaching zero. But it is interesting to note where the significant relationships occur. Primarily, they involve Presidential competence items and the cynicism scale. These may be the most important dependent variables. Several scholars have observed that childhood evaluations of the personal qualities of the President, which here do not relate to family political orientation, are "less functionally relevant" to future adult behavior than are assessments of role-filling capabilities. As stated above, these observers express no alarm at the decline with age of evaluations of Presidential benevolence. Similarly, the fact that parental values do not seem to influence them may not be great evidence about the inefficacy of familial values in conditioning important childhood orientations.

If political cynicism represents a more developed kind of evaluation, it is significant that it appears to depend upon these parental variables. Regarded as an important encapsulator of youthful political affect, this construct may be a crucial indicator whose antecedents should be known.

Family political values, then, appear to have some effect on children's political affect. Especially given the fact that the affective variables in question appear to be among the most significant, the direct transmission hypothesis takes on some credibility. This suggests the desirability of more detailed investigations of the content of intra-familial political communication.

V. THE FAMILY AS PROTOTYPICAL AUTHORITY STRUCTURE

A totally different kind of dynamic is implied in the notion of relations with the family as a model for political affect. It is not, however, incompatible with the notion that the family transmits specific value content to the young. It is entirely possible that both processes operate simultaneously. Moreover, since the relationships are relatively small, our data on value transmission fairly demand that additional explanatory tacks be taken. Table 4 demonstrates the effects of father-image and integrity of the family on Appalachian children's political orientation. Again, evidence is somewhat mixed. Three father image items[43] are placed against their Presidential-image parallels and against cynicism. There is almost a complete lack of relationship. Not only does the "great overlap of the images of father and President"[44] fail to appear among these children, but the more generalized political affect measured by cynicism does not depend on how they see their fathers. In short, there is no evidence at all to support the hypothesis that evaluations of family authority figures are directly projected to regard remote, political ones.

If the father image hypothesis thus suffers, another dynamic by which the family might serve as a model for regime affects fares even worse. The presence or absense of the father might be thought to have political consequences for children. A fatherless home is disrupted and generally thought to have negative implications. Children might project their negative evaluations of such homes onto the political authority.[45] If this were the case, children from fatherless homes should have less positive views. Table 4 reveals exactly the opposite. There are generally low to moderate, but significant, negative relationships between having a father at home and evaluating the President in a favorable light. Fatherless children are more positive toward the political. How can this remarkable result be interpreted? One could argue that there is a cathartic process at work; that there is some sort of psychic neces-

TABLE 4. Relationship Between Family Authority Characteristics and Child's Political Affect

Family authority characteristics	Child's political affect	τ_c	Significance
View of father's liking for people	view of President's liking for people	.05	$p > .05$
	political cynicism	−.07	$p > .05$
View of father's knowledge	view of President's knowledge	.02	$p > .05$
	political cynicism	.02	$p > .05$
View of father as a person	view of President as a person	.05	$p > .05$
	political cynicism	−.03	$p > .05$
Father living with family*	view of how hard President works	−.08	$p < .05$
	view of President's honesty	−.09	$p < .05$
	view of President's liking of people	−.12	$p < .05$
	view of President's knowledge	−.23	$p < .001$
	view of President as a person	.00	$p > .05$
	political cynicism	.05	$p > .05$

*This is a dichotomous variable — either the father lives at home or he does not. However, since father's living at home constitutes a less disrupted family authority structure, we continue to apply ordinal statistics.

sity (possibly anxiety-related) to regard authority as benign. Perhaps unfortunate home life heightens this need which is then manifested in positive evaluations of the political.[46] This does not seem likely, for as we have just seen, specific negative evaluations of their fathers are not related to children's positive political orientations.

Rather than resulting in negative authority orientations, father-absence could interfere with the transfer of specific political value content from family to child. A major agent in the transfer process may be absent. Though mixed, there is some evidence in previous research of "male political dominance" in the family. Fathers may be particularly important communicators of political values.[47] Children from fatherless homes become more dependent upon their mothers. But mothers are not typically strong political cue-givers. Hence, the typical adult political values of Appalachia will not be so effectively transmitted in the fatherless home. These adult values supposedly involve relatively unfavorable assessments of political authority. The fatherless child escapes close contacts with these values and emerges more positively disposed toward political authority. When this agent is absent, perhaps the media, or other agents bearing more favorable cues, assume a more prominent role in the socialization process.

This interpretation, which of course returns us to the transmission-of-

TABLE 5. Relationship Between Family Political Orientation and Child's Political Affect, with Father-Presence Controlled

Family political orientation item	Child's political affect measure	Father-present children τ_c	Father-absent children τ_c	Significance of the difference
I don't think people in the government care much what people like my family think*	view of how hard the President works	.25	.12	$p < .001$
	view of honesty of the President	.12	−.10	$p < .001$
	view of President's liking for people	.23	.04	$p < .001$
	view of President's knowledge	.00	.06	$p < .01$†
	view of President as a person	.10	−.11	$p < .001$
	political cynicism scale	−.18	−.26	$p < .01$†
My family doesn't have any say about what the government does*	view of how hard the President works	.17	−.15	$p < .001$
	view of honesty of the President	.10	−.06	$p < .001$
	view of President's liking for people	.17	−.23	$p < .001$
	view of President's knowledge	.17	.03	$p < .001$
	view of President as a person	−.06	.08	$p < .001$†
	political cynicism	−.13	−.16	$p < .05$†

*Disagreement scored as positive value.
†Relationship not in predicted direction.

specific-values hypothesis, is strongly supported by additional analysis of the data. First, it is clear that there is no unknown process operating to produce more positive adult political values in fatherless families. Fatherless and two-parent families are identical in this regard (*tau's* between father at home and family political value items are −.03 and .00) Though the starting point is the same, it is also clear that the transmission process is greatly attenuated in fatherless homes. This can be seen by imposing a control for father-presence on the relationship between family political orientation and child's political affect (Table 5). The data for father-present children are very similar to the collapsed data shown in Table 3, except that the relationship between family value and child affect is generally somewhat stronger. But for father-absent children, the relationship generally declines and in several cases is actually reversed. Not only can the fatherless family not promulgate its political values, but it seems to leave its children very vulnerable to the socialization of other agents, agents with rather different (more positive) values. To be sure, child political cynicism, which is related to family political values, does not appear to be governed by these considerations. Other family-related roots may affect this variable—perhaps those which relate to generalized cynicism.

VI. CONCLUSION

Children in the relatively poor, rural Appalachian region of the United States are dramatically less favorably inclined toward political objects than are their counterparts in other portions of the nation. Moreover, the image which these children have does not appear to develop with age in the fashion observed for others; there is no indication that a process conducive to the development of political support is operative in Appalachia. Here, children's views appear to be relatively static. These findings have two implications. First, they point to the possibility that the often-emphasized highly positive character of children's views of politics may be a culturally bound phenomenon. One should exercise much caution in accepting such views as a universal norm. Secondly, the occurrence of such divergent findings underscores the desirability of *explaining* children's political orientations.

Since, at the sub-cultural level, these atypical findings are paralleled by 1) atypical adult (parent) political values, and 2) atypical family structure, two broad hypotheses involving the effect of family-related variables on children's political affect were tested. Examination of the hypothesis that parents directly transmit the content of their political values to their children produced some confirming evidence. Reported parental values showed moderate relationship to certain aspects of children's political affect. This was especially true of the competence items in Presidential images (supposedly the most important for subsequent behavior) and of political cynicism, a more generalized kind of system affect.

The thesis which posits the family as prototypical authority structure fares less well, however. There is no support at all for the notion that affect toward the father is extended to remote, political authority. Relationships between specific aspects of children's father images and parallel components of Presidential images are not significant. Nor is there evidence that disrupted family structure, measured by father-absence, contributes to negative political evaluations. In fact, father-absence is associated with more favorable political valuations in Appalachian children! This remarkable result is interpreted as supporting the first hypothesis regarding the direct transfer of value-content from family to child. Where the father is absent, an agent communicating the predominantly negative adult political values to youngsters is lost. This notion seems the more plausible when it is observed that there is a marked relationship between family political values and child political affect among father-present families, but no such relationship — if anything a slight negative gradient—among father-absent families.

Thus, of the two broad hypotheses posited at the outset, our data support the notion of direct value transfer, while leading us to doubt that the family is an effective authority prototype. Though these findings are offered as significant in and of themselves — they certainly suggest the importance of closer examination of parent-child political communication processes in the understanding of regime-free values — there are other implications. The explanatory relationships presented here are of relatively modest magnitudes. The small amount of variance in children's political affect which is explained here by the family suggests that we should search for other agents of socialization, or for other dynamics which may operate within the family. A preliminary view of other of the Knox County data suggests that there may be conditions under which other, less personal agents assume a great role. Fortunately, the move toward cross-cultural and explanatory analysis of childhood socialization will proceed and these and related questions will be joined.[48]

Notes

[1] Robert D. Hess and David Easton, "The Child's Changing Image of the President," *Public Opinion Quarterly,* 14 (Winter, 1960), 632-642; Fred I. Greenstein, *Children and Politics* (New Haven: Yale University Press, 1965), pp. 27-54; Robert D. Hess and Judith V. Tourney, "The Development of Basic Attitudes Toward Government and Citizenship During the Elementary School Years: Part I," (Cooperative Research Project No. 1078; University of Chicago, 1965), pp. 102-105; Dean Jaros, "Children's Orientations Toward the President: Some Additional Theoretical Considerations and Data," *Journal of Politics,* 29 (May, 1967), 368-387.

[2] David Easton and Robert D. Hess, "The Child's Political World," *Midwest Journal of Political Science,* 6 (August, 1962), 243; Greenstein, *op. cit.,* 53.

[3] Roberta S. Sigel, "Political Socialization: Some Reactions on Current Approaches and Conceptualizations," (Paper presented at the 1966 Annual Meeting of the American Political Science Association, New York, Sept. 6-10, 1966), p. 14.

[4] The Chicago area, New Haven, and Detroit provided the research environments for some of the studies cited in Note 1.

[5] Robert D. Hess, "The Socialization of Attitudes Toward Political Authority: Some Cross-National Comparisons," *International Social Science Journal,* 14 (No. 4, 1963), 542-559.

[6] Gabriel A. Almond and G. Bingham Powell, Jr., *Comparative Politics: A Developmental Approach* (Boston: Little, Brown, and Co., 1966), pp. 23-24.

[7] Michael Argyle and Peter Delin, "Non-Universal Laws of Socialization," *Human Relations,* 18 (February, 1965), 77-86.

[8] Several analyses contributory to this assertion are: Virgil C. Jones, *The Hatfields and the McCoys* (Chapel Hill: University of North Carolina Press, 1948); Jack E. Weller, *Yesterday's People* (Lexington: University of Kentucky Press, 1965); Harry M. Caudill, *Night Comes to the Cumberlands* (Boston: Little, Brown and Co., 1963).

[9] Greenstein, *op. cit.,* pp. 45-46; Easton and Hess, *Midwest Journal of Political Science,* 6 (November, 1962), 229-235.

[10] Herbert Hyman, *Political Socialization* (Glencoe, Ill.: Free Press, 1959), Chapter 4; Leonard W. Doob, *Patriotism and Nationalism* (New Haven: Yale University Press, 1964), pp. 119-126.

[11] Weller, pp. 33-56, 163; Also Thomas R. Ford (ed). *The Southern Appalachian Region: A Survey* (Lexington: University of Kentucky Press, 1960), pp. 12-15.

[12] Greenstein, *op. cit.*, p. 44.

[13] Harold D. Lasswell, *Power and Personality* (New York: Viking Press, 1962), pp. 156-159; Sebastian DeGrazia, *The Political Community* (Chicago: University of Chicago Press, 1948), pp. 11-21; James C. Davies, "The Family's Role in Political Socialization," *Annals*, 361 (September, 1965), 10-19.

[14] Easton and Hess, *Midwest Journal of Political Science*, 6 (November, 1962), 242-243.

[15] The effects of widespread unemployment in the coal industry and other economic malaises are well known. Because they are unable to provide, men reportedly invent physical disabilities or contrive "abandonments" of their dependents in order to qualify their families for public assistance. Such men become ciphers: Weller, *op. cit.*, pp. 76-78; Ford, *op. cit.*, pp. 245-256.

[16] At this point, it should be noted that these two general hypotheses do not exhaust the list of suggested socialization processes. In fact, some observers stress the efficacy of altogether different agencies, for example the public school: Hess and Tourney, *op. cit.*, pp. 193-200.

[17] A few schools, not accessible by road, did not participate in the study. The cost of including them would have been very high and the returns realized very small. These schools had a total enrollment of less than fifty and a somewhat smaller number than this in grades five through eight. Knox County was chosen as the site for this study because it to some extent typifies Appalachia. That is, it is isolated, rural, and poor.

[18] For commentary on images of the President, see Fred I. Greenstein, "More on Children's Images of the President," *Public Opinion Quarterly*, 25 (Winter, 1961), 648-654.

[19] For remarks on political cynicism, see Robert E. Agger, Marshall N. Goldstein, and Stanley A. Pearl, "Political Cynicism: Measurements and Meaning," *Journal of Politics*, 23 (August, 1961), 477-506.

[20] Fred I. Greenstein, "The Benevolent Leader: Children's Images of Political Authority," this REVIEW, 54 (December, 1960), 936; Easton and Hess, *Midwest Journal of Political Science*, 6, 241.

[21] Greenstein, *Children and Politics*, p. 54.

[22] Hess and Easton, *Public Opinion Quarterly*, 14, 639.

[23] Jennings and Niemi, *op. cit.*, p. 13.

[24] *Ibid.*, footnote 30.

[25] The evaluation of the Community Action Program in Knox County involved the solicitation of data from a sample of adults. These data can be arranged with those on youngsters to form parent-child pairs. These data are being exploited by Herbert Hirsch.

[26] David Easton and Jack Dennis, "The Child's Acquisition of Regime Norms: Political Efficacy," this REVIEW, 61 (March, 1967), 25-38.

[27] *Ibid.*, p. 32.

[28] Greenstein, this REVIEW, 54, 938-939.

[29] Gabriel A. Almond and Sidney Verba, *The Civic Culture* (Princeton: Princeton University Press, 1963), Chapter 6.

[30] John E. Horton and Wayne Thompson, "Powerlessness and Political Negativism," *American Journal of Sociology,* 67 (March, 1962), 435-493.

[31] Easton and Dennis, *op. cit.*

[32] Hess and Easton, *Public Opinion Quarterly,* 14, 635-642.

[33] On father-absence see: David B. Lynn and William L. Sawrey, "The Effects of Father-Absence on Norwegian Boys and Girls," *Journal of Abnormal and Social Psychology,* 59 (September, 1959), 258-262; George R. Bach, "Father-Fantasises and Father-Typing in Father-Separated Children," *Child Development,* 17 (March, 1946), 63-80.

[34] Hess and Easton, *Public Opinion Quarterly,* 14, 635-642.

[35] *Ibid.*

[36] *Ibid.*, p. 639.

[37] See for example, Greenstein, *Children and Politics.* Chapter 5.

[38] No reliable information on social class could be secured from the children themselves.

[39] Jennings and Niemi, *op. cit.*, p. 15.

[40] Greenstein, *Children and Politics,* pp. 39-40.

[41] This non-variance, a preliminary look at our data suggests, may be due to the homogeneity and isolation of the area. Family, peer groups, schools and other possible agents of socialization indigenous to the region probably manifest substantially the same configuration of values. Thus if families transmit an initial set of political notions to children, subsequent exposure to school, peers, etc., is likely to reinforce rather than change values. The remote location of the county probably insulates it from electronic or printed media and other external stimuli. Any value implications at variance with indigenous norms which such sources might transmit are thus prevented from having a widespread effect on maturing children.

[42] In the absence of additional data, it is difficult to show empirically that the parents of this sample have negative dispositions toward political authority. However, responses to the family political value items, when the distribution is dichotomized, reveal about equal number of agreements (negative dispositions) and disagreements (positive dispositions). Following each item is the percentage of respondents expressing agreement:
"I don't think people in the government care much about what people like my family think," 58%;
"My family doesn't have any say about what the government does," 43%.
The authors are fully aware of the precarious nature of the family value measures. Their proxy nature makes them somewhat suspect. The data they generate are displayed, however, because they are suggestive and because they indicate the kind of research which, in the authors' opinions, should be performed more often. In subsequent publications based on the Appalachian data, direct information on parental values and children's perceptions thereof will be available (See note 25).

[43] The father image items are analogous to the Presidential image items used by Hess and Easton. Though there are five Presidential image items, only three father image analogues are used because of objection to asking respondents to evaluate their fathers' honesty or diligence at work.

[44] Hess and Easton, *Public Opinion Quarterly,* 14, 640.

[45] Davies, *op. cit.,* 13-15.

[46] Judith V. Tourney, *The Child's Idealization of Authority* (unpublished M.A. thesis, University of Chicago, 1962).

[47] Greenstein, *Children and Politics,* p. 119; Kenneth P. Langton, *The Political Socialization Process: The Case of Secondary School Students in Jamaica,* (Unpublished Ph.D. dissertation, University of Oregon, 1965, p. 119. On the other hand, male dominance in the political learning of the young fails to appear in some research: Hyman, *Political Socialization,* pp. 83-89; Eleanor E. Maccoby, Richard E. Matthews, and Anton S. Morton, "Youth and Political Change," *Public Opinion Quarterly,* 18 (Spring, 1954), 23-39.

[48] The forthcoming doctoral dissertation by Herbert Hirsch explores other socialization agents at greater length.

Consensus and Ideology in American Politics

Herbert McClosky

Another ambiguous element in the American conception of democracy relates to the level of political knowledge needed for satisfactory participation, particularly knowledge of the political rules of the game. Some political theorists have concluded that a democratic state requires a body of citizens who have substantial agreement on fundamental political principles. If no such consensus exists, these theorists claim, the culture becomes torn by conflict leading to instability and resulting in governmental paralysis. A handful of empirical studies have aimed to determine the degree to which Americans, in fact, agree on fundamental principles. Herbert McClosky's findings are quite representative of those studies.

The belief that consensus is a prerequisite of democracy has, since deTocqueville, so often been taken for granted that it is refreshing to find the notion now being challenged. Prothro and Grigg,[1] for example, have questioned whether agreement on "fundamentals" actually exists among the electorate, and have furnished data which indicate that it may not. Dahl,[2] reviewing his study of community decision-makers, has inferred that political stability does not depend upon widespread belief in the superiority of democratic norms and procedures, but only upon their *acceptance*. From the findings turned up by Stouffer,[3] and by Prothro and Grigg, he further conjectures that agreement on democratic norms is greater among the politically active and aware—the "political stratum" as he calls them—than among the voters in general. V. O. Key,[4] going a step further, suggests that the viability of a democracy may depend less upon popular opinion than upon the activities and values of an "aristocratic" strain whose members are set off from the mass by their political influence, their attention to public affairs, and their active role as society's policy makers. "If so, any assessment of the vitality of a democratic system should rest on an examination of the outlook, the

Reprinted by permission of the author and publisher from Herbert McClosky, "Consensus and Ideology In American Politics," *American Political Science Review*, 58 (June, 1964), 361-382. Footnotes abridged by editors.

sense of purpose, and the beliefs of this sector of society."

Writers who hold consensus to be necessary to a free society have commonly failed to define it precisely or to specify what it must include. Even Tocqueville[5] does not go deeply enough into the matter to satisfy these needs. He tells us that a society can exist and, *a fortiori*, prosper only when "the minds of all the citizens [are] rallied and held together by certain predominant ideas; ... when a great number of men consider a great number of things from the same aspect, when they hold the same opinions upon many subjects, and when the same occurrences suggest the same thoughts and impressions to their minds" — and he follows this pronouncement with a list of general principles he believes Americans hold in common. Elsewhere, he speaks of the "customs" of the American nation (its "habits, opinions, usages, and beliefs") as "the peculiar cause which renders that people able to support a democratic government." But nowhere does he set forth explicitly the nature of the agreement upon which a democratic society presumably depends.

Later commentators have not clarified matters much. Some, like A. Lawrence Lowell,[6] have avoided Tocqueville's emphasis upon shared ideas, customs, and opinions in favor of the less demanding view that popular government requires agreement mainly "in regard to the legitimate character of the ruling authority and its right to decide the questions that arise." Consensus, in this view, becomes merely a synonym for legitimacy. Others speak of consensus as a sense of solidarity or social cohesion arising from a common ethos or heritage, which unites men into a community.[7] Political scientists have most frequently employed the term to designate a state of agreement about the "fundamental values" or "rules of the game" considered essential for constitutional government. Rarely, however, have writers on consensus attempted to state what the fundamentals must include, how extensive the agreement must be, and *who* must agree. Is agreement required among all men or only among certain of them? Among the entire electorate or only those who actively participate in public affairs? Is the same type of consensus essential for all democracies at all times, or is a firmer and more sweeping consensus needed for periods of crisis than for periods of calm, for newer, developing democracies than for older stable ones?

While certain of these questions are beyond the scope of this paper (no one, in any event, has done the systematic historical and comparative research needed to answer them satisfactorily), something might be learned about the relation of ideological consensus to democracy by investigating the subject in at least one major democracy, the United States. In the present paper I wish to explore further some of the questions raised by the writers I have cited and to present research findings on several hypotheses relating to those questions.

I. HYPOTHESES AND DEFINITIONS

We expected the data to furnish support for the following hypotheses, among others:

That the American electorate is often divided on "fundamental" democratic values and procedural "rules of the game" and that its understanding of politics and of political ideas is in any event too rudimentary at present to speak of ideological "consensus" among its members.

That, as Protho and Grigg report for their samples, the electorate exhibits greater support for general, abstract statements of democratic belief than for their specific applications.

That the constituent ideas of American democratic ideology are principally held by the more "articulate" segments of the population, including the political influentials; and that people in these ranks will exhibit a more meaningful and far reaching consensus on democratic and constitutional values than will the general population.

That consensus is far from perfect even among the articulate classes, and will be evidenced on political questions more than on economic ones, on procedural rights more than on public policies, and on freedom more than equality.

That whatever increases the level of political articulateness—education, S.E.S., urban residence, intellectuality, political activity, etc.—strengthens consensus and support for American political ideology and institutions.

Whether a word like ideology can properly be employed in the American context depends, in part, on which of its many connotations one chooses to emphasize. Agreement on the meaning of the term is far from universal, but a tendency can be discerned among contemporary writers to regard ideologies as *systems* of belief that are elaborate, integrated, and coherent, that justify the exercise of power, explain and judge historical events, identify political right and wrong, set forth the interconnections (causal and moral) between politics and other spheres of activity, and furnish guides for action.[8] While liberal democracy does not fulfill perfectly the terms of this definition, it comes close enough, in my opinion, to be considered an ideology. The elements of liberal democratic thought are not nearly so vague as they are sometimes made out to be, and their coalescence into a single body of belief is by no means fortuitous. American democratic "ideology" possesses an elaborately defined theory, a body of interrelated assumptions, axioms, and principles, and a set of ideals that serve as guides for action. Its tenets, postulates, sentiments, and values inspired the great revolutions of the seventeenth and eighteenth centuries, and have been repeatedly and explicitly set forth in fundamental documents, such as the Constitution, the Declaration, and the Federalist Papers. They have been restated with remarkable unanimity in the messages of Presidents, in political speeches, in the pronouncements of judges and constitutional commentators, and in the writings of political theorists, historians, and publicists. They are so familiar that we are likely to see them not as a coherent union of ideas and principles embodying a well-defined political tendency, but as a miscellany of slogans and noble sentiments to be trotted out on ceremonial occasions.

Although scholars or Supreme Court justices might argue over fine points of interpretation, they would uniformly recognize as elements of American democratic ideology such concepts as consent, accountability, limited or constitutional government, representation, majority rule, minority rights, the principle of political opposition, freedom of thought, speech, press, and assembly, equality of opportunity, religious toleration, equality before the law, the rights of juridical defense, and individual self-determination over a broad range of personal affairs. How widely such elements of American liberal democracy are approved, by whom and with what measure of understanding, is another question—indeed, it is the central question to be addressed in this paper. But that they form an integrated body of ideas which has become part of the American inheritance seems scarcely open to debate.

The term consensus will be employed in this paper to designate a state of agreement concerning the aforementioned values. It has principally to do with shared beliefs and not with feelings of solidarity, the willingness to live together, to obey the laws, or to accept the existing government as legitimate. Nor does it refer to an abstract or universal state of mind, but to a measurable state of concurrence around values that can be specified. Consensus exists in degree and can be expressed in quantitative form. No one, of course, can say how close one must come to unanimity before consensus is achieved, for the cutting point, as with any continuous variable, is arbitrary. Still, the term in ordinary usage has been reserved for fairly substantial measures of correspondence, and we shall take as a minimal requirement for consensus a level of agreement reaching seventy-five per cent. This figure, while also arbitrary, recommends itself by being realistically modest (falling as it does midway between a bare majority and unanimity), and by having been designated in this country and elsewhere as the extraordinary majority required for certain constitutional purposes.

Since I shall in subsequent pages frequently (and interchangeably) employ such terms as the "articulate minority," the "political class," the "political elite," the "political influentials," and the "political stratum," I should also clarify what they are intended to signify. I mean them to refer to those people who occupy themselves with public affairs to an unusual degree, such as government officials, elected office holders, active party members, publicists, officers of voluntary associations, and opinion leaders. The terms do not apply to any definable social class in the usual sense, nor to a particular status group or profession. Although the people they designate can be distinguished from other citizens by their activity and concerns, they are in no sense a community, they do not act as a body, and they do not necessarily possess identical or even harmonious interests. "Articulates" or "influentials" can be found scattered throughout the society, at all income levels, in all classes, occupations, ethnic groups, and communities, although some segments of the population will doubtless yield a higher proportion of them than others. I scarcely need to add that the line between the "articulates" and the rest of the population cannot always be sharply drawn, for the qualities that distinguish them vary in form and degree and no single criterion of classification will satisfy every contingency.

The data for the present inquiry have been taken from a national study of political actives and supporters carried out in 1957-58. I have in a previous paper described the procedures of that study in some detail,[9] and will not trouble to repeat that description here. Perhaps it will suffice for present purposes merely to note the following: national surveys were carried out on two separate samples, the first a sample of over 3,000 political "actives" or "leaders" drawn from the delegates and alternates who had attended the Democratic and Republican conventions of 1956; the second a representative national sample of approximately 1,500 adults in the general population drawn by the American Institute of Public Opinion (Gallup Poll). Gallup interviewers also delivered and introduced the questionnaire to all respondents, discussed its contents with them, and furnished both oral and written instructions for its self-administration and completion....

The party actives may be considered an especially pure sample of the "political stratum," for every person in the sample has marked himself off from the average citizen by his greater political involvement. Although the general population sample may be regarded as a sample of "inarticulates," to be compared with the sample of leaders, there are within it, of course, many persons who by virtue of education, profession, organizational activities, etc. can be classified as "articulates." We shall for certain purposes consider them in this light in order to provide further tests for our hypotheses.

Both samples received the same questionnaire—a lengthly instrument containing questions on personal background, political experiences, values, attitudes, opinions, political and economic orientation, party outlooks, and personality characteristics. Many of the questions were direct inquiries in the standard form, but most were single sentence "items" with which the respondent was compelled to express his agreement or disagreement. While each of these items can stand alone and be regarded in its own right as an indicator of a person's opinions or attitudes, each of them is simultaneously an integral element of one of the 47 "scales" that was expressly fashioned to afford a more refined and reliable assessment of the attitude and personality predispositions of every respondent. Each of the scales (averaging approximately nine items) has been independently validated either by empirical validation procedures employing appropriate criterion groups, or by a modified Guttman reproducibility procedure (supplemented, in some instances, by a "face validity" procedure utilizing item ratings by experts).

Data on the *scale* scores are presented in Table 4 and are to be distinguished from the "percentage agree" scores for *individual items* presented in the remaining tables.

II. FINDINGS

"Rules of the game" and democratic values

Although the so-called "rules of the game" are often separated from other democratic values, the distinction is to some extent arbitrary. One might, for example, reasonably regard as "rules of the game" many of the norms governing free speech, press, social and political equality, political toleration, and the enforcement of justice. For convenience, nevertheless, we shall treat separately those responses that stand out from the general body of democratic attitudes by their particular emphasis upon fair play, respect for legal procedures, and consideration for the rights of others. A sample of items expressing these values is presented in Table 1.

The responses to these items show plainly that while a majority of the electorate support the "rules of the game," approval of such values is significantly greater and more uniform among the influentials. The latter have achieved consensus (as we have defined it) on eight of the twelve items and near consensus on three of the remaining four items. The electorate, by contrast, does not meet the criterion for consensus on a single item.

Although the *scales* (as distinguished from individual *items*) cannot appropriately be used to measure *consensus*, comparison of the scores on those scales which most nearly embody the "rules of the game" furnishes additional evidence that the political class responds to such norms more favorably than does the electorate. The proportion scoring high[10] on a scale of "faith in direct action" (a scale measuring the inclination to take the law into one's own hands) is 26.1 per cent for the active political minority and 42.5 per cent for the general population. On a scale assessing the willingness to flout the rules of political integrity, the proportions scoring high are 12.2 per cent and 30.6 per cent respectively. On "totalitarianism," a scale measuring the readiness to subordinate the rights of others to the pursuit of some collective political purpose, only 9.7 per cent of the political actives score high compared with 33.8 per cent of the general population.

These and other results which could be cited support the claim advanced by earlier investigators like Prothro and Grigg, and Hyman and Sheatsley,[11] that a large proportion of the electorate has failed to grasp certain of the underlying ideas and principles on which the American political system rests. Endorsement of these ideas is not unanimous among the political elite either, but is in every instance greater than that exhibited by the masses.

The picture changes somewhat when we turn from "rules of the game" to items which in a broad, general way express belief in freedom of speech and opinion. As can be seen from Table 2, support for these values is remarkably high for both samples. Both groups, in fact, respond so overwhemingly to ab-

TABLE 1. POLITICAL INFLUENTIALS VS. THE ELECTORATES: RESPONSE TO ITEMS EXPRESSING "RULES OF THE GAME"*

Items	Political Influentials (N = 3020)	General Electorate (N = 1484)
	% Agree	
There are times when it almost seems better for the people to take the law into their own hands rather than wait for the machinery of government to act.	13.3	26.9
The majority has the right to abolish minorities if it wants to.	6.8	28.4
We might as well make up our minds that in order to make the world better a lot of innocent people will have to suffer.	27.2	41.6
If congressional committees stuck strictly to the rules and gave every witness his rights, they would never succeed in exposing the many dangerous subversives they have turned up.	24.7	47.4
I don't mind a politician's methods if he manages to get the right things done.	25.6	42.4
Almost any unfairness or brutality may have to be justified when some great purpose is being carried out.	13.3	32.8
Politicians have to cut a few corners if they are going to get anywhere.	29.4	43.2
People ought to be allowed to vote even if they can't do so intelligently.	65.6	47.6
To bring about great changes for the benefit of mankind often requires cruelty and even ruthlessness.	19.4	31.3
Very few politicians have clean records, so why get excited about the mudslinging that sometimes goes on?	14.8	38.1
It is all right to get around the law if you don't actually break it.	21.2	30.2
The true American way of life is disappearing so fast that we may have to use force to save it.	12.8	34.6

*Since respondents were forced to make a choice on each item, the number of omitted or "don't know" responses was, on the average, fewer than one percent, and thus has little influence on the direction or magnitude of the results reported in this and subsequent tables.

stract statements about freedom that one is tempted to conclude that for these values, at least, a far-reaching consensus has been achieved. These results become even more striking when we consider that the items in the table are not mere clichés but statements which in some instances closely paraphrase the arguments developed in Mill's essay, *On Liberty*. We cannot, therefore, dismiss them as mere responses to familiar, abstract sentiments which commit the respondent to nothing in particular.

Still, as can readily be discerned from the items in Table 3, previous investigators have been partially correct, at least, in observing that the principles of freedom and democracy are less widely and enthusiastically favored when they are confronted in their specific, or applied, forms. As Dahl remarks, it is a "common tendency of mankind ... to qualify universals in application while leaving them intact in rhetoric." This observation, of course, also holds for the political articulates, but to a lesser degree. Not only do they exhibit stronger support for democratic values than does the electorate, but they are also more consistent in applying the general principle to the specific instance. The average citizen has greater difficulty appreciating the importance of certain procedural or juridical rights, especially when he believes the country's internal security is at stake.

TABLE 2. POLITICAL INFLUENTIALS VS. THE ELECTORATE: RESPONSES TO ITEMS EXPRESSING SUPPORT FOR GENERAL STATEMENTS OF FREE SPEECH AND OPINION

Items	Political Influentials (N = 3020) % Agree	General Electorate (N = 1484) % Agree
People who hate our way of life should still have a chance to talk and be heard.	86.9	81.8
No matter what a person's political beliefs are, he is entitled to the same legal rights and protections as anyone else.	96.4	94.3
I believe in free speech for all no matter what their views might be.	89.4	88.9
Nobody has a right to tell another person what he should and should not read.	81.4	80.7
You can't really be sure whether an opinion is true or not unless people are free to argue against it.	94.9	90.8
Unless there is freedom for many points of view to be presented, there is little chance that the truth can ever be known.	90.6	85.2
I would not trust any person or group to decide what opinions can be freely expressed and what must be silenced.	79.1	64.6
Freedom of conscience should mean freedom to be an atheist as well as freedom to worship in the church of one's choice.	87.8	77.0

TABLE 3. POLITICAL INFLUENTIALS VS. THE ELECTORATE: RESPONSE TO ITEMS EXPRESSING SUPPORT FOR SPECIFIC APPLICATIONS OF FREE SPEECH AND PROCEDURAL RIGHTS

Items	Political Influentials (N = 3020) % Agree	General Electorate (N = 1484) % Agree
Freedom does not give anyone the right to teach foreign ideas in our schools.	45.5	56.7
A man oughtn't to be allowed to speak if he doesn't know what he's talking about.	17.3	36.7
A book that contains wrong political views cannot be a good book and does not deserve to be published.	17.9	50.3
When the country is in great danger we may have to force people to testify against themselves even if it violates their rights.	28.5	36.3
No matter what crime a person is accused of, he should never be convicted unless he has been given the right to face and question his accusers.	90.1	88.1
If a person is convicted of a crime by illegal evidence, he should be set free and the evidence thrown out of court.	79.6	66.1
If someone is suspected of treason or other serious crimes, he shouldn't be entitled to be let out on bail.	33.3	68.9
Any person who hides behind the laws when he is questioned about his activities doesn't deserve much consideration.	55.9	75.7
In dealing with dangerous enemies like the Communists, we can't afford to depend on the courts, the laws and their slow and unreliable methods.	7.4	25.5

Findings which underscore and amplify these conclusions are yielded by a comparison of the scale scores. The data presented in Table 4 confirm that the influentials not only register higher scores on all the pro-democratic scales (faith in freedom, faith in democracy, procedural rights, tolerance), but are more likely to reject antidemocratic sentiments as well. Although they are themselves an elite of a sort, they display greater faith in the capacity of the mass of men to govern themselves, they believe more firmly in political equality, and they more often disdain the "extreme" beliefs embodied in the Right Wing, Left Wing, totalitarian, elitist, and authoritarian scales. Their repudiation of anti-democratic attitudes is by no means unanimous either, but their responses are more uniformly democratic than are those expressed by the electorate.

Equalitarian values

If Americans concur most strongly about liberty in the abstract, they disagree most strongly about equality. Examples of equalitarian values are presented in Table 5. Both the political stratum and the public divide sharply on these values, a finding which holds for political, as well as for social and economic equality. Both are torn not only on the empirical question of whether men are *in fact* equal but also on the normative issue of whether they should be *regarded* as equal. Neither comes close to achieving consensus on such questions as the ability of the people to rule themselves, to know their best interests in the long run, to understand the issues, or to pick their own leaders wisely. Support for these equalitarian features of "popular" democracy, however, is greater among the elite than among the masses.

The reverse is true for the values of economic equality. Among the political stratum, indeed, the weight of opinion is against equality — a result strongly though not exclusively influenced by the pronounced economic conservatism of the Republican leaders in the sample. Support for economic equality is only slightly greater among the electorate. The pattern, furthermore, is extremely spotty, with some policies strongly favored and others as strongly rejected. Thus approval is widespread for public policies (such as social security) that are designed to overcome gross inequalities, but is equally strong for certain features of economic life that promote inequality, such as private enterprise, economic competition, and unlimited pursuit of profit.[12] On social and ethnic equality, both samples are deeply split.

In short, both the public and its leaders are uncertain and ambivalent about equality. The reason, I suspect, lies partly in the fact that the egalitarian aspects of democratic theory have been less adequately thought through than other aspects, and partly in the complications connected with the concept itself. One such complication arises from the historical association of democracy with capitalism, a commingling of egalitarian and inegalitarian elements that has never been (and perhaps never can be) perfectly reconciled. Another complication lies in the diffuse and variegated nature of the concept, a result of its application to at least four separate domains: political (*e.g.*, universal suffrage), legal (*e.g.*, equality before the law), economic (*e.g.*, equal distribution of property or opportunity), and moral (*e.g.*, every man's right to be treated as an end and not as a means). Accompanying these are the confusions which result from the common failure to distinguish equality as a *fact* from equality as a *norm*. ("All men are created equal," for example, is taken by some as an empirical statement, by others as a normative one.) Still other complications arise from the differential rewards and opportunities inevitable in any complex society, from the differences in the initial endowment individuals bring into the world, and from the symbolism and fears that so often attend the division of men

TABLE 4. POLITICAL INFLUENTIALS VS. THE ELECTORATE: PERCENTAGES SCORING HIGH AND LOW ON DEMOCRATIC AND ANTI-DEMOCRATIC ATTITUDE SCALES*

Scale	Political Influentials (N = 3020)	General Electorate (N = 1484)	Scale	Political Influentials (N = 3020)	General Electorate (N = 1484)
	(%s down)			(%s down)	
Faith in Democracy			Elitism		
% High*	40.1	18.5	% High	22.8	38.7
% Low	14.4	29.7	% Low	41.0	22.4
Procedural Rights			Totalitarianism		
% High	58.1	24.1	% High	9.7	33.8
% Low	12.3	31.3	% Low	60.1	28.4
Tolerance			Right Wing		
% High	61.3	43.1	% High	17.5	33.1
% Low	16.4	33.2	% Low	45.3	28.9
Faith in Freedom			Left Wing		
% High	63.0	48.4	% High	6.7	27.8
% Low	17.1	28.4	% Low	68.7	39.3
Ethnocentrism			California F-Scale		
% High	27.5	36.5	% Low	14.7	33.5
% Low	46.9	36.3	% High	48.0	23.5

*For explanation of % High and Low see footnote 12 [of original article. ED.]. The middle group has been omitted from this table. Differences between the influentials and the electorate on all the scales in this table are, by Kolmogorov-Smirnov and chi-square tests, statistically significant at or beyond the .01 percent level of significance.

into ethnic compartments. All these confound the effort to develop a satisfactory theory of democratic equality, and further serve to frustrate the realization of consensus around egalitarian values.

Faith in the political system

Another perspective on the state of ideology and consensus in America may be obtained by observing how people respond to the political system. How do Americans feel about the political and social institutions by which they are ruled? Do they perceive the system as one they can reach and influence? Are they satisfied that it will govern justly and for the common good?

Sample items relating to these questions are contained in Tables 6 and 7. An assessment of the responses, however, is confounded by an ambivalence in our tradition. Few will question that Americans are patriotic and loyal, that they accept the political system as legitimate, and that they are inclined to shy away from radical or extreme movements which aim to alter or to overthrow the constitutional foundations of the system. Yet Americans are also presumed to have a longstanding suspicion of government — a state of mind which some historians trace back to the depredations of George III and to the habits of self-reliance forced upon our ancestors by frontier life.

It is impossible in the present context to determine the extent to which the scores contained in these tables signify genuine frustration and political disillusionment and the extent to which they represent familiar and largely ritualistic responses. It is plain, however, that Americans are, verbally at least, both confused and divided in their reactions to the political system. Many feel themselves hopelessly ineffectual politically. Approximately half perceive government and politicians as remote, inaccessible, and largely unresponsive to the electorate's needs or opinions. About the same proportion regard politics as squalid and seamy, as an activity in which the participants habitually practice deception, expediency, and self-aggrandizement. Yet by a curious incon-

TABLE 5. POLITICAL INFLUENTIALS VS. THE ELECTORATE: RESPONSES TO ITEMS EXPRESSING BELIEF IN EQUALITY

Items	Political Influentials (N = 3020)	General Electorate (N = 1484)
	% Agree	
Political Equality		
The main trouble with democracy is that most people don't really know what's best for them.	40.8	58.0
Few people really know what is in their own best interest in the long run.	42.6	61.1
"Issues" and "arguments" are beyond the understanding of most voters.	37.5	62.3
Most people don't have enough sense to pick their own leaders wisely.	28.0	47.8
It will always be necessary to have a few strong, able people actually running everything.	42.5	56.2
Social and Ethnic Equality		
We have to teach children that all men are created equal but almost everyone knows that some are better than others.	54.7	58.3
Just as it is true of fine race horses, some breeds of people are just naturally better than others.	46.0	46.3
Regardless of what some people say, there are certain races in the world that just won't mix with Americans.	37.2	50.4
When it comes to the things that count most, all races are certainly not equal.	45.3	49.0
The trouble with letting certain minority groups into a nice neighborhood is that they gradually give it their own atmosphere.	49.8	57.7
Economic Equality		
Labor does not get its fair share of what it produces.	20.8	44.8
Every person should have a good home, even if the government has to build it for him.	14.9	28.2
I think the government should give a person work if he can't find another job.	23.5	47.3
The government ought to make sure that everyone has a good standard of living.	34.4	55.9
There will always be poverty, so people might as well get used to the idea.	40.4	59.4

sistency which so frequently frustrates the investigator searching the data for regularities, 89.6 per cent express confidence that the government will do what is right. However strongly they mistrust the men and the procedures through which public policies are fashioned, most voters seem not to be greatly dissatisfied with the outcome. They may be cynical about the operation of the political system, but they do not question its legitimacy.

Although the influentials do not unanimously endorse American political practices either, they are substantially less suspicious and cynical than is the electorate. Indeed, they have achieved consensus or come close to achieving it on most of the items in the two tables. These results are further borne out by the *scale* scores: only 10.1 per cent of the articulates score "high" on the political cynicism scale, as contrasted with 31.3 per cent of the general population;

TABLE 6. POLITICAL INFLUENTIALS VS. THE ELECTORATE: RESPONSES TO ITEMS EXPRESSING CYNICISM TOWARD GOVERNMENT AND POLITICS

Items	Political Influentials (N = 3020) % Agree	General Electorate (N = 1484)
Most politicians are looking out for themselves above all else.	36.3	54.3
Both major parties in this country are controlled by the wealthy and are run for their benefit.	7.9	32.1
Many politicians are bought off by some private interest.	43.0	65.3
I avoid dealing with public officials as much as I can.	7.8	39.3
Most politicians can be trusted to do what they think is best for the country.	77.1	58.9
I usually have confidence that the government will do what is right.	81.6	89.6
The people who really "run" the country do not even get known to the voters.	40.2	60.5
The laws of this country are supposed to benefit all of us equally, but the fact is that they're almost all "rich-man's laws."	8.4	33.3
No matter what the people think, a few people will always run things anyway.	30.0	53.8
Most politicians don't seem to me to really mean what they say.	24.7	55.1
There is practically no connection between what a politician says and what he will do once he gets elected.	21.4	54.0
A poor man doesn't have the chance he deserves in the law courts.	20.3	42.9
Most political parties care only about winning elections and nothing more.	28.3	46.2
All politics is controlled by political bosses.	15.6	45.9

TABLE 7. POLITICAL INFLUENTIALS VS. THE ELECTORATE: RESPONSES TO ITEMS EXPRESSING A SENSE OF POLITICAL FUTILITY

Items	Political Influentials (N = 3020) % Agree	General Electorate (N = 1484)
It's no use worrying my head about public affairs; I can't do anything about them anyhow.	2.3	20.5
The people who really "run" the country do not even get known to the voters.	40.2	60.5
I feel that my political leaders hardly care what people like myself think or want.	10.9	39.0
Nothing I ever do seems to have any effect upon what happens in politics.	8.4	61.5
Political parties are so big that the average member hasn't got much to say about what goes on.	37.8	67.5
There doesn't seem to be much connection between what I want and what my representative does.	24.0	43.7
It seems to me that whoever you vote for, things go on pretty much the same.	21.1	51.3

on political suspiciousness the scores are 9.0 per cent high versus 26.7 per cent; on pessimism they are 12.6 per cent versus 26.7 per cent; and on sense of political futility the influentials score (understandably enough) only 3.1 per cent high compared with 30.2 per cent high for the electorate. The active minority also exhibits a stronger sense of social responsibility than the people do (their respective percentage high scores are 40.7 per cent versus 25.8 per cent) and, as previously noted, they are less tolerant of infractions against ethical political procedures.

Should we not, however, have expected these results as a matter of course, considering that the influentials were selected for study precisely because of their political experience and involvement? Possibly, except that similar (though less pronounced) differences emerge when we distinguish articulates from inarticulates by criteria other than actual political activity. Voters, for example, who have been to college, attained high status occupations or professions, or developed strong intellectual interests are, by a significant margin, also likely to possess more affirmative attitudes toward government, politics, and politicians.[13] They display a greater sense of social and political responsibility, are more optimistic, and are less indulgent of shoddy political methods. The political actives who are highly educated exhibit these attitudes even more strongly. Familiarity, it seems, far from breeding contempt, greatly increases respect, hope and support for the nation's political institutions and practices. Inferential support for this generalization is available from the findings turned up by Almond and Verba in all five countries they investigated in their comparative study of citizenship.

Coherence and consistency of attitudes

So far we have explored the question of ideology and consensus mainly from the point of view of agreement on particular values. This, however, is a minimum criterion. Before one can say that a class or group or nation has achieved consensus around an ideology, one should be satisfied that they understand its values in a coherent and correct way. It is a poor consensus in which generalities and slogans are merely echoed with little appreciation of their significance. It seemed appropriate, therefore, to compare the influentials and voters concerning their information and understanding, the relation of their opinions to their party preferences, and the consistency of their views on public affairs.

To begin with, the influentials are more likely than the electorate to have opinions on public questions. For example, 28 per cent of the public are unable (though a few may only be *unwilling*) to classify themselves as liberal, middle of the road, or conservative; while only 1.1 per cent of the articulates fail to make this classification. Forty-eight per cent of the voters, compared to 15 per cent of the actives, do not know in which direction they would turn if the parties were reorganized to reflect ideological differences more clearly. Forty-five per cent of the electorate but only 10.2 per cent of the influentials cannot name any issue that divides the parties. By ratios of approximately three or four to one the electorate is less likely to know which level of government they are mainly interested in, whether they prefer their party to control Congress or the presidency, whether they believe in party discipline and of what type, whether control of the parties should rest at the national or local levels, and so on.

As these and other of our findings suggest, active political involvement heightens one's sense of intellectual order and commitment. This inference is further supported by the data on partisanship. One example may suffice to illustrate the point: when the articulates and the electorate are ranged on a scale assessing their orientation toward 14 current liberal-conservative issues, the political actives tend to bunch up at the extreme ends of the distribution (the

Democratic actives at the "liberal" end, the Republican actives at the 'conservative" end), while the rank and file supporters of both parties fall more frequently into the middle or conflicted category. The political influentials, in short, display issue orientations that are more partisan and more consistent with their party preferences.

Essentially the same effect is achieved among the general population by increases in education, economic status, or other factors that raise the level of articulateness. College-educated Democrats and Republicans, for example, disagree more sharply on issues than grade school Democrats and Republicans do. Partisan differences are greater between the informed than between the uninformed, between the upper-class supporters of the two parties than between the lower-class supporters, between the "intellectuals" in both parties than between those who rank low on "intellectuality."

Increases in political knowledge or involvement, hence, cause men not so much to waver as to choose sides and to identify more unswervingly with one political tendency or its opposite. Inarticulateness and distance from the sources of political decision increase intellectual uncertainty and evoke political responses that are random rather than systematic. We are thus led by the findings to a pair of conclusions that may at first appear contradictory but that in reality are not: the political class is more united than the electorate on fundamental political values but divides more sharply by party affiliation on the issues which separate the two parties. Both facts — the greater consensus in the one instance and the sharper cleavage in the other — testify to its superior ideological sophistication.

Not only are the articulates more partisan, but they are also more consistent in their views. Their responses to a wide range of political stimuli are to a greater extent intellectually patterned and informed. They are, for example, better able to name reference groups that correspond with their party affiliation and doctrinal orientation: approximately twice as many active Democrats as ordinary Democratic voters name liberal, Democratically oriented organizations as groups they would seek advice from (*e.g.*, trade unions, Farmers Union, etc.); and by equally large or larger ratios they *reject* as sources of advice such conservative or Republican oriented organizations as the NAM, the Farm Bureau, and the Chamber of Commerce. With some variations, similar findings emerge when Republican leaders are compared with Republican voters. If we also take into account the liberal or conservative issue-orientation of the respondents, the differential ability of party leaders and followers to recognize reference groups becomes even more pronounced. Clearly, the political stratum has a better idea than the public has of who its ideological friends and enemies are. The capacity to recognize sympathetic or hostile reference groups is not highly developed among the public at large.

Compared with the influentials, ordinary voters also show up poorly in their ability to classify themselves politically. For example, among Democratic actives who score as "liberals" in their views on issues, 82.2 per cent correctly describe themselves as "liberals," while 16.7 per cent call themselves "middle of the roaders" and only 1.1 per cent misclassify themselves as "conservatives." Among Democratic *voters* who actually hold liberal views, only 37.0 per cent are able to label themselves correctly. The disparity is less striking between Republican leaders and followers but bears out no less conclusively that most voters lack the sophistication to recognize and label accurately the tendency of their own political views. Even their choice of party is frequently discrepant with their actual ideological views: as we reported in a previous paper,[14] not only do Democratic and Republican voters hold fairly similar opinions on issues, but the latter's opinions are closer to the opinions of Democratic leaders than to those of their own leaders.

Data we have gathered on patterns of support for individual political leaders yield similar conclusions: the articulates are far better able than the electorate to select leaders whose political philosophy they share. Often, in fact, voters simultaneously approve of two or more leaders who represent widely different outlooks — for example, Joseph McCarthy and Dwight D. Eisenhower. In a similar vein, a surprisingly large number of voters simultaneously score high on a Right Wing scale and a liberal issues scale, or hold other "discrepant" outlooks. Such inconsistencies are not unknown among the political actives either, but they are much less frequent. Not only does the public have less information than the political class but it does not succeed as well in sorting out and relating the information it does possess.

Most of the relationships reported in the foregoing have been tested with education, occupation, and sometimes with other demographic variables controlled, but the introduction of these factors does not change the direction of the findings, although it sometimes affects the magnitude of the scores.

Comparisons of scores for the two samples have also been made with "acquiescent" response-set controlled. Acquiescence affects the results, but does not eliminate the differences reported or alter the direction or significance of the findings. . . .

III. SUMMARY AND DISCUSSION

Several observations can be offered by way of summarizing and commenting upon the data just reported:

1. American politics is widely thought to be innocent of ideology, but this opinion more appropriately describes the electorate than the active political minority. If American ideology is defined as that cluster of axioms, values and beliefs which have given form and substance to American democracy and the Constitution, the political influentials manifest by comparison with ordinary voters a more developed sense of ideology and a firmer grasp of its essentials. This is evidenced in their stronger approval of democratic ideas, their greater tolerance and regard for proper procedures and citizen rights, their superior understanding and acceptance of the "rules of the game," and their more affirmative attitudes toward the political system in general. The electorate displays a substantial measure of unity chiefly in its support of freedom in the abstract; on most other features of democratic belief and practice it is sharply divided.

The political views of the influentials are relatively ordered and coherent. As liberals and conservatives, Democrats and Republicans, they take stands on issues, choose reference groups, and express preferences for leaders that are far more consistent than the attitudes and preferences exhibited by the electorate. The latter's opinions do not entirely lack order but are insufficiently integrated to meet the requirements of an ideology. In contrast to the political elite, which tends to be united on basic values but divided on issues by party affiliation (both of which testify to a measure of ideological sophistication), the voters divide on many basic political values and adopt stands on issues with little reference to their party affiliation.

The evidence suggests that it is the articulate classes rather than the public who serve as the major repositories of the public conscience and as the carriers of the Creed. Responsibility for keeping the system going, hence, falls most heavily upon them.

2. Why should consensus and support for democratic ideology be stronger among the political stratum than among the electorate? The answer plainly has to do with the differences in their political activity, involvement and articulateness.

Some observers complain that Americans have little interest in political ideas because they are exclusively concerned with their own personal affairs. Evidence is becoming available, however, that political apathy and ignorance are also widespread among the populations of other countries and may well be endemic in all societies larger than a city-state. It is difficult to imagine any circumstances, short of war or revolutionary crisis, in which the mass of men will evince more interest in the community's affairs than in their own concerns. This is not because they are selfish, thoughtless, or morally deficient, but because the stimuli they receive from public affairs are relatively remote and intangible. One can scarcely expect ordinary men to respond to them as intensely as they respond to the more palpable stimuli in their own everyday lives, which impinge upon them directly and in ways they can understand and do something about. The aphorism which holds man to be a political animal may be supportable on normative grounds but is scarcely defensible as a description of reality. Political apathy seems for most men the more "natural" state. Although political matters are in a sense "everyone's concern," it is just as unreasonable to hope that all men will sustain a lively interest in politics as it would be to expect everyone to become addicted to chamber music, electronics, poetry, or baseball. Since many voters lack education, opportunity, or even tangible and compelling reasons for busying themselves with political ideas, they respond to political stimuli (if they respond at all) without much reflection or consistency. Their life-styles, furthermore, tend to perpetuate this state of affairs, for they are likely to associate with people like themselves whose political opinions are no more informed or consistent than their own. As inarticulates, they are also inclined to avoid the very activities by which they might overcome their indifference and develop a more coherent point of view.

Many voters, in addition, feel remote from the centers of political decision and experience an acute sense of political futility. They know the political world only as a bewildering labyrinth of procedures and unceasing turmoil in which it is difficult to distinguish the just from the wicked, the deserving from the undeserving. The political questions about which they are asked to have opinions are complex and thorny; every solution is imperfect and exacts its price; measures than benefit some groups invariably aggrieve others. The principles which govern the political process seem vague, recondite and impossible to relate to actual events. All this obviously deters voters from developing ideologically, from acquiring insights into the subtleties of the democratic process, and from achieving consensus even on fundamental values.

Although the influentials face some of the same obstacles, they are better able to overcome them. As a group they are distinguished from the mass of the electorate by their above-average education and economic status, their greater political interest and awareness, and their more immediate access to the command posts of community decision. Many of them participate not only in politics but in other public activities as well. This affords them, among other benefits, a more sophisticated understanding of how the society is run and a more intimate association with other men and women who are alert to political ideas and values. Political concepts and abstractions, alien to the vocabulary of many voters, are for the elite familiar items of everyday discourse.

Consider also that the political stratum is, by almost every social criterion we have examined, more homogeneous than the electorate. This promotes communication among them and increases their chances of converging around a common body of attitudes. As Newcomb[15] has remarked, "The actual consequences of communication, as well as the intended ones, are consensus — increasing." Among many segments of the general population, however, communication on matters of political belief either occurs not at all or is so random and cacophonous as to have little utility for the reinforcement of political values. If Louis Wirth is correct in observing that "the limits of consensus are marked by the range of effective communication," it becomes easier to understand why the active minority achieves consensus more often than the voters do.

Compared with the electorate, whose ordinary members are submerged in an ideological babble of poorly informed and discordant opinions, the members of the political minority inhabit a world in which political ideas are vastly more salient, intellectual consistency is more frequently demanded, attitudes are related to principles, actions are connected to beliefs, "correct" opinions are rewarded and "incorrect" opinions are punished. In addition, as participants in political roles, the actives are compelled (contrary to stereotype) to adopt opinions, to take stands on issues, and to evaluate ideas and events. As *articulates* they are unavoidably exposed to the liberal democratic values which form the main current of our political heritage. The net effect of these influences is to heighten their sensitivity to political ideas and to unite them more firmly behind the values of the American tradition. They may, as a result, be better equipped for the role they are called upon to play in a democracy than the citizens are for *their* role.

The findings furnish little comfort for those who wish to believe that a passion for freedom, tolerance, justice and other democratic values springs spontaneously from the lower depths of the society, and that the plain, homespun, uninitiated yeoman, worker and farmer are the natural hosts of democratic ideology. The mystique of the simple, unworldly, "natural" democrat has been with us since at least the rise of Christianity, and has been assiduously cultivated by Rousseau, Tolstoy, Marx, and numerous lesser writers and social reformers. Usually, the simpler the man, the lower his station in life, and the greater his objective need for equality, the more we have endowed him with a capacity for understanding democracy. We are thus inclined to give the nod to the farmer over the city man, the unlearned over the educated, the poor man over the man of wealth, the "people" over their leaders, the unsophisticated over the sophisticated. Yet everyone of these intuitive expectations turns out, upon investigation, to be questionable or false. Democratic beliefs and habits are obviously not "natural" but must be learned; and they are learned more slowly by men and women whose lives are circumscribed by apathy, ignorance, provincialism and social or physical distance from the centers of intellectual activity. In the absence of knowledge and experience — as we can readily observe from the fidgety course of growth in the newly emerging nations — the presuppositions and complex obligations of democracy, the rights it grants and the self-restraints it imposes, cannot be quickly comprehended. Even in a highly developed democratic nation like the United States, millions of people continue to possess only the most rudimentary understanding of democratic ideology.

3. While the active political minority affirms the underlying values of democracy more enthusiastically than the people do, consensus among them is far from perfect, and we might well inquire why this is so.

Despite the many forces impelling influentials toward agreement on basic ideological values, counteracting forces are also at work to divide them. Not all influentials are able to comprehend democratic ideas, to apply them to concrete contexts, or to thread their way through the complexities of modern political life. Nor is communication perfect among them either, despite their greater homogeneity. Many things divide them, not least of which are differences in education, conflicting economic and group interests, party competition, factional cleavages and personal political ambitions.

In demonstrating that the influentials are better prepared than the masses to receive and reflect upon political ideas, we run the risk of overstating the case and of exaggerating their capacity for ideological reasoning. Some members of the political class obviously have no more intellectual concern with politics than the masses do; they are in it for "the game," for personal reasons, or for almost any reason except ideology.

Then, too, while most democratic ideas are in their most general form simple enough for almost all members of the elite to understand, they become considerably more puzzling when one sets out to explicate them, to relate them to each other, or to apply them to concrete cases. Only a few of the complications need to be cited to illustrate the point; several of the ideas, such as equality, are either inherently vague or mean different things in different contexts. Some democratic (or constitutional) values turn out in certain situations to be incompatible with other democratic values (*e.g.*, the majority's right to make and enforce the laws at times clashes with individual rights, such as the right to stand on one's religious conscience). As this suggests, democratic ideas and rules of the game are ordinarily encountered not in pure form or in isolation but in substantive contexts that are bound to influence the ways in which we react to them. Many businessmen who consider the regulation of business as an unconstitutional invasion of freedom look upon the regulation of trade unions as a justifiable curb upon lawlessness; trade unionists, needless to say, lean to the opposite view.

Consider, too, what a heavy burden we place upon a man's normal impulses by asking him to submit unconditionally to democratic values and procedures. Compliance with democratic rules of the game often demands an extraordinary measure of forbearance and self-discipline, a willingness to place constraints upon the use of our collective power and to suffer opinions, actions, and groups we regard as repugnant. The need for such self-restraint is for many people intrinsically difficult to comprehend and still more difficult to honor. Small wonder, then, that consensus around democratic values is imperfect, even among the political influentials who are well situated to appreciate their importance.

4. We turn now to the most crucial question suggested by the research findings, namely, what significance must be assigned to the fact that democratic ideology and consensus are poorly developed among the electorate and only imperfectly realized among the political influentials?

Our first and most obvious conclusion is that, contrary to the familiar claim, a democratic society can survive despite widespread popular misunderstanding and disagreement about basic democratic and constitutional values. The American political system survives and even flourishes under precisely these conditions, and so, we have reason to think, do other viable democracies. What makes this possible is a more conjectural question, though several observations can be offered by way of answering it.

Democratic viability is, to begin with, saved by the fact that those who are most confused about democratic ideas are also likely to be politically apathetic and without significant influence. Their role in the nation's decision process is so small that their "misguided" opinions or non-opinions have little practical consequence for stability. If they contribute little to the vitality of the system, neither are they likely to do much harm. Lipset[16] has pointed out that "apathy undermines consensus," but to this one may add the corollary observation that apathy also furnishes its own partial corrective by keeping the doubters from acting upon their differences. In the United States, at least, their disagreements are *passive* rather than *active*, more the result of political ignorance and indifference than of intellectual conviction or conscious identification with an "alien" political tendency. Most seem not even to be aware of their deviations from the established values. This suggests that there may, after all, be some utility in achieving agreement on large, abstract political sentiments, for it may satisfy men that they share common values when in fact they do not. Not only can this keep conflicts from erupting, but it also permits men who disagree to continue to communicate and thus perhaps to convert their pseudo-consensus on democratic values into a genuine consensus.

I do not mean to suggest, of course, that a nation runs no risks when a large number of its citizens fail to grasp the essential principles on which its constitution is founded. Among Americans, however, the principal danger is not that they will reject democratic ideals in favor of some hostile ideology, but that they will fail to understand the very institutions they believe themselves to be defending and may end up undermining rather than safeguarding them. Our research on "McCarthyism," for example, strongly suggests that popular support for the Senator represented less a conscious rejection of American democratic ideals than a misguided effort to defend them. We found few McCarthy supporters who genuinely shared the attitudes and values associated with his name.[17]

Whether consensus among the influentials is either a necessary or sufficient condition for democratic stability is not really known. Since the influentials act, make public decisions, are more organized, and take political ideas more seriously, agreement among them on constitutional values is widely thought to be essential for viability. At present, however, we do not have enough information (or at least we do not have it in appropriately organized form) to state with satisfactory precision what the actual relation is between elite consensus and democratic stability. Some democratic governments, e.g., Weimar Germany, crumbled when faced with ideological conflicts among their political classes; others, e.g., post-war Italy and France, have until now managed to weather pronounced ideological cleavages. The opinion has long prevailed that consensus is needed to achieve stability, but the converse may be the more correct formulation, i.e., that so long as conditions remain stable, consensus is not required; it becomes essential only when social conditions are disorganized. Consensus may strengthen democratic viability, but its absence in an otherwise stable society need not be fatal or even particularly damaging.

It should also be kept in mind that the existence of intellectual disagreements—even among the influentials—does not necessarily mean that they will be expressed or acted upon. In the United States (and doubtless elsewhere as well), numerous influences are at work to prevent ideological cleavages from assuming an important role in the nation's political life. This is certainly the tendency of such political institutions as federalism, checks and balances, separation of powers, bicameralism, the congressional committee system, the judiciary's practice of accommodating one discrepant law to another, and a system of elections more often fought around local issues and personalities than around urgent national questions. Our two-party system also functions to disguise or soften the genuine disagreements that distinguish active Democrats from active Republicans. The American social system contributes to the same end, for it is a model of the pluralistic society, a profuse collection of diverse groups, interests and organizations spread over a vast and variegated territory. Consensus in such a society becomes difficult to achieve, but by the same token its absence can also more easily be survived. The complexities of a highly pluralistic social and political order tend to diminish the impact of intellectual differences, to compel compromise, and to discourage the holders of divergent views from crystalizing into intransigent doctrinal camps. Thus it seems, paradoxically enough, that the need for consensus on democratic rules of the game increases as the conflict among competing political tendencies becomes sharper, and declines as their differences become more diffused. Italy, by this reasoning, has greater need of consensus than the United States, but has less chance of achieving it. A democratic nation may wisely prefer the American model to the Italian, though what is ideally desired, as Lipset observes, is a balance between cleavage and consensus—the one to give reality and force to the principle of opposition, the other to furnish the secure framework within which that principle might be made continuously effective. Countervailing power within a structure of shared political values would, by this logic, be the optimal condition for the maintenance of a democratic society.

5. But even giving this much weight to consensus may exaggerate the role attainment of democratic stability. The which intellectual factors play in the temptation to assign a controlling influence to the place of ideas in the operation of democracy is very great. Partly this results from our tendency to confuse the textbook model of democracy with the reality and to assume the high order of rationality in the system that the model presupposes (*e.g.*, an alert citizenry aware of its rights and duties, cognizant of the basic rules, exercising consent, enjoying perfect information and choosing governors after carefully weighing their qualifications, deliberating over the issues, etc.). It is not my purpose to ridicule this model but to underscore the observation that it can easily mislead us into placing more weight than the facts warrant upon cognitive elements—upon ideas, values, rational choice, consensus, etc.—as the cementing forces of a democratic society. An *ad hominem* consideration may also be relevant here: as intellectuals and students of politics, we are disposed both by training and sensibility to take political ideas seriously and to assign central importance to them in the operation of the state. We are therefore prone to forget that most people take them less seriously than we do, that they pay little attention to issues, rarely worry about the consistency of their opinions, and spend little or no time thinking about the values, presuppositions, and implications which distinguish one political orientation from another. If the viability of a democracy were to depend upon the satisfaction of these intellectual activities, the prognosis would be very grim indeed.

Research from many different lines of inquiry confirms unequivocally that the role heretofore assigned to ideas and to intellectual processes in general has been greatly exaggerated and cannot adequately explain many political phenomena which, on *a priori* grounds, we have expected them to explain. Witness, for example, the research on the non-rational factors which govern the voting decision, on the effects—or rather the non-effects—of ideology on the loyalty and fighting effectiveness of German and American soldiers, on the differences between the views of party leaders and followers, on the influence of personality on political belief, and on group determinants of perception. We now have evidence that patriotism and the strength of one's attachment to a political community need not depend upon one's approval of its intellectual, cultural, or political values. Indeed, our present research clearly confirms that the men and women who express "patriotism" in extreme or chauvinistic form usually have the least knowledge and understanding of American democratic ideals, institutions, and practices.

Abundant anecdotal data from the observation of dictatorial and other nations further corroborates the conclusion that men may become attached to a party, a community, or a nation by forces that have nothing to do with ideology or consensus. Many of these forces are so commonplace that we often neglect them, for they include family, friends, home, employment, property, religion, ethnic attachments, a common language, and familiar surroundings and customs. These may lack the uplifting power of some political doctrines, but their ability to bind men to a society and its government may nevertheless be great. This observation, of course, is less likely to hold for the intelligentsia than for the inarticulates, but even the political behavior of intellectuals is never governed exclusively by appeals to the mind.

The effect of ideas on democratic viability may also be diminished by the obvious reluctance of most men to press their intellectual differences to the margin and to debate questions that may tear the community apart. So long as no urgent reason arises for bringing such differences to the surface, most men will be satisfied to have them remain dormant. Although there are men and women who are exceptions to this generalization, and who cannot bear to leave basic questions unresolved, they are likely to be few, for both the principles and practices of an "open society" strongly reinforce tolerance for variety, contingency and ambiguity in matters of belief and conscience. As our data on freedom of opinion suggest, few Americans expect everyone to value the same things or to hold identical views on public questions. The tendency to ignore, tolerate, or play down differences helps to create an illusion of consensus which for many purposes can be as serviceable as the reality.

6. To conclude, as we have in effect, that ideological awareness and consensus are overvalued as determinants of democratic viability is not to imply that they are of no importance. While disagreements among Americans on fundamental values have tended to be passive and, owing to apathy and the relative placidity of our politics, easily tolerated; while they do not follow party lines and are rarely insinuated into the party struggle; and while no extremist movement has yet grown large enough to challenge effectively the governing principles of the American Constitution, this happy state of affairs is not permanently guaranteed. Fundamental differences could *become* activated by political and economic crisis; party differences could *develop* around fundamental constitutional questions, as they have in France and other democracies; and powerful extremist movements are too familiar a phenomenon of modern political life to take for granted their eternal absence from the American scene.

Obviously a democratic nation also pays a price for an electorate that is weakly developed ideologically. Lacking the intellectual equipment to assess complex political events accurately, the unsophisticated may give support to causes that are contrary to their own or to the national interest. In the name of freedom, democracy, and the Constitution, they may favor a McCarthy, join the John Birch Society, or agitate for the impeachment of a Supreme Court Justice who has worked unstintingly to uphold their constitutional liberties. They may also have difficulty discriminating political integrity from demagoguery, maturity and balanced judgment from fanaticism, honest causes from counterfeits. Our findings on the attitudes shown by ordinary Americans toward "extreme" political beliefs (Left Wing beliefs, Right Wing beliefs, totalitarianism, isolationism, etc.) verify that the possibilities just cited are not merely hypothetical. Those who have the least understanding of American politics subscribe least enthusiastically to its principles, and are most frequently "misled" into attacking constitutional values while acting (as they see it) to defend them.

There is, however, reason to believe that ideological sophistication and the general acceptance of liberal democratic values are increasing rather than declining in the United States. Extreme ideological politics of the type associated with Marxism, fascism and other doctrinaire networks of opinion may be waning, as many sociologists believe, but the same observation does not hold for the influence of democratic ideas. On the contrary, democratic ideology in the United States, linked as it is with the articulate classes, gives promise of growing as the articulate class grows. Many developments in recent American life point to an increase in "articulateness": the extraordinary spread of education, rapid social mobility, urbanization, the proliferation of mass media that disseminate public information, the expansion of the middle class, the decline in the size and number of isolated rural groups, the reduction in the proportion of people with sub-marginal living standards, the incorporation of foreign and minority groups into the culture and their increasing entrance into the professions, and so on. While these developments may on the one side have the effect of reducing the tensions and conflicts on which extreme ideologies feed, they are likely on the other side to beget a more articulate population and a more numerous class of political influentials, committed to liberal democracy and aware of the rights and obligations which attend that commitment.

Notes

[1] James W. Prothro and C. W. Grigg, "Fundamental Principles of Democracy: Bases of Agreement and Disagreement," *Journal of Politics,* Vol. 22 (Spring, 1960), pp. 276-94.

[2] Robert A. Dahl, *Who Governs?* (New Haven, 1961), ch. 28.

[3] Samuel A. Stouffer, *Communism, Conformity, and Civil Liberties* (New York, 1955).

[4] V. O. Key, "Public Opinion and the Decay of Democracy," *Virginia Q. Rev.,* Vol. 37 (Autumn, 1961), pp. 481-94. See also David B. Truman, "The American System in Crisis," *Political Science Quarterly,* Vol. 74 (Dec., 1959), pp. 481-97. John Plamenatz, "Cultural Prerequisites to a Successfully Functioning Democracy: a Symposium," this REVIEW, Vol. 50 (March, 1956), p. 123.

[5] Alexis deTocqueville, *Democracy in America* (ed. Phillips Bradley, New York, 1945), II, p. 8; I, pp. 392, 322. The difficulty of specifying the values which underly democracy, and on which consensus is presumed to be required, is illustrated in the exchange between Ernest S. Griffith, John Plamenatz, and J. Roland Pennock, cited above, pp. 101-37. The problem of certifying the "fundamentals" of democratic consensus is directly discussed by Pennock, pp. 132-3. See also Peter Bachrach, "Elite Consensus and Democracy," *Journal of Politics,* Vol. 24 (August, 1962), pp. 449-52.

[6] A. L. Lowell, *Public Opinion and Popular Government* (New York, 1926), p. 9.

[7] *Cf.,* for example, Louis Wirth, *Community Life and Social Policy* (Chicago, 1956), pp. 201-3, 381-2. For a critique of "consensus theory" and the several definitions of consensus see Irving L. Horowitz, "Consensus, Conflict, and Cooperation: a Sociological Inventory," *Social Forces,* Vol. 41 (Dec., 1962), pp. 177-188.

[8] *Cf.* Daniel Bell, *The End of Ideology* (Glencoe, 1960), pp. 369-75; Edward Shils, "Ideology and Civility: on the Politics of the Intellectual," *Sewanee Review,* Vol. 66 (Summer, 1958), pp. 450-1; Louis Wirth, *op. cit.,* pp. 202-3.

[9] Herbert McClosky, Paul J. Hoffmann, and Rosemary O'Hara, "Issue Conflict and Consensus Among Party Leaders and Followers," this REVIEW, Vol. 44 (June, 1960), pp. 406-27.

[10] "High" refers to a score made by the upper third of the popular distribution on the scale in question. For example, in the case of the "political indulgence" scale approximately one-third (actually 30.6%) received scores of five or above. Hence, anyone making a score of five or above on this scale is considered to have scored high on "political indulgence." "Low" refers to scores made by the lower third of the distribution.

[11] Protho and Grigg, *loc. cit.;* Herbert Hyman and Paul B. Sheatsley, "The Current Status of American Public Opinion," in Daniel Katz *et al.* (eds.), *Public Opinion and Propaganda* (New York, 1954), pp. 33-48.

[12] These inferences are drawn not only from the few items presented in Table 5, but from data previously reported by H. McClosky, P. J. Hoffmann, and R. O'Hara, *op. cit.,* p. 413; and from the responses to dozens of items in the present study that express attitudes and opinions toward the private enterprise system, taxes, private property, profits, socialism, etc. On the whole, little enthusiasm is registered among either the elite or the masses for a drastic revision of the economy or a major redistribution of the wealth.

[13] Similar findings are reported by Robert E. Agger, Marshall N. Goldstein and Stanley A. Pearl, "Political Cynicism: Measurement and Meaning," *Journal of Politics,* Vol. 23 (1961), pp. 477-506.

[14] McClosky, Hoffmann, and O'Hara, *op. cit.*

[15] Theodore M. Newcomb, "The Study of Consensus," in R. K. Merton *et al.* (eds.), *Sociology Today* (New York, 1959), pp. 277-92.

[16] Seymour Martin Lipset, *Political Man,* (New York, 1960), p. 27.

[17] Herbert McClosky, "McCarthyism: The Myth and the Reality," unpublished paper delivered at the American Psychological Association, New York, September, 1957. See also Wiebe, *loc. cit.*

The Fear of Equality

Robert E. Lane

Still another point of contention in the American conception of democracy relates to the idea of equality. Many commentators would emphasize that our ideal is much as Ben Franklin saw it, "equality of opportunity." This means that we are presumed to be born equal in the sense that we are all born naked, helpless, and crying, but that we quickly become unequals as we cultivate our different talents. For many holding this viewpoint, the only necessary political equalities along the way are equality at the ballot box and before the law. A quite different vision of needed equality is held by others—particularly those of the "New Left." They express a desire for relatively greater equality in fact — equality of income, of access to political power, of impact on policy outcomes. McClosky's study revealed that his respondents tended more toward the equality of opportunity conception. The psychological dimension of this orientation to equality has been investigated by Yale political scientist Robert Lane. Lane's conclusions are based on a series of depth interviews with fifteen working-class men. During these interviews he was able to probe to discover more complete thought patterns and associations. Lane not only finds a strong resistance to equality among his interviewees, but a fear of it.

We move in equalitarian directions; the distribution of income flattens out; the floor beneath the poorest paid and least secure is raised and made more substantial. Since the demise of Newport and Tuxedo Park, the very rich have shunned ostentatious display. The equality of opportunity, the chance to rise in the world is at least as great today as it was thirty years ago. The likelihood of declining status is less.[1] Where does the energy for this movement come from? Who is behind it?

Since 1848, it has been assumed that the drive for a more equalitarian society, its effective social force, would come from the stratum of society with the most to gain, the working classes. This

Reprinted by permission of the author and publisher from Robert E. Lane, "The Fear of Equality," *American Political Science Review*, 53 (March, 1959), 35-51. Abridged by the editors.

was thought to be the revolutionary force in the world—the demand of workers for a classless society sparked by their hostility to the owning classes. It was to be the elite among the workers, not the *lumpenproletariat*, not the "scum," who were to advance this movement. Just as "liberty" was the central slogan of the bourgeois revolution, so "equality" was the central concept in the working class movement. Hence it was natural to assume that whatever gains have been made in equalizing the income and status of men in our society came about largely from working class pressure.

But on closer investigation the demands for greater liberty or "freedom" turn out to have been of an ambiguous nature. The middle classes sought freedom of speech and action in large part for the economic gains that this would give them, and moralized their action with the theology of freedom. But the freedom that they gained was frightening, for it deprived them of the solidary social relationships and the ideological certainty which often gave order and meaning to their lives. On occasion, then, they sought to "escape from freedom."[2] The older unfree order had a value which the earlier social commentators did not appreciate.

There is a parallel here with the movement toward a more equalitarian society. The upper working class, and the lower middle class, support specific measures embraced in the formula "welfare state," which have equalitarian consequences. But, so I shall argue, many members of the working classes do not want equality. They are afraid of it. In some ways they already seek to escape from it. Equality for the working classes, like freedom for the middle classes, is a worrisome, partially rejected, byproduct of the demand for more specific measures. Inequality has values to them which have been overlooked. It is these attitudes on status and equality that I shall explore here.

I. EXTENDED INTERVIEWS WITH FIFTEEN MEN

This discussion is based upon extended interviews of from ten to fifteen hours each (in from four to seven sessions) with a sample of American urban male voters. The sample is a random selection from the white members on a list of 220 registered voters in a moderate (not low income) housing development where income is permitted to range between $4,000 and $6,500, according to the number of dependents in the family. Out of fifteen asked to participate, fifteen agreed, for a modest cash consideration. The characteristics of the sample, then, are as follows:

They are all men, white, married, fathers, urban, Eastern seaboard.
Their incomes range from $2,400 to $6,300 (except for one who had just moved from the project. His income was $10,000 in 1957.)
Ten had working class (blue collar) occupations such as painter, plumber, oiler, railroad fireman, policeman, machine operator.
Five had white collar occupations as salesman, bookkeeper, supply clerk.
Their ages ranged from 25 to 54; most are in their thirties.
Twelve are Catholic, two are Protestants, one is Jewish.
All are native born; their nationality backgrounds are: six Italian, five Irish, one Polish, one Swedish, one Russian, one Yankee. Most are second or third generation Americans.
All were employed at the time of the interviews.
Their educational distribution was: three had only grammar school education; eight had some high school; two finished high school; one had some college; one completed graduate training.

The interviews with these men were taped, with the permission of the interviewees, and transcribed. They were conducted by means of a schedule of questions and topics followed by conversational improvised probes to discover the underlying meanings of the answers given. The kinds of questions employed to uncover the material to be reported are illustrated by the following: "What do you think the phrase 'All men are created equal' means?" "How would you feel if everyone received the same income no matter what his job?" "Sometimes one hears the term 'social class'—as in working class or middle class. What do you think this term 'social class' means?" "What class do you belong to?" "How do you feel about it?" There were also a number of questions dealing with status, private utopias, feelings of privilege or lack of privilege, and other topics, throughout the interview schedule which sometimes elicited responses bearing on the question of social and economic equality.[3]

II. HOW TO ACCOUNT FOR ONE'S OWN STATUS?

It is my thesis that attitudes toward equality rest in the first instance upon one's attitude towards one's own status. Like a large number of social beliefs, attitudes towards equality take their direction from beliefs about the self, the status of the self, one's self-esteem or lack thereof. It is necessary, therefore, first to explore how people see themselves in American hierarchical society.

The American culture and the democratic dogma have given to the American public the notion that "all men are created equal." Even more insistently, the American culture tells its members: "achieve," "compete," "be better, smarter, quicker, richer than your fellow men"; in short, "be unequal." The men I interviewed had received these inequalitarian messages, some eagerly, some with foreboding. Having heard them, they must account for their status, higher than some, lower than others. They must ask themselves, for example, "Why didn't I rise out of the working class, or out of the 'housing project class,' or out of the underpaid office help class?" And, on the other hand, "Why am I better off than my parents? or than the fellows down the road in the low rental project? or the fellows on relief?" Men confronted with these questions adopt a variety of interesting answers.

Is it up to me?

The problem of accounting for status is personally important for these men only if they think that their decisions, effort, and energy make a difference in their position in life. Most of my subjects accepted the view that America opens up opportunity to all people; if not in equal proportions, then at least enough so that a person must assume responsibility for his own status. Thus O'Hara, a maintenance oiler in a factory, in a typical response, comments that the rich man's son and the poor man's son "have equal opportunity to be President ... if they've got the education and the know how." But, he goes on to say, some of them have a little more help than others." This is the constant theme: "all men can better themselves," the circumstances of American life do not imprison men in their class or station—if there is such a prison, the iron bars are within each man.

There were a few, of course, who stressed the differences of opportunity at birth, the mockery of the phrase "all men are created equal." Here, as only rarely in the interviews, a head of steam builds up which might feed radical social movements—but this is true for only a few of the sample. Three or four angry young or middle aged men deny the Jeffersonian phrase. Rapuano, an auto parts supply man, says:

How could you say we were born equal when, for instance, when I was born, I was born in a family that were pretty poor. You get another baby born in a family that has millions.

And Kuchinsky, a house painter, says:

Are we created equal? I don't believe we are, because everybody's got much more than one another and it's not right, I think. Of course, ah, we have no choice. I mean we can't do nothing about it. So we're not as equal as the next party, that's for sure.

And Ferrera, a salesman, says:

All men created equal? Ah, very hypocritical, cause all men are not created equal—and—I don't know—you really pick some beauties don't you? ... The birth of an individual in a [social] class sort of disputes this.

To these men, then, subordination and life position is attributable not so much to the efforts of the individual, something for which he must assume responsibility, as to the circumstances of birth, over which he has no control. Yet for each of those men the channels of advancement were seen as only partly blocked. Rapuano, for example, says elsewhere that income is generally proportionate to ability. Like the theme of "moral equality," the theme of differential life chances from birth is easily available. What is surprising is not that it is used at all, but rather that it is used so infrequently.

III. REDUCING THE IMPORTANCE OF THE STRUGGLE

When something is painful to examine, people look away, or, if they look at it, they see only the parts they want to see. They deny that it is an important something. So is it often with a person's class status when the reference is upward, when people must account not for the strength of their position, but for its weakness. How do they do this?

In the first place they may *insulate themselves*, limit their outlook and range of comparisons. Ferrera, an insurance salesman, who says, "It's pretty hard for me to think there is anyone in the upper class and I'm not in the upper class," slides into a prepared position of insulated defense:

I think a lot of people place a lot of stress on the importance of social classes [but] I feel that I have a job to do, I have my own little unit to take care of. If I can do it to the best ability that is instilled in me at birth or progress through the years, I feel that I rightly deserve the highest classification you can get. I don't particularly like the headings, "upper, middle, working, and lower."

It is a resentful narrowing of focus in this case: two years at an inferior college may have led to ambitions which life then failed to fulfill. Contrast this to Woodside, a policeman with a Middle-western rural background, who accepts the "categories" of social class rather willingly. He says, after dealing with the moral and intangible aspects of equality:

["Are there any people whom you regard as not equal to you?"] Well, that is a tough question. Well, in fairness, I'd say all people are equal to one another in his own category. When I say category, I mean you couldn't exactly expect a person that had very little knowledge to be, we'll say, should have a position where a person with a lot more education had it.

Equality must be treated within classes, not between them, to be meaningful—and in this way the problem of placing oneself becomes tolerable, or sometimes rather gratifying.

A second device for reducing the importance of class position is to *deny its importance*. This is not to deny the importance of getting ahead, but to limit this to the problem of job classification, or occupational choice—nothing so damaging to the self-esteem as an ordering of persons on a class scale. Rapuano, resisting the class concept, says:

I don't think it [social class] is important. I mean whenever I went and asked for a job, the boss never asked me what class I was in.

They just wanted to know if I knew my business. Oh yes, and I don't think in politics it makes any difference.

Others maintain that for other countries social class is important, but not for Americans. There are rich and poor, perhaps, but not status, class, or deference levels to be accounted for.

A third device for reducing the significance of the struggle for status and "success" is *resignation,* a reluctant acceptance of one's fate. When some men assume this posture of resignation one senses a pose; their secret hopes and ambitions will not down. For others it rings true. When Dempsey, a factory operative, speaks of his situation at the age of 54, one believes him:

It's hard, very hard. We seem to be struggling along now, as it is, right here, to try and get above our level, to get out of the rut, as you might say, that we're probably in right now. . . . [But] After you get to a certain age, there, you stop—and you say, "Well, I can't go any further." I think I've gotten to that point now.

But when Sokolsky reports that he is contented with his station in life, it does not seem authentic:

Being in the average group [He wouldn't assign himself a class status] doesn't bother me. I know I make a living—as long as I make a living, and I'm happy and I have what I want—try to give my family what they want. It doesn't bother me—no. I'm satisfied.

But then he adds: "I hope to God my children will do better than their father did."

Contrast these views with those of Johnson, a plumber, who says, "I feel someday I'll be better off. I feel that way because I believe I have it within me to do it"; and with Flynn, a white collar worker, who answers:

No, I'm nowhere near satisfied. It seems to me every time I start to move up a little bit, all the levels move up one step ahead of me. I can't ever get out this area. I have a certain desire and willingness to do something extra.

IV. THE WORKING CLASS GETS ITS SHARE

When comparing their status with those lower on the scale, however each man may define it, it is easy to point with pride to achievement, material well-being, standing in the community. But satisfaction with one's self and one's friends depends on seeing some advantage in one's situation *vis-a-vis* those who live and work on a higher status level. At first, this seems to be a difficult task, but in many simple ways it can be easily done. Our sample, for example, found ways of ascribing greater happiness, power, and even income to the working class than would be found in the upper class.

The equality of happiness is a fruitful vein. Lower income and status is more tolerable when one can believe that the rich are not receiving a happiness income commensurate with their money income. "Are the rich happier than people who are just average?" O'Hara does not think so:

I think lots of times they're never happy, because one thing is, the majority of them that are rich have got more worries. You see a lot more of them sick than you do, I think, the average. I think a lot of your mental strain is a lot greater in the higher class—in the rich class—than in the other.

And Johnson, a maintenance plumber, says:

Well, even though this rich man can go places and do things that others can't afford, there's only certain things in life that I think make people happy. For instance, having children, and having a place to live — no matter where it is, it's your home ... the majority of these big men — I don't think they devote as much time and get a thrill out of the little things in life that the average guy gets, which I think is a lot of thrills.

Indeed, hardly a man thought the rich were happier. And yet, O'Hara says, on another occasion, "What is the most important thing that money can buy? Happiness, when you come down to it." Perhaps he means that money buys happiness for the average man, but not for the rich. But more likely he means ["I can take care of a gnawing and illegitimate envy by appropriating happiness for me and my kind."][4]

Power, like happiness, is awarded to the working (or lower middle) class. The sheer fact of numbers gives a sense of strength and importance. Costa, a factory operative, says, for example, "People like you [the interviewer] are the minority and people like me are the majority, so we get taken care of in the long run." Whether a person sees himself as middle class or working class, he is likely to believe that most people belong to his class. This being true, his class, people like him, become the most important force in electoral decisions. O'Hara puts it this way:

The biggest part of the people in this country are working class. And I think they've got the most to do with — they've got a big part to do with running this country — because the lower class, a lot of them don't vote, when you come down to it, they don't have the education to vote, and your upper class isn't that much — isn't as great as the other, so really when you come down to it, it's your working class that's deciding one way or the other.

Not only do they "have the biggest part to do with running the country," they are crucial for the economy. This is not only as producers—indeed no one mentioned the theme which romantic writers on the laboring man and the immigrant have often employed—"they cleared the land and built the cities." Rather it is because of their power to shatter the economy and their power to survive in a depression that they are important. Kuchinsky explains this as follows:

I think the lower class of people are the important people. I think so because of the business end of it. Without us, I don't think the businessman could survive. I mean if we don't work — of course, they have the money, but, ah, a lot of times during the crash which was an awful thing, too, I think a lot of 'em lived so high they couldn't stand it any more when they went broke, and they committed a lot of suicides there. But we were used to living that way, it didn't bother us.

Today, as perhaps never before, the working class man can see his status loss compared to white collar workers compensated by income advantages. Thus, De Angelo, a factory operative and shop steward, reports:

You got people working in offices, they might consider themselves upper class, y'know, a little better than the working man. But nine times out of ten the working man is making more money than he is.

. . .

V. MORAL EQUALITY

Another device for dealing with subordination in a society where invidious comparison with others is constantly invited represents, in effect, a borrowing from an older classical or religious tradition — an emphasis upon the intangible and immeasurable (and therefore comfortingly vague) spiritual and moral qualities. The only clearly adequate expression of this religious view was given by McNamara, a gentle and compassionate bookkeeper, who said "All men are created equal? That's our belief as Catholics," implying some sort of religious equality, perhaps such an idea as is captured in the phrase "equality of the soul." Woodside, a Protestant policeman, takes, in a way, a secular 18th Century version of this view when he says that men are equal "not financially, not in influence, but equal to one another as to being a person." Being a person, then, is enough to qualify for equal claims of some undefined kind.

But is seems probable that when men assert their own equality in this vague sense, typically phrased in something like O'Hara's terms: 'I think I'm just as good as anybody else. I don't think there's any of them that I would say are better," something other than moral or spiritual equality is at issue. These moral qualities are what the educated commentator reads into the statement, but O'Hara means, if I may put words in his mouth, "Don't put on airs around me," "I'm trying to preserve my self-respect in a world that challenges it; I therefore assert my equality with all." "I won't be pushed around." "I know my rights," and, to the interviewer: "Just because you're a professor and I'm an oiler, it doesn't mean you can patronize me."] And when Sokolsky, a machine operator and part-time janitor, says, in the interview, "The rich guy—because he's got money he's no better than I am. I mean that's the way I feel," he is not talking about moral or spiritual qualities. He is saying, in effect to his prosperous older brother and his snobbish wife, ["Don't look down on me,"] and to the world at large: ["I may be small, but I will protect my self-esteem."] These men are posting notices similar to the motto on the early American colonies' flags: "Don't tread on me."

Speaking of moral virtues, we must observe how easy it would have been to take the view that the morality of the middle levels of society was superior because the rich received their wealth illegitimately. None of my clients did this. Nor did they stress the immoral lives of the wealthy classes, as did Merton's sample[5] some thirteen years ago — a commentary, perhaps, upon changing attitudes toward the upper classes taking place over this period. The psychic defenses against subordination available in stressing moral equality or superiority were used—but only rarely.

VI. PEOPLE DESERVE THEIR STATUS

If one accepts the view that this is a land of opportunity in which merit will find a way, one is encouraged to accept the status differences of society. But it is more than logic which impels our men to accept these differences. There are satisfactions of identification with the going social order; it is easier to accept differences which one calls "just" than those that appear "unjust"; there are the very substantial self-congratulatory satisfactions of comparison with those lower on the scale. Thus this theme of "just desserts" applies to one's own group, those higher, and those lower.

So Kuchinsky says: " If you're a professor, I think you're entitled to get what you deserve. I'm a painter and I shouldn't be getting what you're getting." Furthermore, confidence in the general equity of the social order suggests that the rewards of one's own life are proportionate to ability, effort, and the wisdom of previous decisions. On ability, Costa, a machine operator, says:

I believe anybody that has the potential to become a scientific man, or a professor, or a lawyer, or a doctor, should have the opportunity to pursue it, but there's a lot of us that are just made to run a machine in a factory. No matter what opportunities some of us might have had, we would never have reached the point where we could become people of that kind. I mean everybody isn't Joe DiMaggio.

And on the wisdom of earlier decisions, Johnson, a plumber, says:

I don't consider myself the lower class. In between someplace. But I could have been a lot better off but through my own foolishness, I'm not. [Here he refers back to an earlier account of his life.] What causes poverty? Foolishness. When I came out of the service, my wife had saved a few dollars and I had a few bucks. I wanted to have a good time. I'm throwing money away like water. Believe me, had I used my head right, I could have had a house. I don't feel sorry for myself—what happened, happened, you know. Of course you pay for it.

But the most usual mistake or deficiency accounting for the relatively humble position is failure to continue one's education due to lack of family pressure ("they should have made me"), or youthful indiscretion, or the demands of the family for money, or the depression of the thirties.

The upper classes deserve to be upper

Just as they regard their own status as deserved, so also do they regard the status of the more eminently successful as appropriate to their talents. Rapuano, an auto parts supply man, reports:

> Your income — if you're smart, and your ability calls for a certain income, that's what you should earn. If your ability is so low, why hell, then you should earn the low income. ["Do you think income is proportionate to ability now?"] I would say so. Yes.

But there is a suggestion in many of the interviews that even if the income is divorced from talent and effort, in some sense it is appropriate. Consider Sokolsky again, a machine operator and part-time janitor, discussing the tax situation:

> Personally, I think taxes are too hard. I mean a man makes, let's say $150,000. Well, my God, he has to give up half of that to the government — which I don't think is right. For instance if a man is fortunate enough to win the Irish Sweepstakes, he gets 150— I think he has about $45,000 left. I don't think that's right.

Even if life is a lottery, the winner should keep his winnings. And De Angelo, a machine operator, comes spontaneously to the same conclusion:

> I think everybody needs a little [tax] relief. I mean, I know one thing, if I made a million dollars and the government took nine-tenths of it — boy, I'd cry the blues. I can't see that. If a man is smart enough to make that much, damn it, he's got a right to holler. I'm with the guy all the way.

Because he is "smart enough" to make money, it is rightfully his. Surely, beyond the grave, there is a spectre haunting Marx.

The concept of "education" is the key to much of the thinking on social class and personal status. In a sense, it is a "natural" because it fits so neatly into the American myth of opportunity and equality, and provides a rationale for success and failure which does minimum damage to the souls of those who did not go to college. Thus in justifying their own positions, sometimes with reference to the interview situation, my clients imply, "If I had gone to college (like you) I would be higher up in this world."

. . .

The lower classes deserve no better than they get

By and large those in the lower orders are those who are paid daily (not weekly) or are on relief; they live in slums or in public housing projects (but not middle income projects); they do not live respectable lives; they have only grammar school education; they may have no regular jobs. Closer to home, those slightly lower in status are people like "The lady next door who has a little less than I have," the man who can't afford to take care of his kids properly in the project, people who spend their money on liquor, the person with less skill in the same line of work.

The rationale for their lower status turns chiefly on two things: their lack of education and therefore failure to know what they want or failure to understand lifesmanship, and their general indifference. It is particularly this "not caring" which seems so salient in the upper working class mind. This is consonant with the general view that success is a triumph of the will and a reflection of ability. Poverty is for lazy people, just as middle status is for struggling people. Thus Ruggiero, an office building maintenance man, accounts for poverty by saying: 'There's laziness, you'll always have lazy people." De Angelo, a factory operative, sees it this way:

A guy gets married and, you know, he's not educated too well, he doesn't have a good job and he gets a large family and he's in bad shape, y'know what I mean. It's tough; he's got to live in a lousy rent — he can't afford anything better.

But De Angelo takes away some of this sympathy the next moment when he goes on to say:

But then you get a lot of people who don't want to work; you got welfare. People will go on living on that welfare — they're happier than hell. Why should they work if the city will support them?

In general, there is little sympathy given to those lower in the scale, little reference to the overpowering forces of circumstance, only rare mention of sickness, death of a breadwinner, senility, factories moving out of town, and so forth. The only major cause of poverty to which no moral blame attaches is depression or "unemployment"—but this is not considered a strikingly important cause in the minds of my clients. They are Christian in the sense that they believe "The poor ye have with you always," but there is no trace of a belief that the poor are in any way "blessed."

VII. WHAT IF THERE WERE GREATER EQUALITY OF OPPORTUNITY AND INCOME?

We have examined here the working (and the lower middle) class defenses of the present order. They are well organized and solidly built. By and large these people believe that the field is open, merit will tell. They may then deprecate the importance of class, limit their perspectives, accept their situation reluctantly or with satisfaction. They may see the benefits of society flowing to their own class however they define it. They tend to believe that each person's status is in some way deserved.

How would these lower middle and working class men feel about a change in the social order such that they and their friends might suddenly be equal to others now higher or lower in the social order? Most of them wouldn't like it. They would fear and resent this kind of equality.

Abandonment of a rationale

Changing ideas is a strain not to be lightly incurred, particularly when these ideas are intimately related to one's self-esteem. The less education one has, the harder it is to change such ideas. Painfully these men have elaborated an explanation for their situation in life; it helps explain things to their wives who take their status from them; it permits their growing children to account for relative social status in school; it offers to each man the satisfactions of social identity and a measure of social worth. Their rationales are endowed with moral qualities; the distribution of values in the society is seen as just and natural. While it gives satisfactions of an obvious kind to those who contemplate those beneath them, it also gives order and a kind of reassurance, oddly enough, to those who glance upwards towards "society" or "the four hundred." This reassurance is not unlike the reassurance provided by the belief in a Just God while injustices rain upon one's head. The feudal serf, the Polish peasant, the Mexican peon believed that theirs was a moral and a "natural order"—so also the American working man.

The problem of social adjustment

Equality would pose problems of social adjustments, of manners, of how to behave. Here is Sokolsky, unprepossessing, uneducated, and nervous, with a more prosperous brother in the same town. "I'm not going to go over there," he says, "because every time I go there I feel uncomfortable." On the question of rising from one social class to another, his views reflect this personal situation:

I think it's hard. Let's say — let's take me, for instance. Supposing I came into a lot of money, and I moved into a nice neighborhood — class — maybe I wouldn't know how to act then. I think it's very hard, because people know that you just — word gets around that you ... never had it before you got it now. Well, maybe they wouldn't like you ... maybe you don't know how to act.

The kind of equality with others which would mean a rapid rise in his own status is a matter of concern, mixed, of course, with pleasant anticipation at the thought of "telling off" his brother.

Consider the possibility of social equality including genuine fraternization, without economic equality. Sullivan, a railroad fireman, deals with this in graphic terms:

What is the basis of social class? Well, things that people have in common ... Money is one, for instance, like I wouldn't feel very comfortable going around with a millionaire, we'll say ... He could do a lot and say a lot — mention places he'd been and so on — I mean I wouldn't be able to keep up with him ... and he wouldn't have to watch his money, and I'd have to be pinching mine to see if I had enough for another beer, or something.

And, along the lines of Sokolsky's comments, Sullivan believes that moving upwards in the social scale is easier if one moves to a new place where one has not been known in the old connection. Flynn holds that having the right interests and conversational topics for the new and higher social group will make it possible—but otherwise it could be painful. Kuchinsky, the house painter, says "I suppose it would feel funny to get into a higher class, but I don't believe I would change. I wouldn't just disregard my friends if I came into any money." Clinging to old friends would give some security in that dazzling new world.

De Angelo, a factory operative, also considers the question of whether the higher status people will accept the *arriviste*, but for himself, he dismisses it:

I wouldn't worry much about whether they would accept or they wouldn't accept. I would move into another class. I mean — I mean — I don't worry much about that stuff. If people don't want to bother with me, I don't bother with them, that's all.

These fears, while plausible and all too human on the face of it, emerged unexpectedly from the interview material designed to capture ideas and emotions on other aspects of class status. They highlight a resistance to equalitarian movements that might bring the working class and this rejecting superior class—whether it is imaginary or not—in close association. If these were revolutionaries, one might phrase their anxieties: "Will my victims accept me?" But they are not revolutionaries.

These are problems of rising in status to meet the upper classes face to face. But there is another risk in opening the gates so that those of moderate circumstances can rise to higher status. Equality of opportunity, it appears, is inherently dangerous in this respect: there is the risk that friends, neighbors, or subordinates will surpass one in status. O'Hara has this on his mind. Some of the people who rise in status are nice, but:

You get other ones, the minute they get a little, they get big-headed and they think they're better than the other ones — where they're still — to me they're worse than the middle class. I mean, they should get down, because they're just showing their illiteracy — that's all they're doing.

Sokolsky worries about this possibility, too, having been exposed to the slights of his brother's family. But the worry over being passed by is not important, not salient. It is only rarely mentioned.

Deprivation of a meritorious elite

It is comforting to have the "natural leaders" of a society well entrenched in their proper place. If there were equality there would no longer be such an elite to supervise and take care of people —especially "me." Thus Woodside, our policeman, reports:

I think anybody that has money — I think their interest is much wider than the regular working man.... And therefore I think that the man with the money is a little bit more educated, for the simple reason he has the money, and he has a much wider view of life — because he's in the knowledge of it all the time.

Here and elsewhere in the interview, one senses that Woodside is glad to have such educated, broad-gauged men in eminent positions. He certainly opposes the notion of equality of income. Something similar creeps into Johnson's discussion of social classes. He feels that the upper classes, who "seem to be very nice people," are "willing to lend a helping hand—to listen to you. I would say they'd help you out more than the middle class [man] would help you out even if he was in a position to help you out." Equality, then, would deprive society, and oneself, of a group of friendly, wise, and helpful people who occupy the social eminences.

The loss of the goals of life

But most important of all, equality, at least equality of income, would deprive people of the goals of life. Every one of the fifteen clients with whom I spent my evenings for seven months believed that equality of income would deprive men of their incentive to work, achieve, and develop their skills. These answers ranged, in the sophistication and approach, across a broad field. The most highly educated man in the sample, Farrel, answers the question "How would you feel if everyone received the same income in our society?" by saying:

I think it would be kind of silly ... Society, by using income as a reward technique, can often insure that the individuals will put forth their best efforts.

He does not believe, for himself, that status or income are central to motivation—but for others, they are. Woodside, our policeman, whose main concern is not the vistas of wealth and opportunity of the American dream, but rather whether he can get a good pension if he should have to retire early, comes forward as follows:

I'd say that [equal income] — that is something that's pretty — I think it would be a dull thing, because life would be accepted — or it would — rather we'd go stale. There would be no initiative to be a little different, or go ahead.

Like Woodside, Flynn, a white collar worker, responds with a feeling of personal loss—the idea of such an equality of income would make him feel "very mad." Costa, whose ambitions in life are most modest, holds that equality of income "would eliminate the basic thing about the wonderful opportunity you have in this country." Then, for a moment the notion of his income equaling that of the professional man passes pleasantly through his mind: "don't misunderstand me—I like the idea"; then again, "I think it eliminates the main reason why people become engineers and professors and doctors."

Rapuano, whose worries have given him ulcers, projects himself into a situation where everyone receives the same income, in this case a high one:

If everyone had the same income of a man that's earning $50,000 a year, and he went to, let's say 10 years of college to do that, why hell, I'd just as soon sit on my ass as go to college and wait till I could earn $50,000 a year, too. Of course, what the hell am I going to do to earn $50,000 a year — now that's another question.

But however the question is answered, he is clear that guaranteed equal incomes would encourage people to sit around on their anatomy and wait for their pay checks. But he would like to see some levelling, particularly if doctors, whom he hates, were to have their fees and incomes substantially reduced.

That these sacrifices shall
not have been in vain

The men I talked to were not at the bottom of the scale; not at all. They were stable breadwinners, churchgoers, voters, family men. They achieved this position in life through hard work and sometimes bitter sacrifices. They are distinguished from the lower classes through their initiative, zeal and responsibility, their willingness and ability to postpone pleasures or to forego them entirely. In their control of impulse and desire they have absorbed the Protestant ethic. At least six of them have two jobs and almost no leisure. In answering questions on "the last time you remember having a specially good time" some of them must go back ten to fifteen years. Nor are their good times remarkable for their spontaneous fun and enjoyment of life. Many of them do not like their jobs, but stick to them because of their family responsibilities — and they do not know what else they would rather do. In short, they have sacrificed their hedonistic inclinations, given up good times, expended their energy and resources in order to acheive and maintain their present tenuous hold on respectability and middle status.

Now in such a situation to suggest that men be equalized and the lower orders raised and one's hard-earned status given to them as a right and not a reward for effort, seems to them desperately wrong. In the words of my research assistant, David Sears, "Suppose the Marshall Plan had provided a block and tackle for Sisyphus after all these years. How do you think he would have felt?" Sokolsky, Woodside, and Dempsey have rolled the stone to the top of the hill so long, they despise the suggestion that it might have been in vain. Or even worse that their neighbors at the foot of the hill might have the use of a block and tackle.

The world would collapse

As a corollary to the view that life would lose its vigor and its savor with equality of income, there is the image of an equalitarian society as a world running down, a chaotic and disorganized place to live. The professions would be decimated: "People pursue the higher educational levels for a reason—there's a lot of rewards, either financial or social," says Costa. Sullivan says, "Why should people take the headaches of responsible jobs if the pay didn't meet the responsibilities?" For the general society, Flynn, a white collar man, believes that "if there were no monetary incentive involved, I think there'd be a complete loss. It would stop all development —there's no doubt about it." McNamara, a bookkeeper, sees people then reduced to a dead level of worth: with equal income "the efforts would be equal and pretty soon we would be worth the same thing." In two contrasting views, both suggesting economic disorganization, Woodside believes "I think you'd find too many men digging ditches, and no doctors," while Rapuano believes men would fail to dig ditches or sewers "and where the hell would we be when we wanted to go to the toilet?"

Only a few took up the possible inference that this was an attractive, but impractical ideal — and almost none followed up the suggestion that some equalization of income, if not complete equality, would be desirable. The fact of the matter is that these men, by and large, prefer an inequalitarian society, and even prefer a society graced by some men of great wealth. As they look out upon the social scene, they feel that an equalitarian society would present them with too many problems of moral adjustment, inter-personal social adjustment, and motivational adjustment which they fear and dislike. But perhaps, most important, their life goals are structured around achievement and success in monetary terms. If these were taken away, life would be a desert. These men view the possibility of an equalitarian world as a paraphrased version of Swinburne's lines on Jesus Christ, "Thou hast conquered, oh pale equalitarian, and the world has grown gray with thy breath."

VIII. SOME THEORETICAL IMPLICATIONS

Like any findings on the nature of men's social attitudes and beliefs, even in such a culture-bound inquiry as this one, the new information implies certain theoretical propositions which may be incorporated into the main body of political theory. Let us consider seven such propositions growing more or less directly out of our findings on the fear of equality:

(1) The greater the emphasis in a society upon the availability of "equal opportunity for all," the greater the need for members of that society to develop an acceptable rationalization for their own social status.

(2) The greater the strain on a person's self-esteem implied by a relatively low status in an open society, the greater the necessity to explain this status as "natural" and "proper" in the social order. Lower status people generally find it less punishing to think of themselves as correctly placed by a just society than to think of themselves as exploited, or victimized by an unjust society.

(3) The greater the emphasis in a society upon equality of opportunity, the greater the tendency for those of marginal status to denigrate those lower than themselves. This view seems to such people to have the factual or even moral justification that if the lower classes "cared" enough they could be better off. It has a psychological "justification" in that is draws attention to one's own relatively better status and one's own relatively greater initiative and virtue.

(4) People tend to care less about *equality* of opportunity than about the availability of *some* opportunity. Men do not need the same life chances as everybody else, indeed they usually care very little about that. They need only chances (preferably with unknown odds) for a slightly better life than they now have. Thus: Popular satisfaction with one's own status is related less to equality of opportunity than to the breadth of distribution of some opportunity for all, however unequal this distribution may be. A man who can improve his position one rung does not resent the man who starts on a different ladder half way up.

These propositions are conservative in their implications. The psychological roots of this conservatism must be explored elsewhere, as must the many exceptions which may be observed when the fabric of a social order is so torn that the leaders, the rich and powerful, are seen as illegitimate—and hence "appropriately" interpreted as exploiters of the poor. I maintain, however, that these propositions hold generally for the American culture over most of its history—and also, that the propositions hold for most of the world most of the time. This is so even though they fly in the face of much social theory—theory often generalized from more specialized studies of radicalism and revolution. Incidentally, one must observe that it is as important to explain why revolutions and radical social movements do *not* happen as it is to explain why they do.

The more I observed the psychological and physical drain placed upon my sample by the pressures to consume—and therefore to scratch in the corners of the economy for extra income—the more it appeared that competitive consumption was not a stimulus to class conflict, as might have been expected, but was a substitute for or a sublimation of it. Thus we would say:

(5) The more emphasis a society places upon consumption—through advertising, development of new products, and easy installment buying—the more will social dissatisfaction be channeled into intra-class consumption rivalry in-

stead of inter-class resentment and conflict. The Great American Medicine Show creates consumer unrest, working wives, and dual-job-holding, not antagonism toward the "owning classes."

As a corollary of this view: (6) The more emphasis a society places upon consumption, the more will labor unions focus upon the "bread and butter" aspects of unionism, as contrasted to its ideological elements.

We come, finally, to a hypothesis which arises from this inquiry into the fear of equality but goes much beyond the focus of the present study. I mention it here in a speculative frame of mind, undogmatically, and even regretfully:

(7) The ideals of the French Revolution, liberty and equality, have been advanced because of the accidental correspondence between these ideals and needs of the bourgeoisie for freedom of economic action and the demands of the working class, very simply, for "more." Ideas have an autonomy of their own, however, in the sense that once moralized they persist even if the social forces which brought them to the fore decline in strength. They become "myths"—but myths erode without support from some major social stratum. Neither the commercial classes nor the working classes, the historical beneficiaries of these two moralized ideas (ideals or myths), have much affection for the ideals in their universal forms. On the other hand, the professional classes, particularly the lawyers, ministers, and teachers of a society, very often do have such an affection. It is they, in the democratic West, who serve as the "hard core" of democratic defenders, in so far as there is one. It is they, more frequently than others, who are supportive of the generalized application of the ideals of freedom and equality to all men. This is not virtue, but rather a different organization of interests and a different training. Whatever the reason, however, it is not to "The People," not to the business class, not to the working class, that we must look for the consistent and relatively unqualified defense of freedom and equality. The professional class, at least in the American culture serves as the staunchest defender of democracy's two greatest ideals.

Notes

[1] See Natalie Rogoff, *Recent Trends in Occupational Mobility* (Glencoe, Ill.: Free Press, 1953), pp. 61-63.

[2] Erich Fromm, *Escape from Freedom* (New York: Rinehart, 1941).

[3] One way of finding out whether these working class men reported their "true feelings"—the ones which form the basis of their relevant behavior and thought—to the listening professor, is to find out how they talk to each other. Fortunately, we have some evidence on this in the transcribed protocols of discussions where two groups of three men each, selected from the fifteen reported on here, argued with each other, without an interviewer present, on the job performance of certain public officials. In these discussions the main themes reported on below are apparent. Illustrative of one of these themes is Costa's remark to Woodside and O'Hara: "If you're the business man and I'm the working man, I don't care if you make a hundred million dollars a year as long as I make a living. In other words, you got your money invested. You're supposed to make money." And O'Hara then chimes in "That's right."

[4] Brackets are used here and below to distinguish inferred meanings or imputed statements from direct quotations.

[5] Robert K. Merton, *Mass Persuasion; The Social Psychology of a War Bond Drive* (New York: Harper, 1946).

Political Cynicism: Measurement and Meaning

It is a popular conclusion that there is widespread apathy in this country. Exactly what proportion of the populace may be so characterized is problematic. A later article in this anthology argues that voting apathy is not nearly so general as usually assumed. Yet there can be no doubt that a number of our citizens feel alienated, estranged from political life. Or, as it is often said, they have a low sense of "efficacy," i.e. they feel their participation makes no real difference in the political process. Feelings of alienation can produce several reactions; withdrawal is one reaction, cynicism another. The following article is based upon a study of the several dimensions of political apathy and takes a significant step toward explaining cynicism.

Robert E. Agger
Marshall N. Goldstein
Stanley A. Pearl

INTRODUCTION

The extent of which people hold *politicians* and *politics* in disrepute, the extent to which these words symbolize something negative rather than something positive, is a matter of some concern to political theorists concerned with the relationships of the governed to the governors as well as to political reformers and professional politicians interested in changing or maintaining the relationships. The purpose of this analysis is to explore some of the causes and consequences of political cynicism in the body politic of a small metropolis in the state of Oregon in 1959.

Of particular interest in this analysis are four sets of factors which, in the folklore of American politics, are related to political cynicism among the citizens: partisanship, social class, age, and personality. As with other elements of political folklore, that is, of apparently logical but empirically unverified notions of cause and effect, contradictory, inconsistent views may be held with great confidence or even with unshakeable faith, sometimes by the same person.

Some observers, for instance, have suggested that after eight years of Republican control of the White House,

Reprinted by permission of the authors and publisher from Robert E. Agger, Marshall N. Goldstein and Stanley A. Pearl, "Political Cynicism: Measurement and Meaning," *Journal of Politics*, 23 (August, 1961), 477-506. Abridged by the editors.

Democrats are more cynical about politics and politicians than are Republicans. Others conjecture that such themes as businesslike government, the value of businessmen in politics, the corruption of the professional politician, etc., are all more appealing to partisans of the party of business than to partisans of the party of the working class. Some suspect that it is the self-proclaimed Independents who are most disdainful of politics and politicians, particularly those Independents who do not remain aloof from the political process out of apathy or ignorance but join the fray as knights uncommitted to organized political party warfare. Still others think that the highly educated Democrats, the liberal-left or the eggheads in current political slang, harbor a distrust for politics and politicians born of frustrated ideals or a sense of intellectual superiority that sets them apart from the mass in the origin and degree of their political cynicism. Then there is the point of view that political cynicism, at least of the verbal kind, is a widespread American trait, found equally among the rank and file of both major parties and among those who proclaim their independence from any and all parties. Former Senator William Benton of Connecticut asserted that:

> ... one of the gravest problems the American people face is the public cynicism about politics and government. We are paying a frightful cost for this unjustified cynicism. Many decent — including many prominent — citizens shy away from assuming civic responsibilities because they mistakenly believe politics and government are generally corrupt and evil. Our entire society suffers.[1]

Comparable notions are extant in regard to varying degrees of political cynicism among people located in different portions of the socio-economic structure, in different age categories along the birth-death continuum, and among people who differ on such psychological attributes as general cynicism about people and a sense of personal potency. Some of these notions will be mentioned and examined below.

THE SAMPLE AND THE MEASURING INSTRUMENT

During the summer of 1959, a random sample survey was conducted as a part of a study of community politics in the two major cities of a standard metropolitan area in Oregon. The smaller city is an industrial, working class community of about 20,000 people, while the larger city of about 50,000 population is a university, retail trading center of a distinctly white collar, middle class character. At the end of an interview the respondent was asked to fill out and return in an addressed, stamped envelope an additional attitudinal inventory containing 62 statements, most of which were in an agree-disagree format. Our measure of political cynicism is based on the responses to six of these statements. The respondents were asked to indicate the extent to which they agreed or disagreed—strongly, slightly, or somewhat—with each item.

Of the 1,230 respondents who were interviewed in the survey, 779 (63%) returned the attitudinal inventory containing the political cynicism items.[2] The items, with the percent selecting each category are found on page 380.

Guttman-scaling procedures were used and a composite political cynicism score was assigned to each person (ranging from 0 to 6) which tells us, with a high degree of precision, what his answer is to each of the six items. We are not assuming that our data are representative of the population in this metropolitan area since only 63 per cent of the respondents in the sample survey returned the mail-back questionnaire containing the responses to the political cynicism items.[3] We have investigated a number of characteristics of those who mailed back the questionnaire and those who did not. There is the expected response rate dif-

	Strongly (a)	Agree Somewhat (b)	Slightly (c)	Slightly (d)	Disagree Somewhat (e)	Strongly (f)	No Answer	Total*
1. In order to get nominated, most candidates for political office have to make basic compromises and undesirable commitments.	11%	17	18	14	18	16	6	100%
2. Politicians spend most of their time getting re-elected or reappointed.	11%	15	19	18	22	10	4	99%
3. Money is the most important factor influencing public policies.	17%	23	20	12	16	7	3	98%
4. A large number of city and county politicians are political hacks.	8%	14	19	16	20	12	10	99%
5. People are very frequently manipulated by politicians.	6%	25	29	9	14	7	11	101%
6. Politicians represent the general interest more frequently than they represent special interests.	9%	27	22	18	12	6	6	100%

*The Total N is 779.

ferential by social class. For example, 53 percent of the respondents who did not complete grade school returned their inventories compared to 69 percent of the college graduates. Seventy three percent of the business and professional people in the sample mailed back the inventory compared to 46 percent of the unskilled workers. The differences in the mail-back rates for different socio-economic groups are sufficient to preclude treating the unweighted returns as a representative sample.

However, within educational levels, for example, there were no significant differences between the returners and non-returners on such characteristics as their authoritarianism, their manipulativeness, their personal morality, the extent to which they think politics is important in their lives, as well as a number of other factors which were measured by means of the basic interview schedule administered to those who did not return the questionnaire as well as to those who did.[4] Thus, while the mail-back is not representative of the entire sample, and we cannot extrapolate about the magnitude of political cynicism from the unweighted returners to the large sample nor to the population of the entire metropolitan area, we expect that relationships between political cynicism and other variables among the returners to hold also for the non-returners.

In developing the scale of political cynicism based on the pattern of people's responses to the six items, we divided the respondents into three categories according to the degree of their political cynicism. Those who scored zero or one (18 percent) we classified as politically cynical, those with scores of two or three (31 percent) as politically neutral, and those with scores of four, five, or six (51 percent) as politically trusting.[5]

POLITICAL CYNICISM, PARTY AND CLASS

Dividing the respondents by the party with which they identify themselves we find that the null hypothesis—that there are no differences in the degree of political cynicism among Republicans, Democrats and Independents—appears to be substantially correct (Table 1). Democrats are slightly less trusting and more neutral than either Republicans or Inde-

TABLE 1. POLITICAL CYNICISM AMONG PARTY SELF-IDENTIFIERS

POLITICAL CYNICISM	PARTY SELF-IDENTIFICATION		
	Republicans	Democrats	Independents
Cynical	19%	22%	18%
Neutral	29	37	32
Trusting	52	41	50
Totals %	100	100	100
N	207	100	100

pendents, a finding we shall return to shortly.

Turning now to the possible relationship between social class and political cynicism we are faced with three logical possibilities. Upper class position may be associated with political cynicism, lower class people may be the more cynical, or political cynicism may not be related to social class. The first possibility rests on the assumption that the more affluent, advantaged and educated naturally accord low status and little respect to a profession open to the non-affluent, disadvantaged and poorly educated who operate in open violation of upper class codes of conduct and even of American middle class mores. In this view contracting covenants covertly in smoke-filled rooms is a political custom more acceptable to, or at least more accepted by, the working man than the corporation executive. The white collar class may avert disquieting feelings about business ethics by focusing on political immorality whereas blue collar workers may expect both political and business ethics to be comparably hypocritical. The working class may accept both philosophically, and even be more trusting of politicians than business management since politicians may represent their interests in opposition to management. Politics may also be conceived by workers as a channel of upward mobility which some of their friends may have already taken given the relative impermeability of the business class for adult members of the working class.

The second possibility rests on the assumption that moral indignation about the practice of politics is more concentrated in the lower classes who are prone to perceive politics in simple black and white terms, with black the dominant conceptual-perceptual shade. Lipset suggests a possible reason for this in commenting upon what he believes to be the empirically established authoritarianism of the lower classes:

... The extent to which the lower strata are *isolated* from the activities, controversies, and organizations of democratic society — an isolation which prevents them from acquiring the sophisticated and complex view of the political structure which makes understandable and necessary the norms of tolerance.[6]

A stereotyped political cynicism might be viewed as another such norm of intolerance on the part of the presumably unsophisticated lower classes. He cites as the second major reason for lower class authoritarianism their "relative lack of economic and psychological security" leading to personal insecurity, high states of tension and the venting of hostility against scapegoats. Politicians might serve as such scapegoats for lower class people.

Someone who does not share Lipset's enchantment with American politics might add that it is the lower classes who have the most cogent reasons for being hostile towards politicians not as scapegoats but as the representatives, agents, or principals of other than lower class interests. One might conclude that it is indeed the lower classes who have the most legitimate, the most just,

TABLE 2. Relationship of Educational Level to Political Cynicism

Educational Level	Cynical	Neutral	Trusting	Totals %	N
Low Education	35%	30	35	100	174
Medium Education	19%	32	49	100	218
High Education	10%	37	53	100	239

reasons for being other than politically trusting in this day and age.

It is, of course, always possible that political cynicism is not related to social class, but to chance factors in life histories, such as an encounter with an unpleasant politician, or to non-class linked personality variables. It is easy to list cogent reasons for thinking that the lower classes are more, or less, or equally, cynical about politics and politicians compared to people in the upper classes. We shall test these alternative propositions with two indices of social class position: educational level and income level.

We find that the highly educated are much more politically trusting than the least educated (Table 2).[7]

The politically trusting outnumber the political cynics by 5 to 1 among the highly educated, while the ratio is 1:1 among the least educated. In our sample, at least, the second possibility noted above is clearly the correct one, whatever the reasons, if educational level is used as the index of social class.

Was the greater political cynicism of the poorly educated the reason for Democrats being slightly less politically trusting than Republicans or Independents? In this as in other samples the Democrats were more poorly educated than Republicans, with Independents in between. Controlling on educational level, we find that among the poorly educated there is no difference in the extent of the

TABLE 3. Political Cynicism Among Party Self-Identifiers by Educational Level

Educational Level* Political Cynicism	Republicans	Democrats	Independents
Low Education			
Cynical	39%	34%	37%
Neutral	26	31	26
Trusting	35	35	37
Totals %	100	100	100
N	49	74	43
Medium Education			
Cynical	19%	20%	19%
Neutral	23	39	30
Trusting	58	41	51
Totals %	100	100	100
N	59	87	63
High Education			
Cynical	10%	14%	5%
Neutral	32	38	38
Trusting	57	48	57
Totals %	99	100	100
N	99	66	63

*Low education includes those with less than three years of high school; medium education includes those with three or four years of high school; and high education includes all those who went beyond high school.

political cynicism of Democrats, Republicans, or Independents (Table 3).

At both the medium and high education levels, Democrats, while not more cynical, are the least trusting. The original small difference among the partisans and Independents is therefore largely a function of social class differences, though at the medium and high education levels Democrats are slightly less politically trusting. We cannot be sure whether the mistrust of the more educated Democrats is an indication of a general liberal-intellectual feeling of contempt for the politician, an indication that the more aware Democrats identify politicians with Republicans in a state where the latter have been until recently the dominant party, or simply a chance finding.

In this connection, it is revealing to find that in a special sample of precinct committeemen and committeewomen and members of political clubs in the Eugene-Springfield area (N=250), Democratic party activists are less cynical than the self-identified Democrats in the random sample. By contrast, the Republican activists are more cynical than Republicans in the random sample, and much more cynical than Democratic activists (Table 4).

TABLE 4. POLITICAL CYNICISM AMONG PARTY ACTIVISTS

POLITICAL CYNICISM	PARTY SELF-IDENTIFICATION	
	Republicans	Democrats
Cynical	25%	13%
Neutral	45	63
Trusting	30	24
Totals %	100	100
N	111	140

Both sets of partisan activists are more neutral and less trusting than their fellows in the random sample. While familiarity does not seem to breed an uncritical trust of one's colleagues or adversaries, it also does not necessarily breed contempt, as evidenced by the relatively low degree of political cynicism among the Democratic activists. Many of these Democratic activists were found to be highly educated, (64% of these activists had at least some college compared to 29% of the self-identified Democrats in the random sample) connected with the university in Eugene, and extremely liberal in their orientations towards issues, so that any liberal-intellectual feelings of contempt for the politician is at the most a very minor characteristic of the liberal-intellectuals actively involved in politics in this area.

Once again, however, the class differential found in the citizenry holds for both sets of these party activists. The poorly educated activists are more cynical than the highly educated by identical 2½:1 ratios for both Democratic and Republican party workers.

Turning to the second indicator of social class, we find that there is also a relationship between the level of income and political cynicism. In order to see whether there is an independent effect of income level on political cynicism education again needs to be controlled. Higher incomes result in increasing proportions of politically trusting, although the increases are not great (Table 5). Viewed in another way, the same data show clearly that within every income level, the higher the level of education, the lower the proportion of political cynics. The relationship here is both strong and consistent. It appears that educational attainment is more strongly related to political cynicism than is income.[8]

To what extent might political cynicism be a function of age rather than educational level? The educational level-political cynicism relationship might be spurious since in this, as in other community samples, the aged tend to be poorly educated while the younger adults tend to be more highly educated.

Classifying those under 35 years of age as the young adults, those between 35 and 54 years as the middle-aged, and those over 55 years as the elderly,[9] we find that both age and educational level have independent effects on political cynicism (Table 6).

TABLE 5. RELATIONSHIP OF FAMILY INCOME TO POLITICAL CYNICISM BY EDUCATIONAL LEVEL

EDUCATIONAL LEVEL FAMILY INCOME	POLITICAL CYNICISM				
	Cynical	Neutral	Trusting	%	N
Low Education					
Under $3,000	41%	26	33	100	58
$3,000-4,999	26%	45	28	100	42
$5,000-6,999	34%	25	41	100	44
Over $7,000	33%	24	43	100	21
Medium Education					
Under $3,000	22%	26	52	100	23
$3,000-4,999	22%	29	49	100	55
$5,000-6,999	18%	39	43	100	91
Over $7,000	17%	26	57	100	46
High Education					
Under $3,000	12%	42	44	100	25
$3,000-4,999	16%	31	53	100	51
$5,000-6,999	8%	45	47	100	72
Over $7,000	7%	33	61	101	89

TABLE 6. RELATIONSHIP OF AGE TO POLITICAL CYNICISM BY EDUCATIONAL LEVEL

EDUCATION LEVEL AGE	POLITICAL CYNICISM			Totals	
	Cynical	Neutral	Trusting	%	N
Low Education					
Under 35	28%	24	48	100	25
35-54	28%	33	39	100	72
55 and over	45%	28	27	100	78
Medium Education					
Under 35	17%	33	50	100	82
35-54	19%	34	46	99	98
55 and over	22%	28	50	100	40
High Education					
Under 35	10%	36	54	100	95
35-54	5%	39	56	100	108
55 and over	22%	37	41	100	37

Within the low and high educational categories, the elderly are the most politically cynical, and within every age category the poorly educated are the most politically cynical. Among the content sensitive the elderly are more cynical than any other age group at all levels of education.

We may summarize our findings to this point. The acquisition of formal education tends to produce political trust regardless of social class background. Political cynicism levels tend to remain relatively constant for people with different levels of education regardless of how much money they make. Aging tends to produce more political cynicism.

Is it possible that aging, or factors and experiences in the process of aging, does not cause increased political cynicism, but that the society is more positive in its political images than it was at the time the elderly were growing up? This explanation would account for the relatively high political cynicism of the elderly equally as well as the explanation that people become more politically cynical with age. . . .

CONCLUSIONS

This study of the correlates of political cynicism leads to a model of the processes contributing to the maintenance of, or changes in, the level of political cynicism in the polity. This model is different than alternative models implicit in the political folklore. Projecting these processes over time, and assuming no drastic changes in the way in which politicians actually behave or in the images of them projected to the citizens, these processes are conceived as contributing to a more or less stable level of political cynicism in this small portion of the American body politic. The reasons for expecting this dynamic equilibrium are as follows.

People from lower class backgrounds who have not themselves attained more than a minimum education retain the presumably high level of political cynicism of their lower class parents. Although children of poorly educated parents tend to remain more poorly educated than the children of upper class parents, a sizeable proportion do attain a higher educational level than their parents. The increasingly widespread distribution of secondary and higher education in society generates a higher level of political trust in the polity. At the same time there are two counter-trends, one minor and one major. The minor trend is due to the relatively few people from well-educated families who do not themselves attain much education and are extremely cynical. The major counter-trend is the increasing political cynicism that comes with increasing age. With the aged constituting an increasingly larger proportion of the citizenry the dissipating effect on political cynicism of an increasingly educated citizenry may be effectively offset.

Comparative research on political cynicism is needed not only for producing generalizations that may hold for larger numbers of people than this sample in Oregon. It is also needed in order to establish with more precision the relevant conditions under which the relationships that were found hold. If, for example, there is actually more political cynicism in large, Eastern metropoli than in small, Western cities, would we find younger people in the East to be as cynical as older people?[10] Is Eastern politics a less open, populist-type, popular sport than it is in the West, and, if so, with what consequences, if any, on the processes generating political trust and mistrust?[11]

The need for comparative research over time within politie as well as among polities is underlined when we consider the finding that political cynicism was related to the level of political participation. We found that, in general, the politically trusting reported a generally higher level of political discussion than did the politically cynical. There have been instances, however, both in the politics of Eugene and Springfield and elsewhere in the nation, of sharply increased involvement in particular elections and in political movements over a period of time on the part of ordinarily non-participant, politically cynical, politically impotent people. It also should be recalled that the Republican party activists in this area were comparatively a highly cynical group.

We have found in a national sample of American law students that while there was generally no relationship between their present level of political activity nor their interest in going into politics in the future on the one hand, and the degree to which they were politically cynical on the other, political cynicism was positively related to political involvement and aspirations among Negro law students in the South. The Negro law students who were the most politically cynical on the same measure as used in the Eugene-Springfield study were more active and more interested in going into politics themselves than the Negro law students who were most trusting of (white?) politicians. Like activists of the relatively far right, these Negroes, who adhere to an almost diametrically opposite political philosophy, may be attracted to politics partly because of felt needs to improve their own political, social and economic status by improving a "pathological" political system. A pessimistic, cynical view of politics may push people towards drastic solutions much as a pessimistic prognosis may lead to drastic surgery on the part of physicians. Comparative research is needed to establish the conditions, particularly the conditions of political leadership and structure, under which such "deviant" dynamics occur.

Political participation has been treated so far as a dependent variable. It may be that it is an independent variable affecting political cynicism, or the two may be interacting and reinforcing with each other in a causal sense. It is plausible that as people participate in political discourse, as they become at least minimally involved in the polity, they become sensitized to politics in a way that may dilute an earlier cynicism or may help to keep it at a lower level than otherwise might be the case. Our findings on the more participant party activists suggests that if a certain threshold of involvement is reached, even the degree of political trust may be reduced. At the same time the relatively high level of political cynicism of Republican party activists suggests that active involvement may not be a causal factor of the level of political cynicism, at least for certain people under certain conditions. Further studies of a longitudinal nature are indicated to clarify the character of the cause and effect complex.

Special attention needs to be devoted to another theoretical problem pointed up by our findings. Among indicators of social class, the level of formal education was the one relating most strongly to political cynicism. What is the meaning of this? Does it mean that social class lines are affected more by one's educational experiences than by one's type of job or level of income, at least in this area in the West? Does it mean that the more education a person acquires, the more he is exposed to positive images of politics and politicians, or the more he becomes trained to be less negative in general or to beware of using negative symbols? Does it mean that the treatment of the political culture and the use of political symbols vary according to educational institution: primary, secondary, or college?

Or does this mean that the amount of formal education a person is able to acquire, rather than financial or occupational achievements later in life, is the basic determinant of one's self-evaluation as a success or failure? The more a person feels himself to be a failure, the more he may decide that it is the politicians who are most responsible for the gap between the promise of America and his own relatively unenviable position in the world. A person who has failed to attain what the society reiterates is accessible to every one who has the necessary ambition: a college degree, may, upon reflection, decide that the spokesman for the society, its politicians, are deceitful because such is not really the case.

Such feelings of personal impotence may, less "rationally," generate a generalized cynicism about people as well as a feeling that politicians are to blame for the failure of the system. Feelings of failure may lead to some degree of self-hate, which can be projected outwards onto a culturally sanctioned substitute target of hostility, politicians and the political process. The leaders of the economic structure may share in some of this hostility, but since there is always the chance that one's fortune may be made without a great deal of formal education, there may be less channeling of aggression in this direction. The leaders of business and industry generally do not seem to be treated by the press and in the popular literature as venal, manipulative, corrupt men to the extent that politicians are so treated. Thus, whatever the social-economic class composition of his future work group peers, of his friends and of neighbors, the person who is poorly educated may remain a member of a cultural class that shares in common a cynical attitude towards politics and politicians. Carefully designed studies of the political symbolism in various formal educational environments, its influence in shaping people's political attitudes, and the relative effects of home, school, friends, work, associates, and media consumption are in order as well as simultaneous studies of economic, religious and other relevant symbolism in such environments in order to establish which of these, not mutually exclusive, possibilities are correct.

Notes

[1] Quoted in *Fair Play in Politics,* The Fair Campaign Practices Committee, Inc., (1960), pp. 3-4.

[2] Webster's Collegiate Dictionary, Fifth Edition: cynical . . . contemptuously distrustful of human nature.

[3] Of the 779 attitudinal inventory returns from the 1230 people who were interviewed 73 refused or failed to answer two or more of the six political cynicism items, making our data still more unrepresentative of the population of these cities than it otherwise might be. We have not weighted the responses from the cities of Eugene and Springfield and the suburban areas (which were sampled separately) in relation to their share of the population, so that we do not have a metropolitan sample in the sense of its being proportionately representative of the different parts of the total metropolitan area.

[4] About 10 percent of the attitudinal inventories were administered in a personal interviewing situation. We have found that the responses did not appear to vary as a function of the type of inventory administration. See the comment on non-response to mail surveys and non-response in personal approach situations by Arnold M. Rose, "Attitudinal Correlates of Social Participation," *Social Forces,* Vol. 37, No. 3 (March, 1959), p. 3, Footnote No. 3.

[5] Using the fold-over technique, an intensity analysis indicates that the politically cynical (those scoring 0 or 1 points) were the most intense in their evaluations of politics-politicians while there was relatively little difference in the intensity of feeling among those who were less cynical (those scoring 2-6 points). The least intense were those who scored 2 or 3 points, the category we have labelled the politically neutral.

[6] Seymour Martin Lipset, *Political Man,* (Doubleday & Company, Inc. New York, 1960), p. 112.

[7] The relationship between educational level and political cynicism holds almost identically for Eugene and Springfield when the metropolitan sample is divided by city of residence.

[8] Educational level is also more strongly related to political cynicism than is both respondent's and father's occupation. Parental interest in politics, as measured by the respondents' own reports, is not related at all to the latter's degree of political cynicism. This does not mean that parents have not affected their children's political attitudes in this regard; it means that other factors are more important and have presumably overcome whatever parental influences there may have been.

[9] Categorizing those between 55 and 64 years of age with those over 65 years of age as the "elderly" was done only because of the small number of people in the sample in the latter age bracket.

[10] Christie and Merton report "some evidence that worldly sophistication and high scores on the Mach scale appear to be related . . . college

students in the Midwest score significantly lower on the scale than college students in the East." . . . Christie and Garcia report that respondents from a Southwest city have higher authoritarianism scores than respondents from Berkeley, California, and suggest as an explanation for this the "relatively authoritarian sub-culture" in terms of the dominant political ideology of the city in the Southwest rather than differences in toilet training or in other child-rearing practices. See their "Subcultural Variation in Authoritarian Personality." *Journal of Abnormal and Social Psychology,* Vol. 46, No. 4, (October, 1951), pp. 457-69.

[11] Levin says that "cynicism with respect to Boston politicians is widespread in the Hub. Voters . . . are predisposed to view those in power as actually or potentially corrupt." . . . He suggests that the most significant factors in the 1959 mayoralty race in Boston were "the profound cynicism of the electroate toward professional politicians and the deep-seated feeling that the voters are politically powerless." . . . Although this is very plausible and he argues persuasively, his own data are inconclusive.

A Critique of the Theory of Democratic Elitism

Peter Bachrach

The empirical studies of political participation in the United States paint the average citizen as something less than the ideal model of traditional democratic thought. Yet, few political scientists are willing to conclude that we are not a democracy. One explanation of these behavioral findings might be that they simply verify what we already know, that man seldom realizes his ideals in practice. Those who make this analysis then conclude that we need more and better citizenship training, more programs exhorting participation. An alternative attempt to reconcile behavioral findings with democratic theory would lead us to modify our understanding of what constitutes democracy. Many political scientists argue that democracy requires only political activists and a few others who are attentive to political matters to make operative the democratic "rules of the game." This is the fundamental point of the interpretation which has come to be called "elitist democracy" by some, "pluralism" by others. Whatever the name applied, it is a clear implication of this interpretation that mass involvement in politics is unnecessary to the health of the system. Peter Bachrach is one of a number of political scientists who find both of these explanations unacceptable. In this excerpt, he critically evaluates "elitist democracy" and offers his own alternative explanation and prescription.

While it is true that there are many theories of democracy,[1] it is also true that there is a general theory of democracy which is supported by most leading theorists and which reflects the main currents of thought in social science today. It is a theory largely explanatory rather than normative in approach; directed toward clarifying on-going democratic systems rather than suggesting how they ought to operate. Yet it is a theory which reflects, on the one hand, a receptiveness toward the existing structure of power and elite decision-making in large industrial societies, and

"An Alternative Approach," Chapter 7 from Peter Bachrach, *The Theory of Democratic Elitism: A Critique,* pp. 93-106. Copyright © 1967, Little, Brown and Company (Inc.). Reprinted by permission of the publisher. Abridged by the editors.

on the other, an impatience with old myths and sentiments associated with phrases such as "will of the people," "grass-roots democracy," and "the dignity of the common man."

This general theory purports to be above ideology but is in reality deeply rooted in an ideology, an ideology which is grounded upon a profound distrust of the majority of ordinary men and women, and a reliance upon the established elites to maintain the values of civility and the "rules of the game" of democracy. It is an ideology which is closely attached to and protective of the liberal principles embodied in the rule of law and in the rights of the individual to freedom of conscience, expression, and privacy. While embracing liberalism it rejects, in effect, the major tenet of classical democratic theory—belief and confidence in the people. The suspicion that liberalism and classical theory are fundamentally incompatible is manifested in the key explanatory concepts of democratic elitism.

Democracy conceived solely as a political method is one of these concepts. Since democracy is not seen as embodying an overriding objective, such as enhancing the self-esteem and development of the individual, the democratic-elite theorist frees himself from the charge that democratic means have failed to achieve democratic ends. He holds only that democracy must be self-perpetuating as method, and thus able to secure the open society through time. In focusing upon openness *qua* openness —avoiding the question of openness for whom—he is in a position to show that the system is in good health, while acknowledging at the same time that a large number of people are probably alienated from the social and political life around them.

While the concept of democracy as political method is not inherently elitist, it does serve as a formidable defense of the elite-mass structure of on-going democratic systems. The charge, for example, that the common man is not given sufficient opportunity to participate in meaningful decision-making and is therefore deprived of an essential means to develop his faculties and broaden his outlook is, under this concept, irrelevant. For, conceived as political method, the standard for judging democracy is not the degree of centralization or devolution in the decision-making process but rather the degree to which the system conforms to the basic principles of the democratic method: political equality (universal suffrage), freedom of discussion, majority rule, free periodic elections, and the like. When these principles are adhered to, the system is characterized by the accountability of political elites to non-elites. And in being held accountable, the former, owing to the phenomenon of anticipated reactions, normally rules in the interests of the latter. Thus, although democracy as a political method is defined in terms of procedural principles, it invariably is defended today on the basis of its service to the interests of the people.

This defense of democracy construes the interests of the people narrowly and the democratic elite theorist has little difficulty in accepting it. He posits that the value of the democratic system for ordinary individuals should be measured by the degree to which the "outputs" of the system, in the form of security, services, and material support, benefit them. On the basis of this reasoning, the less the individual has to participate in politics on the "input" and demand side of the system in order to gain his interests on the output side, the better off he is. With rare exception elites are available to represent his interest in the decision-making process, relegating to him the comparatively painless task of paying nominal dues and occasionally attending a meeting and casting a ballot. By assuming a one-dimensional view of political interest, the democratic elitist is led to the conclusion that there is a natural division of labor within a democratic system between elite rule and non-elite interest.

By conceiving of man's political interest solely in terms of that which accrues to him from government, the democratic elitist implicitly rejects the contention of classical theorists that interests also include the opportunity for development which accrues from participation in meaningful political decisions. This two-dimensional view of political interests—interests as end results and interest in the process of participation—is rejected by the democratic elitists on the ground that it has little relevance to the reality of political life in large-scale industrial societies, and that it is based on the concept of equality of power in decision-making which is completely at odds with existing practices in modern democracies, where key political decisions must of necessity be made by a small minority. The main thrust of the elitist argument is incontestable. However, although participation in key political decisions on the national level must remain extremely limited, is there any sound reason, within the context of democratic theory, why participation in political decisions by the constituencies of "private" bureaucratic institutions of power could not be widely extended on those issues which primarily affect their lives within these institutions?

The answer to the question turns on what constitutes "political." If private organizations, at least the more powerful among them, were considered political—on the ground that they are organs which regularly share in authoritatively allocating values for society — then there would be a compelling case, in terms of the democratic principle of equality of power, to expand participation in decision-making within these organizations.[2] This could be achieved by radically altering their hierarchical structures to facilitate the devolution of the decision-making process. However, if one holds, as the democratic elite theorist does, to a narrow and institutional concept of political (when referring to political elites and political equality), this line of reasoning is effectively excluded from democratic theory. If "political" is confined to governmental decision-making and that which relates to it, the clearly nongovernmental institutions, irrespective of the power which they may wield and the impact of their decisions on society, are not political. And in being not political, they are exempt, as far as the reach of democratic theory goes, from democratization.

The importance to the theory of democratic elitism of interpreting narrowly the integral and key concept "political" cannot be overemphasized. First, on the basis of this interpretation, the argument for expanding democracy to encompass a portion of the economic sector can be discarded out of hand as irrelevant. Democracy is a *political* method, neither intended nor designed to operate beyond the political realm. Second, this narrow concept supports the legitimacy of the elite decision-making process within the corporations and other large private institutions. It is common knowledge that corporate elites, who regularly make decisions directly affecting social values, are accountable largely, if not solely, to themselves. But this is not considered to be an irresponsible exercise of political power since corporate managers act as private citizens on nonpolitical matters. Finally, and most important, by accepting a rigid and narrow concept of political, the elite theorist removes from consideration (within the context of democratic theory) the question of the feasibility of increasing participation in decision-making by enlarging the political scope to include the more powerful private institutions. The existing elite-non-elite relationship is consequently made immune to attack by democratic theorists loyal to the classical tradition.

If the area of politics is conceived narrowly for purposes of democratic theory, then it is understandable that the principle of equality of power, long identified as an ideal of democracy, must give way to the more realistic principle of equality of opportunity to obtain a position of power. For the former principle is only meaningful as an ideal to strive for in a society in which there is hope of obtaining a more equalitarian base for decision-making. The latter principle is suited to a political system in which power is highly stratified.

In sum, the explanatory side of democratic elite theory, in the form of its conceptualization of "method," "interest," "political," and "equality," unmistakably leads to a twofold conclusion: (a) on-going democratic systems, characterized by elite rule and mass passivity, handsomely meet the requirements of democratic theory; and (b) any suggestion that a departure from the system in the direction of obtaining a more equalitarian relationship between elites and non-elites is, on objective grounds, unrealistic.

These conclusions are in harmony with and support the normative judgment, as reflected in the writing of democratic elitists, that the illiberal propensity of the masses is the overriding threat to the free society, which, if it does survive, will do so because of the wisdom and courage of established elites. The theory of democratic elitism is not a theory of the status quo. For on the one hand it is completely in tune with the rapid change toward greater concentration of power in the hands of managerial elites, and on the other, it manifests an uneasiness that, in the absence of the creation of an elite consensus, the system is doomed.

II

Classical theory, as I emphasized at the outset of this essay, is based on the supposition that man's dignity, and indeed his growth and development as a functioning and responsive individual in a free society, is dependent upon an opportunity to participate actively in decisions that significantly affect him. The psychological soundness of this supposition has in recent years been supported by the well-known experiments contrasting the impact of authoritarian and democratic leadership on group behavior, conducted by Kurt Lewin and associates in the late 1930's,[3] by the subsequent testing of the "participation hypothesis" by numerous small group researchers,[4] and in the more speculative writings of Eric Fromm and others.[5] But surely one does not have to rely upon hard data to share in the belief of Rousseau, Kant, Mill, Lindsay, and others, that man's development as a human being is closely dependent upon his opportunity to contribute to the solution of problems relating to his own actions.

Although firmly grounded on what I consider to be a sound ethical position, classical theory falls short of being a viable political theory for modern society. For in underscoring the importance of widespread participation in political decision-making, it offers no realistic guidelines as to how its prescription is to be filled in large urban societies.

On its face it would appear that the democrat is left with a Hobson's choice: a theory which is normatively sound but unrealistic, or a theory which is realistic but heavily skewed toward elitism. It is my contention that he should reject both and instead accept the challenge to create a democratic theory for the twentieth century; one that is founded on the self-development objective and one that at the same time firmly confronts the elite-mass structure characteristic of modern societies. This approach to democracy can perhaps best be understood by contrasting it with the position of the democratic elitists in reference to certain key concepts and empirical statements that closely relate to the role of elites in a democracy. Table 1 is, in summary form, an attempt to make this contrast.

At the outset the democratic theorist must abandon explanatory theory as an approach to his subject. By adhering to it he tends to accept as unalterable the configuration of society as shaped by impersonal forces. In accepting the growing concentration of elite power as given, he has been left with the task of pruning democratic theory in accord with changing conditions. Invariably this leads to support for an ideology that is strongly

TABLE 1. THE CONTRAST BETWEEN DEMOCRATIC ELITISM AND
SELF-DEVELOPMENTAL THEORY OF DEMOCRACY

Concepts & Empirical Statement	Democratic Elitism	Modern Self-Developmental
Democracy	political method	political method and ethical end
Interest	interest-as-end-results	interest-as-end-results and interest-as-process
Equality	equality of opportunity	equality of power
Political	governmental decision-making and that which relates to it	decision-making which significantly affects societal values
Elite-mass structure of modern industrial societies	unalterable	alterable
Anti-liberal propensity of a great number of non-elites	reliance upon elites to safeguard the system	reliance upon broadening and enriching the democratic process

elitist in character. Instead, what we must acquire, as Richard Crossman has suggested, is a healthy dose of Promethean defiance against the illiberal and impersonal forces which tend to devastate us.[6] To submit to those forces which threaten to emasculate democracy, to adjust values eagerly to facts as the latter turn against us, is not the attitude of the scientist but of the defeatist.[7]

Stripped of normative ends, political theory, including democratic theory, cannot perform the crucial function of providing direction to man's actions. To argue that we must be content to struggle modestly forward by combating social evil as it arises is to assume that a series of incremental moves to combat various evils will add up over time to a step forward. That need not be and often is not the case. In any event, the fundamental issue is not whether democracy should or should not have an overriding objective; it is rather whether its objective should be implicitly dedicated to the viability of a democratic elitist system or explicitly to the self-development of the individual.

In opting for the latter objective, I believe that a theory of democracy should be based upon the following assumptions and principles: the majority of individuals stand to gain in self-esteem and growth toward a fuller affirmation of their personalities by participating more actively in meaningful community decisions;[8] people generally, therefore have a twofold interest in politics — interest in end results and interest in the process of participation; benefits from the latter interest are closely related to the degree to which the principle of equality of power is realized; and progress toward the realization of this principle is initially dependent upon the acceptance by social scientists of a realistic concept of what constitutes the political sector of society.

The elite-mass structure of present-day society is very much a reality. But it is an unalterable structure only if political decision-making is viewed narrowly, as governmental decision-making. I have argued that such a view is untenable, that the evidence will simply not support a *twofold* definition of political. To define political broadly for general purposes and then, when concerned with the meaning of political elites or political equality to retreat to a nineteenth-century notion of the concept is to remove an important area of politics from political research. If the political scientist is to be realistic, he must recognize that large areas within existing so-called private centers of power are political and therefore potentially open to a wide and democratic sharing in decision-making.

It is true that political scientists of all persuasions are very willing to analyze both the power structure of "private governments" and the interaction of these units with government policy. But these institutions are distinguished from government on the ground that they, unlike the latter, do not possess the exclusive and legitimate right to exercise force. Of course this is a valid distinction, but is it sufficient to exempt private governments from scrutiny within the context of the democratic norms of political equality, popular participation in the formulation of basic policy, and accountability of leaders to lead? I do not believe so. Obviously General Motors is not the United States government. However, there is a basic similarity between the two: they both authoritatively allocate values for the society. It is on the basis of this similarity that General Motors and other giant private governments should be considered a part of the political sector in which democratic norms apply. Within the context of constitutional law, a private firm which performs a public function is subject, like the government, to the limitations of the Constitution.[9] The expansion of the concept of "state action" by the Supreme Court, which has had a significant effect in constitutionalizing private governments, reflects the Court's insistence that the Constitution will be a viable instrument to meet the needs of the present. It is time that democratic theorists emulate the spirit of their judicial brethren. They may begin by holding that when a private government performs a public function — such as authoritatively allocating values for society or a large part of it — that for purposes of democratic theory as well as constitutional law, it is considered a political institution and thus within the reach of the Constitution *and* democratic principles.

It might be asked, why is it necessary to politicize private centers of power in order to broaden the base for participation? Does not the argument erroneously assume that ordinary men and women actually desire a greater share in shaping policies which affect them? If this were the case, one would think that the people would have already exploited to the fullest every opportunity to engage in politics within existing political institutions. As one study after another has shown, a comparatively large portion of the public is indifferent to politics, they abstain from voting, they are virtually ignorant of public affairs, and they lack a strong commitment to the democratic process. Would not this same pattern of indifference exist within a broadened political area?

If the newly recognized political sector were the factory, the office, the enterprise, I do not believe this would be the case. For many individuals political issues and elections appear either trivial or remote and beyond the reach of their influence. Of a different magnitude are issues which directly affect them in their place of work, issues which are comparatively trivial, yet are overlaid with tensions and emotions that often infuriate and try men's souls. It is here — despite the legitimatizing effects of bureaucratic forms—that the ugliness of man's domination of man is fully revealed, and it is here, consequently, that democracy must become established and put to use. I am not suggesting that the average worker, for example, if given the opportunity to share in the making of factory decisions, would be magically transformed, in the fashion of Rousseau's common man, from an unimaginative, parochial, selfish human being to a broad-minded, intelligent public-spirited citizen. I am saying that political education is most effective on a level which challenges the individual to engage cooperatively in the solution of concrete problems affecting himself and his immediate community. In the past this task was ideally performed in the New England town meeting; in twentieth-century America it can effectively be performed in the factory community.

Clearly the highly complex, mammoth industrial corporate structure of today has little resemblance to the town meetings of eighteenth-century America. This does not mean, however, that the modern corporation could not, to a significant extent, be democratized in line with the principles and objectives that I have outlined above. Admittedly at this point it is a matter of conjecture whether such an undertaking, from both a political and economic standpoint, is workable. However, in my view, it borders on dogmatism to reject this challenge out of hand, on the assertion, for example, that the principles of accountability and equality of power are irreconcilable, or that the devolution of decision-making is, without serious loss of efficiency, impossible within the modern industrial firm. We cannot, with any degree of confidence, extrapolate a democratic scheme for modern industry from on-going oligarchic institutions. It seems equally evident that we cannot, with any degree of confidence, conclude from observation of oligarchic practices that such a democratic scheme, if put into practice, would be doomed to failure. If democracy is to be taken seriously, we cannot remain on dead center on this issue. What is called for, at minimum, is discussion and debate on various aspects of the question with the view of possible experimentation with nationalization of one or a few corporate political giants. Serious consideration of such a proposal can no longer be left to socialists, nor should controversy centering on such a proposal be fought along traditional socialist-capitalist lines of argument. Today, argument along those lines would border on the irrelevant. For the fundamental issue no longer relates to the problem of production or distribution but to the problem of power.

The illiberal and anti-democratic propensity of the common man is an undeniable fact that must be faced. But to face it realistically is not, as I have attempted to show, to rely upon elites to sustain the system. For in the first place, there is little evidence that elites, any more than non-elites, are prepared to defend procedural rights at the risk of jeopardizing their own personal status, prestige, and power. Secondly, to assume a harmony between the vested interests of elites and the well-being of democracy is to sap the latter of the boldness and imaginativeness characteristic of democracies of the past. To do so would be to confine the expansion of democracy to an area where it does not threaten the basic substantive interests of dominant elites. Thirdly, it is difficult to understand how elites, who have conflicting substantive interests, can reach a consensus sufficiently effective to safeguard democracy from attack. Finally, assuming elites can reach such a consensus, it seems doubtful that they could generate sufficient power *democratically* to restrain the excessive demands and actions of the undemocratic mass and its leaders.

If it is time to abandon the myth of the common man's allegiance to democracy, it is also time that elites in general and political scientists in particular recognize that without the common man's active support, liberty cannot be preserved over the long run. The battle for freedom will be lost by default if elites insulate themselves from the people and rely on countervailing forces, institutional and social barriers, and their own colleagues to defend the system from the demagogic leader of the mob. Democracy can best be assured of survival by enlisting the people's support in a continual effort to make democracy meaningful in the lives of all men.

Notes

[1] Robert Dahl, *Preface to Democratic Theory* (Chicago, 1951), p. 1.

[2] The problem of what interests should be included within the corporate constituency is a difficult one, but certainly it would include the

stockholders (if the corporation were privately owned), various categories of employees, suppliers, customers (would usually include the federal government), and the general consumers.

[3] For these experiments, see Kurt Lewin, Ronald Lippitt, and R. White, "Patterns of Aggressive Behavior in Experimentally Created Social Climates," *Journal of Social Psychology* (vol. 16, 1939), pp. 271-99.

[4] For a review of these studies, see Sidney Verba, *Small Groups and Political Behavior* (Princeton, 1961), pp. 216-25.

[5] See especially *Escape from Freedom* (New York, 1941); and *The Sane Society* (New York, 1955); also see A. H. Maslow, "Power Relationship and Patterns of Personal Development," and sources cited in A. Kornhauser (ed.), *Problems in Power* (Detroit, 1957), pp. 92-131; Christian Bay, *Structure of Freedom* (Stanford, 1958), pp. 155-240.

[6] *The New Fabian Essays* (New York, 1952), pp. 14-15.

[7] For as Mannheim argued, the determinist—and the positivist can be included—"overlooks the fact that every major phase of social change constitutes a choice between alternatives." *Essays on the Sociology of Culture* (London, 1956), p. 169.

[8] I am fully aware that participation will not necessarily in all cases lead to salutary results. Clearly under some conditions participation may feed the pathological needs of the participants and thereby impede development rather than facilitate it. Under other conditions, what appears to be free, meaningful discussion may in reality be a subtle process of manipulation in which the feelings and thoughts of those participating are induced by the leader. [Eric Fromm, *Escape from Freedom* (New York, 1941), p. 210.] This technique is an effective way of controlling without revealing the source of control. [See Sidney Verba, *Small Groups and Political Behavior* (Princton, 1961), p. 217-25.] In an age where individuals are particularly sensitive to the demands and values of others, participation that is free of manipulation may nonetheless contribute to the prevalent tendency to "cut everyone down to size who sticks up or sticks out in any direction." [David Riesman, *The Lonely Crowd* (New Haven, 1950).]

Admittedly these dangers exist. But they do not vitiate the assumption regarding the value of participation. They do however raise two important questions: Under what concrete conditions will man's capacities be developed and under what conditions will development be frustrated? How will democratic theory provide the development conditions? Definitive answers to these questions must await empirical research. Tentatively, however, I would suggest that beneficial results from participation can best be assured if two conditions are present: (*a*) that the participants are roughly equal in the power they are capable of exerting in the decision-making process, (*b*) that diverse interests are represented within the participating group. The first condition would tend to prevent manipulation and the second would tend to prevent the pressures of conformity from being overbearing on those sharing in the decision-making process. Democratic theory must therefore include among its principles equality of power and pluralism.

[9] See *Marsh v. Alabama,* 326 U.S. 501 (1946); *Perry v. Adams,* 345 U.S. 461 (1953), and Arthur Miller, *Private Governments and the Constitution* (Center for the Study of Democratic Institutions, Santa Barbara, Cal., 1959).

Is There a Ruling Elite in America?

William A. Schultze

Some commentators on American political life reject the interpretation that our system is democratic in any sense. They would argue that our political process is unvarnished elitism. In this view American politics is dominated by an "establishment" or "power structure" composed of a few powerful individuals or groups which are able to consistently dictate policy on important public issues. There has been much recent research and writing aimed at verifying or denying the existence of such a ruling elite. The following bibliographic and interpretative essay reviews and critiques the common arguments of several of the most influential of these writings.

At the core of many American political controversies is the question: Is there a power elite or establishment which holds the ultimate political power of the country? It is momentarily provocative to realize that both radical right and radical left agree that the answer to this question is a resounding "yes." The similarity is superficial, however, beginning and ending with that common response. Fundamental divergence develops as to the personnel who compose and the policy intent of the elite. To the extreme right the rulers of America are agents of the "enemy without," the world communist conspiracy. To the left, the enemy is within and is variously characterized, most often as either the business and financial aristocracy or the military-industrial complex.

A large number of scholars and practicing politicians would simply dismiss this question as absurd or unanswerable or both. Yet the persistence and pervasiveness of the *belief* that an elite exists is enough to make the question important enough for serious consideration. For beliefs may influence actions, whatever the truth of those beliefs. Moreover, it is an important question because an affirmative answer to it would have radical impact on our understanding of American government. If it can be demonstrated that there is an elite, then

This article was prepared especially for this volume. Permission to reprint should be obtained from Charles E. Merrill Publishing Company.

discussion of the Congress, the Presidency and the Courts become devoid of meaning; they become, in Senator Clark's phrase, "sapless branches." However, I shall contend that we do not yet have adequate evidence that there is a ruling elite. This contention can be supported by a critical examination of representative writings on American elites.

WORLD COMMUNIST CONSPIRACY

The position of the far right is that world communism's current strategy is to subvert America by infiltrating and destroying its institutions. This much is agreed upon, despite the fact that there is organizational diversity among the far right, to name the most prominent: The John Birch Society, The Minutemen, media organizations like Texas millionaire H. L. Hunt's *Life Line*, *The Dan Smoot Report* and *The Manion Forum*, and several Christian anti-communist groups, the largest of which is Billy James Hargis' *Christian Crusade*.

Most leaders of these organizations would agree with the estimate of the house organ of the John Birch Society, *American Opinion* magazine, that the United States is 60 percent to 75 percent under communist influence and control.[1] The Society also claims that "communist domination of many departments of the federal government is too obvious to require much comment."[2] Particularly the State Department is singled out as "Communist headquarters in Washington."[3]

Individual "conspirators" have been readily named; Robert Welch, founder of the Birch Society, reportedly called President Eisenhower a "dedicated, conscious agent of the communist conspiracy" and claimed that Milton Eisenhower was "Dwight Eisenhower's superior and boss within the Communist Party."[4]

Somewhat more moderate accusations of "usurpation" of political power have been made by Medford Evans, an Associate Editor of *American Opinion*. In his recent book, Evans has named the "would-be conquerors" of the United States—Clark Clifford, Abe Fortas, Lyndon Johnson, Walt Rostow, Nicolas deB. Katzenbach, Robert McNamara, Dean Rusk and others.[5]

Seemingly every American institution bears the stamp of the conspiracy; in a 1961 speech, Welch declared that "about 3% of the Protestant clergy can now be described as Comsymps."[6] Even popular music has been subverted, according to Reverend David Noebel of the Christian Crusade. Noebel's pamphlet *Communism, Hypnotism and the Beatles* argues that there is a communist "music master plan" calling for the creation and distribution of popular music which will make American youth mentally ill and emotionally unstable.

It is difficult to take these ideas seriously enough to offer refutation. They sound absurd to most of us. Yet, and this is an important point regarding all conspiracy theories, decisive proof of its falsehood is difficult to muster since it must be presumed that conspirators by their very nature operate in secret and seek to manipulate us without our knowing it. Thus, *there is virtually no way to disprove the existence of a conspiracy to the satisfaction of someone who chooses to believe in one*. Commitment becomes religious in character, a matter of taking the "leap of faith."

To one who has not chosen to leap however, at least until the evidence is more compelling than it currently is, the central difficulty with the right wing analysis is that it rests upon a rather broad definition of "communist." In fact, there are many on the right whose implicit definition seems to be, "a communist is someone whose ideas I find disagreeable," using the logic: one who disagrees with me is my enemy; all enemies are communists. True, the spokesmen of the right have attempted to respond to this kind of criticism on many occasions by retreating to the position that Mr. X, if not a communist, is "communist controlled" or "communist influenced" or, at the very least, a "dupe" of the conspiracy. Medford Evans seems to have been forced back even farther when he says that he doesn't believe America's top men are traitors in the "classical sense";

I think that many of our top leaders in government and business have participated in a usurpation of power through which they hope to manage rather than represent the American people. I think further that they hope to participate in the management of the world and that they do not envisage this as possible without ultimately merging with the communist bloc.[7]

That any particular American leader is motivated by this vague cluster of intents is more than the right has demonstrated.

THE BUSINESS ELITE

Among the earliest and most persistent interpretations of the American left has been that there exists an aristocracy of wealth with the ability to translate that wealth into political dominance. The quality of these interpretations has ranged from superficial to careful and systematic. The writings most deserving of attention are those of Baltzell,[8] Sweezy,[9] Kolko,[10] Hunter,[11] Lundberg,[12] and Domhoff.[13]

Although there is some variety in terminology and findings among these authors, I shall nonetheless allow Domhoff's book *Who Rules America?* to represent this view. Domhoff's work is recent, responsive to the kinds of criticisms which have long been leveled at other of these studies, and is more concise and systematic. Essentially, Domhoff marshalls evidence which is reasonably convincing that there exists an American social and economic upper class,

... which (upper class) receives a disproportionate amount of [the] country's income, owns a disproportionate amount of [the] country's wealth, and contributes a disproportionate number of its members to the controlling institutions and key decision-making groups in [the] country.[14]

He identifies this upper class as those who meet one or more of the following criteria: (1) listing in a *Social Register*, (2) attendance at certain prep schools (e.g. Lawrenceville, Groton, etc.), (3) membership in one of a small number of exclusive men's clubs (e.g. California Club in Los Angeles, Somerset in Boston), (4) a particularly high level of family wealth, and (5) marriage or other close attachment to those meeting the above criteria.[15] Having identified an upper class, Domhoff has little difficulty in demonstrating that they hold numerous controlling positions in the corporate economy.

Where he has most serious difficulty is in establishing that this "upper class" is a *ruling* class, that is, that the business aristocracy (which Domhoff uses as a synonym for upper class) translates its corporate wealth into political power. In attempting to establish that the upper class achieves political dominance, Domhoff is content to demonstrate that upper class members have a predominant representation in many of the organizations which seek, and seem to have, influence on American political decisions — organizations like the Council of Foreign Relations, the National Association of Manufacturers, the Council for Economic Development, the large foundations, the universities, the major media, etc.

As for the federal government itself, Domhoff attempts to show that the upper class provides the major financial backing for both of the major political parties, that it is an important source of recruitment for the Cabinet, and occasionally — though not usually — the Presidency, and the upper echelons of the diplomatic corps and the regulatory agencies. Still, Domhoff concedes that the upper class ". . . does not control every aspect of American life," nor does it permeate every locus of political power. He finds the Congress, state and local governments, and certain agencies of the federal government (e.g. the F.B.I.) to be relatively free from upper-class control. On balance, however, he feels his analysis justifies the conclusion that his upper class, by virtue of its corporate wealth, income, and institutional leadership earns it the title of "governing class."

Domhoff's technique for ascribing control to those who hold formal positions is particularly offensive to the political behavioralist who has long argued that one must know a great deal more than who holds the office to comprehend who holds power. Ribbon-cutting, weak mayors do not necessarily run their cities. Even though the Secretary of State be of the upper class, this does not mean the upper class will is impressed on all or any of the decisions that he will make. As Robert Dahl has pointed out, to discover who is powerful it is necessary to examine the *actual scope of control* of any particular decision-maker by observing his actions in specific, key issues.[16] In short, Domhoff's work is provocative, but incomplete. His conclusion that the upper class is in fact a ruling class is thus premature.

THE MILITARY-INDUSTRIAL COMPLEX

Similar in many respects to the works finding a business elite are those which conclude that the United States is presently dominated by a "military-industrial complex." A recent count disclosed twenty-one books published in this area in the last few years.[17] Among the most prominent of these works are Cook, *The Warfare State;*[18] Perlo, *Militarism and Industry;*[19] and the best known work on American elites, C. Wright Mills, *The Power Elite.*[20] Since Mills' work remains the best expression of the position, let us discuss it more fully.

Mills asserts that the major decisions affecting Americans—especially those having to do with war and peace—are made by a small number of persons he calls the power elite. Instead of finding an exclusive business aristocracy, which is the pool from which the "ruling class" is drawn, as does Domhoff, Mills says instead that three groups comprise the elite, corporation executives, military men, and high-ranking politicians. This elite is not accountable to the general public. Their decisions are a product of their common perspective on life and common interests, not popular will. Free from accountability, the elite often exercises power in "immoral" and "irresponsible" ways.

Mills, in contrast to Domhoff, is not concerned with systematic identification of the individual members of this elite. It is thus impossible, using Mills as a guide, to know which decision-makers are members, to chart their activities, or appraise their degree of interdependence. In fairness to Mills, it should be pointed out that the failure to name names may not be a hedge. Pilisuk and Hayden point out that Mills refrains from discussing individuals precisely because his emphasis is on institutions as the basic elements in his analysis.

If the military, political, and economic *institutional* orders involve a high coincidence of interest, then the groups composing the institutional orders need not be monolithic, conscious and coordinated, yet exercise elite power. This means specifically that a military-industrial complex could exist as an expression of a certain fixed ideology (reflecting common institutional needs), yet be "composed" of an endless shuffle of specific groups.[21]

Below the Power Elite are two substrata, the "middle levels of power" and the "powerless masses." The middle level is composed of Congress, state political machines, and regional interest groups, all of which hold some power, but practically none over major decisions. The "masses" of American society Mills sees pursuing meaningless lives, manipulated by the elite controlled media of communication. The mass thus becomes apathetic and cynical toward politics.

Superficially, it might appear that Mills has met the criticism that was made of Domhoff's failure to analyze actual decision-making, since Mills discusses five issues: (1) steps leading to intervention in World War II, (2) decision to drop the atomic bomb, (3) declaration of war in Korea, (4) the indecisions over Quemoy and Matsu in 1955, and (5) decision regarding possible intervention in Dien Bien Phu when that city was about to fall in the French Indo-China War. Yet, Mills' treatment of these issues is unsatisfying for he does not carefully examine the concrete behaviors of decision-makers, demonstrating that the most influential ones are members of the power elite or that elite will is continuously impressed on the policies. He is instead content to point out that "(m)ore and more of the fundamental issues never came to any point of decision before Congress ... much less before the electorate."[22] Even if this point were conceded—and it is debatable—it would not constitute *prima facie* evidence that an elite *is* making these decisions. In fact, Richard Rovere has proceeded issue by issue with Mills to demonstrate that elite involvement was not decisive in any of the issues Mills has used.[23] The inadequacy of Mills' mode of analysis leaves vulnerable, or at least empirically undemonstrated, his whole thesis. Finally, Mills is subject to the same criticism as leveled at Domhoff, that his conception of "power" ("control" in Domhoff) is imprecise and thus, an inadequate guide to who has it and how they exercise it.[24]

THE PLURALIST CRITIQUE AND ALTERNATIVE

Most of the criticisms of the elite literature that have been made thus far have also been made by those who would call themselves pluralists. By pluralism they mean, "Instead of a single center of sovereign power there must be multiple centers of power, none of which is or can be wholly sovereign."[25] And while this definition poses pluralism as a value to be sought, their research has generally found pluralism to be a fact of American political life.

Pluralists tax the elite studies for beginning with the assumption that there is a single dominant group. That, they say, is taking as a given what is to be empirically verified. Pluralist technique proceeds to an analysis of actual participation in the making of key decisions.

If a man's major life work is banking, the pluralist presumes he will spend his time at the bank, and not in manipulating community decision. This presumption holds until the banker's activities and participations indicate otherwise . . .[26]

We should note that this presumption could also be assailed as likely to have a dramatic impact on research findings. If one begins assuming no structure exists, the scholarly dice are loaded for finding no structure.

Most of the research done by pluralists has been on cities, which they have consistently found to be more pluralistic than elite dominated.[27] Thus far, the only work claiming the pluralist frame of reference which is national in scope is Arnold Rose's *The Power Structure*.

As the pluralists recommend, Rose avoids beginning with the assumption that there are classes in America and instead proceeds to investigate particular issues—political structure in Texas, the Kennedy nomination, the passage of the Medicare Bill. In examining these issues, Rose makes the point rather convincingly that there are a variety of participants in the resolution of these issues; that a business elite, to be sure, is often importantly involved, but that their influence is limited in scope, focusing "... mainly on issues affecting production, occasionally on issues affecting consumption and distribution of wealth, and ordinarily very little on issues that do not affect wealth directly or primarily."[28]

In fact, Rose argues, there are "many power elites," each specializing in particular issues of interest to them, each elite manifesting its power over public policy within its particular domain, but occasionally making temporary alliances with other interests. He acknowledges that within each of these several elites a small number of persons hold power, estimating that as little as one percent of the total population hold leadership positions within these elites, but nonetheless he asserts that ". . . the rank and file voters exercise some restraining and modifying power over the elite."[29]

To meet Mills' contention that a military-industrial complex has developed which exercises elite control, Rose offers little that is new. He develops only short sketches of issue participation and, finally, relies heavily on the work of Morris Janowitz who concludes "the military is not a monolithic power group. A deep split pervades its ranks in respect to its doctrine and viewpoints in foreign affairs, a split which mirrors civilian disagreements."[30]

Superficially, Rose's position is rather satisfying, especially to those of us who know that political realities are far too complicated to be easily reduced to a pat formulation wherein the elite, however defined, say jump and we all do. However, satisfaction gives way to criticism upon more careful examination of Rose's alternative interpretation. Most fundamentally, it is disconcerting to conclude that an unstated premise of the book seems to be: *if we can find conflict, then there is no elite.* When the proposition is made explicit, it has an obvious false ring to it. Conflict, even severe conflict, can occur within a context of fundamental agreement. The best clarifying analogy is to the game — wherein complete agreement on the fundamentals (rules) enables complete opposition of interests which seek the rewards of the game. This game competition is a quite different form from competition to change the rules themselves. What Rose describes in his issue discussions, and this criticism may be made of the pluralists generally, may be only game competition. To demonstrate that it is a more thoroughgoing competition that is involved in the issues he examines would necessitate systematic discussion of the grounds of *agreement* among opponents as well as disagreement. This Rose does not do. In a review of Rose's book, Robert Heilbroner makes much the same criticism:

The trouble is that Rose does not explain the nature of the interests that *bind* the contestants, over and above the issues that divide them. He does not see . . . that the politician who struggles against a businessman . . . may also be a representative of the interests of the upper class.[31]

More broadly, it has been suggested that the pluralist frame of reference leaves unexamined what Peter Bachrach and Morton Baratz have called the other face of power, "nondecision-making." They contend that the pluralist, by examining issue participation, ". . . takes no account of the fact that power may be, and often is, exercised by confining the scope of decision-making to relatively 'safe' issues."[32] In other words, elites may be able to influence or control the active decision-makers in an issue to the extent that conflict is restricted to alternatives and issues that are acceptable to the elite. If I (a nondecision-maker) can put you (a decision-maker) in a position in which you must choose between death by drowning and death by hanging, my will has had, most would agree, a more profound impact on the outcome than yours.

That the nondecision-making process occurs in fact, in American political life is still an unverified hypothesis. There have been no empirical studies using its concepts, and recent criticism of the nondecision-making hypothesis makes clear how difficult research will be that might attempt verification.[33] Still, it seems premature to make conclusions before the attempt to discover nondecision-making has been made.

CONCLUSION

In sum, then, the leading attempts to demonstrate the existence and assess the machinations of a ruling elite in America fall short. The radical right is blinded by its ideology; Domhoff fails to demonstrate that the upper class impresses its will on actual decisions; Mills makes substantially the same omission, but Rose is also unsuccessful in his attempt to demonstrate than no single, dominant elite exists because he fails to examine all pertinent aspects of decisional behavior. Unless we are prepared to make a leap of faith, we must proceed with the assumption that we do not yet know how to answer the question: Is there a ruling elite in America?

Where does this leave us? There is no easy way to reconcile these strongly held diverging views. But one suspects, as in many disagreements, that the disputants are talking past each other on important issues. Perhaps the most useful and appropriate step to take at the present is to clearly state the conditions precedent to reconciliation of these contending viewpoints in future elite studies. I make no pretense to be exhaustive, but the most important conditions to be met, it would seem, are four:

1. *Agreement on the meanings of central terms.* This is not to say there have been no such attempts, only that each of the elite studies done so far has used either an ambiguous or a particularlized definition of terms like elite, pluralism and power. For example, the elitists conception of power emphasizes its relational character. They feel that to comprehend power a researcher must examine not only the capacities and dispositions of the power holder but also those of the recipients in the power relationship as well as the situational context in which power is applied. The pluralists move toward a more individualized conception of power, presuming that power is an attribute of a particular decision-maker.[34]

The conceptions of elitism and pluralism seem to badly overlap, allowing the same findings to be interpreted both as evidence of elitism and of pluralism. Does Rose's observation that only one percent of the population holds leadership positions constitute evidence of elitism or pluralism? We will only be able to answer that question when we have made a full conceptualization of these terms and have greater agreement upon their operational dimensions.[35]

2. *A Classification of Issues.* Which are the *fundamental* issues? Those involving war and peace, perhaps those that allocate wealth or power, or those that attract most public attention? Since the studies undertaken so far deal with different issues (when they deal with issues at all) it becomes difficult to say whether the process they describe pertains to important or merely peripheral issues. Until we are able to make such a distinction it will be possible to contend that a finding of plural participation in any decision is unimportant because the issue is trivial. Future elite studies will need to be more self-conscious about qualifying the issues to be studied as fundamental.

3. *Research strategies which enable description of the relationships between local and national leaders.* To focus exclusively on either national or local leadership is to leave room for serious doubts as to the meaning of any set of findings. It can always be argued that a national elite dissolves into local pluralism (as Domhoff claims in reconciling his with Dahl's findings), or the reverse, that national pluralism is rendered meaningless by

local elitism. Examination of the full decisional process on any given issue will have to account for the whole complex of decision-making in the federal system.

4. *Satisfactory operationalizing and testing of the nondecision-making hypothesis.* To avoid some of the criticisms of the nondecision-making hypothesis it would seem advisable to pursue verification of it by relying on the research strategies and leading assumptions of the pluralists; i.e. by focusing on actual decisional behavior. However, to determine what forces (if any) are acting to limit the scope of actual decision-making it would be necessary to obtain additional information about the rationales of active decision-makers. To examine a decision-maker's role concept, for example, would be particularly useful since this would provide his orientation to a variety of groups and interests external to his immediate decisional setting.[36] In addition, more careful examination of the values of decision-makers and the means by which values are mobilized would enable better grounded generalizations about the nature of consensus.[37]

Notes

[1] "Notes on the Scoreboard," *American Opinion,* July-August, 1965, pp. 68-69.

[2] *Ibid.*

[3] Quoted in Benjamin R. Epstein and Arnold Forster, *Report on the John Birch Society, 1966* (New York: Random House, 1966), p. 17.

[4] For a discussion of the authenticity of this quotation and the reaction by the Birch Society to public criticism of it, see George Thayer, *The Farther Shores of Politics* (New York: Simon and Schuster, 1967), pp. 186-187.

[5] Medford Evans, *The Usurpers* (Boston: Western Islands, 1968).

[6] Reported in Thayer, *op. cit.,* p. 188.

[7] Evans, *op. cit.*

[8] E. Digby Baltzell, *An American Business Aristocracy* (New York: The Free Press, 1958) and *The Protestant Establishment* (New York: Random House, 1964).

[9] Paul Sweezy, "The American Ruling Class" in *The Present as History* (New York: The Monthly Review Press, 1964).

[10] Gabriel Kolko, *Wealth and Power in America* (New York: Praeger, 1962).

[11] Floyd Hunter, *Top Leadership: USA* (Chapel Hill: University of North Carolina Press, 1960).

[12] Ferdinand Lundberg, *The Rich and the Super-Rich* (New York: Bantam Books, 1968).

[13] G. William Domhoff, *Who Rules America?* (Englewood Cliffs: Prentice-Hall, Inc., 1967).

[14] *Ibid.,* p. 142.

[15] *Ibid.,* pp. 34-37. There are two other, more minor, criteria not included in this summary.

[16] Robert A. Dahl, "Critique of the Ruling Elite Model," *American Political Science Review,* Vol. 52 (June, 1968), 463-69. Also see Nelson

Polsby, *Community Power and Political Theory* (New Haven: Yale University Press, 1963), pp. 42-44.

[17] Marc Pilisuk and Thomas Hayden, "Is There a Military-Industrial Complex Which Prevents Peace?: Consensus and Countervailing Power in Pluralistic Systems," *Journal of Social Issues,* Vol. XXI, 67-117.

[18] Fred J. Cook, *The Warfare State* (New York: Macmillan Company, 1962).

[19] Victor Perlo, *Militarism and Industry* (New York: International Publishers, 1963).

[20] C. Wright Mills, *The Power Elite* (New York: Oxford University Press, 1958).

[21] Pilisuk and Hayden, *op. cit.,* p. 77.

[22] Mills, *op. cit.,* p. 255.

[23] Richard Revere, "The Interlocking Overlappers," *The Progressive,* Vol. 20 (June, 1968), 33-35. Revere's treatment here is quite brief, however, and could also be faulted for not specifying concrete behavior of participants.

[24] These and other criticisms of Mills' work are more completely developed in the works already cited and Daniel Bell, "The Power Elite—Reconsidered," *The American Journal of Sociology,* Vol. 64 (November, 1958), 238-250; and Talcott Parsons, "The Distribution of Power in American Society," *World Politics,* Vol. 10 (October, 1957), 123-143.

[25] Robert Dahl, *Pluralist Democracy in the United States: Conflict and Consent* (Chicago: Rand-McNally, 1967), p. 24.

[26] Nelson Polsby, "How to Study Community Power: The Pluralist Alternative," *Journal of Politics,* Vol. 22 (August, 1960), 480-481.

[27] The leading work here is Robert Dahl, *Who Governs?* (New Haven: Yale University Press, 1961). Also see Wallace Sayre and Herbert Kaufman, *Governing New York City* (New York: W. W. Norton, 1960), "Introduction" for a simple statement of pluralist assumptions.

[28] *The Power Structure* (New York: The Oxford University Press, 1967), p. 89.

[29] *Ibid.,* p. 484.

[30] Quoted by Rose, p. 151. Original source is Morris Janowitz, *The Professional Soldier* (Glencoe: The Free Press, 1960), p. viii.

[31] Robert L. Heilbroner, "Who's Running This Show?" *The New York Review of Books,* 9 (January 4, 1968), 18-21.

[32] Peter Bachrach and Morton Baratz, "Two Faces of Power," *American Political Science Review,* LVI (December, 1962), 949.

[33] See Richard Merelman, "On the Neo-Elitist Critique of Community Power," *American Political Science Review,* LXII (June, 1968), 451-460. Merelman's contentions are: (1) that the existence of a "false consensus" is nonfalsifiable; i.e. there is no way to put an empirically testable opposite hypothesis; (2) it will be necessary to observe actual application of "force" to verify that actual decision-makers anticipate elite reactions; and (3) "we also have reason to believe that no elite can operate for long solely on the basis of nondecision-making" (p. 460).

[34] See the influential discussion of power in Harold Laswell and Abraham Kaplan, *Power and Society* (New Haven: Yale University Press, 1950), Ch. 5.

[35] Robert Presthus, *Man at the Top* (New York: Oxford University Press, 1964), pp. 10-32.

[36] For discussion of the role concept and its applicability to political research see John C. Wahlke, Heinz Eulau, William Buchanan and LeRoy Ferguson, *The Legislative System* (New York: John Wiley and Sons, 1962), Ch. 1.

[37] Value study poses some complex problems; for discussion and useful bibliography, see Phillip E. Jacob and James J. Flink, "Values and Their Function in Decision-Making," *The American Behavioral Scientist,* 5, supplement (May, 1962); and John R. Tisdale, *Psychological Value Theory and Research: 1930-1960* (Unpublished doctoral dissertation, Boston University Graduate School, 1961).

The Political Behavior of the Electorate

Warren E. Miller

Traditional democratic theorists have made a great many assumptions about the voter: that he is rational, sufficiently informed to make an enlightened choice, that he votes a concept of public interest. Studies of voting behavior cast bright, though not always flattering light on the voters' reasons. Most of our findings about the American voter have been made using some variation of the technique called survey research. Simply, survey research involves drawing a representative sample, writing standardized wordings for questions, and administering the questions to informants in a uniform manner. Modern survey research relies often on computer processing of responses to enable quick handling of the vast amount of data gathered in national-sized samplings. One of the best developed centers studying American voting behavior is the Survey Research Center, in operation at the University of Michigan since 1948. The most striking finding of the Center to date has been that the single most important influence on the voting choice is the party identification of the voter. In other words, self-identified Democrats vote for candidates of the Democratic Party. Party loyalty is found to develop early in life and to persist in the face of dramatic social and political change. Exceptions to this pattern and additional insights into voting behavior are contained in the following summary, written by a political scientist prominently involved in the work of the Survey Research Center, who is also co-author of what is widely considered the best treatment of voting yet produced, The American Voter (New York: John Wiley and Sons, 1964).

To the casual observer, the results of a Presidential election may contain a striking contrast between the personal and the impersonal in politics. On the one hand a single person, an Eisenhower or a Truman or a Roosevelt, has been elected to office. On the other, he is elected by 33 million votes, or 21 million or 23 million. A single well-known man and millions of faceless voters. Some pro-

Reprinted by permission of the publisher from Warren E. Miller, "The Political Behavior of the Electorate," in Earl Lathem *et al., The American Government Annual: 1960-61,* pp. 41-61. © 1960, Holt Rinehart and Winston, Inc. Abridged by the editors.

fessional students of politics find it satisfying to do their work with such different entities. They scan the histories and the election returns and try to match this personal attribute or that economic event with variations of so many votes from one election to the next.

The politician is likely to have a much different view of life. To be sure, the final vote totals are the pay-off in his effort to be elected, but his campaign for election or re-election cannot be run on such gross terms. He must identify at least the major groups of people who contribute to his strength at the polls. He cannot simply ask, "How many thousand or million voters will be favorably impressed by my support of Policy Q?" The estimate will be, instead, of how many farmers or mothers or taxpayers or internationalists will be impressed. And will he gain rural support at the expense of his big-city vote or will his support of labor cost him the good will of business?

. . .

Ten years ago, sociological classification of the members of the American electorate resulted in rather striking classification along political lines as well. Knowledge of a man's income or occupation or religion told us a good deal about his politics. Or, conversely, we could describe Democratic voters and Republican voters as quite different people socially and economically. Between the election of 1948 and that of 1956, many changes in voting behavior took place.[1] These changes are not yet well understood by the sociologist or the political statesman, and least of all by the politician who only wants to know how to get elected. We will now proceed to look at some of these changes and comment on them. At times we will speak for the sociologist in trying to explain the sociological meaning of observed political differences among various groupings of people. Occasionally we may try to be political statesmen and speculate about the significance of these changes for the future of our country. Quite often, however, we will share with the unhappy politician his bewilderment upon discovering that things really aren't the way they used to be at all. When such is the case we will try to find new ways of making sense out of the behavior of the voters.

GROUP DIFFERENCES IN POLITICS

Sex Differences in Participation

In addition to its many other implications, sex is a human characteristic of considerable fascination in political life. Granting women the right to vote was one of the last changes in federal election controls — and it took a Constitutional amendment to bring it about. The women's vote has been overtly courted by office seekers; and party organizations give special attention to women by creating a "Women's Division" to encourage their political participation. Nevertheless, from one viewpoint this is one of the better examples of a classification extremely important to the sociologist, but one which should be of relatively limited interest to the candidate for office. As Table 1A suggests, the partisan preference of female voters does not differ markedly from that of the males. And what the simple table does not disclose is that those differences which can be observed probably are not attributable to the political uniqueness of women.

TABLE 1A. REPUBLICAN PROPORTION OF THE TWO-PARTY VOTE, 1948-1956, IN RELATION TO SEX
(in percent)

Sex	1948	1952	1956
Male	44	57	57
Female	47	59	63

TABLE 1B. PROPORTION NOT VOTING, 1948-1956, IN RELATION TO SEX
(in percent)

Sex	1948	1952	1956
Male	31	21	20
Female	40	31	33

The slightly greater Republican vote among females is largely the result of three factors: age, region of residence, and sex differences in mortality. As we shall see in a moment, older people tend to vote Republican more often than do younger people. And there are substantially more older women than there are older men. Because men die younger than women, there are somewhat fewer old male Republicans than elderly Republican women. Finally, in the South, women tend to vote considerably less often than men, and since most Southerners are Democrats, the nonvoting female there is a nonvoting Democrat. The combination of deceased Republican husbands and nonvoting Democratic wives creates a disparity resulting in more Republican women voters than men and more Democratic men voters than women—but age differences in voting choices, regional differences in voting rates, or sex differences in mortality are not what people have in mind when they talk about a distinctive women's vote.

The one basic fact of married life that politicians seem to overlook is that husbands and wives share many important personal and social values and agree on many questions that provoke widespread controversy among larger social units. Most husbands and wives are in complete political agreement. And, in the minority of instances where there is disagreement, it is as likely to be between a Democratic-voting wife and a Republican-voting husband as it is other way around.

Part B of Table 1 illustrates an important political difference between men and women: women do not turn out and vote as often as do men. To explain this we may turn again to the sociologist, this time not to the demographer but to one who specializes in the study of the role of women in modern society. One of the first things that he can tell us is that many American women of today still reflect in their own behaviors and attitudes the expectations which society had for women of another generation. For example, if we travel into rural areas, particularly in the South, we will find women who will tell us "politics is a man's business; I don't pay any attention to that sort of thing." The suffragette's desired role for emancipated womanhood is still not realized, and not wanted, by many women.

Other American women find themselves handicapped by an earlier generation's attitude toward education for females. Participation in politics is facilitated by formal education; among college-educated men and women there is a uniformly high voting rate. But many middle-aged and elderly women have not had educational opportunities equal to those of their husbands or male counterparts. The resulting differences in life experiences of men and women are reflected in their differing rates of political participation.

In yet another way the role of women restricts their political activity. The commonplace but time- and energy-consuming task of child rearing is very heavily the mother's responsibility. Among parents of young children, wives consistently vote less regularly than do their husbands, even though their interest in politics and their readiness to participate may be every bit as high.

In short, the roles which our society defines for men and women still result in limiting the political participation of women. In the matter of equipping them for political activity through education, in giving approval to their actions as interested and would-be effective citizens, and in assigning them responsibilities which restrict their activities outside the home, the expectations of the members of our society still work against complete equality of political participation.

Age and Politics

Age-related differences in voting behavior are among those which changed substantially between 1948 and 1956. In the Truman-Dewey election of 1948, the preferences of people under 45 years of age differed markedly from those over 45. Four years later, Mr. Eisenhower made his greatest gains over Mr. Dewey in his effective appeal to the younger

TABLE 2A. REPUBLICAN PROPORTION OF THE TWO-PARTY VOTE, 1948-1956, IN RELATION TO AGE
(in percent)

Age	1948	1952	1956
Under 34	37	55	59
35-44	39	55	58
45-54	53	58	61
55 and over	55	64	62

TABLE 2B. PROPORTION NOT VOTING, 1948-1956, IN RELATION TO AGE
(in percent)

Age	1948	1952	1956
Under 34	44	32	37
35-44	34	24	25
45-54	25	21	23
55 and over	37	23	22

voters. The swing to the Republican column continued in the younger groups into the 1956 elections. All told, the 1948 to 1956 increases in Republican voting, from youngest to oldest voters, were 60 percent (a 22-point increase from 37 to 59 percent), 49 percent, 15 percent, and 13 percent, respectively. One consequence was the virtual elimination of the earlier rather gross age differences in political preference.

The politician may be disappointed to learn he cannot always tell friend from foe by estimating ages. The rest of us, however, should be intrigued by the possible implications of this change in the age-relatedness of voting choices. The American electorate is quite heavily pro-Democratic in its basic partisan loyalties; despite the Eisenhower victories of 1952 and 1956, a constant six out of every ten political partisans continued to assert they were Democratic throughout this period. If at a given period of history the minor party draws relatively more of its strength from the old folks, it would be reasonable to expect that it might be in danger of dying out. The fact that its Presidential candidate could more than redress the balance by his attraction for the younger members of the electorate raises the possibility of renewed and prolonged life for the Republican party.

If age-related differences in the vote choice were largely eliminated by 1956, quite visible differences still persisted in the rate of voting. The older people, who tended to stay at home in 1948, voted with a will during the next two elections and thereby emphasized the low turnout of the youngest voters. To some extent, of course, the poor voting record of the young adults is a function of situations like that of the young mother with children noted above. This is not the full explanation, however. The most intensive study suggests that man-for-man, or woman-for-woman, young people just do not vote as regularly as do older adults. This is true, however, only as long as we treat all people 55 years old and older in one group. If we extend our analysis to an inspection of the turnout among people over 65 or over 75 we discover that their rate of participation drops rather sharply. The infirmities of old age do not diminish interest in politics, but they apparently do decrease the regularity with which high interest is translated into votes. Consequently, among persons over 75 the voting rate in any given election is lower than for any group other than the very youngest of eligible adults.[2]

Rural-urban Voting Patterns

Of all the distinctions among voters, that which separates the big-city voter from his farmer cousin is one of the most familiar. For the past thirty years one of the stereotyped dichotomies of political analysis is that between urban Democrat and rural Republican. As with so many stereotypes, the facts frequently belie the supposition. In 1948, for example, Mr. Truman did better among rural voters than among any others. And in neither of the next two elections did the Democratic candidate, Mr. Stevenson, do markedly better in the cities than elsewhere. In part, the data of Table 3

TABLE 3A. REPUBLICAN PROPORTION OF THE TWO-PARTY VOTE, 1948-1956, IN RELATION TO SIZE OF COMMUNITY
(in percent)

Community Size	1948	1952	1956
Big city	41	57	56
Small city and town	52	58	65
Rural	33	62	57

TABLE 3B. PROPORTION NOT VOTING, 1948-1956, IN RELATION TO SIZE OF COMMUNITY
(in percent)

Community Size	1948	1952	1956
Big city	17	21	21
Small city and town	37	27	28
Rural	59	32	32

obscure matters by lumping together the North and the South. But even with the heavily rural South removed, Republican strength in the rural North is not as impressive as is sometimes imagined. More elaborate analysis confirms what Table 3A only hints at—in all three elections Republican strength at the polls was greatest in the towns and small cities of the nation.

A few paragraphs back we suggested that rural residents vote less than do citizens of the central cities. This was true in all three elections, but much more so in the election of 1948. In that election the Democratic majority in rural areas was actually smaller in absolute numbers than that in the metropolitan centers because so few rural residents voted. The combination of information about preference and turnout in Table 3 presents a rather vivid contrast between the Truman election and the victories of Mr. Eisenhower. The urban character of Mr. Truman's election is particularly apparent when we note that nonvoting outside the metropolitan centers ran two and three times as high as it did within them. Not only did Mr. Eisenhower draw support quite equally from all sectors of the population, but the discrepancies in turnout had been substantially reduced. In the absence of completely comparable data from 1944 and 1960, it is difficult to tell which pattern is more normal. It is clear, however, that the population size of one's place of residence is no certain key to whether or how a man will vote.

Income and the Vote

We deliberately chose to begin this discussion by looking for sex differences in political behavior. The brief review of relevant information illustrated a set of unchanging relationships between a very stable social characteristic and political behavior over the period of time examined. The second characteristic, age, is almost equally stable over a short span of time, but here we observed temporal variations in its relationship with voting. A detailed analysis of rural-urban differences in voting behavior immediately discloses that *both* the sociological factor (place of residence) and the political factor have undergone considerable change as people have moved from farm to city and from city to the suburbs. Thus the dynamic quality of sociopolitical relationships is even more explicitly displayed in the analysis of the electoral behavior by place of residence.

As we turn to a review of the political implications of income we encounter a set of extremely volatile relationships. In the period from 1948 to 1956, the distribution of income in the United States underwent great change. Where one in every four families received less than $2000 annual income in 1948, only one in six had a similarly low income in 1956; and where only 13 percent received over $5000 in 1948, 46 percent were in the same upper bracket by 1956. During the same period, the distribution of Democratic and Republican votes also changed markedly. One result of the two sets of changes is depicted in Table 4. The major message of the table is that the partisan meaning of income has changed dramatically. As a result of relatively orderly and systematic changes in voting behavior within income groups, a once-strong correlation between income and

TABLE 4A. REPUBLICAN PROPORTION OF THE TWO-PARTY VOTE, 1948-1956, IN RELATION TO INCOME
(in percent)

Income	1948	1952	1956
Under $2000	36	58	59
$2000 - 2999	31	54	49
$3000 - 3999	51	54	61
$4000 - 4999	52	51	55
$5000 and over	68	67	62

TABLE 4B. PROPORTION NOT VOTING, 1948-1956, IN RELATION TO INCOME
(in percent)

Income	1948	1952	1956
Under $2000	54	47	48
$2000 - 2999	39	32	40
$3000 - 3999	26	24	31
$4000 - 4999	25	17	25
$5000 and over	18	12	17

voting preference has disappeared. In 1948 the pattern born in the 1930s persisted; low-income families voted heavily Democratic while high-income families voted equally heavily Republican. Between 1948 and 1956 the vote division within the lowest income group underwent a major shift, resulting in a 64-percent increase in the Republican proportion of the vote (a 23-percentage-point increase from 36- to 59-percent Republican). Persons in the $2000-$3000 range increased their contribution to a Republican victory by 58 percent. Those in the next income interval increased their Republican vote by only 20 percent, the next bracket increased by only 6 percent, and the Republican vote among families receiving over $5000 actually dropped about 10 percent.

From one viewpoint this constitutes an impressive description of the increase in the Republican vote. When we consider the income distribution as of 1956, it is apparent that Mr. Eisenhower benefited greatly from a shift in the votes of people on the bottom half of the income ladder. On the other hand, he did less well than Mr. Dewey had four years earlier among the remainder of the population. As a consequence the once standard relationship between income and the vote was virtually destroyed. It is now necessary to locate persons receiving over $10,000 a year before discovering an income group which divides its vote in a manner substantially different from the others. Among this top 5-10 percent of the people, the Republican proportion does increase rather sharply.

Nevertheless, at the same time the *partisan* implications of income have been changing, the relationship between income and turnout has remained as regular and dependable as death and taxes. Part B of Table 4 illustrates the absence of any systematic change in this political meaning of income. Family income, as an indicator of a person's position in the social structure of society, has been positively related to turnout throughout the entire period.

The absence of any major 1948-1956 increase in turnout within an income category suggests that changes in individual turnout must accompany individual changes in income. In each of the preceding tables, the drop in nonvoting between 1948 and 1956 is clearly located: for example, an 11-percent drop among men, a 15-percent drop among persons over 55 years of age, and a 27-percent drop among rural residents. With regard to income, changes in income have quite apparently been accompanied by changes in voting habits. In each of the three elections from 1948 to 1956, only every other person in families receiving less than $2000 a year was a voter. But as the same people moved into the $2000-$3000 bracket or up to the $3000-$4000 level, more of them voted—matching the turnout rate of people already in that bracket. By and large, as an individual moved up, his voting rate increased. The result by 1956 was more people in higher turnout groups, and an increase in total turnout despite the fact that the turnout rate within any income category had not changed appreciably.

Education and the Vote

Formal education means many different things to Americans. To some it means training for better jobs, to others the development of talents and self-improvement; for some it is the opportunity to learn so that life will be richer and more interesting; for others, it is merely the fulfillment of expectations held by family and friends. The political analyst is aware of this multiplicity of meaning, but he is likely to think of three important ways in which formal education contributes to the individual's political behavior. First and perhaps most important, education provides intellectual training. Even without taking courses designed primarily for these purposes, students learn how to think logically, how to be critical in appraisal and evaluation, how to use abstraction and generalization to simplify the task of understanding. Skills are developed in the use and comprehension of words so that communications about many things the individual has never seen or experienced can nevertheless be understood. It is unhappily true that many persons manage twelve years of grade school and high school and another four years of college without developing much in the way of intellectual ability. It is also true, however, that each major step in the educational process does find larger and larger proportions growing and developing along these lines. The result seems to be that people with more education are more often able to understand and appreciate the complexities of politics. They feel greater confidence in their ability to be effective citizens. They respond to political events more intelligently, and, in short, come closer to behaving as the theory of self-government holds everyone should.

In addition to the development of intellectual skills and abilities, education encourages the growth of interests which utilize these skills. Awareness and information are important additions to the mental equipment which a person is going to use in dealing with the economic, social, cultural, and political problems of life. In the absence of more than minimal educational experiences, even people with a good deal of native intelligence tend to be poorly informed, unaware of many things that better educated people take for granted.[3] This is probably particularly true with regard to politics. An individual certainly has many social and economic experiences every day; even without formal training he comes to know a good bit about those aspects of life which he experiences himself. It is much more difficult to imagine instances in which a person is exposed to politics and government in a way in which he necessarily learns very much about them. So much of political affairs is completely removed from the life of rank-and-file citizens. Even city hall and the state capitol remain unknown to most people unless they read or hear something about them.

Thus the second contribution of formal education is that of supplying facts and figures, information about how government works, about what politics means, and so on. With an organized introduction to civics or American government or the political parties or international relations, the student is given a framework within which he may understand the facts he knows. As he becomes aware of the problems which people in government and public affairs think important, he is able to understand and give meaning to additional, more specific information he picks up on his own later on. One of the functions of education is to enhance the individual's understanding of government and thereby provide a basis for a continuing interest in and comprehension of the events related to governmental affairs.

The third important meaning which can be assigned to education is somewhat less direct and obvious. Whatever the goals and purposes a student may have in mind, his education is related to his eventual position in society. His occupation, his values, and his interests are going to be similar to those of other persons with educational experiences similar to his own. In part this will be true because education is a means of transmitting and maintaining the values and interests which his parents and their friends have developed. It is assumed, and doubtless correctly in many cases, that unless the child has a very different education from that of his parents, he will carry on many elements of the family's style of life. Thus, the common expectation of parents who have been to college is that their children will also go to college and, more precisely, to the same colleges attended by the parents. Where the parents or the child want the child to have a life different from that of the parents—different job, better income, and so forth—a decision to bring this about through schooling may follow. The increasingly widely shared view that all children should have a chance to go to college is doubtless based less on a vague and general sense that education is "good for one" and more on recognition that education is a prerequisite to the maintenance or improvement of one's lot in life. Education has very real meanings in terms of social functions and rewards as well as in terms of individual intellectual abilities and gratifications.

TABLE 5A. REPUBLICAN PROPORTION OF THE TWO-PARTY VOTE, 1948-1956, IN RELATION TO EDUCATION
(in percent)

Education	1948	1952	1956
Some college (or completed college)	76	73	69
Some high school (or completed high school)	46	57	58
Some grade school (or completed grade school)	32	51	58

TABLE 5B. PROPORTION NOT VOTING, 1948-1956, IN RELATION TO EDUCATION
(in percent)

Education	1948	1952	1956
Some college (or completed college)	21	10	10
Some high school (or completed high school)	33	20	26
Some grade school (or completed grade school)	45	38	40

Because of this, we can view the voting behavior of people of different education as one index of the social implications of political choice. Table 5 illustrates something of the extent to which the vote was tied to social status in 1948, and the extent to which position in the social hierarchy had ceased to discriminate between Democratic and Republican voters by 1956.

Social Status and Political Behavior

One of the historically important themes of political analysis has been the division of society into social levels or stata. One extreme formulation of the stratification thesis has been advanced by the Marxists who see capitalist society divided into self-conscious groups or classes ranging from the elites, the rulers of the masses who must rebel, to the inert bottom layer composed of people so degraded they must be taught their own self-interest. The intellectual battle among scholars as to the importance, indeed as to the very existence of class politics in America is an enduring debate. However, recent studies suggest that the relationship between class or status and political preference is a fluid, rapidly changing relationship. At times, as in 1948, much political behavior takes on meaning in terms of social class. At other times, as in 1956, very few people appear to behave politically in terms of class interests.

The Truman election may well have been the last election based on the social and economic coalitions formed in the days of the New Deal, fifteen to twenty years earlier. Throughout that era the two major parties drew their support from very different strata of society. The Democratic vote was very heavily a vote of the economically disadvantaged; the core of Democratic strength came from people who had not received all of the rewards the American way of life promised. The Republican strength, on the other hand, came largely from the successful and relatively well-placed voters. Throughout the 1930s and 1940s the policies and programs of the candidates of both parties were calculated to emphasize social-class differences among their supporters. In contrast, part of the magic of Mr. Eisenhower's appeal rested on his popularity among all classes of Americans. This popularity increased between 1952 and 1956 among the less well educated. At the same time, although no more than a small minority of the college educated ever voted for Mr. Stevenson, the minority of Democratic votes cast by this group increased visibly over the 1948 figures. The small loss of Republican votes among the college educated and the large gain of Republican votes among those educated only in grade school wiped out a major part of the class distinctions between party supporters.

One of the other political consequences of education may be seen in Part B of Table 5. If changes in vote preferences between 1948 and 1956 eliminated much of the status- or class-relatedness of the vote, persistent differences in rate of turnout continued to mark the impact of education on voting behavior. The election of 1948 was obviously not a very exciting affair (at least not until election eve when it became apparent that Mr. Dewey was not going to win in a Republican landslide). The turnout of voters was only slightly better than it had been four years earlier when millions of Americans were in uniform or otherwise far removed from domestic politics. But where the excitement of the campaign of 1952 stirred half of the college-educated nonvoters in 1948 into action, only one in seven of the grade-school-educated nonvoters of 1948 were moved to come out and vote.

Quite apart from these variations in the two elections, the constant difference in rating of voting among grade-school, high-school, and college people is striking. Nonvoting among the grade-school group runs from two to four times as great as it does among the college educated. This is, of course, quite consistent with what we have suggested about the differences in intellectual training and ability and interest necessary for an active response to the stimuli of politics. The college graduate's interest and involvement in the affairs of the nation and the world is sharply reflected in his rate of political participation. The narrower horizons, the feeling of impotence when confronted with the big problems of society, the absence of a socially reinforced tradition of regular voting all combine to restrict the activity of people with limited educational background.

Status Polarization

If education is an antecedent to one's eventual station in life, occupation is a more obvious badge of the status attained. Both education and occupation seemed to relate in the same way to voting from 1948 to 1956. Although some of the particulars differ slightly, the conclusions drawn about the voting behavior of people classified by education can be repeated for the occupational groupings in society.

TABLE 6A. REPUBLICAN PROPORTION OF THE TWO-PARTY VOTE, 1948-1956, IN RELATION TO OCCUPATION
(in percent)

Occupation	1948	1952	1956
Professional and Business	80	69	68
White collar	50	65	62
Skilled and semiskilled	22	44	55
Unskilled	26	31	45

TABLE 6B. PROPORTION NOT VOTING, 1948-1956, IN RELATION TO OCCUPATION
(in percent)

Occupation	1948	1952	1956
Professional and business	25	12	17
White collar	19	19	22
Skilled and semiskilled	29	26	28
Unskilled	50	40	47

There are, of course, still other ways of defining or describing social status and class. We can, for example, move from deductions about the relation of education or occupation to class, and we can ask each person directly about his or her sense of belonging to a social class. We find, when we do this, that about two out of every three Americans think of themselves as being in the working class or the middle class. And although the other third say that they don't usually think of themselves as belonging to a social class, most of them can place themselves in one class or the other if asked to do so. The sociologist and the social psychologist have indicated still further information useful to know about the ties between individual and social class.

On the other side of the question, we can also provide many political elements other than the vote to define and describe the individual's political commitment. We can turn to his sense of belonging to a political party—a matter quite different from a particular choice between the candidates of the two parties. Or we may be concerned with the citizens' view of political issues. We can distinguish degrees to which the Republican or Democratic position is preferred, or we can look more directly to the content of issues and separate citizens into those with "liberal" preferences and those with "conservative" preferences.

Confronted with many different aspects of both social status and political preference, the social analyst needs a means of simplifying his view of the many interrelationships which may be observed. Such a means has been suggested by the concept of *status polarization*.[4] The central idea is that a society is completely "polarized" when classification of people by social status also results in perfect classification on other dimensions, such as the political, economic, or cultural. Complete depolarization results when social class is not systematically related to any other components of social significance. Our inspections of education and occupation in relation to the vote are thus inspections of specific instances of status polarization. They suggest, as a general conclusion, that polarization diminished considerably between 1948 and 1956.

Other much more elaborate analyses bear out the same conclusion.

Group Membership and Voting

At various times the relationship of the individual to his class is only one example of the broad range of memberships which people maintain in social groups. Except for social class, few of the sociological categories we have examined thus far ever constitute psychologically real groups for the individual. Few of us think of ourselves as members of the *Amalgamated Residents of Cities between 10-000 and 50,000 in Population, of Voters Less Than 35 years Old, Ltd.*, or of the *Incorporated Families with Less Than $5000 Income*. These various classifications may lump together people who have similar interests or who have had similar life experiences—but the grouping is done by the analyst, and the people so grouped are probably unaware of each other, and of each other's political values and commitments. The same, however, is scarcely true of members of a labor union, or of Catholics, or of Negroes, or of the members of any other collectivity to which members have a sense of belonging.

The study of the political impact of groups on their members is too complex to be included in this discussion. We can, however, look very briefly at the patterns of voting behavior among four of the most prominent groups in American politics: farmers, union members, Catholics, and Negroes.

Two groups which sometimes are treated as variations of the occupational classification are farmers and union members. In 1948, these two groups clearly reflected the pattern of rural-urban differences we have already observed. Despite the so-called Green Revolution of that year which saw the rural Republican vote drop rather precipitously, one out of every three voting farm operators voted Republican, while only one in five union voters cast a vote

TABLE 7A. REPUBLICAN PROPORTION OF THE TWO-PARTY VOTE, 1948-1956, IN RELATION TO GROUP MEMBERSHIP
(in percent)

Group	1948	1952	1956
Farm operators	35	63	54
Union	19	43	52

TABLE 7B. PROPORTION NOT VOTING, 1948-1956, IN RELATION TO GROUP MEMBERSHIP
(in percent)

Group	1948	1952	1956
Farm operators	50	33	26
Union	27	23	24

TABLE 8A. REPUBLICAN PROPORTION OF THE TWO-PARTY VOTE, 1948-1956, IN RELATION TO RACE
(in percent)

Race	1948	1952	1956
White	48	60	61
Negro	*	20	36

*Too few cases to provide a reliable estimate.

TABLE 8B. PROPORTION NOT VOTING, 1948-1956, IN RELATION TO RACE
(in percent)

Race	1948	1952	1956
White	34	21	24
Negro	64	67	64

TABLE 9A. REPUBLICAN PROPORTION OF THE TWO-PARTY VOTE, 1948-1956, IN RELATION TO RELIGION

Religion	1948	1952	1956
Protestant	53	64	65
Catholic	35	49	55

TABLE 9B. PROPORTION NOT VOTING, 1948-1956, IN RELATION TO RELIGION

Religion	1948	1952	1956
Protestant	42	28	30
Catholic	21	15	20

for Governor Dewey. At the same time, only two of every four farmers actually voted, while three of every four union members managed to get to the polls.

The first Eisenhower-Stevenson contest saw the party differential between the groups maintained, even though both groups voted much more heavily Republican than they had four years before. Four years later, in 1956, the differences in Presidential preference and in turnout had both been eliminated. If the voting behavior of these group members in 1948 emphasized the geographic and economic differences in the responses to Democratic and Republican appeals, their votes in 1956 attested to the uniformity with which Mr. Eisenhower's popularity covered the nation.

The analysis of racial and religious differences in political behavior is quite thoroughly confused by the regional differences which still permeate American politics. But despite the high rate of nonvoting among southern Negroes and despite the heavily Democratic vote of southern Protestants, some gross differences in behavior set both Negroes and Catholics apart from the dominant white Protestant population. Tables 8 and 9 also document rather dramatically the extent to which the partisan behavior of Negroes and Catholics, once dependable citadels of Democratic support, continued to change between 1952 and 1956 while the voting sentiment remained almost constant in the larger social categories. Although the Negro vote was still pro-Democratic by a ratio of two to one in 1956, the Republican vote in the group had apparently nearly doubled over that of 1952. The Catholic vote, at the same time, also became less distinctively Democratic; even though Catholics still voted Democratic more often than did Protestants, a solid majority of their votes went to Mr. Eisenhower in 1956.

Although three of the four membership groups we have just examined do not fit neatly into social class or status hierarchies, the changes in their behavior fit the general pattern established by the changes we observed in status polarization. Indeed, with the exception of the stability of the politically meaningless gross differences in partisanship of men and women, the partisan divisions within each and every scheme of social classification we have examined underwent dramatic changes between 1948 and 1956. We have documented a very sharp decline in social differences in partisan choice at the polls.

With another pair of Presidential candidates, a new set of political issues, and a new context of national and international events, old differences may be reasserted or new differences may emerge. In the meantime we are confronted with a set of facts which have serious implications for political analysis. We have seen political changes occur despite the absence of change in social and economic classification. Dramatic alteration of partisan choice occurred between 1948 and 1956; but in this short span of time, the educational background, the occupational status, the race and religion of the electorate did not change. We have also seen political shifts take place in the face of social and economic change, running strongly counter to what might have been presumed to be the patterning of interrelated sociopolitical changes. Family income did change very substantially in the eight-year span — the proportion of incomes over $5000 nearly quadrupled. But the change in vote took place largely in the low-income group; in the over-$5000 bracket the vote, in fact, was more heavily Democratic in 1956 than it had been in 1948. We have thus witnessed electoral developments which cannot be understood in the simple socioeconomic terms of New Deal politics, political changes which cannot be explained by a simple extrapolation of the meaning of social change. The old guide posts to the byways of American electoral behavior were, in 1956, at least temporarily outmoded. This may be as much a commentary on Mr. Eisenhower and the epiphenomena of the Eisenhower Presidency as it is a clue to fundamental changes in the social and political structure of America. Nevertheless, even a temporary eclipse of the old order urges the political analyst on to different modes of analysis.

THE CONTEXT OF INDIVIDUAL POLITICAL CHOICE

The rather simple categories of group identification just discussed cannot tell us all we need to know to understand the political behavior of the electorate. Other factors than these, or other factors in combination with these, may determine the behavior of voters. Let us see where we can go using another scheme of explanatory categories, one which contains five great classes of phenomena.

The first category is the environment which surrounds the individual—the external world of people and events to which the potential voter responds. The second category is the means by which the citizen is informed of political events—the media of mass communication, the conversations he holds with other people, the experiences which he has with other persons and with affairs external to himself. The third is his store of past experience, reflected in the social categories we have already examined—age, education, occupation, religion—and others which we might introduce. Among these others would be the voter's interest and involvement in politics and his sense of being a political partisan. The interaction of the outside world with the social, economic, and political predispositions of the voter —an interaction made possible by the existence of the communications channels—produces the fourth class of phenomena, his political attitudes of the moment. These attitudes are then expressed in the fifth and final class of phenomena—his political behavior. Thus, our categories would be the environment or events, communication, social factors, attitudes, and behavior. They are the context of individual political choice. The paths by which external events acquire political meaning and lead to political behavior are illustrated in Figure 1.

The very act of indicating that at least five different classes of phenomena can be treated separately in an electoral analysis suggests ways in which the group description of the vote may be modified. We may note, first, that a group description of the vote explicitly involves only two of the five classes of politically relevant phenomena, that is, social factors and political behavior. The partisan *attitudes*—by which the policy intentions, or their absence, among voters could be specified—are not disclosed by such analysis and can only be inferred. Second, the importance of actions and *events* of the external world which may influence individual political choice but which do not have unique significance for special groups is hard to estimate when we ask only about the voting behavior of groups. A stimulating Presidential campaign which increases turnout by 3 or 4 percent in every group or which decreases the Republican vote across the board is not well reflected in an analysis of the voting behavior of sociological classes. Finally, the fact that all of the members of a given group or classification do not receive their *information* and interpretations of an event from the same source may produce differences of political behavior. An individual's access to information may be an important factor in his response to an event. And the nature of his response will frequently be understood in terms of his personal experiences and political predispositions, in terms of attitudes which are generated outside the context of his social or economic position in society.

Thus, three kinds of phenomena—events, communications and attitudes—may all be more or less independent of group memberships and social classifications. They all make important contributions to the individual's political behavior. But their importance is inevitably minimized or neglected in group-oriented descriptions of electoral behavior.

Political Participation

Let us now apply our new fivefold scheme of analysis to the problem of political participation. Why do people vote? There may be many explanations but two have had wide currency. The first is the notion that people in a democratic society should and do act to advance their self-interest. A considerable amount of political theory presumes that citizens participate on behalf of their own social values and economic goals. In this view, the parties and their candidates are but the vehicles for conveying the policies of government. It is presumed that the active citizen is active on behalf of issues to which he is devoted. The devotion may be born of narrow self-interest or of a broad concern for the public weal, but the object of his action is to influence governmental policy. This is a persuasive argument, and one which has been sup-

FIGURE 1. ILLUSTRATIVE PATHS BY WHICH EXTERNAL EVENTS ACQUIRE POLITICAL MEANING AND LEAD TO AN INDIVIDUAL'S POLITICAL BEHAVIOR

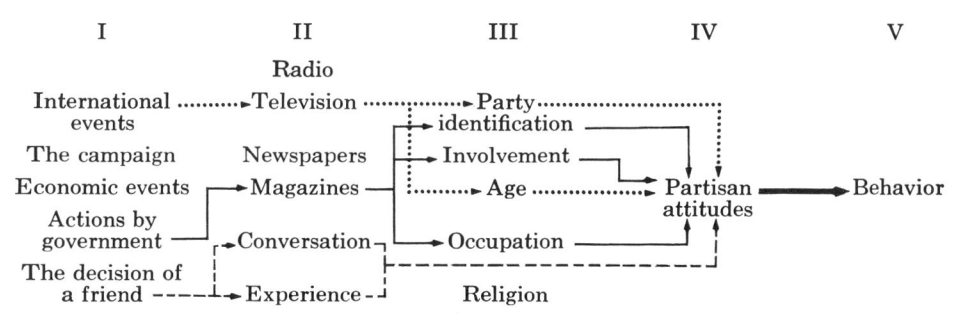

I	II	III	IV	V
International events	Radio	Party identification		
The campaign	Television	Involvement		
Economic events	Newspapers	Age	Partisan attitudes	Behavior
Actions by government	Magazines	Occupation		
The decision of a friend	Conversation	Religion		
	Experience			

Source: The somewhat more elaborate theoretical formulation from which this scheme of organization has been abstracted may be found in Chapter 2, "Theoretical Orientation," of *The American Voter, op. cit.*

ported in the past by the obviously important role of interest groups in politics. And, as we have suggested, the group-oriented view of the electorate has been pervasive. In part it has been popularized because presumably it has been relatively easy to identify the interests which the group and its members have in the implementation of governmental policy. Students of the legislative process have also emphasized the role of organized groups. Much of our literature on politics deals with the farm lobby or the NAM or organized labor or the AMA or other so called pressure groups. In this theory government is seen as a broker which achieves the general good through skillfully amalgamating the interests of the groups which make up our society.

A second popular explanation of voting is the normative thesis that citizens *should* vote because it is their civic duty to take part in the public affairs of the society. People vote out of a sense of the responsibilities and obligations of citizenship. People vote because they are good citizens.

Both of these explanations of electoral participation are indeed valid—but they are only partial explanations, derived from sophisticated theories of politics. What other clues to the making of the decision to cast a vote can we find? Our fivefold analytical scheme supplies some help in understanding the complex elements that sometimes go into the making of a decision as seemingly simple as casting a ballot for one party or candidate, or another.

Some of the other important explanations of participation have already been foreshadowed by our earlier discussion of such factors as age, sex, and formal education. To return for a moment to our consideration of the political implications of education: courses in civics and social studies or in American government and economics doubtless instruct some students in the realization of their personal goals through participation in the political process. Other people, however, develop, in the course of their education experiences, an interest in politics which is really much less political. It may have little to do with the political gratification of personal, social, and economic interests, but may be greatly involved in the excitement of nation-wide biennial battles for victory. Participation in politics based on such an interest has been described as participation inspired by "spectator interest."[5] Or, in another vein, given the fact that many people inherit political partisanship much as they are born into and learn a religion, education may make the nature of annual or biennial political competition more understandable. It may thereby simply foster a continuation of interest in that aspect of the family's social tradition which has to do with politics.

In discovering why people vote, there is another element to be considered. Education and occupation, let us suppose,

TABLE 10. VOTE TURNOUT BY INVOLVEMENT, EFFICACY, AND EDUCATION, OUTSIDE THE SOUTH, 1956

	Grade School	High School	College
High efficacy, high involvement			
Proportion voting	96%	89%	96%
Number of cases	48	197	137
High efficacy, low involvement: or low efficacy, high involvement			
Proportion voting	81%	83%	87%
Number of cases	158	287	59
Low efficacy, low involvement			
Proportion voting	53%	68%	92%
Number of cases	156	173	36

Source: From Chapter 17 of *The American Voter,* reproduced by permission of John Wiley and Sons, Inc., New York.

have fixed the status of the young adult in the social structure. His associates are the carriers of traditional or habitual ways of behaving. In the upper middle class he will quickly note that practically everyone who is physically and legally able to vote does so. In fact, a college education, without necessarily leading one into the top strata of society, seems to be the prelude to a social location which is characterized by regular participation in elections. Among persons who had been to college, variations in personal interest and involvement in politics, in one's own sense of personal effectiveness through political action or even variations in one's sense of the civic obligation to vote are almost totally unrelated to variations in turnout. Practically speaking, almost everybody who has been to college votes. We may well conclude that social pressures, whether overt or subtle, enforce a very high rate of political participation among members of such groups.

On the other hand, political participation in the lower strata of society is quite a different matter. Here, apparently, social traditions of consistent participation have not been developed and consequently are not uniformly enforced. Individual differences in frequency of voting are much greater, and they appear to be strongly influenced by a host of different factors. Among people whose education ended in grade school, personal attitudes toward politics are very important. A personal sense of involvement and effectiveness in politics, or a sense of civic duty, is quite necessary if the person is to vote regularly. Membership in groups which attempt to establish political participation as a group norm—as in many labor unions—also may be associated with a higher rate of voting, but personal political factors, as well as social and economic factors, play an important role in determining whether the manual laborer goes to the polls.

In short, participation in politics may have many uniquely personal and social roots as well as origins more manifestly political. Indeed, the thesis may be expanded to embrace peoples' interest in some of the objects of national politics themselves. The candidates, in particular, evoke sympathies and attachments which lead people to vote for them, but which do not necessarily carry implications for subsequent governmental action. A Presidential campaign is scarcely underway before it becomes apparent that two men are engaged in a gigantic contest for national favor. Those attributes of the candidates which attract attention and command approval or disapproval *may* relate to foreign and domestic policy, to the welfare of the farmer or the Negro or the business man —or they may relate to the nobility, the honesty, the sincerity, the intelligence, or the family life of the candidate. Is he

TABLE 11. THE DISTRIBUTION OF PARTY IDENTIFICATION

	Oct. 1952	Sept. 1953	Oct. 1954	April 1956	Oct. 1956	Nov. 1957	Oct. 1958
Strong Rep.	13%	15%	13%	14%	15%	10%	13%
Weak Rep.	14	15	14	18	14	16	16
Ind. Rep.	7	6	6	6	8	6	4
Independents	5	4	7	3	9	8	8
Ind. Dem.	10	8	9	6	7	7	7
Weak Dem.	25	23	25	24	23	26	24
Strong Dem.	22	22	22	19	21	21	23
Apolitical; don't know	4	7	4	10	3	6	5
Total	100%	100%	100%	100%	100%	100%	100%

Source: From Chapter 6 of *The American Voter*, reproduced by permission of John Wiley and Sons, Inc., New York. A detailed discussion of the origins and impact of party identification may be found in Chapters 6 and 7 of *The American Voter*.

a good speaker, does he have a warm smile, is he too pushy and aggressive, or is he too indecisive?

The general point of our argument is that from the perspective of the individual, the forces impelling him to be a participant in politics have extremely diverse origins. Behavior in response to many of these factors is not necessarily a response to group forces nor necessarily political in intent. The satisfactions the individual is attempting to realize through political participation may be essentially similar to those he realizes through other forms of individual or social behavior. He tells the truth, he votes Republican, he is kind to children, and he is interested in politics because, in each instance, he has learned that such behavior brings personal gratification when carried out.

Party Identification

One of the most important specific components of our fivefold system for analyzing electoral behavior has only been alluded to in the discussion up to now. It is the enduring political partisanship of four out of every five voters. When we center our attention on the vote, as we very largely have up to this point, we tend to emphasize the fluidity and propensity for change within the electorate. We think of the new candidates and the new issues which dominate the news of each election. We overlook the fact that the parties—the Republican and the Democratic parties—are among the most enduring political institutions known to Western civilization. And we tend to overlook the possibility that a sense of being a Democrat or being a Republican is not necessarily at all the same as voting for the candidate which a party has sponsored. In point of fact, considering oneself to be a Democrat while voting for Mr. Eisenhower was a very common phenomenon both in 1952 and 1956. The President could not have been elected nor re-elected had it not been for millions of Democrats who voted for him. And voting for him at least once, and sometimes twice, apparently did not convince many of these Democrats that maybe they were really Republicans after all.

Moreover, between 1952 and 1958 there was virtually no net change in the basic partisan loyalties of the entire American electorate. Before the election of 1952 there were three Democrats for every two Republicans among the citizens of the nation, and after the election of 1958 — with no appreciable change, year-by-year, in between — Republicans were still outnumbered by the same margin. The fact that this was so makes the Congressional elections of 1954, 1956, and 1958 considerably easier to understand. It seems clear that, by and large, voters voted their party loyalties when they voted for Congressmen, but they voted for many other reasons when they voted for a President in the same period.

These enduring party loyalties may be located in the third category of the fivefold analytical scheme as a special case of persistent group affiliation. People see themselves belonging to a political party much as they think of themselves as belonging to other social groups—church, union, or social class. In the case of the party, of course, the unique political implication of membership is quite obvious. The more general nature of the individual's sense that he is a strong and loyal Republican, or Democrat, is psychologically the same as his feeling that he is a good Catholic or a staunch union member. In each instance the person identifies himself with his group; what happens to his group happens to him, he flourishes or wanes with the group's triumphs and defeats.

Identification with party normally begins early in life and grows stronger with the passing years. Despite the fact that a large part of the present adult population experienced or took part in the political upheaval that followed the Great Depression of the 1930s, 80 percent of the adult citizens do not recall ever changing their party identification. This massive recollection of stable and endur-

TABLE 12. RELATION OF AGE TO PARTY IDENTIFICATION*

Party Identification	21-24	25-29	30-34	35-39	40-44	45-49	50-54	55-59	60-64	65-69	70-75	Over 75
Strong Dem.	16%	20%	21%	21%	24%	22%	25%	23%	23%	26%	28%	25%
Weak Dem.	32	29	29	31	29	24	23	22	21	18	17	17
Independent	31	26	24	23	22	23	19	20	19	15	14	16
Weak Rep.	13	18	16	15	15	16	17	16	18	19	16	16
Strong Rep.	8	7	10	10	10	15	16	19	19	22	25	26
	100%	100%	100%	100%	100%	100%	100%	100%	100%	100%	100%	100%
Proportion of strong identifiers	24	27	31	31	34	37	41	42	42	48	53	51
Number of cases	552	1038	1201	1221	1081	977	915	741	677	473	354	297

*These data are combined from seven national samples interviewed by the Survey Research Center between 1952 and 1957.

Source: From Chapter 7 of *The American Voter*, reproduced by permission of John Wiley and Sons, Inc., New York.

ing partisan commitments is consistent with the short-term stability we have seen for the 1952-1958 period in Table 11. Moreover, the age distribution of party identifiers by and large fits the thesis that Republicans tend to be persons who came of political age in the Republican era of the early 1900s or else are children of such families. Democrats, at the same time, tend to be the younger adults who have entered the electorate during and following the Depression and under the influence of the Democratic predominance of the present era. One possible influence of the preponderance of Democratic identifiers in the electorate is reflected in the almost overwhelming Democratic-to-Republican ratio among the youngest adults, those under 25 years of age.

The fundamentally important question of how stable party identification is cannot, however, be definitively answered as yet. The historical argument and the age-related differences in Democratic and Republican identification would tend to suggest that Republican strength must decline as death claims Republicans and Democrats in equal numbers while new adults enter the electorate at the rate of slightly less than one Republican for every two Democrats. And yet, over the seven-year span of our measurement of party identification in the electorate, the Republicans have not suffered any net decline in relative strength. Although the evidence on this point is not clear, it may well be that a persistently greater defection from Democratic ranks (among the small minority who do change their basic party loyalties) makes up for the Democratic advantage among new members of the electorate. Contrary to some popular theories, this defection is demonstrably not necessarily connected with upward social mobility, but it may have other as yet unspecified origins.[6]

Party identification is of tremendous importance as a factor shaping political behavior. This is so in large part because it establishes an underlying partisan predisposition which does much to shape attitudes toward the new and constantly changing phenomena of national politics. The events of the day, as they are somehow communicated to the citizen, acquire political meaning for him. And this political meaning is in large part a product of the fact that he perceives and evaluates the events as a partisan and through a partisan's eyes. The Republican-party identifier responds to news about national government, or an international crisis, as a Republican—not as an uncommitted, independent, and thoroughly objective recipient of the information. And where *his* interpretations are likely to fit his pre-existing commitment to Republicanism, his Democratic counterpart is probably going to respond to the same news as a Democrat. Short of great provocation, neither of them is going to discard all that he has come to believe and know merely to avoid a partisan interpretation to new information.

A good example of the extent to which prior partisan commitments influence new political attitudes was provided by popular reaction to the Suez crisis of 1956. In the middle of the Presidential campaign, war threatened in the Middle East. There was much speculation about the impact which this might have on the voting at election time. Because we interviewed the same people both before and after the election, it was possible to assess quite precisely what the voters' response to the crisis actually was. Only a small minority of the voters responded at all — less than 10 percent. But those who did respond did so in a fashion that was least disruptive and disturbing to the commitments which they had already made prior to the crisis. Most of the voters who had planned to vote for Stevenson said something like, "See, the Suez problem proves that Eisenhower is not doing a good job and we need Stevenson to resolve the crisis and prevent war." Most of the voters who had planned to vote for Eisenhower replied at the same time, "See, the Suez crisis is just the sort of emergency I had in mind, one which demands the skill and experience of a soldier like Eisenhower; we must re-elect him if we want somebody who knows about these things leading our country." To be sure, an occasional voter intending to vote for Eisenhower saw the Suez crisis as a failure of American foreign policy and switched to Stevenson; and a few Stevenson intenders were afraid to lose the advantage of Eisenhower's military experience abroad and switched their votes to support the President. But most voters merely fitted the new information into an old partisan frame, used the new situation further to justify their previous decision, and voted the way they had intended to vote all along.

Identification with a political party provides the same sort of "standing decision" regarding partisan politics. Year in and year out it is a powerful determinant of the political attitudes of the 80 percent of the Americans who consider themselves to be Democrats or Republicans.

Partisan Attitudes

Although a person's educational background or his religion or his party identification seldom undergo any change between two elections, some of his partisan attitudes toward the affairs of politics do change in response to new events and new situations. It is true that most of his attitudes will probably be conditioned by his education or his social class or his party identification—or any of the other politically relevant but stable attributes—but it is also true that his attitudes will sometimes reflect changing events on the political scene. The fourth class of political phenomena—the political attitudes — are crucially important because they are sensitive reflections of the many factors — both stable and changing—which lie behind the vote decision. In the attitudes of the citizens we can see the impact of a popular Republican candidate on Democratic-party identifiers, or the effect of a recession on Republicans. If an increase in income, or a promotion on the job, has any political significance it will be mirrored in the accompanying changes of political attitudes.

The vote, on the other hand, is, in many ways, a very crude measure of a man's political hopes and fears, his aspirations and commitments. The voter who is tremendously excited about the election cannot cast more votes nor a stronger vote than the voter who gets to the polls only because somebody persuaded him to go and offered him a ride to get there. The voter with a wide range of interests must somehow express all of them in a single vote. He can't cast one vote labeled "for foreign policy," another for his favorite candidate, and a third for the party of his choice. And if all three of his causes for political concern favor one party's candidate, he still cannot cast a vote that is more unequivocally partisan and therefore different from the vote of his confused neighbor who likes one thing about one party but also likes something else equally well about the opposite party. A vote is a vote is a vote. Each person casts only one and it counts no more and no less than any other. It will be for one party's candidate and no more partisan when cast by the fanatic partisan identifier than when cast by a man who mentally flips a coin to decide his vote.

The range and complexity of each person's political interests may, however, be captured in the political attitudes of the voter. If all of the considerations that go into each single vote decision are put down, and if the relative contribution of each to the vote can be assessed, we can in a manner of speaking "decompose" the vote into its attitudinal components. Each attitudinal component can then be taken up in turn in a search for the factors which lie behind it. Our fundamental task of comprehending the meaning of the vote, both in terms of the voter and in terms of governmental decisions subsequent to the election, is thereby greatly facilitated.[7]

Even if we are not self-consciously interested in ferreting out the antecedents of specific attitudes, a comparison of the attitudes provoked by two different election situations may do much to inform us of the elements important in the elections. A comparison of selected attitudes toward Mr. Eisenhower and Mr. Stevenson in 1952 and 1956, for example, tells us a good bit about the basis for Eisenhower's second triumph and Stevenson's second defeat. In 1952, Stevenson, the man, was not widely known; people made three comments about Mr. Eisenhower's personal attributes to every two such references made to Mr. Stevenson. But on the matter of drawing favorable or unfavorable comment, Stevenson fully matched the very positive appeal of Eisenhower; 70 percent of the comments about each candidate were favorable and supportive. By 1956 the Eisenhower margin in sheer volume of attitudinal response had been reduced somewhat. But more important than his still commanding the lead in prominence and familiarity was the dramatic shift in public favor. In their second campaign, Eisenhower's popularity held steady at the 1952 level while the negative references to Stevenson increased and the positive references decreased to the point that slightly more than half of all responses to his personal attributes were unfavorable. . . .

A relatively full discussion of these attitudes has been provided elsewhere. For our present discussion it is enough to note that attitudes of this kind, pertaining to the parties and the issues of the day as well as to the personal attributes of the candidates, can be and have been used to represent the fourth class of political phenomena. From the full array of immediately contemporary partisan attitudes we can ascertain the attitudinal components of the electoral decision. They can be usefully employed to describe an election, to compare two or more elections, or to provide the foundation for a complex analysis of electoral behavior.

STABILITY AND CHANGE IN THE ELECTORAL DECISION

To place the relatively stable political, social, and economic classifications (the third category of phenomena) side by side with the more fluid mixture of changing attitudes toward the events and actors of the national political scene (the fourth category of phenomena) suggests an important problem in the analysis of political behavior. The problem is that of ascertaining the balance that exists between elements of stability and elements of change in the political reactions of the electorate. Group and class categories of behavior do not help to ascertain this balance because the rates and directions of social change have not kept pace with the changes in political behavior that we want to explain. On the other hand, if we concentrate just on the role of political attitudes in determining individual behavior, the view of politics we derive may be as completely fluid as the other is static. If we ignore the social and psychological continuities which in fact characterize much of human action, we may even become entranced with the possibility of manipulated change. We may imagine that a cleverly designed campaign, or the proper response to the adventitious appearance of a crisis in public policy, or the appeal of a striking candidate may have such an all-important impact on the outcome of an election as to provide us with our explanation of political behavior.

Many who are actively involved in politics, particularly a political candidate or his advisor, are too ready to accept such a view of politics. It is, of course, partly true that influence can be exerted over the formation of the attitudes which are a prelude to behavior. But active political people tend to exaggerate the possibility, and to believe that with enough money or time or television talent, a candidate can assure himself victory at the polls. And it is equally persuasive for the defeated partisan to attribute his defeat to the superior resources of the opposition.

On the other hand, much evidence can be assembled to illustrate the ponderous slowness with which political attitudes actually do change. And it can be suggested that the dominant source of change which does occur is not to be found in the deliberate act of a publicist or a campaign manager, but in the nonpolitical events which impinge on the daily routine of the voter.

Research in elections tends to show that the electoral decision has an enduring nature at least for most voters, and in the historical short run. In support of V. O. Key's concept of the "standing decision," there is much evidence that the elections of a given era show a basic sameness. Many research findings confirm the impression that a great constancy characterizes the intent and the deed of most voters.

But many practitioners of the art and science of governance are convinced that their daily acts—the decisions of candidate, party, or government—make and break tomorrow's political fortunes. It seems equally clear from the record that much, if not most, of the variation in political fortune lies beyond the control of individual decision makers. The major secular changes in the behavior of the electorate have been the unanticipated consequence of national crisis rather than the purposeful attainment of partisan political advantage. Although we lack definitive proof, it is likely that the Civil War and the Great Depression each resulted in establishing party loyalties which persisted for decades thereafter. The Civil War made the United States a predominantly Republican nation for the seventy years between 1860 and 1930, and the Depression made us a Democratic nation from 1930 until the present and perhaps beyond. Even the shorter shifts in the balance of political power have tended to be the result of largely fortuitous circumstance—the short-run financial panic of the turn of the century, a first World War which followed on the heels of a schism within Republican leadership, and a Korean war which gave twentieth-century Democratic Presidents an unhappy monopoly on the responsibility of directing a nation at war. This is not to say that the considered acts of political leadership have no consequence in subsequent tests at the polls; it *is* to say that the events of greatest political significance for modern American politics were not fashioned by those in power with the intent of producing the results we have observed. In retrospect first one party and then the other has benefited from the basic constancy of individual partisan loyalties, or has reaped a sometimes undeserved reward as the result of the misadventure and misfortune of others. Recent studies have disclosed few portents of future change in this state of affairs. The nature of American politics of tomorrow, the forces which will make for its stability and change, are not likely to be radically different from those of the recent past.

Just as the basic shaping of the electorate may be viewed as a product of epochal social and economic events, individual, short-run changes may be due to nonpolitical, social, and economic circumstances. The preceding comments on the role of party identification and partisan attitudes emphasized the central role which is properly assigned to completely *political* attitudes. The political attitudes of the citizen *are* of prime importance because they present the political evaluations which lie immediately prior to the vote and which are derived from the individual's interpretation of public and semipublic events. Nevertheless, despite the preoccupation of many political analysts with the daily circuit of the Washington merry-go-round, and despite the wealth of reported detail describing the plans and performances of political VIPs across the country, there is good reason to believe that most singularly political events are of minor, limited, immediate importance as antecedents to the decision at the polls. There is only meager evidence that the political actions of partisan leaders have the *immediate* electoral consequences which are traditionally presumed.

It can easily be shown that many nonpolitical events have unintended political consequences. For example, against the backdrop of Gilbraltarlike partisan loyalties, the geographical movement of people remakes local and even regional political alignments. The movers' search for new social and economic opportunities results, for some few, in the finding of new political commitments as well; but for most, the principal result is to provide a partially new setting in which to manifest old political values. The consequences for local party organizations and leaders, or even for politicians on the national scene, may be considerable, but the implications for the attitudes and the vote of the individual are almost negligible.[8]

Although individual political commitments are strikingly stable, changes do take place because of certain kinds of group membership. These exceptions, however, do not weaken our conclusions about the nonpolitical origins of important political developments. The new union member doesn't join the organization so that he can be coached in the political postures of his union, but time and propinquity nevertheless operate to accomplish a considerable political education. The southern Negro who moves North may have a predisposition to change his politics. But, again, the data support the conclusion that change in his political attitudes and behavior occurs only relatively slowly *after* exposure to new norms. More broadly, the establishment of political norms for a group may well be an important act of political leadership by the elite of the group, but the individual member responding to those norms is usually responding more as a social animal than as political man.

Without denying the importance of external political events, one may affirm and reaffirm the political importance of nonpolitical phenomena. Such affirmations are cumulative. They leave little alternative to the conclusion that much of political stability, and perhaps most short-run political change, originate at points in life not obviously labeled as the first causes of political behavior. For those readers with a sense of the worth of ancient seers, this may be no more than long overdue recognition of the declared wholeness of man and the seamlessness of the web of government.

Notes

[1] For descriptions of national electoral behavior, see A. Campbell and R. Kahn, *The People Elect A President* (Ann Arbor, Mich.: Institute for Social Research, 1952); Campbell, G. Gurin, and W. E. Miller, *The Voter Decides* (Evanston, Ill.: Row, Peterson and Co., 1954); and Campbell and H. Cooper, *Group Differences in Attitudes and Votes* (Ann Arbor, Mich.: Institute for Social Research, 1956). Comprehensive discussions of the voting behavior of groups are also contained in P. Lazarsfeld, B. Berelson, and H. Gaudet, *The People's Choice* (New York: Columbia University Press, 1948); Berelson, Lazarsfeld, and W. McPhee, *Voting* (Chicago: University of Chicago Press, 1954); and E. Burdick and A. J. Brodbeck (eds.), *American Voting Behavior* (Glencoe, Ill.: The Free Press, 1958).

[2] A detailed analysis of age-related voting behavior may be found in Chapter 17 of A. Campbell, P. E. Converse, W. E. Miller, and D. E. Stokes, *The American Voter* (New York: John Wiley and Sons, 1960).

[3] See, for example, the discussion of "Sam Hodder," pp. 196-203, in M. B. Smith, J. S. Bruner, and R. W. White, *Opinions and Personality*, (New York: John Wiley and Sons, 1956).

[4] The development of this concept and a full discussion of its relationship to theories of social class may be found in Chapter 13, "The Role of Social Class," *The American Voter, op. cit.*

[5] See W. S. Robinson, "The Motivational Structure of Political Participation," *Amer. Soc. Rev.*, 17 (1952), pp. 151-156.

[6] Neither intergenerational nor intragenerational mobility appear to be related to changes in party identification. See Chapter 16, *The American Voter, op. cit.*

[7] See D. E. Stokes, A. Campbell, and W. E. Miller, "Components of Electoral Decisions," *Amer. Pol. Sci. Rev.*, 52, 3 (June 1958), pp. 367-387. Also, Chapters 3, 4, and 5 of *The American Voter, op. cit.*

[8] See Chapter 16, "Population Movement," *The American Voter, op. cit.*

While presidential elections consistently attract a higher percentage of the potential electorate to the polls than do state or local elections, the generally accepted figure of those eligible to vote who do vote in presidential elections is only 60 percent. The use of the terms "potential" and "eligible" illustrate a problem in analyzing voting data. They are nonsynonymous terms. This confusion might be little more than a semantic problem hardly worthy of mention if it had not resulted in a prevailing assumption that a large percentage (approximately 40 percent) of the American adult citizenry are politically apathetic. Because of this assumption, invidious, and also erroneous, comparisons have been drawn between the American adult citizenry and the "eligible" electorate of other Western democracies. William Andrews explores the implications of this confusion of terms and suggests that legal barriers, not apathy, are the primary cause of "non-voting." Once Americans are "eligible" to vote, their turn-out percentages compare very favorably with other nations.

American Voting Participation

William G. Andrews

It is generally assumed that about two-thirds of the American electorate vote in a presidential-year election. This is the figure that is used in the standard American government textbooks, in most specialized studies, and by public officials.[1] It is calculated by dividing the civilian voting-age population into the total number of votes cast for President and increasing the result arbitrarily by several percentage points to account for persons of voting age who are legally excluded from the electorate. Research for the present article suggests that the two-thirds figure is too low. In 1960, at least, probably between 80 and 85 per cent of persons who were legally and physically able to vote did so. This suggests that much of the discussion about apathetic, uninterested, lazy, and alienated voters rests on false information. It also indicates that some of the unfavorable comparisons made with voting participation in other countries may not be valid.[2]

Reprinted by permission of the University of Utah, copyright owners, William G. Andrews, "American Voting Participation," *Western Political Quarterly,* 19 (December, 1966), 639-654.

The two-thirds figure is low for three principal reasons: (1) The number of persons excluded from the electorate by law is higher than is usually assumed. (2) The figure does not take into account persons unable to vote because of a combination of personal circumstances and legal requirements, especially the requirement that one vote at a polling place near his residence unless he anticipates an impediment that is legally acceptable as grounds for issuing an absentee ballot. Nor does it take into account Negroes who are excluded from the electorate by intimidation. (3) The number of persons who vote in an election is greater than the number who cast valid ballots for President.

Some estimates used in this study must be very rough approximations. In the first place, available election statistics are incomplete and often not comparable among states. For instance, very few states report the number of spoiled ballots and others do not report the total number of valid ballots. Secondly, official or authoritative statistics on some relevant population characteristics are incomplete or unavailable. The number of persons who do not meet state residence requirements, for instance, can be estimated only in a very general way, and there is even less basis for estimating the number of persons who are traveling or ill on election day and are not eligible for absentee ballots.[3] Thirdly, there are some sticky problems of definition. What is a pauper? What is an insane person? Finally, there seems to be no easy way to estimate with confidence the extent of overlap among different categories. An alien, illiterate prison inmate is thrice excluded from the electorate, yet he is counted only once in the total civilian voting-age population. Nor is it feasible to estimate the number of legally excluded persons who actually do vote, or the amount of "ballot box stuffing," or deliberately uncounted valid votes. With so many uncertainties and calculated guesses the following estimates can make only limited claim to definitiveness. It seems unlikely, however, that the main point of this article is undermined as a result. In any case, the available data do seem to provide a more precise estimate of electoral participation than has been made previously.

The figures 106,974,000 and 68,836,355 are the ones usually used in reaching the two-thirds estimate for the 1960 election.[4] My research shows that the first figure is larger than the actual legal, effective electorate and that the second figure is lower than the actual number of voters. The next two sections of this article will whittle away at the first figure. The third section will augment the second figure.

The Bureau of the Census estimates that there were 106,974,000 civilians of voting age in the United States on November 1, 1960. This includes all non-military persons residing in the fifty states and the District of Columbia, whether or not residing on federal reservations or in institutions. It does not include persons living abroad or in the dependencies whether or not they are civilian dependents of military personnel. The Clerk of the House of Representatives reported that 68,836,385 valid votes were cast for President in 1960. This includes all valid votes cast for legal elector candidates as far as reported by the appropriate state authorities. It omits spoiled and blank ballots and many write-in votes.[5]

LEGAL EXCLUSIONS

Residence Requirements

The most numerous group of persons excluded from the electorate by law is composed of those who do not meet residence requirements. All states in 1960 had some type of residence requirements for voting, although three states[6] permitted persons to vote for President without meeting the residence requirements imposed as prerequisites to voting for state and local offices. There was great variation in the states' requirements. The most restrictive state was Mississippi which required residence of two years in the state and one year in the election district.[7] The most liberal was Idaho, which permitted voting after residing six months in the state and 30 days in the county. Typically, the prospective voter must have resided in the state one year and, less often, in the county 90 days and in the precinct 30 days.[8]

Key estimates the percentage of otherwise qualified voters who are excluded from the electorate for failure to meet residence requirements at 5 per cent.[9] Another scholar sets the figure at 4.3 for the 1950 election.[10] In 1960, 5 per cent of the estimated civilian voting-age population was 5,348,700 persons and 4.3 per cent was 4,599,882. The American Heritage Foundation estimates that in the year preceding the 1960 elections, 33 million Americans moved, of whom about 8 million were thereby disfranchised.[11] The census bureau estimated that from March 1, 1960, to March 1, 1961, 6,510,000 persons twenty-one years of age or over moved between counties, 3,319,000 moved between states, and 13,806,000 moved within counties.[12] It may be assumed from these figures that about 1,627,500 persons moved between counties during the 90 days preceding the election and were thereby disfranchised in most cases. The 3,319,000 may similarly be presumed to have been disfranchised. The intra-county movers moved at the rate of 1,150,500 per month, but, of course, not all of them changed precincts. If we assume that one-third of them (550,000) did, we arrive at a total figure of 5.5 million. Some of them — let us say 100,000 — escaped disfranchisement in one way or another. This leaves a total very close to the Key estimate mentioned above, 5.4 million.

Aliens

A second major group excluded legally is composed of adult aliens, of whom there were about 2.75 million in 1960:[13] No state has permitted aliens to vote since 1928.[14] Also, in 1960, three states[15] excluded aliens naturalized less than 90 days before the election.[16] In addition, of course, aliens naturalized after the end of the registration period were excluded. Twenty-six states closed registration more than 30 days before polling day. New Hampshire and Rhode Island closed their books 60 days before election day. Mississippi's lead time was four months and Georgia's was six months. In Texas and Arkansas the poll tax rolls served as a substitute for registration. The Texas rolls closed for the 1960 election on January 1, 1960. In Arkansas they closed on October 1, 1960. Based on the average rate of naturalization in these states and on the percentage of all naturalized citizens who were twenty-one years or older as reported by the Immigration and Naturalization Service, about 53,000 recently naturalized citizens may have been excluded by these stipulations, raising the total number of persons excluded because of citizenship requirements to about 2.8 million.

Illiterates

Twenty states excluded persons illiterate in English from the suffrage in 1960. The number of illiterates in any language of voting age residing in those states in 1960 was about 1.37 million.[17] Other states— Kansas and Ohio, for instance — effectively exclude illiterates by denying them assistance in marking their ballots.[18]

There were 101,000 illiterates of voting age in Kansas and Ohio alone in 1960.[19] If all adult illiterates, regardless of legal eligibility, are considered excluded, the number would be 2.75 million. Furthermore, the Census Bureau defines illiteracy as "inability to read and write a simple message either in English or any other language," whereas every state, except Hawaii, requiring literacy specifies English, and most of them require an understanding of at least part of the state constitution.[20] As one example of the discrepancy between the literacy standards of the Census Bureau and those of a state, 9.21 per cent of the persons taking the New York test in 1945 failed, whereas in 1960 only 2.9 per cent of New York's population over fourteen years old was classified as illiterate. Such a difference in 1960 would have accounted for about 685,000 persons of voting age.[21] It seems likely, therefore, that the total number of persons excluded because of illiteracy (not including literate Negroes in the South) in 1960 was at least 3.4 million: 1.4 million counted by the Census Bureau in 20 states; 1.5 million literate but not in English, in the same states; 0.5 million illiterates unable to vote in the other 30 states because of the unavailability of assistance.

Mental Incapacity

Thirty-eight states have some provision in their election laws to exclude persons with impaired mental faculties. In the others, judicial decisions have produced the same result.[22] On April 1, 1960, there were 697,371 adult persons in mental hospitals or institutions for the mentally handicapped.[23] There were also about 300,000 adult persons "unable to carry on a major activity because of mental or nervous condition" who were not confined to institutions.[24] It seems impossible to estimate the number of mentally ill persons who are legally excluded. As the leading authority on the question points out, however, practical problems effectively exclude those who are confined to institutions or otherwise unable to go to the polls.[25]

Prisoners

All states exclude prison inmates[26] and six of them exclude the inmates of all penal institutions.[27] The total number of persons so confined on April 1, 1960, was 208,947.[28] In many states a convicted felon who is no longer confined is permanently deprived of his voting rights unless they are expressly restored by formal, official action by the state governor, legislature, or special commission. About 1.5 million persons seem to fall in the category of ex-convicts. Some have had their voting rights restored through executive pardons. Data on the number are very fragmentary, but indicate that there are about two pardons for every 100 releases.[29] Making liberal allowance for them, it is probably safe to assume about 1.4 million persons were unable to vote in 1960 because they had been convicts.

District of Columbia Residents

In the 1960 elections residents of the District of Columbia were still without the suffrage. At that time there were approximately 0.5 million persons of voting age residing in the District.

Paupers

Paupers are specifically excluded from suffrage in eleven states.[30] The term "pauper" is subject to wide variation in interpretation. It would seem to include persons receiving care in homes for the aged and dependent and persons receiving public relief payments (general assistance). In 1960 there were 80,075 persons twenty years and older in homes for the aged and dependent in those eleven states, and in December 1959, 52,606 persons were receiving general assistance welfare payments in the same states. It is reasonable to assume that there must be many additional persons —the skid row derelicts, town bums, etc., —who do not find a spot in those data. Their number, however, can hardly be estimated. A very modest guess would suggest that the total number of "paupers" in the eleven states might be about 150,000.

OTHER EXCLUSIONS

In addition to those persons excluded from the electorate by express legal or constitutional provision, there is a large group excluded for other reasons. This category includes persons who were ill, traveling, or in the military service on election day. It also includes intimidated Negroes and, because they exclude themselves for religious reasons, members of the Jehovah's Witnesses religious sect.

Absentees

Some of the persons who were ill, traveling, or in military service voted by absentee ballot. There were about 3.4 million absentee ballots cast in 1960.[31] Some persons were unable to cast absentee ballots, because state law did not permit them to do so, because they were too ill, or because their illness developed or their plans to travel were made so shortly before election day that they could not apply for absentee ballots before the legal deadline. State-by-state breakdowns of statistics on illness and traveling are not available. It has been necessary, therefore, to make some assumptions that obviously are not wholly valid but that, on balance, would seem to provide as close an approximation to the truth as is possible with such statistics as are available. These are: (1) that all states permitted absentee voting on grounds of illness or travel;[32] (2) that all chronically ill persons, students, and travelers were able to cast absentee ballots; and (3) that no persons suffering from acute illnesses voted by absentee ballot.[33]

About 2,464,000 adult persons each day, on the average, October through December 1960, were at home suffering from acute illnesses so severe as to prevent them from engaging in their regular major activity (work or housework in most cases). It is assumed that one of these was able to vote.[34]

From July 1959 through June 1961, an average of about 3,818,000 adult persons each day suffered at home from chronic illnesses that prevented them from engaging in a major activity. This number includes about 304,000 with mental or nervous conditions who have been accounted for elsewhere in this study. The net total of non-institutionalized chronically ill persons, therefore, is about 3,514,000.[35]

There was, in 1958 through 1960, a daily average of 378,060 adult patients in short-stay hospitals.[36] It may fairly be assumed that these patients were suffering from acute conditions and were unable to vote by absentee ballot.[37]

On April 1, 1960, there were the following patients of voting age in other types of hospitals: 60,297 in tuberculosis hospitals; 40,815 in hospitals for chronic illness, except tuberculosis and mental illness; 2,189 in homes and schools for the physically handicapped; 463,432 in homes for the aged and dependent; 918 in detention homes; 139 in diagnostic and reception centers; and 651 in homes for unwed mothers—a total of 568,441. Some in that population would fail to qualify because of mental incompetence or indigence and others were simply too ill to vote. We may speculate that some were able to vote in person at the polls. Most of them, however, could have voted only by absentee ballot and, in most cases, they would have been able to obtain such ballots.[38]

About 500,000 full-time college students twenty-one years and over were living away from their legal residence in 1960. In most states they were eligible for absentee ballots.[39]

Some 3.3 million persons of voting age were members of the armed forces, wives of servicemen, or dependent parents residing with servicemen.[40] Because of their failure to meet residence requirements at their military stations, state laws preventing active-duty military families from establishing legal residence, the serviceman's preference to maintain his legal residence at his pre-military residence, or overseas assignment, most of those persons could vote only by absentee ballot.

Also, about 300,000 civilians and their adult dependents were overseas employees of the national government in 1960.[41]

About 1.6 million adult persons were traveling on election day.[42] The estimate may be low because it includes only journeys of at least 200 miles round-trip or overnight and because the tendency of the interviewees to forget trips "has lowered the general estimate of the total number of trips . . . by perhaps as much as one-third."[43] On the other hand, it is based on a quarterly total for October through December and probably there was more traveling during the holiday season than on election day.

About 0.1 million adult persons were confined in penal institutions but not legally deprived of their voting rights.[44]

The groups assumed to be eligible for absentee ballots totaled about 9.9 million persons. The institutionalized or ill persons assumed not to be able to vote by absentee ballots totaled about 3.8 million. The entire voting-age population, including about 900,000 military and civilian government personnel and dependents overseas,[45] was 107.9 million. Thus, about 94.2 million persons of voting age were physically able to vote in person. Of these, about 66.4 million (70.5 per cent) did so.[46] If the eligible absentees had voted at the same rate, 7.0 million would have done so. As only 3.4 million absentee ballots were cast, it seems that about 3.6 million persons failed to vote because of the difficulty or impossibility of casting absentee ballots.[47]

Southern Negroes

A major group that is excluded without the use of express legal provisions is composed of Negroes, especially in the South, who are prevented from voting by intimidation or the discriminatory enforcement of election laws. Calculations based on the 1961 United States Commission on Civil Rights Report indicate that about 1.9 million Negroes were so excluded.[48] That figure was deduced by determining the number of Negroes who would have been registered to vote in thirteen southern or border states[49] if they were registered at the same rate as the white residents in those states and subtracting from that figure the number who actually did register.[50]

Jehovah's Witnesses

Finally, there are some 239,418 adult Jehovah's Witnesses whose religious beliefs prevent their taking part in elections.[51]

Total

The total of the groups excluded indirectly or illegally was about 8.6 million persons. When this is added to the 14.85 million who were excluded legally, one arrives at a total of 23.45 million who could not vote.

OVERLAP AND ILLEGAL VOTERS

No doubt the figures in the two preceding sections conceal a certain amount of overlap. This is impossible to measure with exactness. Some categories do not overlap at all; others do. The illiterate group, those ill at home, traveling, in the military service, or attending college do not overlap any of the institutionalized groups. On the other hand, the excluded group must be reduced by about 0.5 million if the illiteracy rate is the same in the whole population as it is in these groups: those lacking residence eligibility, aliens, non-institutionalized mentally disabled, ex-convicts, paupers, Jehovah's Witnesses, the acutely ill, travelers, and jailees. It must be reduced a further 0.4 million to take into account aliens in all categories except illiterates and southern Negroes. Subtract another 0.5 million for movers who have been otherwise excluded.

None of the other categories would seem to contain significant overlap. If one adds 0.1 million to the 1.4 million so far identified, overlap would seem to be accounted for sufficiently. Subtraction of the 1.5 million overlap from the 23.45 million persons excluded leaves a 21.95 million remainder.

Another of the insoluble problems raised by this study is an estimate of the number of persons who vote, though not legally eligible. There must be a certain number of persons who do so because the enforcement of the exclusions depends on a challenge. For instance, an ex-convict who has broken with his past may vote to avoid embarrassing questions as to why he does not.

THE NUMBER OF VOTERS

As the number of potential voters has often been overestimated, so has the number of actual voters been underestimated. More persons vote in an election than are reported as having voted for President. This is especially true if one accepts the Supreme Court's interpretation that most primary elections are integral parts of the electoral process. Once again, the fragmentary nature of the evidence makes it very difficult to estimate with confidence the number of additional voters. They fall into three main categories: (1) those who cast invalid ballots; (2) those who cast valid ballots but no presidential vote; and (3) those who vote in primaries but not in general elections and are not otherwise accounted for in this study.

Accurate and complete data are exceedingly difficult to obtain for the first two categories. Large numbers of invalid ballots are probably never reported from the precincts or counties and, in some cases at least, the total number of ballots cast is not reported either. Even when they are, they are often inaccurate.[52] Rhode Island officials placed counters on the voting booths and learned that a number of voters equal to 2 per cent of the presidential vote entered the polling booths in the 1960 general elections but cast no valid ballot for President. The corresponding figure while paper ballots were being used was from 8 to 10 per cent.[53] Indiana election data for 1960 support those conclusions. In 58 counties only paper ballots were used, in 27 counties only voting machines were used, and in the remaining 6 counties some ballots were paper and some machine, with the latter heavily predominating (194 precincts to 37). In 21 of the paper-ballot and 7 of the voting-machine counties the returns were obviously erroneous. In the remaining 37 paper-ballot counties the difference between the total vote cast and the presidential vote was 7.2 per cent of the presidential vote. In the remaining 20 voting-machine counties the comparable figure was 0.7 per cent, and in the mixed counties it was 2.3 per cent. The statewide figure for those 63 counties was 2.6 per cent.[54]

In 1960 about half the votes in the general election across the nation were cast by machine and half by paper ballot.[55] Generalizing from the Rhode Island and Indiana experiences, one would conclude that the number of persons who entered voting booths but had no vote counted for President in 1960 was equal to about 5 per cent of the presidential vote, that is, about 3.6 million voters.[56]

On the other hand, an examination of all published official state election returns discloses that twenty-one states have reported some data, varying considerably in completeness, on total votes cast and invalid ballots. They ranged from 0.7 per cent in Utah to 2.6 per cent in Indiana, the median being 1.2 and the cumulative average, 1.4.[57] Probably states using voting machines extensively are disproportionately represented among them. For instance, they include no southern states. Taking into account this probability and the incompleteness of much of the data, a figure of 1.5 per cent nationally, 1.0 million votes, would seem reasonable. Thus, we may conclude that the number of general election voters who failed to cast valid ballots for President probably numbered between 1.0 million and 3.6 million persons in 1960.

About 0.9 million persons in the South voted in the primary but not in the general elections of 1960. This figure is obtained from a close analysis of county-by-county primary and general election returns in Georgia, Alabama, South Carolina, Tennessee, Texas, Louisiana, North Carolina, Mississippi, and Florida. No primary election results are published by Arkansas. Only primary election results for congressional contests are published by Virginia. Louisiana was the only state in 1960 in which more votes were cast in the primary than in the general election. The net difference was 93,222 votes. However, in three parishes at least one office in the general election received more votes than did any office in the primary election, for a total difference of 7,083. This means that in the remaining parishes 100,305 more votes were cast in the primary than in the general election.[58]

In North Carolina there was only one county with a higher primary than general election vote and the difference was only 22 votes. In Mississippi there were no such counties. In each of the other states on which data are available at least 30 counties had higher primary votes with the differences totaling at least 18,000 in every case. Table 1 summarizes this information.

It seems fair to assume that Arkansas and Virginia also have in the neighborhood of 20,000 more votes reported by counties in primaries than in general elections. This would raise the aggregate to about 290,000. Furthermore, it is very likely that, if precinct returns could be inspected, a similar number of votes would be found concealed at that level. That is, another 290,000 votes or more have probably been cast in the primaries than in the general elections in precincts of counties in which more general election than primary votes were cast; or were canceled out at the county level in the 315 counties mentioned above by other precincts in those counties that had more general than primary election votes. Finally, there must certainly be a substantial number of southern voters— let us say another 290,000 — who voted in the primary but not in the general election, yet who do not appear in either

TABLE 1. SOUTHERN COUNTIES IN WHICH THE VOTES CAST FOR AN OFFICE IN THE PRIMARY ELECTION NEAREST THE 1960 GENERAL ELECTIONS EXCEEDED THAT OF ANY OFFICE IN THE 1960 GENERAL ELECTIONS AND TOTAL OF SUCH VOTES IN EACH OF THE STATES.

State	Number of Counties	Total Difference
Alabama	31	19,989
Florida	29	19,120
Georgia	63	39,704
Louisiana	61	100,305
Mississippi	—	—
North Carolina	1	22
South Carolina	30	30,157
Tennessee	32	18,062
Texas	68	23,275
Total	315	250,612

Sources: *World Almanac 1964*; Florida, Secretary of State, *Report, 1959-1960*; *Louisiana Almanac and Fact Book 1962*; *Georgia's Official Register, 1959-1960*; *North Carolina Manual 1962*; *Mississippi Official and Statistical Register 1960-1964*; (Tennessee) "Democratic Primary, August 4, 1960" (mimeo): *Texas Almanac 1961-1962*; and *Alabama Official and Statistical Register 1959*. As the results of the 1960 primaries in South Carolina and Alabama had not yet been published, it was necessary to rely on those of the 1958 in the former state and 1956 in the latter.

of the above figures, their performance having been concealed by an equal number who voted in the general but not in the primary election in the same precincts. Add to that number a relatively small category of northern voters who went only to the primary polls, and appear nowhere else in our calculations, and it would seem safe to assume that roughly 1.0 million Americans who did not vote in the general election of 1960 voted in the nearest primaries.

CONCLUSIONS

The above inventory contains gaps and guesses. Some of the statistics on which it is based are square pegs driven into not-so-square holes. Additional research including, it is planned, use of the one-in-a-thousand-household questionnaires of the 1960 census and questionnaires to secretaries of state and other state election data-gathering officials may remove some of the remaining uncertainties. The present state of available data, however, makes it unlikely that conclusive and exact statistics can be calculated.

Nevertheless, we are able to define the size of the electorate more closely than has been done before. About 14.85 million of the 107 million persons of voting age were legally excluded from the electorate. Another 8.6 million persons were unable to vote because of illness, absence from their legal residences, intimidation, or religious beliefs. About 1.5 million persons have been accounted for more than once in different categories. This indicates a legal, able electorate of 85.1 million persons. Of that number, 68.8 million persons cast valid ballots for President in the general elections, 1.0 million voted in the general elections without casting valid presidential ballots, and 1.0 million voted in the primaries but not in the general election and are otherwise unaccounted for in the inventory. This means that about 83.2 per cent of the eligible, able electorate voted in 1960 — a figure nearly 20 per cent higher than the one generally used to indicate voting participation in the United States. One can reasonably conclude that between 80 and 85 per cent of the American electorate voted in 1960.

Furthermore, it cannot be assumed that the remaining 15 to 20 per cent was indifferent or alienated. It must include a sizable number of voters who were neither ill nor absent yet were prevented from voting by forces beyond their control. The doctor who plans to vote after supper but is called out on an emergency case, the fisherman who expects to return from the sea before the polls close but is held up by a storm, the mother whose small child has suddenly come down with the measles, the telephone lineman called out to repair a broken line, the motorist involved in a fender-bender on his way home from work or en route to the polls are only a few examples that can be multiplied in each reader's mind. The total number of persons in that category is, of course, impossible to measure. One may assume that when it is eliminated there would remain only some 10 to 15 per cent of the electorate that was unwilling to vote or uninterested in voting.

This probably compares closely to most other democratic electorates. While this analysis does not eliminate a sizable group of alienated, apathetic, or indifferent citizens in the United States, it seems to indicate that it is substantially smaller than has usually been assumed.

Notes

[1] Some examples: Robert K. Carr, et al., *American Democracy in Theory and Practice* (4th ed.; New York: Holt, 1963), p. 274; James MacGregor Burns and Jack Walter Peltason, *Government by the People* (5th ed.; Englewood Cliffs: Prentice-Hall, 1963), p. 254; E. E. Schattschneider, *The Semi-Sovereign People* (New York: Holt, 1960), p. 97; Claudius O. Johnson and Associates, *American National Government* (5th ed.; New York: Crowell, 1960), p. 395; Thomas H. Eliot, *Governing America* (2d ed.; New York: Dodd, Mead, 1964), p. 234; William Goodman, *The Two-Party System in the United States* (2d ed.; Princeton: Van Nostrand, 1960), p. 574; V. O. Key, *Parties, Politics, and Pressure Groups* (5th ed.; New York: Crowell, 1964), pp. 576-78; Clinton Rossiter, *Parties and Politics in America* (Ithaca: Cornell U. Press, 1962), 28-32; Hugh A. Bone and Austin Ranney, *Politics and Voters* (New York: McGraw-Hill, 1963), p. 44. Bone and Ranney estimate 75.8 per cent in 1960. Rossiter says "75 per cent of the electorate outside the South voted in 1952."

[2] Great Britain, 78.7 per cent in 1959; West Germany, 87.5 in 1961; France, 68.8 in 1962; Switzerland, 66.1 in 1963. D. E. Butler and Richard Rose, *The British General Election of 1959* (London: Macmillan, 1960),

p. 205; Press and Information Office of the German Federal Government, *The Bulletin,* September 19, 1961; *Année politique,* 1962 (Paris: P.U.F., 1963), p. 126; *Le Monde diplomatique,* October 27, 1963. On the other hand: Italy 92.9 per cent in 1963, and New Zealand, 90.5 per cent in 1963. Italian Information Center, *Italy's General Elections 1963,* Part II (New York), p. 6; *Le Monde diplomatique,* November 30, 1963. Most countries based their estimates of electoral turnout on official lists of eligible voters, including those ill or traveling. In some cases, these lists may not be complete. One study covering France indicates that perhaps 15 per cent of the voting-age population is not enrolled on the official voting lists. René Rémond, "Participation électorale et participation organisée," in Georges Vedel (ed.), *La dépolitisation* (Paris: Colin, 1962), p. 75. This 15 per cent probably includes ineligible persons, but no doubt also includes a substantial number of eligible voters who are not inscribed on the official register.

A systematic comparative study of voting participation would be interesting and invaluable, but lies far outside the scope of this paper. Much close study remains to be done before comparable data on other countries can be produced.

[3]This inadequacy remains despite a thorough search of relevant materials in the superb collection of election data assembled by the library of the Littauer School of Public Administration under the guidance of the late Professor V. O. Key, Jr.; in the library of the Harvard Law School; in Harvard College's Widener Library; in the library of the State Capitol, Boston; in the Boston Public Library; in the Eaton and Ginn libraries of Tufts University; and in the Education Libraries at Tufts and Harvard.

[4]The 1960 election has been used because it is recent and coincided with a census.

[5]U.S. Congress, Clerk of the House, *Statistics of the Presidential and Congressional Election of November 8, 1960.*

[6]Ohio, Oregon, and Wisconsin.

[7]Data on state election laws has been drawn from Constance E. Smith, *Voting and Election Laws* (New York: Oceana, 1960), and from the relevant state statutes in effect in 1960. South Dakota had the additional, unusual requirement of five years' residence in the United States.

[8]The residence requirements also exclude Americans living abroad. The American Heritage Foundation estimates that they numbered 500,000 in 1960. See Brendan Byrne, *Let's Modernize Our Horse and Buggy Election Laws!* (Washington, Connecticut: Center for Information on America, 1961), p. 4. Those persons, however, are not included in the civilian population figure cited above and have not, therefore, been subtracted from it.

Another residence qualification excludes fewer than 4,000 residents of the Uintah Indian reservation in Utah, apparently the only persons still denied the suffrage because they live on an Indian reservation. John H. Allen, "Denial of Voting Rights to Reservation Indians," *Utah Law Review,* Fall 1956, 244-56; Murline Jean Worth, "Restrictions of Indian Suffrage by Residence Qualifications," *Oklahoma Law Review,* February 1968, 67-69. Also, apparently some residents on other federal property are excluded from the suffrage. Judicial and statutory interpretations regarding such exclusions are so diverse and ambiguous as to make a reasonable estimate of their number virtually impossible. Robert Gerwig, "The Elective Franchise for Residents of Federal Areas," *George Washington Law Review,* March 1956, 404-21.

[9]Key, *op. cit.,* p. 621.

[10]W. Ross Yates, "The Functions of Residence Requirements for Voting," *Western Political Quarterly,* 15 (September 1962), 469-88.

[11]Byrne, *op. cit.*, p. 3.

[12]*Current Population Reports,* Series P-20, No. 118, August 9, 1962. See also U.S. Bureau of the Census, *Census of Population, 1960. General Social and Economic Characteristics. U.S. Summary Final Report PC (1)-IC* (Washington, D.C.: G.P.O., 1962), 1-205: Lott H. Thomas, "Federal Elections—The Disfranchising Residence Requirements," *U. of Illinois Law Forum,* Spring 1962, pp. 101-9, especially his discussion of the constitutional law problems; Yates, *Residence Requirements for Voting: Ten Years of Change,* delivered to 1962 meeting of the American Political Science Association; John R. Schmidhauser, "Residency Requirements for Voting and the Tensions of a Mobile Society," *Michigan Law Review,* February 1963, 823-40, especially his discussion of recent liberalization of residency requirements and his argument that federal regulation of residency requirements is constitutional; Senator Samuel J. Ervin, Jr., of N.C., "Literacy Tests for Voters: A Case History in Federalism," *Law and Contemporary Problems,* 1962, pp. 481 ff., for a defense of the position that constitutional law reserves the domain of suffrage to the states; I. Ridgeway Davis, "Reappraisal of the Residence Requirements for Voters," *Social Science,* January, 1960, p. 33; Elmo Roper, "How to Lose Your Vote," *Saturday Review,* March 18, 1961, 14-15.

[13]*Current Population Reports,* Series P-25, No. 221, October 7, 1960, p. 1.

[14]Key, *op. cit.*, p. 620.

[15]California, Minnesota, and Utah.

[16]*Book of the States,* 1962-63 (Chicago: Council of State Governments, 1962), pp. 20-22.

[17]*Current Population Reports,* Series P-23, No. 8, February 12, 1963. The states are Maine, New Hampshire, Massachusetts, Connecticut, New York, Delaware, Virginia, North Carolina, South Carolina, Georgia, Alabama, Mississippi, Louisiana, Wyoming, Arizona, Washington, Oregon, California, Alaska, and Hawaii. Hawaiian was an alternative language on the island state.

The number of illiterates, fourteen years of age and over, in the twenty states was 1,519,000. About 10 per cent of the population was fourteen through twenty years of age.

[18]Richard D. Haney, "Elections—Assistance to Illiterates," *U. of Cincinnati Law Review,* March 1956, 302-4. Earl J. Reeves, *Kansas Voters Guide 1960* (Lawrence: Government Research Center), p. 10.

[19]*Current Population Reports,* Series P-23, No. 8, February 12, 1963.

[20]The relevant state statutes, as of 1956, are listed in Ralph R. Blume, "Use of Literacy Tests to Restrict the Right to Vote," *Notre Dame Lawyer,* March 1956, pp. 251-64, fns. 27 through 32. Blume states (p. 257) that in "Massachusetts and California the literacy requirement is no longer enforced." For Massachusetts, at least, that statement is not correct. I took—and passed—the test myself in 1964.

[21]*Current Population Reports,* Series P-23, No. 8, February 12, 1963; Blume, *loc. cit.*, p. 256. Furthermore, Blume's figures do not include illiterate persons in New York who did not take the test.

[22]Smith, *op. cit.*, p. 23.

[23]U.S. Bureau of the Census, *U.S. Census of Population: 1960, Subject Reports, Inmates of Institutions.* Final Report PC(2)-8A (Washington, D.C.: G.P.O., 1963), 83-108, 171-73.

[24]U.S. Department of Health, Education, and Welfare, Public Health Service, *Health Statistics from the U.S. National Health Survey; Chron-*

ic conditions causing limitations of activities, U.S., July 1959-June 1961, Series B-No. 36, October 1962, 10, 19. Apparently about 172,000 of these were mentally retarded. *Health Statistics . . . : Impairments by type, sex, and age, U.S., July 1957-June 1958,* Series B-9, April 1959, calculated from 8-9.

[25]Frank T. Lindman and Donald M. McIntyre, Jr. (eds.), *The Mentally Disabled and the Law* (Chicago: U. of Chicago Press, 1961), pp. 268-69, 291-96, which reviews state legal and constitutional restrictions on voting by the mentally disabled.

[26]Smith, *op. cit.,* p. 23.

[27]Alabama, Colorado, Indiana, Kentucky, Maine, and Michigan. *State of Connecticut Register and Manual,* 1963 (Hartford: Secretary of State, 1963), pp. 657-59.

[28]*U.S. Census of Population: 1960 Inmates of Institutions, op. cit.,* p. 4.

[29]*Ibid.,* Bureau of Prisons, *National Prisoner Statistics,* 1950, 1951, 1952 and 1953, 1960; *Message of Governor Leslie Jensen to the Twenty-sixth Legislative Session of the South Dakota Legislature,* 1939; Arizona, Board of Pardons, *Reports,* annual from 1935 to 1963; Alabama, Special Legislative Committee Investigating Pardons and Paroles, *Report,* Legislative Document No. 4, 1951 (covering 1939 through 1950); Georgia, State Board of Pardons and Paroles, *Biennial Reports,* 1943-44 through 1961-62; California, *Acts of Executive Clemency,* annual or biennial reports 1931-32 through 1962.

[30]Delaware, Louisiana, Maine, Massachusetts, Missouri, New Hampshire, Oklahoma, South Carolina, Texas, Virginia, and West Virginia.

[31]Data on absentee voting is very incomplete. The 3.4 million figure was obtained by extrapolation from eight states (Alaska, California for 1962, Connecticut, Missouri, New Hampshire, Pennsylvania, Rhode Island, and Washington), which published absentee ballot totals in their official statistics abstracts.

[32]Mississippi (with a few exceptions) and South Carolina permit no civilian absentee voting. All others do. See Smith, *op. cit.,* pp. 89-99.

[33]Some persons covered by the second assumption could not vote, either because they were too ill or they were not eligible under absentee ballot laws in their states. Some covered by the third assumption were able to obtain absentee ballots. It is impossible to break down these categories further.

[34]*Health Statistics . . . : Acute Conditions, Seasonal Variations, United States, July 1957-July 1961,* Series B. No. 33, June 1962, 22-23.

[35]Estimated from *Health Statistics . . . : Chronic Conditions . . .* , p. 19.

[36]General; maternity; eye, ear, nose, and throat; osteopathic; or the hospital department of an institution.

[37]Estimated from *Health Statistics . . . : Hospital Discharge and Length of Stay: Short Stay Hospitals, United States 1958-1960,* Series B, No. 32, April 1962, p. 14.

[38]The above data are based on *U.S. Census of Population: 1960, Inmates of Institutions, op. cit.,* pp. 5-7, 9-11, 87-88, 91, 109, 139, 163, 165, 175-77, 187, 189, 202, 204, 302, 303.

[39]Bureau of the Census, *Current Population Reports,* Series P-20, No. 93, March 27, 1959; Office of Education, *Opening (Fall) Enrollment in Higher Education 1960; Analytic Report* (Washington D.C.: G.P.O., 1961). (See also Bureau of the Census, *U.S. Census of Population:*

1960 School Enrollment). Final Report PC (2)-5A (Washington, D.C.: G.P.O., 1964). The decennial census report is less useful than the sources cited, however, as it presents data as of April 1 rather than for the autumn. Note comments on comparability, *ibid.,* p. x.

[40] *Department of Defense, Annual Report for Fiscal Year, 1961* (Washington, D.C.: G.P.O., 1962), p. 375, for data on dependents as of March 31, 1961; Department of Defense estimate on October 19, 1960, *New York Times,* October 20, 1960, for data on voting-age servicemen. There were undoubtedly some wives under voting age but also some of the 2,337,520 children and "other" dependents must have been of voting age.

[41] *U.S. Statistical Abstract 1963,* p. 409. This does not include data on the Central Intelligence Agency or the National Security Agency. Nor does it include non-government employees residing temporarily abroad, but counted in the census.

[42] Estimate based on Donald E. Church, *Travel Survey, 1957* (Washington, D.C.: Bureau of Census, September 1958), adjusted to exclude children and to take into account the population increase from July 1, 1957, to November 1, 1960. *Current Population Reports,* Series P-25, No. 253, August 16, 1962; *U.S. Statistical Abstract 1962,* p. 6.

[43] Church, *op. cit.,* p. 9.

[44] *U.S. Census of Population: 1960 . . . Inmates of Institutions, op. cit.,* pp. 67-82.

[45] Department of Defense, *Annual Report, 1961,* pp. 370, 375; *U.S. Statistical Abstract, 1963,* p. 409.

[46] Calculated from 68.8 million presidential votes plus 1.0 million valid ballots without presidential votes or invalid ballots minus 3.4 absentee ballots.

[47] If all ill persons were eligible for absentee ballots and had voted at the same rate as those able to go to the polls, 9.5 million absentee ballots would have been cast, 6.1 million more than the estimated actual figure.

[48] The literature on discrimination against Negroes in exercise of the suffrage is, of course, vast. *Inter alia,* see *1961 U.S. Commission on Civil Rights Report: Voting* (Washington, D.C.: G.P.O., n.d.); V. O. Key, Jr., *Southern Politics* (New York: Knopf, 1950); "Elections and Voting Rights," *Northwestern University Law Review,* July-August 1959, 367-76; Donald R. Matthews and James W. Prothro, "Social and Economic Factors and Negro Voter Registration in the South," *APSR,* 57 (March 1963), 24-44, and "Political Factors and Negro Voter Registration in the South," *APSR,* 57 (June 1963), 355-67, and references cited therein.

[49] Alabama, Arkansas, Delaware, Florida, Georgia, Louisiana, Maryland, Mississippi, North Carolina, South Carolina, Tennessee, Texas, and Virginia.

[50] *Voting, op. cit.,* pp. 252-311. That figure may be somewhat low. It may be that a smaller proportion of registered Negroes than registered whites actually goes to the polls. Exact figures on Negro and white registrations were not available for the following: 41 of 254 counties in Texas (with a total voting-age population of 1,136,768); Mississippi; 146 of 159 counties in Georgia (with a total voting-age population of about 1,884,000); 32 of 95 counties in Tennessee (with a total voting-age population of 743,420); and South Carolina. Total figures for Texas and Tennessee were estimated by projecting from the available data. The figures for South Carolina and Georgia were calculated from 1958 figures. *Congressional Record,* March 15, 1960, p. 5613, and February 27, 1960, p. 3682. Because Mississippi does not keep statewide registration figures, total 1960 presidential voting figures and an estimate of 8,000 Negro voters

were used. *Ibid.,* March 15, 1960, p. 5597. See also *New York Times,* September 15, 1960, and September 24, 1961; *Book of the States,* 1962-63, p. 30. As Matthew and Prothro have pointed out, *loc. cit.,* part of the difference between white and Negro registration rates results from the depressed social and economic status of the Negroes. It seems irrelevant here whether the difference in voting participation is a result of direct political or indirect social and economic intimidation.

[51] *Yearbook of American Churches, 1961* (New York: National Council of the Churches of Christ in the U.S.A., October 1960), p. 57; F. E. Mayer, *The Religious Bodies of America* (St. Louis: Concordia Publishing House, 1958), p. 466.

[52] For instance, in the official election report for Indiana in 1960, 28 of the 91 counties made obvious errors in reporting the total vote cast. Typically, they have reported a total vote identical with the total presidential vote or the major-party presidential vote, but in some cases the reported total is even less than the major-party presidential vote. They also report that Posey County had a total vote of 143,031 but it had a 1960 population of only 19,214 and a presidential vote of 9,857.

[53] State of Rhode Island, Board of Elections, *Official Count of the Ballots Cast . . . , November 8, 1960,* p. 333.

[54] *1960 General Election Report of Indiana.* It should be noted that apparently persons entering the voting-machine booth but not casting valid ballots would not be included in the total vote-cast figures whereas they were included in the Rhode Island total.

[55] Key, *Politics, Parties, and Pressure Groups,* p. 648, citing the Automatic Voting Machine Corp.

[56] About 0.5 per cent has been added to take into account invalid ballots in Indiana.

[57] The states and percentages are Indiana, 2.6 (not including the obviously erroneous returns); Minnesota and Arizona, 2.4; Alaska, 2.3; Rhode Island, 2.0; North Dakota, 1.9; Illinois 1.8; Nevada, 1.7; Washington and California, 1.3; New York and Vermont, 1.2; Ohio and Massachusetts, 1.1; New Jersey, Nebraska, and Wyoming, 1.0; Connecticut and New Hampshire, 0.7; Oregon, 0.5; and Utah, 0.07.

[58] In all comparisons between primary and general election voting, the available vote total was used in each county or parish for the office obtaining the largest vote for each type of election.

Electoral Myth and Reality: The 1964 Election

Philip E. Converse
Aage Clausen
Warren E. Miller

Americans have tended to assume that there are real differences between the ideologies of the two major political parties. Still, recent candidates have been able to start heads nodding in agreement by charging that there is not a "dime's worth" of difference between the Republicans and the Democrats. Which is the more adequate perspective? Can a candidate win a national election who takes, for example, conservative ideology seriously and attempts to fashion his issue stances so as to conform to that ideology? The Survey Research Center of the University of Michigan has found that only slightly more than 10 percent of the electorate can be classed as ideological in their political orientation. The 1964 presidential election in which Senator Barry Goldwater met such overwhelming defeat would seem to bear out the accuracy and importance of that finding. In the following article Philip Converse, Aage Clausen, and Warren Miller analyze the 1964 election and assess its implications for the ideological party.

On Election Day, 1964, the aspirations of Senator Barry Goldwater and the conservative wing of the Republican Party were buried under an avalanche of votes cast for incumbent President Lyndon Johnson. The margin of victory, approaching 16 million votes, was unprecedented. Historical comparisons with other presidential landslides are left somewhat indeterminate by the intrusion of third parties. However, it is safe to observe than Johnson's 61.3 percent of the two-party popular vote put him in the same general range as the striking victories of Franklin Delano Roosevelt in 1936, Harding in 1920, and Theodore Roosevelt in 1904.

Before the fact, the election was also expected to be the most intensely ideological campaign since 1936, in no small measure because of Goldwater's reputation as a "pure" conservative. After the fact, doubt existed as to whether this expectation had been fulfilled. Goldwater supporters, in particular, expressed dis-

Reprinted by permission of the publisher and authors from Philip E. Converse, Aage R. Clausen and Warren E. Miller, "Electoral Myth and Reality: The 1964 Election," *American Political Science Review,* 59 (June, 1965), 321-336. Abridged by the editors.

appointment that President Johnson had refused to join battle on any of the fundamental ideological alternatives that were motivating the Goldwater camp. However, as we shall see, the mass public had some sense that "important differences" between the two major parties were heightened in 1964 compared with parallel data from either 1960 or, as is more impressive, the relatively tense election of 1952.[1] And certainly no one questioned the importance of ideological differences in the factional dispute that split the Republican Party along liberal-conservative lines with an enduring bitterness unmatched in decades.

Indeed, these three prime elements of the 1964 election—faction, ideology and the contest for votes—became intertwined after the manner of a classic script. That is, the "outer" ideological wing of a party captures its nomination, leaving a vacuum toward the center of gravity of national opinion. This vacuum is gleefully filled by the opposing party without any loss of votes from its own side of the spectrum. The outcome, logically and inexorably, is a landslide at the polls.[2]

With a script so clearly written in advance, the outsider would naturally ask why any party controlled by rational strategists should choose a course likely to lead to such massive repudiation in its name. The answers to this question in the 1964 case are not particularly obscure, although they can be made at numerous levels. One answer, of course, is that Republican Party strategists were themselves in deep disagreement as to just what script was relevant: many recognized the classic script and predicted the eventual outcome, with all of its attendant losses for other Republican candidates, in deadly accuracy.

For the factional dispute within Republican ranks involved not only an ideological clash, but also major differences in the perception of that political reality which becomes important in winning votes and elections. The Goldwater faction was told by its Republican adversaries, as the conservative wing had been told for years, that a Goldwater could not conceivably defeat a Democratic President, and would instead greatly damage the party ticket at all levels. The Goldwater groups countered that a victory for their man was entirely plausible despite the danger signals of the spring polls and the normal difficulties of challenging an incumbent. It is not clear how sincere or widespread this confidence was: some statements sounded as though the Goldwater candidacy had little chance of winning but would at least provide a forum for the conservative philosophy, along with control of the Republican Party. But even in their more pessimistic moments, the Goldwater people would argue that while victory might be difficult, they certainly saw no reason to believe that Goldwater would do worse than any other Republican challenger, or encounter the electoral disaster the liberals were predicting.

Similarly, at the San Francisco nominating convention, his opponents vehemently charged that Goldwater was a "minority candidate," even among Republicans in this country. In another direct clash of perceptions, Senator Goldwater is said to have remarked to a group of Midwestern delegates, "What the minority [the convention liberals] can't get through their heads is that this is a true representation of the Republican Party."[3]

In this article we wish to examine the relationship between such conflicting perceptions and what is known of the relevant reality in the context of the 1964 election. Our information comes primarily from sample survey studies of the mass public that formed the electorate in 1964, and whose reactions represent one level of political reality about which so many conflicting opinions and predictions were made. While the most important aspect of that reality was unveiled by the election outcome, there remained some of the customary latitude of interpretation as to its full significance. And with respect to the interplay between the stratagems of party elites on one hand and the grass-roots American voters on the other, the chronology of the 1964 election does indeed provide a fascinating composite of sheer myth, genuine but discrepant reality worlds, and self-fulfilling prophecies.

I. THE MYTH OF THE STAY-AT-HOME REPUBLICANS

The first theory of electoral reality on our agenda may be rapidly disposed of, for it lies more simply and unequivocally in the realm of myth than any of the others we shall treat. It should not be overlooked, however, both because of its historical persistence and because of its enshrinement in the battle cry of 1964 Goldwater supporters: "A choice, not an echo!"

In the quadrennial competition between liberal and conservative wings of the Republican Party for the presidential nomination throughout the 1940s and 1950s, the conservatives were consistently bested. One of the prime contentions of the liberals was that all of the entries of the conservative wing were so distant from the "middle-of-the-road" that they had no hope of attracting the independent votes necessary for victory over the Democrats. At an ideological level, the conservative wing coined the epithet "me-tooism" to ridicule the liberals for their refusal to reject Democratic innovations of the New and Fair Deal eras root and branch. The liberals, it was charged, were slowly selling out the fundamental principles on which earlier days of G.O.P. ascendancy had been based.

This accusation of ideological "flabbiness" was not, however, compelling of itself without some further comment on the problem of winning votes. As a consequence, a theory became widely current among conservative Republicans that G.O.P. difficulties in maintaining much contact with the White House were in fact directly tied to the "me-tooist" flavor of its presidential candidates. Republicans running for that office tended to lose not because there was any lack of potential Republican votes (as the superficial observer might have thought), but because many of the "real" Republicans were sufficiently offended by "me-tooism" that they simply didn't bother to vote at all. Nominate a true Republican rather than a Tweedledee, the theory went, and enough of these stay-at-homes would return to the polls to put him into the White House.

As such theories go, this contention was remarkably verifiable. That is, the critic need not argue that few Republicans were disappointed by the nominees of their party, for disappoinment in itself is irrelevant for argument. The question is simply whether or not Republicans, however disappointed, did continue to turn out and vote even for "me-tooist" candidates through this period—a matter much easier to ascertain. Nor is there any point in arguing that there were *never* any stray Republicans who in the last analysis vented their frustrations by refusing to go to the polls. Undoubtedly there were. But the theory hinges less on the question as to whether such people existed, than on the contention that they existed in significant numbers: not merely several hundred or several thousand or even a few hundred thousand, but in the millions needed to overcome the persistent Democratic majorities.

Such a pool of potential voters would be large enough to be discriminated reliably in most sample surveys. And we know of no reputable sample surveys at any time in this period that gave any shred of reason to believe that this significant pool of stay-at-home Republicans existed. Indeed, such findings as were relevant pointed massively in the opposite direction. From 1944 on, for example, one can contrast turnout rates between Democrats and Republicans of comparable strengths of identification. And over election after election featuring "me-tooist" Republican nominees, one finds that turnout rates are consistently higher—and often much higher—on the Republican side. Indeed, each time we isolate that polar minority who not only have an intense commitment to the Republican Party, but whose commitment is of a highly sensitive ideological sort, turnout typically reaches proportions staggering for the American system: 96 percent, 98 percent—levels almost implausible in view of registration difficulties, travel, sickness and other accidents which can keep the most devoted American from the polls upon occasion. More impressive still, we find that in 1952 those Republicans who reported during the campaign that they would have preferred the "conservative" Taft over the "liberal" Eisenhower—exactly those Republicans to whom the theory refers—actually turned out at much *higher* rates to vote for Eisenhower in the November election (94 percent) than did the set of Republicans who indicated satisfaction with Eisenhower's nomination (84 percent).[4]

These brief observations do not begin to exhaust the evidence, none of which lends any support whatever to the theory of a silent pool of frustrated conservative Republicans. Hence it is scarcely surprising that the Goldwater cause in 1964 was not buoyed up by some sudden surge of new support at the polls which other strategists had overlooked; for the hitherto silent people expected to provide such a surge existed principally in the imaginations of conservative strategists who in time of adversity needed desperately to believe that they were there. It is less of a wonder that this theory was generated, particularly before sample survey data took on much scope or stature in the 1940s, than that it persisted with greater or lesser vigor into the 1960s in the face of repetitive contradictory evidence readily available to any proponents with an edge of interest as to what the facts actually were.

II. THE MINORITY CANDIDATE OF A MINORITY PARTY

On the eve of the Republican nominating convention, an irate Goldwater supporter wrote to the Paris edition of the *Herald Tribune*, upbraiding it for the doubts it had expressed as to the extent of Goldwater sentiment beyond the convention delegates themselves, and pointing out that a massive groundswell of support had built up for Goldwater throughout the country "west of Madison Avenue."

The charge of the liberal wing of the G.O.P. that Goldwater not only was unattractive to Democrats and Independents but was not even the majority preference of Republicans was a particularly severe allegation in view of the constraints under which the Republican Party has been obliged to operate in recent years. It has been the consensus of observers for quite some time that the Republican Party is a minority party in the affections of the American public. Our relevant data collections at frequent intervals since 1952 have left little question in our minds both as to the minority status of the Republicans, and as to the stability of that status during this epoch. For most of this time, our estimates would suggest that in terms of underlying loyalties, the Democrats could expect to receive, all other things equal, something in the neighborhood of 54 percent of the national popular vote; and if any change has been occurring in this figure in the past 15 years, it is that this Democratic majority is slowly increasing.[5] In practical terms, this means that a Democratic candidate need not have much attraction for grass-roots Republicans: he can win easily if he can but carry the votes of a reasonable share of independents, and has general appeal for Democrats. A Republican candidate, on the other hand, can only win at the national level by drawing nearly monolithic support from Republicans, attracting the votes of a lion's share of independents, and inducing unusual defection among the less committed Democratic identifiers as well. The latter was the Eisenhower formula, and one which Nixon had nearly succeeded in following in 1960. More generally, the liberal wing of the Republican Party had sought candidates with this kind of broad appeal throughout this period. In this light, the question of Goldwater's popularity was serious: for if a minority party nominates a figure enjoying only minority support within his own party, it is an obvious invitation to disaster.

In the spring and early summer of 1964, the opinion polls lent much weight to the contention that Goldwater enjoyed no broad support even among Republicans. The Goldwater supporters tended to counter this kind of evidence either (1) by ignoring the polls; or (2) by questioning the validity of the polls (some Goldwater placards were to read "Gallup didn't count us!"); or (3) by questioning the immutability of the early poll readings. Of these reactions, certainly the last-mentioned was entirely appropriate. That is, in the very early stages of a push toward the presidency, even a person who has been something of a "national" figure as Senator or major Governor for a considerable period may not be recognized by very large portions of the public. Until he has received much more intense national exposure in the limelight of presidential primaries and the nominating convention, "straw polls" as to his popularity can be highly misleading and unstable, particularly if the polling pits such a candidate against other figures with more longstanding national prominence and "household" names.[6]

However, survey data gathered over the course of 1964 can be put together with "hard" data from the presidential primaries to provide an illuminating picture of Goldwater's general popularity and, in particular, the reactions of grass-roots Republicans to him. In January, 1964, before the beginning of the spring primaries, we asked a national sample of the electorate:

Many people are wondering who will run for President on the Republican side this fall. . . . If you had to make a choice, which Republican leader do you think would be best for our country in 1964?
Who would be your second choice?
Are there any of the leading Republicans that you think would make very bad candidates?

Table 1 summarizes the responses to this sequence of questions. The open-ended nature of the questions meant that individuals only rated those Republicans whom they were aware of at the time, and thought of as plausible candidates. The table excludes a thin scattering of other mentions. Since the scoring used reflects both the breadth and the intensity of support, a Republican receiving relatively few mentions could not achieve any very high score. Thus, for example, another possible scoring could have shown Henry Cabot Lodge vastly outdistancing all other aspirants, as his references were almost unanimously positive, whereas the other Republicans suffered numerous descriptions as "very bad candidates." However, at this time he was not commonly regarded as an aspirant for the nomination, and the scoring deliberately puts this warm but limited positive feeling toward him in perspective.[7]

The table speaks for itself as to Goldwater's attractiveness as a candidate. Clearly Goldwater's problem was not that he was still too little known: he received mentions from a wider proportion of the electorate than any of his competitors. But for much of the electorate he was an object of antagonism even in January, 1964. And among grass-roots Republicans, where his strength was concentrated, he remained fourth in a field of six.

The sequence of Republican primary elections in the succeeding months tended, with some local variation, to fit the lines suggested by these January reactions. The table presages the startling Lodge write-in victory over both Goldwater and Rockefeller among New Hampshire Republicans in March, as well as his numerous subsequent strong showings. It contains ample warning as well of the amazingly poor Goldwater record in the primaries throughout the spring, including the scattered victories in such seemingly congenial states as conservative Nebraska, where by standing alone on the ticket he managed to win about half of the votes cast over a flood of Nixon and Lodge write-ins. It even renders intelligible the crucial Goldwater victory in California, where write-ins were not permitted, where the sole opponent was Rockefeller, and where Democrats had a hotly fought primary of their own. Indeed, there is room to wonder whether any presidential aspirant has ever contested so many primaries with as disastrous a showing and still captured the nomination of his party's convention.

No evidence from polls of the period, moreover, suggests that Goldwater's popularity showed any sudden increase, even among Republicans, in the short interval between the final primary and the San Francisco convention. In interviewing our sample of the national electorate in September and October, we asked respondents to recall their reactions to the decisions of the Republican convention, including the identity of the candidates they had preferred at the time the convention began, as well as their gratification, indifference or disappointment at the outcome. While these responses suffer the inevitable frailties of any retrospective accounts that go back over an evolving situation, the social and political lines of support and antagonism for the various major contestants in July as reported during the campaign bear so close a resemblance to the lines of support visible in the January, 1964 data, as to make it unlikely that they are badly distorted by selective recollection, *post hoc* rationalization, and the like.

It is most instructive, perhaps, to set these popular reactions to the 1964 Republican convention against a fairly comparable set of data collected in 1952 after the conservative wing had lost its bid to nominate Senator Taft for the presidency against the liberal wing's offering of General Eisenhower, for the bitterness engendered in the 1952 struggle came closer to matching that of 1964 than either of the intervening conventions. Our question in 1952 asked respondents irrespective of partisan allegiance whether they would have preferred to have seen any other candidate nominated in either of the major-party conventions held in Chicago. Thus Republicans could focus their remarks on the Democratic convention in a way that the 1964 questions did not permit. However, partisans tended to comment primarily on the outcomes of their own party's nominating conventions.

Among Republican identifiers in the fall of 1952, about one in five recalled having felt a preference for Taft at the time of the convention. Another eight percent had preferred some third candidate. The vast majority of the remaining 72 percent indicated that they had been indifferent to the choices at either convention, or expressed gratification in the selections of Eisenhower as the Republican candidate. Some other Republicans responded that they would have preferred a candidate other than Stevenson from the Democratic convention. Presumably, however, these citizens were satisfied with the Republican convention,

TABLE 1. Preferences for the Republican Presidential Nomination among Selected Segments of the Electorate, January, 1964

	Per cent mentiona	Score across total electorateb	Score within "Minimal Majority": all Independents and Republicansb	Score among all Republicansb
	(%)			
Nixon	42	+25	+32	+37
Lodge	10	+11	+13	+13
Romney	11	+ 9	+11	+10
Rockefeller	49	+19	+10	+ 1
Scranton	11	+ 7	+ 6	+ 5
Goldwater	54	− 8	− 5	+ 9

aThe percentage entered represents the proportion of individuals in the total sample mentioning the Republican leader indicated, either as one of two best or one of two very bad candidates.

bEach mention of a leader as the "best" candidate received a score of +2. Each mention as second best received a score of +1. The first-mentioned "bad" candidate received a score of −2. Any negative second mentions were scored −1. The entries in the table represent the net balance of positive or negative scores for the leader, expressed as a proportion of the maximum possible positive score an individual would have received had he been awarded all of the "best" choices given by the indicated segment of the electorate.

and it seems reasonable to conclude that a maximum of some 30 percent of all Republicans in 1952 had ground to recall any disappointment over their party's nomination.

The picture from 1964 is remarkably similar in one respect, and drastically different in another. Among Republican identifiers in this latter year, slightly less than 20 percent of all Republicans recalled having preferred Goldwater at the time of the convention. This figure is only one percent less than the proportion of Taft supporters among Republicans in 1952. What was different, of course, was that in 1952 Taft lost the nomination on the first ballot, whereas in 1964 Goldwater won it handily on the first ballot. Although in our 1964 data a large segment (30 percent) of Republican identifiers indicated that they had held no preference for a specific candidate at convention time, very nearly half of all of our Republicans did recall some preference other than Goldwater. Thus these grass-roots Republicans with non-Goldwater choices outnumbered the Goldwater supporters within Republican ranks by a margin of better than two and one-half to one. A clear majority (60 percent) of those with other preferences, when asked "Were you particularly happy that Goldwater got the nomination, or did you think that he was nearly as good as your man?" expressed their lingering unhappiness about the outcome.

In sum, then, it is hard to turn up any bit of evidence to challenge the conclusion that Goldwater was, in rather startling degree, a minority candidate within a minority party. If his camp actually believed that the San Francisco delegates represented a true cross-section of grass-roots Republican sentiment, then they had grossly misunderstood the situation. There was, however, at least one extenuating circumstance: the support among Republican citizens for other candidates than Goldwater was split badly among the four or five other leading candidates. Thus while any of several pairs of other candidates had grass-roots party support at convention time which would have outnumbered the Goldwater faction quite readily, the fact remains that the 20 percent Goldwater support represented a plurality for any single candidate.

However this may be, disappointment at the convention outcome in 1964 had radically different consequences in November than the comparable disappointments among Republicans in 1952. As we have seen above, the former Taft supporters in that year turned out at the polls in near-perfect proportions and cast a very faithful Republican vote for Eisenhower. In 1964, however, the widespread defections among Republicans necessary to account for the Johnson landslide tended to follow rather closely the lines of lingering discontent with the nomination.

These recollections of San Francisco varied according to the different camps in which rank-and-file Republicans had located themselves at the time. So, for example, about three Lodge supporters in four reported they were unhappy with the Goldwater nomination; for Rockefeller supporters, the figure was closer to two in three. Slightly over half of the Nixon supporters, however, indicated that they thought Goldwater was "nearly as good" as their man, Nixon. With minor departures, similar patterns marked the ultimate defections to Johnson among these varying Republicans. Since Nixon supporters were, like Goldwater's, more frequent "strong" Republicans than the adherents of some of the other camps, lower defection rates here were only to be expected. However, defections to Johnson among Republicans who had preferred Nixon at convention time remained about double what could be expected from past norms for Republicans of this particular mixture of strengths of identification. Over three times as many Republicans for Lodge and Scranton defected to Johnson as parallel "normal" expectations would suggest, and—perhaps surprisingly—defections among Republicans who expressed no pre-convention favorite at all were in this range as well. Most extreme were the Rockefeller and Romney supporters, with defection rates at the polls exceeding expectation by a factor of greater than four.[8]

These differences across the several non-Goldwater camps are intriguing, in part because they appear related to reactions of the various G.O.P. leaders to the Goldwater candidacy. That is, of the set of major Republicans under discussion, Nixon took greatest pains to maintain relations with the Goldwater group before the convention, and undertook to help unify the party behind him after the nomination. Therefore it seems fitting that dismay at the nomination was least in his camp, and defections relatively limited. Neither Rockefeller nor Romney made any major show of reconciliation after the nomination, and subsequently went to some lengths to dissociate themselves from the Goldwater aspects of the Republican campaign.

Yet if it were true that nothing more than a "follow-the-leader" response is needed to account for these variations in defection rates among Republicans, the data would cast a somewhat different light on the question of conflicting perceptions between liberal and conservative wings of Goldwater's voting strength. For in such a case the Senator's problem would have been less one of gross overestimates of his strength, than of self-fulfilling prophecy on the part of the disgruntled liberal leaders. In other words, they first refused to support Goldwater on grounds that he could not win enough votes, and then proceeded to withhold in large quantities the votes of their "followers" to assure exactly this outcome.

No airtight way is available to determine whether or not Republican defections at the presidential level might have been reduced significantly had Rockefeller or some of the other liberals effected a more genuine reconciliation with Goldwater to unite the party for the campaign. Nevertheless, if we were to compare the issue positions and ideological persuasions of 1964 Nixon Republicans with those of Rockefeller or Romney Republicans and find no substantial differences, we might be tempted to judge that differences in leader behavior did play some independent role in minimizing or maximizing Republican defections in November. Preliminary analyses suggest rather clearly, however, that substantial ideological differences did exist across the range of Republican factions. Republicans enthusiastic about Goldwater showed a rather unique (or "extreme") pattern of ideological positions. Nixon supporters, while unmistakably different, looked more nearly like the Goldwater people than the adherents of any of the other camps. Next in order moving away from the Goldwater position were the Scranton and Lodge followers, and the Rockefeller and Romney adherents show slightly more liberal positions still. Ideological differences therefore, plainly existed between grassroots supporters of the various factions, and these differences were indeed correlated with defections from a Goldwater vote. This does not exclude the possibility that the defections might have been lessened by a genuine "unity" move on the part of more liberal Republican leaders. It indicates nevertheless that the desertions were rooted not only in leader-follower behavior, but in a more personal sense of ideological distance between many rank-and-file Republicans and the Goldwater faction—a distance that would have produced increased defections quite apart from examples set by the leadership.

However this may be, it was a significant feature of the election that the customary post-convention reconciliation between party factions was in the 1964 Republican case lack-luster at best, and at many levels simply non-existent. Many of the liberals wished to avoid the Goldwater platform. At the same time, Goldwater seemed to do less than most candidates in making it easy for the dissident brethren to return to the fold. Among several possible reasons, one may have been that in the blueprint laid out by Goldwater strategists for a November victory, the support of most of these leaders did not appear to be critical.

III. CAMPAIGN STRATEGY: THE SOUTH AS REPUBLICAN TARGET

The strategy of the Goldwater camp for a November victory was both simple and relatively selective. Goldwater felt, to begin with, that he could hold on to essentially the same states that Nixon had won in 1960. This meant a clean sweep of the populous states of the Pacific Coast, most of the Mountain and Plains states, and a scattering east of the Mississippi. To reap the additional electoral votes for victory, Goldwater believed that the way lay open, under proper circumstances, for the Republican Party to make further major inroads in the once solidly Democratic South. The plan implied that Goldwater could largely afford to write off the populous industrial states of the Northeast and some, if not all, of the Midwest—a matter which greatly reduced the importance of the dissident liberal Republican bloc. And it represented a dramatic departure from any past Republican strategy in making of the South a fulcrum for victory.

Such a strategy was not only unusual but, against the long sweep of American electoral history, it might even be thought of as implausible. Yet it was no hastily devised scheme. For years Goldwater had participated in the Congressional coalition between conservative Republicans and Southern Democrats. The same drive for ideological neatness that led him to call for the reorganization of American politics into "Conservative" and "Liberal" parties impressed upon him the grotesque incongruity of a Democratic South. The South had no reason to be a Democratic bastion; by all of its affinities and traditions, it should long since have become Republican. Part of the problem lay with the national Republican Party, which, in the control of the Northeastern bloc, had failed to present national-level candidates making clear that Republicanism was the natural home of the Southern voter. This had been a frustrating fact since Goldwater's entry into politics—a period during which political observers had frequently predicted an imminent partisan realignment of the South; but gains in the region, while very obvious, had remained rather modest. In discussions of Republican difficulty in recapturing majority status in the land, Goldwater had opined that the Party had to learn to "go hunting in the pond where the ducks are"— the South. As bitterness began to mount in that region toward the civil rights pressures of the Kennedy Administration, the time seemed more ripe than ever for the presentation of a purely conservative Republican candidate who could appeal to the Southern ethos in a most direct way, thereby breaking the Democratic hold on the region in one dramatic and decisive stroke.

This long-planned strategy had suffered two temporary but alarming setbacks. The assassination of President Kennedy suddenly placed a Southerner in the White House, and removed from power the most feared personal symbols of federal intrusions. The continuation of the Kennedy beginnings by the Johnson Administration, however — particularly in the 1964 Civil Rights bill—helped to reset the stage. So did the increased signs of Negro unrest, and the new element of "white backlash" in the North as well as the South that seemed apparent in the spring primaries. The capping touch was Goldwater's vote against the Civil Rights bill. This vote, to be sure, represented no condoning of segregationism *per se*, but rather a blow for states' rights against the encroachment of the federal government. Nevertheless, white supremacists in the South had so long paraded under the states' rights banner as to leave little room for fear lest the

Goldwater gesture go unappreciated. The liberal wing of the Republican Party, having worked for years to prevent the Democrats from "gaining position" on the civil rights issue, was further horrified as it envisioned the G.O P. suddenly transformed into "the party of the white man" at just the moment when the Negro vote was becoming effectively mobilized.

The second setback threatened when Governor Wallace of Alabama decided to enter the presidential race as a states' rights candidate. This was especially alarming, for Wallace would have competed for exactly the same votes that Goldwater had been wooing toward the Republican column. However, Wallace's subsequent withdrawal left the field open again for the original victory blueprint, and the implementation began in force. Mid-campaign accounts of the Goldwater organizational efforts spoke of a high-powered, modernistic campaign apparatus in the South stocked with volunteer labor in numbers that would have been unbelievable for the earlier Eisenhower and Nixon campaigns. While this machine had been humming efficiently from the start, the Goldwater organization in the West was described as effective but less advanced; in the Midwest it was chaotic, and in the Northeast next to non-existent. At few if any points in recent political history have so many campaign resources—in both issue positions taken and organizational efforts made—been devoted to the cultivation of a single region. The first discordant note came when, during the campaign and apparently as the result of new poll data, Goldwater remarked to reporters that he was not as strong in the South as everybody seemed to think.

After the votes were counted, what was the success of this strategy? The verdict must come in two halves. From one point of view, the strategy was a brilliant success, and it left its imprint on the geographical voting returns with greater strength than any other of what we have called "short-term forces" in the 1964 election. One crude way of separating these immediate or new effects from those better attributable to long-term standing loyalties is to create a different kind of electoral map, entering state by state or region by region the departure of a particular presidential vote in a more Republican or more Democratic direction than the normal voting of the area involved. A map so constructed for 1964, with pro-Goldwater deviations regarded as "high ground" and pro-Johnson deviations as "low," would show one primary "tilt" or gradient across the nation. The very lowest ground would appear in the northern reaches of New England, and the gradient would move upward with fair regularity all the way west to the Pacific Coast. The same gradient would appear, but much more sharply tilted still, as one moved southward to the Gulf of Mexico. In other words, Goldwater's regional emphases were indeed profoundly reflected in the vote.

As soon as one leaves the relative question of the regional and the geographic, however, the strategy was a dismal failure. For while the whole continent tilted in the expected direction, the strong Democratic tide nationally left virtually all of the country submerged under what from a Goldwater point of view was "sea level"—the 50-50 mark in popular votes. In terms of electoral votes, Goldwater was stranded on a few islands which remained above the tide on the outer Southern and Southwestern fringe of the continent. These islands represented stunning "firsts" or dramatic historic reversals in states like Georgia, Alabama, Mississippi and South Carolina. But their historic interest did not bring Goldwater any closer to the presidency.

Indeed, while Goldwater scored sharp Republican gains through the "Black Belt" of the deepest South, his assault on the South as a whole produced rather pathetic results. All observers agree, for example, that the South has been drifting away from its old status as a one-party Democratic bastion for at least two decades, if not for five or more.

Hence Goldwater could have hoped to profit from four years more of this drift than Nixon, and a decade more than Eisenhower. Secondly, all observers are equally agreed that not only in the Black Belt but well north into the Border States of the South, civil rights was the prime political issue, and there is no doubt where the mass white population stood on the matter. Our data from the late 1950s and the early 1960s have consistently made clear that the potential of this issue for dramatic partisan realignment in the South had been muffled because of lack of clarity in the eyes of the mass population, prior to 1964, that either of the two major national parties offered much hope to the Southern white. It was exactly this ambiguity that Goldwater set out to remove by providing a clear party differentiation on civil rights at the national level. Putting these two ingredients together, the actual 1964 election results from the South as a whole might seem astonishing. For Goldwater actually did less well in the region than either Nixon in 1960 or Eisenhower in 1952 and 1956. One has to return at least to 1948 to find a comparably poor showing for a Republican presidential candidate; and there are reasonable treatments of the 1948 Thurmond vote which would send one back to 1944 for a parallel. Given the fact that Goldwater wooed the South so straightforwardly, and injected the new and potent ingredient of clear party differentiation on civil rights into the 1964 picture, this retrogression of Republican popular voting strength for a presidential candidate back to levels of the 1940s may seem quite incomprehensible.

A possible explanation, although one that we can summarily reject, would be that the clear party differentiation on civil (or "states'") rights which Goldwater tried to communicate failed to come across to the mass voters.[9] Perhaps to the dismay of the liberal wing of the Republicans, however, the communication was near-perfect. In our 1960 election study, a measure of association between the two parties and the policy extremes of the civil rights controversy showed values of .02 and .05 (the Democrats only very slightly associated with a pro-civil rights position) on two different civil rights policy items.[10] In 1964, the perceived association in the same terms on the same two items had risen to values of .54 and .50. The change in *volunteered* identifications of the two parties with the issue, among the much smaller subset of people so concerned that they brought the matter up themselves, showed even more dramatic change. In 1960 these civil rights-concerned people had tended to associate Kennedy somewhat with a pro-civil rights position, and Nixon with more of a "go-slow" approach (an association of .30). For Johnson and Goldwater in 1964, the association had mounted to .84, approaching consensus. The same volunteered materials include images of the parties, as well as of the candidates, and it is a matter of some interest to know in what measure Goldwater's 1964 position "rubbed off" on the Republican Party as a whole. In 1960, the civil rights association appeared to lie more clearly with the Kennedy-Nixon pairing (.30) than with any differences between the two parties, for these volunteered references to the parties showed only an association of .08. The comparable figure for the two parties in 1964 was .86. In short, we cannot explain why Goldwater produced a retrogression of Republican presidential voting strength in the South by suggesting that his key civil rights position failed to get across.

The Southern vote for Goldwater becomes intelligible if we add three elements to the consideration. First, while civil rights lent an important new pro-Goldwater force to the situation, various strong short-term forces which had pushed the Southern electorate in a pro-Republican direction in 1952, 1956 and 1960 were no longer present. We have argued elsewhere that the popular vote for Eisenhower and Nixon in the South was a very misleading index of the degree of solid Republican advance there.[11] While our data do show the Republican party inching forward in the affections of mass Southern voters, the pace has been slow; the South remains a preponderantly Democratic region. In 1952 and 1956, the Southern presidential vote swung far to the Republican side of normal for the region, just as it did in all other parts of the United States. In 1960, with the Eisenhower appeal gone, most other regions moved back toward the Democrats as we expected. This return toward normal was almost invisible in the South, since a new and offsetting short-term force—Kennedy's Catholicism—had arisen which was peculiarly repugnant to the Southern population with its concentration (Louisiana excepted) of devout and fundamentalist Protestants.[12] Thus if any other of the Republican aspirants had run in 1964, we might have expected a delayed return toward a much more normally Democratic vote in the South. From this point of view, the injection of a new civil rights differentiation by Goldwater did not occur in a void, but was something of a replacement for other forces which had kept the Southern vote extended in a remarkably pro-Republican direction for three consecutive presidential elections.

Once we take this into account, the Republican retrogression is less perplexing, although intuitively we would expect civil rights to have an impact on the Southern voter more potent than either Eisenhower's appeal or fear of a Catholic president. It is here that the second and third considerations enter. While Goldwater's civil rights position drew Southern whites toward the Republicans, Negroes both South and North moved monolithically toward the Democrats. Although Southern Negro voting was still limited by registration difficulties, it increased over 1960 and was almost unanimously Democratic for the first time.[13] If this sudden new increment of Negro votes could be removed from the Southern totals, the Goldwater vote proportion would undoubtedly appear to be a slight progression, rather than a retrogression, over the Eisenhower and Nixon votes.

Finally, it must be recognized that civil rights, while the primary issue in the South, was not the only one. Beyond civil rights, Southerners reacted negatively to the Goldwater positions much as their fellow citizens elsewhere. Many Southern white respondents said in effect: "Goldwater is right on the black man, and that is very important. But he is so wrong on everything else I can't bring myself to vote for him." From this point of view, the civil rights issue did indeed have a powerful impact in the South: without it, the 1964 Goldwater vote probably would not only have slipped to normal Republican levels, but would have veered as elsewhere to the pro-Democratic side. The more general ideological appeal to what Goldwater saw as Southern "conservatism" aside from the Negro question, did not have major impact.

Much the same comments hold for the failure of "white backlash" to develop in the way many expected outside the South. Our data show that civil rights feeling did not lack impact elsewhere. But for many non-Southern whites who resented the advance of the Negro cause and the summer of discontent, the election involved other important issues as well; and Goldwater's positions on them struck such voters very negatively. Thus "white backlash" feelings were translated into Goldwater votes by Democrats only where fear of the Negro was so intense as to blot out virtually all other considerations. Voters fitting this description existed in fair number and geographic concentration in the deepest latitudes of the South. Elsewhere, they were thinly scattered.

IV. THE ELECTION "POST-MORTEM"

Up to this point we have referred only vaguely to the many negative reactions

Goldwater occasioned in all sectors of the country, which tended to dim out isolated attractions he did present. The Goldwater "image" was indeed phenomenally unfavorable. We have measured such images in the past, among other ways, by tallying the simple number of favorable and unfavorable references made by respondents to broad questions inviting them to say what they like and dislike about each of the candidates. Typically, American voters have tended on balance to speak favorably, even about candidates they were about to send down to defeat. The least favorable image we have seen—in Adlai Stevenson's second try in 1956—involved only about 52 percent of all responses that were favorable. Less than 35 percent of the Goldwater references were favorable.

Just after the election, Goldwater observed that "more than 25 million people" voted "not necessarily for me, but for a philosophy that I represent. . . ." At another time, in assessing the magnitude of his defeat, he chastised himself for having been a personally ineffective spokesman for that philosophy. This seemed particularly odd against the descriptions of Goldwater before his nomination, in which even opponents concurred that at long last the right wing had found an articulate spokesman with a magnetic personality.

The candidate references we collect are a mixture of observations concerning the personality and leadership qualities of the individuals themselves as well as reactions to policy positions they represent in the public eye. Ideally, we could take this image material and split it cleanly into references to personal attributes as opposed to policy positions, in order to judge the accuracy of the proposition that what the public repudiated was the spokesman, and not the philosophy. Practically speaking, such divisions present many difficult coding decisions.[14]

Nevertheless, we have sifted Johnson and Goldwater references into categories more or less purely reflecting "policy" as opposed to "personality" significance. Among the most pure policy references, Johnson's were favorable by an 80-20 margin, visibly ahead of the 69-31 balance of his total image. Mentions of Goldwater policies ran less than 30-70 favorable, thereby trailing the rest of his image slightly. In general, the farther one moves from pure policy to pure personality, Johnson's advantage declines. His "wheeler-dealer" style and the aura of conflicts-of-interest which dogged him during the campaign came through to dilute his attractiveness. Against this backdrop, Goldwater's personal "integrity" and "sincerity" drew praise. Throughout, the data suggest that Johnson was carried along to an image nearly as positive as Eisenhower's best, less by his personal characteristics than by the policies with which he was associated (many of them identified by respondents as continuations from the Kennedy Administration). For Goldwater, if anything, the reverse was true.

Aside from civil rights and a faint flutter of approval brought by Goldwater's latter-day stand against immorality, none of his major positions was attractive to voters outside the most hard-core Republican ranks. In general, the mass of public opinion has been quite unsympathetic to traditional Republican thinking in areas of social welfare and other domestic problems for several decades. A major Goldwater theme involved attacks against the increasingly heavy hand of "big government," yet this struck little in the way of a responsive chord. Most Americans in the more numerous occupational strata do not appear to feel the governmental presence (save for local civil rights situations) in any oppressive or day-to-day manner, and as a consequence simply have no reactions to the area which have any motivational significance. Among those more aware of the practices and potentials of federal government, a slight majority feels that if anything, governmental services and protections are inadequate rather than overdone. Thus for better or for worse, such contentions on

Goldwater's part had little popular resonance.

Goldwater's failure to make much capital of domestic policy was not uncharacteristic of a Republican presidential candidate. What was new for a Republican, however, was his performance in the area of foreign policy. In a degree often overlooked, the 1950s were a period during which, from the point of view of many Americans inattentive to the finer lines of politics and reacting to the parties in terms of gross associations and moods, something of an uneasy equilibrium prevailed between the two major parties. Much more often than not, for these Americans the Democratic Party was the party of prosperity and good times, but also the party more likely to blunder into war. The Republican Party, conversely, was more skilled in maintaining peace, but brought with it depression and hard times.

The foreign policies proposed by Goldwater and refracted through the press and other commentators, shifted this image more dramatically than one might have thought possible (Table 2). Setting aside the large mass of voters who throughout the period did not see any particular differences between the parties in foreign policy capability, the balance of expectations in the area favored the Republicans by better than a 5-1 margin in 1956. This margin deteriorated somewhat in the late stages of the Eisenhower Administration, but remained at an imposing 2-1 edge. During the Goldwater campaign it reversed itself to a 3-1 margin favoring the Democrats.

Thus to the many ways of describing the public's repudiation of the Goldwater candidacy, another may be added: between a party of prosperity and peace, as against a party of depression and war, there is little room for hesitation.

. . .

V. CONCLUSIONS

It should be apparent that the phenomena we have examined in this paper have a significance that stretches considerably beyond the 1964 election, or questions of the credibility of public opinion polls, or the playing of games with the epistemologies of practicing politicians, fascinating though each of these subjects may be.

But the more important implications flow from the reflection that while these opinion worlds may be discrepant from one another in many regards, and it behooves us not to confuse them, it is not a simple matter of fact *vs.* fantasy: both worlds are real, and have real effects on the political process. Save for the obvious fact that the reality of "one man, one vote," governs the mass election with greater or lesser modification, while other public-opinion realities like the letter-writing world tend to hold sway otherwise, we know all too little empirically about the counterpoint between the two in actual political systems, and the normative significance of motivation-weighted votes is largely unexamined.

However this may be, if the reality of one of these worlds was manifest on Election Day, 1964, then the reality of the other was equally apparent in the San Francisco convention. For it is obvious that the intense levels of political motivation which underlie the letter-writing of the ultra-conservative wing are part and parcel of the ingredients which led

TABLE 2. PERCEPTIONS AS TO THE PARTY MOST LIKELY TO KEEP THE UNITED STATES OUT OF WAR IN THE ENSUING FOUR YEARS

	1956	1960	1964
	(%)	(%)	(%)
Democrats would handle better	7	15	38
No party difference	45	46	46
Republicans would handle better	40	29	12
Don't know, not ascertained	8	10	4
	100	100	100

to a Republican convention delegation so markedly discrepant from either the rank-and-file of the Party or its customary leadership. What had been lacking around the country in bodies was made up for in dedication; but the outcome of the convention was in no sense the less real for it. And from this juxtaposition of two worlds, the oddities of the 1964 election grew.

Notes

[1] The collection of data from a national sample of the electorate around the 1964 election was made possible by a grant to the Survey Research Center of the University of Michigan from the Carnegie Corporation of New York, which had also supported the 1952 election study.

[2] The most fertile elaboration of this classic script is of course contained in Anthony Downs, *An Economic Theory of Democracy* (New York, 1957).

[3] *The New York Times,* July 19, 1964.

[4] This datum is not as absurd as it might appear if the reader has failed to grasp the import of the preceding text. That is, in 1952 it was the most intense and ideologically "pure" Republicans who tended to prefer Taft to Eisenhower, much as 12 years later their counterparts chose Goldwater over the other Republican alternatives. It was the less ideologically committed (either by persuasion or by lack of ideological sensitivity) who were more satisfied with the Eisenhower candidature. The erstwhile Taft supporters did not perversely turn out at higher rates because they were disappointed in the convention choice, but because their striking commitment to Republicanism compelled them to more ardent support of its candidate whatever his ideological position.

[5] See "The Concept of a 'Normal Vote,'" ch. 1 in A. Campbell, P. Converse, W. Miller and D. Stokes, *Elections and the Political Order* (New York, 1965.)

[6] In our estimation, some challengers of this description have been prematurely discouraged from competition by poll results which might well have changed radically with greater exposure.

[7] Lodge's strong grass-roots popularity was one of the untold stories of the 1960 election, when he ran for vice-president. Well-known for his televised confrontations with the Russian delegation in the United Nations, he was far and away the most widely recognized and warmly regarded first-time vice-presidential candidate in the elections we have studied. Given the tarnish which seems to accompany second efforts at the presidency in American elections and which would undoubtedly have hurt Nixon, it may well be that Lodge, had he been acceptable to the Republican Party leadership, could have pushed Lyndon Johnson to a closer race than any other of the Republican hopefuls.

[8] While these rates may sound mountainous, it should be remembered that the expected defection rates for most of these groups are rather low —in the vicinity of 10 percent. Nonetheless, 40 percent of the Rockefeller Republicans in our sample voted for Johnson.

[9] We have examined this possibility in some seriousness simply because often in the past we have found public perceptions of party differences on major issues totally confused and muddy. Even on issues where the politically sophisticated see marked party differences, general public inattention and the ambiguities which politicians exploit to blur the edges of their positions combine to produce either lack of recognition of differences, or very conflicting impressions of what those differences are at any given point. See Campbell et al., *The American Voter* (New York, 1960), pp. 179ff.

[10] The statistic is such that if all citizens in the sample agreed that the Democrats represented one side of the issue and the Republicans the other, the figure would be 1.00 (perfect association). A figure of .00 represents the case of no aggregate association whatever.

[11] Philip E. Converse, "A Major Political Realignment in the South?" in Allan P. Sindler, ed., *Change in the Contemporary South* (Durham, N. C., Duke University Press, 1963).

[12] These religious effects were described in Converse *et al.*, "Stability and Change in 1960: a Reinstating Election," this REVIEW, Vol. 55 (June, 1961), pp. 269-80.

[13] In our data, expressions of party loyalty from the South which had been slowly losing Democratic strength throughout the 1950s show a sudden rebound in 1964. However, all of the rebound can be traced to Southern Negroes; the downward trend among Southern whites continued and at about the same pace.

[14] Take, for example, the charge hung on Goldwater by Democrats and some Republicans that he was "impulsive." This allegation reverberated in the public and came to make up one of our largest single categories of negative references to Goldwater. "Impulsiveness" is a personality trait that on one hand might have been less plausible for some other right-wing leader. Yet the charge took roots and began to flourish with respect to a cluster of policies that Goldwater shared with other Republican leaders of similar persuasions. It seems quite arbitrary to decide that it is exclusively either the person or the policy which is "impulsive."

How well did our established assumptions about American voting behavior stand up in the 1968 presidential election? So much about that contest seemed atypical — President Johnson's surprise decision not to seek re-election, George Wallace's third party candidacy, Eugene McCarthy's success with the Viet Nam issue, the Kennedy assassination. The first blush reaction is that the election must have been totally aberrant. The following analysis of that election by the researchers at the University of Michigan's Survey Research Center describes and assesses both the continuities and discontinuities in the voting behavior that emerged.

Continuity and Change In American Politics: Parties and Issues in the 1968 Election

Philip E. Converse
Warren E. Miller
Jerrold G. Rusk
Arthur C. Wolfe

Without much question, the third-party movement of George C. Wallace constituted the most unusual feature of the 1968 presidential election. While this movement failed by a substantial margin in its audacious attempt to throw the presidential contest into the House of Representatives, in any other terms it was a striking success. It represented the first noteworthy intrusion on a two-party election in twenty years. The Wallace ticket drew a larger proportion of the popular vote than any third presidential slate since 1924, and a greater proportion of electoral votes than any such movement for more than a century, back to the curiously divided election of 1860. Indeed, the spectre of an electoral college stalemate loomed sufficiently large that serious efforts at reform have since taken root.

At the same time, the Wallace candidacy was but one more dramatic addition to an unusually crowded rostrum of contenders, who throughout the spring season of primary elections were entering and leaving the lists under circumstances that ranged from the comic through the astonishing to the starkly tragic. Six months before the nominating conventions, Lyndon Johnson and Richard Nixon had been the expected 1968 protagonists, with some greater degree of uncertainty, as usual, within the ranks of the party out of power. The nominat-

Reprinted by permission of the authors and publisher from Philip E. Converse, Warren E. Miller, Jerrold G. Rusk, Arthur C. Wolfe, "Continuity and Change in American Politics: Parties and Issues in the 1968 Election," *American Political Science Review,* 63 (December, 1969), 1083-1105.

ing process for the Republicans followed the most-probable script rather closely, with the only excitement being provided by the spectacle of Governors Romney and Rockefeller proceeding as through revolving doors in an ineffectual set of moves aimed at providing a Republican alternative to the Nixon candidacy. Where things were supposed to be most routine on the Democratic side, however, surprises were legion, including the early enthusiasm for Eugene McCarthy, President Johnson's shocking announcement that he would not run, the assassination of Robert Kennedy in the flush of his first electoral successes, and the dark turmoil in and around the Chicago nominating convention, with new figures like Senators George McGovern and Edward Kennedy coming into focus as challengers to the heir apparent, Vice President Hubert Humphrey.

No recent presidential election has had such a lengthy cast of central characters, nor one that was kept for so long in flux. And under such circumstances, there is an inevitable proliferation of "what ifs?" What if Lyndon Johnson had decided to run again? What if Robert Kennedy had not been shot? What if George Wallace had been dissuaded from running, or had remained simply a regional states-rights candidate? What if Eugene McCarthy had accepted party discipline and closed ranks with Humphrey at the Chicago convention? What if Hubert Humphrey had handled the interaction with Mayor Daley and the Chicago demonstrators differently?

Strictly speaking, of course, there is no sure answer to questions of this type. If the attempt on Kennedy's life had failed, for example, an enormous complex of parameters and event sequences would have been different over the course of the campaign. One can never be entirely confident about what would have happened without the opportunity to live that particular sequence out in all its complexity. Nonetheless, given sufficient information as to the state of mind of the electorate during the period in question, plausible reconstructions can be developed which do not even assume that all other things remained constant, but only that they remained *sufficiently* constant that other processes might stay within predictable bounds. And answers of this sort, if not sacrosanct, carry substantial satisfaction.

One of our purposes in this paper will be to address some of these questions, as illuminated by preliminary analyses from the sixth national presidential election survey, carried out by the Survey Research Center of the University of Michigan.[1] An effort to develop answers gives a vehicle for what is frankly descriptive coverage of the 1968 election as seen by the electorate. At the same time, we would hope not to miss along the way some of the more theoretical insights which the peculiar circumstances of the 1968 election help to reveal. In particular, we shall pay close attention to the Wallace campaign, and to the more generic lessons that may be drawn from this example of interplay between a pair of traditional parties, potent new issues, and a protest movement.

THE SETTING OF THE ELECTION

The simplest expectation for the 1968 election, and one held widely until March of that year, was that President Johnson would exercise his option to run for a second full term, and that with the advantages of incumbency and the support of the majority party in the land, he would stand a very good chance of winning, although with a margin visibly reduced from his landslide victory over Barry Goldwater in 1964.

We will probably never know what role public opinion may have actually played in his decision to retire. But there is ample evidence that the mood of the electorate had become increasingly surly toward his administration in the months preceding his announcement. When queried in September and October of 1968, barely 40% of the electorate thought that he had handled his job well, the rest adjudging the performance to have been fair to poor. A majority of Democratic and independent voters, asked if they would have favored President Johnson as the Democratic nominee had he decided to run, said they would not have. Affective ratings elicited just after the election for all the prominent political figures of the campaign showed Johnson trailing Robert Kennedy in average popularity by a wide margin, and lagging somewhat behind Humphrey and Muskie as well, among other Democrats (see Table 2). Given the normal head-start that a sitting president usually enjoys in such assays of opinion, Johnson completed his term amid a public bad humor matched only in recent elections by the cloud under which Harry Truman retired from the presidency in 1952. It is correspondingly dubious that Lyndon Johnson could have avoided the embarrassment of defeat had he set his sails for another term.

Indeed, the pattern of concerns exercising the voters and turnover in the players on the presidential stage combined to produce a shift in popular preferences between 1964 and 1968 which was truly massive. It is likely that the proportion of voters casting presidential ballots for the same party in these two successive elections was lower than at any time in recent American history. Among whites who voted in both elections, a full third switched their party. Almost one Goldwater voter out of every five turned either to Humphrey or to Wallace four years later (dividing almost 3 to 1 for Wallace over Humphrey); at the same time, three in every ten white Johnson voters switched to Nixon or Wallace, with Nixon the favorite by a 4-to-1 ratio. A full 40 percent of Nixon's votes came from citizens who had supported Lyndon Johnson in 1964! Much of this flood, of course, came from Republicans who were returning home after their desertions from Goldwater.

Nevertheless, Democrats and Independents who had voted for Johnson and then turned to Nixon four years later made up nearly half of *all* the remaining vote switches, more than matching the combined flow of Johnson and Goldwater voters who supported Wallace, and almost equalling the total Wallace vote. The Johnson-Nixon switchers easily outweighed the flow away from Goldwater to Humphrey and Wallace, and the Republican presidential vote rose from 39% to 43% in 1968 as a consequence. At the same time, the loss of more than a quarter of the total Johnson vote to Wallace and Nixon was scarcely offset by the trickle of votes from Goldwater to Humphrey, and the Democratic proportion of the vote across the land dropped a shattering 19 percentage points from more than 61 percent to less than 43 percent.

Such a massive drain from the Democratic ranks establishes a broader parallel with 1952, for in both cases an electorate professing to be of Democratic allegiance by a considerable majority, had arrived at a sufficient accumulation of grievances with a Democratic administration as to wish it out of office, thereby producing what we have labelled elsewhere a "deviating election."[2] Indeed, the frantic motion of the electorate in its presidential votes between 1964 and 1968 may be ironically juxtaposed against the serene stability of party identifications in the country, for the overall proportions of self-proclaimed Democrats, Independents and Republicans have scarcely changed over the past twenty years, much less in the past four. Of course this juxtaposition calls into question the predictive value of party identification, relative to other kinds of determinants of the vote, and we shall undertake a more intensive discussion of this matter presently. For now, however, let us simply point out that while the inert distribution of party loyalties cannot by definition explain the complex flows of the presidential vote between 1964 and 1968, it was handsomely reflected in the 1968 congressional elections, as it has been in virtually all of the biennial congressional contests of the current era. Despite widespread dissatisfaction with Democratic performance, the Republican proportion of seats in the House rose only a minute 1 percent, from 43 in 1966 to 44 percent on the strength of the Nixon victory. Even at more local levels, the continuing dominance of Democratic partisanship across the nation is documented by the results of thousands of races for state legislative seats. Prior to the election, Democrats controlled 57.7 percent of all legislative seats. After the election, which saw contests for some or all seats in 43 states, Democratic control had dropped from 4,269 seats (or 57.7%) to 4,250 seats (57.5%).[3]

In view of such continued stability of partisanship, it is clear we must turn elsewhere to account for the remarkable changes in voting at the presidential level between 1964 and 1968. The classic assumption is, of course, that such change must spring from some flux in "short-term forces" — the impact of the most salient current issues, and the way in which these issues interlock with the leadership options, or the cast of potential presidential figures in the specific year of 1968. These terms obviously best define the setting of the 1968 election.

When asked on the eve of the presidential election to identify the most important problem facing the government in Washington, over 40% of the electorate cited the war in Vietnam. The salience of this issue provided another striking parallel with 1952. In both presidential elections, widespread public discouragement with the progress of a "bleeding war" in the Far East, seen as initiated by a Democratic administration, was a major source of indignation.

But the Vietnam issue did not, of course, stand alone. Offering vivid testimony to another bitter current of controversy was a simple, though little-noted, pattern in the popular presidential vote itself: while some 97% of black voters in the nation cast their ballots for Humphrey, less than 35% of white voters did so. Thus the presidential vote must have been as sharply polarized along racial lines as at any time during American history.[4] One major irony surrounding this cleavage was the fact that it was the comfortable white majority that was agitating to overturn control of the White House, while the aggrieved black minority was casting its vote as one in an effort to preserve the partisan status quo.

Indeed, this irony is compounded when the role of the Vietnam issue is jointly taken into account. We have indicated above that the public was deeply impatient with the Johnson administration, in part because of the handling of the war. Blacks stood out as the major demographic grouping most exercised about the entanglement in Vietnam. They were more likely than whites to opine that the government should never have undertaken the military commitment there. They also were more likely to feel that American troops should be brought home immediately, a position not generally associated with the Johnson administration. Nonetheless, as Table 2 (below) will document, Negro enthusiasm not only for Hubert Humphrey but for Lyndon Johnson as well remained high to the very end. It seems quite evident that when black citizens were making decisions about their vote, Vietnam attitudes paled into relative insignificance by contrast with attitudes toward progress on civil rights within the country; and that where such progress was concerned, the Johnson-Humphrey administration was seen as much more friendly than the other 1968 alternatives.

Because of the near-unanimity of the black vote, many of our analyses below have been focussed on differences within the white vote taken alone.[5] At the same time, this treatment must not be allowed to obscure in any way the deep imprint of racial cleavage on the election outcome. The additional "between-race" variance in the vote, concealed when data are presented only for whites, remains extreme, and is a faithful reflection of the crescendo to which civil rights tumult had risen over the four preceding years. It should be kept in mind.

To say that Vietnam and civil rights were dominant issues for the public in 1968 is not equivalent, however, to saying that voter positions on these issues can account for the large-scale voting change we have observed for whites between 1964 and 1968. As the comparisons provided by Table 1 suggest, changes in

TABLE 1. COMPARISON OF ATTITUDES ON CURRENT VIETNAM POLICY AND RACIAL DESEGREGATION, 1964, AND 1968, FOR WHITES ONLY

"Which of the following do you think we should do *now* in Vietnam?
1. Pull out of Vietnam entirely.
2. Keep our soldiers in Vietnam but try to end the fighting.
3. Take a stronger stand even if it means invading North Vietnam.

Northern Democrats

	Pull Out	Status Quo	Stronger Stand	Don't Know, Other	Total
1964	8%	25	29	38	100%
1968	20%	39	35	6	100%

Northern Republicans

| 1964 | 8% | 19 | 38 | 35 | 100% |
| 1968 | 20% | 39 | 36 | 5 | 100% |

Southern Democrats

| 1964 | 8% | 25 | 28 | 39 | 100% |
| 1968 | 17% | 36 | 38 | 9 | 100% |

Southern Republicans

| 1964 | 10% | 18 | 42 | 30 | 100% |
| 1968 | 15% | 29 | 48 | 8 | 100% |

"What about you? Are you in favor of desegregation, strict segregation, or something in between?" (This was the fourth question in a series asking about others' attitudes toward racial desegregation.)

Northern Democrats

	Desegregation	Mixed Feelings	Strict Segregation	Other	Total
1964	31%	50	17	2	100%
1968	38%	45	14	3	100%

Northern Republicans

| 1964 | 32% | 51 | 13 | 4 | 100% |
| 1968 | 35% | 50 | 10 | 5 | 100% |

Southern Democrats

| 1964 | 12% | 35 | 52 | 1 | 100% |
| 1968 | 18% | 45 | 30 | 7 | 100% |

Southern Republicans

| 1964 | 15% | 44 | 40 | 1 | 100% |
| 1968 | 15% | 60 | 20 | 5 | 100% |

public thinking about strategic alternatives in Vietnam or civil rights outcomes over this period were rather limited. Where Vietnam was concerned, opinion was somewhat more crystallized in 1968 than in 1964 but there had been no sweeping shift of sentiment from hawk to dove in mass feeling. On civil rights, the drift of white opinion had been if anything toward a more liberal stance, and hence can hardly explain a vote which seemed to vibrate with "blacklash." Thus public positioning on these two central issues taken alone seems no more capable of illuminating vote change from 1964 to 1968 than the inert partisan identifications.

What *had* changed, of course, was the public view of the success of Administration performance in these areas. As we have discussed elsewhere, throughout the 1950's citizens who felt the Republicans were better at keeping the country out of war outnumbered those who had more confidence in Democrats by a consistently wide margin, much as the Democratic Party tended to be seen as better at keeping the country out of economic depression. In 1964, however, the pleas of Barry Goldwater for an escalation of the Vietnam War in order to produce a military victory served to frighten the public, and rapidly reversed the standing perception: by the time of the November election more people felt the Democrats were better able to avert a large war.[6] But this novel perception was transient. President Johnson himself saw fit to authorize an escalation of bombing in Vietnam almost immediately after the 1964 election. By the time of the 1966 congressional election, the balance in popular assessments had already shifted back to the point where a slight majority chose the Republicans as more adept in avoiding war. By 1968, exasperation at the handling of the war had increased sufficiently that among people who felt there was a difference in the capacity of the two parties to avoid a larger war, the Republicans were favored once again by a margin of two to one.

To the bungled war in Vietnam, the white majority could readily add a sense of frustration at a racial confrontation that had taken on increasingly ugly dimensions between 1964 and 1968. Although national opinion had evolved in a direction somewhat more favorable to desegregation, largely through the swelling proportions of college-educated young, some persistently grim facts had been underscored by the Kerner Commission report in the spring of the year: forbidding proportions of the white citizenry outside of the South as well as within it had little enthusiasm for the redress of Negro grievances to begin with. And even among whites with some genuine sympathy for the plight of blacks, the spectacle of city centers aflame had scarcely contributed to a sense of confidence in the Administration handling of the problem.

From Vietnam and the racial crisis a corollary discontent crystallized that might be treated as a third towering issue of the 1968 campaign, or as nothing more than a restatement of the other two issues. This was the cry for "law and order" and against "crime in the streets." While Goldwater had talked in these terms somewhat in 1964, events had conspired to raise their salience very considerably for the public by 1968. For some, these slogans may have had no connotations involving either the black race or Vietnam, signifying instead a concern over rising crime rates and the alleged "coddling" of criminal offenders by the courts. More commonly by 1968, however, the connection was very close: there were rallying cries for more severe police suppression of black rioting in the urban ghettos, and of public political dissent of the type represented by the Vietnam peace demonstrations at Chicago during the Democratic convention.

In view of these latter connotations, it is not surprising that people responsive to the "law and order" theme tended, like George Wallace, to be upset at the same time by civil rights gains and the lack of a more aggressive policy in Vietnam. Therefore it might seem redundant to treat "law and order" as a third major issue in its own right. Nevertheless, we have found it important to do so, even where the "order" being imposed is on black militants or peace demonstrators, for the simple reason that many members of the electorate reacted as though the control of dissent was quite an independent issue. This becomes very clear where support for blacks and opposition to the war are accompanied with a strong

TABLE 2. AVERAGE RATINGS OF MAJOR 1968 POLITICAL FIGURES BY A NATIONAL SAMPLE, NOVEMBER-DECEMBER, 1968

	TOTAL SAMPLE	NON-SOUTH White (N's of 785-843)	NON-SOUTH Black (N's of 54-64)	SOUTH White (N's of 315-340)	SOUTH Black (N's of 55-66)
Robert Kennedy	70.1	70.4	94.1	60.5	91.2
Richard Nixon	66.5	67.7	53.0	67.8	56.6
Hubert Humphrey	61.7	61.2	86.1	53.4	85.8
Lyndon Johnson	58.4	56.6	81.9	53.7	82.7
Eugene McCarthy	54.8	56.5	59.1	49.8	54.0
Nelson Rockefeller	53.8	54.4	61.6	50.7	53.5
Ronald Reagan	49.1	49.6	42.9	50.0	41.8
George Romney	49.0	50.4	48.3	45.6	50.2
George Wallace	31.4	27.7	9.4	48.2	13.2
Edmund Muskie	61.4	62.7	71.0	54.7	68.9
Spiro Agnew	50.4	50.9	37.7	52.9	42.4
Curtis LeMay	35.2	33.6	21.1	43.9	22.9

revulsion against street protest and other forms of active dissent. And this combination occurs more frequently than an academic audience may believe.

One would expect, for example, to find support for peace demonstrations among the set of people in the sample who said (a) that we made a mistake in getting involved in the Vietnam War; and (b) that the preferable course of action at the moment would be to "pull out" of that country entirely. Such expectations are clearly fulfilled among the numerous blacks matching these specifications. Among whites, however, the picture is different. First, a smaller proportion of whites—about one in six or seven—expressed this combination of feelings about Vietnam. Among those who expressed such feelings it remains true that there is relatively less disfavor vented about some of the active forms of peace dissent that had become customary by 1968. What is striking, however, is the absolute division of evaluative attitudes toward peace dissenters among those who were themselves relative "doves," and this is probably the more politically significant fact as well. Asked to rate "Vietnam war protestors" on the same kind of scale as used in Table 2, for example, a clear majority of these whites who themselves were opposed to the Administration's Vietnam policy located their reactions on the negative side of the scale, and nearly one-quarter (23%) placed them at the point of most extreme hostility.

Even more telling, perhaps, are the attitudes of these same whites toward the peace demonstrations surrounding the Democratic convention at Chicago, for in this case the protestors were given undeniably sympathetic coverage by the television networks. Keeping in mind that we are dealing here with only those whites who took clear "dove" positions on Vietnam policy, it is noteworthy indeed that almost 70% of those giving an opinion rejected the suggestion that "too much force" was used by Chicago police against the peace demonstrators, and the *modal* opinion (almost 40%) was that "not enough force" had been used to suppress the demonstration.[7]

It should be abundantly clear from this description that the white minority who by the autumn of 1968 felt our intervention in Vietnam was a mistake and was opting for a withdrawal of troops turns out to fit the campus image of peace sentiment rather poorly. Such a disjuncture between stereotypes developed from the mass media and cross-section survey data are not at all uncommon. However, as certain other aspects of the election may be quite unintelligible unless this fact has been absorbed by the reader, it is worth underscoring here. This is not to say that the more familiar Vietnam dissent cannot be detected in a national sample. Among whites resenting Vietnam and wishing to get out, for example, a unique and telltale bulge of 12% gave ratings of the most extreme sympathy to the stimulus "Vietnam war protestors." Now this fragment of the electorate shows all of the characteristics expected of McCarthy workers or the New Left: its members are very young, are disproportionately college-educated, Jewish, and metropolitan in background and register extreme sympathy with civil rights and the Chicago convention demonstrations. The problem is that this group represents such a small component (one-eighth) of the 1968 dove sentiment on Vietnam being singled out here that its attitudes on other issues are very nearly obscured by rather different viewpoints held by the other 88% of the dove contingent. On the larger national scene, in turn, those who opposed Vietnam policy and were sympathetic to Vietnam war protestors make up less than 3% of the electorate —even if we add comparable blacks to the group—and law and order were not unpopular with the 97 percent.

In the broad American public, then, there was a widespread sense of breakdown in authority and discipline that fed as readily on militant political dissent as on race riots and more conventional crime. This disenchantment registered even among citizens who apparently were sympathetic to the goals of the dissent on pure policy grounds, and everywhere added to a sense of cumulative grievance with the party in possession of the White House. Thus the "law and order" phrase, ambiguous though it might be, had considerable resonance among the voters, and deserves to be catalogued along with Vietnam and the racial crisis among major issue influences on the election.

While the 1968 situation bore a number of resemblances to the basic ingredients and outcome of the 1952 election, the analogy is far from perfect. In 1952, the public turned out to vote in proportions that were quite unusual for the immediate period, a phenomenon generally taken to reflect the intensity of frustrations over the trends of government. It is easy to argue that aggravations were fully as intense in 1968 as they had been in 1952, and more intense than for any of the elections in between. Yet the proportion turning out to vote in 1968 fell off somewhat from its 1964 level.[8]

Of course any equation between indignation and turning out to vote does presuppose the offering of satisfactory alternatives, and there was somewhat greater talk than usual in 1968 that the candidate options in November were inadequate. Certainly the array of potential candidates was lengthy, whatever the actual nominees, and our account of the short-term forces affecting the electorate would be quite incomplete without consideration of the emotions with which the public regarded the dramatis personae in 1968. Just after the election, respondents in our national sample were asked to locate each of twelve political figures on a "feeling thermometer" running from zero (cold) to 100° (warm), with a response of 50° representing the indifference point. Table 2 summarizes the mean values for the total sample, as well as those within relevant regional and racial partitions.

Numerous well-chronicled features of the campaign are raised into quantitative relief by this tabulation, including Wallace's sharply regional and racial appeal, Muskie's instant popularity and near upstaging of Humphrey, and the limited interest that McCarthy seemed to hold for Negroes compared to other Democratic candidates. At the same time, other less evident comparisons can be culled from these materials, although the reader is cautioned to keep in mind that these scores refer to the period just after the election, and not necessarily to the period of the spring primaries or the summer conventions.[9] This may be of particular importance in the case of the ratings of Eugene McCarthy. When respondents were asked before the election which candidate from the spring they had hoped would win nomination, over 20 percent of Democrats and Independents recalling some preference mentioned McCarthy. However, many of these citizens gave quite negative ratings to McCarthy by November, so it appears that some disenchantment set in between the primaries and the election.

The question of timing poses itself acutely as well where Robert Kennedy is concerned.

Taken at face value, the data of Table 2 imply that aside from the tragedy at Los Angeles, Kennedy should have been given the Democratic nomination and would have won the presidential election rather handily. Yet how much of this massive popularity is due to some posthumous halo of martyrdom? It seems almost certain that at least some small increment is of this sort, and that the harsh realities of a tough campaign would have eroded the bright edges of Kennedy appeal. Nevertheless, both in contested primaries and poll data of the spring period,[10] as well as in the retrospective glances of our autumn respondents, one cannot fail to be impressed by the reverberations of Kennedy charisma even in the least likely quarters, such as among Southern whites or among Republicans elsewhere. And rank-and-file Democrats outside the South reported themselves to have favored

Kennedy for the nomination over Humphrey by two-to-one margins, and over McCarthy by nearly three-to-one. Clearly a Kennedy candidacy could not have drawn a much greater proportion of the black vote than Humphrey received, although it might have encouraged higher turnout there. But there is evidence of enough edge elsewhere to suggest that Robert Kennedy might have won an election over Richard Nixon, and perhaps even with greater ease than he would have won his own party's nomination.

As it was, Humphrey received the mantle of party power from Lyndon Johnson and, with Robert Kennedy missing, captured the Democratic nomination without serious challenge. At that point he faced much the same dilemma as Adlai Stevenson had suffered in 1952: without gracelessly biting the hand that fed him, how could he dissociate himself from the unpopular record of the preceding administration? In 1952, Stevenson did not escape public disgust with the Truman administration, and was punished for its shortcomings. The 1968 data make clear in a similar manner that Humphrey was closely linked to Lyndon Johnson in the public eye through the period of the election. For example, the matrix of intercorrelations of the candidate ratings presented in Table 2 shows, as one would expect, rather high associations in attitudes toward presidential and vice presidential candidates on the same ticket. Thus the Humphrey-Muskie intercorrelation is .58, the Nixon-Agnew figure is .59, and the Wallace-LeMay figure is .69. But the highest intercorrelation in the whole matrix, a coefficient of .70, links public attitudes toward Lyndon Johnson and those toward Hubert Humphrey. Humphrey was highly assimilated to the Johnson image, and his support came largely from sectors of the population for which the administration had not "worn thin."

When we consider the relative strength of Kennedy enthusiasts as opposed to loyal Humphrey-Johnson supporters among identifiers with the Democratic Party within the mass public, the line of differentiation that most quickly strikes the eye is the noteworthy generation gap. As we have seen above, Kennedy supporters enjoy a marked overall plurality. However, this margin comes entirely from the young. For Democrats under thirty, only about one in five giving a pre-convention nomination preference picks Humphrey or Johnson, and Kennedy partisans outnumber them by nearly three to one. Among Democrats over fifty, however, Humphrey-Johnson supporters can claim a clear plurality.[11] The "wings" of the Democratic Party that emerged in the struggle for the nomination had an "old guard" and "young Turk" flavor, even as reflected in a cross-section sample of party sympathizers.[12]

This completes our summary of the setting in which the 1968 election took place. We have seen that despite great continuity in party loyalties and a surprising constancy in policy positions of the public, there was an unusual degree of change in partisan preference at the presidential level by comparison with 1964. This change occurred in part as a response to increased salience of some issues, such as the question of "law and order," and in part because of the way in which contending leadership cadres had come to be identified with certain policies or past performance. The Democratic party lost, as quickly as it had won, its perceived capacity to cope with international affairs and the exacerbating war in Vietnam. Hubert Humphrey, long a major figure in his own right, could not move swiftly enough to escape his links with a discredited regime.

Let us now pursue some of the more obvious analytic questions posed by the general discontent among voters in 1968, and by the Wallace movement in particular. We shall first consider influences on the actual partitioning of the vote on Election Day, and then examine some of the attitudinal and social bases underlying the outcome.

HYPOTHETICAL VARIATIONS ON THE VOTE OUTCOME

Impact of the Wallace Ticket

There were signs of some concern in both the Nixon and Humphrey camps that the success of George Wallace in getting his name on the ballot might divert votes and lower their respective chances of success. Nixon was more alarmed by the prospective loss of the electoral votes in the Deep South that Goldwater had won in 1964, while Humphrey was alarmed in turn by intelligence that Wallace was making inroads outside the South among unionized labor that had been customarily Democratic since the New Deal. At the very least, the Wallace ticket was responsible for the injection of unusual uncertainty in a game already replete with unknowns. Now that the dust has settled, we can ask more systematically how the election might have been affected if Wallace had been dissuaded from running.

Numerous polls made clear at the time of the election that Wallace voters tended to be quite disproportionately nominal Democrats, and data from our sample are congruent with this conclusion, although the differences were more notable in the South than elsewhere. For the South, 68% of Wallace voters considered themselves Democrats, and 20% Republicans.

Outside the South, proportions were 46% Democratic and 34% Republican. Yet these proportions taken alone do not address in any satisfying fashion what might have happened if Wallace had not run. In the first place, these partisan proportions among Wallace voters do not differ very markedly from those which characterize the regional electorates taken as a whole. Indeed, as we shall see, the overall association between partisanship and attitudes toward Wallace (the rating scale) shows Republicans slightly more favorable across the nation as a whole, although this fact is faintly reversed with blacks set aside, and the main lesson seems to be that the "true" correlation is of utterly trivial magnitude (.05 or less). More important still, however, is the obvious fact that Democrats voting for Wallace were repudiating the standard national ticket, as many as a third of them for the second time in a row. If Wallace had not run, we can have little confidence that they would have faithfully supported Humphrey and Muskie.

It is clear that the crucial datum involves the relative preferences of the Wallace voters for either Nixon or Hum-

TABLE 3. DISTRIBUTION OF THE WALLACE VOTE, BY TRADITIONAL PARTIES AND CANDIDATES

		Democratic	Independent	Republican
Rating of Two Major Candidates	HUMPHREY over NIXON	4% (347)	26% (23)	21% (24)
	Tied	24% (79)	9% (11)	6% (17)
	NIXON over HUMPHREY	26% (132)	15% (53)	7% (314)

The percentage figure indicates the proportion of all voters in the cell who reported casting a ballot for Wallace. The number of voters is indicated between parentheses.

phrey, assuming that these preferences would have been the same without Wallace and that these citizens would have gone to the polls in any event. This information is available in the leader ratings used for Table 2. In Table 3 we have arrayed the total sample according to whether Humphrey or Nixon was given the higher rating, or the two were tied, as well as by the respondent's party identification. Within each cell so defined, we indicate the proportion of the vote won by Wallace, and the number of voters on which the proportion is based. The latter figures show familiar patterns. Of voters with both a party and a candidate preference, more than four-fifths prefer the nominee of their party. And while Democrats are in a majority, it is clear that the tides are running against them since they are suffering the bulk of defections.

It is interesting how the Wallace vote is drawn from across this surface. While the numbers of cases are too small to yield very reliable estimates in some of the internal cells, it is obvious that Wallace made least inroads among partisans satisfied with their party's nominee, and showed major strength where such partisans were sufficiently disgusted with their own party nominee actually to prefer that of the opposing party. Conceptually, it is significant that these protestors included Republicans unenthusiastic about Nixon as well as the more expected Democrats cool to Humphrey. Practically, however, Nixon Democrats so far outnumbered Humphrey Republicans that while Wallace drew at nearly equal rates from both groups, the majority of his votes were from Democrats who otherwise preferred Nixon rather than from Republicans who might have given their favors to Humphrey.

This in turn provides much of the answer to one of our primary questions. While the data underlying Table 3 can be manipulated in a variety of ways, all reasonable reconstructions of the popular vote as it might have stood without the Wallace candidacy leave Nixon either enjoying about the same proportion of the two-party vote that he actually won or a slightly greater share, depending on the region and the detailed assumptions made. In short, unless one makes some entirely extravagant assumptions about the mediating electoral college, it is very difficult to maintain any suspicion that the Wallace intrusion by itself changed the major outcome of the election.

Impact of the McCarthy Movement

If he was ever tempted at all, Eugene McCarthy decided against mounting a fourth-party campaign for the presidency. At the same time, he withheld anything resembling enthusiastic personal support for Hubert Humphrey. In view of his devoted following, some observers felt that McCarthy's refusal to close party ranks after Chicago cost the Democratic nominee precious votes, and conceivably even the presidency.

In order to understand the basis of McCarthy support at the time of the election, it is useful to trace what is known of the evolution of McCarthy strength from the time of the first primary in the spring. It will be recalled that McCarthy was the sole Democrat to challenge the Johnson administration in the New Hampshire primary. With the aid of many student volunteer campaign workers, he polled a surprising 42% of the vote among Democrats, as opposed to 48% drawn by an organized write-in campaign for President Johnson. Although he failed to upset the president in the vote, most observers saw his performance as remarkably strong, and a clear harbinger of discontent which could unseat Lyndon Johnson in the fall election. This reading was plainly shared by Robert Kennedy, who anounced his own candidacy for the nomination four days later, and probably by Johnson himself, who withdrew from any contention less than three weeks later.

Sample survey data from New Hampshire at the time of the primary show some expected patterns underlying that first McCarthy vote, but also some rather unexpected ones as well. First, the vote among Democrats split toward Johnson or McCarthy in obvious ways according to expressions of satisfaction or dissatisfaction with Administration performance and its Vietnam policy in particular. The McCarthy vote in New Hampshire certainly reflected a groundswell of anger at the Johnson administration, and an expression of desire for a change which was simply reiterated in November. Surprisingly, however, in view of McCarthy's clear and dissenting "dove" position on Vietnam, the vote he drew in New Hampshire could scarcely be labelled a "peace vote," despite the fact that such a conclusion was frequently drawn. There was, of course, some hard-core peace sentiment among New Hampshire Democrats that was drawn quite naturally to McCarthy. Among his supporters in the primary, however, those who were unhappy with the Johnson administration for not pursuing a *harder* line against Hanoi outnumbered those advocating a withdrawal from Vietnam by nearly a three to two margin! Thus the McCarthy tide in New Hampshire was, to say the least, quite heterogeneous in its policy preferences: the only common denominator seems to have been a deep dissatisfaction with the Johnson administration.[13] McCarthy simply represented the only formal alternative available to registered Democrats. This desire for an alternative was underlined by the fact that most of the 10 percent of the Democratic vote that did not go to Johnson or McCarthy went to Nixon as a write-in candidate on the Democratic ballot.

The entry of Robert Kennedy into the race did provide another alternative and, as we have seen, a very popular one as well. He made major inroads into the potential McCarthy strength, and by the time our autumn sample was asked what candidate of the spring would have been preferred for the Democratic nomination, 46% of those Democrats with some preference cited Kennedy first while only 18% mentioned McCarthy. Nevertheless, even this 18% cannot be thought of as constituting hard-core McCarthy support at the time of the actual election, since almost two-thirds of this group had turned their attention elsewhere, giving at least one of the other presidential hopefuls a higher rating than they gave McCarthy in the responses underlying Table 2. The remainder who reported McCarthy as their preconvention favorite and awarded him their highest ratings just after the election make up some 6% of Democrats having some clear candidate preference, or 3% of all Democrats. Along with a handful of Independents and Republicans showing the same reiterated McCarthy preference, these people can be considered the McCarthy "hard-core."

While it is this hard-core whose voting decisions interest us most, it is instructive to note where the other two-thirds of the pre-convention McCarthy support among Democrats went, over the course of the campaign. If these migrations are judged according to which presidential aspirant among the nine hopefuls of Table 2 was given the highest rating in November, one discovers that a slight plurality of these erstwhile McCarthy backers found George Wallace their preferred candidate in the fall. Slightly smaller groups favored Kennedy and Nixon, and a scatter picked other Republicans like Reagan and Rockefeller, despite their own Democratic partisanship. Very few of these McCarthy Democrats—about one in seven—migrated to a preference for Hubert Humphrey. Where the actual presidential vote was concerned, the choice was of course more constrained.

Since the McCarthy movement was commonly thought of as somewhat to the left of Humphrey and the administration, while Wallace was located rather markedly to the right, a major McCarthy-to-Wallace transfer of preferences may seem ideologically perplexing. Were McCarthy supporters so furious with the Humphrey nomination that pure spite overcame issue feelings and led to a protest vote for Wallace? Although there were rumors of such a reaction at the time, our data suggest a somewhat simpler interpretation. We have already noted the attitudinal heterogeneity of McCarthy voters in New Hampshire. Those in our autumn sample who recall a preconvention preference for McCarthy are similarly heterogeneous. Indeed, on some issues of social welfare and civil rights, preconvention McCarthy supporters are actually more conservative than backers of either Humphrey or Kennedy.

This heterogeneity declined markedly, however, as the size of the McCarthy group eroded over the summer to what we have defined as the hard-core. If we compare the attitudes of that hard-core on major issues with those of the professed early backers of McCarthy who subsequently supported Wallace, the differences are usually extreme. The McCarthy-Wallace group was against desegregation, in favor of an increased military effort in Vietnam, and was highly indignant with the situation in the nation where "law and order" was concerned (see Table 4). People supporting McCarthy to the bitter end took opposite positions on all of these major issues. Similarly, the winnowing down of the McCarthy support operated very sharply along demographic lines. Among non-Southern white Democrats who reported a preconvention McCarthy preference, for example, the hard-core that remained enthusiastic about McCarthy through to the actual election were 60% of college background, whereas, of those whose ardor cooled, only 18% had had any connection with college.

In short, then, it is evident again that among Democrats particularly, McCarthy was an initial rallying point for voters of all policy persuasions who were thoroughly displeased with the Johnson administration. When the Wallace candidacy crystallized and his issue advocacies became more broadly known, that portion of the discontented to whom he spoke most directly flocked to him. Hence it seems very doubtful that Humphrey would have won many votes from this group even if McCarthy had lent the Vice President his personal support in a whole-hearted fashion. The main motivation of this group was to register its disgust with incumbent leaders concerning civil rights advances, timidity in Vietnam and outbreaks of social disorder. It may well be that by September, with the far more congenial candidacy of Wallace available, Senator McCarthy would already have become a relatively negative reference point for this two-thirds of his early support, especially if he had joined forces with Humphrey. Therefore if we are to search for votes withheld from Humphrey because of the kinds of discontent McCarthy helped to crystallize, they are much more likely to be found among the McCarthy hard-core.

We persist in looking for such withheld votes, not simply because of rumors they existed, but also because there are rather tangible signs in the data that they were present in 1968. Such votes could take any one of four major alternative forms: they could be located among citizens who went to the polls but did not vote for president; they could be reflected in votes for minor party candidates; they could involve staying at home on election day; or they could take the form of votes spitefully transferred to Humphrey's chief rival, Mr. Nixon. Easiest to establish as "withheld votes" are the first two categories. Although their incidence is naturally very limited, both types can be discerned in the sample and do occur in conjunction with strong enthusiasm for McCarthy. Projected back to the nation's electorate, perhaps as much as a half-million votes are represented here, lying primarily outside the South. This is only a faint trace when sprinkled across the political map of the nation, however, and taken alone would probably have made little or no difference in the distribution of votes from the electoral college.

It is more difficult to say that specific instances of abstinence from any voting in 1968, or "defection" to Richard Nixon, reflect an abiding loyalty to McCarthy that Humphrey could not replace, and would not have occurred but for the McCarthy intrusion. There is a faint edge of non-voting that looks suspiciously of this sort, but it is again very limited: most ardent McCarthy fans were too politically involved to have thrown away a chance to vote at other levels of office. Far more numerous are the defections to Nixon on the part of voters of liberal and Democratic predispositions, who reported sympathy toward McCarthy. Here, however, it is difficult to be confident that McCarthy made any necessary contributions to the decision equation: the situation itself might have soured these people sufficiently, McCarthy or no. Nevertheless, when one begins to add together putative "withheld votes" from the preceding three catgories one does not need to factor in any very large proportion of these defectors to arrive at a total large enough to have provided Humphrey with a tiny majority in the electoral college, without requiring any gross maldistribution of these new-found popular votes outside the South.

We should reiterate, of course, that any such hypothetical reconstructions must be taken with a grain of salt. If McCarthy had embraced Humphrey on the final night in Chicago, not all of his most fervent supporters would necessarily have followed suit, and Humphrey would have needed most of them for a victory. Or if Humphrey had catered more dramatically to the McCarthy wing in terms of Vietnam policy after the

TABLE 4. Issue Differences Among Whites Preferring McCarthy as the Democratic Nominee, According to November Preferences for McCarthy or Wallace

		McCarthy "Hard Core"[a]	Voted Wallace[b]
"Are you in favor of desegregation, strict segregation, or something in between?"	DESEGREGATION IN BETWEEN SEGREGATION	79% 21 0	7% 50 43
		100% (24)	100% (14)
"Do you think the (Chicago) police (at the Democratic Convention) used too much force, the right amount of force, or not enough force with the demonstrators?"	TOO MUCH FORCE RIGHT AMOUNT NOT ENOUGH	91% 9 0	0% 50 50
		100% (23)	100% (12)
"Which of the following do you think we should do now in Vietnam: pull out of Vietnam entirely, keep our soldiers in Vietnam but try to end the fighting, or take a stronger stand even if it means invading North Vietnam?"	PULL OUT STATUS QUO STRONGER STAND	50% 50 0	7% 7 86
		100% (24)	100% (13)

[a] This column is limited to whites whose pre-convention favorite was Eugene McCarthy and who continued to give him top rating after the November election.
[b] It is to be emphasized that this column includes *only* those Wallace voters who said that in the spring of 1968 they had hoped Eugene McCarthy would win the Democratic nomination. This fact explains the small case numbers. However, in view of the relative homogeneity of respondents in the table—all are whites who reported a pre-convention McCarthy preference and most happen in addition to be nominal identifiers of the Democratic Party—the disparities in issue position are the more impressive.

election, he might have suffered losses of much greater proportion to Wallace on his right, for there is simply no question but that Democrats sharing the circle of ideas espoused by Wallace outnumbered the Democrats attuned to McCarthy by a very wide margin—perhaps as great as ten to one. Morever, it is appropriate to keep in mind our earlier suggestion that the Wallace intrusion hurt Nixon's vote more than Humphrey's: if we now remove Wallace as well as McCarthy from the scene, the net result might remain a Nixon victory.

However all this may be, it seems probable that the entire roster of prominent Democratic candidates—McCarthy, Wallace, Kennedy, McGovern —who were in their various ways opposing the administration, must have contributed cumulatively to Humphrey's problem of retaining the loyalty of fellow Democrats in the electorate. Certainly the failure of liberal Republican leaders to rally around the Goldwater candidacy in 1964, itself an unusual departure from tradition, had contributed to the Republican disaster of that year. 1968 provided something of a mirror image, and the result was an inordinate movement of the electorate between the two consultations.

. . .

THE SOCIAL BASES OF WALLACE SUPPORT

A variety of facts already cited about the Wallace movement of 1968 makes clear that while there was some modest overlap in support for Goldwater in 1964 and Wallace in 1968, it was at best a weak correlation and the Wallace clientele differed quite notably from Goldwater's. Thus, for example, almost exactly half of our 1968 Wallace voters who had participated in the 1964 election reported that they had voted for Johnson. Or again, we have seen that the majority of Wallace voters, like the electorate as a whole, was identified with the Democratic party, while it is obvious that most Goldwater voters were Republican identifiers. Similarly, we have just noted that the Wallace movement had a much less clear ideological focus among its sympathizers than marked Goldwater supporters in 1964.

This discrepancy in clientele may seem perplexing. After all, in the terms of conventional analysis in political sociology both candidates were "darlings of the radical right." Yet the limited degree of overlap between Goldwater and Wallace voters is confirmed in equally impressive fashion when one compares their social backgrounds or even their simplest demographic characteristics. Among Goldwater voters, for example, women both South and non-South showed the same slight majority they enjoy in the electorate; Wallace voters in the South showed a similar balance, but elsewhere were rather markedly (almost 60-40) male. The Goldwater vote had been much more urban, while the Wallace vote was relatively rural and small-town, particularly in the South. Outside the South, the age distribution of Wallace voters departed markedly from that shown by Goldwater in 1964, with the proportion under 35 being about twice as great and that over 65 only half as large.

The well-publicized appeal of Wallace to the unionized laboring man is clearly reflected in our data: outside the South, the proportion of white union members preferring Wallace over the other major candidates was more than three times as great as it was within households having no unionized members (19% to 6%); even in the South, where other appeals were present and the unionization of labor is more limited, the contrast between the preferences of union members and non-union households remains dramatic (52% to 28% giving top preference to Wallace over the conventional candidate). Indeed, in both regions the occupational center of gravity of Wallace popularity was clearly among white skilled workers. Nationwide, only about 10% of the Wallace vote was contributed by the professional and managerial strata, whereas persons of these occupations had given Goldwater almost half of his vote (46%). Needless to say, the proportion of unionized labor supporting Goldwater was very low. Along with these class differences, marked discrepancies in educational background can be taken for granted. In the South, one-third of Wallace's support came from whites with no more than grade school education, while the national figure for Goldwater was 13%. The proportion of voters of college experience backing Goldwater was about double that found voting for Wallace either in the South or elsewhere.

All of these comparisons help to underscore the major disparities in the social bases of support for Goldwater and Wallace, despite the apparent common policy ground of the relatively extreme right. While one should not lose track of the fact that there was a small and systematic overlap in clientele, it is abundantly clear that neither candidate exhausted the potential support for a severely conservative program in matters of civil rights, law and order or Vietnam. In a very real sense, it can be seen that Wallace was a poor man's Goldwater. As we suggested at the time, Goldwater pitched his campaign on an ideological plane which rather escaped some members of the electorate who might otherwise have found his positions congenial.[14] Wallace's perfectly direct appeal to citizens of this latter description, along with the undercurrent of populism alien to the Goldwater conservatism, apparently sufficed to put off some of the Arizona senator's more well-to-do supporters.[15] The Goldwater support was drawn from a relatively urbane and sophisticated conservatism; Wallace appealed to many similar instincts, but the style was folksy and tailored to the common man.

In a significant way, too, Wallace remained a regional candidate despite his discovery that he could win more than scattered votes in the North and his consequent presence on every state's ballot. Over half of his popular votes came from the states of the Confederacy. Everything, from his lack of political experience at a federal level to his marked Southern accent, suggested a parochial relevance that had rarely been salient where Goldwater was concerned. While electoral maps leave no doubt as to the regional nature of the response, sample survey data show that even these visible effects have been diluted by inter-regional migration. Thus, for example, while much has been written about the Wallace appeal in various European ethnic communities of northern cities, little has been said about the "American ethnic group" of southern white migrants, most of whom are blue-collar and frequently in a position to take special pleasure in the spectacle of a Southern compatriot coming north to give the Yankees what for. Our data indicate that Wallace drew over 14% of the vote from these migrants, and less than 7% otherwise outside the South. On the other hand, the significant stream of migration of Yankees into the South, the political implications of which we have described elsewhere,[16] provided something of a barrier to further Wallace successes. Heavily Republican in a non-Southern sense and now constituting better than one-seventh of white voters in the region, these migrants were even less interested in voting for Wallace than were Southern whites in the North, and gave the former Alabama governor only 10% of their vote while their native Southern white colleagues were casting almost one vote in every three for him.

. . .

There can be no question but that dramatic and persistent displays of dissent on the campuses between 1964 and 1968 helped to place question marks around "consensual" national policies which might otherwise have continued to be taken for granted by most of the citizenry. At the same time, disregard for the occasional junctures of electoral decision when the mass public has some say in the political process may mean that a battle was won but a war was lost. For some few, this *politique de pire* is quite intentional, being thought to help "radicalize" the electorate in ways that can be controlled and manipulated. For most student activists, however, success in raising questions is of little value if one is helping in the same stroke to elect "wrong people" to answer them. And quite apart from the nature of the leadership elected in 1968, it is obvious to any "rational" politician hoping to maximize votes in 1970 or 1972 that there are several times more votes to be gained by leaning toward Wallace than by leaning toward McCarthy.

If these facts were inevitable consequences of "raising the issues" from the campuses, the dilemma would be severe indeed. It is not clear to us, however, that any intrinsic dilemma is involved. Much of the backlash expressed in the 1968 voting received its impetus less from irreconcilable policy disagreement —although on civil rights there is more than a modicum of that—than from resentment at the frequency with which the message of dissent from the campuses was clothed in "bait" conventional opinion. In the degree that the feelings and opinion reflexes of the common man, including age peers of lower circumstances, were comprehended at all by campus activists, they tended to be a subject for derision or disdain. Strange to say, such hostile postures communicate with great speed even across social gulfs, and are reciprocated with uncommon reliability. Fully as often, of course, there was simply no comprehension of the dynamics of public opinion at all.

Whether one likes it or not, the United States does retain some occasional elements of participatory democracy. A young and well-educated elite-to-be that it too impatient to cope with this bit of reality by undertaking the tedium of positive persuasion may find its political efforts worse than wasted.

Notes

[1] The 1968 national sample survey (N = 1559) was made possible by a grant from the Ford Foundation, whose support we gratefully acknowledge. A total of 1559 citizens of voting age were interviewed, most of them both before and after Election Day. The preliminary nature of this report is to be emphasized, since the data on which it is based had not been fully cleaned at the time of writing. When the study is released through the Inter-University Consortium for Political Research, interested analysts may discover small discrepancies from the statistics reported here. Readers should also remember that all sample statistics are subject to varying amounts of sampling error in relation to the number of cases on which they are based.

[2] A deviating election is one in which the party commanding the identifications of a majority of the electorate is nonetheless voted out of power temporarily. See A. Campbell, P. Converse, W. Miller, and D. Stokes, *The American Voter* (New York: John Wiley, 1960), Chapter 19.

[3] *Congressional Quarterly,* November 22, 1968, p. 3177.

[4] The percentage difference of 62% in candidate preference between blacks and whites is substantially larger than class differentiation or other social cleavages and partisanship within the United States in recent history or for democracies of Western Europe.

[5] Such segregation is indicated simply because of the fact that within the black vote in 1968 there is next to no meaningful "variance" to be "accounted for." When categories of "Nixon voters" and "Wallace voters" are presented, they are necessarily "lily-white" in composition. Therefore when "Humphrey voters" are contrasted with them, it is confusing if differences may be totally a function of the large admixtures

of blacks in the Humphrey support, as opposed to differences which would stand up even with comparisons limited to whites.

[6] See "Voting and Foreign Policy," by Warren E. Miller, Chapter 7 in James N. Rosenau (ed.), *Domestic Sources of Foreign Policy* (New York: The Free Press, 1967).

[7] A separate analysis, carried out by a colleague in the Survey Research Center Political Behavior Program and using the same body of data from the SRC 1968 election study, suggests, moreover, that many voters who thought the police used too little force deserted Humphrey in the course of the campaign while the minority who objected that too much force was used voted more heavily for the Democratic nominee. See John P. Robinson, "Voter Reaction to Chicago 1968," Survey Research Center (1969), mimeo.

[8] The decline was only on the order of 1½ percent nationally, but the overall figures are somewhat misleading. Enormous efforts devoted to voter registration projects among Southern blacks between 1964 and 1968 appear to have paid off by increasing voter participation in that sector from 44% to 51%. Perhaps in counterpoint, Southern whites increased their turnout by 2%, thereby inching ever closer to the national norm. Thus the decline in turnout was concentrated outside the South, and there approached the more substantial drop of 4%. Even this figure is misleading, since whites outside the South showed a 3% loss in percentage points of turnout, while nonwhites declined by almost 11 percentage points! See *Current Population Reports,* "Voter Participation in November 1968," Series P-20, No. 177, December 27, 1968. Although such turnout figures, apart from the more general mobilizing of Southern blacks, are consistent with a proposition that whites were more eager to "throw the rascals out" than blacks, and that among whites, Southerners had the fiercest grievances of all, there is no hiding the fact of anemic turnout in most of the country in 1968. Interestingly enough, the decline from 1964 was uniformly distributed across the entire spectrum of party allegiances from loyal Democrats to strong Republicans.

[9] The reader should also keep in mind several other things about Table 2. The "South" here refers, as it will throughout this paper, to the Census Bureau definition of the region that includes 15 states and the District of Columbia. Hence such border states as Maryland or West Virginia are included along with the deeper southern states of the old confederacy. Presumably, for example, George Wallace's rating among whites of a more hard-core South would be correspondingly higher. Secondly, it should be remembered for some of the lesser candidates that respondents knowing so little about a candidate as to be indifferent to him would end up rating him "50°." Thus it would be questionable to conclude from Table 2 that LeMay was more popular than George Wallace, except in a very limited sense. Actually, three times as many respondents (nearly one-third) left LeMay at the indifference point as did so for Wallace. Thus lack of visibility helped to make him *less unpopular.* But among those who reacted to both men, LeMay was less popular than Wallace. Similarly, Wallace's low rating must be understood as a compound of an admiring minority and a hostile majority. The variance of Wallace ratings is much greater than those for other candidates, even in the South.

[10] Just after the decision of Robert Kennedy to run and before Lyndon Johnson's withdrawal, the Gallup poll showed Democrats favoring Kennedy as the party's nominee by a 44-41 margin.

[11] Interestingly enough, the same generational cleavages among Southern white Democrats occur at an earlier age than those elsewhere. In that region, Humphrey-Johnson preferences hold a plurality in all age cohorts over 30, despite the fact that Kennedy support has an edge of better than three to one among those under 30 (N of 34), perhaps because the latter group has less of a memory of the fury in the deep South

at the Kennedy family prior to the assassination of President John Kennedy in Dallas in 1963.

[12] Although there is some slight tendency for pre-convention supporters of McCarthy to be relatively young, the distribution by age is more homogeneous than expected, and much more so than is the case for Kennedy. It is possible that young people supporting McCarthy as the only alternative to the Administration switched more heavily than the middle-aged to Kennedy when he announced his candidacy.

[13] See also the account for New Hampshire by Louis Harris, "How Voters See the Issues," *Newsweek,* March 25, 1968, p. 26.

[14] P. Converse, A. Clausen, and W. Miller, "Electoral Myth and Reality: The 1964 Election" this REVIEW, 59 (June, 1965), 321-336.

[15] It is quite possible, however, that some of this support might have moved to Wallace had the Republican Party nominated anybody but Nixon or Reagan, among the main contenders.

[16] A. Campbell, P. Converse, W. Miller, and D. Stokes, *Elections and the Political Order* (New York: John Wiley, 1965), Chapter 12.

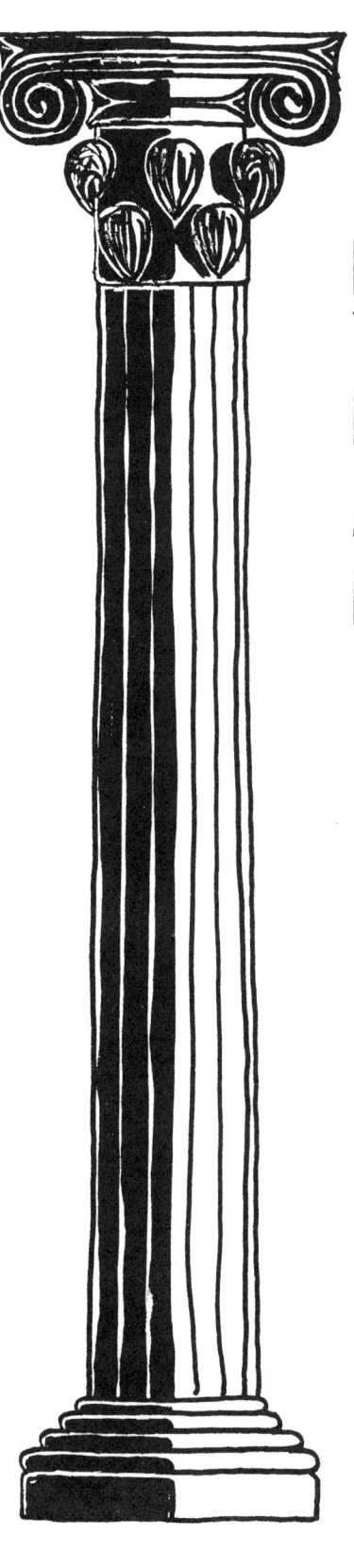

Part Four

Issues of American Politics

Extension of the Bill of Rights to the States

William J. Brennan, Jr.

Among the many issues which the American political process is called upon to resolve are a cluster of controversial questions arising from recent judicial application of the Bill of Rights. The first ten amendments, the Bill of Rights, were added to the Constitution as part of a compromise to secure the ratification of the key states of New York and Virginia and contain guarantees of both substantive and procedural rights—substantive rights like free speech, free press, free exercise of religion, the right to peaceable assembly, and procedural rights like the prohibition of unreasonable searches, against requiring a person to testify against himself, and against a person being put twice in jeopardy for the same crime. Since there are many guarantees in the Bill of Rights, we have selected just one for more careful examination: the substantive guarantee of the right to free speech. But a prior question of "judicial federalism," affecting both substantive and procedural due process determinations of the courts, must be faced first. The federal courts have developed over a long period of time a set of rules which guide them in their potentially sensitive relations with the constitutionally autonomous state courts. One difficult determination the court must make in particular cases is whether it may pass upon the conformity of the laws of the states (and their local governments) with the federal Constitution. The earliest decisions of the Supreme Court had upheld the autonomy of the state courts in matters pertaining to the Bill of Rights. More recent interpretation, however, looks to a second "due process" clause contained in the Fourteenth Amendment (ratified in 1868) to alter those early decisions. Section 1 of that Amendment reads

AMENDMENT XIV [1868]

SECTION 1. All persons born or naturalized in the United States and subject to the jurisdiction thereof, are citizens of the United States and of the State wherein they reside. No State shall make or enforce any law which shall abridge the privileges or immunities of citizens of the United States; nor shall any State deprive any

Reprinted by permission of the publisher from William J. Brennan, Jr., "Extension of the Bill of Rights to the States," *Journal of Urban Law,* 44 (Fall, 1966), 11-24.

person of life, liberty, or property, without due process of law; nor deny to any person within its jurisdiction the equal protection of the laws.

As Justice Black has put it: "My study of the historical events that culminated in the Fourteenth Amendment . . . persuades me that one of the chief objects of the provisions of the Amendment's first section . . . was to make the Bill of Rights applicable to the states." A fuller discussion of this viewpoint, sometimes referred to as the "incorporation" doctrine, is contained in the following article by Associate Justice William J. Brennan, Jr.

We are all familiar with Alexis de Tocqueville's remark over a century and a half ago that "Scarcely any question arises in the United States which does not become, sooner or later, a subject of judicial debate. . . ." America's constitutional development in the lifetimes of most of you in this audience attests to the perceptiveness of that observation. The last 25 years has been primarily a time of defining what claims to personal freedom must be respected by government. Controversies between such claims and the powers of the federal government have been many and important, but perhaps the more significant cases have involved such claims in collision with the powers of the States. For the great questions in the areas of free speech and press, of freedom of religion, of racial equality, of legislative apportionment, of fair trial for those accused of crime, have arisen in cases in which the exercise of state powers, by state executives, state legislatures and state courts have been challenged as overstepping limitations in favor of personal liberty imposed by the Federal Constitution. The question has been: What in the Federal Constitution supports the decisions requiring the States to apportion their legislatures according to the standard of "one man, one vote"; forbidding the States to maintain school systems segregated on the basis of race; denying the States the power to convict a man of crime on evidence illegally seized from him, or on confessions obtained from him in disregard of his privilege against self-incrimination; barring the States from using state prescribed prayers to open the school day; and narrowly limiting the application of a State's libel laws in favor of a public official? . . .

The seeds of a controversy over federal constitutional limitations upon state power were sown before the Nation was formed. When the Declaration of Independence severed the tie that bound the colonies to the Throne of England, each colony fell back upon its own inherent sovereignty, and the people of each, with the exceptions at first of Connecticut and Rhode Island, formed for themselves a Constitution, local, separate, and apart. Each State, formerly a colony, took fierce pride in its separate sovereignty. The States formed a Confederation, but so jealous was each of its sovereign prerogatives that too few powers essential to union were surrendered, and the enterprise foundered.

The Constitution of the original States anticipated the national Constitution in declaring the doctrine that there are human liberties which are inalienable. This doctrine has ever since been the center and core of the American idea of limited government. The government of each State was the creation of the people of the State; the source of power was the people of that State. The only end and aim of government was to secure the people in their natural and civil rights. However, union, under the Articles of Confederation, and later under the Constitution, was not effected by the people as a mass, but by the several peoples of the several States. In other words, the Nation was created by the States and the people of the States, and not by the people separate from the States. The States remained possessed of every power of sovereignty which the several peoples of the several States had not delegated to the United States. This feature was basic to both the Articles of Confederation and to the Constitution. A purpose of the Constitution was to improve upon the Articles of Confederation, and "to form a more perfect union" of States. The Framers' aim was to grant the national government only such powers of sovereignty as were necessary to attain ends better secured by a national government than by the States individually or in confederation. Powers of sovereignty as they affected only a State and the people of the State were reserved to the State.

In contrast, the national government might exercise only the powers enumerated in the Constitution, together with the power to make all laws necessary and proper for carrying into execution the enumerated powers. Even these limitations were not enough for the peoples of some of the States. So widespread was the fear that the national government might encroach upon the sovereignty of the States, and the sovereign rights of the peoples of the several States, that a number of States were reluctant to ratify the new Constitution without an express limitation on the authority of the national government to exercise certain powers. This was the genesis of the Bill of Rights.

It is natural then that the first ten Amendments should have been conceived only as a bulwark to the States, and the peoples of the States, against encroachments of the national government upon the sovereignty which the people of each State reserved to themselves and to their state government. Protection against encroachment on individual rights by a state government was a matter for the state Constitution.

But immediately upon ratification of the first ten Amendments in 1791 voices were heard to say that the Bill of Rights "form parts of the declared rights of the people, of which neither the state powers nor those of the Union can ever deprive them . . ."[1] As a result, a case testing that proposition soon came to the Supreme Court. This was *Barron v. Baltimore*, 7 Pet. 243, decided in 1833. Maryland had taken a citizen's private property for public use, but had not paid for it. The property owner argued that this violated the provision of the Fifth Amendment, "nor shall private property be taken for public use, without just compensation." That provision, the owner argued, "being in favour of the liberty of the citizen, ought to be so construed as to restrain the legislative power of a state, as well as that of the United States." Chief Justice Marshall dismissed the argument as "not of much difficulty." The Bill of Rights, he said, did not operate against state, but only federal power. The Federal Constitution, Marshall went on, "was ordained and established by the people of the United States for themselves, for their own government, and not for the government of the individual States. Each State established a constitution for itself, and, in that constitution, provided such limitations and restrictions on the powers of its particular government as its judgment dictated. The powers . . . conferred on [the national] government were to be exercised by itself; and the limitations on powers, if expressed in general terms, are naturally and, we think, necessarily applicable to the government created by the instrument. They are limitations of power granted in the instrument itself; not of distinct governments, framed by different persons and for different purposes."

This holding that the restraints of the Bill of Rights did not apply to the States was to stand up for 64 years until 1897. In that year the identical question presented in *Barron v. Baltimore* again came to the Court, this time from Illinois. Illinois had taken a citizen's private property for public use, but had not paid for it. The Court held that this denied the property owner a right to compensation secured him by the Federal Constitution. What had happened in the meantime? Well, what had happened was the adoption in 1867 of the Fourteenth Amendment providing that "No state shall make or enforce any law which shall abridge the privileges or immunities of citizens of the United States; nor shall any state deprive any person of life, liberty or property without due process of law; nor deny to any person within its jurisdiction the equal protection of the laws." That language does not displace the powers of the States to legislate directly upon all their citizens in regard to life, liberty and property, but obviously it imposes some limits upon the exercise of that traditional authority. Do those limitations embrace the restraints of the Bill of Rights applicable up to that time only against the federal government?

Promptly after the adoption of the Fourteenth Amendment cases came to the Supreme Court in which it was contended that the logical referrent of "privileges or immunities of citizens of the United States" mentioned in the Amendment were the privileges and immunities declared in the Bill of Rights, and therefore that the Amendment effected a wholesale extension of the specific restraints against the States. The Supreme Court rejected that proposition. In case after case beginning in 1875—each case presenting the question as to a different specific—the Court held that the guarantees in the federal Bill of Rights were not "privileges and immunities of citizens of the United States," within the meaning of those words in the Amendment. There have been strong dissents within the Court from this view. Indeed, ten Justices of the sixty who have sat since 1892, including two of my present colleagues, have disagreed. However, the dissenters have never mustered a majority for their view. But its rejection, and the disregard of the Privilege and Immunities Clause, did not end the story. I mentioned that in 1897 the Court in effect bound the States to the obligation of the Just Compensation Clause of the Fifth Amendment when taking private property for public use. That decision rested on the Due Process Clause of the Fourteenth Amendment. Ten years later in 1908, the Court articulated a standard under which particular specifics of the Bill of Rights might be held to constitute restraints against the States because denial of them would amount to a denial of due process of law in violation of the Due Process Clause. The test announced in 1908 was whether a particular restraint could be characterized as a "fundamental right." Now the phrase "fundamental right" is not to be found anywhere in the Constitution. It has been left to the Court to say which of the specifics in addition to the Just Compensation Clause constitute "fundamental rights."

I count 27 specific guarantees in the first eight Amendments. In the interval from 1897 to 1956, approximately 60 years, in addition to the Just Compensation Clause of the Fifth Amendment, only the specifics contained in the First and Fourth Amendments, a total of eight, were held to be "fundamental rights" and therefore binding on the States. Six are the First Amendment— the prohibitions against making a law respecting an establishment of religion, or prohibiting the free exercise thereof; or abridging the freedom of speech, or of the press; or the right of the people peaceably to assemble, and to petition the government for a redress of grievances. The two in the Fourth Amendment secure the right of the people against unreasonable searches and seizures; and provide that no warrants shall issue, but upon probable cause. Since 1956, however, four more specifics have been held to be "fundamental rights" binding upon the States. They include the privilege against self-incrimination of the Fifth Amendment, extended by a decision in 1964; the provision of the Sixth Amendment guaranteeing the assistance of counsel, extended by a decision in 1963; the provision of the Sixth Amendment guaranteeing an accused the right to be confronted with the witnesses against him, extended by a decision in 1965; and the provision of the Eighth Amendment prohibiting cruel and unusual punishments, extended by a decision in 1962.

Of course, each of these decisions extending a specific of the Bills of Rights against the States has far reaching consequences. For example, the decision holding the States to the command of the First Amendment, rendered in 1925, became the predicate of the decisions barring state required prayers in public schools and limiting the availability of state libel laws to public officials claiming to have been libeled by criticism of their official conduct. Again, the decision in 1964 requiring the States to respect the privilege against self-incrimination became the predicate of last Term's decision barring the use of confessions obtained from suspects without first informing them of their right to silence. Again, the 1963 decision requiring the States to comply with the command of the Sixth Amendment to afford an accused the assistance of counsel at trial has brought on the provisions of various States providing compensation to lawyers appointed to defend the indigent accused of crime. And finally, the 1949 decision requiring the States to comply with the Fourth Amendment's provision against unreasonable searches and seizures culminated in the 1964 decision barring the States from using illegally seized evidence to convict a suspect of crime. Parenthetically, I should note that the decisions in the racial desegregation and reapportionment cases do not result from the application of any of the specifics of the Bill of Rights to the States. They rest on the Equal Protection Clause of the Fourteenth Amendment.

I said earlier that I find 27 specifics in the first eight Amendments and that only 12 of these have so far been held to constitute "fundamental rights" binding on the States. We must expect other cases urging that the remaining 15 specifics should also be held to be "fundamental rights." The 15 include the provision of the Second Amendment that the right of the people to keep and bear arms shall not be infringed: the provision of the Third Amendment that no soldier shall, in time of peace, be quartered in any house without the consent of the owner, nor in time of war, but in a manner to be prescribed by law; the remaining provisions of the Fifth Amendment that no person shall be held to answer for a capital, or otherwise infamous crime, unless on a presentation or indictment of a Grand Jury, nor shall any person be subject for the same offense to be twice put in jeopardy of life or limb; the remaining provisions of the Sixth Amendment that in all criminal prosecutions, the accused shall enjoy the right to a speedy and public trial, by an impartial jury, and to be informed of the nature and cause of the accusation and to have compulsory process for obtaining witnesses in his favor; the provision of the Seventh Amendment that in suits at common law, where the value in controversy shall exceed $20, the right of trial by jury shall be preserved; and the remaining provisions of the Eighth Amendment that excessive bail shall not be required, nor excessive fines imposed.

I cannot predict the outcome as to any of these specifics. I can only suggest that, as in the other cases, careful, conscientious and considered judgment will be brought to bear on the history, function and significance of each as to which a decision may be required.

In each of the instances where the Court has already reached the conclusion that a specific embodies a "fundamental right," the deecision represented a judgment contrary to that reached by the Court when the same question regarding that specific came before it during the period from 1897 to 1922.

Some scholars of the work of the Court have voiced the view that some of these decisions therefore disregard the doctrine of *stare decisis*. May I respectfully demur. When a decision finds that a specific not deemed 60 or 70 years ago to be a "fundamental right" now has that character, has the Court really overruled the old precedent or, rather, has the Court appraised the specific in today's context of the necessity for restraining arbitrary action by governments more powerful and more pervasive than in our ancestor's day? In other words, does not the common thread of the holdings extending the restrictions against the States—none arrived at until after a long series of decisions grappling with the pros and cons of the issues—simply enforce the conclusion that in today's America the guarantees in question are essential to the preservation and furtherance of the constitutional structure of government for a free society? For the genius of the Constitution resides not in any static meaning that it had in a world that is dead and gone, but in its adaptability of its great principles to cope with current problems and current needs.

The aspiration to social justice and human brotherhood is the most powerful force in the world today. It is not new in our country because in a very meaningful way that aspiration brought this Nation into being. The Declaration of Independence, the Constitution and the Bill of Rights solemnly committed the United States to be a country where the dignity and rights of all persons were equal before all authority. In all candor we must concede that part of this egalitarianism in America has been more pretension than realized fact. Although we recognize the Bill of Rights as the primary source of expressed information as to what is meant by constitutional liberty, and also recognize that its safeguards secure the climate which the law of freedom needs in order to exist, we should remind ourselves that we haven't fully appreciated, indeed don't yet fully appreciate, the potency of the Bill of Rights as an arsenal for achieving human brotherhood at home. In a world in revolt, the full realization of the guarantees of the Bill of Rights for all of us will do more to achieve the aspiration of all people for social justice and human brotherhood than all our wealth or all our military might.

Do not the Nation and the World indeed present vastly different problems and needs today? The mists which have obscured the light of freedom and equality for countless millions are dissipating, and the unity of the human family is becoming more and more distinct on the horizon of human events. The gradual civilization of all people replacing the civilization of only the elite, the rise of mass education and mass media of communications, the formation of new thought structures due to scientific advances and social evolution—all these hasten that day. Our own Nation has shrunk its distances to hours, its population is becoming primarily urban and suburban, its technology has spurred an economy capable of fantastic production, and we have become leader of a world composed of a host of new countries which are ready to follow but also quick to reject the path that we take.

Moreover, until the end of the nineteenth century, freedom and dignity in our country found meaningful protection in the institution of real property. In a society still largely agricultural, a piece of land provided men with the means of economic independence, the necessary precondition of political independence and expression. Not surprisingly, property relationships formed the heart of litigation and of legal practice, and lawyers and judges tended to think stable property relationships the highest aim of the law.

But the days when common-law property relationships dominated litigation and legal practice are past. To a growing extent economic existence now depends on less certain relationships with government—licenses, employment, contracts, unemployment benefits, welfare, and the like. Government participation in the economic existence of individuals is pervasive and deep. Adminstrative matters and other dealings with government are at the epicenter of the exploding law. We turn to government and to the law for controls which would never have been expected or tolerated before this century, when a man's answer to economic oppression or difficulty was to move 200 miles west. Professor Arthur E. Sutherland in his perceptively named "Apology for Uncomfortable Change" has said: "The amazing dimensions of ... change in the sheer numbers of our people and in the concomitant reorganization of existence ... have called for wholly new means of government, have exacted wholly new tolerance of government by the citizen, have occasioned wholly new expectations of the services government should perform for its people." Problems of the relationship of the citizen with government have therefore multiplied and thus have emerged some of the most important constitutional issues of our day. As government acts ever more deeply upon those areas of our lives once marked "private" there is an even greater need to see that individual rights are not curtailed or cheapened in the interest of what may temporarily appear to be the "public good." To put this another way, the possibilities for collision between government activity and individual rights will increase as the power of government itself expands, and this growth in turn heightens the need for constant vigilance at such collision points. If free government is to endure, those who govern must recognize human dignity and accept the enforcement of constitutional limitations on their power conceived by the Framers to be necessary to preserve that dignity and the air of freedom which is our proudest heritage. Such recognition will not come from a technical understanding of the organs of government, or the new forms of wealth they administer. It requires something different, something deeper—a perspective which comes from personal confrontation with the wellsprings of our society. Solutions of constitutional questions from the perspective have become the great challenge of our time and of the years that lie ahead.

It is essentially, of course, a challenge to the capacity of our constitutional structure to foster and protect the freedom, the dignity and the rights of all our citizens, which it is the great design of our system to secure. Indeed, more than the evolution of constitutional doctrine has felt the impact of this social revolution; law itself has been compelled to rethink its role. None of us in the ministry of the law, whether teacher, practitioner or judge, can deny that law has sometimes given cause for the complaint that law too long isolated itself from the boiling and difficult currents of life as life is lived. Under the influence of legal thinkers who dominated legal thought in the nineteenth century, the vogue of isolating law from the other disciplines, particularly from theology and from philosophy that was not expressly legal philosophy, had its day. This was admittedly a notion of law wholly unconcerned with the broader extralegal values pursued by society at large or by the individual. It lived in a heaven of abstract technicalities and legal forms, and found its answers to human problems in an aggregation of already existing rules, or found no answers at all. The substantive problems of human living were left for adjustment to the psychologists, sociologists, educators, economists, bankers and other specialists.

But law is again coming alive as a living process responsive to changing human needs. The shift is to justice and away from fine-spun technicalities and abstract rules. We find this in a 1964 American Bar Association report:[2]

"[T]his new jurisprudence constitutes ... a recognition of human beings, as the most distinctive and most important feature of the universe which confronts our senses, and of the function of law as the historic means of guaranteeing that pre-eminence. ... In a scientific age it asks, in effect, what is the nature of man, and what is the nature of the universe with which he is confronted .... Why is a human being important; what gives him dignity; what limits his freedom to do whatever he likes; what are his essential needs; whence comes his sense of injustice?"

This echoes what Mr. Justice Holmes said for the Court 45 years ago:

"The law has grown, and even if historical mistakes have contributed to its growth, it has tended in the direction of rules consistent with human nature." *Brown v. United States*, 256 U.S. 335, 343.

Perhaps some of you may detect, as I think I do, the philosophy of St. Thomas Aquinas in the New Jurisprudence. Call it a resurgence if you will of concepts of natural law—but no matter. St. Thomas, you will remember, was in complete agreement with the Greek tradition, both in its aristotelian and platonic modes, that law must be concerned with seeing things whole, that it is but part of the whole human situation and draws its validity from its position in the entire scheme of things. It is folly to think that law, any more than religion or education, should serve only its own symmetry rather than ends defined by other disciplines.

Of course, this shift of law away from emphasis upon abstract rules to emphasis upon justice has profound significance for judicial decision making. It has not only brought on cases requiring reappraisal of particular specifics in the light of the "fundamental rights" standard; it has also resulted in the Court's holding that a provision of the Bill of Rights, which is enforced against the States under the Fourteenth Amendment, is enforced according to the same standards as it is enforced against federal encroachment.[3]

It is true, as Justice Brandeis said, that "it is one of the happy incidents of the federal system that a state may serve as a laboratory, and try novel social and economic experiments."[4] But this does not include the power to experiment with the fundamental liberties of citizens safeguarded by the Bill of Rights. Furthermore, to deny the State the power to impair a fundamental constitutional right is not to increase federal power, but, rather, to limit the power of both federal and state governments in favor of safeguarding the fundamental rights and liberties of the individual. This, I think promotes rather than undermines the basic policy of avoiding excess concentration of power in government, federal or state, which underlies our concepts of federalism.

In sum, "freedom is an unstable compound. Because one man's liberty can be another man's constraint, because conditions of life in our dynamic society continue to change and because freedom at large is grand but elusive in the particular, the task of formulation is never ending . . . We must bear in mind that our Bill of Rights was written in another age for another society. This heritage with its noble concepts of liberty and freedom has to be re-defined and re-defended by every generation." Pedrick, 49 Cornell L. Q. 581, 608 (1964). The constant for Americans, for our ancestors, for ourselves, and we hope for future generations, is our commitment to the constitutional ideal of libertarian dignity protected through law. Crises in prospect are creating, and will create, more and more threats to the achievement of that ideal—more and more collisions of the individual with his government. The need for judicial vigilance in the service of the ideal will not lessen. It will remain the business of judges to protect fundamental constitutional rights which will be threatened in ways not possibly envisaged by the Framers or even by us. Justices yet to sit, like their predecessors, are destined to labor earnestly in that endeavor—we hope with wisdom—to reconcile the complex realities of their times with the principles which mark a free people. For as the Nation moves ever forward towards its goals of liberty and freedom, and new and different constitutional stresses and strains emerge, the role of the Supreme Court will be ever the same—to justify Madison's faith that "independent tribunals of justice will consider themselves in a peculiar manner the guardians of [constitutional] rights."[5]

Notes

[1] See, *e.g.*, Rawle, A View of the Constitution of the United States of America 120-121 (1825).

[2] ABA Section of International and Comparative Law, Report of Committee on New Trends in Comparative Jurisprudence and Legal Philosophy (Rooney, Chairman), August 10, 1964.

[3] *Malloy v. Hogan, supra,* 378 U.S., at 10-11.

[4] *New States Ice Co. v. Liebmann,* 285 U.S. 262, 280, 311.

[5] I Annals of Congress 439 (Gales & Seaton ed. 1834).

"Selective Incorporation" in the Fourteenth Amendment

It is not universally agreed among legal scholars that the doctrine of "incorporation" rests on firm ground. There is dispute as to the historical contention that the Fourteenth Amendment was intended to make the Bill of Rights applicable to the states at all, and there is contention as to which provisions, and what standards of guarantee are wisely demanded of the states. Louis Henkin, on the faculty of the Columbia University Law School, is one such critic of a doctrine of total incorporation.

Louis Henkin

During recent Terms, four justices of the Supreme Court of the United States espoused a doctrine of "selective incorporation"; the fourteenth amendment incorporates specific provisions of the Bill of Rights, and those that are "absorbed" at all are incorporated whole and intact, providing protections against the states exactly congruent with those against the federal government.[1] Of the other justices presently sitting, one has rejected this view, while the others have not felt compelled to address themselves directly to it.[2] Students of the Court have been strangely silent about this interpretation of the Constitution, perhaps holding breath while it hovers on the brink of obtaining a majority in a changing Court. Since this doctrine would be a major tenet of constitutional jurisprudence, relevant to the resolution of issues which come regularly before the Court, it seems appropriate to draw attention to it, to examine its credentials, to consider its implications.

Before examining the doctrine of selective incorporation, it may help to recall its background. From the beginning, the Court has rejected the claim that the fourteenth amendment subjected the states to all the limitations in the Bill of Rights, which were originally written to govern the federal government only.[3] In 1947, in *Adamson v. California*,[4] three Justices joined Mr. Justice Black in a strong bid to overrule the accepted view and hold that the fourteenth amendment did apply to the states the whole of the Bill of Rights. Of the four dissenters in

Reprinted by permission of the Yale Law Journal Company and Fred B. Rothman and Company from the *Yale Law Journal*, Vol. 73, pp. 74-88. Abridged by the editors.

Adamson, Justices Black and Douglas remain on the Court and have maintained their views, but no others have seen fit to join them.[5]

In rejecting the suggestion that section one of the fourteenth amendment, or any of its clauses, made the entire Bill of Rights applicable to the states, the Supreme Court did not hold that the amendment afforded no similar protections at all. The Court has developed "substantive due process," imposing limitations on the states which include some similar to the prohibitions in the first and fourth amendments. The Court has also found in the due process clause "procedural due process": this requires of the states those procedures which, in Mr. Justice Cardozo's phrases, are "so rooted in the traditions and conscience of our people as to be ranked as fundamental," which are "of the very essence of a scheme of ordered liberty"; it forbids to the states that which "is repugnant to the conscience of mankind."[6] Procedure by procedure, case by case, the Court has decided whether particular actions of the state did or did not conform to "ordered liberty," to due process of law. Recent years have seen the Court increase steadily the procedural content of the due process clause and its limitations on the states.[7] In other cases, dissenting Justices would have had the Court increase still further the requirements of procedural due process, sometimes to make them coterminous with limitations imposed by the Bill of Rights on the federal government.[8]

Selective incorporation would apply to the states the substantive provisions of the first and fourth amendments, imposing the same limitations that these amendments place on the federal government.[9] The principal target of the proponents of incorporation has been criminal procedure and the ordered liberty approach of the *Adamson* case. If the due process clause forbids only that which violates "ordered liberty," every challenged procedure must make its own way into the conscience of mankind as the Court reads that conscience. In each case it is necessary to decide whether what was done is so gross as to be unfair or uncivilized. Even where a safeguard is found to be required by due process, it may not be as extensive as the procedural safeguards required of the federal government by the appropriate, specific provision of the Bill of Rights. The doctrine of selective incorporation might make it possible to increase the procedural protections of the due process clause in substantial leaps. Under this doctrine, the Court apparently would not look at the procedure followed by a state in a particular case to determine whether it shocks the conscience of mankind. Rather it would hold to the light of due process the various provisions of the Bill of Rights.[10] If a particular provision is incorporated within the due process clause, that provision applies to the states to the same extent and in the same ways as it does to the federal government. Thus, not only the freedoms of the first amendment and the right to be secure from unreasonable search and seizure, but also the right to counsel, the provision against cruel and unusual punishment, even the freedom from double jeopardy and the privilege against self-incrimination, might apply to the states in their full, federal measure.

"Selective incorporation" may represent a compromise with Mr. Justice Black's view of incorporation of the whole Bill of Rights. Perhaps, indeed, it is an effort to achieve, more acceptably, substantially what Mr. Justice Black's position in *Adamson* sought to achieve and failed to achieve. It might be more acceptable in that it does not depend on Justice Black's views of the history of the amendment and the intention of its draftsmen, views which historians have challenged.[11] Selective incorporation does not so clearly require overruling the consistent, often reaffirmed, and almost unanimous jurisprudence of the Court for nearly a hundred years. And since it does not involve automatic absorption of the whole of the Bill of

Rights, selective incorporation permits the abandonment, as regards the states, of one or more provisions of the Bill of Rights that seem less important and would be too onerous—say, that dated provision in the seventh amendment requiring a jury trial in civil cases where the value in controversy exceeds twenty dollars. For the rest, selective incorporation could apply to the states all the "important" provisions of the Bill of Rights in their full and growing vigor. Moreover, unlike Mr. Justice Black's position, this view, presumably does not preclude the Court from finding in the due process clause additional protections not found in any of the specifics of the Bill of Rights.[12]

In addition to its promise to raise the standards of individual protection against the states to the higher, federal level, the proposed doctrine has other claims. It is difficult, says Justice Brennan, the chief proponent, to "follow the logic which applies [to the states] a particular specific [of the Bill of Rights] for some purposes and denies its application for others," or to perceive what warrant there is for applying to the states only a "watered-down subjective version of the individual guarantees of the Bill of Rights. . . ."[13] The suggested doctrine also appears to avoid the impression of personal, ad hoc adjudication by every court which attempts to apply the vague contents and contours of "ordered liberty" to every different case that comes before it. Finally, in respects here relevant, the citizen does not distinguish between state and federal government;[14] he may not understand why the same standards should not apply. If he reads his Constitution, most of the Bill of Rights is addressed at large, not expressly to the federal government alone; he may not understand why he should not enjoy against the states what the Bill of Rights says is his right. Similar standards for state and nation, moreover, would simplify constitutional jurisprudence, the administration of justice, and cooperation between state and federal agencies.

The thesis, and its consequences, are appealing. That it has not, to date, obtained a majority may reflect its difficulties. Principally, perhaps, it is difficult to find it in the Constitution, as it was written or as it has developed. Even leaving aside considerations of federalism that might militate against such interpretation of the amendment, the burden in logic and in law, surely, is not on those who would claim that the states are subject to lesser limitations than were imposed on the federal government. Initially, at least, the burden is on those who would invalidate action of a state to find in the Constitution some relevant limitation. And the burden of showing that specifics of the Bill of Rights, admittedly written only as limitations on the federal government, are at all relevant to the powers of the states, and in what way, is on those who would assert such relevance. Selective incorporation finds no support in the language of the amendment, or in the history of its adoption. Indeed, it is more difficult to justify than Justice Black's position that the Bill of Rights was wholly incorporated. There is some evidence that some persons associated with the adoption of the amendment contemplated that it might apply the Bill of Rights to the states.[15] There is no evidence, and it is difficult to conceive, that anyone thought or intended that the amendment should impose on the states a selective incorporation. In the absence of any special intention revealed in the history of the amendment, we have only the language to look to. It is conceivable, again, that the phrase "privileges and immunities of citizens of the United States" might include a reference to the whole Bill of Rights.[16] Surely there is no basis for finding that some "specifics" of the Bill of Rights are, while others are not, privileges and immunities of national citizenship. Even the phrase "due process of law" might conceivably be a short-hand expression for the whole Bill of Rights. It is hardly possible to see in that phrase some purpose to select some specifics of the Bill of Rights and an insistence that they be selected whole.

In fact, it should be clear, the Court has not read "due process of law" as a short-hand way of referring to specifics of the Bill of Rights. (It could hardly have so read a clause which restates, identically, only one single provision of only one of the early amendments) To find in that phrase any limitations at all it had to give meaning and content to the phrase "due process of law." It found protection for "liberty," including the liberties mentioned in the first and fourth amendments, in notions of "substantive due process." Of this, we treat separately later. In regard to procedural due process, the Court held that the "process" that is "due"—say, in criminal proceedings—is what is required by the conscience of mankind. *That is the essential link* between the constitutional language and purport and all the procedural limitations which the Court applies to the states under this provision. So far as here relevant, then, all that is required of the states is that which is due because it is "fundamental," because its denial would shock the conscience of mankind. There is no relation — historical, linguistic or logical—between that standard and the specific provisions, or any specific provision, of the Bill of Rights.[17] At bottom, it is difficult even to ask meaningfully whether a specific of the Bill of Rights is incorporated in ordered liberty. That a particular procedure or action is required of, or forbidden to, the federal government by a provision of the Bill of Rights is some evidence that it may be required, or forbidden, by the conscience of mankind. But this indirect relevance of the Bill of Rights to determine the content of "due process of law" cannot support the view that any provision of the Bill of Rights, in its total federal import, is either all in, or all out of, this standard of ordered liberty. Some specifics of the Bill of Rights, in all their manifestations, may indeed be "process" which is required by the conscience of mankind; others may not. Some elements or aspects of a specific may be required by the conscience of mankind; others may not.

So far as it would incorporate, in procedural due process, procedural provisions of the Bill of Rights, then, the proposed doctrine does not appear to be one that can be reasonably arrived at from the language and history of the fourteenth amendment, or from its development in the constitutional jurisprudence of the Supreme Court. It does find its roots in language used by the Supreme Court in some of the cases. Where a claimant urged that the state had denied him due process—say by denying him a right to be represented by counsel in a criminal case—the issue properly raised was whether the right to counsel, in the circumstances, was a fundamental right, essential to ordered liberty. That the claimant would have counsel as of right in a comparable federal proceeding would be, we have said, some evidence that it may be fundamental. But counsel, as well as the Justices, sometimes framed the issue as whether "the right to counsel" was "incorporated," "absorbed," or "applied" to the states by the fourteenth amendment. If the question is whether a right contained in the Bill of Rights is "incorporated," one may argue that the right "incorporated," as if by reference, must be the same right with the same meaning and the same scope.

In order to determine whether a particular procedural safeguard, in a particular case or in all cases, is "due" process, *i.e.*, is required by the conscience of mankind, it does not appear apt or relevant to ask whether a particular provision of the Bill of Rights is "incorporated" in due process. In any event, in regard to standards of criminal procedure at least, no case has said that a specific provision in the Bill of Rights, or a federal standard, is being "incorporated."[18] A right of counsel, one might say, was incorporated in the fourteenth amendment, but not necessarily the same right of counsel given in the fifth amendment.[19] What is clear, too, is that the court could — and did—justify any such "incorporation" only by finding it in the concept of ordered liberty that is due process.[20] Incorporation then does not, and cannot, avoid reference to the uncertain, debatable, changeable touchstone of ordered liberty. And incorporation, by reference to ordered liberty, cannot claim that specific procedural provisions in the Bill of Rights are incorporated "whole." Ordered liberty, indeed, may for some safeguards require exactly what is required by the Bill of Rights. But it can as well require less, or more. Nothing in that concept suggests that if it includes some procedure akin to one in the Bill of Rights, it must be of exactly the same size, shape, scope as the federal protection.

It has sometimes been claimed that this doctrine of selective incorporation derives from Justice Cardozo's opinion for the Court in *Palko v. Connecticut*.[21] We shall deal later with the dictum of Mr. Justice Cardozo about "absorption" within the Fourteenth Amendment of basic substantive freedoms like those in the First Amendment.[22] But in regard to the criminal procedures required in the later amendments, for which the doctrine is now invoked, *Palko* was not applying a doctrine of incorporation as distinguished from a touchstone of "ordered liberty." It was in this case, involving criminal procedure, that Justice Cardozo coined "ordered liberty." Nor did the Court ask whether some specific of the Bill of Rights was incorporated in "ordered liberty." In fact, in setting forth ordered liberty as the meaning of due process, Justice Cardozo said that whether procedure claimed to be required of a state would have been required of the federal government by a specific provision in the Bill of Rights was not the question. Speaking, with apparent approval, of *Powell v. Alabama*, he said:

The decision did not turn upon the fact that benefit of counsel would have been guaranteed to the defendants by the provisions of the Sixth Amendment if they had been prosecuted in federal court. The decision turned upon the fact that in the particular situation laid before us in the evidence the benefit of counsel was essential to the substance of the hearing.[23]

Most important, Mr. Justice Cardozo quite clearly rejected the principal focus of the proposed doctrine—that specifics must be incorporated whole. In that case the Court held that it was not a denial of due process for the State of Connecticut to appeal error in Palko's first trial and upon reversal to bring him to trial again and convict him. Since the Court assumed that this would be forbidden to the federal government as "double jeopardy," it is sometimes said that the Court held that the provision against double jeopardy in the fifth amendment was not incorporated into the fourteenth amendment. In fact, the Court held, and could have held, nothing of the kind. It held nothing with regard to the fifth amendment; it held only that what Connecticut did was not a violation of due process. But if it be deemed to have held anything about the incorporation of the provision against double jeopardy, it held only that federal double jeopardy in all its aspects and reach was not incorporated in due process. It expressly reserved the possibility that some parts of the federal protection against double jeopardy might—if you will—be incorporated in due process: "What the answer would have to be if the state were permitted after a trial free from error to try the accused over again or to bring another case against him, we have no occasion to consider."[24] One could hardly doubt, indeed, that such "true" double jeopardy would have been held by Justice Cardozo, and that Court, to be a violation of due process.[25] If so,

Palko clearly does not support a doctrine that procedural "specifics" which are incorporated at all must be incorporated whole. In fact, since "hard core" double jeopardy would almost certainly be "incorporated," once the Court, so held, the doctrine of selective incorporation would require the Court to apply the double jeopardy provision whole, and to overrule *Palko!*

The Court has also consistently negated the doctrine of "incorporation whole" in the cases involving the so-called privilege against self-incrimination. It is sometimes said—even by the Justices—that the Court has refused to find that the fourteenth amendment incorporated the fifth amendment's provision that no person shall be compelled to be a witness against himself. In fact, the Court *held* only that the state did not violate due process if it permitted the prosecution to comment on the failure of Twining, or Adamson, to take the stand.[26] If it held that to this extent the privilege of the fifth amendment was not "incorporated," so be it. At the same time, and with full awareness, the Court has—if one would speak in terms of incorporation of specifics—repeatedly held applicable to the states that part of the privilege not to be compelled to testify against oneself which bars the use of coerced confessions.[27] These two strands of self-incrimination cases have existed side by side, and have been applied consistently by the Court, including many of the Justices who sat in *Palko*. There was never any suggestion that these cases were inconsistent with each other, or with some constitutional doctrine of selective incorporation.[28]

These difficulties suggest that the proposed doctrine would seek possible additional protections for the individual on the wings of inadequate analysis, in the face of the language and history of the hundred years of constitutional jurisprudence. One may well ask, moreover, what is gained. In fact, selective incorporation cannot avoid the difficulties of the traditional doctrine. Try as one might to avoid the phrase, "ordered liberty" or something much like it remains as the principle of selection, to determine which specifics are "incorporated," and which are not. (Some such standard is applied, too, where there is a challenge to a procedure which does not correspond to any federal specific.) That judgment of selection is as likely to be "subjective" as is the application of the traditional standard. And if the traditional approach sometimes applies a "watered-down" version of some federal procedural specific, one can as well challenge selective incorporation as a watered-down version of incorporation of the entire Bill of Rights.

Most important, perhaps, accepting the need or the desirability of increasing constitutional protections against the states, one may yet ask whether this doctrine is really necessary. If the federal standard is indeed the goal in some instances, the Court can, without any difficult new doctrine, find the federal standard to be required by ordered liberty or by other elements in the Court's jurisprudence. That is now the case with the right to counsel.[29] The Court has also found it possible to justify identical standards in regard to exclusion of the fruits of unreasonable search and seizure, not from any notion of total incorporation, but because of convenience in administration and in federal-state cooperation in the enforcement of criminal law.[30] Federalism and *stare decisis* apart, without any new doctrine the flexibility and vitality of the concept of ordered liberty[31] would permit the extension today to the states of the heart of concepts against double jeopardy, perhaps even against self-incrimination — the only safeguards now apparently in issue— without necessarily saddling all the states with what may be peripheral survivals or accretions in the Bill of Rights.[32] Of course, if the Justices are not to be imposing their own notions of what is desirable procedure, they can only find these new protections in the fourteenth amendment if they are satisfied that they are indeed required by some impersonal, objective, determinable (if difficult to determine) standard of community conscience. But a similar reference to some similar standard, we have said, could not be avoided if the Court asked anew, for example, "whether the privilege against self-incrimination is incorporated." There is no constitutional language, no established doctrine, no old case, that can be invoked to avoid the inevitable question of ordered liberty.

There is indeed a kind of inversion about attempting today to increase the content of procedural due process vis-à-vis the states through wholesale incorporation of complete provisions of the Bill of Rights. For in regard to the federal government the Court has also been extending constitutional liberties and protections. It has done so in part by recognizing distinct content in the due process clause of the fifth amendment and applying notions of fairness and ordered liberty there.[33] It has done so even more by developing the flexible standards of some of the provisions—"unreasonable" search and seizure, "cruel and unusual" punishment, even "double jeopardy."[43] The Court, surely, is aware that though it is ostensibly applying a "specific," the specific is not very specific; and in seeking a standard for developing these and other ambiguities the Court has inevitably applied contemporary notions of fairness—not very different from "ordered liberty." Sometimes, it seems, the Court has stretched quite far the language of one of the specifics to achieve in effect what it thought required by new communal enlightenment. One may wonder, then, whether in regard to both state and federal governments, the Court might not better look less to the procedural specifics of the Bill of Rights and exploit rather the more flexible notion of due process in both the fifth and fourteenth amendments to achieve identical and contemporary standards of liberty under ordered government. To Mr. Justice Black this approach may still be abhorrent because it leaves the courts at large with too much discretion.[35] Most of the Justices, one might guess, would not find this discretion distressingly larger than is in play when the Court develops the mentioned ambiguities of the Bill of Rights, or applies the due process clause of the Fifth Amendment, or decrees notions of propriety under the Court's supervisory powers, where there is no applicable specific.[36]

SUBSTANTIVE DUE PROCESS AND THE SUBSTANTIVE AMENDMENTS

Palko v. Connecticut, it seems clear, is not authority for any general doctrine that specifics of the Bill of Rights are incorporated into the Fourteenth Amendment. It is surely not authority—indeed it negates—a doctrine that insists that any federal specific which is at all reflected in "due process" must be incorporated whole. Neither *Palko* nor any other case, nor independent inquiry, has suggested any acceptable basis for incorporating whole federal specifics in the procedural amendments. But Cardozo's dictum in *Palko* may suggest incorporation, possibly incorporation whole, of "the privileges and immunities that have been taken over from *the earlier articles* of the federal bill of rights and brought within the fourteenth amendment by a process of absorption."[37] For these important substantive rights—the freedom of speech, press and religion, separation of church and state, privacy against unreasonable search and seizure—protection against encroachment by the states has also been found in the due process clause, in "substantive due process." That these freedoms are protected against the states to exactly the same extent as against federal abridgment has been asserted, and questioned.[38] I venture to suggest that as to these provisions—the origin and perhaps a principal motivation for "selective incorporation" —one might arrive where that doctrine would take us, though by another path.

Substantive due process in concept and in its development is, of course, quite different from "procedural due process," although the Court has found them both in the same clause. Due process of law in the original Bill of Rights, while its total impact is less than clear, surely had procedural connotations. The same phrase was probably designed to impose some procedural limitations on the states when it was written into the fourteenth amendment. To determine the scope of these safeguards the Court interpreted the words "due process," holding that the process that is due is that which conforms to accepted notions of "dueness," to the demands of civilized conscience.

"Substantive due process," on the other hand, may be wholly a judicial creation. It was first found in the fifth amendment in the *Dred Scott* case.[39] However, when "due process of law" appeared in the fourteenth amendment, it is far from agreed that it intended substantive limitations on what state legislatures might do. Substantive due process, as is well known, found its origin and its wild and questionable growth in regard to economic regulation; only comparatively recently has it begun to protect political and civil liberties. In regard to the latter, when the Court decided, say, that freedom of speech enjoyed protection from state encroachment, it was asserting that the "liberty" of which a person may not be deprived includes the freedom of speech. Liberty, it later held, included other freedoms, indeed "the full range of conduct which the individual is free to pursue."[40] Surely, the Court has found, it included those liberties whose significance was expressly honored in the first and fourth amendments.

One may say, then, that the liberties mentioned in the Bill of Rights were, in this sense, "incorporated" or "absorbed" in the "liberty" protected by the fourteenth amendment.[41] It remained to be determined what is the standard of protection accorded to these liberties. The scope of the protection has indeed been found in the phrase "due process," but here it means something different from what it means as procedural due process. The standard of substantive due process is not "conscience" or "fairness" as in the procedural cases. Substantive due process, we know, has suggested to the modern Court standards for permissible limitations on property different from those on liberty, and perhaps, too, different standards for limitations on different liberties. In regard to property, or even "economic liberties," the standard has been reduced to mere "reasonableness" of end and means. For "civil liberties" it has meant much greater protection. For property or liberty the standard has reflected developing values, developing attitudes on the relation of government and individual, of order and liberty, applied to the issues of a new day. Except to those who think that the first amendment speaks clearly and absolutely,[42] however, these same developed values in fact determine the protection accorded by the substantive amendments too — the scope of "respecting an establishment" or "prohibiting the free exercise" of religion, of "abridging" the freedom of speech or of the press, and other ambiguities in the first amendment, as of "the right to be secure" against "unreasonable searches and seizures" in the fourth amendment. To those who see in these amendments flexible standards reflecting respective needs of order and of liberty, it is easy to suggest that there is no reason to assume different values in this regard as concerns the actions of the states.[43] In terms of incorporation, then, one may say that the liberties mentioned in the first and fourth amendments are incorporated in "liberty" in the fourteenth, and that the values of order and liberty which determine the protection accorded against the federal government by the substantive amendments are the same as—are congruent with if not "incorporated" in — substantive "due process of law" applicable to the states.

This suggestion, I emphasize, does not depend merely on linguistic parsing of the different phrases of the due process clause. The point is that if the fourteenth amendment is deemed to afford substantive protection for "liberty," it should surely protect the fundamental and established liberties. And if the Court is creating a standard of protection for these liberties, it may well look to the standards of protection which it has developed for these liberties in regard to the federal government. Surely it may look to those same standards if, as most of the Justices accept, the substantive provisions are "specific" only in identifying the right protected, but not as to elaborating the standard of protection, and the latter must derive from contemporary enlightenment. The fact is that without having explicitly accepted incorporation, the Court never seems to have found in the explicit provisions of the early amendments some standard higher than that to be applied to the states. And even the individual Justices who have insisted that the standard is different have not been able to articulate and justify two different standards.[44] Whether one calls in incorporation or not, identical standards for federal and state governments apparently are established. Incorporating the procedural provisions of the Bill of Rights, on the other hand, would automatically apply to the states provisions of considerable specificity, including the accretions those amendments have acquired in the history of their application to the federal government. Some of these may not fall within the notion of fairness and ordered liberty that is the core of procedural due process. True, in some situations, as in the right to counsel, there may indeed be congruity with federal protection. In others, congruity may not be required by "due process." There seems no occasion to seek it by an artificial process of incorporation.

I am suggesting, then, that the concept of incorporation might be applied to the substantive liberties in the Bill of Rights, though difficult to accept as to the procedural provisions.[45] (Perhaps, indeed, this distinction accords with the view of Mr. Justice Cardozo, although he apparently saw both kinds of due process as aspects of "ordered liberty.")[46] Incorporating some provisions of the Bill of Rights and not others needs no special justification. There is, of course, no necessary logical link or relation between the substantive provisions of the early amendments and the procedures later in the Bill of Rights. Nor has the Bill of Rights any necessary logical unity. Its historical unity and significance (which would apply also to the tenth amendment) has no relevance to the fourteenth amendment. What must be remembered is that for the states we start with the fourteenth amendment, not with the Bill of Rights. Unless, with Justice Black, one relies on some special intention of the draftsmen of the amendment, that amendment has no relation to the Bill of Rights as a whole. If one finds in the fourteenth amendment protection for the freedoms in the early amendments, but cannot find in it a requirement for judicial procedures like those in the latter part of the Bill of Rights, it is not because the former amendments "secure more important individual rights."[47] It is rather that one must find some basis for finding in the fourteenth amendment any relation to the Bill of Rights at all. And in the fourteenth amendment, where any incorporation must lie, one may readily find that the "liberty" protected includes the liberties of the early amendments, but it seems difficult to find that the judicial "process" that is "due" relates to the later provisions of the Bill of Rights, incorporates some of them but not all of them, and incorporates them whole. Language aside, the distinction we have suggested appears to accord with the separate and different development and significance of substantive due process from that of procedural due process in the history of the Constitution.

Whether or not one accepts this suggested distinction between the protections afforded to substantive rights and the concept of fairness applied to criminal procedure, one may still conclude that, within the established standard of "ordered liberty," some safeguards contained in provisions of the Bill of Rights might in fact be applied equally to the states, others might not. The suggestion that protection of the Bill of Rights must in all cases be applied exactly to the states, if they be applied at all, is difficult to support as a matter of constitutional language or of the jurisprudence of the Court, or to justify on any other relevant considerations. It creates its own rigidities and runs counter to the direction of growth of the Constitution to embody flexible standards permitting the increase of individual safeguards with the growing enlightenment of contemporary civilization. Even the strongest libertarian instincts do not need such a doctrine to increase protection for the rights of the criminally accused when greater communal enlightenment suggests higher standards to be required of the states as of the federal government.

Notes

[1] This view was expounded by Mr. Justice Brennan, joined by the Chief Justice and Justices Black and Douglas, in an opinion in Ohio *ex rel.* Eaton v. Price, 364 U.S. 263, 274-76 (1960), and again in Justice Brennan's dissenting opinion in Cohen v. Hurley, 336 U.S. 117, 154 (1961). Compare Douglas, J., concurring in Gideon v. Wainwright, 372 U.S. 335, 345-47 (1963). It may have been suggested earlier by Mr. Justice Black in his dissent in Adamson v. California, 332 U.S. 46, 85-86 (1947), but to him and to Justice Douglas this was a compromise, less desirable than complete incorporation of the Bill of Rights in the fourteenth amendment. See text accompanying note 4 *infra*. We shall call the latter the Black doctrine as distinguished from the Brennan doctrine which is the subject of these pages.

[2] During the last term of Court, eight Justices held that the standards for permissible search and seizure were the same for the states as for the federal government. Ker v. California, 374 U. S. 23 (1963). A unanimous Court also held in effect that the states must provide counsel to the indigent in criminal cases, as is required of the federal government. Gideon v. Wainwright, 372 U.S. 335 (1963). In both cases the opinion of the Court reached the result while skirting the doctrine of incorporation. Mr. Justice Harlan's concurrence in the latter case and his dissent in the former indicate that he definitely rejects incorporation. See also Justice Harlan's concurrence in Lanza v. New York, 370 U.S. 139, 147 (1962), and note 38 *infra*.

[3] *E.g., in* Hurtado v. California, 110 U.S. 516 (1884); Twining v. New Jersey, 211 U.S. 78 (1908). The leading contemporary cases are Palko v. Connecticut, 302 U.S. 319 (1937), and Adamson v. California, 332 U.S. 46 (1947). Mr. Justice Frankfurter has been the leading contemporary spokesman for the traditional interpretation of due process, for example in his concurring opinion in *Adamson, supra* at 59-68.

[4] 332 U.S. 46 (1947).

[5] Justice Douglas reasserted his *Adamson* view last term, expressing the hope that it may yet obtain a majority. See his concurring opinion in Gideon v. Wainwright, 372 U.S. 335, 345 (1963). In Ohio *ex rel.* Eaton v. Price, 364 U.S. 263, 275 (1960), Mr. Justice Brennan and the Chief Justice indicated that they "have neither accepted nor rejected that view."

[6] Snyder v. Massachusetts, 291 U.S. 97, 105 (1934); Palko v. Connecticut, 302 U.S. 319, 325 (1938); *id.* at 323.

[7] See Ker v. California, 374 U.S. 23 (1963); Gideon v. Wainwright, 372 U.S. 335 (1963). And see, Rochin v. California, 342 U.S. 165 (1952); Thompson v. Louisville, 362 U.S. 199 (1960); Robinson v. California, 370 U.S. 660 (1962).

[8] In addition to Adamson v. California, 332 U.S. 46 (1947), and Cohen v. Hurley, 366 U.S. 117 (1961), see, *e.g.,* Louisiana *ex rel.* Francis v. Resweber, 329 U.S. 459 (1947); *cf.* Frank v. Maryland, 359 U.S. 360 (1959), and Ohio *ex rel.* Eaton v. Price, 364 U.S. 263 (1960). And see Mapp v. Ohio, 367 U.S. 643 (1961), and Gideon v. Wainwright, 372 U.S. 335 (1963), which overruled earlier cases setting lower standards for the states.

[9] See text accompanying note 37 *infra.*

[10] Presumably, if the state action complained of does not correspond to any rubric in the Bill of Rights, Mr. Justice Brennan would apply the test of ordered liberty directly, finding in it some limitations beyond the specifics of the Bill of Rights. In this respect he would join Justices Murphy and Rutledge. *Compare* their dissenting opinion in Adamson v. California, 332 U.S. 46, 124, *with* that of Justices Black and Douglas, *id.* at 68.

[11] See Fairman, *Does the Fourteenth Amendment Incorporate the Bill of Rights?*, 2 STAN. L. REV. 5 (1949); and Morrison, *Does the Fourteenth Amendment Include the Bill of Rights?, id.* at 140.

[12] See note 10 *supra.* Since *Adamson,* Justices Black and Douglas, too, have been willing to find state violations of due process that do not readily correspond to any specific provision in the Bill of Rights. . . .

[13] Cohen v. Hurley, 366 U.S. 117, 158 (1961); see Ohio *ex rel.* Eaton v. Price, 364 U.S. 263, 275 (1960). Justice Brennan argues also that the First and Fourth Amendments have been absorbed and that there is no reason to consider the rights secured by some later amendments less important. See note 47 *infra.*

[14] *Cf.* Black, J., dissenting in Bartkus v. Illinois, 359 U.S. 121, 155 (1959).

[15] See Mr. Justice Black's dissenting opinion and Appendix in Adamson v. California, 332 U.S. 46, 68, 92 (1947).

[16] This was argued, and rejected, in Twining v. New Jersey, 211 U.S. 78, 93-99 (1908). . . .

[17] See note 20 and text accompanying note 23 *infra.*

[18] The Court may have said that a specific provision of the Bill of Rights—say, the privilege against self-incrimination—was *not* incorporated. Twining v. New Jersey, 211 U.S. 78 (1908). That, too, was careless and unnecessary. The issue before the Court in that case was only whether what the state there did—permitting the prosecution to comment on the defendant's failure to take the stand—was consistent with fairness and ordered liberty. See text accompanying note 26 *infra.* In any event, that a particular provision of the Bill of Rights may not be incorporated at all, does not imply that other provisions, which may be incorporated, must be incorporated whole.

[19] *Cf.* Powell v. Alabama, 287 U.S. 45 (1932); compare Betts v. Brady, 316 U.S. 455 (1942), *overruled,* Gideon v. Wainwright, 372 U.S. 335 (1963).

[20] As to the rights "incorporated," the Court in *Twining* said: "If this is so, it is not because those rights are enumerated in the first eight amendments, but because they are of such a nature that they are included in the conception of due process of law." Twining v. New Jersey,

211 U.S. 78, 99 (1908). See, too, Mr. Justice Cardozo in Palko v. Connecticut, 302 U.S. 319, 327 (1937). See text accompanying note 23 *infra*.

[21]302 U.S. 319 (1937). See the opinions of Mr. Justice Brennan in the cases cited in note 1 *supra*. See also Mr. Justice Black's dissent in Adamson v. California, 332 U.S. at 46, 85-86 (1947). "If the choice must be between the selective process of the *Palko* decision applying some of the Bill of Rights to the States, or the *Twining* rule applying none of them, I would choose the *Palko* selective process." *Id.* at 89. Mr. Justice Black, of course, did not feel limited to this choice.

[22]Palko v. Connecticut, 302 U.S. 319, 326, quoted at note 37 *infra*.

[23]*Id.* at 327, referring to Powell v. Alabama, 287 U.S. 45 (1932); see also 302 U.S. at 324-25.

[24]*Id.* at 328. Earlier the Court emphasized that it was talking only about the particular kind of double jeopardy in the case: "Is double jeopardy in such circumstances, if double jeopardy it must be called, a denial of due process forbidden to the states?" *Id.* at 323. And later: "Is that kind of double jeopardy to which the statute has subjected him a hardship so acute and so shocking that our polity will not endure it?" *Id.* at 328.

[25]Compare Hoag v. New Jersey, 356 U.S. 464, 468-69 (1958); United States v. Furlong, 18 U.S. (5 Wheat.) 184, 197 (1820).

[26]Twining v. New Jersey, 211 U.S. 78 (1908); Adamson v. California, 332 U.S. 46 (1947). See note 18 *supra*. Both Mr. Justice Brennan and Mr. Justice Black recognized the limits of the holding, urging that *Twining* did not conclude the case before the Court, in their dissents in Cohen v. Hurley, 366 U.S. 117, 134-35 n.10, 159 (1961). Mr. Justice Black had also recognized earlier that in these self-incrimination cases the Court was negating any notion of total incorporation, applying to the states part of the federal privilege but not all of it. See his dissent in *Adamson*, 332 U.S. at 86.

[27]Brown v. Mississippi, 297 U.S. 278 (1936); Chambers v. Florida, 309 U.S. 227 (1940).

[28]These self-incrimination and double jeopardy cases, of course, reveal the corollary of the proposed doctrine. Selective incorporation means that the Fourteenth Amendment takes all of a federal provision, or it takes none of it. The Court could not, then, keep both *Adamson* and the coerced confession cases, both *Palko* and a rule against "hard-core" double jeopardy. Overruling *Adamson* and *Palko*, even on their limited facts, may indeed be what the Brennan doctrine intends. But this all-or-nothing doctrine could, with equal logic, lead to the opposite conclusion. If some part of a "specific" is *not* included in due process, none of it can be; or, since whether a provision is to be incorporated must still depend on its conclusion in "ordered liberty," if a federal specific includes elements which are shocking and elements which are not, it may be as reasonable to exclude the provision from the fourteenth amendment as to include it. Thus, the Court, having long ago decided *Twining* and *Palko*, might be held to have decided that the *whole* federal privilege against self-incrimination, and the *whole* rule against double jeopardy, are excluded from the Fourteenth Amendment. Repeated trials and coerced confessions, then, should not be barred to the states either. And new applications involving self-incrimination or double jeopardy should also be permitted although these may, in fact, shock the conscience.

[29]Gideon v. Wainwright, 372 U.S. 335 (1963).

[30]Ker v. California, 374 U.S. 23 (1963); *cf.* Mapp v. Ohio, 367 U.S. 643 (1961). And, as the *Ker* case shows, getting the federal standard does not assure that the result will be different; a majority of the Court found that it was not violated.

Security against unreasonable search and seizure is, in the first instance, a substantive right, part of substantive due process. See *infra* note 44 and accompanying text.

[31] See, *e.g.,* Mr. Justice Brandeis, dissenting, in Olmstead v. United States, 277 U.S. 438, 472 (1928); compare his dissent in United States v. Moreland, 258 U.S. 433, 451 (1922). See Mr. Justice Frankfurter concurring in Malinksi v. New York, 324 U.S. 401, 414 (1945), and in Joint Anti-Fascist Refugee Comm. v. McGrath, 341 U.S. 123, 162-63 (1951); and see Hurtado v. California, 110 U.S. 516, 530 (1884).

[32] If selective incorporation accepts that some specifics — like the twenty-dollar rule in the seventh amendment—are outdated, one might leave open the possibility that some specific provision retaining vitality may have accumulated insignificances or anachronisms that should not be imposed on the states. . . .

[33] See, *e.g.,* Crain v. United States, 162 U.S. 625, 645 (1896); Japanese Immigrant case, 189 U.S. 86, 100-01 (1903); Morgan v. United States, 304 U.S. 1, 18-19 (1938); Wong Tang Sung v. McGrath, 339 U.S. 33, 50 (1950); *cf.* Hannah v. Larche, 363 U.S. 420 (1960). The invocation of due process against the federal government has become less frequent as the Court began to expand the specifics, note 34 *infra,* and to require even higher standards under its supervisory powers over federal courts and federal administration of justice. McNabb v. United States, 318 U.S. 332 (1943); Rea v. United States, 350 U.S. 214 (1956); Mallory v. United States, 354 U.S. 49 (1957).

[34] See, *e.g.,* Chapman v. United States, 365 U.S. 610 (1961); Trop v. Dulles, 356 U.S. 86 (1958); United States v. Green, 355 U.S. 184 (1957); Fong Foo v. United States, 369 U.S. 141 (1962); see also United States v. Lovett, 328 U.S. 303 (1946).

[35] See, *e.g.,* his dissent in Adamson v. California, 332 U.S. 46, 90-92 (1947).

[36] For examples of the latter, see cases cited *supra* note 33.

[37] 302 U.S. at 326. (Emphasis added.) Justice Cardozo goes on to speak in particular of the importance of "freedom of thought, and speech." *Id.* at 326-27. See also note 46 *infra.*

[38] See Beauharnais v. Illinois, 343 U.S. 250, 288 (1952) (Jackson, J. dissenting) (questioning the view of the other dissent that the first amendment is incorporated in the fourteenth); Roth v. United States, 354, U.S. 476, 505-06 (1957) (Harlan, J. separate opinion) (dangers of a uniform standard as to pornography under the First Amendment applied to the state). The opinions of the Court may have applied the same substantive standard as would apply to the federal government under the Bill of Rights, but have avoided explicit language of incorporation. See Cohen v. Hurley, 366 U.S. 117, 156 (1961) (Brennan, J., dissenting). See also note 47 *infra.* Compare, *e.g.,* the Court's opinion in Lanza v. New York, 370 U.S. 139, 142 (1962), *with* Justice Harlan's concurrence, 370 U.S. at 147.

[39] Scott v. Sandford, 60 U.S. (19 How.) 393 (1856).

[40] Bolling v. Sharpe, 347 U.S. 497, 499 (1954).

[41] See text accompanying note 37 *supra.* There is no problem of selection here; all substantive rights, even those perhaps outdated ones in the second and third amendments are liberties entitled to some protection. The Court has apparently also treated breach by the states in the separation of church and state, or state establishment of religion, as deprivations of "liberty" which affected individuals have standing to vindicate. *E.g.,* Engel v. Vitale, 370 U.S. 421 (1962). . . .

[42] Mr. Justice Black, of course, applies the first amendment to the states as part of his total incorporation of the Bill of Rights, *supra* note 4. Alternatively, he might say that the provisions of the first amendment are within the "liberty" protected by the fourteenth amendment. On either basis, Mr. Justice Black might say the "absolute character of the prohibition of the first amendment applies equally to the states."

[43] To say that the standard is the same for the states as for the federal government is to suggest the same process of balancing and the same values in the balance. It does not mean that all governmental interests, state or federal, weigh the same. The interest of the United States in advance military censorship in time of war might outweigh the liberty to speak or publish, where a state's concern to prevent libel, by advance censorship, might not.

[44] See note 38 *supra*.

[45] One need not become enmeshed in difficult distinctions between substance and procedure which elsewhere trouble the law. Substantive due process and procedural due process are phrases of recognized content describing different constitutional limitations on government. And there appears to be no difficulty in separating those provisions of the Bill of Rights which may be called liberties (and deemed incorporated in "liberty" in the fourteenth amendment) from those provisions which prescribe procedures required of the federal government (to which the fourteenth amendment does not speak). Some of the liberties incorporated may raise special procedural problems. The right to be secure from unreasonable search and seizure is an incorporated liberty and the standard of protection applies in the same manner against the states as against federal authorities. . . .

[46] At least, in this way one can give literal meaning to his dicta about the "absorption" of the freedoms in the early provisions of the Bill of Rights, and square them with his decision in *Palko,* his reservation of other double jeopardy cases (see note 24 *supra*), and his treatment of Powell v. Alabama, 287 U.S. 45 (1932) (see note 23 *supra*). But Justice Cardozo seems rather to distinguish what is fundamental from what is not, and puts on his higher plan of values, note 47 *infra,* not only freedom of speech but also the concept of a trial, a fair trial. Palko v. Connecticut, 302 U.S. 319, 326-27 (1937).

[47] [A] cloud has plainly been cast on the soundness of *Twining* and *Adamson* by our decisions absorbing the first and fourth amendments in the fourteenth. There is no historic or logical reason for supposing that those amendments secure more important individual rights.

Cohen v. Hurley, 366 U.S. 117, 159 (1960) (Brennan, J., dissenting). Under the views suggested in this Note the comparative "importance" of the substantive and the procedural rights is irrelevant. Incorporation of the substantive provisions, it is suggested, is consistent with the language and development of the Constitution; incorporation of the procedures is not. . . .

The first amendment to the Constitution is seemingly simple and clear reading:

Schenck v. United States

AMENDMENT I

Congress shall make no law respecting an establishment of religion, or prohibiting the free exercise thereof; or abridging the freedom of speech, or of the press; or the right of the people peaceably to assemble, and to petition the Government for a redress of grievances.

Yet, like much of the Constitution, it presents some severe problems in interpretation and application. Is all speech privileged? Would it be a violation of the right to free speech to prevent a sound truck from blaring through residential neighborhoods advertising a sale on aspirin? Can the guarantee of free speech be used to protect someone who advocates assassination of a public official or violent overthrow of the government? At some point, many of us would answer one of those questions, "No," and at that point we would be implying the existence of a line of distinction between acceptable and unacceptable speech—between constitutionally protected and unprotected speech. How and where to draw that line, and what principles make it a defensible line are the questions which the courts face in free speech and other First Amendment cases.

One of the landmark decisions on the free speech question was rendered on a set of facts which developed during World War I. The following opinion was delivered by one of the most famous Justices of the Supreme Court, Oliver Wendell Holmes, who is generally associated with libertarian principles.

249 U.S. 47 (1919)

Mr. Justice Holmes delivered the opinion of the court:

This is an indictment in three counts. The first charges a conspiracy to violate the Espionage Act of June 15, 1917, ... by causing and attempting to cause insubordination, etc., in the military and naval forces of the United States, and to obstruct the recruiting and enlistment service of the United States, when the

United States was at war with the German Empire; to wit, that the defendant willfully conspired to have printed and circulated to men who had been called and accepted for military service under the Act of May 18, 1917, a document set forth and alleged to be calculated to cause such insubordination and obstruction. The count alleges overt acts in pursuance of the conspiracy, ending in the distribution of the document set forth. The second count alleges a conspiracy to commit an offense against the United States; to wit, to use the mails for the transmission of matter declared to be nonmailable by title 12, §2, of the Act of June 15, 1917, to wit, the above-mentioned document, with an averment of the same overt acts. The third count charges an unlawful use of the mails for the transmission of the same matter and otherwise as above. The defendants were found guilty on all the counts. They set up the 1st Amendment to the Constitution, forbidding Congress to make any law abridging the freedom of speech or of the press, and, bringing the case here on that ground, have argued some other points also of which we much dispose.

It is argued that the evidence, if admissible, was not sufficient to prove that the defendant Schenck was concerned in sending the documents. According to the testimony Schenck said he was general secretary of the Socialist party and had charge of the Socialist headquarters from which the documents were sent. He identified a book found there as the minutes of the executive committee of the party. The book showed a resolution of August 13, 1917, that 15,000 leaflets should be printed on the other side of one of them in use, to be mailed to men who had passed exemption boards, and for distribution. Schenck personally attended to the printing. On August 20 the general secretary's report said, "Obtained new leaflets from the printer and started work addressing envelopes," etc.; and there was a resolve that Comrade Schenck be allowed $125 for sending leaflets through the mail. He said that he had about fifteen or sixteen thousand printed. There were files of the circular in question in the inner office which he said were printed on the other side of the one-sided circular and were there for distribution. Other copies were proved to have been sent through the mails to drafted men. Without going into confirmatory details that were proved, no reasonable man could doubt that the defendant Schenck was largely instrumental in sending the circulars about. . . .

The document in question, upon its first printed side, recited the 1st section of the 13th Amendment, said that the idea embodied in it was violated by the Conscription Act, and that a conscript is little better than a convict. In impassioned language it intimated that conscription was despotism in its worst form and a monstrous wrong against humanity, in the interest of Wall street's chosen few. It said: "Do not submit to intimidation"; but in form at least confined itself to peaceful measures, such as a petition for the repeal of the act. The other and later printed side of the sheet was headed, "Assert Your Rights." It stated reasons for alleging that anyone violated the Constitution when he refused to recognize "your right to assert your opposition to the draft," and went on: "If you do not assert and support your rights, you are helping to deny or disparage rights which it is the solemn duty of all citizens and residents of the United States to retain." It described the arguments on the other side as coming from cunning politicians and a mercenary capitalist press, and even silent consent to the Conscription Law as helping to support an infamous conspiracy. It denied the power to send our citizens away to foreign shores to shoot up the people of other lands, and added that words could not express the condemnation such cold-blooded ruthlessness deserves, etc., etc., winding up, "You must do your share to maintain, support, and uphold the rights of the people of this country." Of course the document would not have been sent unless it had been intended to have some effect, and we do not see what effect it could be expected to have upon persons subject to the draft except to influence them to obstruct the carrying of it out. The defendants do not deny that the jury might find against them on this point.

But it is said, suppose that that was the tendency of this circular, it is protected by the 1st Amendment to the Constitution. Two of the strongest expressions are said to be quoted respectively from well-known public men. It well may be that the prohibition of laws abridging the freedom of speech is not confined to previous restraints, although to prevent them may have been the main purpose, as intimated in Patterson v. Colorado, 205 U.S. 454, 462. We admit that in many places and in ordinary times the defendants, in saying all that was said in the circular, would have been within their constitutional rights. But the character of every act depends upon the circumstances in which it is done. . . . The most stringent protection of free speech would not protect a man in falsely shouting fire in a theater, and causing a panic. It does not even protect a man from an injunction against uttering words that may have all the effect of force. . . . The question in every case is whether the words used are used in such circumstances and are of such a nature as to create a clear and present danger that they will bring about the substantive evils that Congress has a right to prevent. It is a question of proximity and degree. When a nation is at war many things that might be said in time of peace are such a hindrance to its effort that their utterance will not be endured so long as men fight, and that no court could regard them as protected by any constitutional right. It seems to be admitted that if an actual obstruction of the recruiting service were proved, liability for words that produced that effect might be enforced. The Statute of 1917, in §4, punishes conspiracies to obstruct as well as actual obstruction. If the act (speaking, or circulating a paper), its tendency and the intent with which it is done, are the same, we perceive no ground for saying that success alone warrants making the act a crime. . . . Indeed, that case might be said to dispose of the present contention if the precedent covers all media concludendi. But as the right to free speech was not referred to specially, we have thought fit to add a few words. . . .

The First Amendment Is an Absolute

Alexander Meiklejohn

Alexander Meiklejohn, a philosopher, has been long and prominently associated with a position on the First Amendment which contrasts sharply with the principle of the Schenck decision. The rule of decision in Schenck is generally given the shorthand name, the "clear and present danger doctrine." Meiklejohn's reading of the First Amendment leads him to favor an "absolutist" interpretation. In the following article, he defends that position against a variety of criticisms.

Forty-two years ago the *Schenck* opinion,[1] written by Mr. Justice Holmes for a unanimous Court, opened a judicial controversy that still rages. It has taken many forms. In recent years it has divided the Supreme Court Justices into two groups which seem unable to understand each other well enough to formulate with clarity the issue about which they differ. Their discussion of that issue, which is indicated by the title of this paper, has been unclear because the contending parties have not been able to agree on the sense in which the word "absolute" shall be used.

The first portions of this paper will seek a needed clarification of the issue in controversy. For that purpose it will use Mr. Justice Black's recent James Madison Lecture, *The Bill of Rights*[2] and that section of Mr. Justice Harlan's *Konigsberg*[3] opinion which discusses theoretically the meaning of the First Amendment. Relevant opinions of Justices Holmes and Frankfurter will also be taken into account. I shall then attempt an expression of my own thesis.[4]

I. MR. JUSTICE BLACK'S POSITION

Mr. Justice Black's absolutist thesis is stated by his lecture in one sentence: "I take no law abridging to mean *no law abridging.*"[5] With that general statement in mind, he examined and interpreted, one by one, the ten provisions of the Bill of Rights. And, on historical and

Reprinted by permission of the publisher from Alexander Meiklejohn, "The First Amendment Is an Absolute," in Philip B. Kurland, ed., *The Supreme Court Review—1961* (Chicago: The University of Chicago Press, 1961), pp. 245-265. Abridged by the editors.

philosophical grounds, he found them all to be "absolutes" in the sense that "they mean what they say." It should be noted however, that this assertion does not imply that in all respects they say fully and clearly what they mean. The Framers of the Constitution suffered from the same semantic difficulties as do its present-day interpreters. The following quotations illustrate the point at issue.

Concerning the Eighth Amendment, Mr. Justice Black said:[6]

The Eighth Amendment forbids "excessive fines," or the infliction of "cruel or unusual punishments." This is one of the less precise provisions. The courts are required to determine the meaning of such general terms as "excessive" and "unusual." But surely that does not mean that admittedly "excessive bail," "excessive fines," or "cruel punishments" could be justified on the ground of "competing" public interest in carrying out some generally granted power like that given Congress to regulate commerce.

And part of his discussion of the Fourth Amendment was as follows:[7]

The use of the word "unreasonable" in this Amendment means, of course, that not *all* searches and seizures are prohibited. Only those which are *unreasonable* are unlawful. There may be much difference of opinion about whether a particular search or seizure is unreasonable and therefore forbidden by this Amendment. But if it *is* unreasonable, it is absolutely prohibited.

About the Fifth Amendment he said:[8] "There has been much controversy about the meaning of 'due process of law.' Whatever its meaning, however, there can be no doubt that it must be granted." And, finally, as he declared the First Amendment to be absolute, Mr. Justice Black supported his assertion by singling out only one phrase of that very complicated statement: "The phrase 'Congress shall make no law' is composed of plain words, easily understood."[9]

With regard to the ambiguity of other phrases of the Amendment, he was not explicit, as he was in dealing with the Eighth and Fourth and Fifth Amendments. But it may, I think, be taken for granted that the words "abridging the freedom of speech, of the press; or the right of the people peaceably to assemble, and to petition the Government for a redress of their grievances" are not "plain words, easily understood." Together with such expressions as "excessive fines" or "cruel or unusual punishments" or "due process of law," they have been subject to "much controversy." We have inherited them from ages of bitter conflict over civil liberties. "The courts are required to determine [their] meaning."[10]

That constitutional effect of a combination of absolutist language with terms of partial ambiguity, Mr. Justice Black summed up in this statement:[11]

To my way of thinking, at least, the history and language of the Constitution and the Bill of Rights, which I have discussed with you, make it plain that one of the primary purposes of the Constitution with its amendments was to withdraw from the Government *all* power to act in certain areas— *whatever the scope of those areas may be.*

It is clear, I think, that Mr. Justice Black, as an absolutist, is here saying, and is saying only, that the provisions of the Bill of Rights are "universal" statements. In affirmative form they say "all are"; when negative, they say: "none are." And such statements are "not open to exceptions." As universals, they refer, validly or invalidly, clearly or unclearly, to every member of the class which their terms designate. If you believe that "all are," it is nonsense to say that "some are not." If you believe that "none are," you thereby believe, whether you know it or not, that "some are" is false. The "absolute" assertion, like every other intelligible assertion "means what it says" or, at least, what it tries to say.

II. MR. JUSTICE HARLAN'S REJECTION OF THE BLACK POSITION

As one reads the opinions of the "non-absolutists," "balancers," or "operationalists" who undertake to refute the thesis that Mr. Justice Black advocated in his lecture, one is amazed at the extent to which they substitute caricature for refutation. A striking example of this intellectual irrelevance may be found in the opening words of Mr. Justice Harlan's discussion of the constitutional issue in his *Konigsberg* opinion:[12]

> At the outset we reject the view that freedom of speech and association . . . , as protected by the First and Fourteenth Amendments are "absolutes," not only in the undoubted sense that where the constitutional protection exists it must prevail, but also in the sense that the scope of that protection must be gathered solely from a literal reading of the First Amendment. Throughout its history this Court has consistently recognized at least two ways in which constitutionally protected freedom of speech is narrower than an unlimited license to talk. . . .

That statement not only flatly rejected the absolutist theory but also gave two different accounts of what that theory is. The first of these two accounts might be accepted by any absolutist as a clear and accurate statement of his belief about the First Amendment. But, in sharp contrast, the second was a caricature which, for forty-two years since Mr. Justice Holmes, in *Schenck*, initiated and then discarded it, has confused and defeated the intention of the Court to confer reasonably about what the First Amendment means to say.

As he drew the caricature which made possible an easy victory over his opponent, Mr. Justice Harlan claimed the support of Mr. Justice Holmes, who had said of the provisions of the Constitution:[13] "Their significance is vital not formal; it is to be gathered not simply by taking the words and a dictionary, but by considering their origin and the line of their growth." He might also have quoted from Mr. Justice Frankfurter's concurring opinion in *Dennis v. United States*,[14] where the same accusation of historical illiteracy was made:[15] "The language of the First Amendment is to be read not as barren words found in a dictionary but as symbols of historic experience illumined by the presuppositions of those who employed them." But Mr. Justice Harlan's own misunderstanding of his opponent goes further than that of his predecessors. His words misconstrue not only the methods of absolutist thinking but also the conclusion at which such thinking arrives. To the accusation that his opponent relies "solely" on a dictionary, he now adds the charge that he interprets the First Amendment as establishing "an unlimited license to talk."

The absolutist interpretation, when it is thus misstated, is, of course, easily destroyed. The supposed belief in "an unlimited license to talk" is casually refuted by a footnote observation that it "cannot be reconciled with the law relating to libel, slander, misrepresentation, obscenity, perjury, false advertising, solicitation of crime, complicity by encouragement, conspiracy, and the like. . . ."[16] But who, among Mr. Justice Harlan's colleagues, believes in "an unlimited license to talk"? Who interprets the words of the First Amendment without "considering their origin or the line of their growth"? Who reads the text as "barren words found in a dictionary" rather than as "symbols of historic experience"?

The records of judicial debate, including Mr. Justice Black's lecture, show these allegations to be mere irrelevancies. Mr. Justice Harlan could not have made them if he had kept in mind what Mr. Justice Holmes wrote in the *Frohwerk* case in 1919:[17] "The First Amendment

... obviously was not intended to give immunity for every possible use of language. ... We venture to believe that neither Hamilton nor Madison, nor any other competent person then or later, ever supposed that to make criminal the counselling of a murder ... would be an unconstitutional interference with free speech." In these words, Mr. Justice Holmes effectively told us that the notion of "an unlimited license to talk" is not worthy of serious consideration. No "competent" person accepts it.

This section cannot, however, be closed without noting that other "balancers" have similarly caricatured the absolutist contention. This is especially true of Mr. Justice Frankfurter in his *Dennis* opinion, where he referred to my book on free speech.[18] He there described an "absolute" as "a sonorous formula which is in fact only a euphemistic disguise for an unresolved conflict."[19] He also represented it as claiming to be "self-defining and self-enforcing."[20] And he further characterized absolute statements as "dogmas too inflexible for the non-Euclidean problems to be solved."[21]

In relation to these inaccurate characterizations, Mr. Justice Black has said that his "absolutes" are not "self-defining"; they make use of terms whose meanings must be "determined by the courts."[22] Nor are they "self-enforcing." No general principle, whether absolute or not, is enforced except as it is found to "fit the facts." The generalizing and particularizing elements in any intellectual activity must always join forces if they are to be effective. To think without facts is as ineffectual as to think without principles. Again, the absolute provisions are not "inflexible." Mr. Justice Black knows, as well as do his antagonists, that the Constitution did not exist two centuries ago. It provides for its own amendment and, through the courts, for its reinterpretation. How long it will last and how it may be changed no one knows. And, finally, absolute statements are not in themselves "dogmas." They may be either true or false, certain or uncertain, wise or foolish. For example, an assertion that "Congress has unlimited authority to abridge political freedom" is absolute in exactly the same sense as is the assertion that "Congress has no authority to abridge political freedom." Their only relevant difference is that one of these propositions is supported by the Constitution, while the other is repudiated by it.

III. MR. JUSTICE HARLAN'S POSITION

Having refuted an assertion which Mr. Justice Black did not make, Mr. Justice Harlan might next be reasonably expected to attempt to refute the assertion which his opponent did make. But at that point the *Konigsberg* opinion branches off in another direction. It offered a new and more theoretical version of the "balancing" doctrine:[23]

On the one hand certain forms of speech, or speech in certain contexts, has [sic] been considered outside the scope of constitutional protection. ... On the other hand, general regulatory statutes, not intended to control the content of speech but incidentally limiting its unfettered exercise, have not been regarded as the type of law the First or Fourteenth Amendment forbade Congress or the States to pass, when they have been found justified by subordinating valid governmental interests, a prerequisite to constitutionality which has necessarily involved a weighing of the governmental interest involved.

These words have interest for this inquiry because in his restatement of the "balancing" doctrine, Mr. Justice Harlan used "contrast" terms which, by implication, suggest the positive meaning of the First Amendment. "Regulatory" suggests, by contrast, "prohibitory"; "not intended to control the content of thought" suggests "intended to control the content of thought"; incidentally" suggests "by deliberate intention." Here are the elements which, properly fused, might tell us what the First Amendment forbids. But more immediately relevant to the present discussion is the fact that Mr. Justice Harlan here turned from the consideration of "the abridgment of the freedom of speech" to a study of the "regulation of speech." And he did so without determining the relation between "regulation" and "abridgment of freedom." Are these two terms identical? I think not. Nor are freedoms and regulation antithetical. For example, a man may be denied the privilege of speaking at a meeting because someone else "has the floor." But the freedom of discussion is not thereby abridged. Members of Congress are guaranteed freedom "on the floor of either House." But their speaking is regulated under "rules of order." A citizen has authority to "petition" Congress or the Supreme Court. But the time, place, circumstances, and manner of the presentation are determined, not by his own choice, but by carefully prescribed regulations. In 1953 I wrote:[24] "Speech, as a form of human action, is subject to regulation in exactly the same sense as is walking, or lighting a fire, or shooting a gun. To interpret the First Amendment as forbidding such regulation is to so misconceive its meaning as to reduce it to nonsense." In the intervening years I have found no reason to change that assertion.

The freedom that the First Amendment protects is not, then, an absence of regulation. It is the presence of self-government. Our argument now proceeds to define, as clearly as it can, the intention of the Constitutional provision that begins with the words: "Congress shall make no law abridging...."

IV. "RATIONAL PRINCIPLES TO MARK THE LIMITS OF CONSTITUTIONAL PROTECTION"

In his *Free Speech in the United States*[25] Professor Chafee stated the dilemma which confronts our inquiry and which divides the Supreme Court so evenly: "The question whether such perplexing cases are within the First Amendment or not cannot be solved by the multiplication of obvious examples, but only by the development of a rational principle to mark the limits of constitutional protection." Professor Chafee was too much involved in the complexities of balancing to formulate the needed principle of which absolutists speak. But he indicated the goal toward which every interpreter of the First Amendment should now be trying to make his way.[26] We are looking for a principle which is not in conflict with any other provision of the Constitution, a principle which, as it now stands, is "absolute" in the sense of being "not open to exceptions," but a principle which also is subject to interpretation, to change, or to abolition, as the necessities of a precarious world may require.

Apart from the First Amendment itself, the passages of the Constitution which most directly clarify its meaning are the Preamble, the Tenth Amendment, and Section 2 of Article I. All four provisions must be considered in their historical setting, not only in relation to one another but, even more important, in relation to the intention and structure of the Constitution as a whole. Out of such consideration the following principles seem to emerge:

1. All constitutional authority to govern the people of the United States belongs to the people themselves, acting as members of a corporate body politic. They are, it is true, "the governed." But they are also "the governors." Political freedom is not the absence of government. It is self-government.

2. By means of the Constitution, the people establish subordinate agencies, such as the legislature, the executive, the judiciary, and delegate to each of them such specific and limited powers as are deemed necessary for the doing of its assigned governing. These agencies have no other powers.

3. The people do not delegate all their sovereign powers. The Tenth Amendment speaks of powers that are reserved

"to the people," as well as of powers "reserved to the States."

4. Article I, § 2, speaks of a reserved power which the people have decided to exercise by their own direct activity: "The House of Representatives shall be composed of members chosen every second year by the people of the several States. . . ." Here is established the voting power through which the people, as an electorate, actively participate in governing both themselves, as subjects of the laws, and their agencies, as the makers, administrators, and interpreters of the laws. In today's government, the scope of direct electoral action is wider than the provisions made when Article I, § 2, was adopted, but the constitutional principle or intention is the same.

5. The revolutionary intent of the First Amendment is, then, to deny to all subordinate agencies authority to abridge the freedom of the electoral power of the people.

For the understanding of these principles it is essential to keep clear the crucial difference between "the rights" of the governed and "the powers" of the governors. And at this point, the title "Bill of Rights" is lamentably inaccurate as a designation of the first ten amendments. They are not a "Bill of Rights" but a "Bill of Powers and Rights." The Second through the Ninth Amendments limit the powers of the subordinate agencies in order that due regard shall be paid to the private "rights of the governed." The First and Tenth Amendments protect the governing "powers" of the people from abridgment by the agencies which are established as their servants. In the field of our "rights," each one of us can claim "due process of law." In the field of our governing "powers," the notion of "due process" is irrelevant.

V. THE FREEDOM OF THOUGHT AND COMMUNICATION BY WHICH WE GOVERN

The preceding section may be summed up thus: The First Amendment does not protect a "freedom to speak." It protects the freedom of those activities of thought and communication by which we "govern." It is concerned, not with a private right, but with a public power, a governmental responsibility.

In the specific language of the Constitution, the governing activities of the people appear only in terms of casting a ballot. But in the deeper meaning of the Constitution, voting is merely the external expression of a wide and diverse number of activities by means of which citizens attempt to meet the responsibilities of making judgments, which that freedom to govern lays upon them. That freedom implies and requires what we call "the dignity of the individual." Self-government can exist only insofar as the voters acquire the intelligence, integrity, sensitivity, and generous devotion to the general welfare that, in theory, casting a ballot is assumed to express.

The responsibilities mentioned are of three kinds. We, the people who govern, must try to understand the issues which, incident by incident, face the nation. We must pass judgment upon the decisions which our agents make upon those issues. And, further, we must share in devising methods by which those decisions can be made wise and effective or, if need be, supplanted by others which promise greater wisdom and effectiveness. Now it is these activities, in all their diversity, whose freedom fills up "the scope of the First Amendment." These are the activities to whose freedom it gives its unqualified protection. And it must be recognized that the literal text of the Amendment falls far short of expressing the intent and the scope of that protection. I have previously tried to express that inadequacy:[27]

We must also note that, though the intention of the Amendment is sharp and resolute, the sentence which expresses that intention is awkward and ill-constructed. Evidently, it was hard to write and is, therefore, hard to interpret. Within its meaning are summed up centuries of social passion and intellectual controversy, in this country and in others. As one reads it, one feels that its writers could not agree, either within themselves or with each other, upon a single formula which would define for them the paradoxical relation between free men and their legislative agents. Apparently, all that they could make their words do was to link together five separate demands which had been sharpened by ages of conflict and were being popularly urged in the name of the "Freedom of the People." And yet, those demands were, and were felt to be, varied forms of a single demand. They were attempts to express, each in its own way, the revolutionary idea which, in the slowly advancing fight for freedom, has given to the American experiment in self-government its dominating significance for the modern world.

What I have said is that the First Amendment, as seen in its constitutional setting, forbids Congress to abridge the freedom of a citizen's speech, press, peaceable assembly, or petition, whenever those activities are utilized for the governing of the nation. In these respects, the Constitution gives to all "the people" the same protection of freedom which, in Article I, § 6(1), it provides for their legislative agents: "and for any speech or debate in either House, they shall not be questioned in any other place." Just as our agents must be free in their use of their delegated powers, so the people must be free in the exercise of their reserved powers.

What other activities, then, in addition to speech, press, assembly, and petition, must be included within the scope of the First Amendment? First of all, the freedom to "vote;" the official expression of a self-governing man's judgment on issues of public policy, must be absolutely protected. None of his subordinate agencies may bring pressure upon him to drive his balloting this way or that. None of them may require him to tell how he has voted; none may inquire by compulsory process into his political beliefs or associations. In that area, the citizen has constitutional authority and his agents have not.

Second, there are many forms of thought and expression within the range of human communications from which the voter derives the knowledge, intelligence, sensitivity to human values: the capacity for sane and objective judgment which, so far as possible, a ballot should express. These, too, must suffer no abridgment of their freedom. I list four of them below.

1. Education, in all its phases, is the attempt to so inform and cultivate the mind and will of a citizen that he shall have the wisdom, the independence, and, therefore, the dignity of a governing citizen. Freedom of education is, thus, as we all recognize, a basic postulate in the planning of a free society.

2. The achievements of philosophy and the sciences in creating knowledge and understanding of men and their world must be made available, without abridgment, to every citizen.

3. Literature and the arts must be protected by the First Amendment. They lead the way toward sensitive and informed appreciation and response to the values out of which the riches of the general welfare are created.

4. Public discussions of public issues, together with the spreading of information and opinion bearing on those issues, must have a freedom unabridged by our agents. Though they govern us, we, in a deeper sense, govern them. Over our governing, they have no power. Over their governing we have sovereign power.

VI. A PARADOX

Out of the argument thus far stated, two apparently contradictory statements emerge. Congress may, in ways carefully limited, "regulate" the activities by which the citizens govern the nation. But no regulation may abridge the freedom of those governing activities. I am sure that the two statements are not contradictory. But their combination is, to say the least, paradoxical. It is that paradox that I must now face as I try to respond to Professor Kalven's challenge.[28] As a non-lawyer, I shall not discuss in detail the difficulties and puzzlements with which the courts must deal. I can only suggest that, here and there, seeming contradictions are not real.

First. A distinction must be drawn between belief and communication in their relations to Congressional authority. A citizen may be told when and where and in what manner he may or may not speak, write, assemble, and so on. On the other hand, he may not be told what he shall or shall not believe. In that realm each citizen is sovereign. He exercises powers that the body politic reserves for its own members. In 1953, testifying before the Senate Committee on Constitutional Rights, I said:[29]

... our First Amendment freedom forbids that any citizen be required, under threat of penalty, to take an oath, or make an affirmation, as to beliefs which he holds or rejects. Every citizen, it is true, may be required and should be required, to pledge loyalty, and to practice loyalty, to the nation. He must agree to support the Constitution. But he may never be required to *believe* in the Constitution. His loyalty may never be tested on grounds of adherence to, or rejection of, any *belief*. Loyalty does not imply conformity of opinion. Every citizen of the United States has Constitutional authority to approve or to condemn any laws enacted by the Legislature, any actions taken by the Executive, any judgments rendered by the judiciary, any principles established by the Constitution. All these enactments which, as men who are governed, we must obey, are subject to our approval or disapproval, as we govern. With respect to all of them we, who are free men, are sovereign. We are "The People." We govern the United States.

However far our practice falls short of the intention expressed by those words, they provide the standard by which our practice must be justified or condemned.

Second. We must recognize that there are many forms of communication which, since they are not being used as activities of governing, are wholly outside the scope of the First Amendment. Mr. Justice Holmes has told us about these, giving such vivid illustrations as "persuasion to murder"[30] and "falsely shouting fire in a theatre and causing a panic."[31] And Mr. Justice Harlan, referring to Holmes and following his lead, gave a more extensive list:[32] "libel, slander, misrepresentation, obscenity, perjury, false advertising, solicitation of crime, complicity by encouragement, conspiracy. ..." Why are these communications not protected by the First Amendment? Mr. Justice Holmes suggested an explanation when he said of the First Amendment in *Schenck*:[33] "It does not even protect a man from an injunction against uttering words that may have all the effect of force."

Now it may be agreed that the uttering of words cannot be forbidden by legislation, nor punished on conviction, unless damage has been done by them to some individual or to the wider society. But that statement does not justify the imputation that all "words that may have all the effect of force" are denied the First Amendment's protection. The man who falsely shouts "Fire!" in a theatre is subject to prosecution under validly enacted legislation. But the army officer who, in command of a firing squad, shouts "Fire!" and thus ends a life, cannot be prosecuted for murder. He acts as an agent of the government. And, in fact, all governing communications are intended to have, more or less directly, "the effect of force." When a voter casts his ballot for a tax levy, he intends that someone shall be deprived of property. But his voting is not therefore outside the scope of the First Amendment. His voting must be free.

The principle here at stake can be seen in our libel laws. In cases of private defamation, one individual does damage to another by tongue or pen; the person so injured in reputation or property may sue for damages. But, in that case, the First Amendment gives no protection to the person sued. His verbal attack has no relation to the business of governing.

If, however, the same verbal attack is made in order to show the unfitness of a candidate for governmental office, the act is properly regarded as a citizen's participation in government. It is, therefore, protected by the First Amendment. And the same principle holds good if a citizen attacks, by words of disapproval and condemnation, the policies of the government, or even the structure of the Constitution. These are "public" issues concerning which, under our form of government, he has authority, and is assumed to have competence, to judge. Though private libel is subject to legislative control, political or seditious libel is not.

Third. In discussions of the First Amendment too little attention has been given to the regulatory word "peaceable" in relation to "assembly." It suggests principles of limitation which apply also to speech, press, petition, and to the other forms of communication which support them. This limitation is significant in demonstrating that a citizen's governing is often both "regulated" and "free."

Peaceableness in governing may serve either one or both of two purposes. It provides protection for an assembly against external violation of rules of public order. It also seeks to ensure that relations within the assembly shall succeed in serving the governing function which warrants its protection by the First Amendment. The first of these purposes has to do with relations between the assembly and "outsiders" who, disagreeing with its ideas and intentions, may seek to disrupt the discussion and, in various ways, to render it ineffectual. In this situation, both the local authorities which have authority to "regulate" and the police who seek to apply the regulations are held responsible by the intention of the First and Fourteenth Amendments. No ordinance may be based upon disapproval of policies to be discussed or decreed by the assembly. And the police must, to the limit of their power, defend the meeting from interruption or interference by its enemies. But basically more important are the conditions of peaceableness within an assembly itself. It is, of course, impossible that everyone should be allowed to express his point of view whenever and however he chooses. In a meeting for discussion, as contrasted with a lecture, however, no one may be "denied the floor" on the ground of disapproval of what he is saying or would say. And, if the interests of a self-governing society are to be served, vituperation which fixes attention on the defects of an opponent's character or intelligence and thereby distracts attention from the question of policy under discussion may be forbidden as a deadly enemy of peaceable assembly. Anyone who persists in it should be expelled from the meeting, and, if need be, the police should give help in getting it done.

I cannot, however, leave those words on record without noting how inadequate, to the degree of non-existence, are our public provisions for active discussions among the members of our self-governing society. As we try to create and enlarge freedom, such universal discussion is imperative. In every village, in every district of every town or city, there should be established at public expense cultural centers inviting all citizens, as they may choose, to meet together for the consideration of public policy. And conditions must be provided under which such meetings could be happily and successfully conducted. I am not thinking of such lunatic-fringe activities as those in Hyde Park in London. I am thinking of a self-governing body politic, whose freedom of individual expression should be cultivated, not merely because it serves to prevent outbursts of violence which would result from suppression, but for the positive purpose of bringing every citizen into active and intelligent sharing in the government of his country.

Fourth. Largely because of our failure to make adequate provision for free and unhindered public discussion, the courts are called upon to judge the constitutionality of local ordinances which forbid or limit the holding of public meetings in public places. Such ordinances come into effect when individuals or groups assemble in such a way as to interfere with other interests of the community or of its members. The most striking and perplexing cases of this kind occur when meetings are held on the public streets or in parks whose primary use is, in the opinion of the authorities, blocked or hindered to a degree demanding action. Now if such ordinances are based upon official disapproval of the ideas to be presented at the meeting, they clearly violate the First Amendment. But if no such abridgment of freedom is expressed or implied, regulation or prohibition on other grounds may be enacted and enforced.

It must not be assumed that every governmental regulation of a public meeting is, under current conditions, destructive of political freedom. Conditions of traffic on a city street are very different from those in the relatively open spaces of a country village. Parks may be needed for rest, quiet, and release from excitement and strain. Just as an individual, seeking to advocate some public policy may not do so, without consent, by interrupting a church service, or a classroom, or a sickroom, or a session of Congress or of the Supreme Court, or by ringing a doorbell and demanding to be heard, so meetings must conform to the necessities of the community, with respect to time, place, circumstance, and manner of procedure. And, unless those considerations are dishonestly used as a cover for unconstitutional discrimination against this idea or that, there is no First Amendment complaint against the ordinances which express them. The Amendment, I repeat, does not establish an "unlimited right to talk."

It must further be noted that in "emergency" situations, when something must be said and no other time, place, circumstance, or manner of speech will serve for the saying of it, a citizen may be justified in "taking the law into his own hands." In the famous example of Mr. Justice Holmes, a man is not allowed to shout "Fire!" *falsely* in a theatre. But, if during a performance in a theatre, a person sees a fire which threatens to spread, he is not only allowed, he is duty-bound, to try to find some way of informing others so that a panic may not ensue with its disastrous consequences. The distinction between "falsely" and "truly" is here fundamental to an understanding of what freedom is.

Fifth. In the current discussions as to whether or not "obscenity" in literature and the arts is protected by the First Amendment, the basic principle is, I think, that literature and the arts are protected because they have a "social importance" which I have called a "governing" importance. For example, the novel is at present a powerful determinative of our views of what human beings are, how they can be influenced, in what directions they should be influenced by many forces, including, especially, their own judgments and appreciations. But the novel, like all the other creations of literature and the arts, may be produced wisely or unwisely, sensitively or coarsely, for the building up of a way of life which we treasure or for tearing it down. Shall the government establish a censorship to distinguish between "good" novels and "bad" ones? And, more specifically, shall it forbid the publication of novels which portray sexual experiences with a frankness that, to the prevailing conventions of our society, seems "obscene"?

The First Amendment seems to me to answer that question with an unequivocal "no." Here, as elsewhere, the authority of citizens to decide what they shall write and, more fundamental, what they shall read and see, has not been delegated to any of the subordinate branches of government. It is "reserved to the people," each deciding for himself to whom he will listen, whom he will read, what portrayal of the human scene he finds worthy of his attention. And at this point I feel compelled to disagree with Professor Kalven's interpretation of what I have tried to say. In his recent article on obscenity, he wrote:[34]

> The classic defense of John Stuart Mill and the modern defense of Alexander Meiklejohn do not help much when the question is why the novel, the poem, the painting, the drama, or the piece of sculpture falls within the protection of the First Amendment. Nor do the famous opinions of Hand, Holmes, and Brandeis. The emphasis is all on truth winning out in a fair fight between competing ideas. The emphasis is clearest in Meiklejohn's argument that free speech is indispensable to the informed citizenry required to make democratic self-government work. The people need free speech because they vote. As a result his argument distinguishes sharply between public and private speech. Not all communications are relevant to the political process. The people do not need novels or dramas or paintings or poems because they will be called upon to vote. Art and belles-lettres do not deal in such ideas — at least not good art or belles-lettres. . . .

In reply to that friendly interpretation, I must, at two points, record a friendly disavowal. I have never been able to share the Miltonian faith that in a fair fight between truth and error, truth is sure to win. And if one had that faith, it would be hard to reconcile it with the sheer stupidity of the policies of this nation—and of other nations—now driving humanity to the very edge of final destruction. In my view, "the people need free speech" because they have decided, in adopting, maintaining and interpreting their Constitution, to govern themselves rather than to be governed by others. And, in order to make that self-government a reality rather than an illusion, in order that it may become as wise and efficient as its responsibilities require, the judgment-making of the people must be self-educated in the ways of freedom. That is, I think, the positive purpose to which the negative words of the First Amendment gave a constitutional expression. Moreover, as against Professor Kalven's interpretation, I believe, as a teacher, that the people do need novels and dramas and paintings and poems, "because they will be called upon to vote." The primary social fact which blocks and hinders the success of our experiment in self-government is that our citizens are not educated for self-government. We are terrified by ideas, rather than challenged and stimulated by them. Our dominant mood is not the courage of people who dare to think. It is the timidity of those who fear and hate whenever conventions are questioned.

VII. CONCLUSION

Professor Leonard W. Levy, in a stimulating book,[35] has recently given strong evidence that the Framers of the Constitution were not, for the most part, explicitly concerned with those aspects of the First Amendment's meaning and application which now especially concern us. If we assume that his thesis has been established, what bearing does it have upon the contentions of this paper?

In answer to that question, two different statements can be made which properly supplement each other. First, the Framers initiated a political revolution whose development is still in process throughout the world. Second, like most revolutionaries, the Framers could not foresee the specific issues which would arise as their "novel idea" exercised its domination over the governing activities of a rapidly developing nation in a rapidly and fundamentally changing world. In that sense, the Framers did not know what they were doing. And in the same sense, it is still true that, after two centuries of experience, we do not know what they were doing, or what we ourselves are now doing.

In a more abstract and more significant sense, however, both they and we have been aware that the adoption of the principle of self-government by "The People" of this nation set loose upon us and upon the world at large an idea which is still transforming men's conceptions of what they are and how they may best be governed. Wherever it goes, that idea is demanding — and slowly securing — a recognition that, with respect to human dignity, women have the same status as men, that people of all races and colors and creeds must be treated as equals, that the poor are at least the equals of the rich. In popular language the idea finds expression in such phrases as "the land of the free," or "government by consent of the governed," or "government of the people, by the people, for the people shall not perish from the earth."

In our discussions of the Constitution, we commonly think that the clearest and most compelling expression of the "idea" of political freedom is given by the First Amendment. But in theory, and perhaps in practice, more penetrating insights are given by the Preamble's declaration that "We, the people of the United States . . . do ordain and establish this Constitution . . . ," or by the Tenth Amendment's assertion that, while we have delegated some limited governing powers to our agents, we have reserved other powers to ourselves, or, finally, by the provision of Article I, Section 2, that we have authority to exercise direct governing power in electing our representatives.

If what we are saying here is true, then *Robertson v. Baldwin* seems to me to contain the most disastrous judicial pronouncement that I have found:[36] "The law is perfectly well settled that the first ten amendments to the Constitution, commonly known as the Bill of Rights, were not intended to lay down any novel principles of government, but simply to embody certain guaranties and immunities which we had inherited from our English ancestors. . . ." In 1951, in his opinion in *Dennis*, Mr. Justice Frankfurter, in quoting that statement, said of it,[37] "That this represents the authentic view of the Bill of Rights and the spirit in which it must be construed has been recognized again and again in cases that have come here within the last fifty years."

In 1953, in a comment on that concurring opinion,[38] I quoted that dictum and criticized it. To sum up what I have been trying to say in this paper, I wish to repeat some part of that criticism. Mr. Justice Frankfurter, it must be noted, does not here speak as one expressing his own opinion. He is telling us of a contention which has prevailed for a long time in the Court. Is that contention valid? Is it true, for example, that the religion clause of the First Amendment was "inherited" from a nation which had, and still has, an established church. However that may be, a ringing dissent by the first Mr. Justice Harlan in *Robertson v. Baldwin* seems to me to cut into meaningless bits the assertion that no "novel principles of government" were in mind when the Bill of Rights was adopted. Arguing, in his dissent, about the constitutionality of involuntary servitude, he said:[39] "Nor, I submit, is any light thrown upon the question by the history of legislation in Great Britain. The powers of the British Parliament furnish no test for the powers that may be exercised by the Congress of the United States." The distinctive feature of our Constitution, he declared, that marks it off from British political institutions, is that it is established, not by the legislature, but by the people. And he summed up the novelty of our system:[40] "No such powers have been or can be exercised by any legislative body under the American system. Absolute, arbitrary power exists nowhere in this free land. The authority for the exercise of power by the Congress of the United States must be found in the Constitution. Whatever it does in excess of the powers granted it, or in violation of the injunctions of the supreme law of the land, is a nullity, and may be so treated by every person." To a teacher of freedom in the United States that seems to be good law. I wish it would seem so to those who now have authority to determine what good law is.

Notes

[1] Schenck v. United States, 249 U.S. 47 (1919).

[2] 35 N.Y.U.L. REV. 882 (1960).

[3] Konigsberg v. State Bar, 366 U.S. 36, 49-56 (1961).

[4] For several reasons, much of this paper is written in the first person. First, in his *Konigsberg* dissent, 366 U.S. at 56, Mr. Justice Black, taking the absolutist position, speaks of "some people" of the same school whose view of the First Amendment differs from his own. And, in an appended note, he mentions me as one of them. *Id.* at 65 n. 19, referring to: Meiklejohn, *What Does the First Amendment Mean?* 20 U. CHI. L. REV. 461 (1953). In the words which follow, I must, therefore, speak not for absolutism in all its forms, but only for my own version of it.

Second, my book *Free Speech and Its Relation to Self-Government* (1948) has a closing chapter entitled "Reflections" that begins: "No argument about principles is, I suppose, ever finished. But the argument of these lectures seems to the writer of them, peculiarly incomplete. They constitute, it seems to me, not an inquiry, but only the beginning of an inquiry. Even if it be agreed that the 'clear and present danger' formula denies rather than expresses the meaning of the Constitution, even if we are convinced that the guarantee of the freedom of public discussion which is provided by the First Amendment admits of no exceptions, we are, because of those very conclusions, plunged at once into a multitude of bewildering questions. Those questions relate both to theory and to practice. And this book makes no pretense of having specifically dealt with them." *Id.* at 92. That frankly acknowledged incompleteness has often been called to my attention and I need, in reply, to say about it whatever a non-lawyer can say.

Third, the writing of this paper is largely due to the friendly insistence of Professor Harry Kalven, Jr., of the Law School of the University of Chicago. He and I have had, in recent years, a continuing exchange of ideas. Professor Kalven tells me that he is not sure that my interpretation of the First Amendment can stand the test of lawyer-like application to the many specific situations which the courts must handle. In response to that challenge, I cannot presume to offer fully specific answers to specific problems. I can only suggest principles, bringing them as near as I can to the actual issues with which the courts deal.

[5] Black, *supra* note 2.

[6] *Id.* at 871-72.

[7] *Id.*, at 873.

[8] *Ibid.*

[9] *Id.* at 874.

[10] *Id.* at 871. I am not sure that Mr. Justice Black will accept this reading of what he means.

[11] *Id.* at 874-75. (Emphasis added.)

[12] 366 U.S. at 49-50.

[13] Gompers v. United States, 233 U.S. 604, 610 (1914), quoted at 366 U.S. at 50 n. 10.

[14] 341 U.S. 494, 517 (1951).

[15] *Id.* at 523.

[16] 366 U.S. at 49 n. 10.

[17] Frohwerk v. United States, 249 U.S. 204, 206 (1919).

[18]341 U.S. at 524 n. 5.

[19]*Id.* at 519.

[20]*Id.* at 523.

[21]*Id.* at 525.

[22]See text *supra,* at note 10.

[23]366 U.S. at 50-51.

[24]Hearings before the Subcommittee on Constitutional Rights of the Senate Committee on the Judiciary, 84th Cong., 2d Sess., at p. 17 (1955).

[25]15 (1941).

[26]That Chafee was, in 1942, a "balancer" is shown by the first chapter of his book to which I already have made reference. There he said in summation: "That is, in technical language, there are individual interests, and social interests, which must be balanced against each other, if they conflict, in order to determine which interest shall be sacrificed under the circumstances and which shall be protected and become the foundation of a legal right." *Id.* at 32. . . .

[27]Meiklejohn, *supra* note 4, at 463.

[28]See *supra* note 4.

[29]*Supra* note 24, at p. 20.

[30]Abrams v. United States, 250 U.S. 616, 627 (1919).

[31]Schenck v. United States, 249 U.S. 47, 52 (1919).

[32]366 U.S. at 49 n. 10.

[33]249 U.S. at 52.

[34]Kalven, *Metaphysics of the Law of Obscenity,* 1960, Sup. Ct. Rev. 1, 15-16.

[35]Legacy of Suppression (1960).

[36]165 U.S. 275, 281 (1897).

[37]341 U.S. at 524.

[38]Meiklejohn, *supra* note 4.

[39]165 U.S. at 296.

[40]*Ibid.*

On the Meaning of the First Amendment: Absolutes in the Balance

Wallace Mendelson

The absolutist position has never commanded a consistent majority on the Supreme Court. Justices Douglas, Black, and Murphy have, in particular cases, come close to the Meiklejohn position; Justice Black, for example, in Wieman v. Updegraff *(1952) held that the First Amendment invalidates the ". . . slightest suppression of thought, speech, press, or public assembly." Still, in other factual situations they have been moved to observe, as did Justice Murphy in* Chaplinsky v. New Hampshire *(1942) that "It is well understood that the right of free speech is not absolute at all times and under all circumstances." In short, the Court seems never to have unequivocally accepted any single rule of decision to be applied in all First Amendment cases. This more pragmatic approach to the First Amendment guarantees has occasionally been referred to as "balancing of interests" in the specific case. In the following article, Wallace Mendelson defends the balancing stance and in doing so relates the legal to the political process.*

Doctrines are the most frightful tyrants to which men ever are subject, because doctrines get inside of a man's reason and betray him against himself. —W. G. Sumner[1]

In a recent article, Mr. Laurent Frantz criticizes the Supreme Court's "balancing of interests" approach in free speech cases. In the course of his argument, he also lampoons the "absolutist" approach of the dissenters, and chides its chief spokesman for putting his argument "largely in the form that the first amendment 'means what it says.' "[2] Yet in criticizing the Court, Mr. Frantz himself rests largely on what he seems to assume is a clear meaning in the "constitutional text"—and its history.[3]

In support of the Court's balancing position, I suggest that the language of the first amendment is highly ambiguous, and that this ambiguity is at best compounded by history. Professor Chafee put it in a thimble: "The truth is, I think, that the framers had no very

Reprinted by permission of the publisher, Wallace Mendelson, "On the Meaning of the First Amendment: Absolutes in the Balance," *California Law Review,* 50 (December, 1962), 821-828. Copyright © 1950, California Law Review, Inc. Abridged by the editors.

clear idea as to what they meant by 'the freedom of speech or of the press.' "[4] Indeed, perhaps it is not going too far to suggest that there is no more equivocal word in the English language than "freedom." What Lincoln said of "liberty" is relevant here: "The world has never had a good definition of [it]." He also pointed out that what is freedom for the lion is death for the lamb. In short, however clear the thou-shalt-not part of the amendment may be, its chain of meaning cannot transcend the fogginess of its weakest link. Surely the framers would have communicated more clearly if they had omitted the weasel-word, and provided simply, "Congress shall pass no law abridging (or restricting) speech." This suggests, of course, that they used the word "freedom" as a limiting or qualifying, not an enlarging, term—a reference presumably to the narrow conception of free utterance that prevailed in the late eighteenth century. Finally, it is noteworthy that even so stout a libertarian as Alexander Meiklejohn has chided those who insist that the words "abridging the freedom of speech or of the press" are "plain words, easily understood."[5]

Of course, as Mr. Frantz suggests, we are entitled to seek clarification in history. Doing so, he cites Jefferson's statement that "it is time enough for the rightful purposes of civil government for its officers to interfere when principles break out into overt acts against peace and good order."[6] But this is not only selective history, it is selective Jefferson. Referring to the "licentiousness" of the press that opposed him, the first of the Jeffersonians observed:

This is a dangerous state of things, and the press ought to be restored to its credibility if possible. The restraints provided by the laws of the States are sufficient for this, if applied. And I have, therefore, long thought that a few prosecutions of the most prominent offenders would have a wholesome effect. . . . Not a general prosecution, for that would look like persecution; but a selected one.[7]

Some of us may be excused for finding in these combined statements as much equivocation as in the undefined terms of the first amendment itself.

Holmes presumably was one of the greatest of legal historians. Yet he gave at different times opposite interpretations of the historic meaning of the amendment. Speaking for himself and Brandeis, he observed that "History seems to me against the notion [that] the First Amendment left the common law of seditious libel in force."[8] A few years earlier he had written for the Court: "[T]he main purpose of such constitutional provisions is "to prevent all such *previous restraints* . . . as had been practiced by other governments,' and they do not prevent the subsequent punishment of such as may be deemed contrary to the public welfare."[9] In this statement Holmes had the support of Cooley, who maintained that its Blackstonian outlook "has been followed by American commentators of standard authority as embodying correctly the idea incorporated in the constitutional law of the country by the provisions in the American Bill of Rights."[10] To support this proposition Cooley justifiably cites Kent, Story, and Rawle.

While Holmes' switch suggests that the historic purpose of the first amendment is something less than obvious, Mr. Frantz may find comfort in the fact that the Justice's later position was the more liberal one. Professor Chafee also seems to support the charge of vagueness, but by a switch from a generous to a more restricted view. Thus he first asserted that the framers intended "to wipe out the common law of sedition, and make further prosecutions for criticism of the government, without any incitement to law-breaking, forever impossible."[11]

It would be ironical if Holmes reversed himself under the influence of Chafee,[12] because Chafee later appears to have altered his own position:

[The] argument that all the freedoms within the First Amendment are not open to any governmental restrictions . . . leans far too heavily on the absolute nature of its language. . . . Especially significant is the contemporaneous evidence that the phrase "freedom of the press" was viewed against a background of familiar legal institutions which men of 1791 did not regard as objectionable, such as damage suits for libel. Many state constitutions of this time included guarantees of freedom of speech and press which have been treated as having approximately the same scope as the federal provisions. Some of these, as in Massachusetts, were absolute in terms, while others . . . expressly imposed responsibility for abuse of the right. The precise nature of the state constitutional language did not matter; the early interpretation was much the same. *Not only were private libel suits allowed, but also punishments for criminal libel and for contempt of court.* For instance, there were several Massachusetts convictions around 1800 for attacking the conduct of the legislature and public officials. . . .

The truth is, I think, that the framers had no very clear idea as to what they meant by "the freedom of speech or of the press," but we can say . . . with reasonable assurance . . . . [that] the freedom which Congress was forbidden to abridge was not, for them, some absolute concept which had never existed on earth.[13]

Henry Schofield's "Freedom of the Press in the United States," which appeared in 1914, seems to be the seedbed of the modern libertarian conception of the first amendment. It begins, however, with the admission that the "nearly if not quite unanimous expressed view of our judges always has been, and is, that the constitutional declarations of liberty of the press are only declaratory of the English common-law right protected by the English courts at the time of the Revolution. . . ."[14] Of course, it may be that Professor Schofield, writing 123 years after adoption of the amendment, had a truer insight into that history than judges and commentators who witnessed or participated in it, but surely there is room for respectful doubt.

So far, I have meant only to suggest that at best (from the liberal point of view) history is a somewhat less than obvious key to the meaning of the first amendment. Surely, however, no such discussion can fail to mention Leonard Levy's powerful (if reluctant) case that history speaks clearly in these matters—but in a way that contradicts the libertarian position.[15]

For those who are not moved by his "textual and historical" arguments, Mr. Frantz offers three "fundamental policy reasons" for a more active judicial role in expression, than in economic, cases:

An economic mistake or injustice [by Congress] does not interfere with the political process and that process therefore remains open for its correction or redress if the courts refuse relief. The same cannot be said where legislation results in infringement of political rights, for the injured can hardly rely for redress on the very weapons of which they are deprived.[16]

This is difficult to follow. By the Interstate Commerce Act, Congress deprives a railroad owner of his "freedom" to charge what the traffic will bear. By the Smith Act, Congress deprives a Communist of his "freedom" to teach and advocate violent overthrow of government. *Yet both the railroad owner and the Communist are perfectly free to seek political redress, i.e., repeal of the measure deemed offensive.* Both may speak freely in favor of a change in the law. Any substantial legislative interference with that kind of freedom would certainly have hard going in the Supreme Court.[17] Even the leader of the antiactivists has made his position clear on that point.[18]

Mr. Frantz's second policy reason for giving free utterance a "preferred place" is that

economic interests are typically represented in legislative bodies—or are able to obtain a hearing from them. Despised ideological minorities typically are not. In extreme situations such as those which give rise to first amendment test cases, their political influence may be less than zero, for it may be better politics for a legislator to abuse them than to listen to their grievances.[19]

Surely we cannot pretend that all economic interests have substantial "political influence," nor that all other interests are politically impotent. Mr. Frantz's distinction then is not between the economic and the non-economic, but between claims which have much political leverage and those which have little or none. On this basis, some economic interests ought to enjoy a "preferred place" (including perhaps a presumption of unconstitutionality for offending legislation), just as some spiritual interests should have only a second-class status. This might entail some difficulties in application. Would the crucial test refer to absolute or relative political influence? How would such values be measured? How much political strength would be required to justify a "deferred" judicial place? Would a politically negligible religious group enjoy an advantage in the courts that would be denied to the Catholic Church? Would the latter have a "preferred place" vis-à-vis protestantism? Ideally, of course, legislators and all of us would give every "despised minority" a respectful hearing, but surely *the first amendment* does not require it.

The final policy reason presented on behalf of libertarianism on the Bench is that while "activism" in economic cases restricts the scope of "popular choice," activism in utterance cases expands it.[20] But surely a judicial veto of anticommunist legislation limits the range of popular government just as effectively as a judicial veto of minimum-wage legislation. Both say to the people these are choices you may not make. And is it absolutely clear that democracy is poisoned by suppressing those who preach violence when all the avenues of peaceful change are open? Men of the Weimar Republic, like those of pre-1948 Czechoslovakia, might have some interesting thoughts on that question.

Having bludgeoned both the balancing and the absolutist gambits in speech cases, Mr. Frantz concludes by insisting that constitutionally protected freedom of speech ought to be "defined."[21] Yet strangely (for one who is so concerned for freedom of popular choice) he thinks this should be done not by a constitutional convention, nor by Congress, but by the Supreme Court. To insist that "freedom of speech" needs defining is to concede what I have been arguing: that it is not adequately defined either in the language of the Constitution, or by history, or by considerations of public policy so unquestionable as to be fit subjects for judicial notice.

It is largely because of the absence of defining standards, I suggest, that the Court has resorted openly to balancing in free speech cases. We have had too many opinions that hide the inevitable weighing process by pretending that decisions spring full-blown from the Constitution — a document written generations ago by men who had not the slightest conception of the world in which *we* live. "It will ever remain a mystery to me," Thomas R. Powell observed, "how intelligent jurists can make these professions of non participation in the judicial process."[22] Open balancing compels a judge to take full responsibility for his decisions, and promises a particularized, rational account of how he arrives at them—more particularized and more rational at least than the familiar parade of hallowed abstractions, elastic absolutes, and selective history. Moreover, this approach should make it more difficult for judges to rest on their predispositions without ever subjecting them to the test of reason. It should also make their accounts more rationally auditable. Above all, the open balancing technique is calculated to leave "the sovereign prerogative of choice" to the people — with the least interference that is compatible with our tradition of judicial review. Absent that tradition in utterance cases, the Court might logically accept Learned Hand's view that the first amendment (like the republican-form-of-government clause[23]) is too uncommunicative — too lacking in guidelines — to be treated as law.[24]

Those who find these thoughts offensive may recall that even modern libertarians are far from agreement on the meaning of free speech. Thus its two leading academic advocates—Chafee and Meiklejohn — are deeply divided on matters of scope and limitation.[25] Similarly, Justices Black and Douglas have found themselves on opposite sides of utterance issues.[26] Indeed the first amendment idea is so obscure that both of them apparently failed to see a free-expression problem in the compulsory flag salute until it was pointed out by Mr. Justice Jackson.[27] The obscurity is also revealed in Mr. Justice Black's change of heart with respect to the validity of libel laws[28]—and in the disagreements of Holmes and Brandeis.[29] So too, as we have seen, Jefferson could not agree with himself on the meaning of free communication. Finally, even those two well springs of Anglo-American freedom, Milton's *Areopagitica* and Mill's *On Liberty*, are deeply at odds on the thing that they both eulogize. For surely Mill could not accept Milton's principle that only "neighboring differences, or rather indifferences" are entitled to toleration.[30]

This brings us to the anguished question that Mr. Frantz puts at least by implication: What good is the first amendment, if it is not to be given a "preferred place" by "activist" magistrates? Madison long ago gave the answer: It is futile to rely on judges and "parchment barriers"; politics is the only reliable protection for basic substantive interests.

Of course, Madison introduced and fought for the Bill of Rights—and, in so doing, referred to judicial review in support of it, as libertarians emphasize ad infinitum.[31] What they fail to mention is that this was Madison under pressure. If the "father of the Constitution" had really wanted a bill of rights, why did he not introduce and fight for one in the constitutional convention? Here is his answer:

> I have never thought the omission [of a bill of rights from the original Constitution] a material defect, nor been anxious to supply it even by *subsequent* amendment, for any other reason than that it is anxiously desired by others. . . .
>
> I have not viewed it in an important light . . . because [among other things] experience proves [its] inefficiency on those occasions when its controul is most needed. . . . In Virginia I have seen the bill of rights violated in every instance where it has been opposed to a popular current. . . .[32]

Before he was pressured into supporting a bill of rights, Madison insisted the only use of a formal declaration was that "the political truths declared in that solemn manner acquire by degrees the character of fundamental maxims of free government, and as they become incorporated with the national sentiment, counteract the impulses of interest and passion."[33] If the government should act improperly, a bill of rights would be "a good ground for an appeal to the sense of the community."[34] How far this is from judicial review! And how close to Learned Hand's thought that the Bill of Rights is not law, but a moral admonition.[35]

Madison was unenthusiastic about the Bill-of-Rights-Judicial-Review approach because he foresaw a far more reliable, and far more sophisticated, shield for civil liberty: the structure and process of politics.[36] For him the constitutional diffusion of power and the vast expanse of the nation with its multiplicity of regional, economic, religious, and other interests were the true safeguards. Faction would resist faction; ambition would weigh against ambition. The hopes and fears of each subgroup would check and balance those of all the others. Government could act only after political compromise had found the common denominator of a host of mutually suspicious minorities. In the extended, pluralistic republic of the United States this could not be an easy, overnight venture. No program that had survived the give and take necessary to attain support by a concurrent majority of our incredibly varied factional interests could depart substantially from the Nation's moral center of gravity. No governmental system could be expected to achieve more; certainly not by idealistic fiats from the Bench that fly in the face of deeply felt community needs. In short, as Madison saw it, majority rule—given a vast empire of diffused socio-political power—was the only reliable security against governmental inhumanity.[37]

Of course, some free speech "indiscretions" might survive the shifting of the social and political processes—the Sedition Act of 1798, the Espionage Act of 1917, the Smith Act of 1940 come to mind. But these (assuming they were unjustified) would necessarily reflect such deep and widespread feelings as to defy judicial veto. The upshot is that Congress has killed thousands of bills reflecting every imaginable form of bigotry, intolerance, and demagogery; the Supreme Court has not yet struck down a national measure on the basis of any provision in the first amendment.[38] As Madison anticipated, the congressional batting average is about .999; the Court's is .000.

My point is that liberals appreciate the political processes far too little, and expect far more from judicial review than it has ever been able to deliver. Conservatives no longer make this mistake. They know the cost and frailty of a preferred place in court. Accordingly, since 1937, they have concentrated on legislatures, and have carried off all but a few of the prizes.

Meanwhile a select little company of libertarians—with far less social support than conservatives had in the old days—is trying to repeat all of the Old-Guard mistakes: the twisted history, the tortured parchment, the sugar-coated bias called public policy, the preferred place that can hope only to delay defeat. Sooner or later libertarians will have to face it—the real victories are won in legislatures and at the polls.[39] Man after all is a political, not a legal, animal.

Notes

[1] Hitchner & Harbold, Modern Government 509 (1962).

[2] Frantz, *The First Amendment in the Balance,* 71 Yale L.J. 1424, 1432 (1962).

[3] *Id.* at 1433-44, 1446.

[4] Chafee, Book Review, 62 Harv. L. Rev. 891, 898 (1949).

[5] Meiklejohn, *The First Amendment Is an Absolute,* 1961 Sup. Ct. Rev. 245, 247.

[6] Frantz, *supra* note 2, at 1446.

[7] Letter from Thomas Jefferson to Thomas McKean, Feb. 19, 1803, in 8 *The Writings of Thomas Jefferson* 216, 218-19 (Ford ed. 1897).

[8] Abrams v. United States, 250 U.S. 616, 630 (1919).

[9] Patterson v. Colorado, 215 U.S. 454, 462 (1907).

[10] Cooley, *Constitutional Limitations* 420 (3d ed. 1874).

[11] Chafee, *Freedom of Speech in Wartime,* 32 Harv. L. Rev. 932, 947 (1919).

[12] Chafee's initial position appeared in the June issue of the *Harvard*

Law Review in 1919. Holmes' switch found expression in the *Abrams* case which was argued in October; and decided in November, 1919.

[13] Chafee, Book Review, 62 Harv. L. Rev. 891, 897-98 (1949). (Emphasis added).

[14] Schofield, *Freedom of the Press in the United States*, in 2 *Essays on Constitutional Law and Equity* 510, 511 (1921).

[15] Levy, Legacy of Suppression (1960).

[16] Frantz, *supra* note 2, at 1446.

[17] See De Jonge v. Oregon, 299 U.S. 353, 365-66 (1937).

[18] West Virginia Bd. of Educ. v. Barnette, 319 U.S. 624, 664 (1943); Minersville School Dist. v. Gobitis, 310 U.S. 586, 600 (1940).

[19] Frantz, *supra* note 2, at 1447.

[20] *Ibid.*

[21] *Id.* at 1449-50.

[22] Powell, *Vagaries and Varieties in Constitutional Interpretation* 28 (1956).

[23] See Luther v. Borden, 48 U.S. (7 How.) 1 (1849).

[24] Hand, *The Spirit of Liberty* 177-78 (1st ed. 1952).

[25] See Chafee, Book Review, 62 Harv. L. Rev. 891 (1949).

[26] See, *e.g.*, Communist Party v. Subversive Activities Control Bd., 367 U.S. 1 (1961); Barr v. Mateo, 360 U.S. 564 (1959); Tenney v. Brandhove, 341 U.S. 367 (1951).

[27] *Compare* their position in Minersville School Dist. v. Gobitis, 310 U.S. 586 (1940), *and* Jones v. Opelika, 316 U.S. 584 (1942), *with* West Virginia Bd. of Educ. v. Barnette, 319 U.S. 624, 643 (1943).

[28] *Compare* his position in Chaplinsky v. New Hampshire, 315 U.S. 568, 572 (1942), *with Justice Black and First Amendment "Absolutes": A Public Interview*, 37 N.Y.U.L. Rev. 549, 557 (1962).

[29] See Meyer v. Nebraska, 262 U.S. 390 (1923); Gilbert v. Minnesota, 254 U.S. 325, 334 (1920).

[30] 4 The Works of John Milton 349-50 (Patterson ed. 1931).

[31] See, *e.g.*, Frantz, *supra* note 2, at 1448 n. 100.

[32] Letter from James Madison to Thomas Jefferson, Oct. 17, 1788, in Padover, *The Complete Madison* 253-55 (1953).

[33] *Id.* at 254.

[34] *Id.* at 255.

[35] See note 24 *supra*. . . .

[36] His thoughts on this, very inadequately summarized below, will be found in *The Federalist* Nos. 10, 51 (Madison).

[37] Madison recognized that the sociopolitical check and balance system might not be an adequate restraint upon a state because of the relative paucity of interests at play within its boundaries. This may explain why the Supreme Court has been more willing to impose first amendment ideals upon the states than upon the Nation.

[38] Mr. Frantz criticizes the Court for not enforcing the first amendment as "absolutely" as it enforces some other Bill-of-Rights provisions.

Frantz, *supra* note 2, at 1436-38. The answer is presumably that these other provisions are directed largely against judges, administrators, and police officers. It is one thing for the Supreme Court to override them; it is quite another to override the National Legislature *acting in its lawmaking capacity.* See also note 37 *supra.*

[39] Brown v. Board of Educ., 347 U. S. 483 (1954), was costly indeed, if it convinced libertarians that the judicial process is an effective tool of libertarianism. Eight years after the original decision, *all the public schools of one of the defendants* (Prince Edward County, Virginia) *remained closed.* Only .4% of the South's Negro public school pupils were in classes with whites—and they were concentrated largely in the border states. Alabama, Mississippi, and South Carolina still had no integrated public schools. What Georgia and Louisiana had achieved could not fairly be called even token integration. See generally *Is the South Really Integrating Now?,* U.S. News & World Report, Dec. 10, 1962, p. 78.

Black Power: Its Need and Substance

Stokely Carmichael
Charles Hamilton

Most of us realize that we are witnesses to dramatic developments in our time. The triumphs and tragedies of technology, the noisy violence of protest and the quiet violence of injustice, the majesty and filth of our cities make us all uneasy. We find it increasingly difficult to understand the origins and anticipate the consequences of the seemingly endless flow of stressful events. Perhaps this has been so of all ages, but it is certainly no less so of our own. Everyone has his own explanation for contemporary turmoil. The most common view is that we have lost the vision that made America great; that our moral and religious standards are in decay; that we have lost respect for law, authority, and the flag; and that the communists or anarchists are the promoters of our plight. To many of those holding this position, the solution is comfortably simple: punish offenders. Many others, and probably a majority of social scientists, are equally troubled by events and our inability to cope adequately with them, but have a greater respect for the complexity of social phenomena than to prescribe patent medicine. Many of those agitating for change analyze our situation not as decay, but as a time in which our traditional values, pegged as they are to competitiveness, materialism, and exploitation of human and physical resources, are no longer adequate guides to behavior. They seek alternatives, believing that revolution is necessary to shake us free of the "death grip" of those values. There are, of course, many other versions of the meaning of contemporary ferment, but these two describe the poles. Both the militant civil rights advocates and the militant student movement tend toward the latter pole. For example, let us examine the "black power" strategy associated with such groups as the Student Coordinating Committee (formerly the Student Nonviolent Coordinating Committee), the Black Panthers and US. Stokely Carmichael was an early and persuasive spokesman for black power; here, along with political scientist Charles Hamilton, he defines and defends that position.

Reprinted by permission of the publisher from Stokely Carmichael and Charles Hamilton, *Black Power: The Politics of Liberation in America* (New York: Random House, Inc., 1967), pp. 34-56. © Copyright 1967 by Stokely Carmichael and Charles V. Hamilton.

"To carve out a place for itself in the politico-social order," V. O. Key, Jr. wrote in *Politics, Parties and Pressure Groups*, "a new group may have to fight for reorientation of many of the values of the old order" (p. 57). This is especially true when that group is composed of black people in the American society —a society that has for centuries deliberately and systematically excluded them from political participation. Black people in the United States must raise hard questions, questions which challenge the very nature of the society itself: its long-standing values, beliefs and institutions.

To do this, we must first redefine ourselves. Our basic need is to reclaim our history and our identity from what must be called cultural terrorism, from the depredation of self-justifying white guilt. We shall have to struggle for the right to create our own terms through which to define ourselves and our relationship to the society, and to have these terms recognized. This is the first necessity of a free people, and the first right that any oppressor must suspend.

In *Politics Among Nations*, Hans Morgenthau defined political power as "the psychological control over the minds of men" (p. 29). This control includes the attempt by the oppressor to have *his* definitions, *his* historical descriptions, *accepted* by the oppressed. This was true in Africa no less than in the United States. To black Africans, the word "Uhuru" means "freedom," but they had to fight the white colonizers for the right to use the term. The recorded history of this country's dealings with red and black men offers other examples. In the wars between the white settlers and the "Indians," a battle won by the Cavalry was described as a "victory." The "Indians'" triumphs, however, were "massacres." (The American colonists were not unaware of the need to define their acts in their own terms. They labeled their fight against England a "revolution"; the English attempted to demean it by calling it "insubordination" or "riotous.")

The historical period following Reconstruction in the South after the Civil War has been called by many historians the period of Redemption, implying that the bigoted southern slave societies were "redeemed" from the hands of "reckless and irresponsible" black rulers. Professor John Hope Franklin's *Reconstruction* or Dr. W. E. B. Dubois' *Black Reconstruction* should be sufficient to dispel inaccurate historical notions, but the larger society persists in its own self-serving accounts. Thus black people came to be depicted as "lazy," "apathetic," "dumb," "shiftless," "good-timers." Just as red men had to be recorded as "savages" to justify the white man's theft of their land, so black men had to be vilified in order to justify their continued oppression. Those who have the right to define are the masters of the situation. Lewis Carroll understood this:

"When I use a word," Humpty Dumpty said in a rather scornful tone, "it means just what I choose it to mean—neither more nor less."

"The question is," said Alice, "whether you *can* make words mean so many different things."

"The question is," said Humpty Dumpty, "which is to be master—that's all." Lewis Carroll, *Through the Looking Glass*. New York: Doubleday Books, Inc., p. 196.

Today, the American educational system continues to reinforce the entrenched values of the society through the use of words. Few people in this country question that this "is the land of the free and the home of the brave." They have had these words drummed into them from childhood. Few people question that this is the "Great Society" or that this country is fighting "Communist aggression" around the world. We mouth these things over and over, and they become truisms not to be questioned. In a similar way, black people have been saddled with epithets.

"Integration" is another current example of a word which has been defined according to the way white Americans see it. To many of them, it means black men wanting to marry white daughters; it means "race mixing"—implying bed or dance partners. To black people, it has meant a way to improve their lives—economically and politically. But the predominant white definition has stuck in the minds of too many people.

Black people must redefine themselves, and only *they* can do that. Throughout this country, vast segments of the black communities are beginning to recognize the need to assert their own definitions, to reclaim their history, their culture; to create their own sense of community and togetherness. There is a growing resentment of the word "Negro" for example, because this term is the invention of our oppressor; it is *his* image of us that he describes. Many blacks are now calling themselves African-Americans, Afro-Americans or black people because that is *our* image of ourselves. When we begin to define our own image, the stereotypes — that is, lies — that our oppressor has developed will begin in the white community and end there. The black community will have a positive image of itself that *it* has created. This means we will no longer call ourselves lazy, apathetic, dumb, good-timers, shiftless, etc. Those are words used by white America to define us. If we accept these adjectives, as some of us have in the past, then we see ourselves only in a negative way, precisely the way white America wants us to see ourselves. Our incentive is broken and our will to fight is surrendered. From now on we shall view ourselves as African-Americans and as black people who are in fact energetic, determined, intelligent, beautiful and peace-loving.

There is a terminology and ethos peculiar to the black community of which black people are beginning to be no longer ashamed. Black communities are the only large segment of this society where people refer to each other as brother—soul-brother, soul-sister. Some people may look upon this as *ersatz*, as make-believe, but it is not that. It is real. It is a growing sense of community. It is a growing realization that black Americans have a common bond not only among themselves, but with their African brothers. In *Black Man's Burden*, John O. Killens described his trip to ten African countries as follows:

Everywhere I went people called me brother.... "Welcome, American brother." It was a good feeling for me, to be in Africa. To walk in a land for the first time in your entire life knowing within yourself that your color would not be held against you. No black man ever knows this in America [p. 160].

More and more black Americans are developing this feeling. They are becoming aware that they have a history which pre-dates their forced introduction to this country. African-American history means a long history beginning on the continent of Africa, a history not taught in the standard textbooks of this country. It is absolutely essential that black people know this history, that they know their roots, that they develop an awareness of their cultural heritage. Too long have they been kept in submission by being told that they had no culture, no manifest heritage before they landed on the slave auction blocks in this country. If black people are to know themselves as a vibrant, valiant people, they must know their roots. And they will soon learn that the Hollywood image of man-eating cannibals waiting for, and waiting on, the Great White Hunter is a lie.

With redefinition will come a clearer notion of the role black Americans can play in this world. This role will emerge clearly out of the unique, common experiences of Afro-Asians. Killens concludes:

I believe furthermore that the American Negro can be the bridge between the West and Africa-Asia. We black Americans can serve as a bridge to mutual understanding. The one thing we black Americans have in common with the other colored peoples of the world is that we have all felt the cruel and ruthless heel of white supremacy. We have all been "niggerized" on one level or another. And all of us are determined to "deniggerize" the earth. To rid the world of "niggers" is the Black Man's Burden, human reconstruction is the grand objective [p. 176].

Only when black people fully develop this sense of community, of themselves, can they begin to deal effectively with the problems of racism in *this* country. This is what we mean by a new consciousness; this is the vital first step.

The next step is what we shall call the process of political modernization—a process which must take place if the society is to be rid of racism. "Political modernization" includes many things, but we mean by it three major concepts: (1) questioning old values and institutions of the society; (2) searching for new and different forms of political structure to solve political and economic problems; and (3) broadening the base of political participation to include more people in the decision-making process. These notions (we shall take up each in turn) are central to our thinking throughout this book and to contemporary American history as a whole. As David Apter wrote in *The Politics of Modernization*, "... the struggle to modernize is what has given meaning to our generation. It tests our cherished institutions and our beliefs.... So compelling a force has it become that we are forced to ask new questions of our own institutions. Each country, whether modernized or modernizing, stands in both judgment and fear of the results. Our own society is no exception" (p. 2).

The values of this society support a racist system; we find it incongruous to ask black people to adopt and support most of those values. We also reject the assumption that the basic institutions of this society must be preserved. The goal of black people must *not* be to assimilate into middle-class America, for that class —as a whole—is without a viable conscience as regards humanity. The values of the middle class permit the perpetuation of the ravages of the black community. The values of that class are based on material aggrandizement, not the expansion of humanity. The values of that class ultimately support cloistered little closed societies tucked away neatly in tree-lined suburbia. The values of that class do *not* lead to the creation of an open society. That class *mouths* its preference for a free, competitive society, while at the same time forcefully and even viciously denying to black people as a group the opportunity to compete.

We are not unmindful of other descriptions of the social utility of the middle class. Banfield and Wilson, in *City Politics* concluded:

> The departure of the middle class from the central city is important in other ways. ... The middle class supplies a social and political leavening in the life of a city. Middle-class people demand good schools and integrity in government. They support churches, lodges, parent-teacher associations, scout troops, better-housing committees, art galleries, and operas. It is the middle class, in short, that asserts a conception of the public interest. Now its activity is increasingly concentrated in the suburbs [p. 14].

But this same middle class manifests a sense of superior group position in regard to race. This class wants "good government" for *themselves;* it wants good schools *for its children.* At the same time, many of its members sneak into the black community by day, exploit it, and take the money home to their middle-class communities at night to support their operas and art galleries and comfortable homes. When not actually robbing, they will fight off the handful of more affluent black people who seek to move in; when they approve or even seek integration, it applies only to black people like themselves—as "white" as possible. *This class is the backbone of institutional racism in this country.*

Thus we reject the goal of assimilation into middle-class America because the values of that class are in themselves anti-humanist and because that class as a social force perpetuates racism. We must face the fact that, in the past, what we have called the movement has not really questioned the middle-class values and institutions of this country. If anything, it has accepted those values and institutions without fully realizing their racist nature. Reorientation means an emphasis on the dignity of man, not on the sanctity of property. It means the creation of a society where human misery and poverty are repugnant to that society, not an indication of laziness or lack of initiative. The creation of new values means the establishment of a society based, as Killens expresses it in *Black Man's Burden*, on "free people," not "free enterprise" (p. 167). To do this means to modernize—*indeed, to civilize* —this country.

Supporting the old values are old political and economic structures; these must also be "modernized." We should at this point distinguish between "structures" and "system." By system, we have in mind institutions, values, beliefs, etc. By structures, we mean the specific institutions (political parties, interest groups, bureaucratic administrations) which exist to conduct the business of that system. Obviously, the first is broader than the second. Also, the second assumes the legitimacy of the first. Our view is that given the illegitimacy of the system, we cannot then proceed to transform that system with existing structures.

The two major political parties in this country have become non-viable entities for the legitimate representation of the real needs of masses—esspecially blacks —in this country. Walter Lippmann raised the same point in his syndicated column of December 8, 1966. He pointed out that the party system in the United States developed before our society became as technologically complex as it is now. He says that the ways in which men live and define themselves are changing radically. Old ideological issues, once the subject of passionate controversy, Lippmann argues, are of little interest today. He asks whether the great urban complexes—which are rapidly becoming the centers of black population in the U.S.— can be run with the same systems and ideas that derive from a time when America was a country of small villages and farms. While not addressing himself directly to the question of race, Lippmann raises a major question about our political institutions; and the crisis of race in America may be its major symptom.

Black people have seen the city planning commissions, the urban renewal commissions, the boards of education and the police departments fail to speak to their needs in a meaningful way. We must devise new structures, new institutions to replace those forms or to make them responsive. There is nothing sacred or inevitable about old institutions; the focus must be on people, not forms.

Existing structures and established ways of doing things have a way of perpetuating themselves and for this reason, the modernizing process will be difficult. Therefore, timidity in calling into question the boards of education or the police departments will not do. They must be challenged forcefully and clearly. If this means the creation of parallel community institutions, then that must be the solution. If this means that black parents must gain control over the operation of the schools in the black community, then that must be the solution. The search for new forms means the search for institutions that will, for once, make decisions in the interest of black people. It means, for example, a building inspection department that neither winks at violations of building codes by absentee slumlords nor imposes meaningless fines which permit them to continue their exploitation of the black community.

Essential to the modernization of structures is a broadened base of political participation. More and more people must become politically sensitive and active (we have already seen this happening in some areas of the South). People must no longer be tied, by small incentives or handouts to a corrupting and corruptible white machine. Black people will choose their own leaders and hold those leaders responsible to *them*. A broadened base means an end to the condition described by James Wilson in *Negro Politics*, whereby "Negroes tended to be the objects rather than the subjects of civic action. Things are often done for, or about, or to, or because of Negroes, but they are less frequently done *by* Negroes" (p. 133). Broadening the base of political participation, then, has as much to do with the quality of black participation as with the quantity. We are fully aware that the black vote, especially in the North, has been pulled out of white pockets and "delivered" whenever it was in the interest of white politicians to do so. That vote must no longer be controllable by those who have neither the interests nor the demonstrated concern of black people in mind.

As the base broadens, as more and more black people become activated, they will perceive more clearly the special disadvantages heaped upon them as a group. They will perceive that the larger society is growing more affluent while the black society is retrogressing, as daily life and mounting statistics clearly show (see Chapters I and VIII). V. O. Key describes what often happens next in *Politics, Parties and Pressure Groups:* "A factor of great significance in the setting off of political movements is an abrupt change for the worse in the status of one group relative to that of other groups in society.... A rapid change for the worse... in the relative status of any group... is likely to precipitate political action" (p. 24). Black people will become increasingly active as they notice that their retrogressive status exists in large measure because of values and institutions arraigned against them. They will begin to stress and strain and call the entire system into question. Political modernization will be in motion. We believe that it is *now* in motion. One form of that motion is Black Power.

The adoption of the concept of Black Power is one of the most legitimate and healthy developments in American politics and race relations in our time. The concept of Black Power speaks to all the needs mentioned in this chapter. It is a call for black people in this country to unite, to recognize their heritage, to build a sense of community. It is a call for black people to begin to define their own goals, to lead their own organizations and to support those organizations. It is a call to reject the racist institutions and values of this society.

The concept of Black Power rests on a fundamental premise: *Before a group can enter the open society, it must first close ranks.* By this we mean that group solidarity is necessary before a group can operate effectively from a bargaining position of strength in a pluralistic society. Traditionally, each new ethnic group in this society has found the route to social and political viability through the organization of its own institutions with which to represent its needs within the larger society. Studies in voting behavior specifically and political behavior generally have made it clear that politically the American pot has not melted. Italians vote for Rubino over O'Brien; Irish for Murphy over Goldberg, etc. This phenomenon may seem distasteful to some, but it has been and remains today a central fact of the American political system. There are other examples of ways in which groups in the society have remembered their roots and used this effectively in the political arena. Theodore Sorensen describes the politics of foreign aid during the Kennedy Administration in his book *Kennedy:*

No powerful constituencies or interest groups backed foreign aid. The Marshall Plan at least had appealed to Americans who traced their roots to the Western European nations aided. But there were few voters who identified with India, Colombia or Tanganyika [p. 351].

The extent to which black Americans can and do "trace their roots" to Africa, to that extent will they be able to be more effective on the political scene.

A white reporter set forth this point in other terms when he made the following observation about white Mississippi's manipulation of the anti-poverty program.

The war on poverty has been predicated on the notion that there is such a thing as a community which can be defined geographically and mobilized for a collective effort to help the poor. This theory has no relationship to reality in the deep South. In every Mississippi county there are two communities. Despite all the pious platitudes of the moderates on both sides, these two communities habitually see their interests in terms of conflict rather than cooperation. Only when the Negro community can muster enough political, economic and professional strength to compete on somewhat equal terms, will Negroes believe in the possibility of true cooperation and whites accept its necessity. En route to integration, the Negro community needs to develop a greater independence—a chance to run its own affairs and not cave in whenever "the man" barks—or so it seems to me, and to most of the knowledgeable people with whom I talked in Mississippi. To OEO, this judgment may sound like black nationalism. . . .[1]

The point is obvious: black people must lead and run their own organizations. Only black people can convey the revolutionary idea—and it is a revolutionary idea—that black people are able to do things themselves. Only they can help create in the community an aroused and continuing black consciousness that will provide the basis for political strength. In the past, white allies have often furthered white supremacy without the whites involved realizing it, or even wanting to do so. Black people must come together and do things for themselves. They must achieve self-identity and self-determination in order to have their daily needs met.

Black Power means, for example, that in Lowndes County, Alabama, a black sheriff can end police brutality. A black tax assessor and tax collector and county board of revenue can lay, collect, and channel tax monies for the building of better roads and schools serving black people. In such areas as Lowndes, where black people have a majority, they will attempt to use power to exercise control. This is what they seek: control. When black people lack a majority, Black Power means proper representation and sharing of control. It means the creation of power bases, or strength, from which black people can press to change local or nation-wide patterns of oppression—instead of from weakness.

It does not mean *merely* putting black faces into office. Black visibility is not Black Power. Most of the black politicians around the country today are not examples of Black Power. The power must be that of a community, and emanate from there. The black politicians must start from here. The black politicians must stop being representatives of "downtown" machines, whatever the cost might be in terms of lost patronage and holiday handouts.

Black Power recognizes—it must recognize—the ethnic basis of American politics as well as the power-oriented nature of American politics. Black Power therefore calls for black people to consolidate behind their own, so that they can bargain from a position of strength. But while we endorse the *procedure* of group solidarity and identity for the purpose of attaining certain goals in the body politic, this does not mean that black people should strive for the same kind of rewards (i.e., end results) obtained by the white society. The ultimate values and goals are not domination or exploitation of other groups, but rather an effective share of the total power of the society.

Nevertheless, some observers have labeled those who advocate Black Power as racists; they have said that the call for self-identification and self-determination is "racism in reverse" or "black supremacy." This is a deliberate and absurd lie. There is no analogy—by any stretch of definition or imagination—between the advocates of Black Power and white racists. Racism is not merely exclusion on the basis of race but exclusion for the purpose of subjugating or maintaining subjugation. The goal of the racists is to keep black people on the bottom, arbitrarily and dictatorially, as they have done in this country for over three hundred years. The goal of black self-determination and black self-identity—Black Power—is full participation in the decision-making processes affecting the lives of black people, and recognition of the virtues in themselves as black people. The black people of this country have not lynched whites, bombed their churches, murdered their children and manipulated laws and institutions to maintain oppression. White racists have. Congressional laws, one after the other, have not been necessary to stop black people from oppressing others and denying others the full enjoyment of their rights. White racists have made such laws necessary. The goal of Black Power is positive and functional to a free and viable society. No white racist can make this claim.

A great deal of public attention and press space was devoted to the hysterical accusation of "black racism" when the call for Black Power was first sounded. A national committee of influential black churchmen affiliated with the National Council of Churches, despite their obvious respectability and responsibility, had to resort to a paid advertisement to articulate their position, while anyone yapping "black racism" made front-page news. In their statement, published in the *New York Times* of July 31, 1966, the churchmen said:

We, an informal group of Negro churchmen in America, are deeply disturbed about the crisis brought upon our county by historic distortions of important human realities in the controversy about "black power." What we see shining through the variety of rhetoric is not anything new but the same old problem of power and race which has faced our beloved country since 1619.

... The conscience of black men is corrupted because having no power to implement the demands of conscience, the concern for justice in the absence of justice becomes a chaotic self-surrender. Powerlessness breeds a race of beggars. We are faced with a situation where powerless conscience meets conscienceless power, threatening the very foundations of our Nation.

We deplore the overt violence of riots, but we feel it is more important to focus on the real sources of these eruptions. These sources may be abetted inside the Ghetto, but their basic cause lies in the silent and covert violence which white middle class America inflicts upon the victims of the inner city.

... In short, the failure of American leaders to use American power to create equal opportunity *in life* as well as *law*, this is the real problem and not the anguished cry for black power.

... Without the capacity to participate with power, i.e., to have some organized political and economic strength to really influence people with whom one interacts, integration is not meaningful.

... America has asked its Negro citizens to fight for opportunity as *individuals,* whereas at certain points in our history what we have needed most has been opportunity for the *whole group,* not just for selected and approved Negroes.

.... We must not apologize for the existence of this form of group power, for we have been oppressed as a group and not as individuals. We will not find our way out of that oppression until both we and America accept the need for Negro Americans, as well as for Jews, Italians, Poles, and white Anglo-Saxon Protestants, among others, to have and to wield group power.

It is a commentary on the fundamentally racist nature of this society that the concept of group strength for black people must be articulated—not to mention defended. No other group would submit to being led by others. Italians do not run the Anti-Defamation League of B'nai B'rith. Irish do not chair Christopher Columbus Societies. Yet when black people call for black-run and all-black organizations, they are immediately classed in a category with the Ku Klux Klan. This is interesting and ironic, but by no means surprising: the society does not expect black people to be able to take care of their business, and there are many who prefer it precisely that way.

In the end, we cannot and shall not offer any guarantees that Black Power, if achieved, would be non-racist. No one can predict human behavior. Social change always has unanticipated consequences. If black racism is what the larger society fears, we cannot help them. We can only state what we hope will be the result, given the fact that the present situation is unacceptable and that we have no real alternative but to work for Black Power. The final truth is that the white society is not entitled to reassurances, even if it were possible to offer them.

We have outlined the meaning and goals of Black Power; we have also discussed one major thing which it is not. There are others of greater importance. The advocates of Black Power reject the old slogans and meaningless rhetoric of previous years in the civil rights struggle. The language of yesterday is indeed irrelevant: progress, non-violence, integration, fear of "white backlash," coalition. Let us look at the rhetoric and see why these terms must be set aside or redefined.

One of the tragedies of the struggle against racism is that up to this point there has been no national organization which could speak to the growing militancy of young black people in the urban ghettos and the black-belt South. There has been only a "civil rights" movement, whose tone of voice was adapted to an audience of middleclass whites. It served as a sort of buffer zone between that audience and angry young blacks. It claimed to speak for the needs of a community, but it did not speak in the tone of that community. None of its so-called leaders could go into a rioting community and be listened to. In a sense, the blame must be shared—along with the mass media—by those leaders for what happened in Watts, Harlem, Chicago, Cleveland and other places. Each time the black people in those cities saw Dr. Martin Luther King get slapped they became angry. When they saw little black girls bombed to death *in a church* and civil rights workers ambushed and murdered, they were angrier; and when nothing happened, they were steaming mad. We had nothing to offer that they could see, except to go out and be beaten again. We helped to build their frustration.

We had only the old language of love and suffering. And in most places—that is, from the liberals and middle class—we got back the old language of patience and progress. The civil rights leaders were saying to the country: "Look, you guys are supposed to be nice guys, and we are only going to do what we are supposed to do. Why do you beat us up? Why don't you give us what we ask? Why don't you straighten yourselves out?" For the masses of black people, this language resulted in virtually nothing. In fact, their objective day-to-day condition worsened. The unemployment rate among black people increased while that among whites declined. Housing conditions in the black communities deteriorated. Schools in the black ghettos continued to plod along on outmoded techniques, inadequate curricula, and with all too many tired and indifferent teachers. Meanwhile, the President picked up the refrain of "We Shall Overcome" while the Congress passed civil rights law after civil rights law, only to have them effectively nullified by deliberately weak enforcement. "Progress is being made," we were told.

Such language, along with admonitions to remain nonviolent and fear the white backlash, convinced some that that course was the *only* course to follow. It misled some into believing that a black minority could bow its head and get whipped into a meaningful position of power. The very notion is absurd. The white society devised the language, adopted the rules and had the black community narcotized into believing that that language and those rules were, in fact, relevant. The black community was told time and again how *other* immigrants finally won *acceptance:* that is, by following the Protestant Ethic of Work and Achievement. They worked hard; therefore, they achieved. We were not told that it was by building Irish Power, Italian Power, Polish Power or Jewish Power that these groups got themselves together and operated from positions of strength. We were not told that "the American dream" wasn't designed for black people. That while today, to whites, the dream may *seem* to include black people, it cannot do so by the very nature of this nation's political and economic system, which imposes institutional racism on the black masses if not upon every individual black. A notable comment on that "dream" was made by Dr. Percy Julian, the black scientist and director of the Julian Research Institute in Chicago, a man for whom the dream seems to have come true. While not subscribing to "black power" as he understood it, Dr. Julian clearly understood the basis for it: "The false concept of basic Negro inferiority is one of the curses that still lingers. It is a problem created by the white man. Our children just no longer are going to accept the patience we were taught by our generation. We were taught a pretty little lie— excel and the whole world lies open before you. *I obeyed the injunction and found it to be wishful thinking.*" (Authors' italics)[2]

A key phrase in our buffer-zone days was non-violence. For years it has been thought that black people would not literally fight for their lives. Why this has been so is not entirely clear; neither the larger society nor black people are noted for passivity. The notion apparently stems from the years of marches and demonstrations and sit-ins where black people did not strike back and the violence always came from white mobs. There are many who still sincerely believe in that approach. From our viewpoint, rampaging white mobs and white night-riders must be made to understand that their days of free head-whipping are over. Black people should and must fight back. Nothing more quickly repels someone bent on destroying you than the unequivocal message: "O.K., fool, make your move, and run the same risk I run —of dying."

When the concept of Black Power is set forth, many people immediately conjure up notions of violence. The country's reaction to the Deacons for Defense and Justice, which originated in Louisiana, is instructive. Here is a group which realized that the "law" and law enforcement agencies would not protect people, so they had to do it themselves. If a nation fails to protect its citizens, then that nation cannot condemn those who take up the task themselves. The Deacons and all other blacks who resort to self-defense represent a simple answer to a simple question: what man would not defend his family and home from attack?

But this frightened some white people, because they knew that black people would now fight back. They knew that this was precisely what *they* would have long since done if *they* were subjected to the injustices and oppression heaped on blacks. Those of us who advocate Black Power are quite clear in our own minds that a "non-violent" approach to civil rights is an approach black people cannot afford and a luxury white people do not deserve. It is crystal clear to us—and it must become so with the white society— *that there can be no social order without social justice.* White people must be made to understand that they must stop messing with black people, or the blacks *will* fight back!

Next, we must deal with the term "integration." According to its advocates, social justice will be accomplished by "integrating the Negro into the mainstream institutions of the society from which he has been traditionally excluded." This concept is based on the assumption that there is nothing of value in the black community and that little of value could be created among black people. The thing to do is siphon off the "acceptable" black people into the surrounding middle-class white community.

The goals of integrationists are middle-class goals, articulated primarily by a small group of Negroes with middle-class aspirations or status. Their kind of integration has meant that a few blacks "make it," leaving the black community, sapping it of leadership potential and know-how. . . . Those token Negroes—absorbed into a white mass—are of no value to the remaining black masses. They become meaningless show-pieces for a conscience-soothed white society. Such people will state that they would prefer to be treated "only as individuals, not as Negroes"; that they "are not and should not be preoccupied with race." This is a totally unrealistic position. In the first place, black people have not suffered as individuals but as members of a group; therefore, their liberation lies in group action. This is why SNCC — and the concept of Black Power—affirms that helping *individual* black people to solve their problems on an *individual* basis does little to alleviate the mass of black people. Secondly, while color blindness *may* be a sound goal ultimately, we must realize that race is an overwhelming fact of life in this historical period. There is no black man in this country who can live "simply as a man." His blackness is an ever-present fact of this racist society, whether he recognizes it or not. It is unlikely that this or the next generation will witness the time when race will no longer be relevant in the conduct of public affairs and in public policy decision-making. To realize this and to attempt to deal with it does not make one a racist or overly preoccupied with race; it puts one in the forefront of a significant *struggle*. If there is no intense struggle today, there will be no meaningful results tomorrow.

"Integration" as a goal today speaks to the problem of blackness not only in an unrealistic way but also in a despicable way. It is based on complete acceptance of the fact that in order to have a decent house or education, black people must move into a white neighborhood or send their children to a white school. This reinforces, among both black and white, the idea that "white" is automatically superior and "black" is by definition inferior. For this reason, "integration" is a subterfuge for the maintenance of white supremacy. It allows the nation to focus on a handful of Southern black children who get into white schools at a great price, and to ignore the ninety-four percent who are left in unimproved all-black schools. Such situations will not change until black people become equal in a way that means something, and integration ceases to be a one-way street. Then integration does not mean draining skills and energies from the black ghetto into white neighborhoods. To sprinkle black children among white pupils in outlying schools is at best a stop-gap measure. The goal is not to take black children out of the black community and expose them to white middle-class values; the goal is to build and strengthen the black community.

"Integration" also means that black people must give up their identity, deny their heritage. We recall the conclusion of Killian and Grigg: "At the present time, integration as a solution to the race problem demands that the Negro foreswear his identity as a Negro." The fact is that integration, as traditionally articulated, would abolish the black community. The fact is that what must be abolished is not the black community, but the dependent colonial status that has been inflicted upon it.

The racial and cultural personality of the black community must be preserved and that community must win its freedom while preserving its cultural integrity. Integrity includes a pride—in the sense of self-acceptance, not chauvinism—in being black, in the historical attainments and contributions of black people. No person can be healthy, complete and mature if he must deny a part of himself; this is what "integration" has required thus far. This is the essential difference between integration as it is currently practiced and the concept of Black Power.

The idea of cultural integrity is so obvious that it seems almost simple-minded to spell things out at this length. Yet millions of Americans resist such truths when they are applied to black people. Again, that resistance is a comment on the fundamental racism in the society. Irish Catholics took care of their own first without a lot of apology for doing so, without any dubious language from timid leadership about guarding against "backlash." Everyone understood it to be a perfectly legitimate procedure. Of course, there would be "backlash." Organization begets counterorganization, but this was no reason to defer.

The so-called white backlash against black people is something else: the embedded traditions of institutional racism being brought into the open and calling forth overt manifestations of individual racism. In the summer of 1966, when the protest marches into Cicero, Illinois, began, the black people knew they were not allowed to live in Cicero and the white people knew it. When blacks began to demand the right to live in homes in that town, the whites simply reminded them of the status quo. Some people called this "backlash." It was, in fact, racism defending itself. In the black community, this is called "White folks showing their color." It is ludicrous to blame black people for what is simply an overt manifestation of white racism. Dr. Martin Luther King stated clearly that the protest marches were not the cause of the racism but merely exposed a long-term cancerous condition in the society. . . .

Notes

[1] Christopher Jencks, "Accommodating Whites: A New Look at Mississippi," *The New Republic* (April 16, 1966).

[2] *The New York Times* (April 30, 1967), p. 30.

What Can Be Done About Air Pollution?

Edward Edelson
Fred Warshofsky

Public concern over the quality of the environment has recently emerged as a political issue of major proportions. Long term population growth, urbanization, growing use of our technology without serious consideration of the impact upon our physical environment have produced the problem. President Nixon acknowledged the severity of our situation in his State of the Union Message of 1970 when he said, "The great question of the seventies is, shall we surrender to our surroundings, or shall we make our peace with nature and begin to make reparations for the damage we have done to our air, to our land and to our water?" Nearly all agree; who among us is for environmental decay? This is especially so, when the vision of doom includes predictions like:

1. *Air pollution combined with temperature inversion will kill thousands in some U.S. city early in the '80's.*

2. *By 1985 air pollution will have reduced the amount of sunlight reaching earth by one-half.*

3. *In the 1980's a major ecological system—soil or water—will break down somewhere in the U.S.*

4. *Increased carbon dioxide will effect earth's temperature, leading either to flooding or a new ice age.*

5. *Sonic booms from SST's will damage children before birth.*

6. *Residual DDT collecting in the human liver will make the use of certain common drugs impossible and will increase liver cancer.*

While identification of the problem is relatively simple, solutions are inordinately complex and run head-long into some cherished American values and practices. Some have posed solutions as drastic as outlawing the internal combustion engine, a moritorium on housing development, and governmental regulation of family size. In the following section of their book Poisons in the Air, *Edward Edelson and Fred Warshofsky offer suggestions which are less trans-*

Reprinted by permission of Pocket Book Division of Simon & Schuster, Inc., from Edward Edelson and Fred Warshofsky, *Poisons in the Air* (New York: Pocket Books, Inc., 1966), pp. 142-160. Copyright © 1966, by Edward Edelson and Fred Warshofsky. Abridged by the editors.

forming in their consequences, yet hold out hope of meeting this aspect of the problem.

Air pollution is a problem that ignores all the well-established boundaries—geographic, legal and psychological — boundaries that have never before been challenged. But it is not the only problem to cut across these lines. Almost every major need of the modern city — transportation, water, power and a dozen other problems—run beyond the city/town line and demand a regional approach. Clean air is becoming the foremost of these needs, but it also requires a rethinking of basic ideas in other areas. Industry will have to change its ideas about community responsibility. Engineers will have to become acquainted with new design concepts. The public will have to start thinking in new terms about their individual responsibility to the community. Even city planners will have to take new factors in consideration when they plan and approve new construction.

The sphere in which air pollution has most strained traditional thinking is in government. America has a long heritage of rugged individualism and government on a local community basis. Local government is deeply woven into the American fabric and is the bedrock democracy that makes representative government on all levels work. But in an era when the people of Cincinnati must worry about breathing the pesticide that the farmers of Texas spread on their fields, some modification of the attitudes is clearly necessary.

Air pollution respects neither city nor state boundaries. The state line is the most hallowed American boundary, and states rights a classic rallying cry, but wind patterns impose a sovereignty all their own. Nor do the population centers that have grown up in recent years recognize the historic parochialism of state boundaries. Tens of thousands of New Jerseyites cross state lines every day to work in New York City and Philadelphia, with as little concern as the tens of thousands who cross from Berkeley to San Francisco in California. Of the 212 Standard Metropolitan Statistical Areas in 1960, 24 included parts of two or more states and 38 million people lived in them. Another 31 million people lived in S.M.S.A.'s that adjoined state lines. Chicago, Illinois, and Gary, Indiana, breathe the same air, as do St. Louis, Missouri, and East St. Louis, Illinois; and Detroit and Windsor, Ontario. "The need for governmental mechanisms for coping with interstate flow of air pollution is apparent," said Jean J. Schueneman of the Public Health Service in 1962.

The development of these mechanisms is taking place at a snail's pace. In 1936, a compact between New York and New Jersey (five years later Connecticut joined) established the Interstate Sanitation Commission to set standards and enforce rules against water pollution. The I.S.C. did a creditable job, and in 1957 entered the air-pollution mess, but with considerably less success. Still, it was the first interstate agency to come to grips with air-pollution problems. But few others have followed their lead. In 1965, Illinois and Indiana signed an agreement providing that pollution in one state could be curbed by the action of the other. But by and large, the state boundary has loomed as an insurmountable barrier to a unified effort against air pollution.

Local boundaries are almost as troublesome. A few places, such as Los Angeles and San Francisco — the Bay Area Air Pollution Control District includes 89 urban areas—have managed to hurdle these local boundary tangles, but most have not. More typical is Denver, where the regional approach is almost totally lacking, or Cook County, Illinois, where the 145 municipal governments outside Chicago, with a total population near 1.5 million, virtually ignore the city's problem. There exists a Cook County Air Pollution Control Bureau, but the most it can do is try to persuade the local governments to adopt a model ordinance and enforce it. Most have done nothing and probably never will until a truly regional authority, with full control over the Cook County-Chicago area, is established.

This experience is typical of the lack of results in a multi-community program that relies on persuasion and cooperation, with no enforcement powers. Usually, the best that can happen is a sort of mutual acquiescence based solely on the personal friendships of local officials. The New York-New Jersey Cooperative Committee on Interstate Air Pollution is an attempt at this kind of effort. It is an informal group composed of the heads of local and state control agencies who meet periodically to discuss their problems and possible solutions. It has some accomplishments to its credit, but most members confess to a sense of frustration at trying to solve the massive problem this way. After years of effort, the ordinances of the cities and states in the area are still not standardized.

Lack of standardization is one of the most common complaints of adjoining communities that share a pollution problem but refuse to work together toward a solution. "It is patently unjust for a government on one side of a political boundary line to permit levels of air pollution in its air space far greater than those tolerated on the other side," declared a Muskie subcommittee report on *Steps Toward Clean Air*. "Conversely, it is impractical for one jurisdiction to strive for the attainment of higher standards of air quality if its adjoining neighbor, which will inevitably share the same air supply, does little or nothing to prevent wholesale pollution of the atmosphere. What is needed is a set of uniform laws and ordinances, which can be developed by the Department of Health, Education and Welfare, and recommended to the cities and states of the nation, so they can at least have the benefit of the best judgment on matters pertaining to air pollution."

The lack of progress toward either intercommunity action or standardization of pollution-control laws—only nine states have laws authorizing local communities to form area-wide pollution-control agencies—has led some gloomy prophets to predict that nothing less than super-agencies probably on the federal level, will permit solution of the air-pollution problem. The future these experts foresee is one of continued squabbling and mutual dislike between communities and states that are more eager to blame their neighbors than solve their own pollution problems, or who believe that air-pollution control would hurt local interests. Inevitably, the pessimists say, this will culminate in an enormous air-pollution disaster, the seeds of which are the continued growth of population and fuel use, triggered by freak weather conditions that will throttle a large part of the nation. At that point, the public outcry for immediate action will be so great that the federal government will be forced to step in and create a regulatory agency. Air moving across state lines would then be subject to as many federal controls as factory products in interstate commerce, and local agencies would be reduced to mere vestigial appendages of federal offices in Washington.

Only a minority of officials hold this gloomy view. Most believe that there is still time for the trends that have been developing, albeit slowly, into full-scale regional programs to provide effective control of air pollution. But they warn that many traditional ideas will have to be discarded to bring this about. It will be necessary to disregard state lines entirely and, instead, to use the prevailing-wind patterns as guides for new districts. The logical unit for a control agency is the "airshed," a broad region that shares the same air supply.

Airsheds sprawl across county and state and national boundaries with the insolence of the untrammeled wind. As a result, their actual boundaries do not always follow natural geographic forms. Hydrologists can judge with a high degree of precision how long a river will take to cleanse itself of pollution from a given source, but there are too many factors involved for air engineers to say the same about polluted air. A pollutant that can barely be measured can damage plants at a great distance. An airshed may be safe when the wind is blowing briskly, diluting the pollutants; but it can harbor vast forces of destruction when the wind is just slow enough to keep a lingering cloud of polluted air over the region. With a constantly changing danger of this sort, the present type of control agency is outmoded. An approach that is flexible enough to change the rules as the danger changes, and that governs an entire airshed, is the only answer.

Such an approach is not without precedent in American history. In 1889, John Wesley Powell, then head of the U.S. Geological Survey, proposed essentially the same type of plan for the western states where the supply of water, and not artificial boundary lines, determined the value of land. Powell proposed that counties in the new state of Montana be set up along lines determined by watersheds, with the water rights of every resident of a watershed determined locally by democratic methods. It was such a revolutionary proposal in that era of uncontrolled settlement that Congress indignantly rejected it, but Powell's ideas have been proven correct by time. The idea of limiting the use of air is just as revolutionary today, but the problem now demands it. When farmers a score of miles from a city lose a crop to the chemicals a power plant puts into the air, it is unfair to ask the farmer to bear the entire cost of preventing the loss. Only by considering the rights as well as the responsibilities of every air user in an airshed can everyone in the airshed be protected. The Muskie subcommittee report says:

While the subcommittee recognizes the primary responsibility of state and local governments in controlling air pollution, it cannot concur in the concept that each individual entity within an airshed should attempt to control its own problem with regional development of standards and coordination of enforcement efforts confined to limited problems. Air pollution is a "local" problem within the air basin affected. Only those areas which have established an air pollution control program encompassing their entire airsheds are in a position to reach and regulate every source discharging into the air of the basin. Those airsheds not having regional programs operate at a decided disadvantage; even in the unlikely event that a uniform law is attained by each jurisdiction enacting identical ordinances, uniform enforcement still cannot be assured. Furthermore, hard realities compel consideration of the advantages which accrue when the financial burden of control rests on a population and economic base capable of supporting an adequate staff and required services.

The committee recommended that Clean Air Act grants for local programs be allocated to intensify the drive toward the airshed approach to pollution problems. "Special emphasis" should be given to programs that are aimed toward this objective, it said.

The federal government is vigorously pushing this regional approach with financial support in the Clean Air Act. The P.H.S., for example, gives a local community two dollars for every dollar the local agency adds to its budget, but it dangles the lure of three dollars for every dollar if the program is a regional one. This green bait has produced some results. Of the first 80 grants handed out under the Clean Air Act, 31 were for intermunicipal agencies and 18 were for state agencies. But those getting the grants now rarely cover more than a county, and that is far short of the airshed approach. In some cases, airsheds cover several states. The

East Coast, with its "smear city" stretching from Richmond to Boston, is the area of greatest potential danger. The pollution disaster that some experts predict could come about when a supply of polluted air passes over city after city in this area, growing fouler and fouler as it progresses, until the last cities to breathe it will find it unusable.

The barriers to the regional approach are not only the provincialisms common to many communities. Sheer inertia also plays a part, and so do the vested interests of local officials. When pollution-control agencies are merged, someone loses power or prestige, and even a few jobs, and few officials are ready to sacrifice their own interest for the, to them, doubtful advantages of combined operations. Many of these officials have been around since the smoke-abatement days and they resent the Johnny-come-latelies telling them how to stop air pollution. Just as great a barrier is inertia or indifference. Too many public officials simply do not believe that air pollution is a problem of such magnitude that it demands radical approaches.

But pressure for regional action is building up. In the more forward-looking areas, it comes from those adventuresome local governments that coax their neighbors into cooperation. In others, the availability of federal money is a convincing argument. "What we're trying to do," said a federal official, "is to make the lure of the federal dollar so attractive that it overcomes the prejudices and parochialism that are so characteristic of local government."

Vernon MacKenzie, head of the P.H.S. Division of Air Pollution, is hopeful that air pollution can be beaten on the local and regional level, without the mass federal intervention that some people fear, despite the break with tradition that the regional approach means. "I have sufficient faith in the democratic process to believe that the public can be educated and informed enough to make intelligent decisions," MacKenzie said.

But it will not be an easy job. Moving industry will be just as difficult as moving government officials, but it must be done. The argument that good legislation and good enforcement will bring any reluctant industry into line is true, but most legislation is passed on the local level, where the political influence of industry is greatest. The kind of laws that are passed, and often the passage of the laws themselves, depend on how industry swings its weight about. Until now, it has been rare for an industry threatened with the economic bite of air-pollution reform to go along willingly, and almost none have joined the drive for cleaner air. James M. Quigley, assistant secretary of H.E.W., declared:

Industries tend to be very effective lobbyists. That makes it slightly optimistic to hope for really effective state laws.

The attitude of most businessmen is that air pollution is just an unfortunate side effect that has to be put up with. You'll hear some major executives say, "You know you can't make steel without making smoke or paper without a stink. It would cost a fortune to do anything about it. Why should we spend our stockholders' money on this when everyone else is doing the same thing?"

Then there's the auto industry. I just see the automobile manufacturers as so big and so affluent that their social conscience is not as sensitive as it might be. The auto makers are like the rich family in town that lives in a big house on the hill, with French wine at every meal and every winter in Florida. They're just not conscious of how people on the wrong side of the track live. They're not sinister, just insensitive. Some executives at the technical level are concerned, but not many at the top.

But I think the problem is beatable. In industry as a whole, there is some sensitivity to the problem, but not nearly as much as there should be and I think will be. The biggest problem with industry is giving them incentives. These can be positive as well as negative incentives—tax write-offs for pollution-control equipment, or just emphasis on their social responsibility.

After all, industry during the last generation has developed a public awareness that it did not have in the robber baron era. To many companies, the cost of pollution abatement is just part of the cost of doing business, a cost that has to be met. There will always be some shysters who try to do it cheaper, but responsible businessmen are going to try to do the right thing about air pollution.

With the notable exception of the auto industry, the firms doing business directly with the public have been the most sensitive to the problem in the past. "Its just common sense," one public relations man said. "You don't want to spend millions of dollars on advertising and then louse up your image with some news stories about being hailed into court as an air polluter. Take Kimberly-Clark, for instance. They don't want a housewife walking down the supermarket aisle and go right by their tissues because the company has a reputation for being dirty. But then you take a chemical company that sells all its output to other industries. They couldn't care less about public opinion."

But enough public pressure can occasionally be mounted to seep through to even the most far-removed and entrenched industry in America. Thus Chicago was able to get an agreement to install anti-pollution equipment from four major steel companies with plants in the city. The same type of agreement was signed in June, 1965, between United States Steel and the city of Gary, Indiana. The company agreed to complete an abatement program by 1973. The signing was marred only slightly by the fact that Mayor A. Martin Katz had rejected the first agreement offered by U.S. Steel on the grounds that it contained an escape clause that permitted the company to drop the plan if its Board of Directors refused to provide the money for it.

In modest defense of industry, it should be noted that businessmen have a knack of making their air-pollution-control performance seem even worse than it is. The prevailing business attitude is that the fuss about air pollution is a temporary phenomenon that will go away if the companies sit very still and say nothing about it. As a result, very few firms give wide publicity to the efforts they are making to decrease pollution, and then only when they succeed. The company that spends money and fails to solve its problem usually isn't even given credit for trying. One small California steel mill spent a million dollars and ten years trying to solve its pollution problems, and managed only partial success in the end. All it got for its troubles was increasing complaints from its neighbors. Another steel plant spent $5 million on fume-reducing equipment that still refused to work properly a year after its installation. "Is there any question why other steel plant management is reluctant to rush ahead with similar installations elsewhere?" asked Allen D. Brandt of Bethlehem Steel.

To the majority of business executives who are not convinced that air pollution is a clear danger, this type of spending is sheer waste. Few communities and states try to offer the kind of incentives discussed by James Quigley to—if not alter this view—at least make it less economically painful. Only recently did the federal government take this step by doubling the standard 7 percent investment credit for pollution control, and only six states offer a similar tax incentive. Negative controls are also lacking. In many areas, industry is free to install whatever kind of pollution-creating equipment it wants, since most communities do not have the power of review and approval of new equipment. Only three quarters of the agencies serving communities with populations over 200,000 review plans for new equipment. Many of those review only furnaces, ignoring all other equipment with a pollution capability. Only a third of the agencies in smaller communities look over the plans for new equipment. The lack of review authority is the surest sign that the local air-pollution program is mere window dressing, since new sources of pollution are being continually added to these communities with the tacit consent of the control agency.

Industry's complaints always center on the high cost of fighting air pollution as compared to the doubtful, to them, amount of damage caused by polluted air. Businessmen have a direct financial interest in denying pollution damage, but their arguments about the high cost of prevention are sincere and irrefutable. It has been estimated that it would cost upwards of $75 billion to bring the entire industrial plant of the United States to the standards demanded in Los Angeles, where the typical industrialist will spend 25 percent of his basic equipment costs on pollution-control equipment. The high cost of equipment and the ridiculously low fines usually levied by courts on violators of pollution-control laws have led to suggestions that factories be forced to pay a "pollution fee"—so much per pound of pollutants they send into the air—the money to be applied to improving the enforcement of clean-air laws. Supporters of the proposal point out that it is as logical as sewer taxes, since the polluters are using the air as a giant sewer for their fire-created garbage.

Federal officials believe that the emission of pollutants from stationary sources can best be fought on the local or regional level. In general, the sulphur that comes from a smokestack is washed out of the air swiftly enough to be a problem only in the vicinity of the source. Control methods can be applied by a local agency in relation to the prevailing levels of pollution. Any city that wants to pay the price in higher fuel bills by reducing sulphur content can do so, based on its own needs. For the federal government to set broad, national sulphur regulations, P.H.S. officials believe, is premature. But that time may come with the ever-growing spread of cities and the construction of huge power plants with smokestacks a sixth of a mile high that are already blurring the distinction between local and regional problems.

The automobile poses no such local or even regional alternatives for control. The smoking exhaust pipe that is a negligible problem in the deserts of Nevada becomes a serious concern twenty-four hours later when it arrives in the Los Angeles basin. The vacationer from Maine can pollute the air of a dozen cities as he drives down to Florida. The only true solution to the automobile problem, Senator Muskie and other officials believe, is to set one national standard for exhaust emissions. Some will spend money needlessly as a result, but the problem is so universal—automobiles cause an estimated 50 percent of all the air pollution in the nation—that no more equitable means of distributing the financial burden is known. The difficulty is not in the amount of emission reduction that is required, but in the manner in which it is being reduced. There is a growing feeling that drastic changes in the automobile engine will be needed to meet the tougher requirements on emissions that are bound to develop as the number of automobiles hits the 100-million mark by 1980.

"Since the gasoline engine is, on nearly all other counts, the most desirable power plant available, its design has become well standardized in all major respects," said W. E. Meyer, professor of mechanical engineering at Pennsylvania State University. "Now that exhaust emissions have become a matter of concern, the tendency is to attempt to solve this problem by accessories that will remove from the exhaust gases the unwanted components and thereby avoid major engine changes. It is, however, possible that in the long run it may be more desirable to modify the engine itself in such a manner that the exhaust gases will be inoffensive to begin with, or at least much less offensive than they are now."

Such changes are not now contemplated by the auto industry as a whole. Chrysler did make a few modifications that allow a leaner mixture to be burned, while the other auto makers try to burn up the pollutants with blasts of air before they can get into the atmosphere. Understandably, none of the major companies wants to jeopardize the billion-dollar investment it has in the *status quo*. One tentative step, however, was made by Chrysler with its turbine-engine car — about fifty produced to date and lent for a few months to representative drivers across the country — but many industry observers feel there may be more publicity than progress in it for the auto maker. But the turbine engine would be an almost ideal solution to the auto-emission problem. In contrast to the present engine, the turbine burns any fuel—almost anything from kerosene to hair tonic will do—and uses the heat to turn blades like an old-fashioned paddle-wheeler. The resulting emissions are well below the currently allowed limits. But the turbine engine has several faults that to date have not allowed it to compete economically with the gasoline piston engine. Its acceleration is poor and mileage is bad at low speeds. In the stop-and-go and crawl traffic of the cities, where the pollution problem is greatest, they would be very inefficient. Chrysler claims to have licked most of these problems, while Ford and General Motors, who are undoubtedly also hard at work on a turbine design, say nothing. The economic facts of life will keep the turbine-powered car from the assembly lines for some time to come, simply because there is too much money invested in factories to produce conventional engines.

The same factor would prevent the introduction on a mass basis of diesel engines in passenger cars. There are models on the road, mostly in taxicabs, but their big problem is excess weight and noise. And while some experts say the diesel's exhaust is cleaner than that of the gasoline engine, some have said it emits as many pollutants and more nitrogen oxides and cancer-causing benzpyrene.

Thus, the dubious value of the diesel and the economic and design pitfalls of the turbine are unlikely, in the immediate future, to relegate the gasoline engine to the scrap heap, especially not for the simple purpose of making the air fit to breathe.

The best that Detroit is likely to do is to allow its engineers to fiddle with the gasoline engine just enough to satisfy whatever regulations come out of California or Washington. Only one company, Chrysler, seems to be an exception to this rule, mainly because a remarkable man named Charles M. Heinen is in its engineering division. Heinen was largely responsible for the development of the "clean-air package," which did what California wanted several years before it made its demands official. But even Heinen was unable to get the C.A.P. on cars before California put the demand into law, so it is likely that Detroit is going to proceed only as far as it is prodded, kicking and screaming all the way.

Fortunately, quite a bit can be accomplished even within these narrow limits. If the sales lure of huge engines can ever be seen as the nonsense it is, smaller engines could accomplish quite a bit. The streets of our cities are jammed with cars designed to carry a family of five and all their luggage at eighty-five miles per hour. But most of the time these throbbing power plants are crawling through city streets either accelerating or decelerating, the two times during the driving cycle when emissions are at a maximum. Some engineers have suggested that the energy generated when a car is braked be stored and used for accelerating the car when it starts up again; right now that energy is used solely to heat the brake lining. The engine could be shut down as soon as deceleration begins and started up again by the stored energy. A small auxiliary engine could power the radio and other accessories while the main engine was off. A device that would store this breaking energy efficiently would do a lot for clean air.

Another possibility of reducing emissions is based on the fact that fuel near the walls of the combustion chamber tends not to be consumed. It might be possible to cut down on this source of hydrocarbons by changing the surface-to-volume ratio of the cylinders—reducing the amount of wall area — and increasing the amount of combustion. Other factors, such as temperature and pressure, are involved. The area in which fuel is not consumed becomes narrower as temperature and pressure go up and as the vapor in the cylinder grows more turbulent. Another possibility is to do away with the carburetor, which causes two types of emissions. Some of the fuel just evaporates from the carburetor. Also, the mechanics of the carburetor make it necessary to provide an extra amount of fuel when the throttle is wide open, and that is sheer waste. In addition, carburetors become maladjusted fairly easily, and if the result is too much fuel, the driver rarely notices it, save in his bills, but the contribution to air polution is decidedly noticeable. Carburetor substitutes have been developed experimentally, but they did not work as well as hoped, for no major change was made in the rest of the engine. Once again, the weight of a billion-dollar investment, in production facilities and gas stations, is on the side of the *status quo* and against a redesign of the engine.

But such a redesign may become necessary sooner than the worst Detroit nightmare may predict, for the demands for less foul emission from cars have just begun. All the engine changes ordered to date have not effected the creation of nitrogen oxides, which are as undesirable as carbon monoxides and hydrocarbons. It will be necessary to mark time for a while until the major readjustment of present engine changes is made, but the pressures for less nitrogen oxides from autos cannot be resisted for long.

Despite all the innovations, new gadgets and technological advances, it seems probable that the gasoline engine will be the basic power plant for the American car for the foreseeable future, but the speculators, the dreamers and the hardheaded technocrats still look to a radical changeover. One possibility they offer is the electric car, powered by batteries that can be recharged periodically. Such autos were moderately popular at the beginning of the automobile era, but the increasing efficiency of the gasoline engine drove them off the market. Anyone who has driven an electric car can testify to the almost eerie sensation of cleanliness that it gives. Turning on the ignition produces no sound, just the almost imperceptible jump of an ammeter needle. The only sound when the car is in motion is a slight hum that makes the throaty roar of a gasoline engine seem deafening. And of course, there is nothing coming out of the exhaust pipe: there is, in fact, no exhaust pipe. The problems of the electric car are economic, not technical. It just isn't practical to pay the electric bill for a car.

Reporters at an electric car demonstration in New York City in 1965 were impressed by its smooth operation, but stunned by the cost. The car was a Renault, converted to electricity by the simple expedient of ripping out its gas engine and installing storage batteries from an F-105 jet fighter. The batteries had enough juice to run the car for more than a hundred miles, but they had to be replaced every six months or so at a cost of $350—not counting the $300 in silver that was salvaged from the old batteries. Moreover, the car had to be plugged in overnight to keep the batteries charged. The car's promoters acknowledged that it wasn't everyone's cup of tea, said it might be useful for route drivers like milkmen, who had to leave their gasoline engines on continually, because it is less efficient to keep turning them off and on at every doorstep. They might also serve as the second car the housewife uses to do her shopping and keep the family gas burner in the garage save for weekends, thus cutting down exhaust emissions by the simple expedient of not using the gas in the tank.

There are, however, other shortcomings of the electric car. For one thing, it would merely be a shift from one source of pollution to another, since the power to recharge the batteries would be generated by plants that foul the air with sulphur oxides and ash. There would be some gain, since the power would be generated at night, when the pollution potential is at its lowest. In addition, one big stationary source of pollution is a lot easier to control than a million small moving sources. But the heavy weight of investment in the production, servicing and supply of gasoline engines makes the electric car a marginal proposal at best.

Some experts see greater hope in a space-age device called the fuel cell, which is used in satellites and manned spacecraft. The fuel cell is spectacularly efficient since it does not go through the usual process of burning fuel to turn wheels to generate electricity. Instead, it combines two chemicals—usually hydrogen and oxygen — to create electricity directly. There is also a by-product — water — useful in a space craft but not necessarily so in a car. William T. Reid, a senior fellow at the Battelle Memorial Institute, Columbus, Ohio, has reported that a fifteen-horsepower electric motor that could power a small car for short hauls around cities could be hooked up to an 11.2 kilowatt fuel cell that would cost $560 and provide operating costs competitive with existing gasoline engines. Such a hydrogen-oxygen fuel cell would operate for several thousand hours. The technological barrier to the mating of the fuel cell with the automobile are not unassailable; the economic dislocation, however, might be prohibitive at this time.

There remains one pollution-free power source that is right now economically competitive, technologically feasible and not economically destructive to entire industries. That source is the atom. Atomic power plants are as pollution-free as anything man has developed—so much so that one study found that a conventional power plant releases more radioactive material by burning conventional fuels than an atomic plant does by its operation. The atomic plant gets the heat needed to make steam from the energy released by uranium atoms as they split. The United States is making a fair amount of progress on atomic energy, but countries where fossil fuels are not so readily available are ahead of us in some respects. Great Britain, for instance, is well on the way toward getting most of her power from atomic plants, and the newest of these generate electricity at a lower cost than would be possible if coal or oil were used.

Unfortunately, the development of atomic power plants in the United States is held back by the completely illogical fear generated by all thoughts of the atom. When Consolidated Edison proposed an atomic plant in Queens, the residents of that New York City borough were up in arms at the threat to their lives. Con Edison pointed out that every human precaution had been taken, but the opponents insisted that since nothing human was perfect, there was still danger in the plant. Conceding that only God could provide the type of guarantees the anti-atom people demanded, Con Ed went ahead and built the world's largest conventional power plant on the site that had been earmarked for the atomic plant — and got blasted for polluting the air with dust and sulphur from the new facility.

Unfortunately, the clean-air aspects of atomic power are regarded as no more than an unimportant side effect, rather than a very real reason for building atomic plants. If the fight for clean air were being waged more logically, the power industry would be given economic incentives to build atomic plants. Unfortunately, logic has never been a major part of the air-pollution controversy and the all-too-little good works of air-pollution-control agencies is too often undone by the work of other government bureaus....

Still another area of "what can be done" is the enormously fertile field of intelligent city planning. Zoning, which could be a vital ingredient in the fight against pollution, has been virtually neglected in that respect in the United States. The Russians, on the other hand, substituted brains for money during the rebuilding of Stalingrad (now Volgograd) after its destruction in World War II. The prevailing wind patterns were among the major considerations of the Soviet city planners. The city was laid out in two sections perpendicular to the prevailing winds. The two sections were subdivided into multiple bands, with the upwind section zoned for parks, recreation and homes, and the downwind zone containing industrial plants and railways. The two sections were bisected by a green belt through which a freeway ran. The result is that clean air from the countryside blows over the city's homes and parks before it becomes polluted by the freeway, factories and railroad. The unpopulated area downwind from the city gets the polluted air, not the heavily populated residential areas.

Volgograd is just one instance of the Russian clean-air effort. In general they are more concerned about air pollution than we are. Leaded gasoline is forbidden in large Russian cities and no new factory can be built without approval from the local health officer, who studies its effects on the city's air. Dr. Nikolai F. Izmerov, a World Health Organization official and a leading Russian expert on air pollution, claims that Soviet engineers are busy working on a new type of auto engine that would reduce pollution. Soviet scientists are also making a determined effort to study the exact effects of long-term exposure to small amounts of air pollution on human health.

While the dictatorial powers of the Soviet state make enforcement of any program relatively easy, it still requires imagination and intelligence to begin an effective air-pollution-control program. Surely these two elements can flourish even better in a democratic environment, but we have unfortunately paid not nearly enough attention to the zoning of industry and to limitations on the type of equipment that is installed in our cities. But economic considerations seem to take precedent. In New York City, for example, where land is in short supply, the city yielded to temptation and allowed three huge apartment houses to be built over an eight-lane superhighway. Monitoring instruments have shown that levels of nitrogen oxides and carbon monoxide in these buildings are much higher than those in most city streets. The residents of these houses, moreover, have become unwitting guinea pigs in an experiment on the effects of long-term exposure to those levels of pollution.

Despite the inherent dangers, the city is now considering the sale of air rights over super highways for the construction of still more homes and even schools. This is just one glaring example of the complete neglect of air pollution in American city planning. In addition, no factory or private builder should be permitted to install heating or manufacturing equipment that is not up to the best current standards of pollution control. This is probably the most elementary precaution that could be taken, but many cities simply ignore it.

Until basic steps such as these are taken, more advanced measures—zoning on an airshed-wide basis or the designed construction of factory-home complexes to reduce the driving necessary to get commuters to jobs—must wait. But these measures will definitely be a part of the future, despite their radical departure from past procedures. The completely unplanned surge to the suburbs of the past two decades has done more to pollute America's air than anything else, by multiplying the number of cars on the road, destroying systems of mass transportation and making necessary the superhighways that have become simply ribbons capable of valving pollution into the air. No one suggests abandoning the suburbs or breaking up the highways, but someone should be thinking about preventing even worse pollution situations in the future.

The key word in all these requirements is planning — a look ahead at what can be expected and the start of measures to prevent the worst. Not all communities now face an air-pollution crisis, but the day will come when they will. . . .

"We have some time," Senator Muskie said, "but not time to waste." Time is being wasted, though, primarily because most city officials are so immersed in the demanding task of keeping cities going on a day-to-day basis that far-reaching measures for the future get lost in the shuffle. The pressure for better planning must come from the people. The bright spots in the air-pollution picture, such as Pittsburgh and Chicago, show that this kind of pressure can be effective. But either pressure for cleaner air has not developed in most areas or it has not been transmitted effectively to industry and government. In too many areas, the local civic group that fights for clean air consists of a small number of dedicated citizens who gather periodically to tell each other facts they already know. There is some hope now that this pattern is being broken, as the public becomes more aware of the dangers of polluted air. "There has been an unbelievable change in the whole public attitude toward pollution problems," said assistant H.E.W. Secretary Quigley. To turn this new awareness into political action a nationwide network of Action for Clean Air Committees with members from government, industry and the public at large has been launched.

A guide issued by the New York State organization offers these principles:

A local Clean Air Committee should include representatives of local government, the air-pollution-control agency, the medical society, technical associations and civic groups. It should try to cooperate with other local groups, not replace them.

An information program should be established, with its main purpose to inform people that they may be polluters. Unwitting polluters—those who use back-yard incinerators, for example—will usually cooperate when they learn of the effects of their burning. The community in general should be told it has an air-pollution problem, but without creating hysteria.

Start with obvious sources of air pollution and try to get effective action on those. If necessary, make your own surveys and make sure they get wide publicity. Don't go off half-cocked, but don't be afraid to name names when violations are clear. Try not to exaggerate the problem, since that can hurt in the long run.

The key people to enlist are the local doctors and industrialists. Local executives will be much more sensitive to local pressures, and efforts should be made to get technical advice from industry, as well as appealing to industry to clean up its own sources of pollution. Use of industrial knowhow, and sometimes equipment, may help other polluters to clean up.

Work as closely as possible with local officials on enforcing the existing laws, before demanding new ones. Try to take advantage of ordinances that help in the clean-air fight, even though they were passed for other purposes—a fire-department regulation against trash burning, for instance.

Try to have the problems of air pollution mentioned in the appropriate courses in the schools to make students aware that air pollution is a problem.

Enlist local planning-agency members in the organization and work with them to insure that air pollution is one of the considerations taken into account in the development of the area.

Above all, don't lose your head or neglect the simple rules of common sense. Tackle the easiest problems first; don't lose the effectiveness of publicity by exaggerating; follow up every sound proposal; don't let individual frustrations make policy; and don't be ashamed to ask for information or advice from others. The fight is going to be a long one, so take action while it is still manageable.

The cities that are doing the most about pollution are those in which the private groups grew to enlist mass support and the leadership of natural community leaders. The emphasis has got to be on the community approach because the sources of pollution are almost endless.

"Air pollution is the kind of problem that can be dealt with only on a community basis," said Vernon MacKenzie of the Public Health Service. "It can't be left to individual activities to get a job done. Any individual usually doesn't see his particular contribution as being a significant part of the total problem. A solution simply can't be left to the good intentions of the individual."

In the final analysis, the local law and its enforcement are going to play the largest role in determining just what type of air we breathe. Money is one measure of the effectiveness of local programs. The P.H.S. Division of Air Pollution says that a community with an average air-pollution problem should spend 40 cents per resident per year on pollution-control efforts; a level that few cities other than Los Angeles, Chicago and San Francisco even approach. New York City, with the nation's second-worst problem, spends about 15 cents per person per year. The 40-cent level is of course a rule of thumb—Pittsburgh's very effective program costs less — but it is in general a good guide. Money means manpower, and men are needed to keep the air clean.

Another gauge of effectiveness is the type of ordinance the city has in effect. Does it provide for review of new installations by pollution-control engineers? Are the fines set by the ordinance high enough to deter polluters? Is leaf-burning prohibited?

Money and effective ordinances are the two immediate needs. But plans should also be made for the long run. This can only be done if the community knows just what its problem is and what are the sources of its pollution. The Clean Air Act has made federal grants available for monitoring programs to determine what is in the air. In addition, the city should know how weather conditions and geographical features of the area affect patterns of pollution. It should make projections of pollution trends of the future and set levels for the future so that it may determine the nature of the steps it now is taking. Ambient-air standards should be fixed so that tangible goals will exist. On the basis of these goals and monitoring information, it should establish priorities for its program. A city that has only light industry but burns its rubbish on an open dump will require different steps than a city that has several smoking steel mills in its midst. All along the way, an educational program will be needed to keep the public informed of what is being done and why.

Sooner or later, a control program will outrace the boundaries of any local community. Every state should have a law permitting the formation of multi-governmental pollution-control agencies, and planning for such agencies should start as soon as possible. The first step may be the simple matter of getting all the communities sharing the same air supply to coordinate their pollution ordinances. Then would come the establishment of regional districts with enforcement powers over a wider area. Many experts suggest that the pollution-control district be part of a regional agency dealing with many area problems —transportation, water supply, parks and zoning regulations.

At some future time, a group of such regional districts will coalesce to police the air quality in an entire airshed covering thousands of square miles and often crossing state lines. In this final stage, the factory owner or automobile driver will find his actions governed by the potential effects of polluted air on everyone in an area incorporating perhaps a dozen counties. The rights and duties of every air user will be the responsibility of the airshed agency.

The difference between the best- and worst-possible future worlds is being decided in the technological and governmental decisions now being made. If huge power plants will be placed at random with no controls over the sulphur pouring from their smokestacks, if the roads continue to be filled with overpowered cars pouring fumes into the air, if homes, factories and roads are built with no thought to air pollution—in short, if we go on in the old familiar pattern—then an air-pollution crisis of enormous magnitude is inevitable, and so too are the harsh, belated measures that will be necessary to deal with the crisis.

There is another possible future: building well-planned cities, with streets filled with cars specially designed to keep pollution to a minimum; with factories and equipment, subsidized in part by tax relief, that cleanse the poisons from the wastes it dumps into the air, obtaining power from atomic plants that do not produce pollutants; and whose citizens are aware of the need for continual vigilance to keep the air clean.

The desirable future carries a high price tag. But the present cost is just as high, and will become virtually prohibitive in a few more years. And herein lies the great irony of air pollution. Every expert is convinced that a dollar spent on effective air-pollution control now saves several dollars in hidden pollution costs, to local governments, industry and individuals. The great difficulty, they say, is that people have become so accustomed to paying these hidden costs they are no longer aware of them. The hidden costs of pollution, however, are rising faster than the money spent to fight pollution, and in most areas there is no sign of a break in the trend, Senator Muskie declared:

In none of the cities that we have visited have we seen any evidence that convinces us that our state, local and federal governments cannot afford to increase their efforts to clear the air. We have seen a good deal of evidence which suggests that we cannot afford not to increase our efforts.

The costs of uncontrolled air pollution in economic damages alone, not to mention the threat to our health, far exceeds the cost of adequate air pollution control.

In short, if we do not pay enough for the prevention of air pollution, we are doomed to pay a higher price for our neglect. . . .

The techniques of air pollution control may be complex. The problems of dealing with air pollution in an area such as this, where many millions of people and scores of government jurisdictions depend on the same regional air resource, may be formidable, but the choice we face is simple:

We can begin now an earnest cooperative effort to draw back the curtain of smog that too frequently hides our cities, or we can wait and pay a much higher price in human suffering or dollars some time in the future.

This is the essential choice. Whether we are bold and courageous enough to make the right one, right now, will determine the nature of the air we shall be forced to breathe tomorrow.

The Movement

Jack Newfield

The student movement has been another source of militant action in America. To give it a single name, student movement, is to impute more unity to it than is a fact. The highly visible Students for a Democratic Society (SDS) is itself internally split on goals and tactics, and that organization is a manifestation of only the politicized elements of student unrest. There is, in addition, a large group of students whose major symptom is withdrawal—some into drug-using subcultures and some not. What experience and perspectives unite this diffuse student generation? In the opening chapter of his book, A Prophetic Minority, Jack Newfield, a charter member of the Students for a Democratic Society, journalist and author describes the common grievances of the disaffected young.

We want to create a world in which love is more possible.
—CARL OGLESBY, *SDS President*

There is a time when the operation of the machine becomes so odious, makes you so sick at heart that you can't take part; you can't even tacitly take part, and you've got to put your bodies upon the levers, upon all the apparatus, and you've got to make it stop. And you've got to indicate to the people who run it, to the people who own it, that unless you're free, the machine will be prevented from working at all.
—MARIO SAVIO, *leader of the FSM*

I can't get no satisfaction.
—THE ROLLING STONES

A new generation of radicals has been spawned from the chrome womb of affluent America. The last lingering doubts that the Silent Generation had found its voice vanished forever on April 17, 1965, when more than 20,000 of this new breed converged on the nation's capital to protest against the war in Vietnam. It was the largest anti-war demonstration in the history of Washington, D.C.—and it had been organized and sponsored by a student organization—SDS.

Assembled in the warm afternoon sunshine that Saturday were the boys and girls who had "freedom rode" to Jackson, Mississippi; who had joined the

Reprinted by permission of the World Publishing Company from *A Prophetic Minority* by Jack Newfield. An NAL book. Copyright © 1966 by Jack Newfield.

Peace Corps and returned disillusioned; tutored Negro teen-agers in the slums of the great cities; vigiled against the Bomb; rioted against the House Un-American Activities Committee; risked their lives to register voters in the Black Belt; and sat-in for free speech at the University of California at Berkeley.

They were the new generation of American radicals, nourished not by the alien cobwebbed dogmas of Marx, Lenin, and Trotsky, but by the existential humanism of Albert Camus, the Anti-colonialism of Frantz Fanon; the communitarian anarchism of Paul Goodman; the poetic alienation of Bob Dylan; and the grass-roots radicalism of that "prophetic shock minority" called SNCC. They were there not to protest anything so simple as war or capitalism. They came to cry out against the hypocrisy called Brotherhood Week, assembly lines called colleges, manipulative hierarchies called corporations, conformity called status, lives of quiet desperation called success.

They heard Joan Baez sing Dylan's sardonic poem, "With God on Our Side," and cheered spontaneously when she sang, "Although they murdered six million, in the ovens they fried/Now they too have God on their side."

They sang "Do What the Spirit Say Do," the latest freedom hit to come out of the jails and churches of the South, an indication perhaps of their deepest concern—human freedom and expression. Thus, Freedom now, "Oh Freedom," freedom ride, free university, freedom school, Free Speech Movement, and the Freedom Democratic Party.

And the 20,000 listened to the visionary voices of the New Radicalism.

Staughton Lynd, a romantic, a Quaker, and a revolutionary, told them:

We are here today in behalf of Jean-Paul Sartre . . . we are here to keep the faith with those of all countries and all ages who have sought to beat swords into ploughshares and to war no more.

They heard Bob Parris, SNCC's humble visionary, who told them:

Listen and think. Don't clap, please. . . . Don't use Mississippi as a moral lightning rod. Use it as a looking glass. Look into it and see what it tells you about all of America.

And they listened to Paul Potter, the tense, brilliant, twenty-four-year-old former president of SDS, who said:

There is no simple plan, no scheme or gimmick that can be proposed here. There is no simple way to attack something that is deeply rooted in the society. If the people of this country are to end the war in Vietnam, and to change the institutions which create it, then the people of this country must create a massive social movement—and if that can be built around the issue of Vietnam, then that is what we must do.

By a social movement I mean more than petitions and letters of protest, or tacit support of dissident Congressmen; I mean people who are willing to change their lives, who are willing to challenge the system, to take the problem of change seriously. By a social movement I mean an effort that is powerful enough to make the country understand that our problems are not in Vietnam, or China or Brazil or outer space or at the bottom of the ocean, but here in the United States. What we must begin to do is build a democratic and humane society in which Vietnams are unthinkable. . . .

Then, after three hours of speeches and freedom singing, the 20,000 stood in the lengthening shadow of the Washington Monument, linked arms, and, swaying back and forth, sang the anthem of their movement. Reaching out to clasp strange hands were button-down intellectuals from Harvard and broken-down Village hippies; freshmen from small Jesuit schools and the overalled kamikazes of SNCC; curious faculty members and high-school girls; angry ghetto Negroes and middle-aged parents, wondering what motivates their rebellious children; all together, singing and feeling the words, "Deep in my heart/I do believe/We shall overcome someday."

The SDS march, which had drawn twice the participation everyone, including its sponsors, had expected, suddenly illuminated a phenomenon that had been growing underground, in campus dorms, in the Mississippi delta, in bohemian subcultures, for more than five years. It was the phenomenon of students rejecting the dominant values of their parents and their country; becoming alienated, becoming political, becoming active, becoming radical; protesting against racism, poverty, war, Orwell's 1984, Camus' executioner, Mills' Power Elite, Mailer's Cancerous Totalitarianism; protesting against irrational anti-Communism, nuclear weaponry, the lies of statesmen, the hypocrisy of laws against narcotics and abortion; protesting against loyalty oaths, speaker bans, HUAC, *in loco parentis*—and finally, at Berkeley, protesting against the computer, symbol of man's dehumanization by the machine; in sum, protesting against all those obscenities that form the cryptic composite called the System.

In the weeks immediately following the SDS march the mass media suddenly discovered that the Brainwashed Generation, as poet Karl Shapiro had tagged the campus catatonics of the 1950's, had become a protest generation, that a cultural and sociological revolution had taken place while they had been preoccupied with the Bogart cult, J. D. Salinger, and baseball bonus babies. Within an eight-week period, *Time, Newsweek, The Saturday Evening Post, The New York Times Magazine, Life,* and two television networks all popularized the New Left. They smeared it, they psychoanalyzed it, they exaggerated it, they cartooned it, they made it look like a mélange of beatniks, potheads, and agents of international Communism; *they did everything but explain the failures in the society that called it into being.*

The New Radicalism is pluralistic, amorphous, and multi-layered. Its three political strands—anarchism, pacifism, and socialism—mingle in different proportions in different places. It's different in every city, on every campus. In Berkeley there is a strong sex-drug-literary orientation. In New York there is a politically sophisticated component. In the South there is extra emphasis on the non-violent religious element.

At its surface, *political* level, the New Radicalism is an anti-Establishment protest against all the obvious inequities of American life. It says that Negroes should vote, that America should follow a peaceful, noninterventionist foreign policy, that anti-Communism at home has become paranoid and destructive, that the poverty of forty million should be abolished. It is a series of individual criticisms many liberals can agree with.

At its second, more complex level, this new movement is a *moral* revulsion against a society that is becoming increasingly corrupt. The New Radicals were coming to maturity as McCarthy built a movement based on deceit and bullying, as Dulles lied about the CIA's role in the 1954 Guatemala *coup*, as Eisenhower lied to the world about the U-2 flight over the Soviet Union, as Adlai Stevenson lied to the UN about America's support of the Bay of Pigs invasion, as Charles Van Doren participated in fixed quiz shows on television, as congressmen and judges were convicted for bribery. They saw the organs of masscult lie about their movement, the clergy exile priests for practicing brotherhood, older men red-bait their organizations. Feeling this ethical vacuum in the country, the New Radicals have made morality and truth the touchstones of their movement. Like Gandhi, they try to "speak truth to power." Their politics are not particularly concerned with power or success, but rather with absolute moral alternatives like love, justice, equality, and freedom. Practical, programmatic goals are of little interest. They want to pose an alternative vision, not just demand "more" or "better" of what exists. They don't say welfare programs should be better subsidized; they say they should be administered in a wholly different, more dignifying way. They don't say Negroes need leaders with better judgment; they say Negroes should develop spokesmen from their own ranks.

At its third, subterranean level, the New Radicalism is an *existential* revolt against remote, impersonal machines that are not responsive to human needs. The New Radicals feel sharply the growing totalitarianization of life in this technological, urban decade. They feel powerless and unreal beneath the unfeeling instruments that control their lives. They comprehend the essentially undemocratic nature of the military-industrial complex; the Power Elite; the multiversity with its IBM course cards; urban renewal by technocrats; canned television laughter; wire taps; automation; computer marriages and artificial insemination; and finally, the mysterious button somewhere that can trigger the nuclear holocaust.

The New Radicals are the first products of liberal affluence. They have grown up in sterile suburbs, urban complexes bereft of community, in impersonal universities. They are the children of economic surplus and spiritual starvation. They agree with C. Wright Mills when he writes, "Organized irresponsibility, in this impersonal sense, is a leading characteristic of modern industrial societies everywhere. On every hand the individual is confronted with seemingly remote organizations; he feels dwarfed and helpless before the managerial cadres and their manipulated and manipulating minions."

And they can only chant "amen" to Lewis Mumford, who observed in *The Transformations of Man*, modern man has already depersonalized "himself so effectively that he is no longer man enough to stand up to his machines."

From their fury at arbitrary power wielded by impersonal machines (governments, college administrations, welfare bureaucracies, draft boards, television networks) come some of the New Radicals' most innovative ideas. Participatory democracy—the notion that ordinary people should be able to affect all the decisions that control their lives. The idea that social reformation comes from organizing the dispossessed into their own insurgent movements rather than from forming top-down alliances between liberal bureaucratic organizations. The insistence on fraternity and community inside the movement. The passion against manipulation and centralized decision-making. The reluctance to make the New Left itself a machine tooled and fueled to win political power in the traditional battle pits. The concept of creating new democratic forms like the Mississippi Freedom Democratic Party, the Newark Community Union Project, and the *Southern Courier*, a newspaper designed to represent the Negroes of the Black Belt rather than the white power structure or the civil-rights organizations. It is its brilliant insight into the creeping authoritarianism of modern technology and bureaucracy that gives the New Radicalism its definitive qualities of decentralism, communitarianism, and existential humanism.

Historically, the New Radicals' forebearers are the Whitman-Emerson-Thoreau transcendentalists, and the Joe Hill-Bill Hayward Wobblies. Like the IWW mill strikers at Lawrence, Massachusetts, in 1912, the New Left wants "bread and roses too."

The average American, with visions of campus riots fresh in his memory, is quite likely to think of the student movement as largely negative and destructive. The bumper sticker which says "Love it or leave it" testifies to this view. And the answering sticker "Change it or lose it," might seem to validate the charge. The student movement is undeniably critical of contemporary America, but is it justifiable to say, as so many do, that there is no right to criticize unless the protesters have a workable alternative system? Harlan Lewin here develops the view that the contemporary period is a new age of social and political experiment and change. He argues that the increase of dissent in modern societies serves a necessary function: powerful institutions and powerful ideas are exposed to the intrusion of insights springing from new needs in a novel environment. He traces the origins and types of dissenting "counter-cultures" in America, suggesting new dimensions for understanding current political turmoil.

Seedtime of the New Republic: Ideology, Identity and Social Change

Harlan Lewin

CONFRONTATION

Modern democracies have inherited the legacies of two related wars: the war between church and state and the war between science and religion. The good liberal democrat today bears a superego forged in the fights of past centuries. Modern liberalism rests on old fears: the state should be free from priestly edicts and intuitions, and religion should be free from the corruption and interference of the worldly state. The anxieties remain: since values, ethics, conscience and morality are rooted in the unprovable, disputable areas of belief and intuition they may be welcomed in the channels of public rhetoric, but in the corridors of power, in the balancing of interests and incremental policy-making, arguments based on such considerations are "subjective," "irrelevant," and taboo.

As old battles fade and one amazing feat of technology follows another in what is approaching tedium, a new struggle arises and the historic fear of

This article was prepared especially for this volume. Permission to reprint should be obtained from Charles E. Merrill Publishing Company.

conscience and intuition begins to wear off in important sectors of society. This does not mean that contemporary conservatives who look for a revival of reverence for tradition and interest in natural law are correct. Respect for ideas recommended by their longevity alone and identification with natural law tradition do not seem to be hallmarks of the current changes in ideas and ideals. On the contrary, tradition is still suspect as a crutch for self-interested authority. Experiment and search now flow in the direction of direct interpersonal and deeply individual conscience-behavior, and toward a new union of public and private concerns, previously separated by both the religious and scientific traditions.[1]

The administrator-rulers of the new world of bureaucratic government and economy represent what are by now the old values of the Enlightenment and Industrialism. Impersonality, radical pragmatism (it is only real if you taste, see, smell, touch or hear it, and only right if it fills an explicit need), faith in the power of verbal and mathematical logic, definiteness of decision and record, and adherence to precedent are the most important values of the generation who were once the revolutionary "New Turks." The high goals set for man by the liberal administrator-rulers still in power are: progress in worldly satisfaction, protection of private thought, and tolerance of action limited by the primary necessity of maintaining social stability *as defined by the political institutions of the society*. These otherwise admirable goals have been exposed in their narrowness, however, by precisely the social research resulting from the pragmatic-scientific attitude. Research in interest group activity and in the empirical realities of public administration has cast doubt on the *objectivity* of the liberal system, which is its prime claim.[2] It has been shown that in actual practice the setting of goals and the making of judgments and laws becomes through time the *specialty* of a special class of persons. They may originate in different classes, but they learn the passwords and practices that knit them together in bonds of common interest and outlook.

There is no need to assume that the powerful of the day exercise their power with only self-regard or malevolent authoritarianism, nor even that they understand, themselves, the broad picture of the extent and nature of their power. It is probably reasonable to assume, as Gandhi did,[3] and not for any particularly charitable reason, that the authorities, with very few exceptions, operate on the presupposition of their own moral and legal rectitude and subjective good will. Expertise and specialization elevate and integrate today's administrating elites; and elite rule is acceptable to them when conceived of as a self-defined benevolent concern for the correct interpretation of the wishes and needs of the non-specialist citizens by a small number of highly trained administrators. "We can do for the mass," they believe, "what they do not perceive as necessary and what they do not know how to do."

The problem of politics, when it approaches a stage of confrontation, is that not only the administrative, ruling elite assume their own rectitude, but that the rebels, resistors and revolutionaries may also be presumed to operate from a similar conviction of possessing the truth. The problem of moderating social conflict is the problem of mediating not between honest good guys and cynical bad guys, but between two sets of self-nominated good guys. Furthermore, as the two sides now seem to be saying, there are perhaps no neutral arbiters, no "men from Mars" to act as uninvolved and disengaged judges. Entire cultures are so intertwined with political conflicts today that U.N. adjudicators, judges, and "third parties" in general are suspect. The disappearance of neutrality in the world has set the stage for an era of chronic *confrontations* with minimum room for negotiation. The political problem of today is to expand that minimum room.

Efforts at expanding the space for negotiation must take into account the critical difference of powerful resources between the established and the resistors. The difference is important because the basic strategy of creating progress through negotiation is to establish as much of a balance as possible between the negotiating parties. The difference between our two groups (there are, of course, more than two in real life) is the well known difference between the *ins* and the *outs*. The *ins* have access to all the information about the past, present and future which the society has accumulated, information secret and unknown, which tells what has been done, what is being done, and how to use the resources of the society for future plans. The *ins* have all access to loyal power: think of the army and taxation. The *ins make history*, for what the official administration does is *defined* as news without question. With the new technologies of communication and production, one might conclude that the *ins*, in such a society as contemporary America, have almost attained the power to define what *is*, that is, what is truth, and what is to be desired, that is, what the society will create.

For the *ins*, rectitude and power combine. The *outs* possess rectitude, but relatively little power. The problem of political mediation of conflict becomes the problem of mediating between (at least) two morally persuaded groups, one of which has access to various resources which gives it the edge for having its definitions of what is right becoming the socially accepted definitions. These definitions are more likely to be accepted not necessarily because men believe might makes right, but because might *with the conviction of right* is more attractive to ordinary men than the conviction of right, alone, which promises little physical satisfaction and threatens besides suspicion and exile. Since most men are not moral athletes, it is unfair to criticize them for rejecting the exercise of living in the hilly terrain of dissent.

Given the above recognitions, we perceive, with due credit to Gandhi's explorations, an important and perhaps saving qualification to the theory of the structure and functioning of liberal democracy. This qualification is the necessity of permanent, determined, nonviolent resistance from "outsiders" in the private and "common" levels of life to policies and actions of government (and its supporting established elites). We are not merely advocating such resistance, we shall describe its present origins and growth.

This resistance challenges not only the fairness of particular decisions of the authorities, but also expresses the doubt that it is at all possible for institutionalized authority to maintain an unselfish concern for moral justice without the continual and intense challenge of morally committed and self-sacrificing citizens counseled by "specialists" in the concerns of higher justice. Such "specialists," *whose own qualifications are always to be open to doubt*, are exemplified by Socrates, who has achieved an almost mythical position as The Outsider in the Western tradition, and Gandhi. Essentially, the genius and life situations of such men lead them to set the example of attempting to *realize* the ideal in the here and now—a pursuit which has become less and less popular with the increasing popularity of a narrow, here-and-now-worshipping empiricism.

The importance of "outsider" resistance follows from the recognition that intensive *involvement* and isolating expertise tend to drive even the most fair-minded, rule-oriented administrators to institute as much *self*-regulation and distancing from "non-elites" as can be managed. For example, "police brutality" and out-group frustration in dealing with the police in the United States today are to a large extent the results of the law enforcement bureaucracy's unwillingness to surrender its prerogative of self-regulation. Police malfeasance is investigated primarily *within the bureaucracy* of law inforcement, and public police review boards are anathema to the police.

Briefly, some of the most important arguments of contemporary dissenter "outsiders" are the following. (1) Governing elites and specialized expert bureaucracies tend to become stable and in-grown in personnel and thinking. (2) In the modern age of tremendous power resources for the manipulation of both social and natural environments, policy decisions and the implementation of policies tend to become quickly irreversible—and therefore much irremediable harm, for example, a cataclysmic war or commitment of troops, can be done before "the rascals can be thrown out" in periodic elections. And, finally, (3) a narrowly empirical orientation to the solution of social problems, and reliance on constantly changing and basically tentative findings of social and physical sciences lead to good-willed, yet inhuman social policies, as, for example, our notorious mis-adventures in urban renewal in our cities.[4]

IDEOLOGY AND IDENTITY

Contemporary dissenters view with suspicion fixed and firm ideologies, which are usually rooted in the past. The reason they reject fixed ideologies is not, however, because they have replaced older ideologies with an ideology of "better things for better living through science." They confront the generation of pragmatic action with renewed concern for the inner life and tentative experimentation in linking the subjective to the social.

If we examine the meaning of the word "ideology," which originated as a Napoleonic epithet against doctrinaire Enlightenment thinking,[5] we find that it points to a set of doctrines which link strongly held, metaphysical world-views with *action;* the emphasis on the element of action is important. Ideologies, for example, Marxism, Liberalism or Fascism, eventually drive out the philosophically important and complex considerations of ethical and empirical investigation in which they have their origins, supplanting philosophical search with "common sense" dogma and emphasizing the action element of life over the speculative or contemplative. Max Weber, for example, described this general process in the particular case of the *Protestant Ethic and the Spirit of Capitalism*. Marx specifically tried to put Hegel "back on his feet" by deemphasizing the speculative, contemplative element of German philosophy in order to make action—the "changing of the world"—of prime importance for human orientation. The popularity of ideologizing has determined that intellectual search and resulting beliefs are acceptable only if the search is focused on action in the world and the beliefs composed of norms for action. It is difficult for a contemporary reader to conceive of thought otherwise than subordinated to action.

The alternative to this utilitarian thinking is not a retreat from action into pure contemplation, as the West mistakenly believes the philosophies of the East advocate. The alternative, as is so often the case when an orientation reaches its extreme expression, is to redress the balance and recognize the *equal legitimacy* of speculation and action, so that neither rules the other, but rather assume a marriage of equality.

Concern with the formation of *identity* has been the back road by which the contemporary behavioral and social sciences have sneaked in a recognition of the need for and practice of contemplation, of thought not immediately linked to action, of understanding of self and the world for its own sake. Significantly, the psychologist originator of the now popular notion of "identity" theorizes that we form our identities during a "latency" period of adolescence, a period in which demands for significant, responsible action are minimized.[6] Significant, also, is the prolongation of this "latency" period in the more recent study of identity by Kenneth Keniston.[7] Will it be long, we must ask, before the insight is admitted that men are *throughout their lives* concerned at more or less conscious, more or less verbal levels with the contemplative questions of "Who am I? Where am I going? Where have I come from?" How long will it be before it is recognized that the "latent," i.e., nonpressured, speculative life of men continues at all times alongside the necessitous, action-oriented life?

Gandhi, for one, recognized the dialectical relationship between speculative insight and action and the relative equality of these two elements of life. For Gandhi, identity, the cognitive map that stretches from home to universe, is continually formulated through the interaction of contemplation and action. One performs acts based on outer necessity and on one's inner level of moral and worldly understanding, and one alters his inner views in accord with the result of his action in the world. The discovery or recovery of moral truth is based on experiment in the world, especially on action in moral conflicts, while action is authorized by self and society on the basis of the imperfect knowledge of truth already achieved.[8]

Ideological movements, such as the labor movements of the previous century, including Marxism, are based on previous, widely recognized notions concerning the nature of man and the shape of the good society to be achieved. The belief in the natural equality of men and the importance of the material quality of life, for example, was formed during what we would call the *identity-seeking* social movements of the Renaissance and Reformation.

Today, once again in human history, large numbers of men and women find themselves insecure about where to look for truths which can be accepted as foundations for life plans, for stable notions of the nature of man and his suitable purposes, and the description of the good society and the good life.

Once again, personal insecurity expresses itself socially in the rise of *identity-seeking movements*. These movements appear in various guises with various popular titles throughout the world. In the United States, the various elements of the overall search include what the media call The New Left, The Radical Right (young and old), The Youth Rebellion, Hippies, Black Rebels, etc. The common denominator is that these groups are in the process of attempting to define meaningful goals, activities and life styles in the post-industrial or technological, society. They do this with the usual confusion to both insiders and observers attending human exploratory behavior. And, as is usual in human society, the search for identity and meaning, although a lifelong process, is especially the intense function, one might even say social responsibility, of "youth" the "trustworthy" up to the age of thirty.

Today the evidence for identity has become clouded again, as when the first urban immigrants in Europe in the 16th century and in the New World in the 19th century were confused as to whether they were men of the land or men of the city. Today, in the United States, for example, the "souped up" student generation is unsure what "adult" means, since in many areas they successfully compete with their elders; the worker who owns symbolic stock certificates is confused by the complexities of ownership and employment; the citizen who lives in a technologically administered but formally and symbolically democratic state is confused as to whether he is subject or object, citizen or datum.

COUNTER-CULTURES

The core of dissent today centers around the notions of empathy and compassion. Black and white rebels have this in common: the juggernaut of the established organization of society and government and attendant world-views emphasizes the impersonal treatment of humans, organizing them into armies of soldiers to fight wars which are personally meaningless and into armies of the poor dispatched here and there to receive the insufficient benefits and pride-wounding manipulations of mysterious bureaucracies. Empathy and compassion are two "bleeding heart" orientations which the tunnel vision of modern administration and technology finds it impossible so far to accommodate. The counter-cultures of today, in their proliferating varieties find their source in the basic problems created by the size and hyperorganized confusion of contemporary communities; to put it briefly, the essential problems are due to the integration of humans without a *human* authority which is understandable and close to the people, and the anemia of human leadership in the immensely impersonal content of giant political, economic and social institutions.

Counter-cultures are special instances of what sociologists call subcultures. Sub-cultures consist of groups of people who vary consistently enough from the norms of society — in beliefs, values and behavior — to be distinctly visible: they wear their hair differently, or talk in a slang or dialect, possess distinctive mannerisms, pursue peculiar goals — enough different aspects together to be visible once one looks closely enough. We are familiar with ethnic sub-cultures, regional, and even occupational sub-cultures (such as the military). The counter-cultures which we are pointing at often overlap familiar sub-cultures, but their specific difference lies in their resistance to assimilation, their resistance to officialdom's demands, and the political salience of their life and struggles. Where the sub-cultures of the immigrants, successful literateurs, and even the modernized Mafia seek assimilation and inconspicuousness, counter-cultures spun off from such youth movements as rock music, university and war protest, and civil rights work, resist the melting pot and resent the "success" which leads to peace medallions being sold as trinkets in five-and-tens.

The growth of counter-cultures perhaps promises for the future a positive redress for the defects of modern social organization. This may well be achieved in the shape of the development of a new core identity, around which will form the new citizens of coherent communities. Others have posited the "self-actualizing" personality as the goal for modern man, but they have neglected the realistic stages through which the multitude of men will have to travel to reach that goal. The new identity which we see slowly developing about us, which is not a utopian identity but rather an identity with new possibilities for getting off the dead center of today's confusion, we shall call the "counter-bureaucratic personality."

Briefly, a counter-bureaucratic personality can be described as possessing the awarenesses, values and motivations which we shall enumerate immediately below, and he (or she) will be concerned with maturing from a base of negative awareness, i.e., criticism, toward the construction of expanding counter-cultures in which experimentation in the formulation of alternative value-systems and life-styles and their acting out may take place — not as utopian fantasies but as neighborhoods and communities which retain links with the rest of society.

The counter-bureaucratic personality:

1) Recognizes the self-interest and inevitably distorted perceptions of the bureaucrat and the limitations of the bureaucrat's tools with respect to empathy and recognition of individual differences among members of the general classifications of people with which the bureaucracy deals.

2) Recognizes that every exception made to a general rule and every new classification introduced decreases the cost-benefit ratio of a bureaucratic function, places it at a disadvantage to other administrative units with respect to

maintaining and increasing its budget, and thus stimulates defensive actions to protect the unit's self-interest. Therefore, the counter-bureaucratic personality devises strategies such as non-cooperation to increase the costs of *not* making exceptions and *not* refining and expanding classifications. The evolution of selective service policies during the Vietnam War is an example of this.

3) Recognizes the dangers of the *mirror-image phenomenon*: that the exigencies of dividing resources and organizing resistance create the temptation to meet efficiently organized opponents with a parallel division of labor, so that established-leader meets counter-leader, established-department meets counter-department, established-technique meets counter-technique. For example, the arming of student demonstrators in the United States with shielded helmets, obnoxious gases, electrical devices, and, of course guns and knives — a distinct potential given the traditions of gimmickry and violence of the American scene — has been wisely avoided; such arming and the consequent establishment of a hierarchy with control over weapons resources would have turned the protestors into precisely the dehumanized human machine against which they have been protesting.

Since every plan of action involves a technique of some sort, counter-bureaucratic persons must search for techniques which preserve their values and further their goals. Such techniques must be confined to those which, as in Gandhian non-violent, individually accepted non-cooperation, do not develop a life of their own or distort the critical rationality and moral conscience of men to fit the technique. Counter-bureaucratic techniques must help to formulate, communicate and strengthen ideas which can attract men into a community of discourse and action productive of rich individual inner lives.

Techniques of counter-bureaucratic action must suit a double purpose. On the one hand, they must engage and modify the instruments of man which deal with man merely as a natural object (technology and impersonal organization). On the other hand, they must reflect back on their users to clarify counter-identity, increase understanding of the social context and strengthen resolve amid the tensions and temptations raised in humanizing the technological society.

The humanistic goals of counter-bureaucratic techniques may well conflict with traditional goals of efficiency and effect. This conflict may be illustrated by the well-known risks of participation in mass protests; for if the participants are not correctly prepared, and the protest not endowed with correct content and structure, the individual can lose the sense of both his own, his group's, and, yes, his enemy's essential humanity, becoming in this way a non-human vector of social forces, a carrier of the social disease of egocentric hatred. Such preparation and sense of the opponent's humanity may well dull the purely intimidating thrust of a protest, but this limitation must be accepted, repetition of protest taking the place of violent intensity.

Another source of "inefficiency" and often embarrassment to dissenters of shallow understanding is the common fragmentation of social and political resistance into varieties of groups involved in cycles of conflict and cooperation with each other. Fragmentation, it should be admitted and accepted, is inherent in meaningful resistance. Partially, this is due to the domination of instruments creating basic social integration, such as the schools and information media, by "the established," but it is due also to the very substance of the attitude of dissent and resistance. Exactly the elements of spontaneity and tentativeness which counter-cultures wish to celebrate are sources of the fragmentation of counter-politics. To be efficient, integrated, targeted to a set of fixed goals, or merely concerned with a pragmatically pursuable standard of living would be to resemble exactly the ideology and structure of the established order.

There are two essential directions in the growing activity of the counter-bureaucratic personality.

1. The creation and maintenance of "shadow" counter-cultures and counter-politics: art, education, community

The arts, poetry, painting, sculpture, prose, drama, music and cinema, are the most formidable sources of revolutionary ardor in any culture. Attracting those strong personalities which can, on their own, survive the search for altogether new visions of man and nature, the arts should be recognized as "gray eminences" evoking counter-culture and counter-politics.[9] The arts contrast the "conventional wisdom" of any time and place with intuitions of realities beyond the present and the tangible. They challenge the dullness of routine perceptions of the world and the routine deceptions of ethical cowardice. They are the sources of world-views which link the ideal to the present in terms of discontent and will to action.

Although artists rarely function effectively in the area of broad-scale and self-conscious social and political reform, they set the stage with ideas which lead to such reform. Resistance to norms established by either elite or mass pressures finds its early sources in radical criticism expressed in poetry, novels, music (including popular music), painting and the theater (including cinema), as we can see today worldwide, and especially in the United States and the Soviet Union. Consciousness of the domination of society by administrative and technological values and the presentation of counter-values in the modern context has been heralded by a number of artists of varying capacities but convergent effect, such as Ibsen, Picasso, Pasternak, Ionesco, Yevtushenko, Genet, Henry Miller, Warhol and Ginsberg.

Besides their traditional blind patronage of gadfly art, today's elites, perhaps more self-consciously, also support important sectors of a new, vital underground in education, in printed media and in life styles. The highly trained elites of the West (and numbers of them in socialist societies) live in a schizoid ambivalence produced by their high level literacy, native intelligence and curiosity confronting bureaucratic routines and organizational commitments. Evidence of a subtle love-hate relationship of such elites toward the life of the underground is observable in their self-conscious assimilation of fashion, leisure and language styles originating in marginal communities and is also observable in the values and appearance of the children of the elite — one aspect of the notorious "generation gap."[10]

The technological elites in America, aware of the extreme mental flexibility demanded by the top jobs of today and most of the management and research "jobs" of tomorrow, have chosen to create and inhabit our proliferating psuedo-cities, which are actually private school districts in which permissive, creative and individual-centered teaching inspired by Dewey, Montessori, Neil and Quaker individualism is still carried on. Those students who survive and later reject the peer competition underpinnings of this elite education are driven with a critical engine and desire for creativity, providing a source for the ranks of counter-culture and counter-politics.[11] To a growing extent, also, the institutionalized underground of black and brown ghetto schools, once stimulated by dissent, are another source of critical activists for the American society.

The children of modern education are visionary and pragmatic at the same time. They have taken seriously the oft-ignored fraternal and altruistic imperatives of both liberal and religious ethics to set an ideal direction for themselves. And the experience of science and technology from electric toy to jalopy to college physics—has sharpened their empirical rationality and confident command of nature. What the young post-industrial man is demanding is a raising of goals, a deepening of thought and an end to the irrational rhetoric of political paternalism. There *is* an end to ideology as a tool of manipulation, but there is also a new recognition of ideals with an unnerving "let's-get-on-with-it" stridency.

Another counter-activity which the established support is the journalistic underground now blossoming in new and relevant guises in the technically advanced societies. The amazing growth of the underground press in the late fifties and sixties in the United States has been supported by manufacturers and service corporations who are aware of the wealth which youth are collectively able to spend. Fitting into this niche of advertising ecology, the underground papers, supported also by film, phonograph and theatrical entrepreneurs, present information concerning the failings of the technological culture and explore the values of independence and self-realization of the counter-culture. Of course, these journals are not above creating or exaggerating news, since they are not entirely divorced from the crude journalism of the established culture. Nevertheless, the presentation of a counter-reality provides a different, subjectively significant informal education for many of the urban and suburban young, some of whom will themselves join the "free professions" and managerial elites and contribute in their turn to the survival of the counter-cultures which helped produce them.

Related to the existence of counter-education and counter-journalism is the continued existence of the opposition life-style which has traditionally been known as bohemianism. The maintenance of marginal sub-communities with a kind of "academic freedom" accruing to them in their niche is of utmost importance for the origination of creative alternatives and the maintenance of productive tensions in a society. Mere leisure is not the important thing in highly developed societies, as we are beginning to understand in studying the effects of affluence, but rather flexibility and malleability of life space and time, supported by affluence — that is, an *experimental attitude* toward the uses of leisure and affluence.[12]

2. Creative counter-action

Out of the life of the bohemias and the ghettos and youth rebellions of the suburban ghetto have come the beginnings of systems of counter-training, such as the application of Gandhian non-violence and satirical street theater to the American scene. These beginnings are evident in the experiments of SDS (Students for a Democratic Society), SNCC (Student Non-Violent Coordinating Committee), the YIP (Youth International Party), and especially in the program and training of Saul Alinsky's IAF (Industrial Areas Foundation), which contributed to the training of the California grape strike's Gandhian leader, Cesar Chavez and a large number of lesser known organizers of the poor.[13]

The strategies employed by Saul Alinsky, which evolved out of his experiences as a labor union organizer, illustrate some essential aspects of counter-action.[14] Alinsky is committed to action outside of the usual "channels" sanctified by the established. "I do not believe that democracy can survive, except as a formality," he has written, "if the ordinary citizen's part is limited to voting — if he is incapable of initiative and unable to influence the political, social and economic structures surrounding him."

The main thrust of Alinksy's action is to promote the development of home-grown leadership among the disinherited. The primary obstacle to this goal, superseding even the established opposition, is the apathetic condition of those whom he is trying to stimulate into effective participation. "The daily lives of [the poor] leave them with little energy or enthusiasm for realizing principles from which they themselves will derive little practical benefit," he says, meaning, for example, the fight for free speech. "They know that with their educational and economic handicaps they will be exceptions indeed if they can struggle into a middle-class neighborhood or a white collar job."

Instead of the usual civil rights appeals of the conventional neighborhood organizer, Alinsky appeals to the immediate self-interests of the local residents and to their resentment and distrust of the outside world to stimulate local action and leadership. He insists that the aid of his Foundation be used to make the local community self-sufficient, not to keep it dependent. He will not enter a community unless he is invited by something approaching a cross-section of the population, and he usually insists, as a condition of entering, that the community itself, no matter how poor, take over the full financial responsibility for organizing within a period of three years.

Once Alinsky's representatives (who are usually few in number for any project) enter a community, the process of building an organization follows a fairly standard pattern.

Organizers from the Industrial Areas Foundation filter through the neighborhood, asking questions and, more important, listening in bars, at street corners, in stores, in peoples' homes—in short, wherever people are talking—to discover the residents' specific grievances;

At the same time, the organizers try to spot the individuals and the groups on which people seem to lean for advice or to which they go for help: a barber, a minister, a mailman, a restaurant owner, etc. — the "indigenous" leaders;

The organizers get these leaders together, discuss the irritations, frustrations, and problems animating the neighborhood, and suggest the ways in which power might be used to ameliorate or solve them;

A demonstration or series of demonstrations are put on to show how power can be used. These may take a variety of forms: a rent strike against slum landlords, a cleanup campaign against a notorious trouble spot, etc. What is crucial is that meetings and talk, the bedrock on which middle-class organizations founder, are avoided; the emphasis is on action, and on action that can lead to visible results.

As a result of these steps, a new organization begins to take form as a supergroup comprising many existing member groups—churches, block clubs, businessmen's associations — and of new groups that are formed purely as a means of joining the larger organization. As the organization begins to move under its own steam, the IAF men gradually phase themselves out and local leaders and local paid staffers take over.

The main emphases of Alinsky's method are participation, action and visible results. For example, in the Woodlawn project in Chicago:

Wherever a substantial majority of the tenants could be persuaded to act together, a tenants' group was formed which demanded that the landlord, within some stated period of time, clear up physical violations that made occupancy of buildings hazardous or uncomfortable—broken windows, plumbing that did not work, missing steps from staircases, etc. When the landlords ignored the ultimatum, TWO [The Woodlawn Organization] organized a rent strike. To dramatize the strike on one block where several adjoining buildings were involved, residents spelled out "This is a Slum" in huge letters on the outside of the building. If the landlord remained recalcitrant, groups of pickets were dispatched to march up and down in front of the landlord's own home, carrying placards that read "Your Neighbor is a Slumlord." The picketing provided a useful outlet for the anger the tenants felt, and gave them an opportunity, for the first time in their lives, to use their color in an affirmative way. For as soon as the Negro pickets appeared in a white suburban block, the landlord was deluged with phone calls from angry neighbors demanding that he do something to call the pickets off. Within a matter of hours landlords who were picketed were on the phone with TWO, agreeing to make repairs.

Alinsky's development of counter-cultures and counter-bureaucratic personalities is to a degree successful because its main focus is not in the long run on merely increased consumption standards or on narrow-minded "efficiency." Its deepest goal and effect is to develop inwardly in concrete individuals that most difficult to attain dimension of self-perception, which social scientists glibly refer to as a "feeling of efficacy." A "feeling of efficacy" is in reality a complex constellation of perceptions and conceptions which are nourished in the deep roots of identity and personal view of the world. Without developed notions of who one is, where one is, identification of and relation to general values, and a realization of the concerns and actions of others, "efficacy" is a hollow construct of data processors, an attitude which may be alive in a person at one time and yet easily shattered in any real encounter with a resourceful opposition.

The effect of an Alinsky-type action-project is to draw people out of their somnolent routines and activate them in demanding interactions which require self-discipline and a sense of responsibility towards others. The waste of personal disorganization slowly disappears in the community pursuit of a meaningful goal; appointments begin to be kept and the skills of meaningful debate are learned, for example. As one newly evolved leader said in Chicago: "This organization has given me a sense of accomplishing something—the only time in my life I've had that feeling." As individuals learn to organize their own lives they learn to relate to others. "We've learned to live together and act as a community," another recently developed activist commented, "now I know people all over Woodlawn, and I've been in all the churches. Two years ago I didn't know a soul."

This creative action, though by no means perfect, consciously confronts the deep questions of how to awaken people immersed in a mass society to the reality of their own existence and the consequentiality of their own problems; how to organize without destroying the individual or the natural community; and how to establish a communal feeling based neither on simple emotional gratification nor on merely mechanical pursuit of material goals. It may not approach a community of love, but it sets the stage for one.

Possibly the most potentially effective kind of creative counter-action, which many have called for and few engaged in, is the confrontation of established culture at the mid-level by its products — its youth. It has been easier for white youth to go to the poor in the ghettos than for the same youth to act on adult whites in the world of corporations and suburbs which awaits those who cannot take the route of permanent marginality. One avenue which has hardly been explored is transmuting "adult education" in the suburbs to a form of counter-education to combat the stereotyped thinking and political isolation of the white ghettos. This could be accomplished by training those who can "pass" in the suburbs, such as graduate students, in the techniques of patient listening and sensitive dialogue which are necessary for the "socio-therapy" of mass man.

Those who find themselves entering the established culture with strains in conscience and perception should renounce too-easy pessimistic alienation in favor of relating to those who share their values and organizing to make demands on their environment as they grow into it. For example, demands which are in search of support are raised by the ground-up development of "new towns" by corporations such as General Electric, demands for aesthetic quality, human scale, and participatory governmental structures. Public finance, which has been a dull anathema to most free spirits, must be recognized as the life blood of social rehabilitation and justice in progressive reform. The seductions of convenience, comfort and conformity can only be successfully countered by the pleasures and rewards of creatively shaping one's environment. The corporation and the city as *machines* must be humanized by the happy inefficiencies of permanent resistance on the part of those who understand the joys of fellowship and idealism.

Concerning the ultimates, no one has ultimate answers. What perfection is, whether it lies in the future of mankind or in the excellence of individuals, is for each person to answer for himself. Counter-politics does not offer utopia: *it attempts to provide a context of stimulation for individuals in which they can grow through significant experiment to develop their own goals and achievements.*

Counter-politics is a non-oppressive, non-bureaucratic, spontaneous association of individuals developing and acting out experimental strategies of resistance to the coercive, impersonal and inflexible operation of the technological order as it appears in modern and modernizing societies. Counter-politics provides a context for individual development of the personality. To provide such a context it attempts to realize and exploit all the flexibility of ordering, production, distribution and communication that the developing technologies of machines and information are making feasible.

If efficiency and stability are not the hallmark of counter-politics, if lack of production and success depress and disaffect members, there are at least two saving considerations balancing this: Those overly concerned with efficiency, production and stability already have one foot in the opposite camp of petrification and non-being. Secondly, new recruits are perpetually available, the world over, from the young, who still experience that search for personal identity which is the microcosmic reflection of man's search for cosmic identity.

As the philosophies produced by old battles fade in relevance, new ideas and experiments create a vital period of change: the seedtime of a new republic predicated on a human life for human beings.

Notes

[1] Lewis Yablonsky, *The Hippie Trip* (New York: Pegasus, 1968); Paul Jacobs and Saul Landau, *The New Radicals* (New York; Vintage, 1966); Kenneth Keniston, *Young Radicals* (New York: Harcourt, Brace & World, Inc., 1968); Jack Newfield, *A Prophetic Minority* (New York: Signet Books, 1966).

[2] David B. Truman, *The Government Process: Political Interests and Public Opinion* (New York: Alfred A. Knopf, 1951); Lester W. Milbrath, *The Washington Lobbyists* (Chicago: Rand McNally & Company, 1963); E. E. Schattschneider, *Politics, Pressures, and the Tariff* (New York: Prentice-Hall, Inc., 1935).

[3] Joan V. Bondurant, *The Conquest of Violence* (Berkeley: University of California, 1963); Mohandas K. Gandhi, *The Essential Gandhi*, ed. by Louis Fischer (New York: Vintage Books, 1963); Louis Fischer, *The Life of Mahatma Gandhi* (New York: Collier Books, 1962).

[4] Paul Jacobs and Saul Landau, *The New Radicals* (New York: Vintage, 1966); Stephen Spender, *The Year of the Young Rebels* (New York: Random House, 1969).

[5] George Lichtheim, *The Concept of Ideology and Other Essays* (New York: Random House, 1967).

[6] Erik H. Erikson, "The Problem of Identity," in *Identity and Anxiety*, ed. by Maurice R. Stein, Arthur J. Vidich and David M. White (New York: The Free Press, 1960); Erik H. Erikson, *Young Man Luther* (New York: W. W. Norton & Co., 1964).

[7] Kenneth Keniston, *op. cit.*

[8] See note 3.

[9] John Berger, *Art and Revolution* (New York: Pantheon Books, 1969).

[10] John McCabe, ed., *Dialogue on Youth* (New York: The Bobbs-Merrill Company, Inc., 1967); J. I. Simmons and Barry Winograd, *It's Happening: a portrait of the youth scene today* (Santa Barbara, Calif.: Marc-Laird Publications, 1966).

[11] Editors of *Look Magazine, Suburbia* (New York: Cowles Education Corporation, (1968); John R. Seeley, R. Alexander Sim and Elizabeth W. Loosley, *Crestwood Heights* (New York: Basic Books, 1967); Maurice R. Stein, *The Eclipse of Community* (Princeton: Princeton University Press, 1960); Robert C. Wood, *Suburbia* (Boston: Houghton Mifflin Company, 1958).

[12] Robert Theobald, ed., *The Guaranteed Income* (New York: Doubleday & Company, 1966); Erich Fromm, *The Revolution of Hope* (New York: Harper & Row, 1968).

[13] Jack Newfield, *A Prophetic Minority* (New York: Signet Books, 1966); Charles E. Silberman, *Crisis in Black and White* (New York: Vintage Books, 1964); Howard Zinn, *SNCC, The New Abolitionists* (Boston: Beacon Press, 1964).

[14] Most of the following information concerning Alinsky's programs and strategies, including quotations, is drawn from Charles E. Silberman's valuable book, *Crisis in Black and White,* Ch. X.

The demonstrations and activities of the student movement have often led, it is no secret, to violent confrontations between students and authorities. Just who is responsible for initiating the violence is characteristically in doubt in these incidents, the students usually citing police provocation and brutality and the authorities usually claiming that unruly students gave the police ample cause. An entire scenario of charge and countercharge, violence and escalated violence has become predictable in these confrontations. Sidney Hook is a professor of philosophy and well-known author on the faculty of the New York University. In the following article he is critical of the student movement in general. But more particularly, Professor Hook aims to assign responsibility for campus violence.

Responsibility and Violence in the Academy

Sidney Hook

Wherever American educators meet today, there is one theme of overriding concern that shadows their deliberations even when it is not on the agenda of discussion. This is the mounting wave of lawlessness, often cresting into violence, that has swept so many campuses. Shortly after the riotous events at the University of California at Berkeley in 1964, I predicted that in consequence of the faculty's refusal to condemn the student seizure of Sproul Hall, the administration building, American higher education would never be the same again, that a turning point had been reached in the pattern of its development. I confess, however, to surprise at the rapidity of the change, if not its direction, and by the escalation of the violence accompanying it.

Equally significant in determining the changing intellectual climate of our universities are some of the secondary consequences of the accelerating disorders. Among them are infectious, sometimes paralyzing, fear in administrative ranks lest their campuses erupt; confusion, bewilderment, and divided loyalties among faculties, together with some *Schadenfreude* over the humiliation of their administrations at the hands of disre-

Reprinted by permission of the author and publisher from Sidney Hook, "Who Is Responsible for Campus Violence?" *Saturday Review,* April 19, 1969, pp. 22-25, 54, 55. Copyright 1969 Saturday Review, Inc.

spectful student militants; outright encouragement of student violence by disaffected, younger members of teaching staffs; sustained apathy among the majority of students whose education has been interrupted by radical activists; and the mixture of rage and disgust among the general public whose political repercussions already have been damaging to the cause of higher education.

In California, the indignation of citizens over campus violence has brought Governor Reagan to the peak of his popularity. More alarming, proposed bonds for educational expansion have been voted down. Of approximately 186,000 communications received to date by the trustees and colleges in the state system more than 98 per cent were against campus disruption. More than seventy separate bills, some of dubious wisdom, have been introduced in the Senate and Assembly to deal with disruption of campus activities by students and faculty. Similar bills are in the hoppers of other state legislatures, twenty in Wisconsin alone.

The situation in the East, although not marked by the same degree of physical violence (arson, bombings, beatings), educationally is equally grave. Some recent incidents at New York University, and its sister institution in New York City, Columbia, mark the extent to which violence has invaded the university and rational disciplinary restraints have been eroded.

Last December, Nguyen Huu Chi, the Ambassador of South Vietnam, visited New York University as an invited guest speaker. At a given signal, members of the Students for a Democratic Society from NYU and Columbia invaded the hall, stormed the stage, physically assaulted the Ambassador, and completely disrupted the meeting. Thereupon, they proceeded to another floor, battered down the doors leading to the podium of a meeting-hall where James Reston, executive editor of *The New York Times*, was about to deliver the annual Homer Watts Lecture before an audience of 600 under the auspices of the Alumni Association. The rampaging students spurned an invitation from Mr. Reston to state their objections to what they thought he was going to say, and by threats of violence forced the cancellation of the meeting.

Two students were suspended pending action by the University Senate, and after a careful hearing, at which they refused to appear, were expelled in March. The leaders of the SDS publicly applauded the disruptions, declaring that they disapproved of the positions of the government of South Vietnam and *The New York Times* on the Vietnam war. Most shocking of all, nine members of the faculty at Washington Square in a letter to the student paper endorsed the breaking up of the meeting of the South Vietnamese Ambassador. Although they called the disruption of Mr. Reston's meeting "unfortunate" (as if it were an accident!), they strongly condemned President James M. Hester on the ground that, "we do not believe that the disruption of the Reston speech warrants suspension of the students." They had not a single word of forthright or vigorous criticism of the SDS attack on Chi. The effect of their letter can only be to incite further student violence. It is noteworthy that many meetings and rallies *in support* of the Vietcong and North Vietnam have been held without incident.

At Columbia, Acting President Andrew W. Cordier had petitioned the courts through the Dean of the Law School to dismiss the criminal charges against the Columbia students arrested for serious offenses last spring. The court was assured that the University would apply appropriate disciplinary measures to those guilty. The cases were therefore dismissed. In December, a Columbia College disciplinary tribunal of two teachers —one of them an instructor serving as chairman—two students, and an administrator decided to impose no penalties on the students whatsoever, despite the fact that the students proudly admitted violating University regulations and, to boot, denied the authority of the tribunal to judge them. This incredible decision was taken in order "to re-establish student relationship to the university." These students had won complete amnesty for actions that had been deemed worthy of criminal prosecution when they had occurred. Twice hearings in the Law School were violently disrupted by invading SDS students, and the faculty members of the panel were insulted with gutter obscenities. No one even dared to suggest that disciplinary action be taken against this new wave of disruption. The administrators and many of the faculty of Columbia University for months were deeply distraught. It appeared to some observers as if the University petition to have the criminal charges dropped against the students was a ruse by the administration to ingratiate itself with the militant students, to prove its "good will" toward them and, in this way, buy some campus peace. If so, the strategy failed. It provoked only contempt, jeers, and a stream of foul, four-letter epithets from the militants who held out for complete amnesty from the outset.

Encouraged by the amnesty, the Columbia SDS, with aid from outsiders, began to disrupt classes; a leaflet was distributed to justify such "classroom intervention." In some instances, students tore the notes out of their teachers' hands; in others, they shouted them down. By December, according to one source, as many as thirteen "interventions" had been perpetrated. No action was taken either by the faculty or by the administration. An inquiry from an education editor, who had gotten wind of the situation, went unanswered. No one on campus would talk for publication.

Their appetites whetted by the complaisance or timidity of their victims, the students of the SDS escalated the scale of their disruptions. *The Columbia Spectator* of February 27 reported that "Members of the SDS yesterday interrupted nearly forty classes in six University buildings."

Finally, on March 10, a public statement in response to these outrages was issued by a hundred, mostly senior, professors. In it they declared that the University had an obligation to defend itself against hooliganism. Referring to the policy of amnesty, they criticized the abandonment of disciplinary proceedings for previous serious infractions. President Cordier immediately rushed to endorse the statement taking care, at the same time, to minimize the number of class disruptions, but failing to explain why he had remained silent about the breaking up of classes in December, although he was aware of it, and why he had welcomed the abandonment of disciplinary proceedings.

Punitive legislation, either federal or state, would be undesirable in this situation for many reasons. It would tie the Government too closely to campus events and discipline at a time when a section of the academic community believes that governmental presence is already too obtrusive. Further, the effectiveness of such legislation would depend upon the cooperation of administration and faculty in enforcing it. Most important, existing statutes of the University, and the criminal law, already provide sufficient penalties (suspension, expulsion, fines, and jail for trespassing and assault) to meet disruption, if they were enforced.

Why have they not been enforced? Why has the defense of faculties against these brazen attempts to violate their academic freedom, not only by disruption, but by demands to control the content and personnel of instruction, been so feeble and long-delayed? Why, as one professor observed who had helped the Berkeley rebels triumph in 1964, have administrations and faculties behaved like buffalos being shot, "looking on with interest when another of their number goes down, without seriously thinking, that they may be next"?

Although the major causes of student unrest are outside the universities (Vietnam, the urban crisis, the black revolution) and cannot be solved by them alone, the way in which unrest is expressed, whether creatively or violently, can be influenced by the ideas and attitudes brought to it. This is particularly true today. For although comparatively few institutions have been the scene of violent demonstrations as serious as those at Columbia, Berkeley, and San Francisco State, there is hardly a college or university in the country in which there is not some marked uneasiness, some movement among students toward direct action on the verge of exploding into sit-downs, sit-ins, and other forms of mass violations of rules and regulations suddenly discovered to be as silly, anachronistic, or authoritarian as some of them undoubtedly are. But what struck me about the mood of the students in scores of colleges I visited is that even when these rules and regulations were *not* being enforced, and student conduct was as free and uninhibited as on campuses not subject to these objectionable rules, there was an insistence on their abolition — despite evidence that the formal abolition was likely to stir up a hornet's nest among alumni or townsfolk or state legislatures. This testified partly to student impatience with the "hypocrisy" of tolerating laws that were not being enforced, but even more to the presence of a desire to precipate a showdown with authority, to be where the action is, to have the nation's television cameras focused on the local scene and on the local leaders of dissent. One of the undoubted effects of the kind of coverage given campus disorders by the mass media in their alleged desire merely to report these occurrences is to encourage them by exaggerating their scope and glorifying the heroes of the moment.

Frenzy and excitement among student bodies have always been contagious. Last year, events on some campuses, even chants and slogans, broadcast at once, had a direct influence on happenings on other campuses. That is why the universities of this country are in this "all together," and why capitulation to extremism anywhere weakens resistance to extremism everywhere.

To an already volatile situation must be added the Students for a Democratic Society, an explosive element which claims tens of thousands of militant activists in hundreds of chapters. The SDS is an openly social revolutionary organization, dedicated not to educational reform wherever needed, but to a strategy of politicalization of a university by the tactics of physically violent confrontation. Its operating maxim could well be, "the bloodier the confrontation, the better for our cause, and the worse for the Establishment." Its presence is sufficient to convert a situation in which problems exist into a permanent educational crisis. The members of the SDS are ideologically confused but they constitute a hard, fanatical core of highly politicized individuals among student bodies, extremely skillful in the arts of generating conflicts and disruption through agitation and manipulation of mass organizations. They and their congenials among the New Left, including their faculty allies, would be hard to sustain by wise and enlightened administrators and faculties. Unfortunately, these traits have not been conspicuously in evidence even in places where one would expect them. This is suggested by the fact that the worst excesses on our campuses have occurred at the most liberal institutions. The University of California, San Francisco State College, the University of Colorado, Roosevelt College, Columbia University, and New York University—these read like the beginning of a roll call of the centers of intellectual dissent, experiment, and even educational permissiveness in American life. Events on these campuses, as well as at Swarthmore and Oberlin, reveal the absurdity of the claim that the student revolution has been the consequence of dissatisfaction with the educational curriculum.

Educational changes are often desirable, but it was not a failure to introduce them that provoked the recent outbreaks of student violence, or encouraged continuance of these outbreaks. Much more warranted, as an explanation of the failure to meet the initial challenge of student disruption and to stem its growth, is a mistaken theory of liberalism, a reliance upon what I call *ritualistic* rather than realistic liberalism — a doctrinaire view which does not recognize the difference between belief or doctrine and behavior, and which refuses to grasp the fact, obvious in law and common sense, that incitement to violence is a form of behavior. It is a view which does not realize that although order is possible without justice, justice is impossible without order.

The realistic liberal outlook in education cannot be strictly identified with the liberal outlook in politics because the academic community cannot be equated with the political community. Although we may recognize the autonomy of the academic community, such autonomy cannot be complete since the political community in many ways underwrites its operation. But what both communities have in common is the centrality of the notion of due process.

Due process in the political community is spelled out in terms of specific mechanisms through which, out of the clash of public opinions, public policy is forged. Where due process is violated, consent is coerced, and cannot be freely given. The unlimited spectrum of ideas remains unabridged in the political community up to the point of advocacy, but not to the point of violent action or the incitement of violence. The forces of the state, the whole apparatus of restraint and punishment, enter the scene where the freedom of choice of the citizenry is threatened by extralegal activity.

Due process in the academic community is reliant upon the process of rationality. It cannot be the same as the process in the political community so far as the *mechanisms* of determining the outcome of rational activity. For what controls the nature and direction of due process in the academic community is derived from its educational goal — the effective pursuit, discovery, publication, and teaching of the truth. In the political community all men are equal as citizens not only as participants in, and contributors to, the political process, but as voters and decision-makers on the primary level. Not so in the academic community. What qualifies a man to enjoy equal human or political rights does not qualify him to teach equally with others or even to study equally on every level. There is an authoritative, *not* authoritarian, aspect of the process of teaching and learning that depends not upon the person or power of the teacher, but upon the authority of his knowledge, the cogency of his method, the scope and depth of his experience. But whatever the differences in the power of making decisions flowing from legitimate differences in educational authority, there is an equality of learners, whether of teachers or students, in the rational processes by which knowledge is won, methods developed, and experience enriched.

In a liberal educational regimen, everything is subject to the rule of reason, and all are equals as questioners and participants. Whoever interferes with academic due process either by violence or threat of violence places himself outside the academic community, and incurs the sanctions appropriate to the gravity of his offense from censure to suspension to expulsion. The peculiar deficiency of the ritualistic liberal educational establishments is the failure to meet violations of rational due process with appropriate sanctions or to meet them in a timely and intelligent manner. There is a tendency to close an eye to expressions of lawless behavior on the part of students who, in the name of freedom, deprive their fellow students of the freedom to pursue their studies. It is as if the liberal administration sought to appease the challenge to its continued existence by treating such incidents as if they had never happened.

There is no panacea that can be applied to all situations. It is not a question of a hard line or a soft line, but of an intelligent line. It is easy to give advice from hindsight, to be wise and cocksure after the event. But it is always helpful for the faculty to promulgate in advance fair guidelines for action, so that students will know what to expect. In general, no negotiations should be conducted under threat of coercion, or when administrators or faculty are held captive. In general, no amnesty for lawlessness or violence should be offered. In general, organizations that refuse to accept disciplinary principles worked out by official representatives of the student body and faculty should be denied recognition and the use of university facilities.

As a rule, it is the first step which is *not* taken that costs so much. Both at Berkeley and Columbia, failure to act decisively at the first disruption of university functions undoubtedly contributed to the students' expectation that they could escalate their lawlessness with impunity. Sometimes the attempt to retrieve a failure to meet student disruption promptly and fairly results in a greater failure.

When student defiance of reasonable rules and regulations is pointedly and continuously ignored, and then subsequently disciplined, the consequence may be worse than if the first infraction had been totally amnestied. Unnecessary delay in initiating the disciplinary measures, however mild, incurred by the infraction of rules, can make it appear to large numbers of the uninformed that these students are the innocent victims of vindictive and gratuitous punishment.

The fourth and largest illegal trespass at Berkeley—the seizure of Sproul Hall — came as a consequence of the summons to four student leaders to appear before the Disciplinary Committee several weeks after they had committed the violations for which they were being called to account. There was a similar situation at Columbia. The first action which presaged the events of 1968 occurred in 1965 when students forcibly prevented the NROTC award ceremony. In 1967, "the administration canceled the ceremony citing insufficent time to prepare against violence" (*The Cox Report*). Violence seemed to pay off. A handful of students had forced their will on the University at the cost of seven letters of censure. After the ban on indoor demonstrations had been promulgated at Columbia — both because it interfered with the teaching of classes and because of the dangers of violence between opposing groups of demonstrating students — it was not enforced on three important occasions where it was clearly violated. When the ban was finally invoked, it seemed to many who were unaware of the past history of student provocation and university restraint that the disciplinary action, even if feeble, was arbitrary. It is widely believed, even by some of the SDS members, that if the Columbia University authorities had moved vigorously to enforce existing regulations against the lawless trespass and destruction of property by the small group that sparked the seizure of buildings on the first day, subsequent developments would have been avoided. For campus sentiment was overwhelmingly hostile to the student rebels at the outset.

The ironical aspect of the situation is that despite the liberal character of the institutions in question, a false view of what it means to be liberal seems to provoke or to exacerbate disturbances on the campus. In certain faculty quarters especially, it is believed that the very nature of a liberal educational community necessitates, independent of any student action, an absolute taboo against physical or police sanctions. At a large metropolitan university during a student strike called by a small and rabidly fanatical minority to protest the dismissal of an administrator guilty of vicious antisemitic incitement, a faculty group tried to get a resolution adopted pledging the university "not to call upon the police *under any circumstances*." Had such a resolution been adopted it would have given those who made a cult of violence assurances in advance that they could carry on as they pleased no matter what the cost to life, limb, and university property. It would have encouraged the very violence those who favored the resolution professed to deplore. "What's so tragic about the destruction of a little property?" one professor inquired. He only shrugged when a colleague sardonically added, "Or a little fire?" In the academy as elsewhere there is no substitute for common sense. As it was, fire hoses were cut, elevators jammed to a point where their operation was dangerous to life and limb and their operation temporarily suspended, and the auditorium in the student center set afire.

Some faculty members see truly, in the words of a perceptive member of the Columbia staff, that "the authority of a university is not a civil authority, but a moral one." But he mistakenly concludes that the disruptive activities of students "can only be contained by faculty and by other students, not by the police." This is a morality not of this world but of the hand-wringing, ineffectual spirit that leaves this world and its universities in possession of callow, ruthless fanatics prepared to threaten or use violence.

"Confrontation politics" in the moral academic community "is inadmissible," we are assured by those who love everybody and want to be loved by everybody. Excellent! But what if some students do what is inadmissable? What if they resort to pillage, vandalism, personal assault? What if the torch of learning in some hands becomes a torch of arson? To say that only other students can contain them, and not the police, is to forget that once we leave the world of the spirit, this is an invitation to civil war.

Wars of containment, as we know, can be quite bloody. The police may have to be called in to prevent students from containing (and maiming) each other. And like all sentimentalizing in this cruel world, the fear of relying on the police in *any* circumstances to resist the militant politics of confrontation, which brutally scorns the rationalities of academic due process, is to rely upon the politics of capitulation. It is administrative and/or faculty cowardice masquerading as educational statesmanship. It receives and deserves the contempt with which the storm troopers of the SDS greet it as they prepare for the next phase in the escalating cycle of disruption and violence.

In the light of recent events on campuses and the reactions they have inspired, it should be obvious that the SDS is *not* a Trojan horse in American higher education. It is today the "armed warrior" of anti-education. It makes no secret of its desire to destroy American democracy and the universities that it considers as a faithful replica of that iniquitous society. No, the Trojan horse in American higher education is the rickety structure of doctrinaire thought that shelters the SDS even when it takes official responsibility for violent actions, gives it a free field for operation, retreats before the politics of confrontation, and either shrinks from applying fairly and firmly the rules of reason that should bind the academic community, or interprets them as if they had no more restraining force in times of crisis than ropes of sand.

The facts about the SDS are well known. It has the virtues of openness as well as courage. It takes public responsibility for its action of violence, and promises more to come. For it, the campuses are the front-line barricades in total war against American society. Persistent refusal to recognize these facts has prevented administrators and faculties from preparing proper defensive measures to keep the universities free. This refusal is sometimes undergirded by the odd belief that disciplinary action against an organization that officially organizes violence on campus is incompatible with the conception of a university as a "free market place of ideas." The conjunction of attitude and belief is a forerunner of educational disaster. This is illustrated by the pattern of events within the last two years at the University of Colorado. It culminated early this March in the most violent outbreak in the history of the University, when a guest of the University, President S. I. Hayakawa of San Francisco State

College, was almost mobbed by bottle-throwing members of the SDS and their Black Nationalist allies to prevent him from speaking. Despite its previous actions of violence and the absence of any pledge to forswear violence in the future, the SDS had been reinstated on the campus on the ground that the University must serve "as a free market of ideas." The SDS promptly showed that its purpose was precisely to destroy the University as a free market of ideas.

The detailed story is too long to relate here, but it can serve as a paradigm case of high-minded blunder, panicky ineptitude, and self-righteous obtuseness on the part of some regents, administrators, and faculty members who are convinced that true tolerance requires that we tolerate the actively intolerant.

In the last analysis, it is the faculties who are responsible for the present state of American universities—responsible because of their apathy for what has developed in the past, and for missed educational opportunities. Despite what is said by outsiders, the faculties of most universities possess great powers which they have so far been reluctant to use. No policy in education can succeed without their support. Theirs is the primary responsibility for upholding academic freedom. Now that American higher education is at bay, challenged as it has never been before by forces *within* the academic community, the faculties must marshal the courage to put freedom first, and to defend it accordingly.

At the same time, as they move to safeguard the integrity of the educational process, faculties should, wherever they are not already doing so, undertake a critical review of all aspects of the curriculum and university life. Provisions should be made for the airing and public discussion of all student grievances. Students should be invited to assess existing courses, methods of teaching, the effectiveness of their teachers, and to make proposals for new courses.

It is a libel on American educators to imply that they are hostile to educational change. Most past criticism has inveighed against them for making curricular revisions too readily at the first cries of "relevance" by pressure groups. Educational crackpots, including some headline-hunting administrators, are now rushing to claim that had their curricular panaceas been adopted, student violence would have been avoided. They assiduously ignore the fact that the extremist student groups are trying to bring down bigger game.

John Dewey was fond of saying that in the modern world there is no such thing as the "status quo." Change in education, as in society, is inescapable. The only questions are whether the direction and content of change are sound, and what the rate and magnitude of change should be. Men of good will may differ about the answers. But no matter how profound the differences, they do not justify the resort to violence and the threat of violence to impose solutions. In a secular society, the places where human beings assemble to inquire and to reason together should be regarded as sacred ground. Whoever desecrates it, should feel the disapproval of the entire community.

Revolution and Counterrevolution

Do the conditions described in the last chapter — student unrest, urban rioting and black power—add up to a new American revolution? Certainly the rhetoric of blacks and students is liberally seasoned with the term "revolution," and undeniably America is being asked by these dissenters to make many significant changes. But the crucial question is whether the changes being pressed are so fundamental and profound that they necessitate restructuring of our basic institutions. Professor Zbigniew Brzezinski who has studied revolutionary situations in other countries thinks revolution in America is not imminent. A former member of the State Department Policy Planning Council, author of Ideology and Power in Soviet Politics, *and* America in the Technotronic Age, *Professor Brzezinski casts some needed light on the meaning of the concept "revolution" and assesses the prospects of revolutionary forces in America.*

Zbigniew Brzezinski

A revolutionary situation typically arises when values of a society are undergoing a profound change. The crisis in values in its turn is linked to profound socioeconomic changes, both accelerating them and reacting to them. For example, the transition from an agrarian to an industrial society produced very basic changes in outlook, both on the part of the elites ruling the changing societies and also of the social forces transformed by the changes and produced by them. Similarly it can be argued that today in America the industrial era is coming to an end and America is becoming a technetronic society, that is a society in which technology, especially electronic communications and computers, is prompting basic social changes (see "The American Transition," *The New Republic*, December 23, 1967). This automatically produces a profound shift in the prevailing values.

The crisis of values has several political consequences of relevance to revolutionary processes. First of all, it prompts ambivalent concessions by the authorities in power. The authorities do not

Reprinted by permission of the author and publisher from Zbigniew Brzezinski, "Revolution and Counterrevolution," *The New Republic,* 157 (June 1, 1968), 23-25.

fully comprehend the nature of the changes they are facing, but they are no longer sufficiently certain of their values to react in an assertive fashion—concessionism thus becomes the prevailing pattern of their behavior. Secondly, increasingly self-assertive revolutionary forces begin an intensive search for appealing issues. The purpose is to further radicalize and revolutionize the masses and to mobilize them against the *status quo*. Thirdly, limited claims begin to be translated into more fundamental claims. Expedient escalationism of demands is typically a revolutionary tactic, designed deliberately to aggravate the situation and to compensate for initial revolutionary weakness.

A revolutionary situation is thus a combination of objective and subjective forces. Revolutions do not come by themselves, they have to be made. On the other hand, unless a ripe revolutionary situation exists, revolutionary efforts can be abortive. Abortive efforts can contribute to the creation of a revolutionary situation, but a truly revolutionary situation arises only when a society is ill at ease with itself and when established values, legitimacy and authority are beginning to be seriously questioned.

In that setting, confrontations, the test of will and power, begin to be more and more frequent. Revolutionary forces engage in repeated probes to test the reactions of established authorities, while searching for appealing issues around which to rally. The initial phase of the revolutionary process thus involves a protracted game of hide-and-seek. The authorities try as skillfully as they can to avoid a head-on confrontation: they concede in a limited fashion while trying to avoid confronting fundamental issues. The revolutionary leaders, by their probes, seek to identify weak spots and to provoke a head-on, direct clash.

The critical phase occurs when a weak spot has been identified, appealing issues articulated, and the probe becomes a confrontation. At this stage the purpose of revolutionary activity is to legitimize violence. If the initial act of violence is suppressed quickly by established authorities, the chances are that the revolutionary act itself will gain social opprobrium; society generally tends to be conservative, even in a situation of crisis of values. Thus a revolutionary act is likely to be condemned by most, provided it is rapidly suppressed. If the revolutionary act endures, then automatically it gains legitimacy with the passage of time. Enduring violence thus becomes a symbol of the authorities' disintegration and collapse, and it prompts in turn further escalation of support for the revolutionary act.

Simply by enduring defiantly, the initial act of revolutionary self-assertion becomes legitimized and it contributes to further escalation of support as latent social grievances surface and are maximized. In every society latent grievances exist and a social crisis brings them to the forefront. Moreover, equally important is the manufacturing of grievances and demands to express unconscious resentment of authority. Most individuals and groups to some extent resent authority; a defiantly enduring revolutionary situation brings out this unconscious resentment and prompts the manufacturing of grievances and demands which are designed to define an anti-authority posture.

An important role in this revolutionary process is played by legitimist reformers and intellectuals. Intellectuals by their very nature are unwilling to pick sides, since they are better at identifying gray than siding with black and white. In a revolutionary situation, they are particularly concerned with not being stamped as counterrevolutionary conservatives. They are thus desirous of proving their reformist convictions, even at the cost of compromising their posture as reformers and becoming more closely identified with revolutionaries. Moreover, many intellectuals tend to be frustrated power-seekers, and a revolutionary situation creates a ready-made opportunity for the exercise of vicarious statesmanship.

In a revolutionary situation, their desire for power yet their inability to side with one or the other side prompts intellectuals to adopt a third posture, namely that of interposing themselves between the revolutionary and anti-revolutionary forces. In doing so, they often place their intellect in service of emotions rather than using emotions in the service of intellect. Many are highly excitable; their political weakness and lack of organization inclines them increasingly in a revolutionary situation to rely on demagogy. At the same time, accustomed generally to dealing with established authorities, they are more experienced in coping with the authorities than with the revolutionary forces. Thus, in the process of interposing themselves, they are inclined to apply most of their pressure against the established authority, with which they have many links, than equally against established authorities and the revolutionary forces on behalf of reformist appeals. In effect, irrespective of their subjective interests, the legitimist reformers and intellectuals in a revolutionary situation objectively become the tools of the revolutionary forces, thus contributing to further aggravation of the revolutionary situation and radicalizing the overall condition.

When faced with a revolutionary situation, the established authorities typically commit several errors. *First of all*, because they are status quo oriented, they display an incapacity for immediate effective response. Their traditional legalism works against them. Faced with a revolutionary situation, instead of striking immediately and effectively, they tend to procrastinate, seeking refuge in legalistic responses. *Second*, in so doing, they tend to opt for negotiating with the new interposing element, thus obscuring the clear-cut confrontation. An early confrontation would work to the advantage of the authorities, since mass support begins to shift to the revolutionaries only after the situation has been radicalized. *Third*, while negotiating with the interposing element, they tend to dribble out concessions rather than to make them in one dramatic swoop, thereby gaining broad support. *Fourth*, when finally force is employed, the authorities rarely think ahead to post-use-of-force consequences, concentrating instead on the application of force to the specific challenge at hand. They thus neglect the important consideration that the use of force must be designed not only to eliminate the surface revolutionary challenge, but to make certain that the revolutionary forces cannot later rally again under the same leadership. If that leadership cannot be physically liquidated, it can at least be expelled from the country (or area) in which the revolution is taking place. Emigrants rarely can maintain themselves as effective revolutionaries. The denial of the opportunity for the revolutionary leadership to re-rally should be an important ingredient of the strategy of force, even if it is belatedly used. *Fifth*, in the application of force, a sharp distinction should be made between the direct challenge and the masses which the challenge has tended to bring out. Thus, in the event of violence in a specific setting, the first objective of force ought to be the clearing of the area of those not directly committed and not involved in the revolutionary process. Only after the direct revolutionary participants have been fully isolated should force be directed directly against their strongholds. Moreover, if isolated for a period of time, the revolutionaries themselves may be more inclined to bargain. Finally, established authorities often fail to follow up effective violence with immediate reforms. Such reforms ought to be designed to absorb the energies of the more moderate revolutionaries, who can then claim that though their revolution had failed, their objectives were achieved. This is very important in attracting the more moderate elements to the side of the authorities.

For every revolution that succeeds, at least ten fail. It is not always a matter of abortive revolutionary situations. Frequently, the revolutionary leaders are themselves guilty of certain errors, typically tactical ones. Under the pressure of dramatic events, they tend to make more and more excessive demands, designed to radicalize and politicize specific grievances. In so doing, they often outrun their supporters and end up losing mass support. Moreover, they often engage in wrong symbolization, focusing on personalities rather than on basic issues. Such personal symbolization does not have staying power over the long haul, and it gives the other side the option to change or to keep the personalities involved, depending on the other side's judgment of the utility of one or the other tactic. Secondly, revolutionary leaders frequently overdo their reliance on emotionalizing appeals. For example, the condemnation of violence by revolutionaries is too transparent to be long effective. If sincerely meant, it stamps the revolutionaries as naïve, for violence necessarily accompanies a revolutionary process; if used as a tactic to mobilize support, it tends to backfire after a while because it eventually becomes evident that the revolutionaries themselves court violence in the hope of further radicalizing the situation. Finally, there is a tendency, and this is very important, of the revolutionaries to overestimate the revolutionary dynamic that they have set in motion. Revolutionaries tend to operate in a fishbowl atmosphere and to assume that their context and their appeals have universal validity. They thus underestimate the non-revolutionary context of their own specific revolution. The French revolutionaries expected their revolution to sweep all over Europe, so did the Bolshevik revolutionaries. In most cases, this does not happen, and the revolutionaries, because they lose touch with reality, increasingly become separated from the reformers on whose support they desperately depend for their long-range success.

In that setting, the task of the reformers is to isolate both the revolutionaries and the reactionaries as extremists. This is a terribly difficult task, for in a revolutionary situation there is very little room for reformers. Accordingly, they must formulate tangible and attainable reforms, together with highly concrete action programs for their attainment. It is only through positive involvement that the reformers can begin to gain broader support. Moreover, they must not participate in activities designed to keep the pot boiling, for this, if successful, will benefit the extremist revolutionaries; if it fails, it benefits the reactionaries. Accordingly, if the revolutionary process is itself in motion, the reformers must decide whom to trust more. If they trust the promises of the authorities, they have little choice but to side with them until the revolution is crushed; if they do not trust them, they must side with the revolutionaries and eventually let the revolution consume them. In any case, they should not mislead themselves into thinking that by staying in the middle, they will impose a middle solution.

A crucial consideration in judging the validity and significance of the revolutionary process is to determine whether it is historically relevant. Some revolutions, by relating themselves to the future, clearly were. This was the case with the French Revolution, with the 1848 Spring of Nations, and the Bolshevik Revolution. They all were part of, as well as having ushered in, new historical eras. But very frequently revolutions are the last spasm of the past, and thus not really revolutions, but counterrevolutions, operating in the name of revolutions. A revolution which really either is non-programmatic and has no content, or involves content which is based on the past but provides no guidance for the future, is essentially counterrevolutionary.

Indeed, most revolutionary outbreaks are of this character—they respond to the past, not to the future, and ultimately they fail. Examples are provided by the Luddites and the Chartists in England, who reflected the traumas of an agrarian society entering the Industrial Era; their response was spasmodic and irrelevant to the future. Peasant uprisings, whatever the merit of specific grievances, essentially fail for they do not provide a meaningful program for the future. Anarchist revolutions fall into this category. More recently, the Nationalist Socialists, the Fascists, and now the Red Guards in China are essentially counterrevolutionary: they do not provide meaningful programs and leadership for the coming age on the basis of an integrative analysis which makes meaningful the new era. Rather, they reflect concern that the past may be fading and a belated attempt to impose the values of the past on the present and on the future.

If it can be said that America today is ceasing to be an industrial society and is becoming a technetronic society, then it is important to decide whether some—though not all—of the crises and violence of today really add up to a meaningful revolution, or whether at least some manifestations are not counterrevolutionary in their essence. A revolution which has historically valid content for the future and which provides an integrated program for the future is historically relevant. In that sense, the civil rights revolution is a true and a positive revolution. Similarly, the important function of Marxism was that it made meaningful the revolutionary activities of communists by providing them with a sense of historical relevance and a pertinent program.

No such broad integrative ideology exists today in the United States, a country which confronts a future which no other society has yet experienced. On the contrary, it is revealing here to note that some of the recent upheavals have been led by people who increasingly will have no role to play in the new technetronic society. The reaction reflects both a conscious and, even more important, an unconscious realization that they are themselves becoming historically obsolete. The movements they lead are more reminiscent of the Red Guards or the Nazis, than of the Bolsheviks or the French revolutionaries. Thus, rather than representing a true revolution, some recent outbursts are in fact a counterrevolution. Its violence and revolutionary slogans are merely—and sadly—the death rattle of the historical irrelevants.

A Name for Our Age

Eric Hoffer

Eric Hoffer has long been an observer and critic of contemporary life. His book, The True Believer, *which analyzes the origins and social psychology of mass movements has provided him both an academic and a popular audience. His prominence in these endeavors is especially unusual, since Mr. Hoffer has been most of his life a Longshoreman, working on the docks of San Francisco. His perspective on contemporary America is in many respects unique. Although he does not speak in this excerpt specifically to the civil rights and student movements, he nonetheless provides us with another interpretation of the character and direction of change in our age.*

The general impression seems to be that the age in which we live is the age of the masses. Half the time when you open a book or start a discussion you find yourself dealing with mass production, mass communication, mass consumption, mass distribution, mass culture, mass this and mass that. We blame the masses for all our ills: for the vulgarization of our culture and politics, for the meaninglessness of our way of life and, of course, for the population explosion.

Actually, America is the only country in which the masses have impressed their tastes and values on the whole of society. Everywhere else, from the beginning of time, societies have been shaped by exclusive minorities of aristocrats, scribes, businessmen, and the hierarchies of sacerdotal or secular churches. Only in America did the masses have a chance to show what they could do on their own, without masters to push them around, and it needed the discovery of a new world to give them the chance. But in America just now the masses are on their way out. With the coming of automation 90 percent of the common people will become unneeded and unwanted.

Nor is there room any longer for the special aptitudes and talents of the masses. There was a time in this country when the masses acted as pathfinders and pioneers. They plunged into the unknown, cleared the land, built cities, founded states, and propagated new

Reprinted by permision of Harper & Row, Publishers, Incorporated from "A Name for Our Age," from *The Temper of Our Time* by Eric Hoffer. Copyright © 1966 by Eric Hoffer.

faiths. The masses built America and for almost a century shaped its future. But it is no longer so. America's future is now being shaped in fantastically complex and expensive laboratories manned by supermen, and the masses are on the way to becoming a waste product no one knows what to do with.

No. Our age is not the age of the masses but the age of the intellectuals. Everywhere you look you can see intellectuals easing the traditional men of action out of their seats of power. In many parts of the world there are now intellectuals acting as large-scale industrialists, as military leaders, as statesmen and empire builders. By intellectual I mean a literate person who feels himself a member of the educated minority. It is not actual intellectual superiority which makes the intellectual but the feeling of belonging to an intellectual elite. Indeed, the less valid his claim to intellectual superiority the more typical will be the intellectual. In Asia, Africa, and Latin America every student, every petty member of the professions, and every clerk feels himself equipped for national leadership. In Britain and Western Europe the intellectual, though not as assertive in claiming his birthright to direct and order society, nevertheless feels far superior to the practical men of action, the traditional leaders in politics and business. In the Communist countries the intelligentsia constitutes the ruling class.

In America the educated have not until recently developed a clear-cut, unmistakable intellectual type. There has been a blurring of types in this country. The differences are relatively slight between the educated and the uneducated, the rich and the poor, the old and the young, civilians and soldiers. It is remarkable how many topics there are —sports (including hunting and fishing), cars, gadgets, diets, hobbies, the stock market, politics—in which Americans of all walks of life are equally interested and on which they can all talk with some expertise. The paradox is that it is this sameness which gives to every human type in this country a striking singularity in the eye of the foreign observer. When Edmund Wilson went to London some years ago the British intellectuals could not believe their eyes: Edmund Wilson looked like a businessman. In 1963, a delegation of American longshoremen to Latin America found it hard to convince local labor leaders that they were bona fide workingmen. To a foreign observer, the American businessman is classless; "grandee, entrepreneur and proletarian all in one."[1]

The American intellectual has not always been what he is now. When you read what New England intellectuals were saying about common people early in the nineteenth century you are reminded of what British and French colonial officials were saying about the natives when the clamor for independence rose after the last war: "Wait and see what a mess these savages will make of things."

A resemblance between intellectuals and colonial officials strikes us at first sight as incongruous. We associate colonialism with soldiers and businessmen. I remember how when I first read about the Italian Catholic hierarchy in northern Europe during the late Middle Ages, I was struck by how much it resembled a colonial regime. There was a continuous flow of tribute from the North, and cushy jobs for young Italians. It reminded me of the relations between Britain and India in the heyday of the British Raj. I saw the Reformation as a colonial revolution, and it seemed to me quite logical that it should have fostered national as well as religious separatism. Luther was a colonial revolutionary. "In the eyes of the Italians," cried Luther, "we Germans are Teutonic swine. They exploit us like charlatans, and suck the country to the marrow. Wake up Germany!" Though I knew that the hierarchy of the Catholic Church was made up of intellectuals, it did not occur to me at the time that here was an example of colonialism by intellectuals. I could not connect intellectuals with colonialism.

With the lessons of the present before our eyes we know better. We know that rule by intellectuals—whether by an intelligentsia in a Communist country, by native intellectuals in the new countries, or by professors in Portugal—unavoidably approaches a colonial regime. This is a colonialism that begins at home. Hence, too, the obvious fact that the liberation movements in Asia and Africa, which were initiated and won by native intellectuals, have resulted not in democratic governments but in a passage from colonialism by Europeans to colonialism by natives. The typical intellectual everywhere is convinced that common people are unfit for liberty and for self-government. It is instructive to read what Patrice Lumumba wrote about the African masses before he became Saint Lumumba. In his book *Congo My Country*, written before Congo's independence, Lumumba proposed to the Belgian rulers that they assimilate the African intellectual and together form an elite. As to the masses: "The status quo would be maintained for the uneducated masses who would continue to be governed and guided, as in all countries, by the responsible elite—the white and African elite."

What does an economy run by intellectuals look like? It is colossal: big plans, big statistics, gigantic steel plants, factories, dams, powerhouses—the biggest ever! The intellectual cannot be bothered with the prosaic business of producing food, clothing, and shelter for the people. He wants to start at the end and work backward. He pants for the grandiose, the monumental, and the spectacular. Though factories, dams, etc. are practical things, the intellectual sees them as symbols of power and lordship rather than means for utilitarian ends. In Russia they build the biggest steam shovel ever made, while everywhere in the country you see people carrying brick and mortar on wooden platforms, four men lifting at four corners, because there are neither buckets nor wheelbarrows. It would be hardly possible to make sense of rule by intellectuals without taking into account their consuming passion for grandeur. "The human heart," wrote D. H. Lawrence, "needs, needs, needs splendor, gorgeousness, pride, assumption, glory and lordship. Perhaps it needs these more than it needs love; at least even more than bread." Though the intellectual has been preaching the primacy of economics in the historical process, he shows an aristocratic disdain for economic law. He wants to make history himself and let economics catch up the best way it can. Listen to Doctor Sukarno: "How do we become a great nation? Do we need only rice and bread? A nation does not live only on rice and bread. A nation with a flaming spirit is a great nation. Our food is spirit."

In politics, the intellectual who as a "man of words" should be a master of the art of persuasion refuses to practice the art once he is in power. He wants not to persuade but to command. We now realize that government by persuasion has been an invention of the traders rather than of the educated. The trader is usually more interested in the substance of power than its appearance. The intellectual wants not only to possess power but to seem powerful. Of what avail is the possession of power if you have to argue and persuade? Moreover, the intellectual is not satisfied with mere obedience. He wants to obtain by coercion a response as fervent and acclamatory as that obtained by the most effective persuasion. Silence is subversive—the womb of yet unborn cries of rebellion. Thus soul raping has become a feature of government by intellectuals. Euripides did not know the whole story when he said, "A slave is he who cannot speak his thoughts." We now know that a thousand times more a slave is he who is not allowed to keep silent.

It is significant that there should be so many schoolmasters in the ruling intellectual elites. The passion to teach is far more powerful and primitive than the passion to learn; and for all we know the passion to teach may have been a crucial factor in the rise of the revolutionary movements of our time. Now and then, when I look at Russia, Asia, and the new Africa it seems to me that a band of maniacal schoolmasters have grabbed possession of half of the world and turned it into a vast schoolroom with millions of cowed pupils cringing at their feet. This unprecendented infantilization of whole populations has been one of the most fateful consequences of the intellectual's coming to power. It is partly responsible for the primitivization of the social structure—the return to tribalism, medicine men, and charismatic leaders—which in a large part of the world is going hand in hand with rapid technological modernization. These builders of a heaven on earth have made a nightmare of the words of Jesus that "whosoever shall not receive the kingdom of heaven as a child shall in no wise enter therein." And it is in this nightmare that the schoolmaster's wildest dream is coming true: when he speaks the whole world listens. And how these schoolmasters do talk! Four-hour speeches, six-hour speeches—a schoolmaster's heaven.

In international affairs the coming of the intellectual has brought to the fore the cult of naked power. To an intellectual in power liberalism, the readiness to compromise, and moral considerations are the marks of a paper tiger; and the sight of a paper tiger incites him to a most reckless ferocity. Never before has there been such a disdain for truth and "the court of world opinion." The intellectual in power seems to understand only the simple language of divisions, warships, bombers, and missiles. He has a most sensitive nose for iron determination. Who would have dreamed fifty years ago that intellectuals ready to give their lives for the oppressed would make an article of faith of cynicism and the big lie? Who would have thought that power would corrupt the idealistic intellectual more than it does any other type of humanity?

The age of the intellectuals is full of surprises and paradoxes. One would have thought, for instance, that in societies dominated by intellectuals the atmosphere would be ideal for the performance of poets, writers, and artists. What we find instead is that a ruling intellectual hierarchy tends to hamper or even stifle the creative individual. The reason for this paradox is that when intellectuals come to power it is as a rule the meagerly endowed among them who rule the roost. The genuinely creative person seems to lack the temperament requisite for the seizure, exercise, and, above all, the retention of power. If Hitler had had the talents of a great painter or architect, if Lenin and Stalin had had the making of great theoreticians, if Napoleon and Mussolini had had it in them to become great poets or philosophers, they might not have developed an unappeasable hunger for power. Now, one of the chief proclivities of people who hunger for literary or artistic greatness but lack talents is to interfere with the creativeness of others. They derive an exquisite satisfaction from imposing their taste and style on the gifted and the brilliant. Throughout most of history the creative intellectual was at his best in societies dominated not by "men of words" but by men of action who were culturally literate. In Florence of the Renaissance, Cosimo the Elder, a banker who dreamed of having God the Father on his books as a debtor, reverenced talent the way the pious reverence saints. Though he was first in the state, and unequaled in fortune and prestige, he played the humble disciple to scholars, poets and artists.

And how do the common people fare in societies possessed by intellectuals?

It is well to remember that all through history the masses have found the intellectual a most formidable taskmaster. In the past, rule by intellectuals went hand in hand with subjection or even the enslavement of those who do the world's work. In India and China where scholarly Brahmins and Mandarins were at the top for millennia the lot of the masses was oppression, famine, and grinding poverty. In no other societies have the weak been treated so mercilessly. In ancient Greece an aristocracy of intellectuals, unequaled in body and mind, had its foot on the neck of a large population of slaves. Even in Palestine, where after the return from Babylonian exile the scribes and their successors, the Pharisees, were in power, the common people were considered outcasts unfit even for piety. During the Middle Ages a hierarchy of clerks left the common people to sink into serfdom and superstitious darkness.

One cannot escape the impression that the intellectual's most fundamental incompatability is with the masses. In every age since the invention of writing he has given words to his loathing of the common man. Yet, knowing all this, we were not prepared for the fate that has befallen the masses in the present age of the intellectuals. A ruling intelligentsia, whether in Europe, Asia or Africa, treats the masses as raw material to be experimented on, processed, and wasted at will. Charles Péguy saw it long ago, before the First World War. The intellectuals, he said, dealt with people the way a manufacturer deals with wares; they were *capitalists of people*. Yet the ruling intellectuals see themselves as champions and spokesmen of the people, and call their societies "people's democracies."

When the intellectuals come to power they develop a profound mistrust of mankind. They do not trust each other, but their deepest mistrust is of the common people. Tell a Russian, Chinese, or Cuban commissar that the masses, if left to themselves, would perform well, and he will laugh to your face. He knows that the masses are incurably lazy, stupid and dishonest. You have to watch them all the time, breathe down their necks, push them, and crack the whip if you want to get anything done. The ratio between supervisory and producing personnel is always highest where the intellectuals are in power. In a Communist country it takes half the population to supervise the other half.

The intellectual does not believe in high wages. Affluence, he thinks, corrupts the people. He wants them to work not for filthy money but for a holy cause, for the fatherland, for glory, honor, the future. He wants to enoble them by making them work for words. The ability to induce people to work for words can, of course, be of vital importance to poor countries trying to get ahead. But enthusiasm is perishable and cannot serve for the long haul. Sooner or later, the working people in societies ruled by intellectuals refuse to perform. They laborfake, act dumb, and pilfer the cargo the moment the intellectual turns his back. They cannot be frightened with prison since in these societies the difference between life outside and inside prison is one of degree rather than of kind. So you have to introduce the death penalty for economic offenses, and you have to build high wire fences and brick walls to keep the masses from running away.

Closely allied to the intellectual's attitude toward the masses is his incompatibility with America. With rare exceptions, foreign intellectuals, even when their interests incline them toward us, cannot really stomach America. In France some years ago the French writer François Mauriac found himself at a lunch table with Cardinal Spellman. He tells us that all the time he was conscious of a feeling of revulsion. "Most probably," he says, "I would have felt closer to the Dalai Lama." This from a very Catholic French intellectual about an American cardinal. British intellectuals have said they felt more at home in France, Germany, Russia, and even in India than in English-speaking America.

Wherever American influence penetrates it rouses the fear and the hostility of the intellectuals. What is there in American influence that so offends and frightens the foreign intellectual? What happens when a country begins to become Americanized? We have been told so often that America has a business civilization that you would expect American influence to manifest itself first in its effect on foreign businessmen. We find instead that the Americanization of a country means, above all, the de-proletarianization of its working class—the stiffening of the workingman's backbone, and the sharpening of his appetites. He not only begins to believe that he is as good as anyone else but wants to live and look like anyone else. In other words, the Americanization of a country amounts to giving it a classless aspect, a sameness that suggests equality. It is this that the foreign intellectual fears and resents. He feels the loss of the aristocratic climate as a private hurt. It is a drab, uninspiring world where every mother's son thinks himself as good as anyone else, and the capacity for reverence and worship becomes atrophied. This to the intellectual is a truly "godless" world, and this the "vulgarity" and the "debasement" against which he rails.

Nothing so offends the doctrinaire intellectual as our ability to achieve the momentous in a matter-of-fact way, unblessed by words. Think of it: our unprecedented productive capacity, our affluence, our freedom and equality are not the end product of a sublime ideology, an absolute truth, or a Promethean struggle. The skyscrapers, the huge factories, dams, powerhouses, docks, railroads, highways, airports, parks, farms stem mostly from the utterly trivial motivation of profit. In the eyes of the foreign intellectual, American achievements are illegitimate, uninstructive and uninspiring. An Indian intellectual protested that America has nothing to teach the world because all her achievements came about by chance.

Equally galling is the fact that until now America has run its complex economy and governmental machinery without the aid of the typical intellectual, and wherever American influence penetrates, the services of the intellectual somehow cease to be indispensable. When an American consulting firm was brought in to straighten out the affairs of a South American company, the first thing it did was fire two-thirds of the pencil pushers, most of whom were university graduates who would rather starve than perform manual labor.

The intellectual's hostility toward America is of long standing. Heine spoke of this country as "the prison of freedom" and saw in our equality a tyranny more stifling than any despotism. Carlyle and a whole tribe of nineteenth-century British intellectuals were appalled by our commonness and alarmed by our materialism. Renan saw the end product of our democracy as "a degenerate populace having no other aim than to indulge the ignoble appetites of the vulgar."[2] Freud protested: "I do not hate America, I regret it. I regret that Columbus discovered it." In his "Reflections on America" Jacques Maritain tells in vivid words how the foreign intellectuals, out of their fear and hatred of the common man, have been telling each other that the common man's continent is "a great death continent populated only with machines and walking corpses," a world "only intent on sucking all the vitality and creative instinct of the universe in order to foster with them the levelling power of dead matter and a swarm of automatic ghouls."

Thus it seems that the protagonists of our present age are not America and Russia, or America and China, or Russia and China, but America and the intellectuals. Though the indications are that America will somehow manage to come to terms with governments by intellectuals in Europe, the prospects are not promising for a modus vivendi with dominant intellectuals in Asia, Africa, and Latin America. A letter recently received from an American diplomat serving in Asia says: "I am always surprised at the amount of raw, venomous hatred for the U.S. that is displayed by everyone with more than six years of education in this part of the world. Strangely, the poor and illiterate masses remain well disposed toward the U.S., but that will certainly disappear with the next generation.... By recognizing as a constant factor the hostility of the underdeveloped intellectuals, we could avoid the costly effort involved in trying to win world public opinion, and cold-bloodedly realize what they already know—that we are by our basic nature and destiny a subversive force in these societies, and that our own security lies in the transfer of power to the masses and to real mass leaders, not elite class leaders."

Time seems to be working for the intellectuals. With the spread of automation the intellectuals will be everywhere on top, and the common people unneeded and unwanted. In Dostoyevsky's *The Possessed* a brash intellectual shoots his mouth off on the subject: "For my part, if I didn't know what to do with nine-tenths of mankind, I'd take them and blow them up into the air instead of putting them in paradise. I'd leave only a handful of educated people who would live happily ever afterward on scientific principles." I am quite certain that nothing of this sort is going to happen to us. Still, the question remains: How can the common people safeguard themselves against tyranny by an intellectocracy? Strangely enough, the answer, though not easy, is relatively simple. Just as tyranny by an aristocracy or a plutocracy can be most effectively checked by turning everyone into an aristocrat or a capitalist, so tyranny by an intellectocracy can be neutralized by turning everyone into an intellectual. This, of course, means society as a university, with a Berkeley-style "Free Speech Movement" acting as a formidable opposition against tyranny from any quarter.

Since the central concern of the Great Society must be the realization and cultivation of its human resources, it might have to turn itself into a school even if there were no need for a safeguard against any sort of tyranny. But as we try to visualize society as a school—a country divided into hundreds and thousands of small school districts, each charged with the realization of its natural and human resources—we find the pleasant surprise that what we have would be less society as a school than society as a playground. A wholly automated economy would demand only a token effort from the individual and give him back the child's freedom to play. The relatively small number of people in each school district, with their various interests and pursuits, would have the time and the inclination to know each other, learn from and teach each other, compete with and spur each other. There would be no dividing line between learning and living. All that schoolmasters can teach in a schoolroom is as nothing when compared with what we cannot help teaching each other on a playground. "Man," said Walter Bagehot, "made the school; God the playground."

Notes

[1] Richard Hertz, *Man on a Rock* (Chapel Hill: The University of North Carolina Press, 1946), p. 28.

[2] Saul Bellow echoed Renan when he said that affluence has "left us without a system of values" and made of America "a pig heaven."

DATE DUE

DEMCO 38-297

NORTHERN ILLINOIS UNIVERSITY

3 1211 01738872 5